Part Three: Getting a Final Product

Part Three shows you the many options you have in presenting your 3D model. Chapter 13, **Exploring Photoshop**, is geared toward users of AutoCAD and 3D Studio. It shows you the tools in Adobe Photoshop that are most likely to be needed to bring out the best in your 3D model. Chapter 14, **Transferring Your Animations to Video**, is a survey course in getting your animation into videotape format. Chapter 15, **Using Computer Video**, focuses on how you can turn your 3D Studio animations into a finished product, complete with sound, using Adobe Premiere 4.0. And finally, Chapter 16, **Presentations on Computers Only**, explores the opportunities for communicating your design ideas through computer video, virtual reality, multimedia, and the Internet.

The Appendices

Appendix A offers information and tips on the installation of the main software programs discussed in this book. **Appendix B** discusses the material on the companion CD, and presents the installation and use of the utilities and software found there (including the Adobe products). And finally, if you are a Windows NT user, and you have or are planning to obtain *3D Studio MAX*, you will want to read **Appendix C**, which is a discussion and tutorial for 3D Studio MAX aimed at the user who is already familiar with 3D Studio 4.0.

Mastering AutoCAD 3D

Mastering™ AutoCAD® 3D

George Omura

SYBEX®

San Francisco ◆ Paris ◆ Düsseldorf ◆ Soest

Associate Publisher: Amy Romanoff
Acquisitions Manager: Kristine Plachy
Developmental Editor: Richard Mills
Editor: Doug Robert
Technical Editors: Ali Ebtekar, Robin Hansen
Book Designer: Suzanne Albertson
Desktop Publisher: Bob Bihlmayer at London Road Design
Production Coordinator/Desktop Publisher Liaison: Robin Kibby
Indexer: Ted Laux
Cover Designer: Design Site
Photographer: Mark Johann
Cover Photo Art Direction: Ingalls + Associates

Screen reproductions produced with Collage Plus and Collage Complete.

Collage Plus and Collage Complete are trademarks of Inner Media Inc.

SYBEX is a registered trademark of SYBEX Inc.

Mastering is a trademark of SYBEX Inc.

TRADEMARKS: SYBEX has attempted throughout this book to distinguish proprietary trademarks from descriptive terms by following the capitalization style used by the manufacturer.

Every effort has been made to supply complete and accurate information. However, SYBEX assumes no responsibility for its use, nor for any infringement of the intellectual property rights of third parties which would result from such use.

Some of the architectural renderings within are loosely based upon the concepts of Le Corbusier and have been developed from publicly available photographic and other representations. Actual floor plans and designs were not used and illustrations herein are strictly for pedagogical purposes.

Library of Congress Card Number: 96-67845

ISBN: 0-7821-1850-X

Manufactured in the United States of America

10 9 8 7 6 5 4 3 2 1

◆ Warranty

Sybex warrants the enclosed CD-ROM to be free of physical defects for a period of ninety (90) days after purchase. If you discover a defect in the CD during this warranty period, you can obtain a replacement CD at no charge by sending the defective CD, postage prepaid, with proof of purchase to:

Sybex Inc.
Customer Service Department
2021 Challenger Drive
Alameda, CA 94501
(800) 227-2346
Fax: (510) 523-2373

After the 90-day period, you can obtain a replacement CD by sending us the defective CD, proof of purchase, and a check or money order for $10, payable to Sybex.

◆ Disclaimer

Sybex makes no warranty or representation, either express or implied, with respect to this medium or its contents, its quality, performance, merchantability, or fitness for a particular purpose. In no event will Sybex, its distributors, or dealers be liable for direct, indirect, special, incidental, or consequential damages arising out of the use of or inability to use the software even if advised of the possibility of such damage.

The exclusion of implied warranties is not permitted by some states. Therefore, the above exclusion may not apply to you. This warranty provides you with specific legal rights; there may be other rights that you may have that vary from state to state.

◆ Shareware Distribution

This CD contains various programs that are distributed as shareware. Shareware is a distribution method, not a type of software. The chief advantage is that it gives you, the user, a chance to try a program before you buy it.

Copyright laws apply to both shareware and commercial software, and the copyright holder retains all rights. If you try a shareware program and continue using it, you are expected to register it. Individual programs differ on details—some request registration while others require it. Some request a payment, while others don't, and some specify a maximum trial period. With registration, you get anything from the simple right to continue using the software to program updates.

◆ Copy Protection

None of the files on the CD is copy-protected. However, in all cases, reselling or redistributing these files, except as specifically provided for by the copyright owners, is prohibited.

To the memory of Rudy Langer,
Editor in Chief of Sybex from 1981 to 1995,
without whom there would be no Mastering AutoCAD.

Acknowledgments

3D computer graphics is a complex subject, but not nearly as complex as the process of creating a book. I'd like to acknowledge and thank all those involved in the creation of *Mastering AutoCAD 3D*. My gratitude goes to Richard Mills, Manager of Developmental Editors at Sybex, for believing in the project from the beginning, and also to Amy Romanoff, Associate Publisher, who gave much encouragement. My heartfelt thanks go to Doug Robert, who as my editor was a constant companion via e-mail and telephone throughout this project (the voice you hear in this book is his as much as it is mine) and to my technical editors Ali Ebtekar and Robin Hansen.

I'd especially like to thank Bob Bihlmayer at London Road Design and Robin Kibby at Sybex, the production team who had to put up with my excesses in both words and images. On top of his responsibilities for desktop publishing the entire book, Bob had the unenviable task of creating and positioning all the labels and pointers you see in the images. I know this was a painstaking task at best, and I'm sure the fact that there are well over a thousand images in the book didn't make it any easier. Many thanks, Bob. And my thanks to Robin, who, in addition to her regular job of overseeing the entire production process, got to double-check to see that every word, image, and arrow was in its proper place.

At Autodesk, I'd like to thank Lisa Senauke from Autodesk Developer Network, for keeping me informed on what's happening at Autodesk and for providing software when I needed it. And many thanks to Jane Dalisay at Sybex and Sonya Shaefer at Adobe Systems Inc. for teaming up to provide the Adobe tryout software that is included on the companion CD.

And finally, I want to take this opportunity to say thank you to my wife, Cynthia, for understanding, and putting up with, my absences as I was occupied writing this book.

Contents at a Glance

Table of Contents

Chapter 3
Building Rectangular 3D Surfaces

59

Chapter 4
Understanding Surfaces and the User Coordinate System

101

Chapter 5
Surface Modeling

153

Chapter 6
Modeling with Solids

221

Chapter 7
Viewing Your Model for Presentations and Editing

275

Chapter 8

Rendering with AutoVision

337

Part Two: Giving Life to Your World
407

◆

Chapter 9
Introducing 3D Studio

409

Chapter 10
Editing Objects and Assigning Materials

463

Chapter 11
Controlling Lights and Materials

531

Chapter 12
Creating an Animation

625

Part Three: Getting a Final Product
705

◆

Chapter 13
Exploring Photoshop

707

Chapter 14
Transferring Your Animations to Video

789

Chapter 15
Using Computer Video

829

Chapter 16
Presentations on Computers Only

895

Appendices
955

◆

Introduction

Computer 3D modeling has become a common tool in the design industry. Unfortunately, there are few sources to turn to for practical information on the construction and presentation of 3D material. My aim with *Mastering AutoCAD 3D* is to help AutoCAD users master the art of creating and presenting 3D objects and spaces.

Mastering AutoCAD 3D starts with *AutoCAD* for Windows (release 13, revision C4) as the primary tool for 3D modeling. It goes on to cover the basic rendering tools available in Autodesk's *AutoVision 2.0* and *3D Studio 4.0*. The later part of the book explores the various methods available for converting your computer models into hardcopy prints, videotaped animations, and even virtual reality worlds. The book goes well beyond basic modeling tutorials and reference material by showing you how you can integrate your use of AutoCAD with products like *Adobe Photoshop* and *Adobe Premiere*, among others.

◆ How You'll Use This Book

If you are a novice at 3D, you may want to start at the beginning and work through the tutorials from front to back. I assume you already have AutoCAD release 13 for Windows (and know how to work with it for 2D projects), but don't worry if you don't yet own 3D Studio. Since I've provided all the sample files you need for each chapter, you can skip over the 3D Studio material until you are ready for it. For the other chapters, the trial software is provided.

If you already have some experience working with 3D, you can browse the book to find a chapter that contains information you feel you could use and jump right in at that point. Since I cover quite a wide range of topics, it's likely that no matter what level user you are, you will find something valuable in this book that you can bring to your 3D work.

Users at all levels can use this book as a reference. When you run into problems or find you've forgotten how to accomplish a particular task, you'll find that I've included literally hundreds of illustrations to make life easy for those rushing to finish a project. You can also experiment with the numerous sample files we've provided, modifying them to fit your needs.

> **Note**   *The main project I develop throughout the book is based on a villa designed by the architect Le Corbusier, whose work I greatly admire. The results are a testament to the power of the tools available today for 3D modeling and rendering. Without access to the actual floor plans of this wonderful building, I began with a general outline of the structure and some photographs. As you'll see in the chapters, you can use AutoCAD and various other programs to create a representation of a building so realistic it could pass for a photograph of an actual, concrete structure. Of course, the villa as you and I create it in this book does not really exist, but I would hope that, if Le Corbusier were to see it, he would appreciate the process and excuse any variance for the fact that we did not have his actual plans to start with.*

◆ Software on the Companion CD

You've probably already noticed the CD attached to this book. It contains a wealth of data, utility, and program files to help you freely explore the world of 3D. First of all, I've included all of the files you'll need to complete the exercises in this book. With these, you don't have to work your way through the book from the beginning in order to create the files you need in later chapters—you can skip ahead to the tutorials that most interest you.

To help facilitate your experimentation in the chapters on *Adobe Photoshop* and *Adobe Premiere*, Sybex has arranged with Adobe to include special tryout versions of these two programs on the companion CD. These are fully functional versions, with the exception that the Save and Print facilities have been disabled. I've written the tutorials with the expectation that you may be using these versions, so I've put all the files you need to run these programs and to complete the tutorials on the CD as well.

In addition to the Adobe products, I've included software to help you explore the world of VR (virtual reality). The program *Wcvt2pov* is a translation program that will enable AutoCAD and 3D Studio users to convert their models to a format that can be "walked through" in real time, without the need for special hardware. To view your virtual worlds, I've also included a beta version of *WorldView* by InterVista Software Corp. WorldView is a virtual reality "browser" program that lets you visit and navigate through virtual worlds on the Internet or on your own computer.

I've also included a set of AutoLISP utilities that can help you work in AutoCAD with a minimum of frustration. *Eye2eye* is a collection of tools designed to help you visualize your models more easily. Other AutoLISP utilities, like *Splinep* and *Tube*, help you construct complex shapes.

To find out more about the CD, check out Appendix B. There you will find installation instructions and more detailed information about the CD's contents.

System Requirements

3D modeling is one of the most computer-intensive applications you can find. It should be no surprise, then, that we expect that you will have a high-capacity system. You will need a fair amount of RAM and disk storage space.

Minimum Requirements:

486DX 66MHz processor

16 MB of RAM (24 for Windows NT)

High-capacity hard disk with at least 200 MB free

High-resolution 1024×758×256 color monitor

CD-ROM drive

Mouse or tablet

These are *minimum* requirements; they should be raised if you are considering some serious 3D work (like, doing it for money, on a deadline, for instance).

On the software side, I expect that you are using a true 32-bit operating system such as Windows 95 or Windows NT. If you must use Windows 3.1 (I don't recommend it for this book), make sure you have installed the Win32S driver. This is typically installed along with AutoCAD r13 and is included with your AutoCAD package.

◆ Program Requirements

With one exception, all of the tutorials in this book were created using AutoCAD release 13, revision C4, running under Windows 95. I don't recommend trying to run AutoCAD under Windows 3.1 for the computer-intensive work you'll be doing in this book.

In later chapters I also used AutoVision 2.0 running under Windows 95. AutoVision 2.0, the program I discuss in Chapter 8, is included as a trial version in your AutoCAD r13 package. As mentioned earlier, tryout versions of the Adobe products are included on the CD.

Note that 3D Studio 4.0, which I present in Chapter 9 and later, is a DOS program; no Windows 95 version exists. For this book, I simply set it up as a DOS application under Windows 95.

Part One:

Building a 3D World

Welcome to
3D Cyberspace

In this book you are going to find out how computer 3D modeling is real, practical, and fun, and we are going to give you the tools to do it.

This book is about 3D that you can use from the start to the end of a project—3D for design and communication, not just for fancy presentations. It's about computer-aided imagination and creativity. It's about how to bring your ideas down to earth, and how to get the non-designers among your clients to really see what you're talking about.

You'll look at ways to build your ideas in 3D for your own study, and you'll see how you can combine computer 3D modeling with more traditional presentation techniques. Of course, I will also show you how to get the realistic renderings you usually associate with computer 3D. And to give your ideas life, you'll learn how to deliver your computer 3D images, through video, multimedia, and print.

◆ The Foundation: AutoCAD

One of the world's best two-dimensional drafting programs also happens to be one of the best three-dimensional modeling programs. AutoCAD is a flexible and reliable 3D modeling tool with the additional advantage of being the industry-standard program for creating technical drawings. Of all the programs commonly available for 3D construction, AutoCAD offers the greatest accuracy and control.

If you are already familiar with AutoCAD as a drafting tool for two dimensions, you already have most of the skills needed to explore the world of modeling in three dimensions.

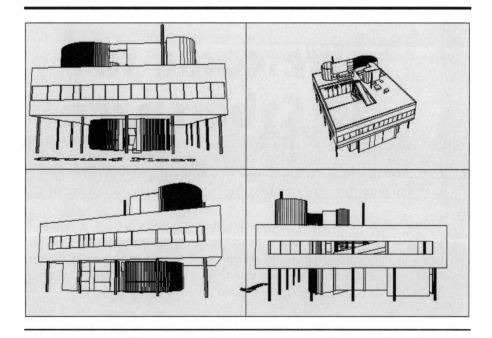

Figure 1.1: AutoCAD can be used to build, view, and study 3D models.

◆ What Is 3D Modeling, Anyway?

When we think of 3D computer modeling, we think of flashy, photo-realistic renderings or eye-popping computer animation as seen in the latest movies or sci-fi television series. But there is a great deal more to 3D modeling than just slick images. Perhaps the most compelling reason for using 3D is to study a design. You may use it, for instance, to find out if your design is just a hare-brained scheme, and not the brilliant yet realistic idea you thought it was. 3D modeling can first help you visualize something that only existed in your imagination; it can help you formulate your ideas into concrete, buildable solutions. Then it can help you communicate your ideas to someone else, like a client or coworker. Once you see your designs unfold in AutoCAD's simulated three-dimensional environment, you will be better equipped to refine them.

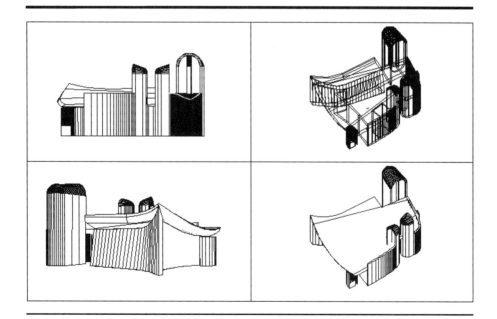

Figure 1.2: Wireframe views of 3D models can be used to study a schematic design.

◆ Why You Need More than AutoCAD

As great a tool as AutoCAD is, it can't do everything you might want it to do. For one thing, you'll need to know about the options you have for *presenting your work*. To get the most from 3D, you'll want to be able to show your rough ideas in a loose, sketched form. Toward that end, I'll show you how to enhance your preliminary 3D models with **_Adobe Photoshop_**. This product can quickly turn an AutoCAD 3D model into presentation-quality images that convey your ideas in a soft, painterly fashion.

a.

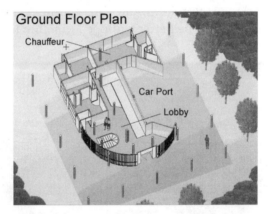

b.

Figure 1.3: Adobe Photoshop can be used to render AutoCAD 3D "sketches" into something more "painterly."

As your design progresses, you'll want to try out *the look of different materials and lighting conditions*. For this, you'll learn how to apply the effects available through Autodesk's **3D Studio** to your AutoCAD model. I'll also show you how you can use 3D Studio to study your ideas in greater detail, through careful placement of your viewpoint as it relates to your model. Once you've gotten your design into 3D Studio, you'll see how easy it is to create animated walk-throughs, to show off the best features of your design.

a.

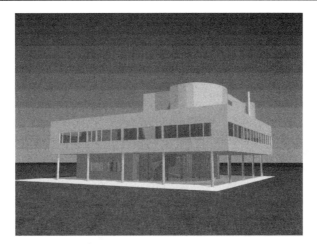

b.

Figure 1.4: Two versions of a study model rendered in 3D Studio

The *delivery of your design ideas* can be crucial to selling them. Once you have all these great 3D images, I'll show you how you can make the best of them. With 3D computer images, you have a bewildering range of delivery methods, from traditional printed material to online web pages on the Internet. I'll also discuss ways that you can create presentations for multimedia and electronic publishing.

◆ You'll learn how ***Adobe Premiere*** can be used to edit and play back your animations from 3D Studio.

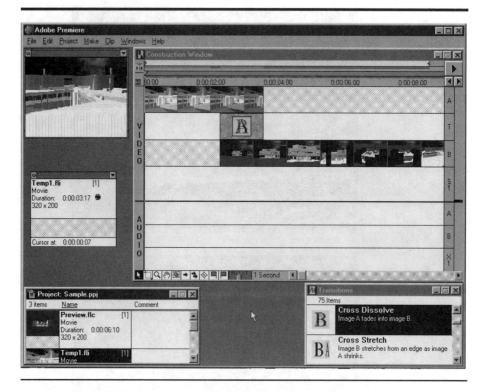

Figure 1.5: Adobe Premiere 4.0 can be used to edit and display your 3D animated walk-through in full 24-bit color.

◆ If you're after higher-quality animations, I'll show you the ins and outs of **video editing** and how to produce your own videotape for industrial presentations or broadcast. You'll also learn about the black art of **video engineering**, things you need to know in order to get the best quality image onto your tape. You'll learn about the different types of video media, from Hi8 to D1-digital videotape.

◆ If you prefer to make your design presentation interactive, I'll show you how **authoring tools** can help you create presentations that let others see your designs in the best light. We'll also look at ways of getting others involved with your design through virtual reality and high-resolution graphics.

Figure 1.6: Waveform monitors and vectorscopes, tools of the video trade

What If I Don't Have These Programs?

Chances are you already have AutoCAD if you're reading this book, but you might not have AutoVision, 3D Studio, Adobe Photoshop, or Adobe Premiere. Actually, you probably *do* have access to AutoVision, because it comes with AutoCAD; you may have simply forgotten about it since the time you first installed AutoCAD. If you don't have 3D Studio, you will want to arrange some way to have access to it when you get to the chapters in Part Two. As for the other programs, you've probably already noticed that the book you are holding came with a CD that includes special tryout versions of Adobe Photoshop 3.0 and Premiere 4.0 for Windows. These tryout versions are fully functional versions of the programs except that their Save and Print features have been disabled. If you don't already have these programs, you can use the tryout versions we've provided to do most of the exercises related to those programs.

In addition to these programs, I've also included all the files you need for each chapter, as well as shareware and tryout versions of other leading imaging, video-editing, and virtual reality software. In short, I've included everything you need outside of AutoCAD, 3D Studio, and a computer.

◆ The Three Biggest Myths That Have Kept You from Computer 3D

This books also sets out to dispel a few myths regarding AutoCAD and 3D modeling, myths that were perhaps true in the not-too-distant past, but are quickly falling away by virtue of greater computer power on the desktop, and better software tools.

Myth 1: It's Too Expensive

One of the greatest misconceptions about 3D modeling is that it is too expensive and time-consuming. Many people regard it as a "luxury." In fact, 3D modeling can help you save time and shorten your development costs. In this age of "get fast or die," getting a product to market quickly is the name of the game, and 3D modeling will help you achieve the speed you need to stay competitive.

3D modeling can also help you avoid costly mistakes by giving you a clear vision of your design before you've committed too many resources and hours.

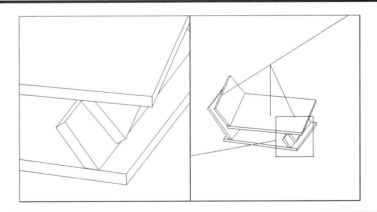

Figure 1.7: This is a 3D model of a platform used to help amateur astronomers track the stars. A careful study of the platform reveals areas that might cause problems.

Myth 2: It's Too Difficult

Chances are, you've heard this statement before. While 3D modeling will help you develop your ideas more fully, you can't do it quickly, especially not with your clients peering over your shoulder. It's true that 3D modeling is not instantaneous, and there is definitely a learning curve, but there are ways to use 3D modeling interactively—once you've created your initial version, you *can* sit down with your associates, your boss, or your clients, and view and edit your computer model in "real time" to get immediate feedback. Using rough models, you can go through a series of "what if" scenarios in front of your computer. You can't "just push a button" and get an instant design, but you can develop and even play with your design ideas more freely, which ultimately helps you to arrive at the design you need more quickly.

Myth 3: Computer Graphics Are Too Cold

Many designers are put off by the hard-edge look of the computer graphics produced by a lot of today's users. This look has its role in giving a sense of "high-tech" to a presentation, but it is in many ways looked down upon by hard-core designers, and is a role best saved for promotional efforts. The thing is, though, that 3D computer renderings don't *have* to be cold and hard-edged. This is where this book departs from other 3D computer books.

I will show you how you can give your 3D models a more loose, "painterly" appearance. Frequently, if you show a client or end user a 3D computer rendering of a building, for example, the viewer interprets the design as fixed and unchangeable. In some cases this might be desirable, but for the most part you don't want to scare your viewer into thinking that what you are showing them is the final word. You don't have to present your 3D model as a fully rendered, detailed image. You can use your AutoCAD 3D model as a starting point in Adobe Photoshop to create presentation-quality design schemes that don't look like the traditional computer image, and you can use virtual reality tools to view your design in a schematic way and in real time.

Figure 1.8: Examples of "soft-edge" 3D images

Figure 1.9: A sample presentation created in Adobe Photoshop using images from AutoCAD and 3D Studio

First Things First

There are numerous ways to accomplish any given task in AutoCAD. I can't show you every permutation of the modeling process, but I'll show you the best way to achieve your goals in the shortest amount of time without sacrificing quality. You will then be equipped to handle any project, regardless of the level of detail or complexity it requires.

The next chapter gives you some hands-on experience in the world of AutoCAD 3D. Think of it as your first step into the virtual world of 3D; a world that you will soon master.

What to Expect

This book is geared toward users of AutoCAD. The first few chapters are directed toward AutoCAD users who have not yet experimented with 3D modeling, but who know the basics of how to open and close files, how to draw basic objects like lines, arcs, circles, and polylines, and how to specify relative and absolute coordinates.

◆ If you already know a little about 3D modeling in AutoCAD, you should still at least skim the first few chapters, just to find out what you are expected to know for the later chapters.

◆ If you are completely new to AutoCAD, I recommend using one of the recent editions of *Mastering AutoCAD* (also from Sybex) to get the basics down. You only need to read the first part of that book, plus the section on polylines and splines, to get enough background to be able to move on to the first 3D exercise in this book.

Exploring the Third Dimension

Note   *The first three chapters in the book are for AutoCAD users who don't know anything about 3D in AutoCAD. If you already have some familiarity with 3D, you may want to skim over these early chapters and go directly to Chapter 4, where we begin to cover more advanced material.*

In this chapter, you will get your first taste of 3D modeling by creating some simple 3D forms. First, you'll turn a 2D rectangle into a box, by *extruding* the rectangle. This process of extruding objects into the third dimension is the most common method for creating walls in floor plans and making other rectangular vertical surfaces. Next you'll see how *polylines* can be used to create more complex shapes. Polylines are an extremely useful object type in 3D modeling with AutoCAD, so getting an early appreciation of their usefulness will give you a head start in creating 3D models in AutoCAD. You'll also find out how to get around in 3D space, using different *coordinate systems*.

◆ Drawing a Box

The following exercises will let you get your feet wet and will expose you to a couple of the most common functions of creating a 3D object: extruding it in the Y axis, and viewing it in a 3D orientation.

> **Note** *The UCS Icon helps you locate the X and Y axes of your drawing. The acronym UCS stands for <u>U</u>ser <u>C</u>oordinate <u>S</u>ystem. See Chapter 4 for more on the UCS.*

1. Start AutoCAD now.

2. If it isn't already on the screen, open the Draw tool palette. Do this by choosing Tools ➤ Toolbars ➤ Draw.

3. If it isn't visible, turn on the UCS Icon by choosing Options ➤ UCS ➤ Icon. (You might notice that choosing the Icon option causes a checkmark to appear next to the word *Icon* in the pull-down menu. The checkmark is an indication that the option is *enabled*, or active.)

4. Click on the Rectangle icon in the Draw palette.

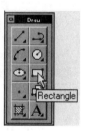

5. For the first corner of the rectangle, enter **7,3**↵ at the prompt. For the other corner, enter **16,10**↵ (see Figure 2.1).

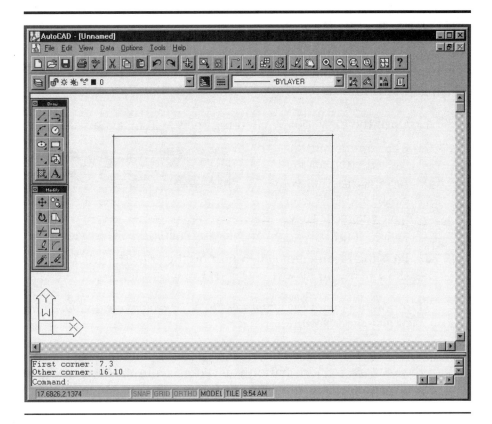

Figure 2.1: Drawing the rectangle

You've created a simple 2D box. You could have picked any two points using your mouse, but I've asked you to select specific points for the purposes of this demonstration.

Getting a 3D View

Next, you'll turn the rectangle into a 3D wireframe box—but before you do that, let's alter our view of the drawing area so you can see the drawing in a 3D format.

1. Open the View tool by choosing Tools ➤ Toolbars ➤ View.

2. Click on the button labeled *SW Isometric View*. Notice that your cursor and UCS icon have changed. They appear angled, as if you are viewing them in a 3D isometric view.

3. Press the F7 function key to turn on the grid. The grid dots also show that your view is now a 3D isometric view.

> *Tip*   *Many of the View options on the View toolbar are also found in the View pull-down menu.*

You can use the UCS Icon to orient yourself to your drawing. The *SW* in the *SW Isometric View* button you clicked on in the View tool palette stands for *Southwest*, so your point of view is "below and to the left" of your rectangle (see Figure 2.2). The orientation of the cardinal directions (North, South, East, and West) on your drawing is the same as it would be on a typical map, with North pointing up.

> *Note*   *You will see numerous prompts and messages in the command-prompt area of the screen as you work. Unless I specifically point these out, however, you needn't bother even looking at what's displayed there. Most of the prompts are equivalents to the easier menu-based approach I'll be using, and indications of the internal workings of AutoCAD. Both are vestiges of the older, DOS approach to issuing instructions.*

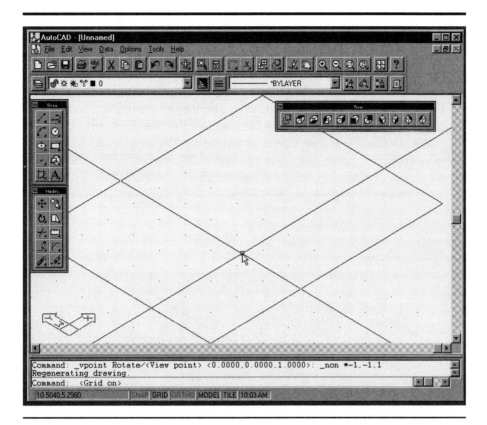

Figure 2.2: The SW Isometric view in relation to the XY plane and the Z coordinate

If you move the mouse pointer slowly over the other options on the View toolbar, you'll see from the ToolTips that you can select from several other views, including the typical engineering top, front, and side views, and three other isometric views. Through other options elsewhere in the menu system, you can "fine-tune" your view by selecting a more specific viewpoint angle. You can also view your drawing in a *perspective mode* that lets you control "camera" and "target" positions, and field of view. You will get a chance to explore these other options later. Now let's move on to the next step: adding 3D depth to your rectangle.

Extruding Your 2D Object into 3D

To add a third dimension to your rectangle, you will *extrude* it. When you extrude an object, you aren't really drawing anything new; instead, you are changing a *property* of an existing object so that it has a "thickness," which in AutoCAD means it has a dimension along the Z axis. In 2D drawings, you don't normally encounter this Z axis, but it's always available. Figure 2.3 shows how a box is formed by adding thickness along the Z axis.

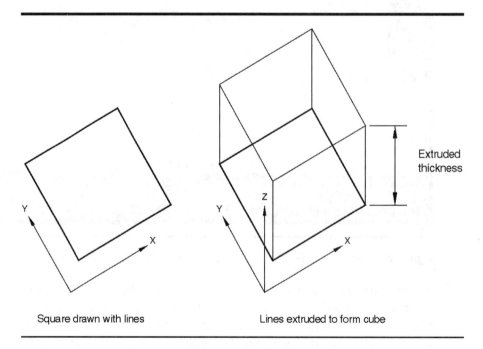

Square drawn with lines   Lines extruded to form cube

Figure 2.3: Extruding a 2D box along the Z axis produces a 3D cube.

In a typical 2D drawing, you never see or use the Z axis, since it is pointing directly toward you, as shown in Figure 2.4. But once you change your viewpoint, as in the previous exercise, you can easily see the Z axis.

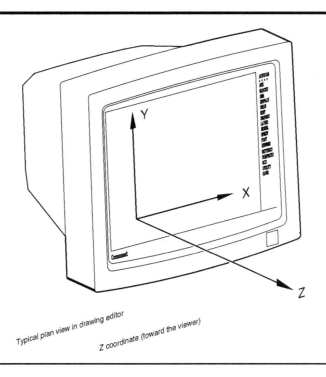

Typical plan view in drawing editor

Z coordinate (toward the viewer)

Figure 2.4: The Z axis points directly at you in a typical 2D AutoCAD drawing.

Now let's see firsthand how changing an object's property can extrude it into the Z axis.

1. Click on the Zoom Out button on the Standard toolbar. This will give you some room to view the changes you will make to your rectangle.

Getting to the Standard and Properties Toolbars

The Standard and Properties toolbars are usually located at the top of the AutoCAD screen, just below the menu bar. If for some reason they do not appear in your AutoCAD window, you can open them by choosing Tools ➤ Toolbar ➤ Standard Toolbar and then Tools ➤ Toolbar ➤ Object Properties. Once they are on the screen, you can click and drag to move them into their docked position just below the menu bar.

2. Click on the Properties button in the Properties toolbar at the top of the AutoCAD window.

Notice that your cursor has now changed to a selection box.

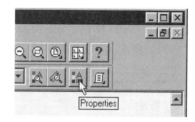

3. Now click on the rectangle and press ↵. The Modify Polyline dialog box appears.

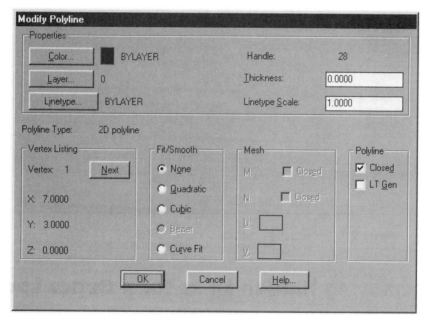

4. Double-click on the input box labeled Thickness, in the upper right corner of the dialog box, then enter **4**.

5. Click OK. Your rectangle changes into a box.

6. Use the scroll bars (or the Pan tool in the Standard toolbar) to center the box in your screen. Your view should look like Figure 2.5.

In step 4, you told AutoCAD to change the thickness of your rectangle to 4 units through the Modify Polyline dialog box. As you saw in the exercise, the thickness of an object gives the object a third dimension.

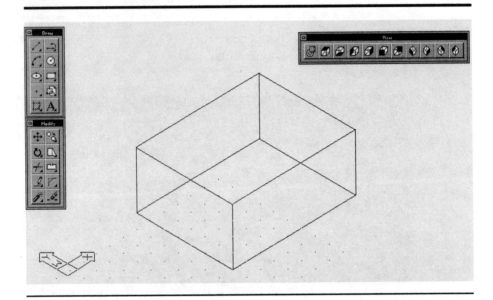

Figure 2.5: The rectangle extruded into a 3D Box

Removing Hidden Lines for a Better Look

Right now, you see the box as a *wireframe view*. To make your cube look more realistic, you can get a view with *hidden lines removed* by using the Hide tool. This hides the lines that are located behind foreground surfaces.

The Hide tool can be found in the Render toolbar.

1. Choose Tools ➤ Toolbars ➤ Render. The Render toolbar appears.

2. Click on the Hide tool.

A hidden line view of your box appears (see Figure 2.6). Notice that your box appears to have an open top. This is because you extruded a *polyline* rectangle, which consisted only of the *lines* of the rectangle; it did not include the area *enclosed* by the polyline. Thus your box has sides, but no top or bottom.

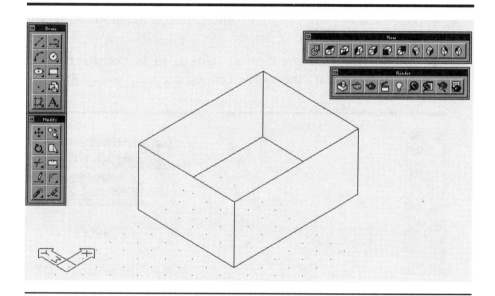

Figure 2.6: The box with hidden lines removed

To close the top of the box, you will need to use another object called a *3D face*. Here's how to add a 3D face to your box to close the top.

1. Choose Tools ➤ Toolbars ➤ Surfaces to open the Surfaces toolbar.

2. From the Surfaces toolbar, click on 3D Face.

3. Shift-right-click to pop up the Osnap menu, and choose the Endpoint Osnap. (I'll discuss this tool later in the chapter, in the section on "object snaps.") Using this tool, select the top four corners of the box in a clockwise sequence (See Figure 2.7). The sequence isn't really important as long as you pick points in a complete clockwise or counterclockwise direction; don't zigzag over the area being covered.

4. Once you've picked all four corners, press ↵ to tell AutoCAD you have finished selecting points.

5. Choose Hide from the Render palette again. Notice that this time, AutoCAD displays the box as a closed one (see Figure 2.8).

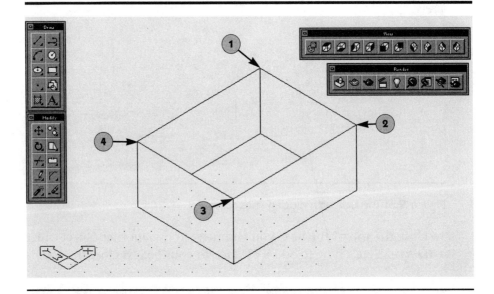

Figure 2.7: Select the top corners in a clockwise sequence to make the top of the box a 3D Face.

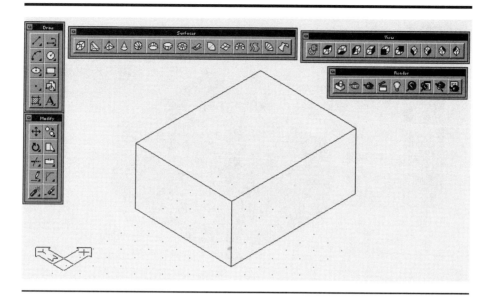

Figure 2.8: The box with a top added and hidden lines removed

If you prefer, you can get a *shaded* view of your box. A shaded view offers some realism to your view by shading the surfaces of the model with gray or another color.

1. Choose Shade from the Render toolbar. After a moment, a shaded view of your box appears (see Figure 2.9).

2. To return to the wireframe view, type **regen**↵.

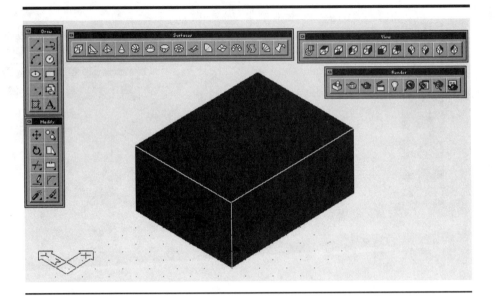

Figure 2.9: A view of the box using the Shade tool

You can control how AutoCAD shades your model by changing the Shadedge system variable. Another option is to use the Render tool. With Render, you can assign representations of different materials to surfaces. You will get a chance to explore the Render tools in depth later in this book. For now, let's look at some other basic 3D modeling operations.

Changing Your Point of View

Now that you have an object in 3D, you will want to see what it looks like from different angles. AutoCAD offers several tools for viewing your drawing in 3D. Some might argue that there are really almost *too* many. You've already seen, for instance, the Isometric tools available in the View toolbar. Those tools allow you to select from four preset 3D views: Southwest, Southeast, Northwest, and Northeast. Next, you'll learn how to use a tool that will give you a bit more freedom in selecting your view.

Moving around Your Model

Suppose you want to change your point of view just slightly to the left, so your view is more perpendicular to the polyline box. To rotate your view, you will use an option from the View pull-down menu.

1. Choose View ➤ 3D Viewpoint ➤ Rotate. The Viewpoint Presets dialog box appears (see Figure 2.10). Notice the two graphics in the dialog box. The one on the left indicates your viewpoint in the XY plane, and the one on the right shows your viewpoint as an angle from the XY plane.

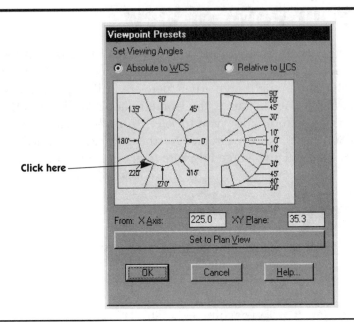

Figure 2.10: Selecting your viewpoint location in the Viewpoint Presets dialog box

2. Place the arrow cursor at the point indicated in Figure 2.10, in the graphic on the left of the dialog box, then click on that point. The line pointer indicating your position in the XY plane changes to the point you clicked on. Also notice that the value in the **From: X Axis** input box changes as well. As you adjust the pointer in the graphic, try to set value in the input box to a value close to 250. If you prefer, you can enter an angle value in this input box instead of using the graphic.

3. Click OK. Your view changes as if you rotated your viewpoint to the left.

4. Click on the Zoom Out button in the Standard toolbar to get a view similar to Figure 2.11.

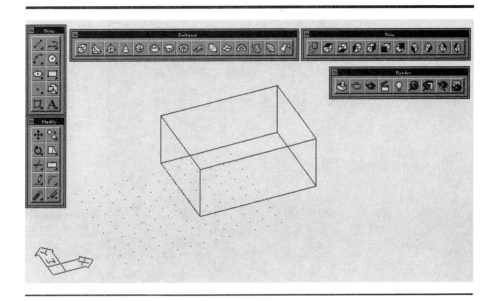

Figure 2.11: Your view after changing the settings in the Viewpoint Presets dialog box

Changing Your Viewpoint Height

Now try adjusting the height of your viewpoint.

1. Choose View ➤ 3D Viewpoint ➤ Rotate again.

2. This time, click on the graphic on the right side of the dialog box as shown in Figure 2.12. Notice the change in the **XY plane** input box. This tells you the exact angle of your viewpoint from the XY plane. Move the pointer in the graphic so the value in the input box reads 60. As before, if you prefer, you can enter an angle value here instead of using the graphic to select an angle.

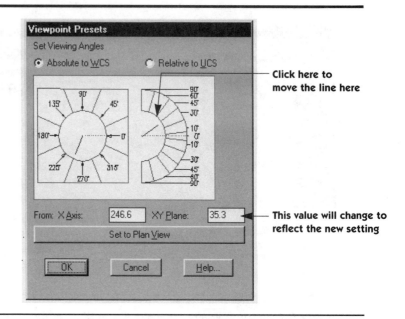

Figure 2.12: Selecting your viewpoint height from the Viewpoint Presets
         dialog box

3. Click OK. Now your point of view is from higher than before.

4. Click on the Zoom Out button on the Standard toolbar to get the
view shown in Figure 2.13.

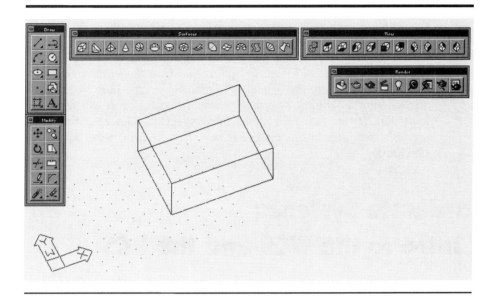

Figure 2.13: The view from your new viewpoint angle

The Viewpoint Presets dialog box offers a quick way to select a viewpoint. You can fine-tune your view by alternately making adjustments in the Viewpoint Presets dialog box and viewing the results.

> **Tip**   *You can right-click anywhere in the AutoCAD drawing area to invoke the last tool you used. This makes going back and forth between the drawing and, say, the Viewpoint Presets dialog box a quick and painless step. To see the differing effects of different adjustments you may be trying in the dialog box, you can simply right-click on the drawing area and the dialog box will open without having to go to the pull-down menu. (Of course, if you use another tool in the meantime, then that tool becomes the default when you right-click on the drawing area.)*

> **Note**   *The tools you've used so far, the Viewpoint Presets dialog box and the standard isometric views, enable you to view your model quickly. Once you get oriented, you can then use the Zoom and Pan tools to get a detailed look at a specific part of you model that you may need to work on. At other times, however, you will want to "get inside" your model, to get an idea of how it will look from the inside out. This will be especially true when you are designing a building or office interior. To do this, you will want to use tools that let you view your model in* perspective. *Those perspective tools are discussed later in this book. For now, let's continue with the introduction to 3D.*

◆ Coordinate Systems: An Intro to the WCS and the UCS

In 2D drawing you probably got so used to the W in the UCS icon that you've forgotten its significance. The W indicates that the UCS you're using is the same as the *World coordinate system*, or WCS, which is typically the base coordinate system for all of your 2D work. It describes the *default drawing surface*.

The WCS includes an X, Y, and Z axis, but as you know, when you draw in 2D the Z axis is fairly unimportant—by default, objects you create in 2D reside at the zero coordinate of the Z axis. For instance, the polyline that you extruded earlier resides on the plane defined by the X and Y axes of the World coordinate system. You extruded it vertically by giving it a *thickness* along the Z axis, but you didn't actually *draw* anything on that vertical plane. Oh, you can draw simple lines, in any direction you want (vertically, parallel, or at any tilt), and move and copy objects in the same way, but you can't *draw* anything *complicated* if it isn't on the XY plane!

Amazing! How then do you explain all those complex 3D models with pictures hanging on the walls?

Well, it's a matter of definition, really. You simply move your XY plane by creating your own UCS. To *draw* objects on any plane other than the XY plane of the WCS (the "default drawing surface"), you have to set up your *own* drawing surface. That's what a UCS is—a *user* coordinate system. You have to set it up in such a way that your drawing surface (your UCS's XY plane) coincides with the plane you want to draw on. Say you want to draw some fancy wallpaper on the wall of a house you're modeling in AutoCAD; to draw *on* that wall, you have to set up a UCS *for* that wall.

A UCS can be defined for any angle relative to the WCS, from flat (parallel to the WCS) to vertical, and any angle in between, like the tilted roof of a house (see Figure 2.14).

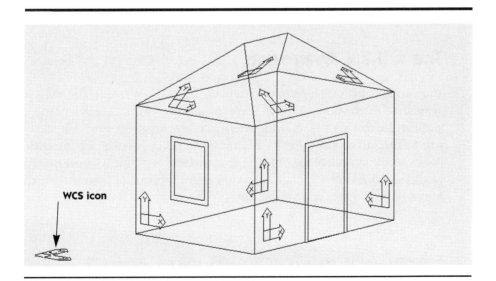

Figure 2.14: A house with a UCS defined for each of its surfaces. The UCS icons on each surface show you the UCS orientation. (The ground, in this case, is the WCS.)

> **Note** *Once you begin to use different UCSes, you'll find that you can't draw or edit any arcs, circles, or polylines that aren't on or parallel to the current UCS. Also, you cannot use the Edit Polyline tool (Pedit) to edit a polyline that was created in another UCS unless it is parallel to the current one. (Actually, these restrictions apply to the WCS as well, but up until now, you would never have noticed them, since you've never used any other coordinate system!)*

User coordinate systems can be defined and stored in a way similar to AutoCAD views. And like text styles and layers, only one coordinate system is ever current at one time. You'll learn more about creating your own user coordinate system later in this chapter, and especially in Chapter 4. For now you will concentrate on working within the WCS in 3D.

Specifying Exact Distances in 3D Space

The @X,Y,Z Approach

You can specify locations and distances in AutoCAD using the *@X,Y,Z approach*. If you want to move something only within the XY plane, you can leave off the Z coordinate in the specification, and AutoCAD will assume that you want to maintain the object's current Z coordinate. For example, to move an object 2 units to the right and 1 unit up, you would select an object, click on a grip point, and press ↵ to invoke the Move option. Then you would enter:

    @2,1↵

at the To point: prompt. In 2D work, you usually specify only the X and Y coordinates and leave off the Z coordinate (because it's usually zero); in 3D you can specify the Z coordinate as needed, as in:

    @2,1,1↵

If you were to enter this at the To point: prompt, your object would not only move 2 units to the right and 1 unit up the screen, it would also move 1 unit "vertically," in the positive direction of the Z axis (see Figure 2.15).

a.

b.

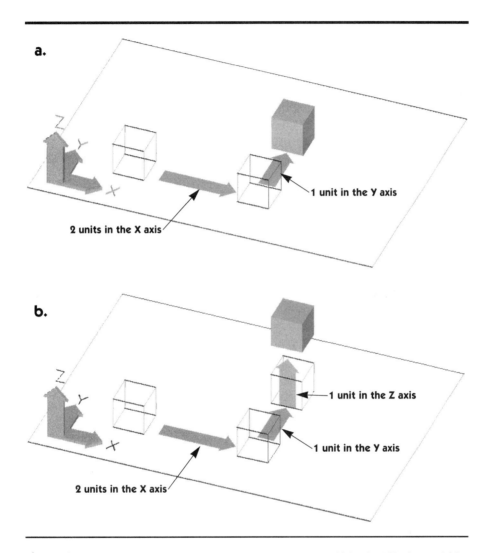

Figure 2.15: The image on top shows an object moved within the XY plane within the WCS. The image on the bottom shows the same move with an additional Z component.

Note   *If you only want to move an object in the Z axis, you would enter a zero for both the X and Y axes, as in @0,0,2↵. This example would move your selected object 2 units in the positive direction of Z axis.*

Just as with the X and Y axes, a negative value for the Z axis will move an object in the negative direction. Figure 2.16 shows the three axes for a typical 2D WCS, with their positive and negative directions.

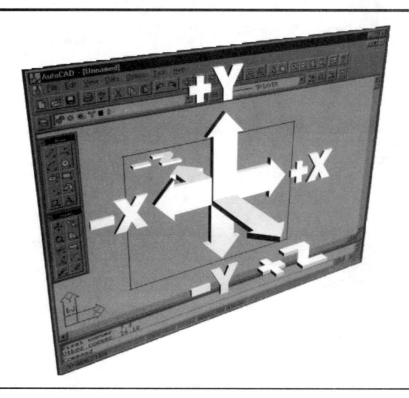

Figure 2.16: The X, Y, and Z axes and their positive and negative directions

Try moving the box vertically 1 unit.

1. Click on your extruded rectangle.

2. Click on a grip, then right-click (or press ↵) to get to the Move grip mode.

3. Type **@0,0,1**↵. The sides of the box move "vertically" 1 unit.

4. Press the Esc key twice to clear the grips.

Notice that the outline of the 3D Face you added earlier to create a box top remained in its original location. Though unintended, this gives you a point of reference, proving that the sides of the box have moved in a positive Z direction.

Other Approaches

You may find it easiest to remember the @X,Y,Z format for specifying distances in 3D, but, in typical AutoCAD fashion, you have the option to use other formats. They are the *Cylindrical* format and the *Spherical* format.

Both of these alternative formats are extensions of the standard AutoCAD *Polar Coordinate* format you would use in 2D drawing. Allow me to digress briefly concerning this standard format. To specify a distance in polar coordinates you enter @, then the distance of the move, then the open angle bracket (<) followed by the angle of the move, as in:

@48<45

This example specifies a displacement of 48 units at a 45-degree angle.

The Cylindrical format approach extends the Polar Coordinate format into the Z axis, by adding a third value for a displacement along the Z axis, as in the following example:

@48<45,20

This example of a Cylindrical format entry produces the same result as the Polar Coordinate format entry above, with, in addition, a displacement of 20 units in the Z direction.

The Spherical format approach differs from the Cylindrical format in that, whereas the Cylindrical format takes one angle and two distances, the Spherical format takes one distance and two angles. For example, to specify a displacement of 48 units in space at an angle of 45 degrees in the XY plane and an angle of 30 degrees *from* the XY plane, you would enter the following:

@48<45<30

Using "Object Snaps" in 3D Space

If you need to place an object in exactly the same place as another object, such as when you want the objects to share endpoints or midpoints, you can do so using *object snaps*, or *Osnaps* for short. Try it out with the following example.

1. Click on the 3D face that we left floating below the top of the box in the last exercise, and select the endpoint grip closest to you, near the middle of the screen (see Figure 2.17a). In this exercise we'll move this face back up to the top of the box.

2. Right-click on the mouse to invoke the Move option, then Shift-right-click to open the Osnap pop-up menu.

3. Select Endpoint from the menu.

4. Pick the top corner of the box, as shown in Figure 2.17b.

5. Press the Esc key twice to clear the grips.

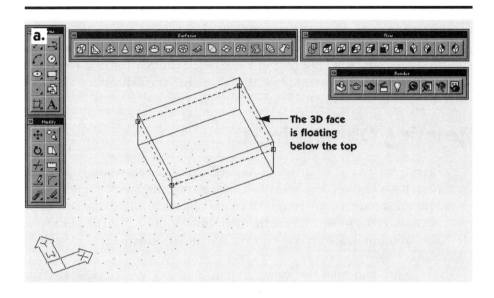

The 3D face
is floating
below the top

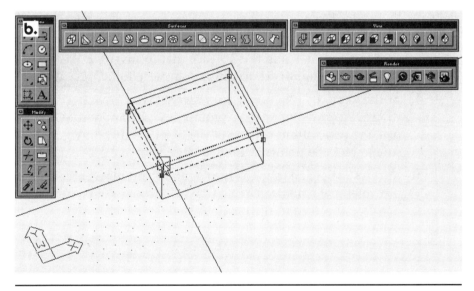

Figure 2.17: Moving the 3D face back up to the top of the box

You can use object snaps in 3D just as you would in 2D drawings, with the added advantage of being able to snap to object-snap points on the top or bottom edges of an extruded object. In this exercise, you were able to snap to the top endpoint of a box, even though the box was originally drawn as a simple rectangle with neither top nor bottom.

Rotating Objects in 3D

Everything you've done so far has been limited to a rectangular orientation. Now suppose you want to create forms that are at angles to the X, Y, and Z axes. One method is to create objects of the shape and size you want and *then* move and rotate them into position. You've already seen how you can move an object. Now try the 3D Rotate tool.

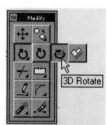

1. Click and hold the Rotate tool in the Modify in the Modify toolbar until the Rotate flyout menu appears

2. Choose 3D Rotate from the Flyout menu.

3. Click on your box and the 3D Face that forms the top, then right-click to finish your selection.

4. At the `Axis by Object/Last/View/Xaxis/ Yaxis/Zaxis/<2points>:` prompt, use the Endpoint Osnap and pick the two bottom corners of the box as shown in Figure 2.18. Be sure to pick the points in the sequence shown.

5. At the `<Rotation angle>/Reference:` prompt, enter **45**. The box rotates at a 45-degree angle about the axis defined by the two points you picked in the previous step.

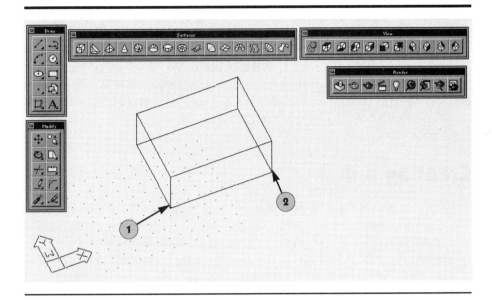

Figure 2.18: Selecting the two points for the 3D rotation

Your box is now standing on edge. With the 3D Rotate tool and the Move and Copy tools, you can position objects in just about any position you want in 3D space.

◆ Working with User Coordinate Systems

When you created the box, you were working off of the World coordinate system, or WCS. The WCS provides the point of reference for your construction. You are not limited to the WCS, however. You can create other coordinate systems oriented in such a way as to help facilitate the construction of objects that are in different orientations.

Creating a UCS

The next exercise will demonstrate how you can create and use a new coordinate system to add an arc that aligns with one of the faces of your now tilted box. In this first set of steps we will begin by choosing one corner of the box to use as the origin for the new UCS and then construct our new X and Y axes to coincide with the edges of the front of your box.

1. Choose Tools ➤ Toolbars ➤ UCS to open the UCS toolbar.

2. Click on the 3 Point UCS tool from the UCS toolbar.

3. At the `Origin point <0,0,0>:` prompt, use the Endpoint Osnap and pick the corner of the box closest to you, as shown in Figure 2.19a.

4. Now your pointer is trailed by a rubber-banding line that represents the new X axis. Anchor it along the bottom front edge of your box by using the Endpoint Osnap to pick the opposite corner as shown in the same figure.

5. Now anchor the new Y axis by picking the top left corner of the front of your box, again, using the Endpoint Osnap (Figure 2.19b).

6. Notice how the UCS icon and grid dots have changed to align with the front face of the box (Figure 2.19c).

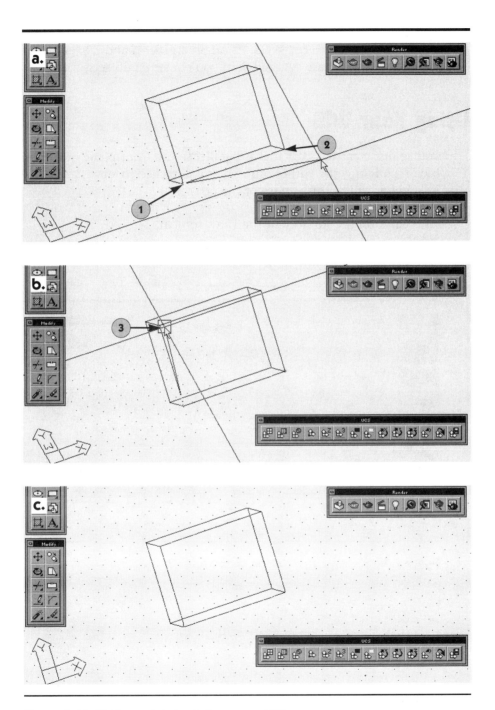

Figure 2.19: Picking points to define a new UCS

The new UCS becomes the default coordinate system until you choose to change it or revert to the WCS. Its origin and X, Y, and Z axes become the default coordinate system when you construct objects.

Using Your UCS

You've just created a UCS that is parallel to the front plane of the tilted box. Its origin is the corner of the box you picked in step 3 above. Now let's add an arc to this surface of the box.

1. Click on the Arc tool in the Draw toolbar.

2. Using Osnaps, select the three points indicated in Figure 2.20. Doing this draws the arc.

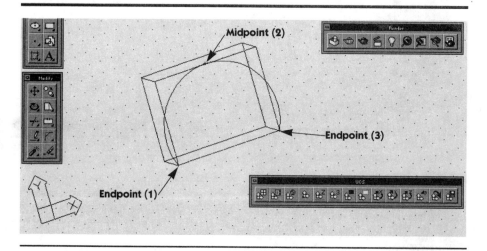

Figure 2.20: Placing the arc on the box surface

To make it more interesting, now let's extrude the arc.

1. Click on the Properties tool in the Properties toolbar.

2. Click on the arc, then right-click the mouse or press ⏎ to finish your selection.

3. At the Properties dialog box, enter **2** in the Thickness input box, then click OK. The arc extrudes 2 units in the positive direction of the current UCS's Z axis (see Figure 2.21).

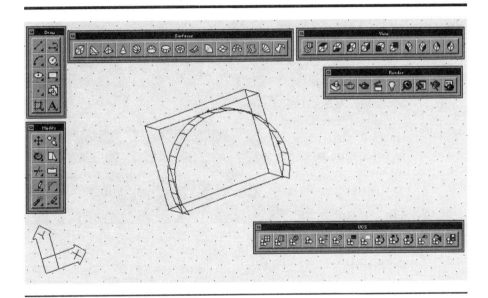

Figure 2.21: Extruding the arc

> **Note** *In the preceding exercise, you used the 3 Point UCS tool and the surface of the tilted box as a template to create the new UCS. There are several other ways to create a UCS; we will explore them later in this book.*

Saving and Restoring Your UCS

Suppose you want to return to the WCS to construct some additional objects that are oriented in the original plane. You can use the UCS Control dialog box to easily return to the WCS to construct those objects. After you've finished with that, you can then go back to the UCS you created when you need the new orientation again.

1. Click on the Named UCS tool in the UCS toolbar. The UCS Control dialog box appears. Notice the options in the list box. The names of available UCSes are listed to the left, and the one currently in use is indicated by the word *Current* to the right.

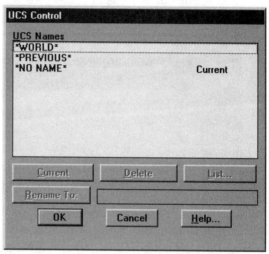

2. Click on the item *World* in the list box, then click on the Current button. The *Current* indicator in the list box moves next to World to show that the World coordinate system is now the current UCS.

3. Click OK. Notice that the UCS icon in your drawing area changes back to its original orientation (that is, to the WCS orientation).

When you finish using the WCS, you can easily revert once again to the UCS you were using previously, by returning to the UCS Control dialog box and clicking the button labeled *Previous*. Notice, though, that this only shows you which UCS was in use before the current one; you still have to click the Current button to make that UCS current again.

Here you've seen how you can switch back and forth between the WCS and your UCS. If you leave things as they are, you can continue to switch between the WCS and your UCS for as long as you have your drawing open. If you close the drawing while in the WCS, however, you will lose the UCS you created. To save your UCS, you need to give it a name.

1. Open the UCS Control dialog box again, then highlight the item labeled *NO NAME*. Notice that *NO NAME* appears in the *Rename To* input box near the bottom of the dialog box.

2. In the *Rename To* input box, change *NO NAME* to **MY-UCS**, then press the button labeled *Rename To*.

3. Press the OK button. You have now saved your UCS for future drawing and editing in this file.

4. Choose File ➤ SaveAs, and save your drawing as **first3d**.

5. Open the UCS Control dialog box once more and restore the WCS.

Now, whenever you open this drawing, you will have this UCS available for quick retrieval.

3D Modeling with Polylines

There is a wealth of tools available in AutoCAD for creating 3D shapes, but none is as versatile as *the polyline*. Polylines are used as the starting point for many of AutoCAD's 3D tools, and they can stand alone as a tool for simulating solid objects. Because they are like a compound object, that is, a single object made up of several segments (line segments and arcs), they reduce the number of objects you have to deal with at one time. This means they can help speed up the creation of your 3D models. Let's take a look at a simple application of this versatile object.

Drawing 3D Curves

The methods you've used so far are enough to let you create 3D models of buildings from floor plans. For example, just by extruding wall lines and using the View toolbar you can better visualize spaces in an office layout. But our world doesn't always fit in a neat rectilinear box. In the following exercise, you'll look at how you can introduce other shapes into your model. The following exercise will show you how you can add a curved polyline to a 3D model.

1. If you haven't done so already, restore the WCS to current status. Click on the *Named UCS* button in the UCS toolbar, then, at the UCS Control dialog box, click on WORLD, then Current, then OK.

2. Turn on the Snap mode by pressing the F9 function key. This will be an aid in drawing the polyline quickly for this exercise.

3. Click on the Polyline button on the Draw toolbar, then select the drawing's WCS origin (0,0,0) to serve as the first point of the polyline.

4. Draw the line segments shown in the bottom left of Figure 2.22a. When you have finished, press ↵.

5. Click on the Properties button on the Properties toolbar, then select the Quadratic radio button in the Modify Polyline dialog box.

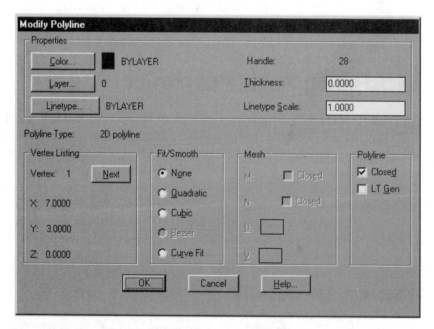

The Quadratic setting converts your polyline into an approximation of a Quadratic B-spline curve.

6. Enter the number **4** in the Thickness input box near the upper right corner of the dialog box, then click on OK. Your polyline becomes an extruded 3D curve (see Figure 2.22b).

7. Turn off the Snap mode by pressing the F9 key.

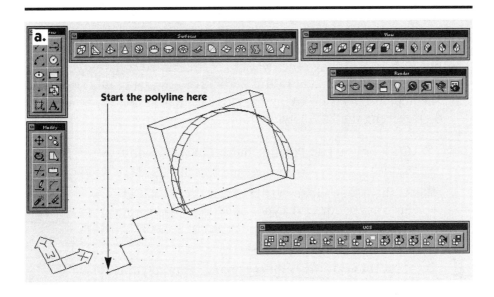

Start the polyline here

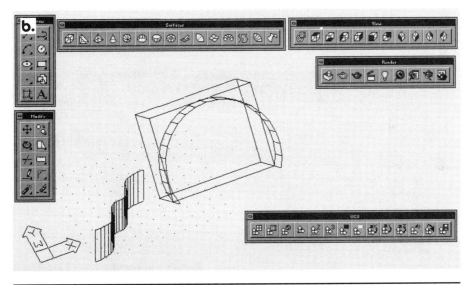

Figure 2.22: Creating a 3D polyline

Giving Polylines a "Solid" Appearance

You've seen how easy it is to create a curved surface by extruding a polyline. (There are many other ways to create curved surfaces; you'll get a chance to see them later in this book.) For now, let's build on our basic 3D modeling skills by giving the curved surface a solid appearance. You do this using the Edit Polyline tool:

1. Click on the Edit Polyline button in the Modify toolbar.

2. At the `Close/Join/Width/Edit vertex/Fit/ Spline/Decurve/Ltype gen/Undo/eXit <X>` prompt, enter **W**↵, then enter **.5**↵ to give the polyline a width of .5 units.

3. Press ↵ to exit the Pedit command (Edit Polyline).

4. Now choose Hide from the Render toolbar. Notice that the polyline appears as a solid shape (see Figure 2.23).

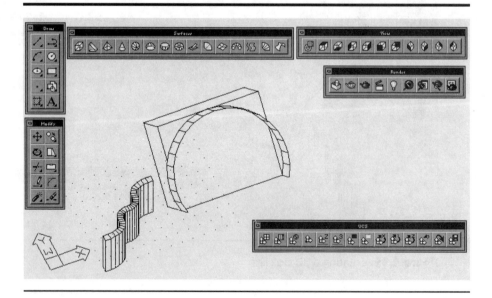

Figure 2.23: The box and polyline with hidden lines removed

Here you can see how an extruded polyline with width appears as a solid object when you use the Hide tool.

All objects, with the exception of 3D polylines (3dpoly), 3D faces, and regions, can be extruded in the way shown in these exercises. Another type of object, the 3D solid, cannot be extruded since such an object is already 3D objects.

The Polyline Paradox

You may have noticed that you've used polylines for two of the four 3D objects in this chapter (rectangles are actually polylines). You've seen firsthand how they can be quickly extruded and shaped. You'll also see, later in this book, how polylines are indispensable for creating other 3D shapes. But with all its power, the polyline is the one of the most constrained objects when it comes to 3D editing. First, their vertex points must be coplanar—other objects, like 3D faces, 3D meshes, lines, and 3D polylines are not limited this way. Second, the ability to edit polylines is dependent on the user coordinate system. Here is a listing of what you can and cannot do with polylines:

You Can...
copy, move, rotate, array, 3D array, scale, mirror, align, and explode polylines while in *any* UCS.

You Cannot...
change properties, edit vertices, or use the Edit Polyline tool (Pedit) unless you are in a UCS that is parallel to the plane defined by the polyline vertices.

Finally, you cannot snap to an apparent endpoint of a wide, extruded polyline like the curve you created in the earlier exercise. For example, if you were to use the Endpoint object snap option to select the endpoint of the curve, it would snap to its actual endpoint, not the apparent corner of the wide curve. Figure 2.24 illustrates this limitation.

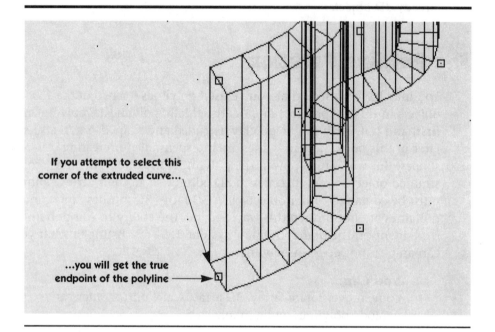

Figure 2.24: Using the Endpoint object snap to select the endpoint of a wide, extruded polyline results in selecting the actual endpoint of the polyline, not one of the apparent endpoints (the corners) of the face of the extruded curve.

Even with these limitations, polylines are essential to constructing your 3D models. This will become more apparent in later chapters.

◆ Summary

In this chapter, you used the main tools needed for working in 3D. If you are the adventurous type, you may want to experiment with what you now know. You'll be surprised at how much you can accomplish with your new-found knowledge. You'll also come up with more questions about 3D modeling, which will be answered in the following chapters.

In the next chapter, you will get a more detailed look at extruding objects. You'll also see how you can manipulate the properties of polylines to create a solid appearance.

Building Rectangular 3D Surfaces

Note *On the CD that is enclosed with this book I've provided a floor plan that you can work with as I present the examples in these next few chapters. Copy the* `Savoye.DWG` *file from the* `Sample` *directory of the CD onto your hard drive before you begin the tutorial section of this chapter.*

In the last chapter you saw how you can extrude an object in the Z axis to get a 3D image. In this chapter, you'll explore the Z axis in more detail by turning a typical 2D AutoCAD floor plan into a 3D model.

The tools and scenarios you will be exposed to in this chapter are fairly common to a majority of 3D modeling projects. In this chapter you'll also explore in more detail the different methods for viewing your model in 3D.

◆ Modeling a Classic Building

For this chapter I've created an AutoCAD floor plan of a building
I've long admired, Le Corbusier's Villa Savoye. Although my rendition
of the floor plan is by no means an exact copy of the original, through
the course of the next few chapters you will see how even with only
an approximate rendition you can create a very realistic 3D model.
My floor plan is shown in Figure 3.1.

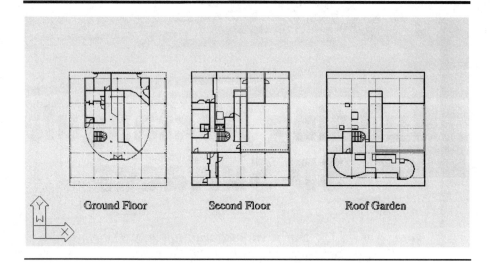

Figure 3.1: The 2D floor plan we'll be using in the next few chapters

Extruding Walls in the Z Direction

Imagine you are a member of an architectural team and you have been asked to model this project based on the latest floor plans. Let's see how you might go about doing this using some of the same tools you were introduced to in Chapter 2. You'll start by extruding the walls and columns of the floor plan.

1. Open the Savoye.DWG file (from the Sample directory on the enclosed CD). Notice there are three plans shown, one for each floor (see Figure 3.1). You'll first focus on the ground floor plan to the far left.

2. Choose View ➤ 3D Viewport Presets ➤ SW Isometric.

3. Click on the Zoom Window button in the toolbar at the top of the AutoCAD window.

4. Using the Zoom Window tool, place a window around the ground floor plan to get a better look (see Figure 3.2).

5. Click on the Layers pop-down list in the Properties toolbar, then turn off the Stair, Wall-head, Colgrid, Overhang, and Ramp layers. (Do this by clicking on the "face" icon in the list so the eyes of the icon appear closed.)

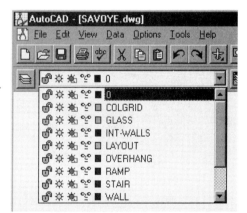

6. Click anywhere in the drawing area to close the pop-down list and return to the drawing. Your drawing should now look like Figure 3.3.

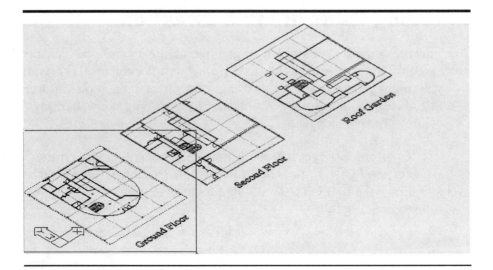

Figure 3.2: Using the Zoom Window tool in a SW Isometric view, zoom to the window indicated here.

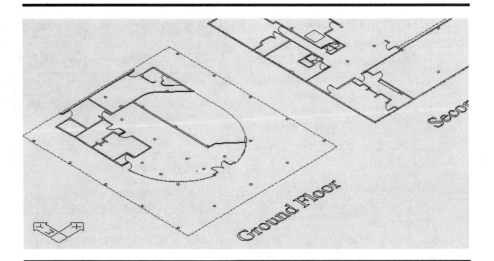

Figure 3.3: Your drawing after turning off the Stair, Wall-head, Colgrid, Overhang, and Ramp layers

You've now turned off all the layers related to parts of the plan that you do not want to extrude:

◆ The stairs and ramps are a bit more complex than the walls, so we will model them separately later.

◆ On the Wall-head layer (the portion of the wall above the door), if you were to extrude the door headers to the full height of the walls, they would fill in the doorways with solid walls, so they are also turned off. (You'll add the door headers later.)

You now have the walls and columns remaining, as well as the vertical mullions of the hall. Let's extrude these components to get a better 3D view of the ground floor.

1. Center the view of the ground floor using the the window's scroll bars.

2. Click on the Properties button in the Properties toolbar, then type **WP.**↵ to use the Window Polygon method for selecting objects.

3. Enclose the ground floor with the window polygon as indicated in Figure 3.4. When you've finished selecting points for the polygon window, press ↵, then press ↵ again to end your selection. The Change Properties dialog box appears.

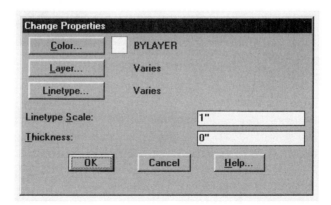

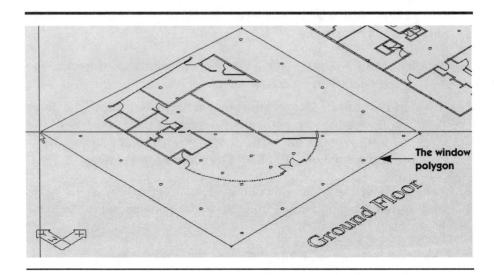

Figure 3.4: The area to select using the Window Polygon selection option

4. In the Thickness input box near the bottom of the dialog box, enter **9'6"**, then click on OK. The walls and columns will extrude nine and a half feet into the Z axis.

5. Use the scroll bars to center your view.

6. Click on the Hide button in the Render toolbar to view your drawing with the hidden lines removed. Your drawing should look like Figure 3.5.

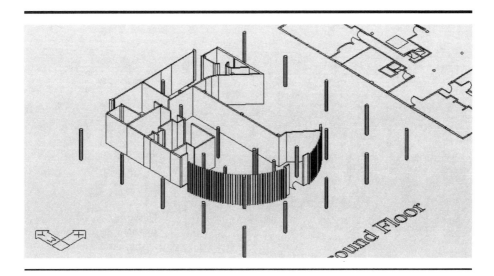

Figure 3.5: The ground floor plan in 3D with hidden lines removed

Adding Window Mullions with Polylines

> **Note** *As you work in 3D you'll begin to notice that it's easy to produce quick massing. The time-consuming part is in developing the details. Knowing the shortcuts to producing model detail can save you lots of time.*

In a very short time, you've built nearly all of the entire ground floor in 3D, just by changing the thickness property of the objects that make up the floor plan. However, you need to attend to a few details. First, let's add some horizontal mullions to the curved hall window. The vertical mullions are already there since they were extruded along with the walls and columns. To create the horizontal mullions, you'll borrow one of the other components in the drawing.

1. Click on the Zoom Window button in the Standard toolbar and zoom to the window indicated in Figure 3.6 to enlarge the view of the curved hall window.

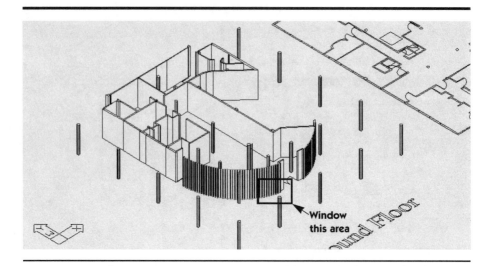

Figure 3.6: Selecting a Zoom Window to enlarge the ground floor window

2. If you need to, adjust your view using the Pan Point button in the Standard toolbar so it matches the view shown in Figure 3.7.

3. Click and hold the Copy button in the Modify toolbar so the fly-out menu appears, then click on the Offset button. This sets AutoCAD up to create a copy of

the curved hall window at a certain distance away from the original.

4. At the Offset distance or Through <0'-0">: prompt, enter **1↵** for a 1-inch offset.

5. At the Select object to offset prompt, click on the cyan-colored line, as shown in Figure 3.7a. This line represents the glass of the window.

6. At the Side to offset prompt, pick a point to the far right of
the view, as shown in Figure 3.7b, then press ↵ to exit the Offset
command.

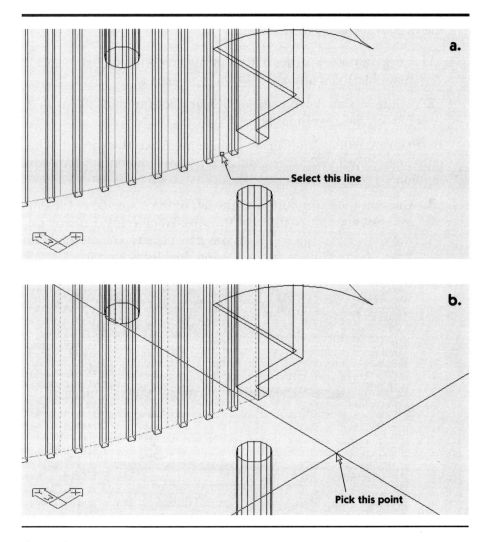

Figure 3.7: Using Offset to create a horizontal mullion

Since you used the Offset command, you know you have an object that conforms to the curve of the glass. I constructed the original 2D drawing with this in mind. Next, you will want to change the height and width of the new object to resemble a horizontal window mullion. First, you will modify its Z-axis thickness to that of a typical window mullion, then you will change its layer.

1. Click on the Properties button in the Properties toolbar, select the new object you just created, and then press ↵.

2. In the Modify Polyline dialog box, replace the value 9'6" with **2** in the Thickness input box.

Here you are telling AutoCAD to change the Z-axis thickness (the height) of the new object to 2 inches, which is a typical dimension for a window mullion.

3. Click on the Layer button to the left of the dialog box. A listing of layers appears. Notice that the selected object is currently on the Glass layer. You will want this new object to be on the Mullion layer. Locate Mullion in the list and double-click on it.

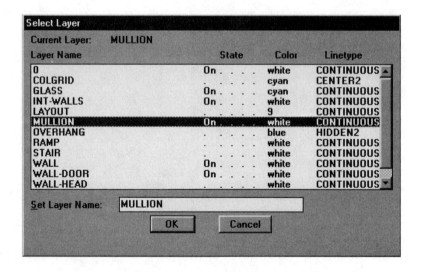

4. At this point you are back at the Modify Polyline dialog box. Notice the label next to the Layer button indicates the new layer for your object. Click OK. The dialog box closes and you see the new mullion (see Figure 3.8).

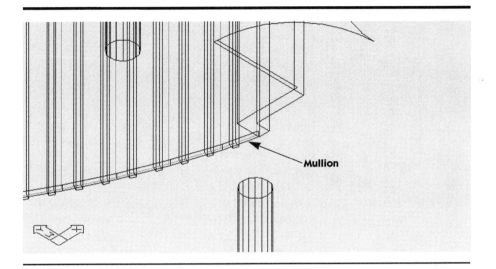

Figure 3.8: The mullion in its new shape after adjusting its layer and Z-axis thickness

In this exercise, you saw that you can adjust the thickness of an object downward from a previously set height. As you can see, then, thickness values are not set in stone. Now the mullion has the right height, but because it has no width, it appears as a ribbon. It needs to be given a width so it will appear as a solid bar. Follow these steps to do that.

1. Click on the Edit Polyline button in the Modify toolbar.

2. At the `Close/Join/Width/Edit vertex/Fit/Spline/Decurve/Ltype gen/Undo/eXit <X>:` prompt, enter **W**↵ for the Width option. This option lets you modify the width of a polyline.

3. At the `Enter new width for all segments:` prompt, enter **2.**↵ to give the mullion a width of 2 inches.

4. Press ↵ to exit the Polyline Edit (Pedit) command. Your drawing will look like Figure 3.9

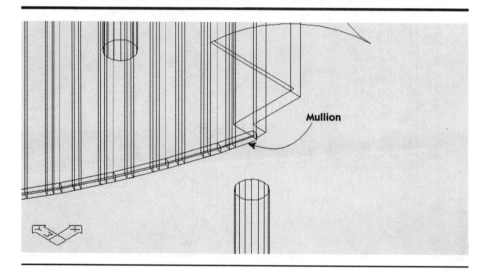

Figure 3.9: The finished mullion

In Chapter 2, I mentioned that the polyline is one of the most useful AutoCAD objects when creating 3D models. In the previous two exercises, you created a mullion by using Offset to create a copy of an existing polyline and adjusting the copy's width and thickness to fit the required size. This demonstrates how polylines can be used to quickly duplicate complex shapes, which can then be converted to 3D shapes that have a solid appearance. Next, you'll make two more copies of the new mullion to add the middle and top edge of the window frame.

1. Change your view to include more of the window by clicking on the Zoom Out button on the Standard toolbar.

2. Click on the Copy button in the Modify toolbar.

3. Click on the new mullion and press ↵ to finish your selection.

4. At the `Base point or displacement:` prompt, enter **0,0**. (Actually, you can simply click on any point in the drawing area instead.)

5. At the `Second point of displacement:` prompt, enter **@0,0,3'**↵ to place a copy of the mullion three feet into the Z axis (a vertical direction).

6. Repeat steps 1 through 4, then at the `Second point of displacement:` prompt, enter **@0,0,9'4"**↵. This places a copy at the top of the window.

7. Click on the Hide button on the Render toolbar to get a better look at your window (see Figure 3.10).

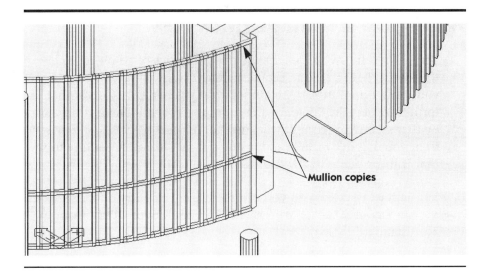

Figure 3.10: The window with the new horizontal mullions

For practice, create the horizontal mullions for the window on the other side of the doorway. Use the same procedures described in the previous exercises.

Careful Layering Can Save Time

You may notice as you work through these tutorials that *layering* plays an important role in helping you work with 3D models. Layers help you distinguish between the different materials and components of the model. As the model becomes more complicated, layers can help you filter out only the objects you want to work on. In later chapters, you will discover that basing your layers on the different *materials* of your project can help you create a more realistic rendering.

Setting Up a Default Thickness

You've seen how you can change the properties of an object to give it a thickness, that is, a dimension ("height") along the Z axis. If you prefer, you can set up AutoCAD to automatically generate objects with a uniform thickness. In the following example, you will draw a door header by first setting the default thickness for all new objects to a new setting, then you will draw the header using a standard AutoCAD line to see that it turns out with a thickness automatically.

1. Adjust your view so you can see the entire entry door as shown in Figure 3.11. You can use the Pan and Zoom Out buttons in the Standard toolbar for this.

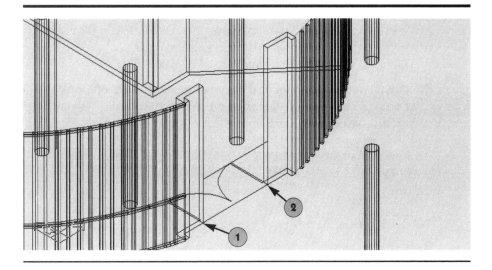

Figure 3.11: By drawing from point 1 to point 2 you'll create a three-foot-thick object.

2. Click on the Object Creation button on the Properties toolbar. The Object Creation dialog box appears.

Notice that you have options in this dialog box for specifying Linetype Scale, Elevation, and Thickness. The Elevation setting refers to the baseline elevation in the Z axis.

3. Enter **3'** in the Thickness input box, then click on OK. You've just set the default thickness for new objects to 3 feet. From now on, every object you draw (with the exception of 3D faces, 3D polylines, and splines) will have a thickness of 3 feet.

4. Now use the Line tool and draw a line across the opening of the doorway as shown in Figure 3.11. Use the Endpoint Osnap to place the line accurately. The line will have a thickness of 3 feet.

This new line will be the header over the doorway once you move it up to the top of the doorway. So with no further ado, let's move it into position.

1. Click on the new line to expose its grips.

2. Click on the upper left grip as shown in Figure 3.12a, then press ⏎ or the spacebar to switch to Move mode. Your command prompt should show ∗∗MOVE∗∗ to indicate that you are in the Move mode.

3. Make sure the Snap mode is off, then use the Endpoint Osnap override and select the top corner of the doorway as indicated in Figure 3.12b. Your header moves into its proper place.

4. With the grips still active, click on the upper left grip of the line again, then press ⏎ or the spacebar to get into the Move mode again.

5. Enter **C**⏎ to prepare to make a copy, then click on the upper corner of the door opening just behind the last corner you picked (see Figure 3.12c). Now you've got both sides (front and back) of the door header in place.

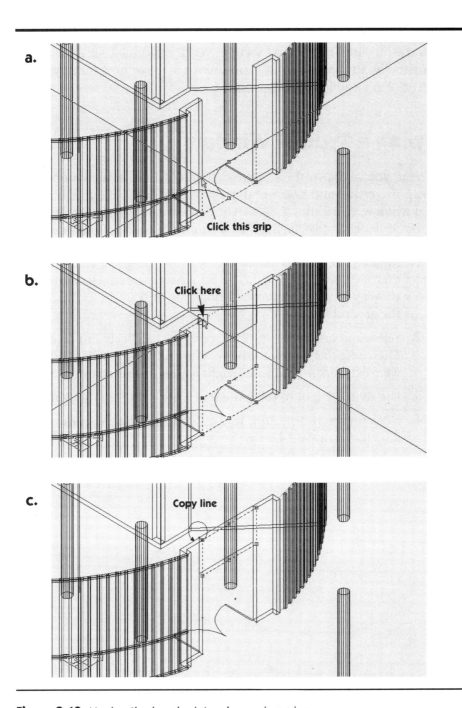

a.

Click this grip

b.

Click here

c.

Copy line

Figure 3.12: Moving the header into place using grips

There are several other door and window headers that need to be added to the drawing. In the next section, you'll continue to use the line drawing tool with the default thickness set to 3' to see how quickly 3D components can be added to a drawing.

Drawing a Typical Window

So far, you've drawn the storefront-style window on the ground floor, with its vertical and horizontal mullions. But what about a more typical window, which has a sill height that is higher than floor level? The ground floor has two such windows on the left side of your current view.

1. Adjust your view to match Figure 3.13a using the Pan button on the Standard toolbar. (The aerial view window in Figure 3.13a shows you where your view should be in relation to the rest of the ground floor plan.)

2. Select and erase the four wall sections as indicated in Figure 3.13b. These sections represent the window sills of the two windows, and were extruded to full wall height earlier in this chapter.

3. Use the Line tool to draw the four lines indicated in Figure 3.13c.

4. Click on the Hide button in the Render toolbar. Your drawing will look like Figure 3.14.

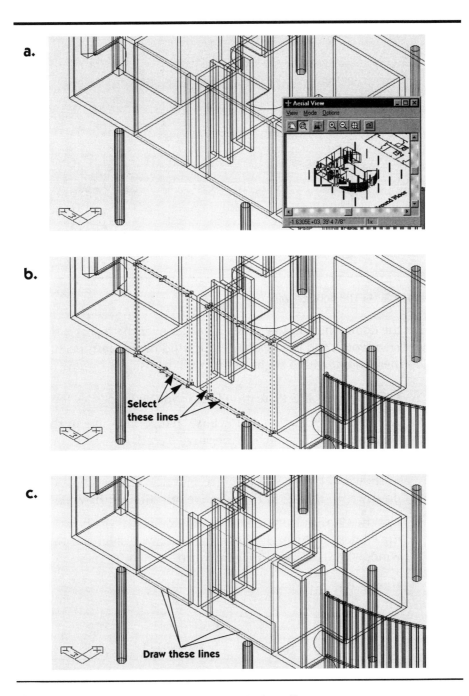

Figure 3.13: Adjusting the height of the window sill

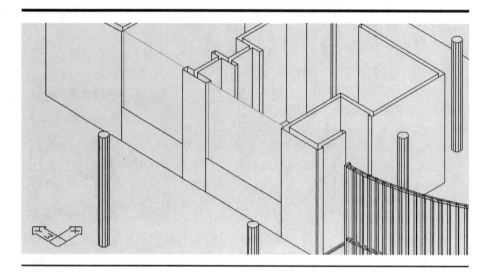

Figure 3.14: The finished window

Like the doors, the window needs a header over the top of it. In these next steps you'll add the header to the window in a fashion similar to the door header, but with a slight twist: you'll be using a *negative thickness*.

1. Click on the Object Creation button in the Properties toolbar.

2. At the Object Creation dialog box, change the value in the Thickness input box to **–3'** (negative 3 feet).

3. Click OK, then draw lines across the very top of the two windows as shown in Figure 3.15a. Notice that now the header is drawn downward—that is, in the negative direction of the Z axis.

4. Use the Copy button on the Modify toolbar or the object grips to draw lines for the back side of the window header and the other window by as shown in Figure 3.15b.

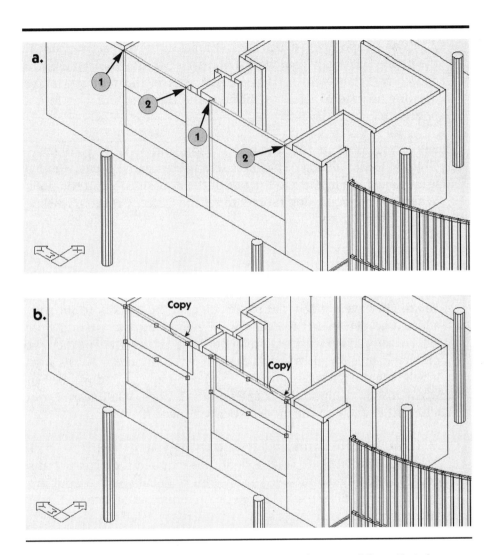

Figure 3.15: Adding headers over the window on the ground floor. First draw the lines from point 1 to point 2 as shown (two lines), then copy the lines to form the backs of the headers.

As you can see from this example, you are not limited to the positive Z axis when specifying a Thickness. In fact, using a negative value for the header will make your work a bit easier because you can use this approach to draw your headers across the *top* of the door or window opening (instead of across the bottom and then moving it up into position).

Before you continue with the next section, and while you still have the Object Creation dialog's Thickness setting at negative 3 feet, you may want to add the headers to the rest of the door opening in the floor plan. When you are done, don't forget to set the Object Creation/Thickness setting back to zero.

Detail vs. Speed

You might have noticed that while you changed the sill height and added a header, we left the glass at full height and did not add a proper sill. For a lot of 3D work, you may not have to worry about such types of detail. Since the glass in this drawing is surrounded by walls anyway, it will be hidden in places where it shouldn't appear and will be exposed where it should appear. In Chapter 6 of this book, you'll learn how to add further detail to the model when you need it.

Much of this book is oriented toward giving you the ability to quickly generate 3D models. To some extent, this required me to leave out some detail in the original model. The amount of detail you leave out in your own drawings, of course, will depend on a number of factors. If you are a kitchen designer, you may want to show more detail than, say, someone designing the shell of a major entertainment complex. Or you may leave out a lot of detail if your model is intended for study only, or for a quick rendering that is intended to convey an impression of your design, rather than a detailed look.

The ability to determine the amount of detail you need for a 3D model will come with experience. These initial exercises will give you some first-hand experience regarding what you can get with a minimum amount of detail.

What Other Options Do I Have?

I've shown you one way to draw windows in a building, but you have other options which may be more preferable. I'm showing you the extrusion method here as an introduction to 3D methods, but later you will learn another way of creating walls using *solid modeling*. Solid modeling can help improve the way you create and edit openings in walls.

◆ Doing a Quick Rendering

Here's the situation: Your boss is leaning over your shoulder and sees the great job you've done on your 3D model. He decides he wants a color rendering. By this afternoon, to show to the clients, who happen to be in town. He'd also like the view to be from a bit higher and slightly to the front. ("You can just press a button, can't you?" he adds.)

Getting the Isometric View You Want

Let's begin by adjusting your view of the overall 3D floor plan. In Chapter 1, you saw how you can use the Viewpoint Presets dialog box to "fine-tune" your view. You'll use it again here.

1. Choose View ➤ 3D Viewpoint ➤ Rotate. The Viewpoint Presets dialog box appears.

2. In the graphic on the left side of the dialog box, click on the first location indicated in Figure 3.16. The input box just below the dial changes to a value of approximately 250. This indicates your new viewpoint is from a location approximately 250 degrees from the 0-degree direction.

3. In the graphic on the right side of the dialog box, click on the second location indicated in Figure 3.16. The input box just below the dial changes to a value of approximately 60. This indicates a view angle that is 60 degrees from the *ground plane* of the model.

4. Click on OK. You will get an overall view of your drawing, including the other two floor plans.

5. Zoom into the ground floor plan so it looks something like Figure 3.17.

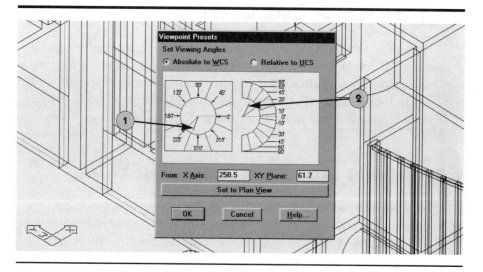

Figure 3.16: Selecting the Viewpoint Preset settings for a higher vantage point

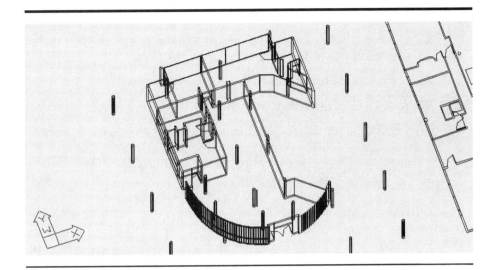

Figure 3.17: The new view of the Ground floor plan

Now you can see the layout of the floor a bit better. You could have entered a value in the input boxes of the Viewpoint Presets dialog box, instead of picking a point from its graphics. Typing the values into the input boxes lets you be more precise about your viewpoint location, though in general you needn't be all that exact.

Exporting Your View to Other Applications

To satisfy your boss's wish, next you will want to quickly render this view. Here is where I will depart from the typical tutorial on 3D rendering and offer an alternative. AutoCAD offers a renderer and a shader that provide a shaded view of 3D models, but instead, you'll use a paint program to add color and notes. First, you will copy a 3D image to the Windows Clipboard, then you'll import the image into Adobe Photoshop. (While I use the example of Adobe Photoshop here, you can use virtually any paint or photo prep software you choose.)

1. Click on the Hide button in the Render toolbar.

2. Choose Edit ➤ Copy View. You now have a copy of your current view in the Windows Clipboard.

3. Start Adobe Photoshop then choose File ➤ New.

4. At the New File dialog box, click OK.

5. Choose Edit ➤ Paste. The image of the 3D Floor plan appears.

As you've just seen, you can easily move an image from AutoCAD to another graphics program within Windows.

At this point, let's save this file in Photoshop and continue with our AutoCAD session. Or if you prefer, go to Chapter 13 to see how you might jazz up this figure for a presentation. (If you decide to skip the rest of this chapter in favor of Chapter 13, be sure you come back to this point and resume the next few exercises.)

◈ Punching Holes in the Second Floor

Let's move on to the second floor. Most of the walls and doors in the second floor can be extruded the same way you extruded the ground floor walls. You can also create the exterior windows in the same way you created the windows in the ground floor.

There is one operation involving the second floor that will require more detailed instruction: You will need to know how to cut holes in the floor to accommodate the stairway and ramp. By creating the floor openings first, you will also avoid the visual clutter that is created by extruded walls.

To create a floor surface with openings, you will need to know how to use *regions*. Regions are AutoCAD objects that have the property of being opaque, flat surfaces. They can be formed into virtually any two-dimensional shape. Regions can be also be joined or subtracted from each other using what are called *Boolean* operations. Don't let the term scare you—Boolean operations in AutoCAD can be considered as simple subtractions or additions to shapes. It's the subtractions that we'll be using in an exercise coming up shortly, in order to create holes.

So before you start to extrude the walls in the second floor, try the following exercises to learn how to accommodate floor openings.

Defining the Floor Plane and Floor Openings

To create a region, you must first create a closed polyline. So the first step in creating a floor with openings is to draw the outline of the entire floor and the outline of the openings. In this exercise, you will use the second-floor plan.

1. Set up your view so it looks like Figure 3.18.

2. Create a layer called **Floor** and make this the current layer.

3. Click on the Polyline button in the Draw toolbar, then click on the four inside corners of the floor plan as shown in Figure 3.18.

4. Once you've selected the last corner, type **C⏎** to close the polyline.

5. Turn the Stair and Ramp layers on.

6. Zoom into the stair area enough so that you can easily select points defining its perimeter.

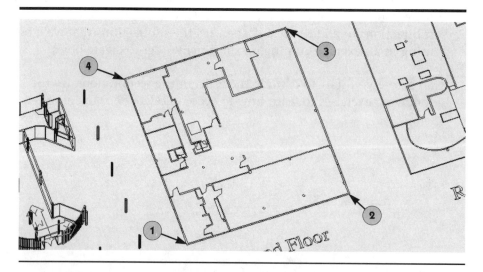

Figure 3.18 Select these points to define the outline of the overall floor area.

7. Start the Polyline command again and outline the stairway, as shown in Figure 3.19a. If you prefer, you may want to draw the linear portions of the outline first, then draw the arc and join it to the rest of the polyline outline.

8. Finally, adjust your view so you can see the ramp behind the stairs and use a polyline to outline it (see Figure 3.19b). Just as with the overall floor area, you can start the Polyline command, click on the four corners of the ramp area, then press **C↵** to close the area.

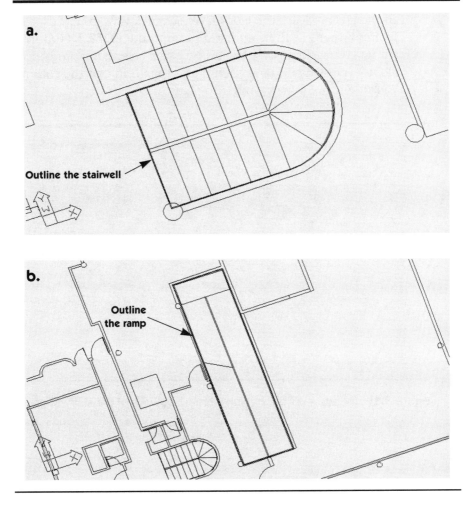

Figure 3.19: Draw the outline of the stairway and ramp.

Converting the Polyline Outlines into Surfaces

Now you've got outlines of both the overall floor area and the floor openings. The next step is to convert these outlines into regions. You can then subtract ("punch out," in my earlier phrase) the openings' shapes from the overall floor shape using the Subtract tool; one of three Boolean tools available in the Modify menu.

1. Zoom out to get an overall view of the second floor, then turn off all the layers except the Floor layer. A quick way to do this is by typing **Layer**↵ at the command prompt, then **Off**↵*****↵ to turn off all the layers, then type **On**↵**Floor**↵ (the layer name) to turn the Floor layer on again (and then press ↵ again to exit the command). You should get a view similar to Figure 3.20.

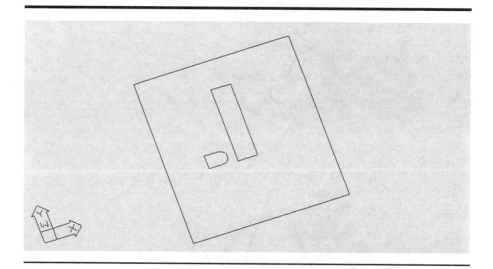

Figure 3.20: The second floor outline with the outlines of the stairway and ramp

2. Click and hold the Polygon button in the Draw toolbar to open the flyout, then click on the Region button.

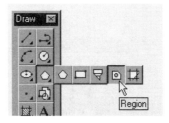

3. At the `Select objects` prompt, select all three polyline outlines you've just drawn (second floor, stairwell, and ramp), then press ↵ to finish your selection.

You've just turned the polylines into regions. The next step is to subtract the stair and ramp region from the overall floor region.

1. Click and hold the Explode button in the Modify menu so the flyout appears.

2. Select the button labeled Subtract.

3. At the `Select solids and regions to subtract from` prompt, click on the overall floor region then press ↵.

4. At the `Select solids and regions to subtract` prompt, select the stair and ramp regions and press ↵. Although it appears that nothing has happened, you have just created a horizontal surface with two holes in it.

To see the result of your work, turn on all the layers, then place a copy of the floor region you just created over the top of the ground floor plan.

1. First zoom out so you can see both the ground floor plan and the second floor together in one view, as shown in Figure 3.21a.

2. Click on the Copy button in the Modify toolbar, then select the floor region. (You can click anywhere on the ramp or stair opening.)

3. Use the Center Osnap override and select the columns shown in Figure 3.21a as reference points for the Copy operation.

4. Click on the Hide button in the Render toolbar. The ground floor plan will appear as shown in Figure 3.21b.

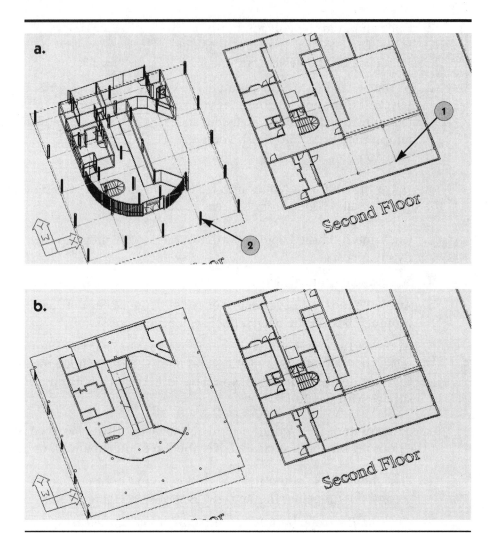

Figure 3.21: (a) Copy from the center of the first column indicated to the center of the second one to see (b), the ground floor plan with the second floor region placed above it.

The exercise you've just finished not only illustrates how you can create complex surfaces using polylines, it also shows that you can easily move or copy objects in 3D space while in an isometric view.

While I used a floor plan as an example of a surface with holes, you can use regions to create any surface you desire. And, as you have seen, you can cut out openings in a region surface using polylines or simple circles converted into regions. A mechanical designer, for example, can quickly draw a surface with holes punched out, simply by creating the outline of the surface and the holes. You could also draw building elevations with window cut-outs using regions.

◆ Building the Rooftop Garden

You now have all the tools and skills needed to construct the rooftop. Since you already have the stairway and ramp cut out for the second floor, you can make a copy of it for the roof area.

1. Adjust your view so you can see both the second floor and the roof plan, then copy the region you created earlier for the second floor over to the roof plan. You can use the columns shown in Figure 3.22 to position the region exactly.

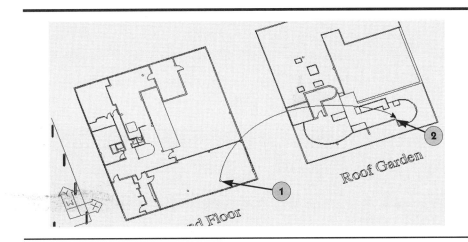

Figure 3.22: Copy the floor region of the second floor from point 1 to the roof plan at point 2.

2. Zoom into the roof plan, then, using a polyline, outline the opening in the roof for the second floor's courtyard area, as shown in Figure 3.23.

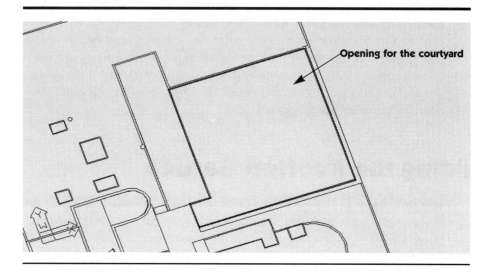

Opening for the courtyard

Figure 3.23: Using a polyline, draw the outline of the opening for the second floor courtyard.

3. Use the Region command to convert the outline into a region.

4. Subtract the new region from the copy of the second floor region.

5. Turn off all the layers except for Wall.

6. Extrude the walls to a height of 8' 6".

7. Turn the Planter layer on, and extrude the planters to a height of 18".

8. Click on the Hide button in the Render toolbar to get a better look at your model (see Figure 3.24).

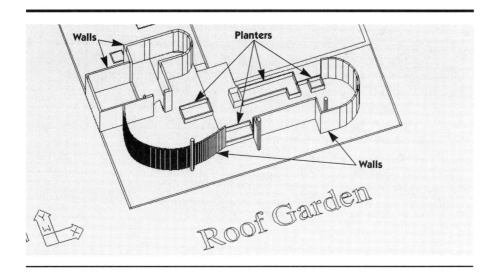

Figure 3.24: Extrude the walls and planters of the roof plan.

You may be wondering why we haven't completed the second floor. The second floor presents some opportunities to show you how to use solid modeling to model in 3D, so I've postponed some of the second floor construction for a later chapter. I'll finish up this chapter with a look at surface intersections in 3D.

A Line Is an Intersection of Two Planes, Except When...

You might notice that the tops of the walls of the ground floor plan show through the floor region. Whenever an object *just* touches a 3D surface, like the second floor region, the outline of the object appears on the surface. If on the other hand, the walls "poke through" the plane of the region, you will not see the intersection of the two surfaces outlined. See Figure 3.25 on the next page for an example illustrating the difference between walls "just meeting" the second floor and walls "poking through" the second floor from the first floor. If you plan to export your drawing to 3D Studio, this is not a problem. On the other hand, if you intend to use a 2D paint or photo-retouching program, the lack of a line showing the intersection of planes can cause problems— for instance, you might mistakenly fill or render both the floor and the walls with the same color or surface material. There are, however, fixes and other alternatives that can help you achieve your goals quickly without having to be too fussy with your modeling.

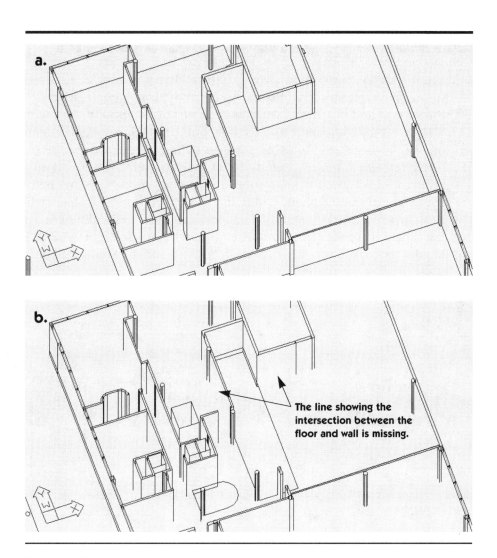

The line showing the intersection between the floor and wall is missing.

Figure 3.25: A comparison of vertical surfaces "just meeting" a horizontal surface (top) and vertical surfaces "poking through" the same surface (bottom)

◆ Understanding Surface Intersections

You might notice that when you use the Hide command, some of the surface intersections do not show up correctly. For example, where the vertical and horizontal window mullions of the ground floor window intersect, you expect to see a line, but AutoCAD does not show one (see Figure 3.26). AutoCAD's hide function is designed for speed, not necessarily accuracy, so it does not indicate surface intersections properly. This is usually not a problem for study models. As an alternative, you can use the Shade command to view your model. Shade will give each surface a different color so you can more easily differentiate the different surface planes and their intersections (see Figure 3.27). The Render tool, the optional AutoVision add-on, and 3D Studio will also show intersections properly.

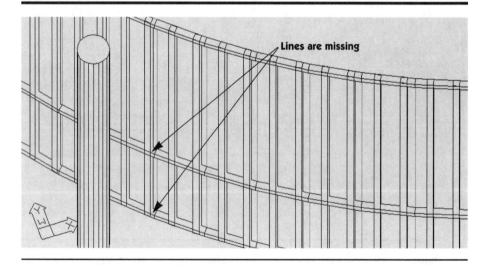

Figure 3.26: A hidden line view of the window mullions. Notice that a line indicating the intersection of two surfaces is missing.

Figure 3.27: A shaded view of the window mullions helps you to visualize the different planes when the intersection lines are missing.

If, however, you intend to plot a hidden-line 3D view for a *presentation* or for a *set of drawings*, you have two options:

◆ You can draw your objects so that they always begin and end at the point of intersection, as shown in Figure 3.28. This can be an appropriate method for simple 3D models.

◆ Or you can convert the 3D hidden-line view into a 2D line drawing. You can then add any missing lines to the 2D image.

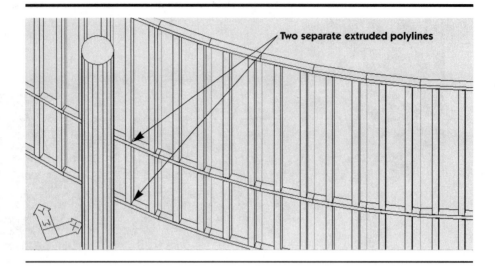

Figure 3.28: To avoid the missing line, you can construct the mullion polyline so that it begins and ends at an intersection (i.e., so it "meets" the horizontal mullion instead of continuing through it).

This method gives you a bit more control over the final result, and although it is not the perfect solution, it does offer other benefits:

◆ You can make minor changes to your image more easily.

◆ Notes can be added easily by anyone familiar with 2D AutoCAD.

◆ The 3D image can be easily combined with 2D schematic drawings for a "presentation" set of drawings.

There are two methods for converting 3D views into 2D drawings. One is to use AutoCAD's PostScript conversion commands: Psout and Psin. Basically, you "plot" your drawing as a PostScript file using the Psout command; then, in a new file, import that PostScript file. The result is a 2D drawing of your 3D view. There are two things you must do, however, to make this process work. First, you must create your view from Paper Space. Create a Viewport using the Mview command and make sure the viewport has its Hideplot setting turned on. Second, when the Psout command prompts you for a drawing size, make it as large as possible. I suggest a size of 60 × 120. This improves the resolution of your output file, making circles and arcs smoother.

The second method is to plot your drawing as a DXB file and then import the DXB plot file into a new drawing. For this method, you must add the AutoCAD ADI plotter driver to your plotter configuration. Appendix A describes how this is done. Once you've set up an ADI plotter, you can plot your drawing in the normal way, with hidden lines removed. Make sure you select the ADI plotter at the Plot Configuration dialog box and have the *Plot to file* checkbox checked.

After you've created your plot file, use the DXBin command to import it into a new drawing. You can also use the File ➤ Import option and select *.dxb for the type of file to import. Once it has been imported, you may want to scale the drawing to an appropriate size.

◆ Summary

Your model is nearly complete, save for the stairs and ramp. These two items will require more-detailed instruction. In the next chapter, you will draw the ramp and stairway, and in doing so, you'll learn how to create shapes that aren't restricted to rectangular forms. You'll also learn how the user coordinate system can be a powerful aid in constructing your model.

Understanding Surfaces and the User Coordinate System

In the last chapter, using some of the simpler 3D tools, you were able to generate a fairly credible model of the ground floor of the Villa Savoye. But everything was based on rectangular forms. In this chapter, you'll learn how to create non-rectangular forms in 3D. To do this, you'll need to understand the *User Coordinate System* (UCS) and AutoCAD's *surface modeling tools*.

To begin this chapter, you'll start with the ramp. While it is still fairly rectangular, you will encounter triangular forms that you cannot easily create using the extrusion method you used in Chapter 3. You'll also use polylines again for windows and mullions. Then you'll move on to a variety of 3D objects that demonstrate different uses for the UCS.

◆ Using 3D Faces to Draw a Ramp

The ramp in Villa Savoye rises through the center of the plan, providing a visual focus. It's a simple geometric form, and you can construct it in a variety of ways in AutoCAD. The methods I'll show you in the following exercise are mainly intended to demonstrate some tools we haven't used yet; they do not represent the only way to construct the ramp.

I've provided a 2D view of the ramp in the sample files on the accompanying CD. You can either use the sample file or construct your own as you follow the steps.

1. Open the Ramp.DWG file from the disk or CD, or create your own Ramp.DWG file with the dimensions shown in Figure 4.1.

2. Choose View ➤ 3D Viewpoint Presets ➤ SE Isometric. (Or enter **Viewpoint**↵ and then **1,–1,1** at the command prompt.)

3. Use the Zoom and Pan commands to set up your view to look like Figure 4.2.

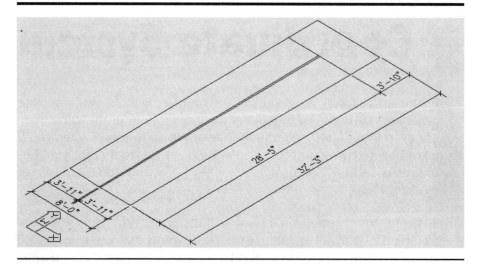

Figure 4.1: The plan of the Villa Savoye ramp

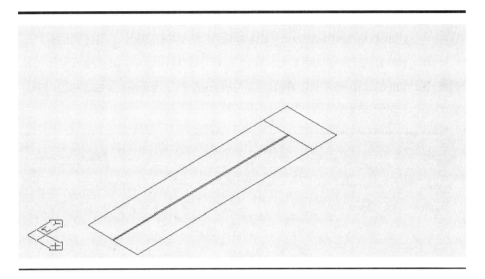

Figure 4.2: An isometric view of the ramp plan

Creating a Layout for the Ramp

Note   To construct the ramp, you cannot extrude objects the way you did for the walls in earlier chapters. When objects are extruded, they form a rect-tangular profile. Since ramps are triangular when viewed from the side, they cannot be simply extruded. You cannot use the 2D plan directly to construct your ramp. Instead, you'll use the ramp plan as a layout tool. The first step is to make copies of the ramp plan at key Z-axis locations that will enable you to construct the ramp. Also, you'll need to know the floor-to-floor dis-tance to construct the ramp accurately—for this tutorial, we'll use a distance of 11 feet. This means that the ramp will rise to 5 feet 6 inches at the land-ing, then rise another 5 feet 6 inches to the next floor.

1. Choose the Copy button from the Modify toolbar, then select the entire ramp.

Press ↵ to finish your selection.

2. At the Base point: prompt, enter **M**↵ to tell AutoCAD that you want to make multiple copies, then pick any point in the drawing area.

3. At the To point: prompt, enter @ **0,0,5'6**↵. This tells AutoCAD that you want to copy the plan 5 feet 6 inches in the Z axis.

4. Next, enter **@0,0,11'**↵. You'll see another copy above the last one.

5. Press ↵ to exit the Copy command. Your view should look like Figure 4.3.

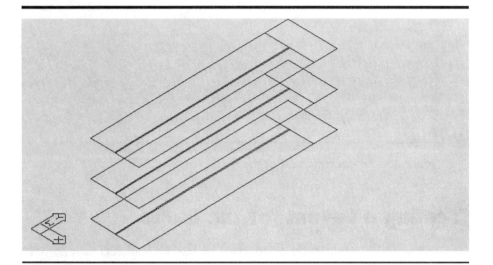

Figure 4.3: The ramp plan copied twice in the Z axis

Since you'll only want to use the 2D ramp plan as a layout tool, you'll want to *lock* the 2D ramp layer so you don't accidentally make changes to it.

1. Click on the Layer drop-down list in the Properties toolbar.

2. Click on the lock icon associated with the Ramp layer (currently unlocked) so the lock changes to look like it is closed. Click on layer 0 in the list to make this the current layer, then click on the drawing area to return to your drawing.

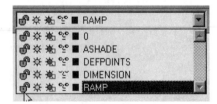

Creating an Inclined Surface with 3D Faces

Now you're ready to start construction of the 3D ramp. You'll start by constructing the ramp surfaces using a 3D face.

1. If the Surfaces toolbar is not already open, open it by choosing Tools ➤ Toolbars ➤ Surfaces.

2. Click on the 3D Face button from the Surfaces toolbar. Alternatively, you can enter **3Dface**↵ at the command prompt.

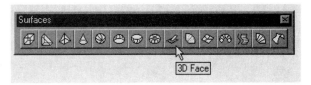

Note *The order in which you select the four points in steps 2 and 3 does not really matter. The point is that you must pick points in a single clockwise or counterclockwise sequence; otherwise you will end up with a "bow tie" shape for a 3D face.*

At the `First point:` prompt, use the Endpoint Osnap to select the first point indicated in Figure 4.4a.

3. At the appropriate prompts, select the next three points in the order indicated in Figure 4.4a. When you have finished, press ↵ to exit the 3D Face command. You have just drawn the top surface of one of the ramps.

4. Click on the Hide button on the Render toolbar to make the 3D face a little more apparent— although there will still be a line visible above the ramp, Hide will hide the lines behind the ramp (Figure 4.4b).

5. Use the 3D Face command again to draw the second run of the ramp on the other side of the landing, as shown in Figure 4.5. Using the Endpoint Osnap, select the corners of the 3D face in the order indicated in Figure 4.5.

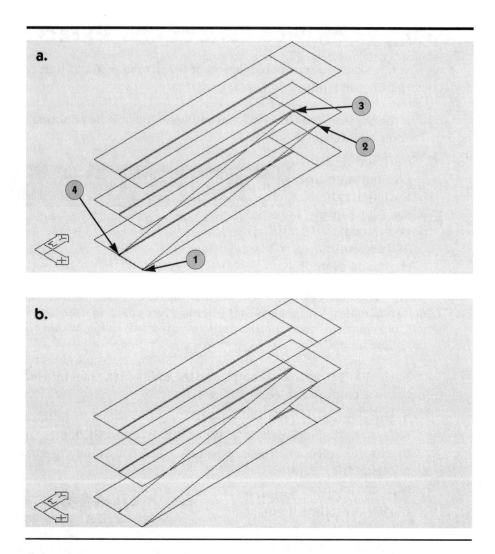

Figure 4.4: Drawing a 3D face for the top surface of the lower ramp

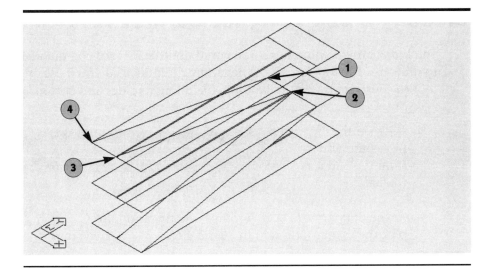

Figure 4.5: Drawing the upper ramp

You may have noticed that in step 4 you have the option to continue to select points while in the 3D Face command. The 3D Face command constructs 3D surfaces that are defined by four points. After one face is created, you have the option of adding more adjoining 3D faces to your drawing to create a more complex surface. While it's good to be aware of this feature, in general it's better to use the Region command in conjunction with polylines to create complex 3D surfaces. Regions let you form complex shapes easily by outlining them with polylines. You can even include curves in regions (something difficult if not impossible to do with 3D faces).

Creating a Box Using the Surface Toolbar

You'll draw the landing next. You could use the 3D Face command again to draw just the top surface of the landing, but instead you'll use another tool to construct the entire landing, including its sides and bottom.

1. Click on the Box command from the Surfaces toolbar.

At the `Corner of box:` prompt, use the Endpoint Osnap and pick the corner indicated in Figure 4.6a.

2. At the `Length and Cube/<Width>` prompts, use the Endpoint Osnap and select the corners indicated in Figure 4.6b.

3. At the `Height` prompt, enter **18** to make the landing 18 inches thick. (Actually, I should have you enter **–18** instead, to give it a depth instead of a height, but I want to use this example to show you some additional techniques.)

4. Finally, at the `Rotation angle about the Z axis` prompt, enter **0** or position the cursor to the right of the pivot point and, with the Orthor mode on, pick a point so the landing is oriented as shown in Figure 4.6c.

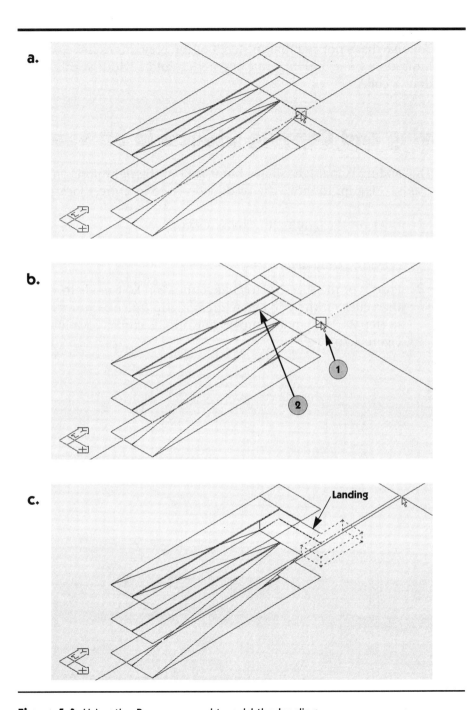

Figure 4.6: Using the Box command to add the landing

The Box command creates a 3D box based on dimensions you provide. You may have noticed that in step 3 of the previous exercise, a prompt indicates a Cube option. You can enter **C↵** and a width at this prompt to draw a cube.

Moving and Copying Objects in 3D Space

The landing is the right shape, but it isn't in the right position in the Z axis. Use grips to move the landing down to its correct location.

1. Click on the landing to expose its grips.

2. Click on the grip at the top corner pointing toward you, as indicated in Figure 4.7a.

3. Press ↵ or the spacebar to change the Grip Edit mode to ✶✶MOVE✶✶, then click on the grip below the hot grip (the one you selected in step 2). The landing moves down to its correct location (see Figure 4.7b).

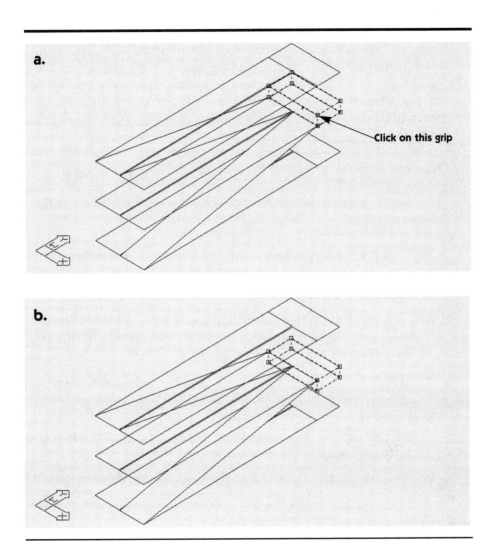

a.

Click on this grip

b.

Figure 4.7: Moving the landing down using its grips

In this simple exercise, you were able to move the landing vertically using its grip points. You can also use the standard Move command in conjunction with the Osnaps. Moving and copying objects in 3D space can be quite tricky, however. This is especially true when you are editing in a 3D isometric view, as you will see as you work through this book, you will be shown some of the pitfalls of 3D editing, and ways to avoid problems.

For now, however, let's draw the bottom and sides of the ramp.

To draw the bottom, you need only copy the top surfaces 18 inches down, as follows.

1. Press the Esc key twice to clear the grip from the landing.

2. Click on the two 3D faces you created earlier to represent the top surfaces of the upper and lower ramps,to expose their grip points.

3. Click on the grip that touches the front left corner of the top of the landing as indicated in Figure 4.8a, then press ⏎ or the space-bar to change the Grip Edit mode to **MOVE**.

4. Type C⏎ to change the Grip Edit mode to Copy. The prompt should change to **MOVE (multiple)**.

5. Use the Endpoint Osnap to select the corner below the previously selected grip, as indicated in Figure 4.8b. Copies of the two ramp surfaces appear.

6. Press the Esc key twice to exit the Grip Edit mode (see Figure 4.8c).

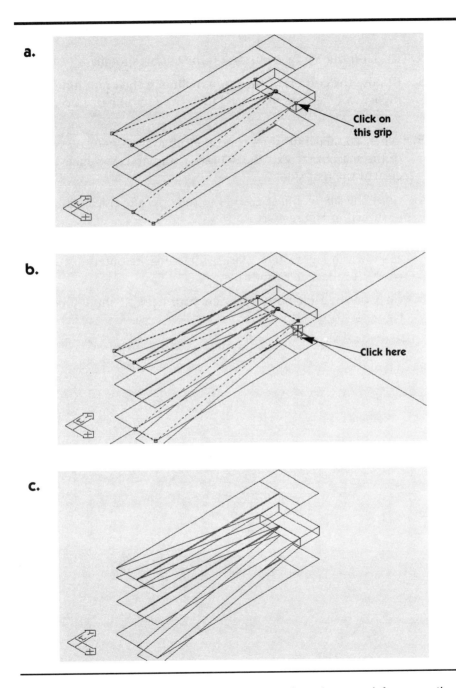

Figure 4.8: Using grips to copy the ramp's top surface downward, for use as the ramp's bottom surface

To finish off the ramps, you'll add the sides using 3D faces.

1. Click on the 3D Face button on the Surfaces toolbar.

2. Choose the corners of the ramp incline in the order indicated in Figure 4.9a. (You may need to use the scroll bars to center your view.)

3. When you have finished choosing the four corners, press ↵ or the spacebar to exit the 3D Face command. You have just created the first side.

4. Copy the side you just created to the opposite side of the incline as shown in Figure 4.9b.

5. Repeat this procedure to add the sides to the other ramp incline, as shown in Figure 4.9c. Start by drawing the outermost side, then copy it to the side closer to you.

6. Click on the Hide button to view your work. It should look like Figure 4.10.

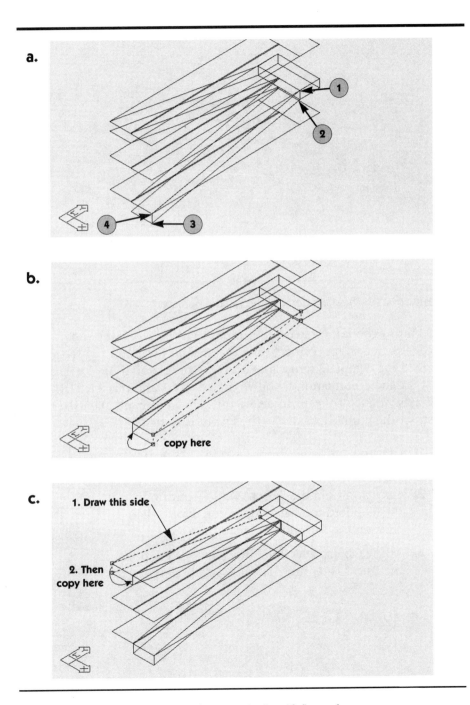

Figure 4.9: Adding the sides to the ramp incline [3 figures]

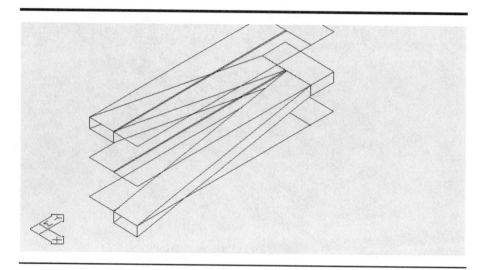

Figure 4.10: The main parts of the ramp completed

So far so good. But have you noticed that the two ramp inclines you've constructed so far connect only the ground floor and the second floor? Since the complete ramp goes up two stories, you'll have to make a copy of the ramp and landing you've drawn so far and place it further up the Z axis. You'll also want to delete the 2D layout you have used to construct the ramp—let's delete the layout data first.

1. Click on the Layer drop-down list, then click on the lock icon of the Ramp layer (to unlock the Ramp layer).

2. Click and hold the Select Window button in the Standard toolbar to open the flyout, then click on the Selection Filters button.

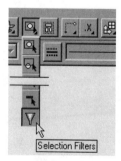

3. At the Object Selection Filters dialog box, open the Select Filter drop-down list and select Layer.

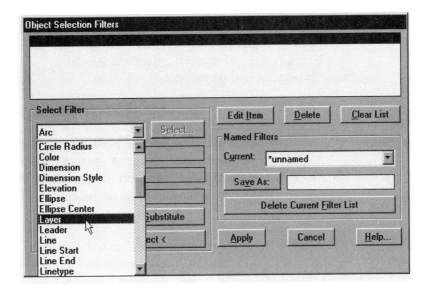

4. Click on the Select... button to the left of the drop-down list, then at the Select Layer dialog box, choose the Ramp layer.

5. Click OK, then click on the Add to List button in the Object Selection Filter dialog box, and then click on the Apply button.

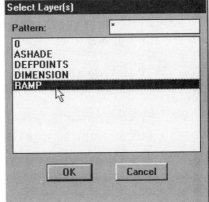

6. Use a selection window to select the entire drawing. The Filter tool will filter out and select only the objects that are assigned to the Ramp layer.

Remember that you constructed your 3D ramp on layer 0 and that your 2D layout is on the Ramp layer. What you've just done with the procedure above is created a *selection set* of the 2D layout using the Filter tool. Now let's delete it.

1. Click on the Erase button in the Modify toolbar.

2. At the Select object prompt, type **P**↵, then press ↵ again to tell AutoCAD you have finished selecting objects. The layout will be deleted.

Since you created a selection set of the objects in the Ramp layer, you need only enter **P**↵ in step 2 to select the previous selection set of objects. AutoCAD "remembers" the last set of objects selected and can select those objects using the Previous option, as long as those objects have not beeen deleted or an Undo operation has canceled the selection set.

Now copy the entire ramp 11 feet vertically up the Z axis.

1. Click on the Copy button in the Modify toolbar.

2. Select the entire 3D ramp, then press ↵ to finish your selection.

3. At the Base point prompt, click on any point in the drawing area or type **@**↵.

Note *Remember that @ when used alone at any Point Selection prompt represents the last selected point.*

4. At the Second point prompt, enter **@ 0,0,11'**↵ to copy the ramp 11 feet in the vertical or Z axis.

5. Zoom out to view the entire ramp. Your drawing should now look like Figure 4.11.

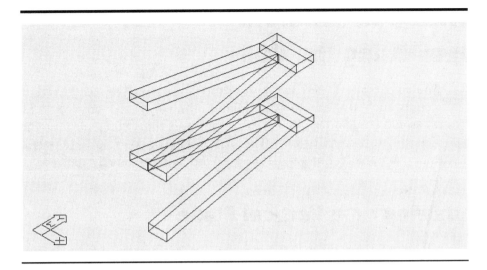

Figure 4.11: The 3D ramp rising two stories

◆ Choosing the Right Object for the Job

Before you continue with the ramp, I'd like to point out some important issues regarding the type of objects you use to construct an object. There is often a trade-off between quick construction of 3D models and your ability to edit them easily later on.

In the example of the ramp, you use 3D faces for the ramp surfaces. You could just as easily have drawn an elevation of the ramp using lines, then extruded the lines to form the ramp surfaces. In fact, this could have been a quicker method. The drawback to this method is that later, if you needed to make adjustments to the width of the ramp, you would have to change the thickness of the lines you used to construct it. Since you used 3D faces, you can easily make changes to the width of the ramp, because 3D faces can be stretched.

Knowing what types of objects to use in a given situation takes practice. Hopefully this book will point you in the right direction.

◆ Working on Different Planes Using the UCS

You've completed the main part of the ramp. Now you need to add a few details, such as the window and hand rails. For these items, you'll return to an old familiar tool, the polyline. But this time, you'll also use the User Coordinate System, or UCS. The UCS will allow you to draw a polyline in a plane that is not parallel to the World Coordinate System.

Drawing on a Vertical Plane

The handrails and the window frame and mullion need to be drawn in a plane that is 90 degrees from the WCS. In the previous chapter, you were able to draw window mullions without having to change your coordinate system. The window enclosing the ramp, however, is not rectilinear. Two of its sides are angled to align with the incline of the ramp. In order to draw such an incline with a polyline, you will have to use a different UCS.

1. Choose View ➤ Preset UCS. The UCS Orientation dialog box appears.

Click on the icon labeled *Right*. The dialog box closes and you see the UCS icon adjust to show you the new UCS orientation (see Figure 4.12).

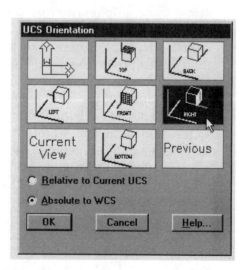

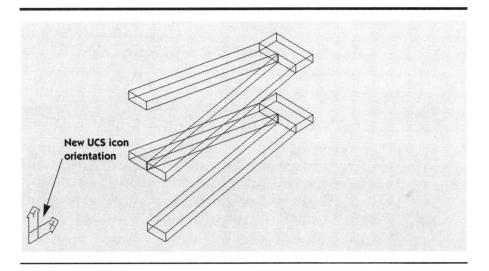

New UCS icon orientation

Figure 4.12: The UCS icon changes to show the new orientation of the UCS.

The UCS Orientation dialog box offers a quick way to select a UCS orientation based on the sides of a cube. By imagining this cube enclosing your model, you can orient the preset UCSes offered in this dialog box to your model.

This dialog box can be used to set up UCSes you'll need most often, but you are not limited to these settings. Later in this chapter, you'll learn how to set up a UCS that is not confined to the cube. For now, let's continue with the window mullion.

1. Zoom into the upper portion of the ramp so your view looks like Figure 4.13.

2. Click on the Polyline button in the Draw toolbar.

3. Use the Endpoint Osnaps and pick the points shown in Figure 4.13.

4. When you've finished selecting the four points, press ⏎ to exit the Polyline tool.

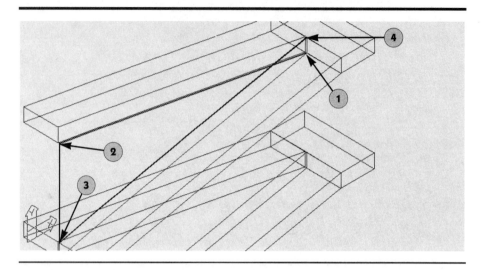

Figure 4.13: Drawing the outline of the ramp window

Notice that with the UCS in its new location, you are able to draw a triangular shape on a vertical plane. In previous exercises, you were limited to drawing such a shape only in the WCS; vertical shapes were limited to rectangles. Now you can draw virtually any shape in this new vertical plane, just as you would in the WCS.

You may have noticed that I asked you to draw the outline of the window with the ends of the polyline extending past the upper point of the window triangle, as shown in Figure 4.14. I had you do this because object snapping at the intersection of 3D faces is not supported in AutoCAD—you have to create a snap point manually at the same place. By using the existing ramp geometry, and drawing your polyline to extend past the window corner, you have created a point you can snap to.

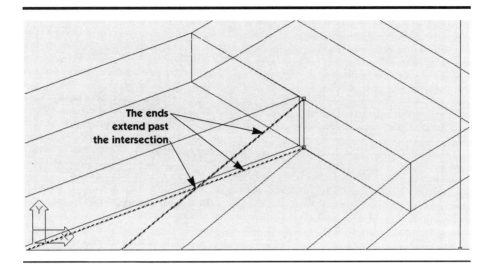

Figure 4.14: Draw the outline of the window so that the ends of the polyline extend past the upper point.

1. Click on the polyline to expose its grips.

2. Click on the endpoint grip of the polyline, then, using the Intersection Osnap, move the grip to the intersection of the two polyline line segments (see Figure 4.15).

3. Move the other endpoint to the same intersection point that you moved to in step 3 so the two endpoints meet end-to-end (also Figure 4.15).

4. Click on the Edit Polyline button of the Modify toolbar and type **C↵** to make sure the polyline is closed.

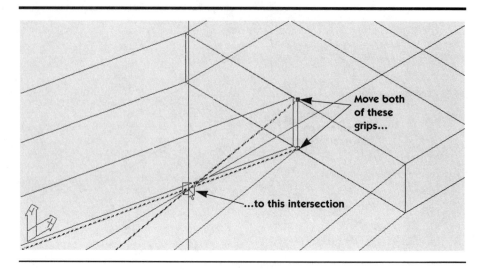

Figure 4.15: Moving the ends of the polyline to the intersection to create a point you can snap to

The polyline you just drew is the outline of the frame of the window. We'll be adding a thickness and width to the frame itself, so you'll want to offset the outline and then change the polyline's properties for thickness and width, just as you did in Chapter 3 for the ground-floor window mullions. This will give the polyline frame the appearance of a solid bar.

1. Click on the Offset button in the Modify toolbar. It can be found on the Copy flyout menu.

2. Enter **1**↙ for the offset distance.

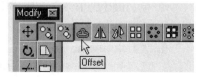

3. Click on the polyline you just drew, then pick a point toward the center of the window (See Figure 4.16).

4. Press ↵ to exit the Offset command.

Notice that the result of the offset is not what you may have expected. Instead of creating an offset copy toward the *center* of the window, the copy appears *outside* the window. This is because the point you selected in step 3, to indicate the direction of the offset, actually lies outside the window frame. How did that happen?

The answer to this is slightly complicated. Whenever you select a point in space, AutoCAD assumes you want a point in the current default Z-axis direction. When you rotated the UCS, although the origin of the UCS remained at 0,0,0, the directions of the axes changed, and virtually all the points on the model ended up in a *negative* direction of the Z axis. When you selected the point you thought you were picking in step 3, then, you were actually picking a point that is quite far from the center of the window frame, and outside of it.

Figure 4.16a shows the relationship of the ramp to the user coordinate systems you are using. You see the World coordinate system with its origin indicated. In the figure I have drawn a line that projects a point from the center of the ramp window to the plane of the UCS. The right endpoint of that line shows the point I *should* have had you pick to offset the window frame in the previous exercise. Instead, and in order to drive the lesson home to you, I directed you to find the location of the point at the *left* end of the line. This put the actual point that much further to the left!

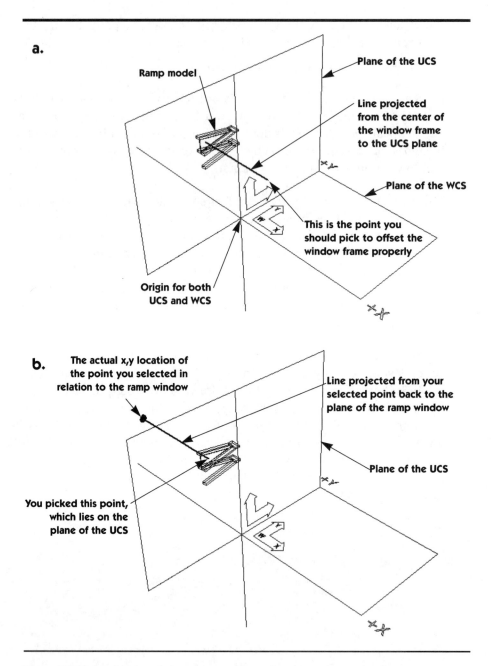

Figure 4.16: Two views showing the relationship of the WCS and UCS to the ramp. The top view shows the UCS's orientation. The bottom view shows how a selected point is not necessarily in the position you might think.

You must take into consideration how the points you pick are translated back to the object you are working on. Since the current UCS is actually in a plane far removed from the plane of the window frame, the points you pick do not necessarily correspond that point's apparent visual location.

To get a better idea of what is going on, try using the ID command to identify the coordinate locations of points on your model versus points you might pick in space.

1. Click and hold the List button on the Properties toolbar, then drag the cursor to the Locate Point button, then let go. Alternatively, you can type **ID**↵ at the command prompt.

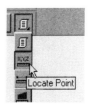

2. Click on the point you selected in step 2 of the previous exercise, to indicate the offset direction.

3. Click on the Locate Point button again, but this time, use the Osnap named *Nearest* and click on the window frame.

4. Press the F2 Button to view the results. Notice that the coordinates of the points you picked vary considerably, especially the Z coordinate.

Now that we've identified the problem, how do we work around it? The solution is to move the UCS so that its Z axis coincides with the object you want to offset. This is easily done using the UCS Origin option.

1. Choose View ➤ Set UCS ➤ Origin.

2. Use the Endpoint Osnap and select the lower left corner of the window-frame polyline.

3. Click on the Offset button in the Modify Toolbar again.

4. Press ↵ to accept the default offset distance of 1".

5. Click on the original polyline outline of the window frame, then click on a point toward the middle of the window. This time the frame moves into the correct position (see Figure 4.17).

6. Erase the other two polylines. You will use the latest one for your window frame.

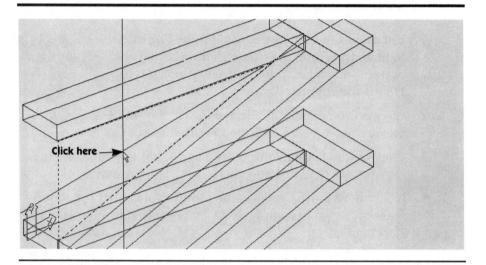

Figure 4.17: Adding the new polyline outline that will become the window frame

Next, adjust the properties of the window frame to give the polyline thickness and depth, just as you did in Chapter 3 for the ground floor's window mullions.

1. Click on the Properties button in the Properties toolbar.

2. Click on the polyline you just created with the Offset command, then press ↵.

3. At the Modify Polyline dialog box, enter **2** in the Thickness input box, then click OK.

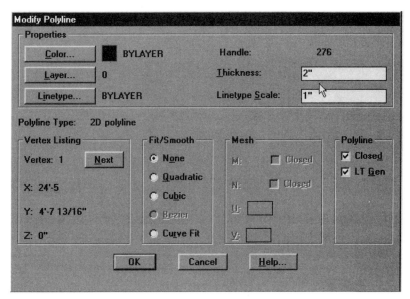

4. Click on the polyline Edit button in the Modify toolbar, then click on the polyline.

5. At the `Close/Join/Width/Edit vertex/Fit/Spline/ Decurve/Ltype gen/Undo/eXit <X>` prompt, type **W↵**.

6. At the `Enter new width for all segments` prompt, enter **2↵**, then press ↵ again to exit the Polyline Edit command.

7. Finally, move the polyline –2" along the Z axis. This places the window frame in the gap between the two ramp inclines.

8. Click on the Hide button in the Render toolbar. Your window should look like Figure 4.18.

Figure 4.18: The finished window frame

Exercise Summary

To help you avoid problems later, here's a brief summary of points to remember as you create and use UCSes:

◆ You can use UCSes when you need to work on a surface or plane other than the WCS.

◆ Once a UCS is created, you can draw any object in that plane, thereby giving you the freedom to draw any shape in any direction in space.

◆ Be aware that when selecting points in a UCS, AutoCAD assumes you want to select points *in the plane of the current UCS*, unless you select a specific geometry on an object using object snaps.

◆ Pay attention to the origin location of your UCS, and if need be, move its origin so the plane of the UCS coincides with the surface plane you are interested in editing.

◆ Understanding How Polylines Are Restrained in a UCS

Let's take a moment to examine the way polylines work in 3D space. If you zoom in to the top corner of your window frame, you'll notice that there is a gap between the corner of the frame and the corner of the ramp incline, even though you used the Endpoint Osnap to select the endpoint of the ramp corner. When you draw a polyline, AutoCAD uses the first point you pick to set the polyline's Z coordinate. The other points of the polyline will then be fixed to that same Z coordinate—they are constrained to the same *plane*. Since you started the window-frame polyline by picking the endpoint of the lower ramp incline, the entire polyline remained in the Z plane that contains that first point (see Figure 4.19). Note that the new UCS has its Z axis pointing to the right, so the window frame polyline is fixed in a plane that is to the right of the upper ramp incline.

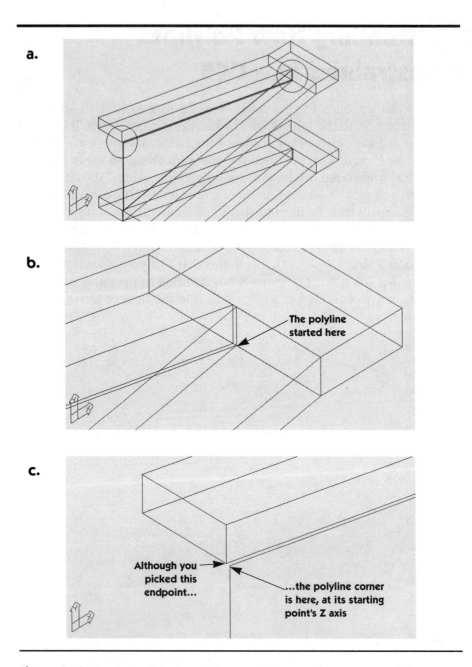

Figure 4.19: The first point of a polyline establishes the Z coordinate of all subsequent points in the polyline. In other words, they all end up in the same Z plane.

Polylines do not like to be edited unless your UCS is parallel to them. Try the following brief exercise and you'll see what I mean.

1. Change the UCS back to the World coordinate system by choosing View ➤ Set UCS ➤ World.

2. Click on the Edit polyline button in the Modify toolbar, then click on the window frame. You see the following error message: "The object is not parallel to the UCS."

3. Press the Esc key to exit the Pedit command.

Since the window-frame polyline is not parallel to the World Coordinate System, AutoCAD will not let you edit it. You must set your UCS to one that is parallel to the polyline you want to edit. In the case of your ramp's window frame, it is fairly simple to find the UCS that is aligned with the window frame, but suppose you have several polylines all aligned at different angles. It would be difficult to keep track of all the different user coordinate systems in a complex 3D model. Here's a quick way to find the UCS of a polyline, or any object.

1. Choose View ➤ Set UCS ➤ Object.

2. At the Select object to align UCS: prompt, click on the window-frame polyline. The UCS aligns itself to the polyline.

You might notice that the UCS is not exactly the same one you used when you created the window frame. The Object option of the UCS command places the UCS in both the exact plane and the exact orientation of the *polyline*. This means the UCS origin is at the beginning vertex of the polyline and the X axis is aligned with the first vector of the polyline (see Figure 4.20).

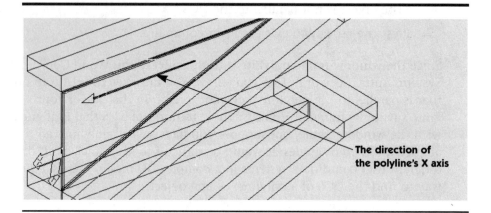

The direction of
the polyline's X axis

Figure 4.20: When you set the UCS to an existing object, the direction of the X axis is determined by the direction of the first line drawn in that object.

In general, the View ➤ Set UCS ➤ Object command (the Object option of the UCS command or **UCS.⏎ O.⏎**) aligns with the plane defined by an object, such as a circle, arc, or polyline. Table 4.1 lists the different types of AutoCAD objects and how the UCS Objects option aligns to these objects.

Table 4.1: UCS Orientation Based on UCS/Objects Option

Object Type	Location of UCS Origin	UCS X-Axis Orientation
Arc	Center of arc	Vector from center of arc and first point
Circle	Center of Circle	Vector from center of circle and first point picked to define circle
Dimension	Midpoint of Dimension text	X axis of the UCS at the time the dimension was created
Line	Endpoint of line nearest selection point	Direction of line
Point	Point location	Orientation of UCS at the time the point was created
2D Polyline	First point of polyline	Vector defined by first and second point of polyline
2D Solid	First point of solid	Vector defined by first and second point of solid
Trace	First point of trace	Direction of trace
3D Face	First point of 3D Face	Vector defined by first and second point of 3D face
Shapes, Text, Blocks, Attributes, Attribute definitions	Insertion point	Angle of rotation

While the UCS is now parallel to the polyline, our work will be made easier if we orient the UCS so that its X axis is aligned with the ground plane. To do this, you will have to rotate the UCS about its current Z axis. Try the following.

1. Choose View ➤ Set UCS ➤ Z Axis Rotate.

2. At the `Rotation angle about Z axis <0>:` prompt, use the Endpoint Osnap to click on the first corner shown in Figure 4.21a.

3. At the `Second point:` prompt, click on the second corner shown in Figure 4.21a. The UCS icon rotates to show that X axis of the UCS is now aligned with the ground plane.

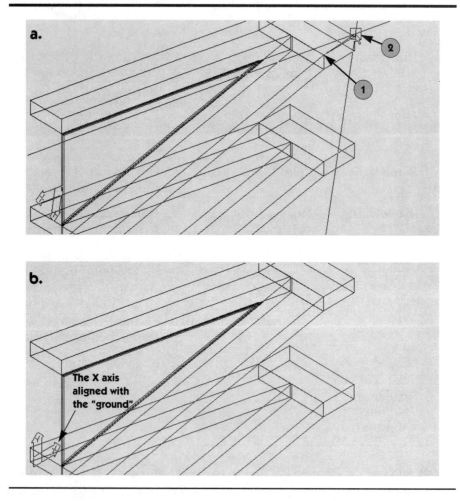

Figure 4.21: Using the UCS Z Axis Rotate option to align the X axis with the ground plane

Now that your UCS is set to be parallel to the polyline window frame, you can add the horizontal mullions for the window.

1. Draw a polyline starting from the midpoint of the vertical portion of the window frame and ending just past the frame to the right as shown in Figure 4.22a.

2. Using the Properties button on the Properties toolbar, change the *thickness* of this mullion polyline to **2**.

3. Using the Edit Polyline button on the Modify toolbar, change the mullion *width* to **2**.

4. Choose the Offset button on the Copy flyout of the Modify toolbar, then set the Offset distance to **18**.

5. Offset the mullion several times in both directions until you have several copies of the mullion as shown in Figure 4.22b (detail is shown in Figure 4.22c).

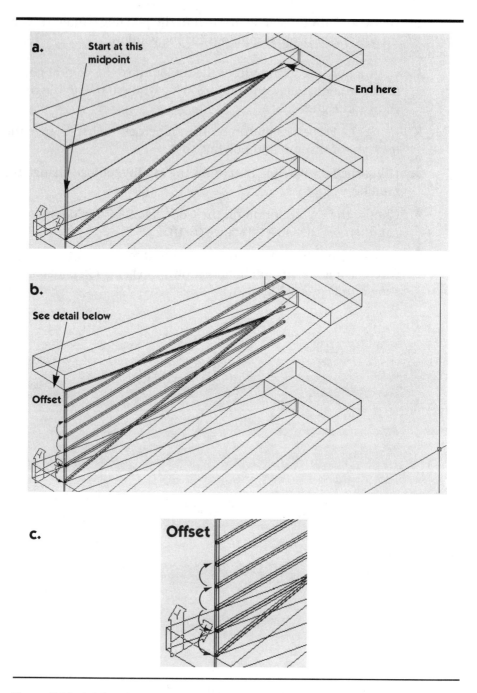

Figure 4.22: Adding the horizontal mullions to the ramp window

6. Choose the Trim button from the Modify toolbar, then select the window frame.

7. Pick the right endpoint of each of the horizontal mullions so they trim back to the frame. When you have finished, press ⏎.

8. Click on the Hide button of the Render toolbar. Your drawing should look like Figure 4.23.

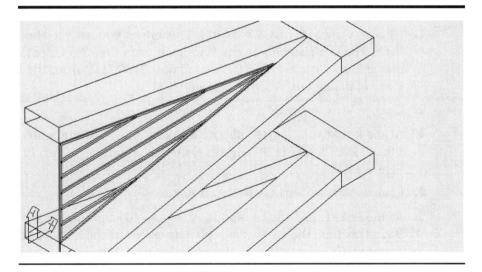

Figure 4.23: The completed ramp window

Just as with the ramp's window frame, the horizontal mullions you just created can only be edited while in a UCS that is parallel to them.

◆ Fine-Tuning the UCS Orientation

Before we move on, you should know about a few of the other options
for the UCS command. Early on in this chapter, you used the UCS
Orientation dialog box (View ➤ Preset UCS) to set up a UCS that was
perpendicular to the WCS in order to draw the ramp window. You can
accomplish the same task using UCS options for rotating the UCS about
the X, Y, or Z axis. The following is the same operation done using the
X Axis Rotate and Y Axis Rotate options.

1. Choose View ➤ Set UCS ➤ World. This brings you back to the
    WCS. You can also choose the WCS icon from the UCS Orientation
    dialog box (View ➤ Preset UCS) or choose *WORLD* from the UCS
    Control dialog box (View ➤ Named UCS).

2. Choose View ➤ Set UCS ➤ X Axis Rotate.

3. At the Rotation angle about X axis <0>: prompt, enter
    90↵. The UCS rotates 90 degrees about the X axis, as shown in
    Figure 4.24a.

4. Choose View ➤ Set UCS ➤ Y Axis Rotate.

5. At the Rotation angle about y axis <0>: prompt, enter
    90↵. This time the UCS rotates 90 degrees about the Y axis of the
    current UCS orientation, as shown in Figure 4.24b.

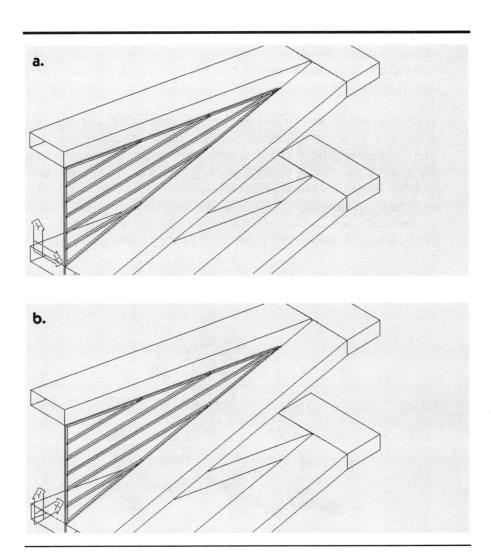

Figure 4.24: Changes to the UCS using the X and Y Axis Rotate option of the UCS command

In this exercise you "manually" rotated the UCS about the X and Y axes, instead of using the UCS Control dialog box. While this method takes a bit longer, it offers more control, because you can specify an angle other than 90 degrees if you so choose.

In an earlier exercise, you rotated the UCS about the Z axis using two points as a reference, which was another way of specifying a rotation angle. Otherwise, the Z Axis Rotation option works in the same way as the X and Y Axis Rotate options in the previous exercise. You can also specify a negative rotation angle to rotate the UCS in the opposite direction shown in the exercise. Figure 4.25 shows you the positive rotation directions for each of the axes of a UCS. Make note of this figure, as it will help you determine the rotation of a UCS when using the X, Y, or Z Axis Rotate option in the View ➤ Set UCS pull-down menu.

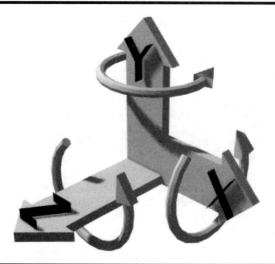

Figure 4.25: The Positive directions for the X, Y, and Z Axis Rotate Option of the View ➤ Set UCS pull-down menu (UCS command)

Drawing a Truss with the UCS

To explore the UCS further, let's take a brief detour from the Villa Savoye model and look at another popular fixture in modern architecture: the truss. Trusses are useful to our exploration of the UCS because, to construct one, you need to be able to manipulate the UCS with some degree of skill. So drawing a truss will help you gain some expertise in using the UCS effectively.

Our particular truss is a typical design that might appear in a commercial building design. In the following exercise, you'll first orient a UCS so that its Z axis is aligned with one of the struts.

1. Save the Ramp file that you created above, then open the `Truss` file from the `Sample` directory on the CD accompanying this book.

2. Zoom into the area shown in Figure 4.26.

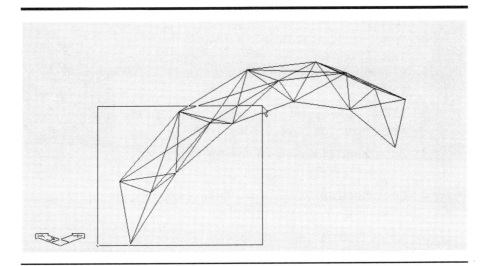

Figure 4.26: The truss file

This truss is shown as a line diagram, much like a diagram a structural engineer might use in his or her design process. Let's pretend that you have received this diagram from your consulting engineer and now want to include it in a 3D model. You'll want to give the truss some thickness by turning the lines in the diagram into 3D *tubes*. You'll have to do this one truss member at a time. The first step is to align a UCS to one of the truss members.

> **Tip**   *You may want to set the Running Osnap option to Endpoint for this exercise. To do this, choose Options ➤ Running Object Snap, then click on the Endpoint checkbox at the top of the Running Object Snap dialog box. Click OK to exit the dialog box. This operation can be done while in the middle of another command.*

1. Choose View ➤ Set UCS ➤ Z Axis Vector.

2. Using the endpoint Osnaps, click on the endpoints of one of the struts of the truss, as shown in Figure 4.27a. You've just aligned the Z axis of a UCS to one of the diagonal members of the truss. (This also means that your UCS is now perpendicular to an axis defined by the strut.)

> **Note**   *I've supplied an AutoLISP macro on the accompanying CD that will automatically draw a "tube" around a line. See Appendix B for details.*

Next, you'll change the strut to a tube segment.

1. Click on the Circle button on the Draw toolbar.

2. Using the Endpoint Osnap, click on the end of the strut you have just aligned to.

3. Enter **2**↵ to indicate a circle with a radius of 2 inches (see Figure 4.27b).

4. Enter **Chprop**↵, then at the `Select object` prompt, type **L**↵ to select the circle you just drew.

5. At the `Change what property (Color/LAyer/LType/ ltScale/Thickness) ?` prompt, enter **T**↵ to bring up the `Thickness` prompt.

6. Using the Endpoint Osnaps, click on the endpoints of the strut you used to align your UCS back in step 1 of the previous set of instructions. The circle extrudes to the length of the strut (see Figure 4.27c).

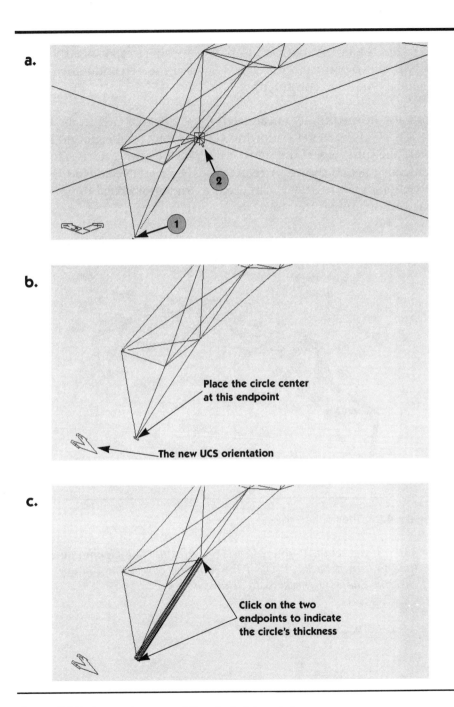

Figure 4.27: Converting one of the struts into a tube

In this exercise, you used the Chprop command to visually set the Z-axis thickness of a truss. With Chprop, you are able to specify a thickness by selecting two points; in this case, you used the two endpoints of the truss member you were constructing.

You also learned that you can align the Z axis of a UCS to the two end-points of a line, thereby allowing you to create a tube around it. To complete the truss, repeat the steps of the previous two exercises for each truss member, as shown in Figure 4.28. Once you've added the tube to a section of the truss, you can use the Array tool's Polar option to copy the section around the truss.

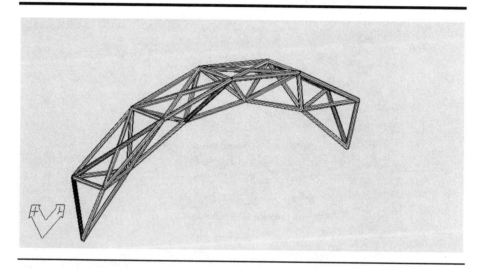

Figure 4.28: The finished truss

Tip   If you set the Running Object Snap feature to Endpoint, now is a good time to turn it back off. Open the Running Object Snap dialog box, then click the Endpoint checkbox to disable it.

Using Object Snaps in 3D

If you do a lot of 2D work in AutoCAD, you know how helpful the Object Snaps can be. They are also an essential tool in 3D modeling, but you need to exercise some care in using them. It's much easier to select the wrong endpoint, for example, while working in 3D space than it is when working in 2D. In addition, we often don't think of the Z axis while using Object Snaps. If you aren't careful, you may select the correct X and Y axis point, but the Z axis will be way off. It is helpful to use the *point filters* in 3D to select specific X, Y, and Z points. You'll learn more about point filters in 3D in Chapters 5 and 8.

Aligning the UCS to a Surface Plane Using Three Points

Earlier in this chapter, you use the Origin option to align a UCS to the surface of the window frame of the ramp. Let's look now at another way to align the UCS to a plane.

Suppose you want to add a skylight to a sloped room. The following exercise shows you how to align a UCS using the three points shown in Figure 4.29.

1. Open the House drawing from the Sample directory on the CD accompanying the book.

2. Choose View ➤ Set UCS ➤ 3 Point.

3. At the Origin point <0,0,0> prompt, use the Endpoint Osnap and click on the closest corner of the roof.

4. At the Point on positive portion of the X-axis prompt, use the Endpoint Osnap again and pick a second roof corner,.

5. At the Point on positive Y portion of the UCS XY plane prompt, use the Endpoint Osnap again to pick the upper corner of the roof. Your UCS is now aligned to the slope of the roof.

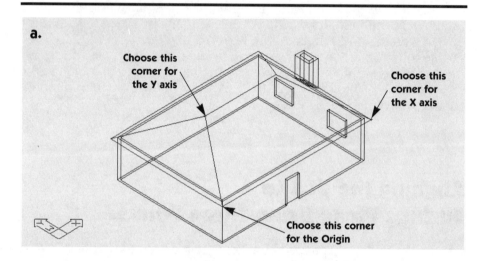

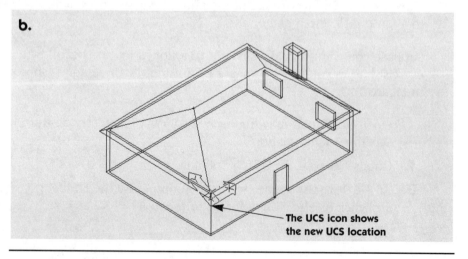

Figure 4.29: Aligning the UCS to a roof slope using the 3 Point option

Notice that the UCS icon moved to the first corner of the roof—the point you selected in step 3. In this drawing, the UCSicon system variable has its Origin option turned on. This causes the UCS icon to appear at its true origin. In this case the origin is at the corner of the roof.

You can set the UCS icon by choosing Options ➤ UCS ➤ Icon Origin. A checkmark appears by this option when it is turned on. You can also use the command line and enter **UCSicon⏎ OR⏎ ON⏎**.

Now that you have the UCS exactly where you want it, you can add the skylight to the roof. One of finer points to remember about the 3 Point option is that it automatically places the origin of the UCS on the first point you pick, as it did in step 3 of the previous exercise. Knowing this, you can place the skylight using the lower corner of the roof as a reference point. For example, suppose you want the skylight to be exactly 5' horizontally and 8' vertically from the lower corner of the roof. Here's how you would do it.

1. Click on the Rectangle button in the Draw toolbar.

   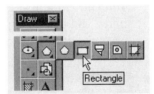

   Enter **10',8'⏎**. Notice that you are not including the usual @ sign at the beginning. This character is left off because you are describing a location in absolute coordinates relative to the current UCS's origin.

2. Enter **@4',4'⏎** for a 4-foot-square skylight.

3. Use the Properties dialog box to change the thickness of the skylight to **1'**.

4. Click on the Hide button of the Render toolbar. Your drawing should look like Figure 4.30.

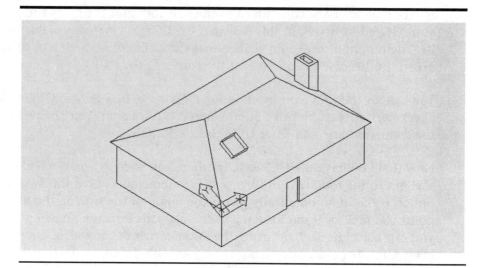

Figure 4.30: The roof with the skylight added

You can embellish the skylight beyond the simple box you've drawn here. The main purpose of this exercise was to show you how the 3 Point option of the UCS command works.

Using the View UCS Option to Add Notes

One last UCS option I haven't covered yet is View. The UCS View option orients the UCS to be parallel to your current view. This can be helpful if you want to add notes to a 3D view. The origin remains in its previous location while the UCS is rotated to coincide with the current view plane. Figure 4.31 shows the House drawing after choosing View ➤ Set UCS ➤ View. You can also choose Current View from the UCS Orientation dialog box (View ➤ Preset UCS). Notice that the origin of the UCS stays at the corner of the roof—only the orientation of the UCS changes.

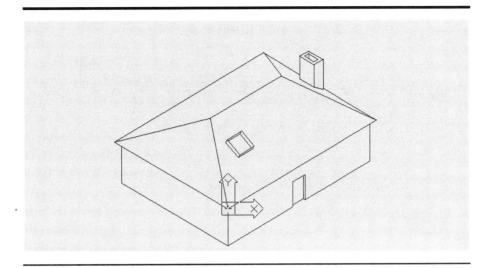

Figure 4.31: Aligning the UCS to your current view

◆ Storing and Recalling a UCS

At times it's a good idea to save a UCS so that you can return to it later. This is especially true for models that have lots of odd angles or are very complex. Saving and recalling a UCS is similar to saving and storing views.

1. Choose View ➤ Named UCS. The UCS Control dialog box appears.

Click on the name *NO NAME* in the list near the top of the dialog box. *NO NAME* appears in the *Rename to* input box near the bottom of the dialog box.

2. Highlight *NO NAME* and in the input box and change it to **ROOF1**.

3. Click on the *Rename to* button. The name ROOF1 replaces *NO NAME* in the listing at the top of the dialog box.

Once you've given a name to a UCS, it is saved and you can easily restore it at any time. You can also use the UCS Control dialog box to go to a stored UCS.

1. Click on *WORLD* in the list to highlight it.

2. Click on the button labeled Current. Notice that the word Current moves to the same line as *WORLD* indicating that the world coordinate system is now current.

3. Click OK and watch the UCS icon. It changes to show that you are indeed in the WCS.

Note *If you prefer using the command prompt, you can enter* **UCS.⌐ W.⌐** *to return to the world coordinate system.*

The UCS Control dialog box lets you save a UCS as well as restore a UCS. You can also rename any UCS with the exception of the WCS.

You may have noticed the *PREVIOUS* option in the UCS Control dialog box. As with the Zoom and View and selection processes in AutoCAD, you can restore the previous UCS by selecting this option. This can be handy for situations where you've created a temporary UCS that you don't necessarily want to save. You can also move back to the previous UCS using View ➤ Set UCS ➤ Previous.

◆ Summary

The UCS is an invaluable tool for creating 3D models in AutoCAD. In this chapter I have shown you some of the more common uses for the UCS. Keep in mind, though, that the examples in this chapter are by no means the only way to use this tool. Try to become as comfortable as you can using the UCS and its options, and you'll discover many other uses you can put it to.

In the next chapter, you'll learn how to use AutoCAD's surface modeling tools. With them, you'll be able to move even further from the rectangular restrictions of extrusions. In addition, you'll be further exercising your skills at using the UCS.

Surface Modeling

The objects you been dealing with up to now have been flat. This chapter will show you how to break out of that flat world and start creating some curved objects. To do this, you'll use AutoCAD's *surface modeling tools*. In addition, you'll see how you can use objects to help you *lay out* your 3D model.

Just as you might use lines to help you lay out a 2D drawing, you can use lines, arcs, and even splines to lay out and construct a 3D model. To see how this works, you'll draw the central stairway of the building that you started earlier in this book.

◆ Drawing the Stair

This stairway has a typical straight run, then arcs around, like half of a circular staircase, then continues with another straight run (see Figure 5.1).

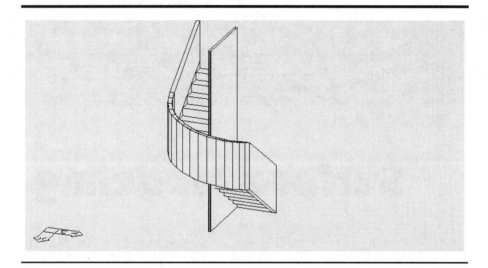

Figure 5.1: The central stair

This design offers an opportunity to explore some ways to create some interesting 3D forms. To begin the stairs, you'll use an existing 2D plan.

1. Open the file called 3dstair.DWG. You will see the plan of the stairway.

2. Choose View ➤ 3D Viewpoint Presets ➤ NW Isometric. This will offer a good viewpoint to start your 3D work (see Figure 5.2).

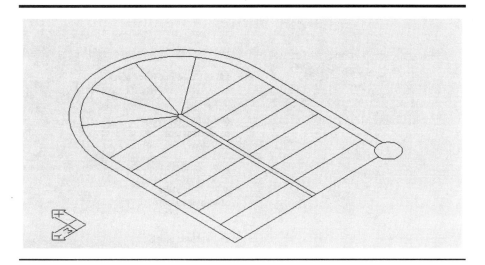

Figure 5.2: The stairway plan

Creating a Layout in 3D

In this exercise, you will make some copies of the plan in the Z axis. You will use these copies as layout points. But before you start copying, you will make some calculations. For any staircase, you will need to know the floor to floor distance, then you will need to calculate the height of the stair risers. Once you've done this, you will want to know the height of the first straight run, then the beginning and ending height of the second run—see Figure 5.3. To save some time, I've already made the calculations for this design.

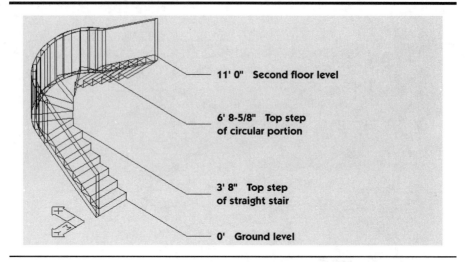

11' 0"   Second floor level

6' 8-5/8"   Top step
of circular portion

3' 8"   Top step
of straight stair

0'   Ground level

Figure 5.3: Locating the heights of key portions of the stairway

Start your 3D stair by making a copy of the stair plan 44 inches in the Z direction. This will bring you to the height at the bottom of the riser that begins the curved part of the stair.

1. Choose Copy from the Modify toolbar.

2. Select the entire stair plan then click on any point in the drawing area to select the base point for the Copy operation.

3. Enter **@0,0,44** to make the copy 44 inches above the original.

The next step is to define the incline angle of the stair. This will help you construct the stair treads and risers.

1. Using the Endpoint Osnap, draw a line from the first stair on the lower stair plan to the top of the straight stair run, as shown in Figure 5.4.

2. Copy the line you just drew 7.33 inches in the Z axis. This second line shows the level of the stair nosing (see Figure 5.4).

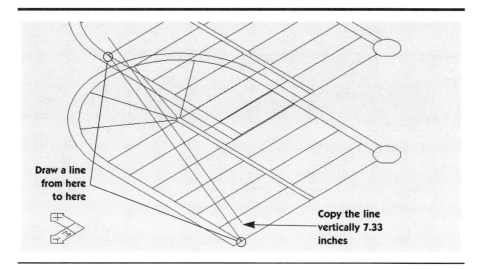

Draw a line
from here
to here

Copy the line
vertically 7.33
inches

Figure 5.4: Drawing the stair incline at the straight run of the stair

Next you'll draw one step of the stair. You'll start by drawing the profile of the step. To make this job easier, rotate the UCS 90 degrees in the X axis, then place the origin of the UCS on the same plane as the side of the stair.

1. Choose View ➤ Set UCS ➤ X Axis Rotate.

2. At the `Rotation angle about X axis` prompt, enter **90**↵.

3. Choose View ➤ Set UCS ➤ Origin, then click on the endpoint of the first stair of the plan view, as shown in Figure 5.5.

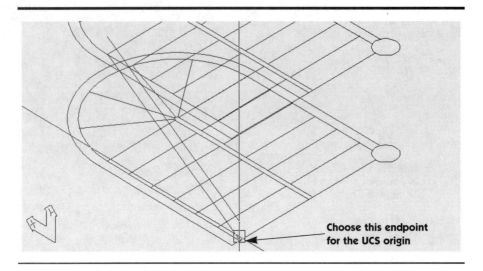

Choose this endpoint
for the UCS origin

Figure 5.5: Placing the Origin of the UCS

Notice that the UCS icon now appears with the Y axis pointing "up."
Also note that you are viewing the UCS from "behind": the X axis points
to the left instead of to the right. Make a mental note of this, as this will
be important when you try to enter coordinate values. Also, you might
remember from Chapter 4, in the Ramp window exercise, that you
moved the origin of the UCS to the same plane as the ramp window.
This was done to allow you to more accurately select points in your
drawing. In the following exercise, you will again want the plane of the
UCS to coincide with the plane on which you are working, to help you
select points.

1. Click on the Line icon in the Draw menu, then, using the Endpoint Osnap, click on the endpoint of the line indicating the second step on the original plan view. See Figure 5.6a to help locate this point.

2. Choose the second point for the line so that it is straight up, as shown in Figure 5.6a.

3. Click on the Polyline button form the Draw toolbar and start the polyline at the intersection of the vertical line and the angled line representing the bottom of the riser. See Figure 5.6b.

4. For the second point of the line, use the Endpoint Osnap and select the endpoint of the upper diagonal line, as shown in Figure 5.6c.

5. Use the Endpoint Osnap and select the end of the line representing the first step in the plan view, as shown in Figure 5.6c, then press ↵ to exit the Pline tool.

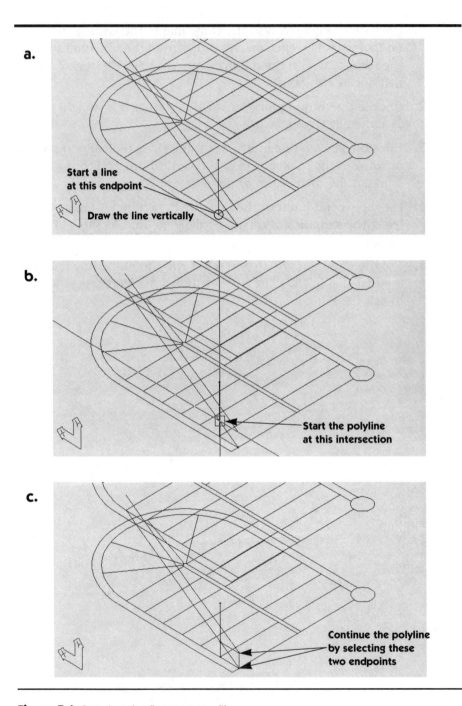

Figure 5.6: Drawing the first step profile

Adding the Steps with the UCS and Array Tools

Let's finish the straight run of stairs and move on to the curved portion. This exercise will show how the UCS and the Array commands work together to quickly construct the straight stair run. You'll extrude the stair profile you just drew to create the first step, then array the step to make the first stair run.

1. Type **chprop**↵, then select the polyline profile of the first stair step you just created and press ↵.

2. At the Change what property (Color/LAyer/LType/ ltScale/Thickness) ? prompt, type **T**↵ to select the Thickness option.

3. At the New thickness <0>: prompt, pick the bottom edge of the stair profile, as shown in Figure 5.7a.

4. At the Second point prompt, pick the other end of the line representing the first step, as shown in Figure 5.7a.

5. Press ↵ at the Change what property prompt. The step extrudes to the width of the stairs, as shown in Figure 5.7b.

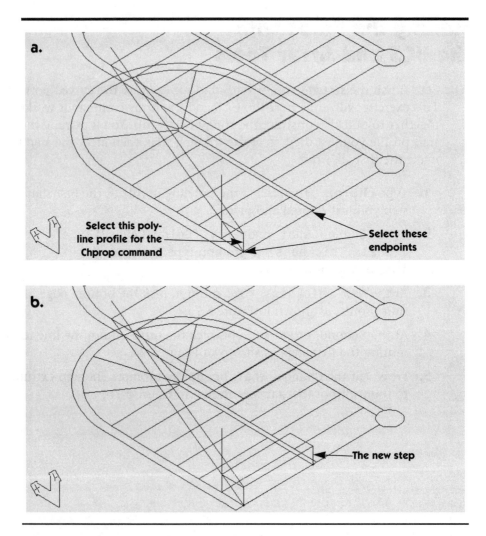

a.

Select this poly-
line profile for the
Chprop command

Select these
endpoints

b.

The new step

Figure 5.7: Extruding the stair step

Next you want to copy each stair to make the stair run. You can use the Array command for that.

1. First rotate the UCS so it its X axis is aligned with the angle of the stair run. Choose View ➤ Set UCS ➤ Z Axis Rotate.

2. At the Rotation angle about Z axis <0>: prompt, use the Endpoint Osnap and pick the bottom of the riser of the first step, as shown in Figure 5.8.

3. At the `Second point:` prompt, turn off the Ortho mode and pick the top of the stair riser line, as shown in Figure 5.8.

4. The UCS X axis aligns with the stair angle, as shown in Figure 5.8.

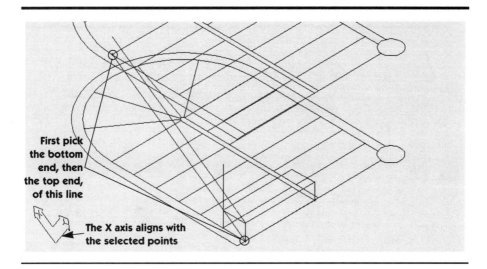

First pick
the bottom
end, then
the top end,
of this line

The X axis aligns with
the selected points

Figure 5.8: Rotating the UCS in preparation to array the step

5. Click and hold the Copy button on the Modify toolbar to open the flyout menu, then, while still holding the mouse button down, drag the cursor to the Rectangular Array button.

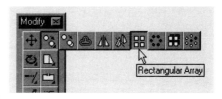

6. At the `Select object` prompt, choose the first step, as shown in Figure 5.9a, then press ↵ to finish your selection.

7. At the `Number of rows (--) <1>:` prompt, press ↵. You only want one row.

8. At the `Number of columns (||||) <1>:` prompt, enter **6**↵, since you want six steps.

9. At the `Distance between columns (||||):` prompt, use the Endpoint Osnap and pick the bottom of the stair riser, as shown in Figure 5.9a.

10. At the Second point prompt, use the Endpoint Osnap again and pick the back of the step, as shown in Figure 5.9a. Your drawing now looks like Figure 5.9b.

11. Choose View ➤ Set UCS ➤ Previous to return to the previous UCS.

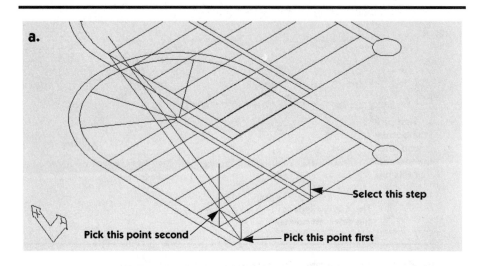

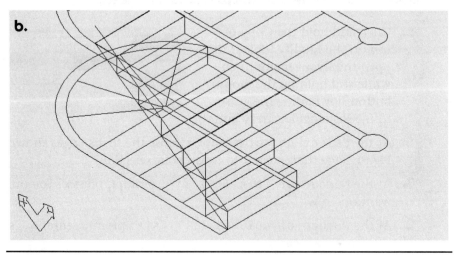

Figure 5.9: Using the Array command to make multiple copies of the step

You could have used the Copy command or the Grips copy mode to make the copies. This exercise demonstrates how arrays are aligned with the UCS.

To finish off the straight run of stairs, you'll draw the wall on the side of the stair. This wall resembles a parallelogram. To create it will be a simple operation, one that may surprise you.

1. Choose View ➤ Set UCS ➤ World to set the UCS to the World coordinate system.

2. Click on the Properties button on the Properties toolbar, then click on the line representing the bottom edge of the stair, as shown in Figure 5.10a, and then press ↵.

3. At the Modify Line dialog box, enter **44** in the Thickness input box, then press OK. Notice what happens to the line (see Figure 5.10b).

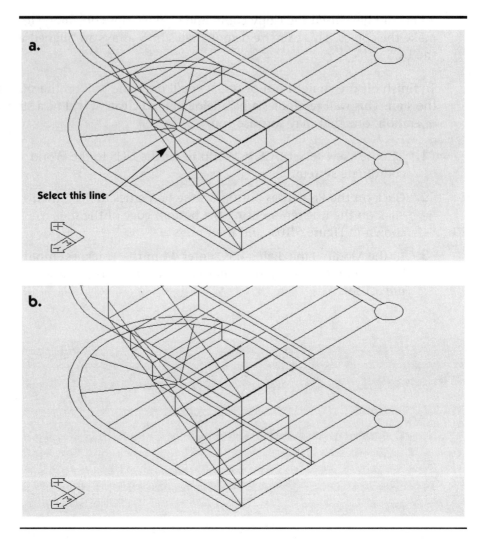

Figure 5.10: Drawing one side of the stair wall

The line extrudes in the positive Z direction to form a parallelogram. This exercise points out that simple lines have unusual properties when used in 3D. As you can see in this exercise, they will extrude in the direction of the Z axis of the UCS in which they were created. Had you left the UCS in its previous orientation and then drawn the line, it would have extruded in the same direction as the stair steps (see Figure 5.11).

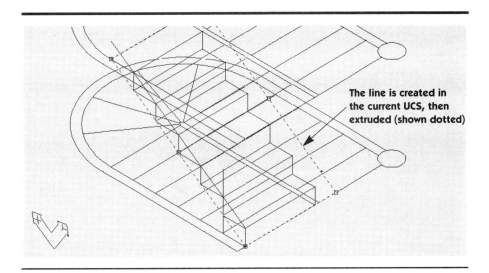

The line is created in the current UCS, then extruded (shown dotted)

Figure 5.11: Extruding a line drawn in the UCS of the stair steps

> **Note** *Remember that freezing a layer causes the layer to be invisible, and that AutoCAD will ignore the material on the frozen layer during operations like Regens and hidden-line removal. To restore a frozen layer, use the Thaw Layer option.*

Now let's complete the stair wall.

1. Adjust your view so you can see the entire wall, as shown in Figure 5.12a.

2. Erase the layout lines you created in the earlier exercise, then click on the Hide button of the Render toolbar. This will help you see what's going on with your drawing.

3. Copy the extruded line to the other side of the wall to form the exterior face of the wall (see Figure 5.12b).

4. Click on the 3D Face button on the Surfaces toolbar and draw the bottom, top, and end surfaces of the wall, as shown in Figure 5.12c.

5. Create a layer called **Stairwall** and move all the components of the stair wall to that layer. Make sure you keep Wall as the current layer.

6. Freeze the Stairwall layer. This will get them out of the way for the next exercise.

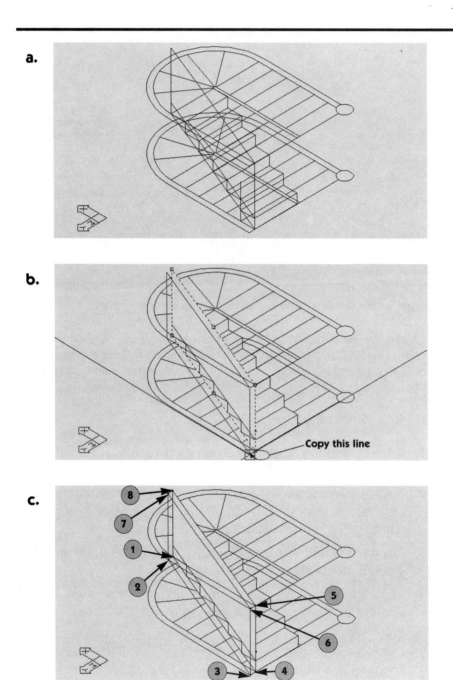

Figure 5.12: Finishing the stair wall

◆ Drawing the Spiral Stair

Now I'll turn to the circular portion of the stair. This part of the stair is a bit more complex and will require the combined use of polylines, 3D faces, and some new tools like the spline and ruled surface.

Using Polar Arrays to Construct the Circular Stair

Now you've come to the circular portion of the stairway. Here, you'll use the Array tool again, but this time it will be used to create circular copies. Start by constructing the first step.

1. Adjust your view so it looks like Figure 5.13a.

2. Using a polyline, trace the straight portions of the stair tread, as shown in Figure 5.13a.

3. Draw an arc tracing the curve of the stair and connecting the two endpoints of the polyline you just drew (see Figure 5.13b).

4. Click on the Edit Polyline button in the Modify toolbar, then select the polyline you drew in step 2.

5. Type **J**↵ to select the Join option, then use a window to select the arc shown in Figure 5.13b and press ↵↵ (that is, press ↵ twice).

6. Move the outline you just drew, **7.33** inches vertically.

7. Click and hold the Polygon button in the Draw toolbar, drag the cursor to the Region button and select it.

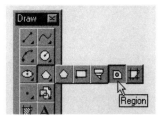

8. At the `Select object` prompt, select the polyline and press ↵. Though nothing seems to have changed, your stair tread is now a surface.

9. Using the 3D Face tool on the Surfaces toolbar, draw the riser for the stair (see Figure 5.13c).

10. Click on the Hide button in the Render toolbar. You now have the first stair tread for the curved stair (see Figure 5.13c).

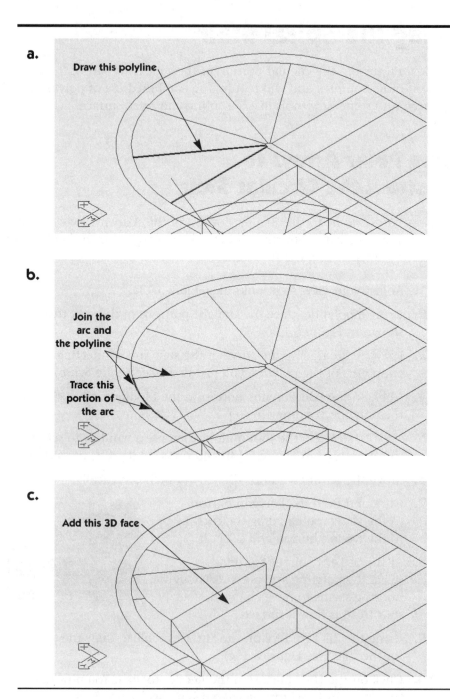

Figure 5.13: Drawing the first tread of the curved stair

Just as with the straight stair, you'll want to array the curved stair step, but you'll use a slightly different method, since this is a circular array.

1. Click and hold the Rectangular Array button in the Modify toolbar, then select the Polar Array button on the flyout.

2. Select the circular stair step, including the 3D Face riser, as shown in Figure 5.14a. Press ⏎ when you've finished selecting.

3. At the `Center point of array` prompt, use the Center Osnap and pick the center of the arc representing the outside curved wall of the stair (see Figure 5.14a).

4. At the `Number of items` prompt, enter **6**. This will give you one more step than you need, but it will allow you to specify a complete semicircle (180 degrees) for the array.

5. At the `Angle to fill (+=ccw, −=cw) <360>` prompt, enter **−180.**⏎ for a minus 180-degree copy.

6. At the `Rotate objects as they are copied? <Y>` prompt, press ⏎ to accept the default Y for Yes. The stairs will array in a semicircle (see Figure 5.14b).

7. Erase the last step and riser shown in Figure 5.14b.

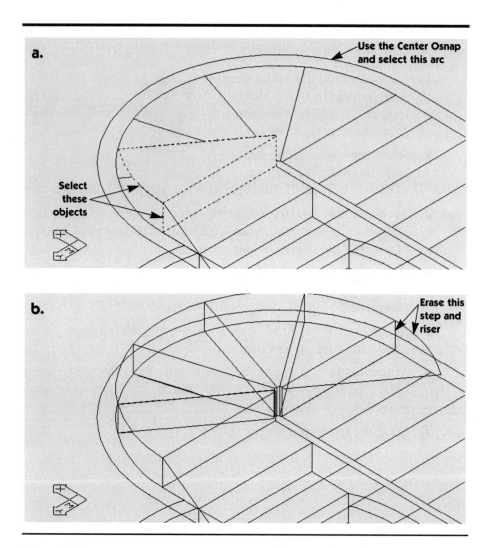

Figure 5.14: Using the Polar Array tool to copy the curved stair step

Now all you need to do is move the stairs vertically into position. The Grips will make quick work of this operation.

1. Adjust your view to show a bit more of the stair as in Figure 5.15a.

2. Click on the last stair tread and riser, as shown in Figure 5.15a to expose their grips.

3. Click on the bottom corner grip of the tread, as shown in Figure 5.15a, then press ↵ once so the command prompt shows the **MOVE** option is active.

4. Using the Endpoint Osnap, click on the corner just above the hot grip on the nosing of the stair tread, as shown in Figure 5.15b. The tread moves into position, as shown in Figure 5.15c.

5. Click on the next stair tread and riser to expose their grips. Now you should see the grips for two of steps, as shown in Figure 5.16a.

6. Click on the grip at the bottom corner of the second stair riser, as shown in Figure 5.16b, then press ↵ so the command prompt shows **MOVE** again.

7. Using the Endpoint Osnap, click on the corner just above the hot grip, as shown in Figure 5.16b. Your drawing should look like Figure 5.16c.

8. Keep repeating steps 4 through 6 until your drawing looks like Figure 5.17.

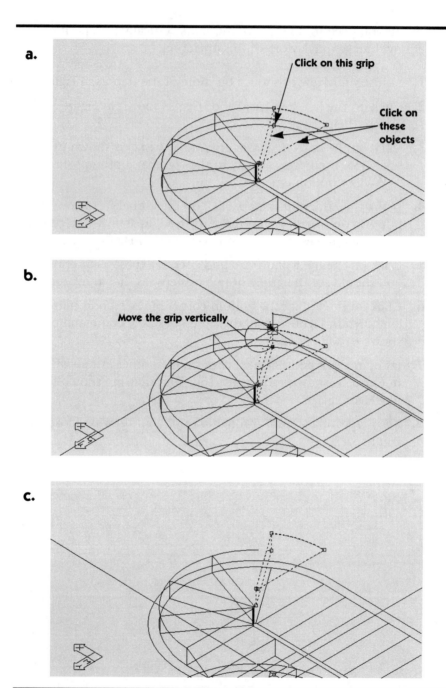

Figure 5.15: Moving the last stair step into position

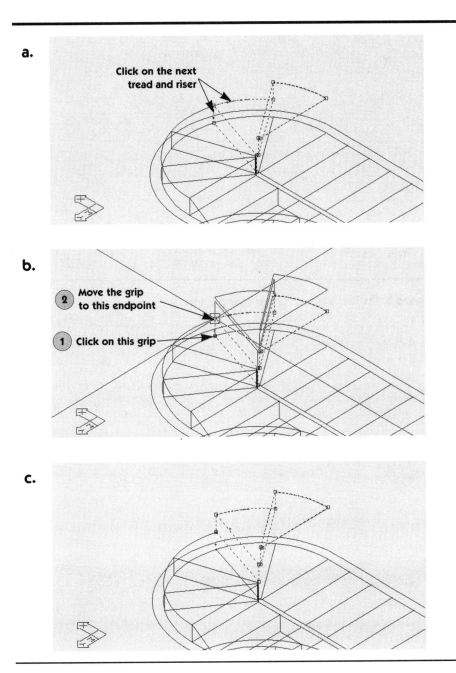

Figure 5.16: Using the Grips feature, continue to move the other steps. Each step moves together with the previous stair step as you add more steps to the grips selection set.

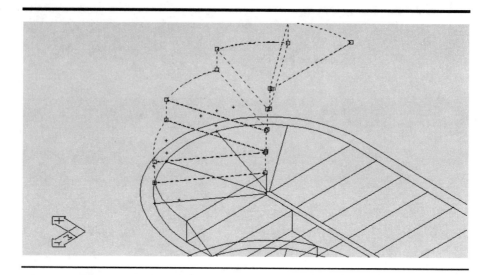

Figure 5.17: The finished curved stair portion

Using the Surface Modeling Tools

The next step is to continue the stair wall around the curved portion of the stairway. Adding the wall was a very simple operation for the straight portion, but the curved portion will take a bit more work. In this section you'll be introduced to the Surface tools. These tools allow you to create curved surfaces with the aid of polylines and splines.

Using Splines and Ruled Surfaces

In the following exercise, you'll use two new tools to create surfaces; the spline and the Ruled Surface tool (the Rulesurf command). First you'll use a spline curve to define one edge of the wall.

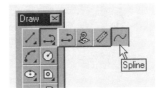

1. Click and hold the Polyline button in the Draw toolbar, then drag to the Spline button and select it.

2. Using the Endpoint Osnap, pick the outside bottom corner of the stair risers, as shown in Figure 5.18a. Start at the bottom step.

3. Select the other stair endpoints, as shown in Figure 5.18a.

4. When you have finished picking the points, press ↵.

5. At the Enter start tangent prompt, press ↵.

6. At the Enter end tangent prompt, press ↵. The last two options let you adjust the tangency of the endpoint of the spline. You now have a spline curve at the base of the stair, as shown in Figure 5.18b.

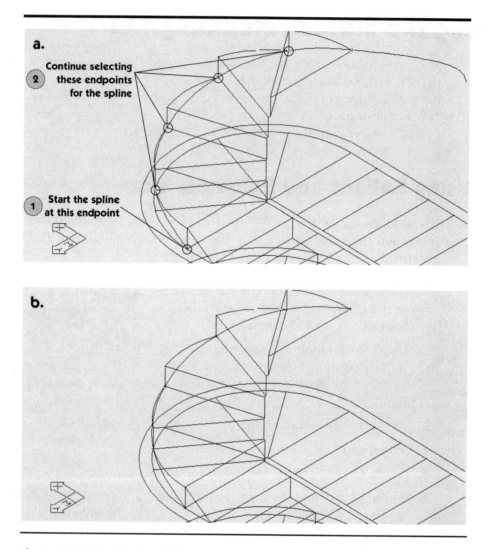

Figure 5.18: Drawing the Spline curve to define the bottom edge of the curved stair wall

Now you need a copy of the spline to define the top edge of the wall.

1. Click and hold the Rectangular Array button in the Modify toolbar, and select the Copy button.

2. Select the spline you just created, and press ↵.

3. Click on any point on the screen.

4. If you have the running object snap turned on, make sure it is turned off, then enter **@0,0,44**↵. A copy of the spline appears above the original.

With the two ends of the wall defined by spline curves, you are ready to add the wall surface.

1. Adjust your view so you can see both splines clearly, as shown in Figure 5.19a.

2. Click on the Ruled Surface button on the Surface toolbar.

3. At the Select first defining curve prompt, click on the first spline curve you created, as shown in Figure 5.19a.

4. At the Select second defining curve prompt, click on the second spline curve at the point shown in Figure 5.19a. A segmented surface appears between the two splines, as shown in Figure 5.19b.

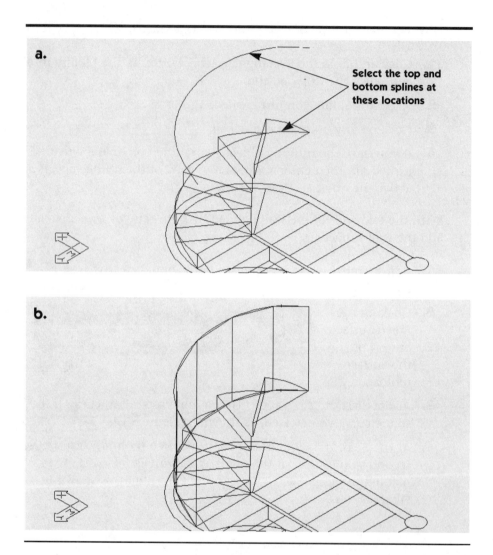

Select the top and
bottom splines at
these locations

Figure 5.19: Using the Ruled Surface tool to generate a curved surface

Tip   *This surface is actually a single object called a* mesh. *It is composed of six 3D faces. In fact, you can use the Explode tool to break the mesh down into its 3D face components. You won't be doing that here, but you may want to keep this little fact in mind for future reference.*

In the previous exercise, I asked you to select the splines by clicking on them at specific points. This is because the location you choose to select the splines will determine how the ruled surface is generated. By selecting points near the same ends of the spline, the surface is generated directly across from spline to spline. If you were to select points at opposite ends of the splines, as shown in Figure 5.20, the Ruled Surface would be "twisted."

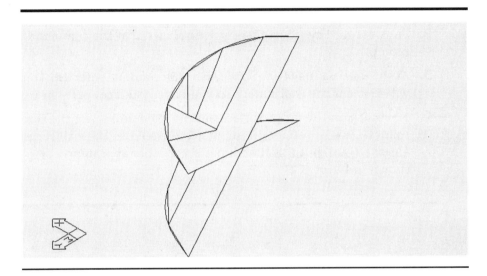

Figure 5.20: The Ruled Surface tool generates a "twisted" surface when points are selected at opposite ends of the defining curves.

While you used splines as your defining curve for the Ruled Surface tool, you can also use polylines, arcs, and standard lines for defining curves.

Getting a Smoother Surface

You may feel that the facets of the curved surface you just created are a bit too rough. A system variable called Surftab1 will allow you to increase the number of facets, thereby creating a smoother appearance. Here's how you would use Surftab1.

1. Erase the surface you just created in the previous exercise, but keep the spline arcs.

2. Press the Esc key twice, then type **Surftab1↵** at the command prompt.

3. At the New value for SURFTAB1 <6> prompt, enter **15**. This will segment the wall surface so you have 3 surfaces per stair tread.

4. Now click on the Ruled Surface button again and select the two splines again as you did in the previous exercise. The wall surface appears again, but this time it has a smoother appearance, as shown in Figure 5.21.

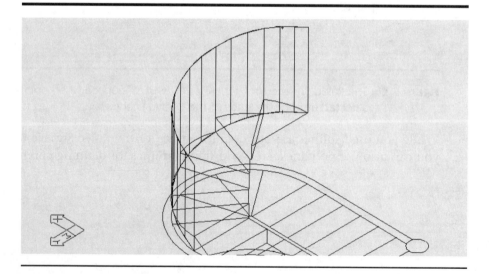

Figure 5.21: The curved wall after Surftab1 is set to a higher value and the wall is redrawn

Another tool called Surftab2 controls the faceting of meshes that form a compound curve. It works in a similar fashion to Surftab1.

In this last exercise, you created a curved surface by using two identical splines to define the surface edges. The defining curves used for the ruled sufrace tool need not be identical, however. You can use a different shape at each side of the surface to generate some fairly complex shapes, as shown in Figure 5.22.

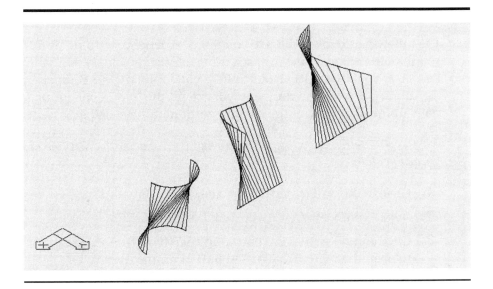

Figure 5.22: Some sample shapes that can be generated using the Ruled Surface tool

Constructing a Spline Using Point Filters

Now let's continue with the stair construction. You need to draw the outer surface of the curved wall. But unlike the inner surface, you don't have the corners of the stairs to help define the location of the spline. But if you consider the model so far, you can extract the data fairly easily using *point filters*. You got a brief glimpse of point filters earlier in this chapter, when you drew the outline of the step for the straight run of stairs. Point filters allow you to "filter" the individual X, Y, or Z component of a point, usually selected by an object snap.

The following exercise will give you direct experience with point filters. You'll draw a spline curve in space using existing geometry and point filters. First, you'll set up a layout to help you locate the XY components of the spline points. To do this, you will extend the lines representing the stairs in the plan view of the circular portion of the stairway.

> **Tip**   *Use selection cycling when attempting to extend the first line of the circular stair.*

1. Change the wall surface to the Stairwall layer.

2. Adjust your view so it looks similar to Figure 5.23.

3. Click and hold the Trim button in the Modify toolbar, then select the Extend button on the flyout.

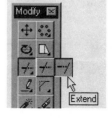

4. At the `Select boundary edge` prompt, select the arc representing the outside curved wall in the plan layout of the stairway (see Figure 5.23), then press ↵.

5. At the `Select object to extend` prompt, click on each of the radial lines representing the stair steps in the plan layout, as shown in Figure 5.23.

6. When you have extended all six lines, press ↵ to exit the Extend tool.

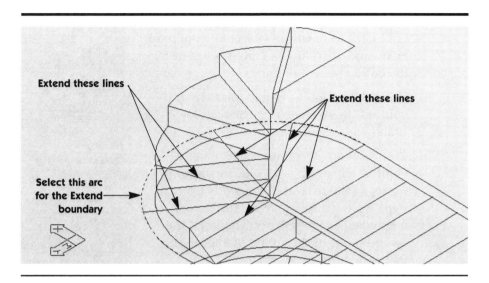

Figure 5.23: Extending the radial lines in the plan layout

Now you are ready to draw the spline using point filters. You will use the endpoints of the lines you extended to locate the spline in the X and Y axis. In addition, you will use the corners of the 3D stair to locate the spline in the Z axis.

> ***Tip*** *You may want to turn on the Endpoint Running Osnap option for this exercise, so you won't have to select it every time you want to select an endpoint. To do this, choose Options ➤ Running Object Snap, then at the Running Object Snap dialog box, click on the Endpoint checkbox. Click OK to exit the dialog box.*

1. Click on the Spline tool in the Draw toolbar.

2. At the `Enter first point` prompt, use the Endpoint Osnap and pick the endpoint of the first stair (see Figure 5.24a).

3. At the Enter point prompt, Shift-right-right-click to open the Object Snap pop-up menu and select the .XY point filter near the bottom of the menu.

4. Using the Endpoint Osnap, pick the end-point of the next step on the plan layout, as shown in Figure 5.24b.

5. At the (need Z) prompt, use the End-point Osnap again, and pick the bottom corner of the riser in the second curved step, as shown in Figure 5.24b. Though it may be hard to tell, you've placed the second point of the spline in a location that is floating in 3D space.

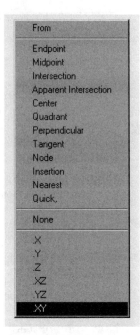

6. At the Enter point prompt, choose .XY again from the Object Snap pop-up menu, then pick the next endpoint, as shown in Figure 5.24c.

7. At the (need Z) prompt, use the Endpoint Osnap and pick the bottom corner of the next 3D stair riser, as shown in Figure 5.24c.

8. Repeat steps 6 and 7 for the rest of the points of the spline curve, as shown in Figure 5.25.

9. When you are done with the last point, press ↵.

10. At the Enter start tangent prompt, press ↵.

11. At the Enter end tangent prompt, press ↵. Your spline will look like Figure 5.25.

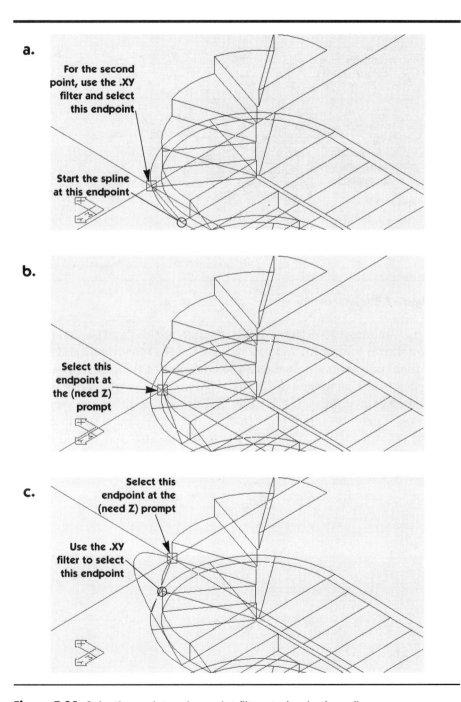

a.

For the second point, use the .XY filter and select this endpoint

Start the spline at this endpoint

b.

Select this endpoint at the (need Z) prompt

c.

Select this endpoint at the (need Z) prompt

Use the .XY filter to select this endpoint

Figure 5.24: Selecting points using point filters to begin the spline

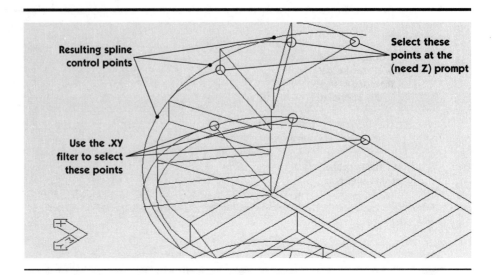

Figure 5.25: Finishing the spline

Take a moment to review what happened in this exercise. In steps 3 and 4, you told AutoCAD you wanted to select just the X and Y component of a geometry, namely, the endpoint of the line representing a step in the plan view (from the top, looking down). By doing this, you restrained the X and Y value to a vertical line that represents that Z coordinate. In step 5, you provided the Z coordinate by clicking on the bottom edge of a stair. The net result was that you picked a point in space that is exactly where you wanted the spline control point.

Now you have the bottom of the outside curved wall. The following exercise will walk you through the steps to finish the wall.

1. Copy the spline you just created 44 inches vertically, just as you did earlier with the spline for the inside of the wall.

2. Click on the Ruled Surface button in the Surfaces toolbar, then select the two splines you just created, as shown in Figure 5.26a. The surface appears.

3. Change the layer for the surface to the Stairwall layer to temporarily move it out of the way.

4. Click on the ruled surface button again, then select the two splines at the bottom of the wall, as shown in Figure 5.26b. This constructs the bottom edge of the wall.

5. Click on the Ruled Surface button a third time, then select the two splines at the top of the wall, as shown in Figure 5.26b. This constructs the top surface of the wall.

6. Change both the bottom and top surfaces to the Stairwall layer, then turn off the Stairwall layer.

7. Thaw the Stairwall layer, then zoom out and click on the Hide button on the Render toolbar, so your view looks similar to Figure 5.26c.

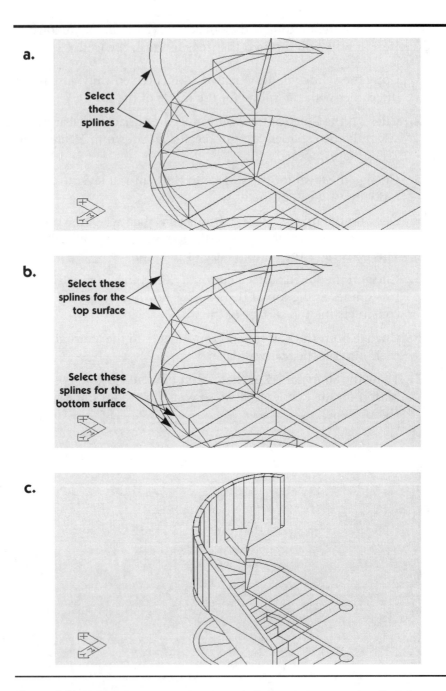

Figure 5.26: Adding the top and bottom surfaces to the curved wall of the stairway

Finishing Off the Stairway

To finish off the stair, you need only copy the straight run of stairs to the opposite side of the stairway. The following images show the steps you need to take to do this. The operation only requires you to copy the straight run of stairs and rotate them. Once this is done, you can move the copy into position.

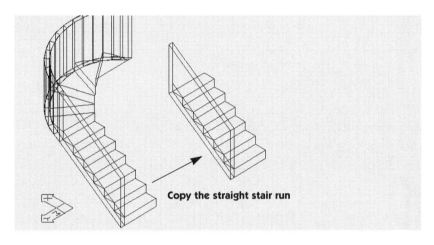

Copy the straight stair run

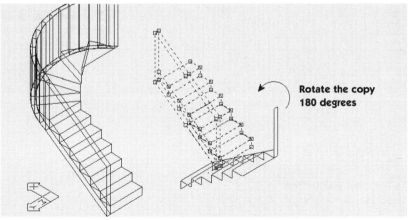

Rotate the copy
180 degrees

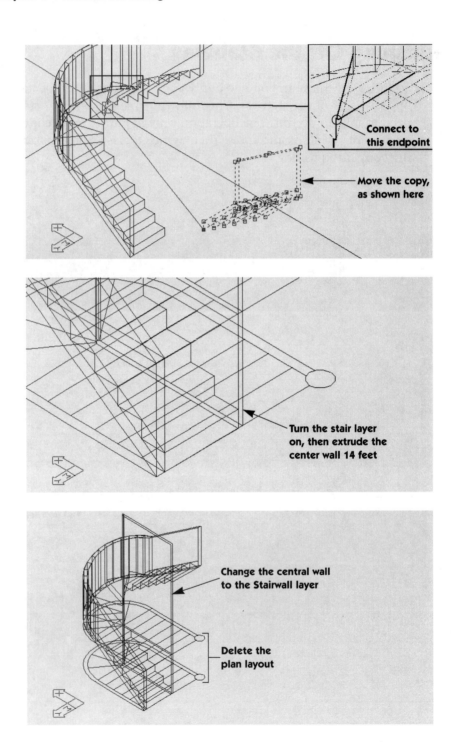

Connect to this endpoint

Move the copy, as shown here

Turn the stair layer on, then extrude the center wall 14 feet

Change the central wall to the Stairwall layer

Delete the plan layout

Once you've completed the stairs, erase the 2D layout of the stairs. To simplify this operation, use the Selection Filter tool in the Standard toolbar and select everything in the Stair layer. See Chapter 4 if you need help with the Selection Filter tool. When you are done, your drawing will look like Figure 5.27.

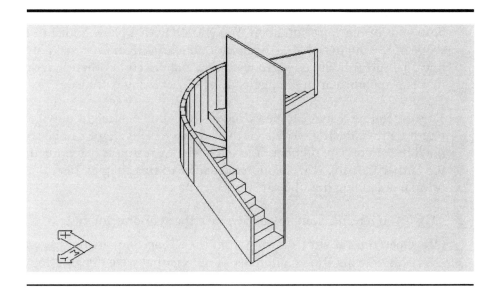

Figure 5.27: The completed stairway

> *Tip*　*The Extrude tools will extrude a shape along a polyline path. Chapter 6 shows you how it's done. For more complex extrusions, I've included on the companion CD-ROM an AutoLISP utility called* SPLINEP.LSP *that will extrude a shape along a curved spline path. Since splines are not restricted to a plane, you can generate complex extrusions very easily.* SPLINEP.LSP *will also allow you to flare or "bulb" the shape as it is extruded along the path. See Appendix B for details.*

Extruding Lines and Curves

In Chapter 4, you used the Extrude command to turn closed polylines into solid masses. The Extrude command only works with closed poly-lines. You may encounter situations, however, where you'd like to be able to extrude an open polyline or arc. The Tabulated Surface tool, or Tabsurf, lets you do just that. It extrudes an object in a straight direction, leaving both ends of the extrusion open. You end up with a plane folded in the shape of the original shape. In addition to extruding non-closed poly-lines, Tabsurf will let you extrude objects in a direction other than one that is perpendicular to the plane of the object being extruded.

Tabsurf requires a shape to be extruded and a line or straight polyline rep-resenting the direction vector for the extrusion. This shape can be a line, polyline, or arc. The number of facets in the extrusion is determined by the Surftab1 setting you encountered earlier in this chapter. Here is a brief tutorial describing how Tabsurf works.

1. If you haven't done so already, save the stair drawing file.

2. Open the Tabsurf drawing from the CD accompanying this book. This drawing shows a number of objects that were drawn using polylines and arcs.

3. Rotate the UCS 90 degrees in the X axis. Do this by typing **UCS.↵** **X.↵ 90.↵** (or choose View ➤ Set UCS ➤ X Axis Rotate, and then enter **90.↵**).

4. Draw a 4-inch line at 45 degrees, as shown in Figure 5.28a.

5. Choose Extruded Surface from the Surface toolbar.

6. At the Select curved path prompt, select the circle.

7. At the Select direction vector prompt, pick the line you drew in step 4 at the location shown in Figure 5.28b. The circle is extruded as a hexagonal prism.

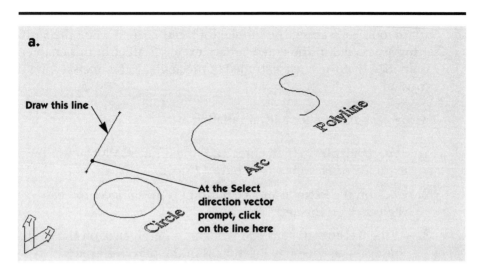

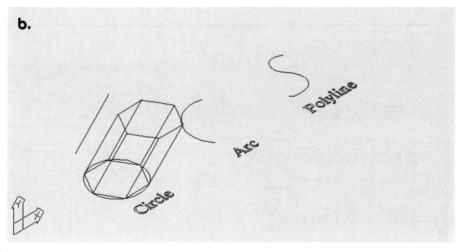

Figure 5.28: Extruding an object using the Extrude button (Tabsurf command)

The Extrude Surface tool creates a faceted mesh, similar to the Ruled Surface tool. You can set the number of facets created using the Surftab1 setting as you did in the Ruled Surface exercise earlier in this chapter. Also notice that the circle extruded at the angle of the line skewing the extrusion.

Try the next exercise for a little variation.

1. Type **Surftab1**↵, then enter **12**↵ to tell AutoCAD you want extruded surface objects to have 12 sides.

2. Click on the Extrude Surface button on the Surfaces toolbar, then click on the arc.

3. At the `Select direction vector` prompt, click on the 45-degree line again, at the same location as in the previous exercise, step 7 (see Figure 5.28). Your arc extrudes, as shown in Figure 5.29.

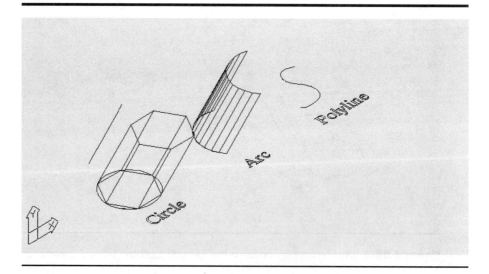

Figure 5.29: The arc extruded with a higher Surftab1 setting

This time the extrusion has 12 facets, giving it a smoother appearance. Notice that the circle remains untouched. All the Surface toolbar tools create new objects from existing ones, leaving the existing objects untouched.

Now try a third extrusion. This time, you'll extrude the polyline in the opposite direction from the circle and arc.

1. Click on the Extrude Surface button again, then click on the polyline.

2. At the `Select direction vector` prompt, click on the 45-degree line again, but this time select a point closer to the top of the line, as shown in Figure 5.30. The polyline extrudes downward.

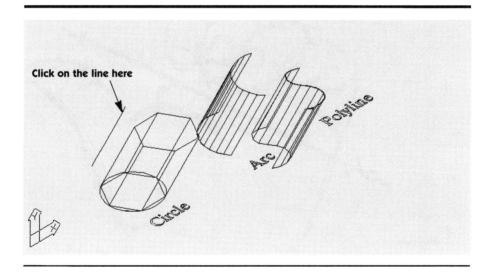

Figure 5.30: The direction of the extrusion is dependent upon the point you select on the direction vector.

Which End Do I Choose?

As you have just seen, the direction of extrusion depends on the point you select on the direction vector. If you select the direction vector closer to the bottom, the object extrudes upward. If you select the direction near the top, the object extrudes downward. A variation of the "right hand rule" can help you remember which end of the direction vector you should pick.

Imagine yourself grasping the direction vector with your right hand, as shown in Figure 5.31. Your thumb is pointing in the direction of the extrusion.

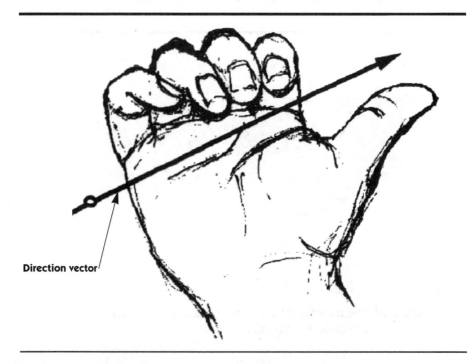

Direction vector

Figure 5.31: The right-hand rule can help you remember which end of the direction vector points toward the extrusion.

Defining Warped Surfaces with the Edge Surface Tool

Both the Extrude Surface and Ruled Surface tools create surfaces that can be defined by a series of adjacent planes. The curvature of the surfaces occur in only one direction. If you want to define a surface that is curved in *two* directions, like a saddle, you can use the Edge Surface tool or **Edgesurf** command. This tool creates a *3D mesh*, which is an array of 3d faces. A mesh looks something like a net.

The following exercise shows you how you can use the Edge Surface tool to create an overstuffed chair. Once again, you'll see how polylines are very useful in creating 3D objects.

1. Open the Stufchr.DWG file from the Sample directory of the CD accompanying this book. You'll see a variety of curved shapes. They are all polylines from which you will construct the chair.

2. Choose View ➤ 3D Viewpoint Presets ➤ SW Isometric to set up for the chair construction.

3. Click and hold the Rotate button on the Modify toolbar, then select the 3D Rotate button on the flyout.

4. At the Select object prompt, click on the curved polyline shown in Figure 5.32a then press ↵ to finish your selection. This polyline represents the profile of the back side of the arm of the chair.

5. At the Axis by Object/Last/View/Xaxis/Yaxis/Zaxis/ <2points>: prompt, click on the endpoint of the polyline, as shown in Figure 5.32a.

6. At the 2nd point prompt, turn on the Ortho mode and pick a point to the right of the first point along the X axis.

7. At the <Rotation angle>/Reference: prompt, enter **80**↵. The polyline rotates into a vertical position, as shown in Figure 5.32b. You may need to adjust your view to the view shown in the figure.

8. Using the 3D Rotate tool, rotate the other two polyline profiles to the angles, as shown in Figure 5.33.

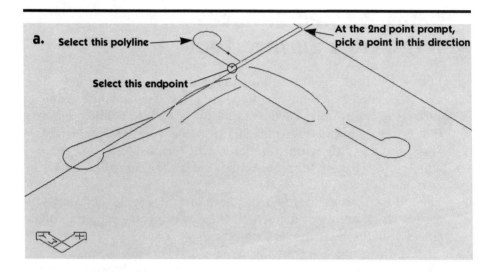

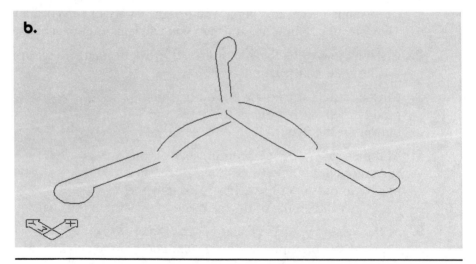

Figure 5.32: Rotating the first polyline profile into position

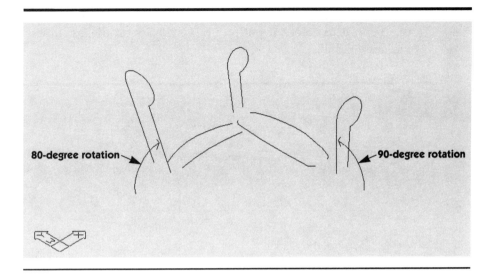

Figure 5.33: Rotating the other two profiles into position

All the polylines in the previous exercise were drawn in a 2D plan view. You've just rotated some of the key profiles into a vertical position. Now you need to make some adjustments.

1. Zoom into the location shown in Figure 5.34a.

2. Move the profile of the front of the chair arm so that its bottom endpoint meets the endpoint of the base profile, as shown in Figure 5.34a.

3. Move the endpoint of the polyline representing the other side of the base to the endpoint of the arm profile, as shown in Figure 5.34b. It is very important the all four polylines meet exactly end-to-end.

4. Zoom into the area shown in Figure 5.35a and move the back profile to meet the base profile, as shown.

5. Click on the other base profile, as shown in Figure 5.35a, to display its grip points.

6. Click on the endpoint grip of the highlighted profile, as shown in Figure 5.35a, then, using the Endpoint Osnap, move it to meet the endpoint of the back profile shown in Figure 5.35a.

7. Click on the base profile to the right, as shown in Figure 5.35b.

8. Click on the grip at the endpoint of the base profile and move
or stretch it to meet the endpoint of the back profile, as shown
in Figure 5.35b.

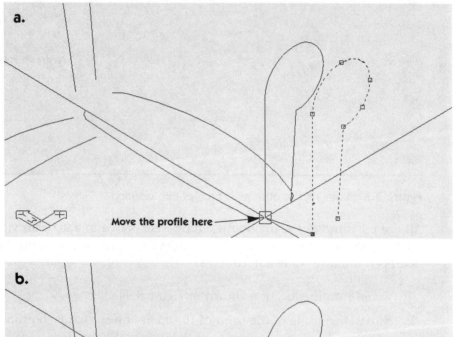

Figure 5.34: Moving the various polyline profiles to meet end-to-end

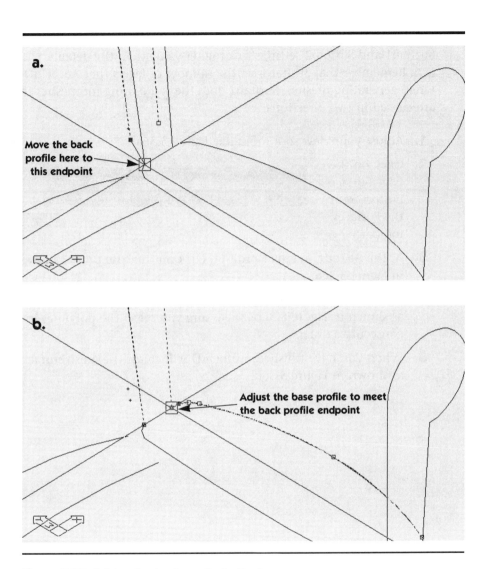

Figure 5.35: Joining the back profile to the base

Now you are ready to create the surface. You will first need to set the Surftab1 and Surftab2 settings to a higher value than the default, which is 6. Remember that Surftab1 set the number of facets that AutoCAD uses when generating meshes. Surftab2 does the same thing for meshes that are curved in two directions.

1. Adjust your view so it looks like Figure 5.36a.

2. Click on the Edge Surface button from the Surfaces toolbar.

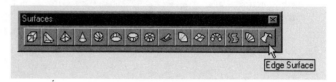

3. At the `Select edge1:` prompt, click on the base profile shown in Figure 5.36a.

4. For the next three prompts, select the other three polyline profiles, as shown in Figure 5.36b. Make sure you select the polylines in consecutive order.

5. When you have finished, AutoCAD will create the mesh surface, as shown in Figure 5.36b.

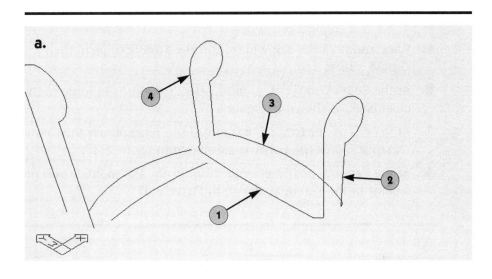

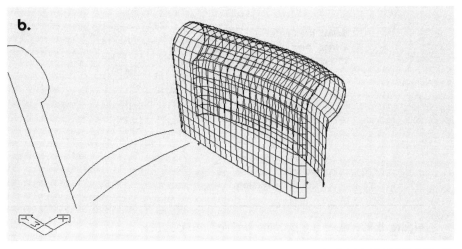

Figure 5.36: Adding the mesh to the chair arm

Now let's move on to the back of the chair.

1. Click and hold the Copy button in the Modify toolbar, then choose Mirror.

2. At the `Select object` prompt, select the vertical profile of the chair back, as shown in Figure 5.37.

3. At the `First point of mirror line` prompt, use the Center Osnap and pick the polyline arc shown in Figure 5.37.

4. At the `Second point` prompt, turn on the Ortho mode and pick a point in the Y axis, as shown in Figure 5.37.

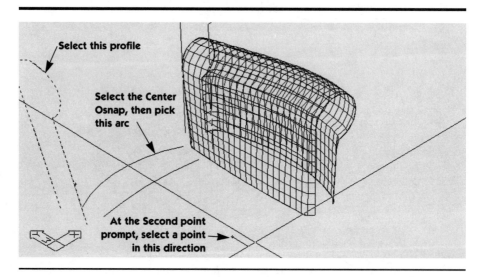

Select this profile

Select the Center Osnap, then pick this arc

At the Second point prompt, select a point in this direction

Figure 5.37: Move the polyline profiles into position.

5. At the `Delete old object` prompt, press ↵. A mirrored copy of the polyline appears to the right of the original.

6. Move the two polyline profiles into position so they touch the front base profile, as shown in the following images.

7. Stretch the back profile into position and adjust its endpoint.

8. Choose the Edge Surface button on the Surfaces toolbar and select the four polyline profiles in sequential order. AutoCAD draws the surface for the back of the chair.

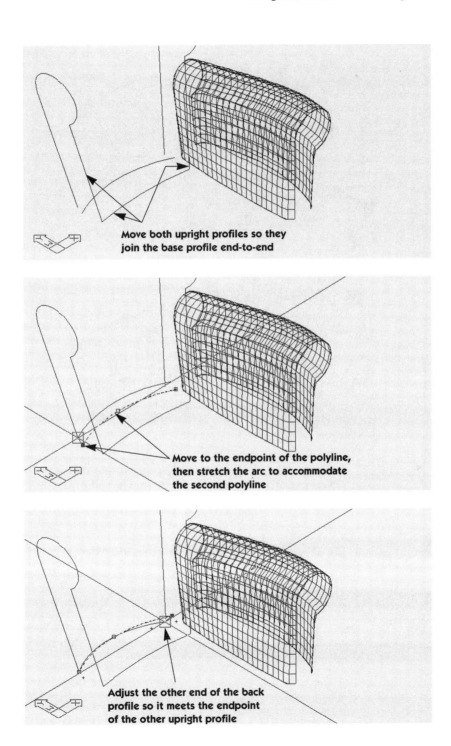

Move both upright profiles so they
join the base profile end-to-end

Move to the endpoint of the polyline,
then stretch the arc to accommodate
the second polyline

Adjust the other end of the back
profile so it meets the endpoint
of the other upright profile

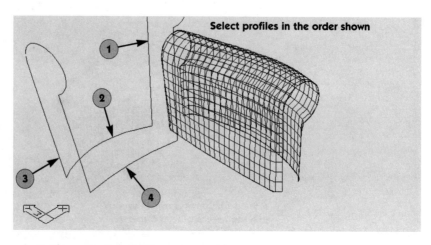

Select profiles in the order shown

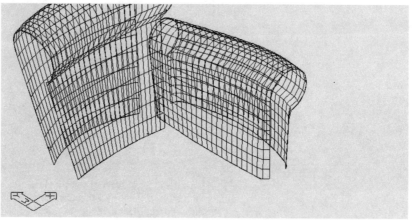

Tip   In this exercise you must first set the UCS to the orientation of a poly-line before you can edit it. The companion CD-ROM includes a utility called 3Dpedit.LSP that will allow you to edit a polyline without having to first align the UCS to it. See Appendix B for details.

To complete the chair, add the other arm and close the ends of the back and arm profiles, as explained in the following steps.

1. Create a layer called **Mesh**, then move all the meshes to the new layer.

2. Turn off the Mesh layer. This will temporarily remove the mesh so you can work more easily with the polyline profiles.

3. Choose View ➤ Set UCS ➤ Object, then click on the arm profile toward the front of the chair, as shown in Figure 5.38. This will allow you to use the Edit Polyline tool to close this polyline.

4. Click on the Edit Polyline tool in the Modify toolbar, then select the same polyline profile you selected in the previous step.

5. Type **C**↵ to close it. In the next step, you will use the Region tool to turn it into a surface. The Region tool will not work unless the polyline is closed.

6. Choose the Region tool from the Polygon flyout of the Draw toolbar, then click on the polyline a third time.

7. Press ↵ once you've selected the polyline. You should see a message in the command area telling you that one region was created. The drawing itself doesn't appear to change.

8. Repeat steps 3 through 7 for the other three polygon profiles indicated in Figure 5.38.

9. Turn the Mesh layer back on and set the UCS to the World coordinate system.

10. Choose the Mirror button in the Modify toolbar, then, using a selection window, select the mesh and the regions representing the arm shown in Figure 5.39a. Press ↵ once you've made the selection.

11. At the `First point of mirror line` prompt, use the Center Osnap and select the center of the arc used for the base profile of the back of the chair, as shown in Figure 5.39b.

12. At the `Second point` prompt, turn on the Ortho mode and select a point along the Y axis, as shown in Figure 5.39b.

13. Zoom back a bit, then click on the Hide button in the Render toolbar. Your chair will look like Figure 5.40.

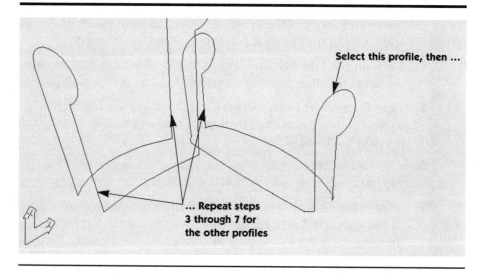

Figure 5.38: Turning the ends of the arm and back into regions so they appear to be closed

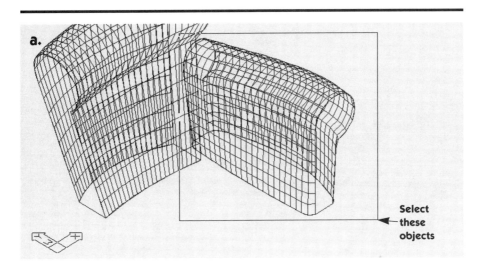

Select
these
objects

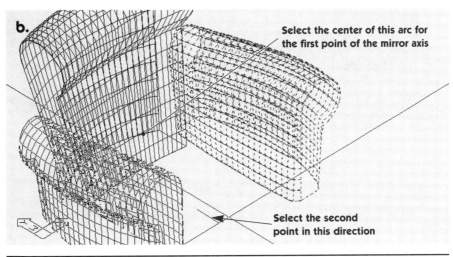

Select the center of this arc for
the first point of the mirror axis

Select the second
point in this direction

Figure 5.39: Mirror the components of one arm to the other side of the chair.

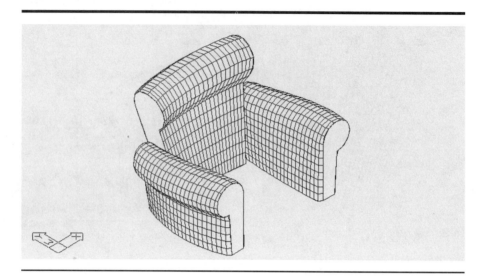

Figure 5.40: The chair thus far, after using the Hide tool

Now the only part missing is the seat cushion. The following images walk you through the process of creating the cushion.

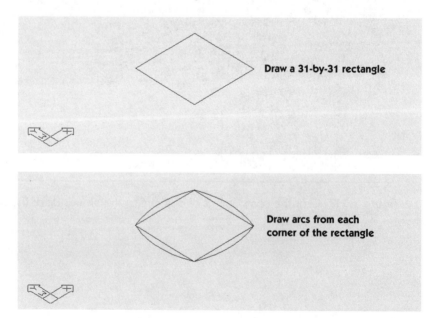

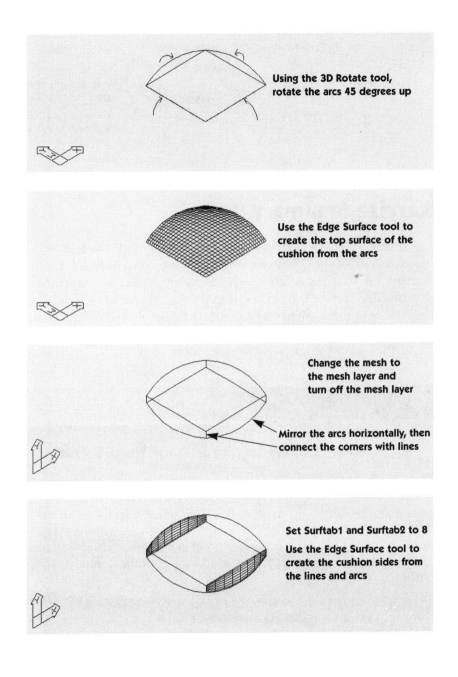

Using the 3D Rotate tool, rotate the arcs 45 degrees up

Use the Edge Surface tool to create the top surface of the cushion from the arcs

Change the mesh to the mesh layer and turn off the mesh layer

Mirror the arcs horizontally, then connect the corners with lines

Set Surftab1 and Surftab2 to 8

Use the Edge Surface tool to create the cushion sides from the lines and arcs

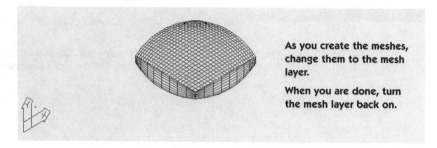

As you create the meshes, change them to the mesh layer.

When you are done, turn the mesh layer back on.

Exercise Summary

In this last set of exercises, you used polylines and arcs as edges for the Edge Surface tool. You can also use splines and 3D polylines to further vary the shape of a surface. Once you've created a mesh surface with the Edge Surface tool, you can make adjustments to the surface. This requires some patience and practice, however. You'll get a chance to see how to edit surfaces later in this chapter. For now, let's take a look at the last of the surface modeling tools—Revsurf.

How Smooth Do the Meshes Have To Be?

Mesh surfaces are essentially a series of flat surfaces joined together to give the appearance of smoothness. When you use the Hidden Line or Shade tool in AutoCAD you see the edges of each and every mesh. But in AutoVision or 3D Studio, you can hide the edges using a feature called Surface Smoothing. Surface Smoothing visually removes the edges of each individual facet of a mesh to give the impression of a smooth curved surface.

If you plan to use your model for export to 3D Studio, or if you plan to use AutoVision for your renderings, you don't have to use high Surftab1 and Surftab2 settings to achieve a smooth appearance on curved surfaces. Both of these programs can smooth out the rough edges.

Extruding a Circular Surface

The Revolved Surface tool (**Revsurf** command) allows you to quickly generate circular extrusions. Typical examples are vases or tea cups. The following exercise shows how the Revolved Surface tool is used to draw a pitcher. You'll use an existing drawing that has a profile of the pitcher already drawn.

1. Save the Stufchr.DWG file from the previous exercise if you haven't done so already.

2. Open the Pitcher.DWG file. This file contains a polyline profile of the pitcher as well as a single line representing the center of the

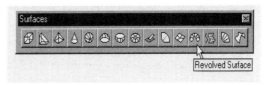

pitcher (See Figure 5.41a). The profile and line have already been rotated to a position that is perpendicular to the WCS. The grid is turned on so you can better visualize the plane of the WCS.

3. Click on the Revolved Surface button on the Surfaces Toolbar.

4. At the Select path curve prompt, click on the polyline profile, as shown in Figure 5.41a.

5. At the Select axis of revolution prompt, click near the bottom of the vertical line representing the center of the vase, as shown in Figure 5.41a.

6. At the Start angle <0> prompt, press ↵ to accept the 0 start angle.

7. At the Included angle (+=ccw, -=cw) <Full circle> prompt, press ↵ to accept the Full Circle default. The pitcher appears, as shown in Figure 5.41b.

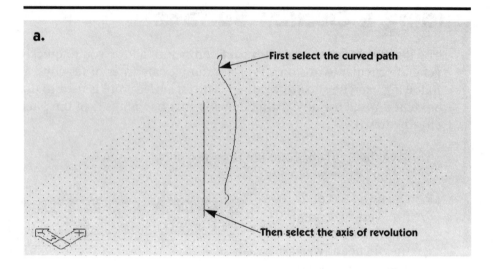

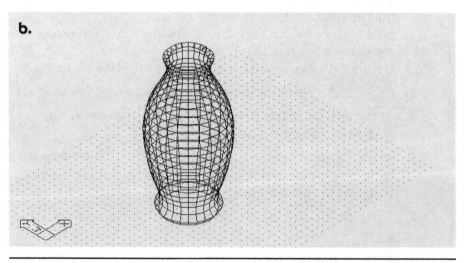

Figure 5.41: Drawing the pitcher using the Revolved Surface tool

Notice that the pitcher is made up of a faceted mesh, like the mesh that is created by the Edge Surface tool. Just as with the Edge Surface tool, you can set the number of facets in each direction using the Surftab1 and Surftab2 system variable settings. Both Surftab1 and Surftab2 were already set to 24 in the Pitcher.DWG file so the pitcher shape would appear fairly smooth.

You may have noticed that in steps 6 and 7 in the previous exercise you have a few options. In step 6, you can specify a start angle. In this case, you accepted the 0 default. Had you entered a different value, 90 for example, then the extrusion would have started in the 90-degree position relative to the current WCS. In step 7, you have the option of specifying the angle of the extrusion. Had you entered 180, for example, you would have gotten half the pitcher. You can also specify the direction of the extrusion by specifying a negative or positive angle.

◆ Editing a Mesh

Once you've created a mesh surface with either the Edge Surface or Revolved Surface tool, you can make modifications to it. For example, suppose you wanted to add a spout to the pitcher. You can use grips to adjust the individual points on the mesh to reshape the object. Here, you must take care how you select points. The UCS will become useful for editing meshes, as shown in the following example.

1. Zoom into the area shown in Figure 5.42a.

2. Choose View ➤ Set UCS ➤ Origin, then, using the Endpoint Osnap, select the point on the rim of the pitcher shown in Figure 5.42a. By placing the UCS origin on this point, you are ensuring that points you select in space are in the plane of the top edge of the pitcher. You'll see why this is important later.

3. Click on the pitcher mesh to expose its grips.

4. Shift-click on the grips shown in Figure 5.42b.

5. Click on the grip shown in Figure 5.42c and move the cursor to the left. As you move the cursor, notice how the lip of the pitcher deforms.

6. When you have the shape of a spout similar to Figure 5.42c, select that point. The spout will be fixed in the new position.

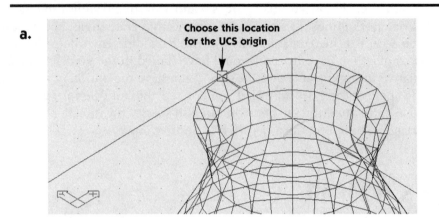

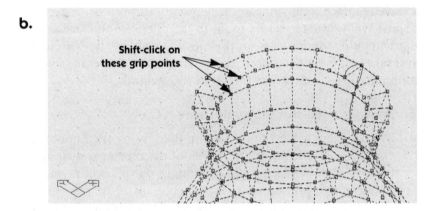

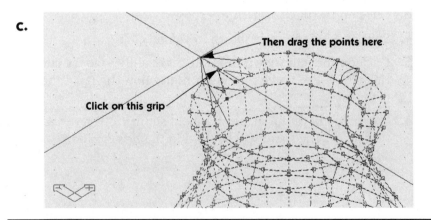

Figure 5.42: Adding a spout to the pitcher mesh

You can refine the shape of the spout by carefully adjusting the position of other grip points around the edge of the pitcher. Later, when you render the pitcher, you can apply a smooth shading value so that the sharp edges of the spout are smoothed out.

In the first part of the previous exercise, you moved the UCS origin to a point at the rim of the pitcher. This was an important step because it allowed you easily place the new location of the mesh grip points by simply clicking on a point in space. Had you left the UCS at the WCS location, the point you picked in step 6 would have been wildly out of place. It would have looked correct from your point of view, but once you looked at your vase from the top down, you would have seen a spout pointing to the far right of the drawing (see Figure 5.43).

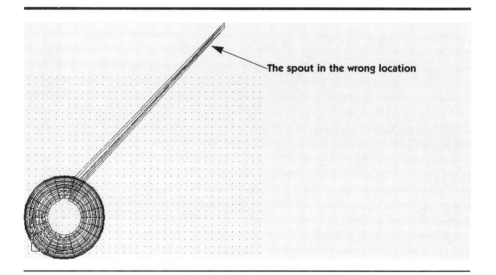

The spout in the wrong location

Figure 5.43: A distorted spout caused by inaccurate placement of the UCS

Another option would be to specify a *relative* distance in step 6, as opposed to selecting a point. By specifying a point, like @.5<50 for example, you would not have to move the UCS. Using this method, however, removes you from the spontaneity of being able to select a point visually.

◆ Summary

This concludes your tour of the surface modeling tools. You haven't actually finished the pitcher; it still needs a handle. In the next chapter, you'll see how you can use some tools from the Solids toolbar to add the handle. You'll also look at how to generate more complex shapes with a combination of surface tools and splines.

Modeling with Solids

AutoCAD's solid modeling tools will help you make quick work of complex designs or shapes that cannot be created with the surface modeling tools. But you have to learn a different method of modeling. Also, solid modeling uses more computer memory than surface modeling and creates larger files. Depending on your system, then, you may want to use solid modeling only sparingly. You can mix solid modeling and surface modeling to achieve nearly any shape you need, quickly and efficiently.

In the last chapter, you used surface modeling tools to develop the stair and wall components of the building you started in the Chapter 3. In this chapter you'll make further additions to that same model. This will give you a sense of how you can mix solid modeling tools and surface modeling tools to speed you through your modeling tasks. You'll also learn how to use other solid modeling features by creating a new building ("Facade") in a more classical style.

◆ Building Complexity from Simple Shapes (Primitives)

Up to now, you have been building 3D shapes using 3D faces and meshes. Essentially, you have been modeling the "skin" of the 3D objects. Solid modeling lets you create 3D shapes by combining 3D shapes together or by subtracting one shape from another. These shapes are called *primitives*, and primitive they are. You have a total of six basic primitive shapes you can use to build your 3D solids. These shapes are the box, cone, cylinder, wedge, torus, and sphere (see Figure 6.1).

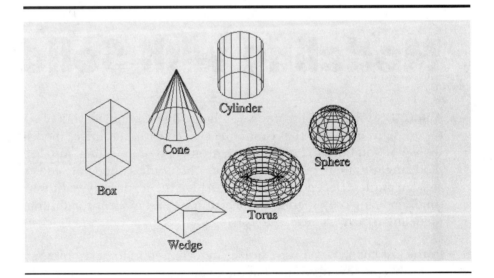

Figure 6.1: The six primitive shapes used for solid modeling

Creating with Unions, Subtractions, and Intersections

Wi+'   tools, you created forms by extruding two-dimensional
                 ing the edge of a surface using different shapes. The
                 'face. You then join surfaces together to give the illu-

                        AutoCAD act like solid objects; you can join
                        iows three very different shapes that can
                        just by joining the objects together in
                        shows the three basic ways you can combine
                        .ion, union, and subtraction. These ways of com-
                        .ed "Boolean operations," are pretty self-explanatory:

        .ntersection of solids produces the shape of the space occupied
    ɔy all the objects.

◆ A subtraction of two solids removes the shape of one solid from
    the other.

◆ A union of solids creates a single object from all the solids.

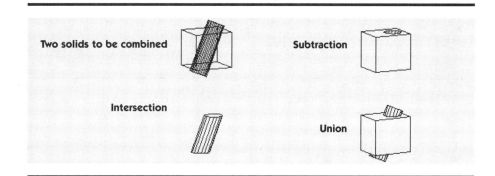

Two solids to be combined   **Subtraction**

Intersection

                                        Union

Figure 6.2: The different ways you can combine solids to get different forms. The
                INTERSECTION of the two creates a solid cylindrical form; the SUBTRAC-
                TION of the cylindrical solid from the box creates a cylindrical hole in
                the box; and the UNION of the original two solids creates a box with
                two round pegs sticking out.

Don Frost
Customer Service

Tel: (250) 382-5184
Fax: (250) 382-4359
Res: (250) 479-8513

UAP/NAPA VICTORIA
555 Ardersier Road
Victoria, BC V8Z 1C8

Figure 6.2 also hints at one of solid modeling's strong points. You can quickly create shapes that are difficult or nearly impossible using any other method. For example, look at Figure 6.3. Creating the circular notch cut out of a cylinder in this figure is a simple operation with solids, but is nearly impossible to create accurately using surface modeling tools.

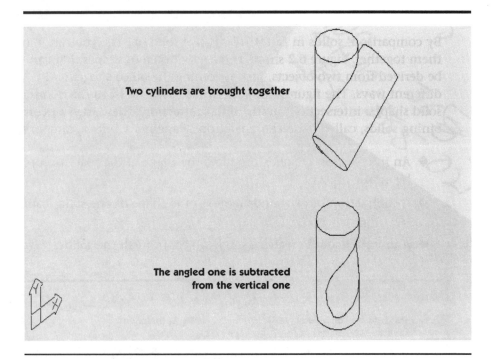

Two cylinders are brought together

The angled one is subtracted
from the vertical one

Figure 6.3: A notch cut out of cylinder is easily accomplished using solid modeling. This same feat would be nearly impossible to accomplish using surface tools.

◆ Using the "Polyline Wildcard"

In addition to the standard primitives, you can also create solids by extruding closed polylines. In fact, if you've been doing the exercises sequentially from the beginning of this book, you've already created some solids by extruding polylines. You've also use Boolean operations using polylines in Chapter 3, when you were introduced to regions. In fact, regions are a sort of 2D primitive.

We call the polylines "wildcards" because you can use them to quickly create any complex 3D solid shape without having to add various primitives. Any shape you can create with a polyline you can extrude into a solid. You can then perform any of the Boolean operations you want to further add complexity and detail. Later in this chapter you'll get a chance to see how polylines are used in solids. First, let's start working with solids using some basic primitives.

◆ Adding Exterior Walls and Floors to Our Model

In this first exercise you'll learn how solid modeling tools will help you quickly model the exterior walls of our model. You'll use a combination of techniques including the use of extruded polylines.

Converting Elevations into Solid 3D Models

Although the shapes in this exercise are simple rectangles, they could be just about any shape you can create with a polyline. The point is that you can subtract a solid from another solid to create a wall with an opening in it.

1. Open the file named Sav-elev.dwg.

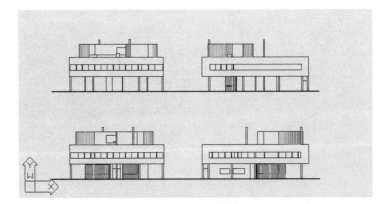

2. Zoom into the elevation in the lower left corner.

3. Click on the Rectangle tool in the Polygon flyout, and "trace" the second story outline with it by picking opposite corners, as shown in Figure 6.4.

4. Use the Rectangle tool again to trace the rectangle for the entire windows area in the second floor (also shown in Figure 6.4).

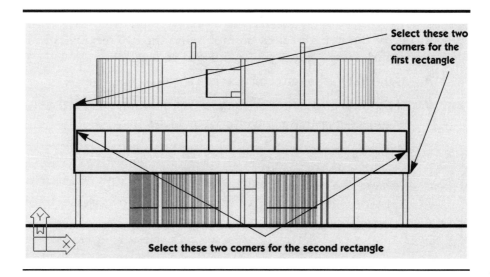

Select these two corners for the first rectangle

Select these two corners for the second rectangle

Figure 6.4: Use the Rectangle tool to select these two rectangles.

5. To help you visualize the next few steps, choose View ➤ 3D View-point Presets ➤ SW Isometric, then zoom in on the same elevation.

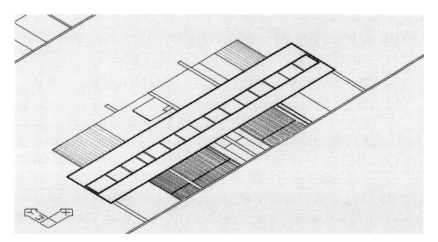

6. Choose the Extrude button from the Solids toolbar.

7. At the `Select objects` prompt, select the two rectangles you just created. Press ↵ when you've finished your selection.

8. At the `Path/<Height of Extrusion>` prompt, enter **6**↵.

9. At the `Extrusion taper angle <0>` prompt, press ↵. The two rectangles appear as 6-inch-thick rectangles.

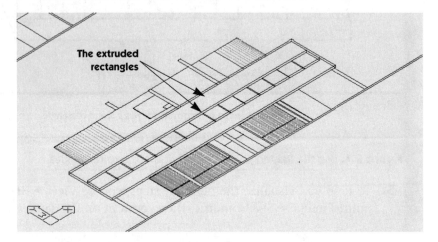

The extruded rectangles

10. Now choose Subtract from the Explode flyout menu.

11. At the `Select solids and regions to subtract from...` prompt, select the larger of the two solids, then press ↵.

12. At the `Select solids and regions to subtract...` prompt, select the smaller rectangle then press ↵. You now have a solid wall with a rectangular opening.

13. Click on the Hide button in the Render toolbar. Your drawing will look like Figure 6.5.

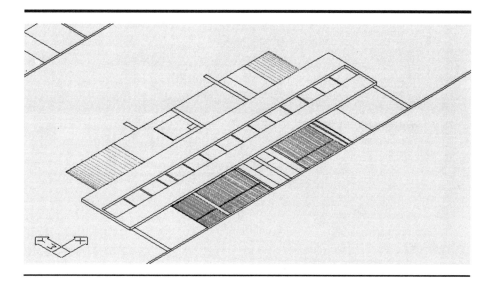

Figure 6.5: The finished wall viewed with hidden lines removed

Notice that, unlike the window you created in Chapter 3 for the ground floor, this window does not show any joint lines where different extruded surfaces meet (see Figure 3.26). The wall is fairly clean and free of unwanted busyness. For example, you don't see any seams between the surface just below the window opening and the full-height portions of the walls at either end.

Now let's continue with another wall.

1. Shift your view so you can see the elevation to the right of the one you just worked on, so your view looks like Figure 6.6a.

2. Trace the outline of the second floor and the second floor window, just as you did in the previous exercise.

3. Extrude both rectangles and subtract the smaller solid from the larger one.

4. Choose the Hide button on the Render toolbar. Your second elevation should look like Figure 6.6b.

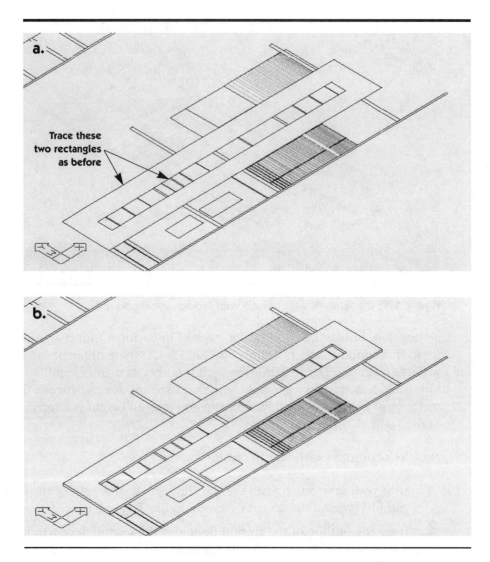

Figure 6.6: Creating a second exterior wall

5. Zoom out so you can see both elevations, then use the 3D Rotate tool to rotate the walls so they are perpendicular to the elevation drawings.

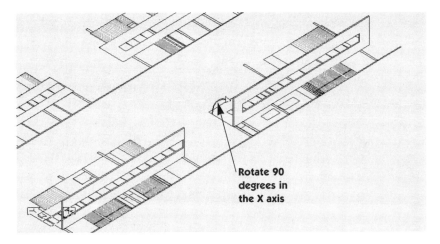

Rotate 90 degrees in the X axis

6. Rotate the newest wall 90 degrees so it is at a right angle to the first wall.

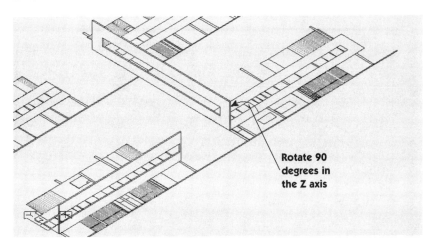

Rotate 90 degrees in the Z axis

7. Adjust your view so it looks like the following image, then move the second wall so its outer corner meets the outer corner of the first wall.

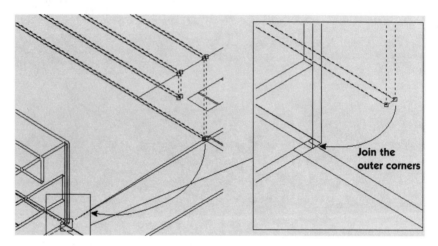

8. Copy both walls and adjust their position so that all the walls meet corner-to-corner, as shown in Figure 6.7.

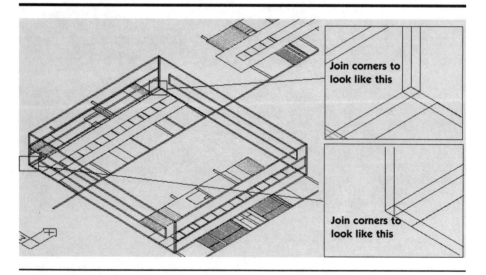

Figure 6.7: Copy both walls and adjust their positions so that all the walls meet corner-to-corner.

9. Click and hold the Subtract button on the Modify toolbar, then select the Union tool.

10. Click on all four upright walls. The walls join to form one object.

11. Click on the Hide button on the Render toolbar. Your drawing will look like Figure 6.8.

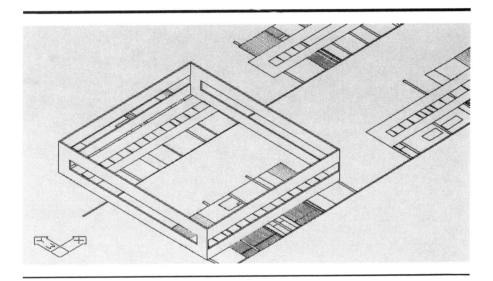

Figure 6.8: The finished exterior walls

You might notice that after you used the Union tool, many of the extraneous lines disappeared. Figure 6.9 shows a before-and-after view of a corner of the wall. Notice that the vertical line representing the wall thickness disappears after the Union.

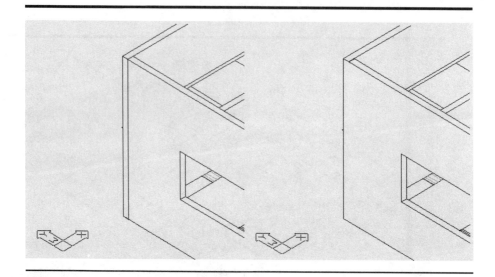

Figure 6.9: The wall corner before and after the Union tool is used. Notice that the vertical joint line disappears.

Using Layers, Xrefs, and Hide as an Editing Tool

As you start to build your 3D model, you'll find that it becomes more difficult to visualize surfaces in a wireframe view. This becomes apparent when you start to stack floors on top of each other or when your line of sight traverses a particularly complex part of your model. To help keep the clutter down, you can sort parts of your model by layers that can be turned on or off depending on where you are working. In a multi-level building, for example, you can provide a layer for each floor and work on only one floor at a time.

You might also employ the use of Xrefs to keep floors in separate files. You can then create a "master" file that combines the floors using the Xref tool. This way, you keep your working files small and manageable and save the "master" file for visualizing and plotting. If you need to export the entire model to a rendering program like 3D Studio, you can bind the Xref floors to the master file.

Another useful tool is Hide. By now you may have noticed that you can continue to work on your 3D model even after you've use the Hide tool. You can use this to your advantage when editing complex models. Issue a Hide every once in a while to help you see the surface you are working on. If you need to see further into your model, use the Regen command (**Regen⏎**) to "unhide" your model.

Joining the Wall to the Original 3D Model

Next, you'll join the exterior walls you just created with the first 3D model you created in Chapter 3. Here, you will be joining two styles of modeling; surface and solid modeling.

1. Choose Edit ➤ Copy, then select the exterior wall and press ⏎.

2. Open the Savoye.DWG file you created in Chapter 3. You may want to save the Savoye-elev.DWG file.

3. Once you are in the Savoye.DWG file, choose Edit ➤ Paste. You will see the wall appear in the drawing.

4. At the Insertion point prompt, select a point so the wall is in the approximate location shown in Figure 6.10a above the ground floor plan. An exact location is not important at this time.

5. Zoom into the lower corner and move the wall so it sits on top of the region you created in Chapter 3 for the second floor area (see Figure 6.10b).

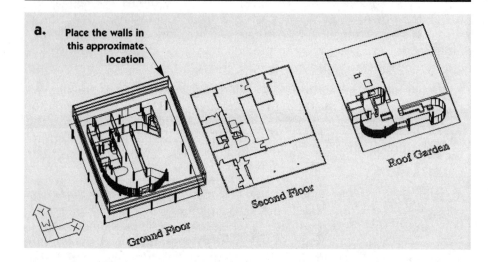

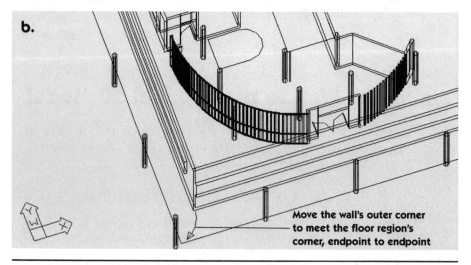

Figure 6.10: Moving the walls into position over the second floor region

As you can see, you can move an object from one file to another using the cut and paste features of Windows. You should be aware, however, that when you cut and paste, the object you paste is actually a block containing the objects you copied from the previous drawing. In the next exercise, you will want to extrude the floor region, then use the Union tool to join it to the walls. But before you can do that, you must explode the walls you pasted into the Savoye.dwg file.

1. Adjust your view to look like Figure 6.11.

2. Click on the Explode button. Remember that it is in the flyout where the Union tool is now located.

3. Click on the exterior walls of the second floor (the ones you just added to the model), then press ↵ (see Figure 6.11).

4. Click on the Extrude button in the Solids toolbar, then click on the second floor region as shown in Figure 6.11. When you've selected the region, press ↵.

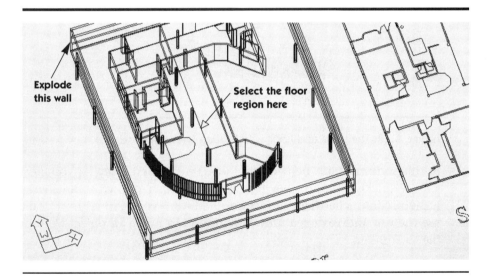

Figure 6.11: Joining the second floor exterior walls with the second floor solid

5. Extrude the region 18 inches, with no taper.

6. Click on the Union button in the Explode flyout, then select the second floor exterior walls you just added to this drawing and the floor solids you created in the previous exercise.

7. Press ↵ when you finish your selection. The walls and floor will join, removing any unwanted seams between the two solids.

8. Click on the Hide button. Your view will look like Figure 6.12.

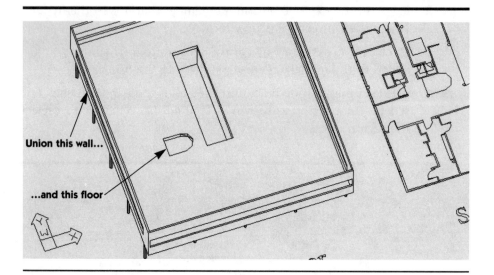

Figure 6.12: The walls and floor with hidden lines removed

In this section, solids helped you in two ways. First, they let you create a mass quickly. Second, they formed complex shapes without leaving unsightly joints between surfaces. In addition, you learned how you can use the Cut and Paste features of Windows to move an object from one file to another.

Now you have worked with all the tools you'll need to finish the model. The following images (Figures 6.13a through 6.13e) will guide you through the steps.

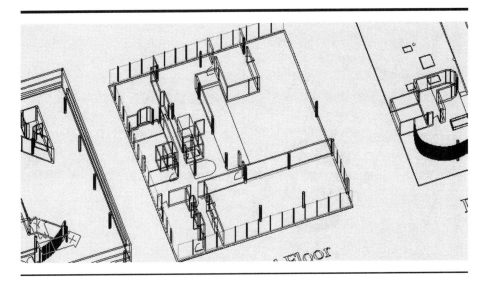

Figure 6.13a: In the second-floor plan, extrude the mullion, interior walls, door jambs, columns, and glass to a height of 9 feet 6 inches, then move the extruded items vertically in the Z axis a distance of 18 inches.

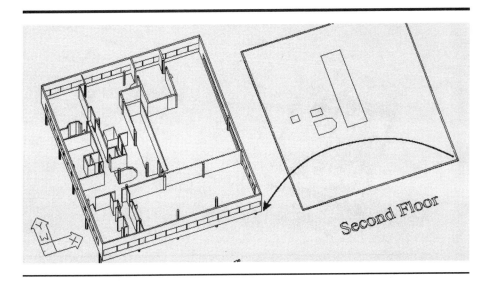

Figure 6.13b: Move the extruded items to the plan with the second-floor exterior wall. Use the corner of the floor as a reference point to align the walls during the move.

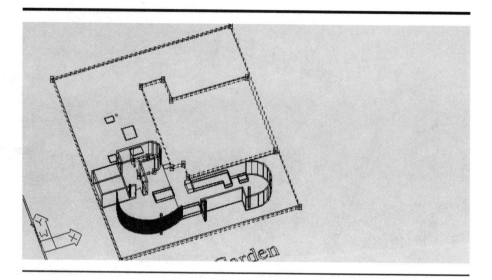

Figure 6.13c: In the roof-garden plan, use the Extrude tool to extrude the roof region a minus 18 inches (shown here highlighted).

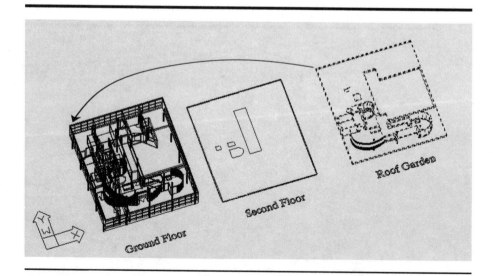

Figure 6.13d: Move the roof-garden plan to a location on top of the second floor plan. Make sure the corners are aligned.

Figure 6.13e: Add the ramp, then use the Hide tool to get a look at your model.

◆ Creating a 3D Elevation with Solids

The Villa Savoye elevation we've worked with so far in this book is a very simple geometric form. It offers a great introduction to solid modeling. But what about modeling something that is considerably more articulated? Figure 6.14 shows an elevation of a building in a classical style. At first glance, it looks like it may have taken a great deal of time to construct. But a few solid modeling tools actually made quick work of this model.

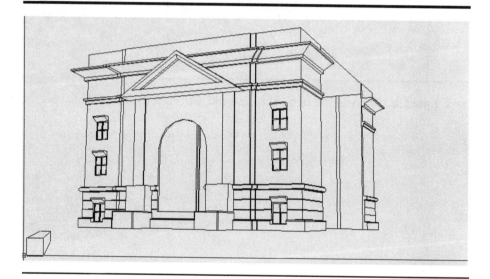

Figure 6.14: A sample building facade created using AutoCAD's 3D Solids tools

Heap Errors and Memory

There is nothing worse than having your program crash, but as you work with AutoCAD Solids, you may encounter an error message mentioning Heap Errors. Without going into a discourse on computer memory, you should know that this error might mean that you don't have enough memory allocated to AutoCAD.

If you are plagued with Heap Error messages, try increasing AutoCAD's memory allocation by selecting Options ➤ Preferences to open the Preferences dialog box. Click on the Environment tab, then increase the value in the Maximum input box (in the Memory options). Click OK to exit the dialog box.

You will also want to make sure you have plenty of free disk space in three places: the drive where AutoCAD is installed, the drive containing the file you are working on, and the Windows swap-file drive. AutoCAD uses the drive it's located on for temporary files, including a file that stores data for Undo's. This Undo file can become quite large. Give AutoCAD around 50 MB breathing room on the drive where it's installed.

AutoCAD also stores, in the location of the file you are editing, temporary data regarding that file. Give it another 50 MB of free disk space there as well. Finally, AutoCAD's RAM requirements are extended through the Windows virtual memory manager. This memory manager makes use of the Windows swap file when memory requirements increase beyond the existing RAM in your system. You can adjust the settings for the Windows swap file in the Control Panel.

Solid modeling is very memory-intensive, so give AutoCAD as much memory as possible while you are working with solids. This goes for rendering and hidden-line removal as well. If you intend to do a lot of 3D work in general, it wouldn't hurt to increase your computer's RAM capacity to at least 32 megabytes or more. It will pay off in the long run with faster rendering, hides, and file loading.

Extruding Polylines along a Path

In previous chapters, you've already used the Extrude tool to turn a closed polyline into a 3D box. In the following exercise, you'll see how you can use Extrude to form some very complex shapes.

1. Open the file entitled `Facade.dwg`. You will see an isometric view of two polylines (see Figure 6.15a). One polyline represents the building plan "footprint" while the other is a closed polyline representing a cross-section of the building wall. Figure 6.15b shows the profile in detail.

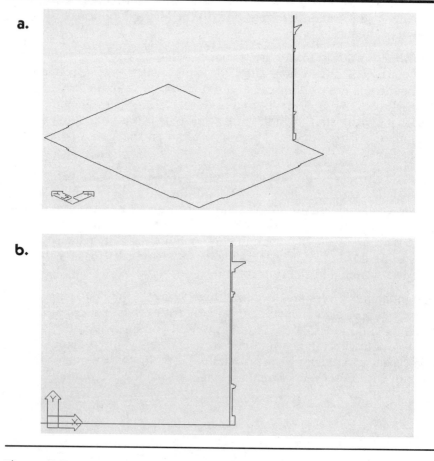

a.

b.

Figure 6.15: The Facade file and a close-up view of the wall cross-section profile.

2. Click on the Extrude tool in the Solids toolbar.

3. At the `Select objects` prompt, select the cross-section profile, then press ↵.

4. At the `Path/<Height of Extrusion>` prompt, enter **P**↵, then select the other polyline representing the building footprint. After a moment, the building facade will appear.

5. Click on the Hide button in the Render toolbar. Your drawing will look like the following:

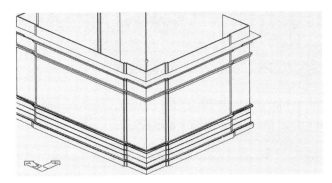

By providing you with the facade cross-section and plan "footprint," you were able to save some time constructing this facade. Still, you can see that polylines in conjunction with the Extrude tool can be a very powerful aid in constructing 3D shapes. There are some points you must be aware of, however, when you extrude polylines along a path:

◆ The profile to be extruded must be a closed polyline or circle.

◆ The path must be an open polyline, arc, or spline restricted to a 2D plane.

◆ If you want the profile to maintain its position in relation to the path, the profile must touch the exact endpoint of the path.

◆ The point at which the profile meets the path must be a vertex point on the profile.

While our example used a polyline made up of straight line segments, you can also use polyline splines, arcs, and spline curves restricted to a 2D plane for an extrusion path. The following images (Figures 6.16a through 6.16f) show an example of how a curved path can be used to model a fluted column.

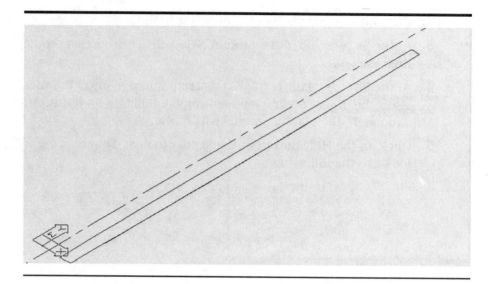

Figure 6.16a: Draw a centerline and polyline profile of the column.

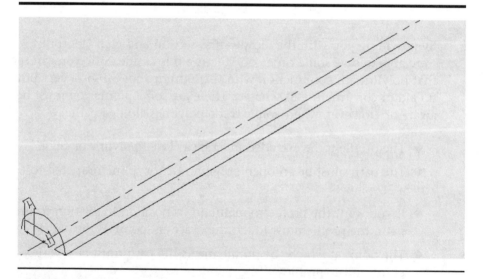

Figure 6.16b: Rotate the UCS 90 degrees in the X axis, then draw an arc representing the path on which you want the column profile extruded. Be sure the arc's endpoint meets one of the profiles vertices exactly.

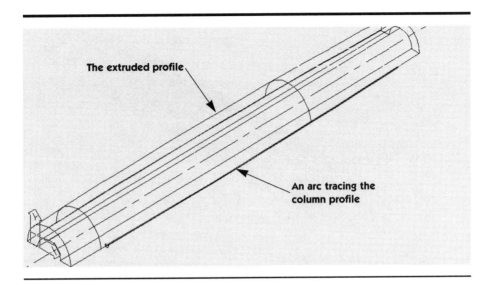

Figure 6.16c: Use the Extrude tool to extrude the profile along the arc path. Next, trace a portion of the column profile with another arc. This will be the path for the fluting.

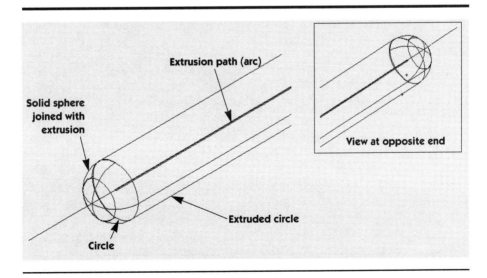

Figure 6.16d: Draw a circle at one endpoint of the arc that traces the profile, then extrude it using the arc as a path. Add a solid sphere to both ends of the extruded circle, and use the Union tool to join both spheres and extrusion.

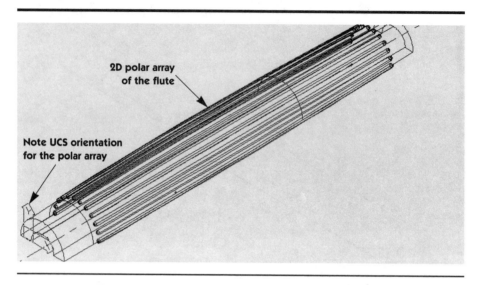

Figure 6.16e: Use the Polar Array tool to make 12 arrayed copies of the extruded flute.

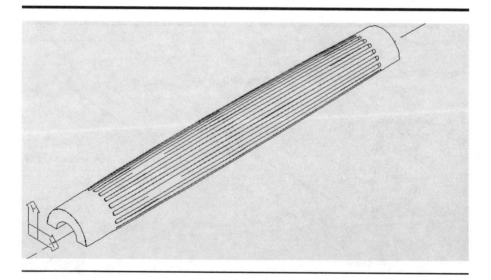

Figure 6.16f: Subtract the the 12 flutes from the main part of the column, then use the Hide tool to view your work.

Figure 6.17 shows how a circle and a polyline can be use to create a handle for the vase from Chapter 5.

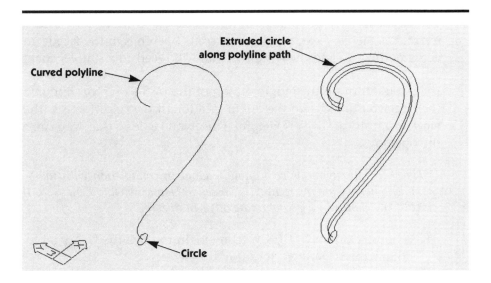

Figure 6.17: A circle is extruded along a curved polyline path to form the handle of the vase from Chapter 5.

Using Solid Modeling to Add Detail to the Facade

The facade is fairly elaborate, but it needs a few windows and other architectural elements. Next, you'll create some openings in the facade and add a portico. To add the windows, you will revert to a simpler shape.

First, you'll turn on the Origin option of the UCS Icon. This option causes the UCS icon to move to the origin location. If that location is within the view area, this can be very helpful. Once you've done that, you can add the openings.

> **Tip**   *Use the dynamic coordinate readout in conjunction with the Snap mode to help locate the rectangles in step 5. Don't use Object snaps, as they will place points in a Z coordinate other than zero.*

1. Choose Options ➤ UCS ➤ Icon Origin to force the UCS icon to follow the UCS origin location.

2. Choose View ➤ Set UCS ➤ X Axis Rotate, then enter **90.**⏎ so the UCS is aligned with the facade.

3. Choose View ➤ Set UCS ➤ Origin, then use the Endpoint Osnap to select the point shown in Figure 6.18a for your new UCS origin.

4. Choose 3D Viewpoint Presets ➤ Plan View ➤ Current. Your view will change to show the elevation of the facade. Zoom back a bit so your view looks like Figure 6.18b.

5. Using the Rectangle tool, draw one of the 5'-by-8' rectangles as shown in Figure 6.18b. Don't worry about its exact location at this point.

6. Copy the rectangles so they are arranged as shown in Figure 6.18b. I've provided coordinates for the lower left corner of each rectangles to help you locate them.

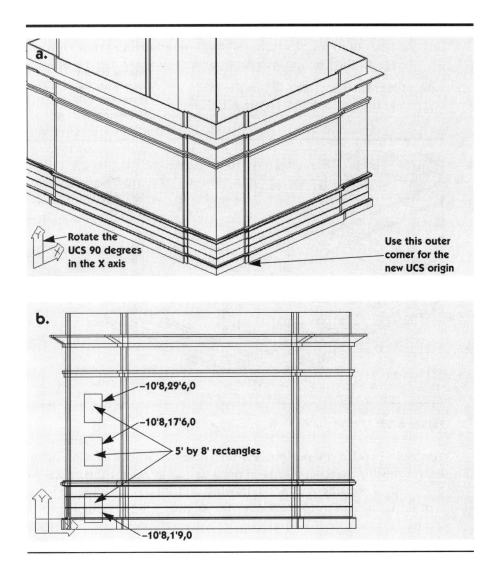

Figure 6.18: Setting up the UCS before adding window openings and locating the window openings in the facade

7. Click and hold the Zoom All button in the Standard toolbar, then select Zoom Previous from the flyout menu twice. Your view will return to the previous isometric view.

8. Mirror the rectangles about the midpoint of the building. Your view should look like Figure 6.19.

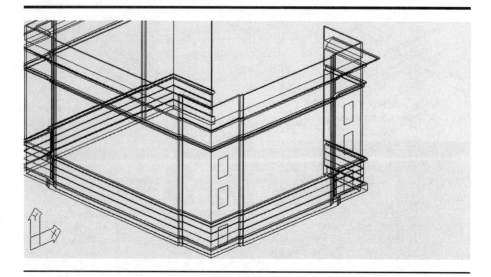

Figure 6.19: Adding the rectangular outlines for the windows

You've just added the outlines for the windows on one portion of the facade. In this exercise, you even drew the windows on the facade elevation, just as you might in a 2D drawing. But in 3D modeling, it is important to pay attention to the Z axis. By aligning the UCS origin to a point whose Z coordinate is well in front of the window surface, you ensure that the solid you create in the next exercise will penetrate the full depth of the facade wall.

Now let's continue by completing the windows.

1. Click on the Extrude button in the Solids toolbar, then select the rectangles you just created.

2. At the `Path/<Height of Extrusion>` prompt, enter **–10'**↵ (minus ten feet), then press ↵ again at the extrusion taper prompt. Your drawing should look like Figure 6.20.

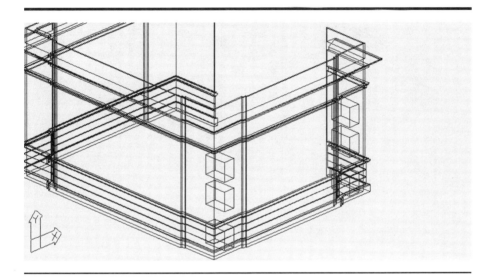

Figure 6.20: Setting up the window solids

You extruded the rectangles in the minus Z direction because you want the rectangular solids to *intersect* the facade. Remember that, in the current UCS, the Z-axis coordinate of the rectangles is zero while the Z-axis coordinate of the wall is less than zero, or a minus direction in the Z coordinate. To make the extruded rectangles intersect the wall, then, they must be extruded in a minus direction toward the wall.

3. Click on the Subtract button in the Explode flyout menu, then select the facade.

4. At the `Select Solids and regions to subtract` prompt, select all the window solids, then press ↵. After a moment, the window openings will appear in the facade (see Figure 6.21a).

5. To get a better idea of what has happened, zoom into the window at the bottom right corner of the facade, then use the Hide tool to get a hidden-line view (see Figure 6.21b).

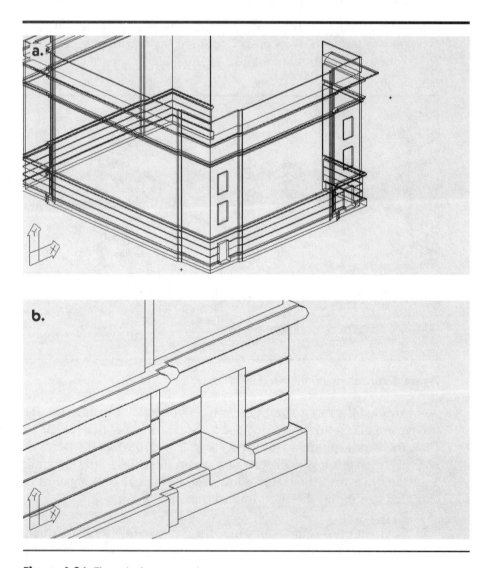

Figure 6.21: The windows openings

You now have the window openings cut out of the facade. Although you used a simple rectangle for the opening shapes, you could have just as easily used a more elaborate shape, such as a pointed arch or perhaps a star shape.

In this exercise, the extrusion dimension of the window rectangles is somewhat arbitrary. It only needs to be thick enough to pass completely through the facade solid.

The windows need a bit of work. We've already constructed windows that you can add to the openings, so the next step is to simply add the windows to your facade drawing.

1. Adjust your view so it looks similar to Figure 6.22 and make sure your UCS is still oriented vertically, as shown in the figure.

2. Click on the Insert Block button in the Draw toolbar.

3. At the Insert dialog box, click on the File button, then at the Select File dialog box, locate `Basewin.DWG`.

4. Click OK at both dialog boxes, then at the `Insertion point` prompt, use the Endpoint Osnap and click on the point shown in Figure 6.22.

5. Copy the inserted window to the remaining openings.

6. When you have finished, click on the Hide button in the Render toolbar. Your drawing should look like Figure 6.23.

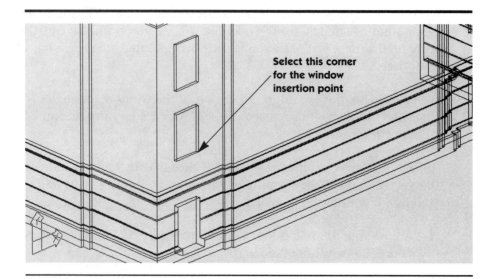

Select this corner
for the window
insertion point

Figure 6.22: Inserting the windows for the facade

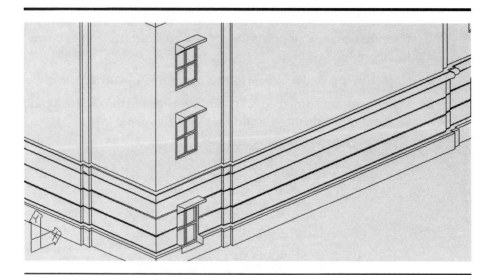

Figure 6.23: The facade with all the windows inserted

Note *The* Basewin.DWG *file was created with its windows perpendicular with the WCS. When you import one 3D model into another, the imported model's WCS will be aligned with the current model's UCS. Since the UCS of the Facade model is rotated 90 degrees in the X axis from the WCS, the Basewin model inserts in the correct orientation for the Facade wall. Had you switched back to the WCS, the Basewin model would have appeared in the wrong orientation, parallel to the WCS.*

The windows you inserted into the facade were constructed using solids. Figures 6.24a through 6.24d show how they were made. For practice, you might want to try duplicating the construction of the windows.

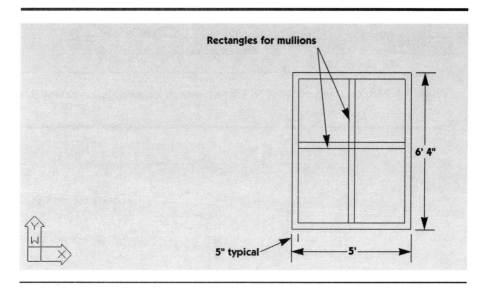

Figure 6.24a: Draw these rectangles using the Rectangle tool.

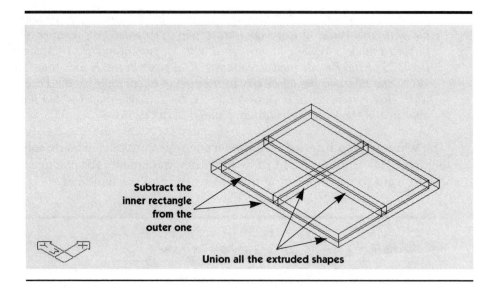

Figure 6.24b: Change your view to SW Isometric, then extrude all rectangles 4".

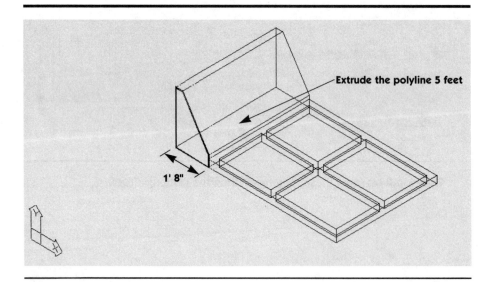

Figure 6.24c: Rotate the UCS to the orientation shown here, and draw the ledge shape using a polyline.

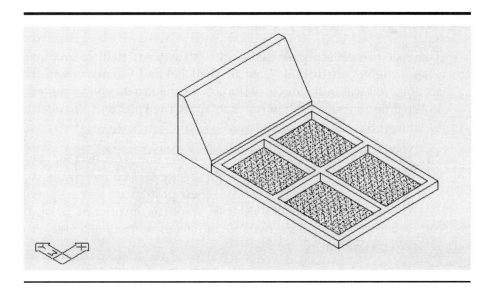

Figure 6.24d: Draw a 3D face tracing the base of the frame and place the 3D face on a layer called *Glass*.

In these exercises, you created holes in the facade surface. You can also use solids to create indentations on a surface. In fact, there are a variety of ways solids can be used to model a surface.

Building the Entry Portico

There are two editing tools that work with solids to help you refine the shapes you've constructed. They are the Fillet and Chamfer tools. In this section, you will build an entry portico for the facade you've started, and in the process you'll see how you can apply the Fillet and Chamfer tools to your work.

1. Save the Facade.DWG file then open the Portico.DWG file. This file contains a few polyline profiles ready for you to extrude. As with other exercise in this book, these profiles are just 2D polylines drawn to the profile of objects we want to construct in 3D. In fact, much of what you see here might be derived from a 2D sketch of an elevation.

2. Choose View ➤ 3D Viewpoint Presets ➤ SW Isometric.

3. Use the Extrude tool to extrude the polylines to the heights indicated in Figure 6.25a.

4. After extruding the shapes, move the small triangle and arch as shown in Figure 6.25b.

5. When you have finished, use the 3D Rotate tool in the Rotate Flyout to rotate all the solids 90 degrees in the X axis (Figure 6.25c).

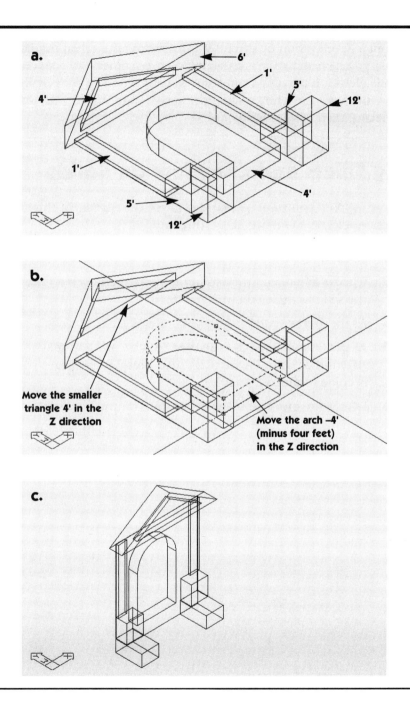

Figure 6.25: Extrude the polylines to these heights.

You can see from this exercise that you can quickly build a 3D elevation from a 2D elevation by carefully constructing the elevation drawing so that you have drawn masses with closed polylines. Even if you've acquired a 2D elevation drawing from someone else, you can convert the 2D drawing into a 3D model by tracing the appropriate shapes with a closed polyline and then extruding them.

Using Fillets and Chamfers on Solids

Now suppose you want to round some of the corners of the portico. For this, you'll use a familiar 2D editing tool.

1. Zoom into the left base of the portico as shown in Figure 6.26.

2. Choose Fillet from the Modify toolbar, then click on the edge of the solid as indicated in Figure 6.26.

3. At the Enter radius prompt, enter **3.**⌐.

4. At the Chain/Radius/<Select edge> prompt, select the other edge indicated in Figure 6.26, then press ⌐. The edges you select become rounded corners.

5. Repeat the process for the other solid on the opposite side.

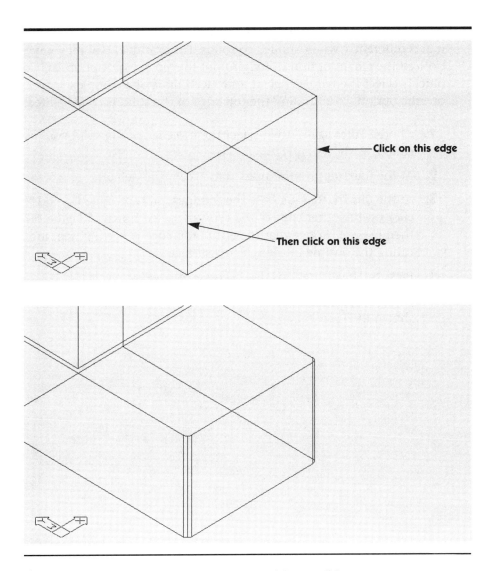

Click on this edge

Then click on this edge

Figure 6.26: Use Fillet to round the corners of these solids.

If you use Fillet frequently in 2D drawings, you'll notice right away that it acts differently when applied to solids. For example, you may nave noticed the Chain option in the prompt in step 4. This option lets you quickly select the whole edge of a surface that is of a complex shape. Try out the option, by rounding the top edge of the solid you just edited.

1. Choose Fillet again, then select the top edge of the solid you just edited, as shown in Figure 6.27a.

2. At the `Radius` prompt, press ↵ to accept the default.

3. At the `Chain/Radius/<Select edge>` prompt, type **C**↵ and then click on the other edge of the top surface as shown in Figure 6.27a, then press ↵. Notice that the entire top edge is highlighted, indicating the outline of the selected surface.

4. Press ↵. The entire top edge becomes filleted.

5. Repeat steps 1 through 3 to fillet the top of the opposite solid, as shown in Figure 6.27b.

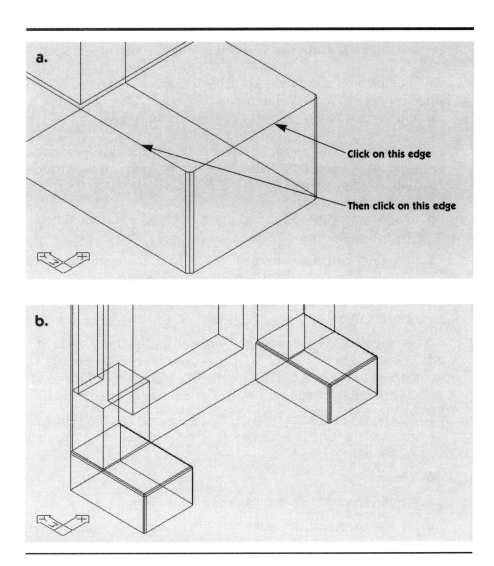

Figure 6.27: Filleting the top edge of the solid

Notice how the corners are rounded, showing that AutoCAD takes into consideration the rounded edge on the vertical corners.

Another interesting feature of the Fillet command is that you have the option to set a different radius for each edge you select. To do this, enter **R**↵ and the new radius, just before you select an edge.

Next, let's add a chamfer to the top edge of the triangular portion of the entryway. Chamfer, like Fillet, acts in a different way when applied to solids.

1. Adjust your view so you can see the triangular portion of the portico as shown in Figure 6.28a.

2. Use the Subtract tool in the Explode flyout of the Modify toolbar to subtract the smaller triangle from the larger one.

3. Click and hold the Fillet button so the flyout appears, then select Chamfer.

4. At the `Polyline/Distance/Angle/Trim/Method/<Select first line>:` prompt, select the front edge of the triangle, as shown in Figure 6.28a. Notice that the whole edge of the solid is highlighted. We'll explain why at the end of this exercise.

5. At the `Select base: Next/<OK>` prompt, type **N**↵. Notice that the surface that is highlighted changes. The `Next/<OK>` prompt remains.

6. Press ↵.

7. At the `Enter base surface distance` prompt, enter **12**↵.

8. At the `Enter other surface distance <12>` prompt, press ↵ to accept the default value of 12 for a symmetrical chamfer.

9. At the `Loop/<Select edge>` prompt, select the edge you want to chamfer, then press ↵. The edge chamfers, as shown in Figure 6.28b.

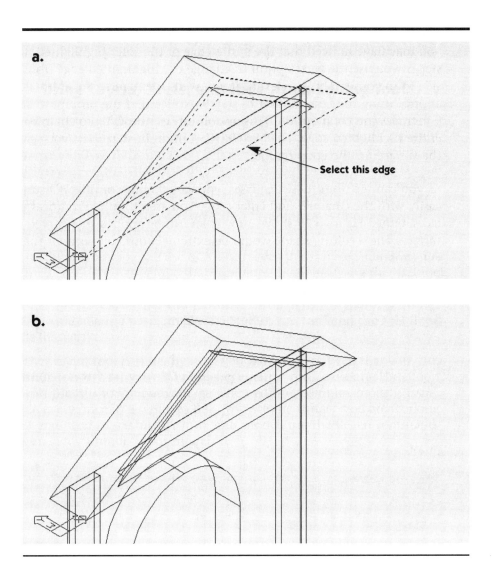

Figure 6.28: The arch with the entire edge chamfered using the Loop option

The Chamfer tool offers a few more options than Fillet. In steps 2 and 3, you may have noticed that the entire edge of the solid highlighted. In step 5, you use the Next option to change the highlighted edge from one side to the other. This is relevant if you want to chamfer the entire edge at once using the Loop option in step 9. Notice that the prompt in step 9 includes the Loop option. This option causes AutoCAD to chamfer the entire highlighted edge. The Next/<OK> option in step 5 lets you select the surface for the Loop option.

As you can see from these exercises, you can chamfer or fillet 3D surfaces easily with the Chamfer and Fillet tools. You aren't limited to linear surfaces, either. Figure 6.29 shows how Fillet can be applied to a curved surface. The resulting shape would be extremely difficult without the Fillet tool.

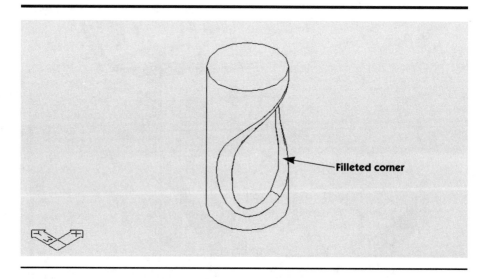

Figure 6.29: A sample of what the Fillet tool can do on non-linear shapes

Let's complete the facade by adding the portico. Here, you will see how the Union tool can combine complex shapes to quickly define the intersection of those shapes.

> **Note** *If you know the exact coordinates you want for your base point, you can use the Drawing Aids dialog box (Options ➤ Drawing Aids) to enter those coordinate values.*

1. At the command prompt, type **Base⏎**. This command lets you assign a specific insertion base point location for a file. The default base point of a drawing is the absolute World coordinate 0,0.

2. At the `Base point` prompt, select the midpoint of the line at the bottom of the portico, as shown in Figure 6.30a.

3. Save the Portico drawing, then open the Facade drawing.

4. Set the UCS to the World coordinate system.

5. Use the Insert Block tool in the Draw toolbar to insert the `Portico.DWG` file.

6. For the insertion point, use the midpoint of the base of the facade, as shown in Figure 6.30b.

7. Use the Explode tool in the Modify toolbar to explode the inserted portico.

8. Use the Subtract tool in the Explode flyout of the Modify toolbar to subtract the arch from the facade, as shown in Figure 6.30c.

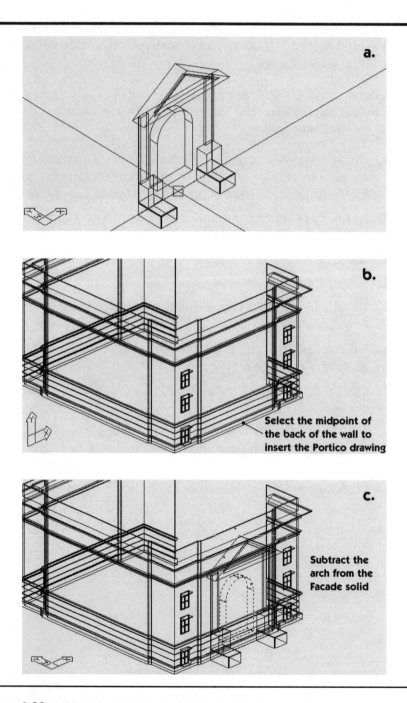

Figure 6.30: Adding the Portico model to the Facade model

9. Use the Union tool in the Explode flyout to combine the portico solids and the facade.

10. Use the Hide tool to get a final look at your facade drawing (see Figure 6.31).

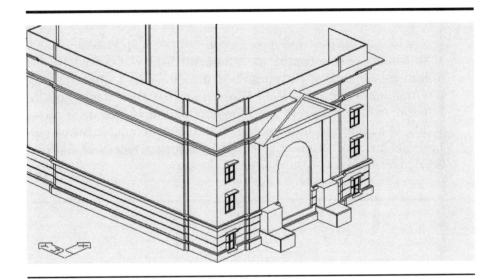

Figure 6.31: Adding the portico to the facade drawing

Notice how the edges where the portico meets the facade are clearly delineated. You may recall from earlier chapters how surface modeling requires objects to meet exactly, edge to edge, before their intersections will render properly in hidden-line views. Here, the Union tool creates the solid geometry necessary to fit all the surfaces perfectly edge-to-edge.

◆ Hiding Unwanted Lines in Solids

Before we end this chapter, you will want to know about a little AutoCAD system variable that can save you a lot of frustration and agonizing over hidden-line views. The *Dispsilh* system variable lets you eliminate unwanted lines from hidden-line views of curved solids.

If you look at the description of Dispsilh in the Help system, you will see that its purpose is to control the silhouette display of curved 3D surfaces. You might notice that curved surfaces are shown in a schematic way with a minimum of line work. With Dispsilh set to 0, the default, no silhouette is drawn. When set to 1, a silhouette outline is shown for curved solids. In addition to showing the outline, however, a setting of 1 also prevents AutoCAD from displaying all the surface faces when a Hide or Shade is issued (see Figure 6.32).

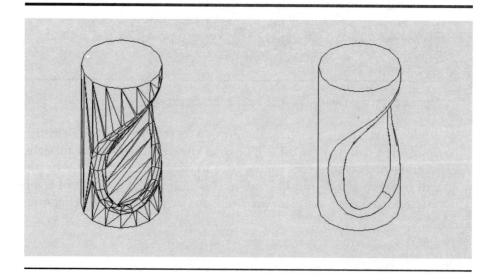

Figure 6.32: A comparison of a curved solid with Dispsilh set to 0 (left) and set to 1 (right)

To make changes to Dispsilh, enter '**Dispsilh**⏎, then enter a 0 or 1 for the option you desire.

If you plan to render your 3D models using the built-in Render tool, or in AutoVision or 3D Studio, you needn't worry about this setting. But if you want to use your models as a line drawing, you will want to set Dispsilh to 1.

◆ Taking Precautions with Solid Modeling

Solids are unforgiving. Once you've created a solid shape, that's it; you cannot make small adjustments. For this reason, you should plan your solid modeling work carefully. You may also want to make use of AutoCAD's Undo command which lets you mark a place in your edit session to which you can return, in case you make errors.

There are really two types of Undo in AutoCAD; the standard Undo that you get when you click on the Undo button in the Standard toolbar or the Edit menu, and the full Undo command. The Undo command is issued by typing **Undo**⏎ at the command prompt. It offers the following set of options in the command line:

```
Auto/Control/BEgin/End/Mark/Back/<Number>:
```

The Mark option will mark the current state of the drawing with a "placeholder" to which you can return in case your editing goes awry. Once you select the Mark option by typing **M**⏎ at the Undo prompt, you can proceed with your creating and editing. In the event that you want to return to the placeholder, you issue the Undo command again by typing **Undo**⏎, then enter **B**⏎ to select the Back option. This restores the drawing to the condition it was in when you used the Mark option.

Of course, you can also use the standard Undo button on the toolbar to undo one operation at a time.

◆ Summary

Solid modeling can make quick work of complex modeling problems, but keep in mind that solids also use up RAM in a hurry. Try to use it sparingly if you have a limited amount of RAM. Also, consider mixing both solid and surface modeling tools when building large models.

In the next chapter, you'll learn how to manipulate your views to help visualize your ideas. You'll also learn how to get perspective views and how the perspective tools can be used to help others visualize your ideas.

Viewing Your Model for Presentations and Editing

So far, you've been creating and editing your drawings from a single *isometric view*. You aren't limited to isometric views, however; nor are you limited to seeing just one view of your model at a time. AutoCAD offers you the ability to split your screen into several views, each with a different viewpoint of your model. In addition, you can view your model in a *perspective mode* which gives a greater sense of what your model will look like in the real world.

In this chapter, you'll explore the different ways AutoCAD lets you view your 3D models. You'll start by looking at how multiple viewports can be created and used for 3D modeling. You'll then take a look at AutoCAD's perspective viewing tool. Along the way, you'll learn how these tools can be used to help others view your work and interactively edit your 3D models.

◆ Creating and Using Viewports for Editing

Many 3D modeling programs offer multiple viewports that allow you to edit your drawing from different points of view. Viewports are like subdivisions of your drawing area. You might, for example, have four equal viewports, each being a separate drawing area displaying different parts of your drawing, as shown in Figure 7.1.

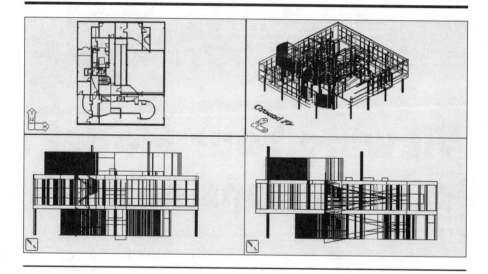

Figure 7.1: A sample of the AutoCAD drawing area divided into four equal viewports

While the trend lately in modeling programs is moving away from this method for displaying 3D models, multiple viewports can be quite useful for a variety of scenarios. In this section you'll learn how to set up multiple viewports in AutoCAD in both Paper Space and Model Space.

Setting Up Model Space Viewports

We'll start by looking at how to create Model Space viewports to help us model the chair shown in Figure 7.2. Model Space is typically the display mode in which we do most of our creating and editing, so it may seem the most likely mode to set up working viewports. While this isn't necessarily true, Model Space provides the best mode to introduce the viewport concept.

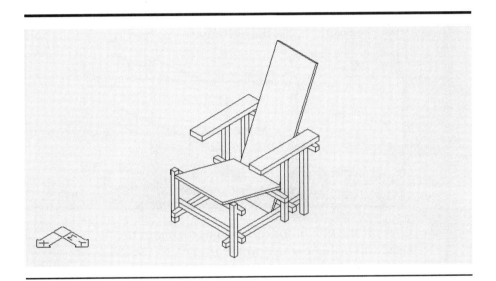

Figure 7.2: The chair we'll be modeling in this chapter

> **Note** *You can quickly get four equal viewports by selecting View ➤ Tiled Viewports ➤ 4 Viewports. The Tiled Viewports dialog box, however, offers more options and shows you what is available.*

1. Open the Rvchair.dwg file.

2. Choose View ➤ Tiled Viewports ➤ Layout. You'll see the Tiled Viewports Layout dialog box appear.

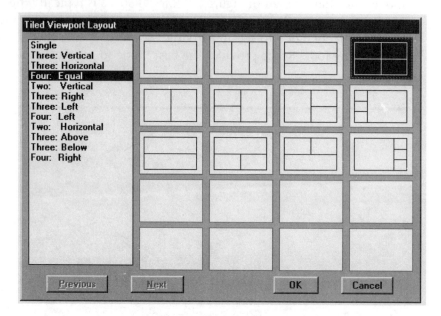

3. Click on the box in the upper right corner of the dialog box. *Four: Equal* will be highlighted in the list box to the left.

4. Click OK. The dialog box closes and your screen divides into four equal views of the drawing, as shown in Figure 7.3.

5. Move your cursor over the different viewports. Notice that when your cursor is in the lower right viewport, you see the standard cross-hair cursor. When moving the cursor over the other viewports, you see the arrow cursor.

6. Place the arrow cursor in the upper left viewport then click on it. Notice that the cursor changes to a cross-hair cursor.

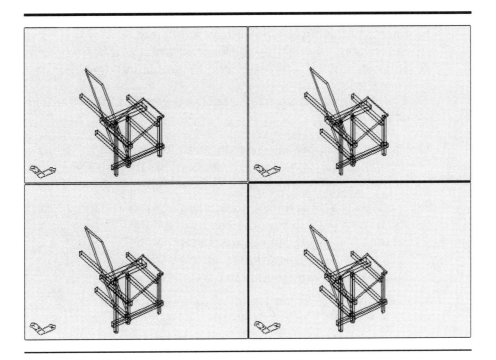

Figure 7.3: The drawing divided into four equal viewports

Only one viewport can be active and editable at a time; you can't pass your cursor over a viewport and expect to have access to it. It's a simple matter of clicking on a viewport to make it active, however.

As you can see from the Tiled Viewport Layout dialog box, you have a variety of viewports to choose from. And if you don't like the arrangements offered in the dialog box, you can set up your own using the Viewport keyboard command. We'll discuss the fine-tuning of the viewport arrangement later. For now, let's explore what we can do with multiple viewports.

All the viewports show the same image of the chair. Let's make some adjustments to the display so you have a different view of the drawing in each viewport. You'll set up the views to a typical top, front, right side, and isometric view typically used in mechanical drawings.

> **Tip** *For a quick way to obtain a plan view of a UCS, type* **Plan**↵ *at the command prompt.*

1. Click on the upper left viewport and then choose View ➤ 3D Viewpoint Presets ➤ Plan View ➤ Current. This gives you a plan view of the WCS, which is the current UCS.

2. The view is a bit cramped, so you will want to zoom out a bit. Click on the Zoom Scale button on the Zoom All flyout of the Standard toolbar, then enter **.9x**↵. This adjusts your view so there is a bit more room around the edge of the image.

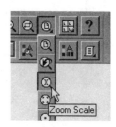

3. Click on the lower left viewport, then choose View ➤ Set UCS ➤ X Axis Rotate.

4. Enter **90**↵ for the rotation angle. This will set up the UCS for a front view of the model.

5. Choose View ➤ 3D Viewpoint Presets ➤ Plan View ➤ Current. You'll see the outline of the chair profile. Use the Zoom Scale button as you did in step 2 to give your view a little more room.

6. Click on the upper right viewport to make it active.

7. Choose View ➤ Set UCS ➤ Y Axis Rotate.

8. Enter **90**↵ for the rotation angle. This will set up the UCS for a right-side view of the model.

9. Choose View ➤ 3D Viewpoint Presets ➤ Plan View ➤ Current, then zoom out a bit so your view looks like the one in Figure 7.4.

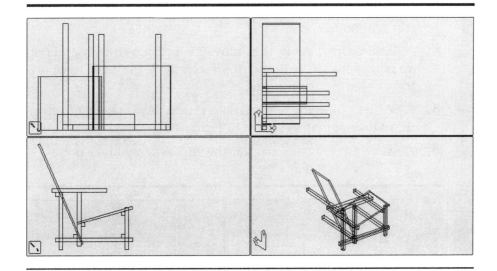

Figure 7.4: The top, left, and right side views in three viewports

This exercise demonstrates that you must take care to click on the viewport you want to use before you issue display commands. Zoom and Pan will affect the currently active viewport only. You cannot switch viewports once you've started either of these commands.

Editing and Drawing with Viewports

Unlike the display-related tools, many tools will allow you to switch viewports while they are active. For example, you can use the move or copy tools to select a base point in one viewpoint and then select the second point in another viewport. Let's see how we might use a few editing tools to construct this chair.

1. Choose View ➤ Set UCS ➤ World to return to the WCS.

2. Click on the lower left viewport, then click on the small square in the lower right corner of the chair to expose its grips (see Figure 7.5).

3. Click on one of the grips, then press ⏎ to shift to the **MOVE** grip edit mode.

4. Make sure Ortho is off, then move the square vertically and notice what happens to the isometric view in the lower right viewport. You can see the bar moving.

5. Type **C**⏎ to copy the selected object, then place a copy directly above the original, as shown in Figure 7.5.

6. Press the Esc key twice to clear the grips when you are done.

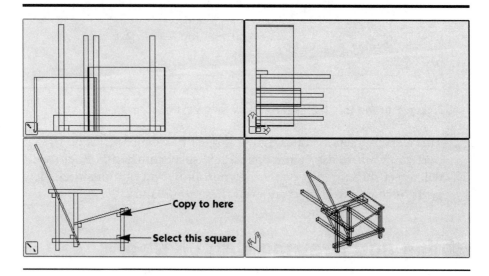

Figure 7.5: Using grips to make a copy of the chair component

If you look carefully at the position of the new bar you created, you'll see that it is not quite aligned with the original shown in the upper left plan view. It has shifted one snap unit in the Y axis. What this exercise has shown you, then, is that while it appeared that you made a vertical copy, the object in fact shifted in an unexpected way. When you are editing objects in 3D using viewports, therefore, you need to take a few extra steps as you edit, as discussed below.

To edit in an orthogonal viewport without getting undesirable surprises, you will want to set the UCS to be parallel with the viewport view.

Let's try moving the seat and back of the chair using grips again, but this time, you'll set the UCS parallel to the view plane.

> **Tip** *Remember that the F8 key toggles the Ortho mode on and off, while the F9 key toggles the Snap mode.*

1. Click on the upper right viewport to make it active.

2. Choose View ➤ Set UCS ➤ View.

3. With the Snap and Ortho modes on, click on the chair's back to expose its grips.

4. Click on any one of the grips, then press ↵ to go to the **MOVE** mode.

5. Move the chair's back three snap units to the right, then select that point. Your chair should look like Figure 7.6a.

6. Using the grips, move the seat of the chair two snap units to the right, then move the horizontal members to the left 1 snap unit. Your chair should now look like Figure 7.6b.

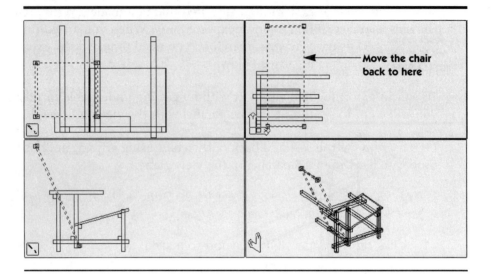

Figure 7.6a: Moving the back of the chair into its new position

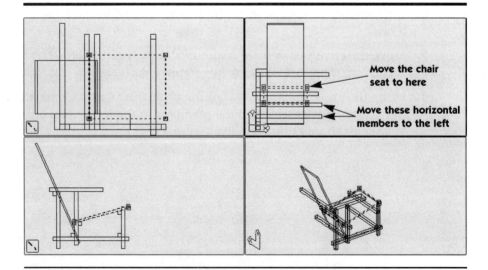

Figure 7.6b: Moving the seat of the chair into its new position

Now that you've set the UCS to be parallel to the plane in which you are working, moving objects accurately is fairly easy. You can edit objects as if you were working in 2D, using the Snap and Ortho modes.

But there are other quirks to editing in viewports you should know about. In a previous exercise, you were able to move a component of the chair horizontally by changing the UCS to match that of your view plane. You also had the Snap and Ortho modes on. Let's see what happens when we try the same thing in the plan view, but this time you'll turn the Ortho mode off.

1. Choose View ➤ Set UCS ➤ World to return to the WCS, then click on the upper left viewport to make it active.

2. With the Ortho mode off, click on the chair arm, as shown in Figure 7.7.

3. Click on the upper right grip, then press ↵ to use the **MOVE** grip mode.

4. Move the cursor upward and notice what happens to the arm in the isometric view. It jumps downward to the "floor level" as you move it (see Figure 7.7).

5. Turn the Ortho mode on.

6. Move the arm downward one snap unit, then select that location. The arm moves into the correct position.

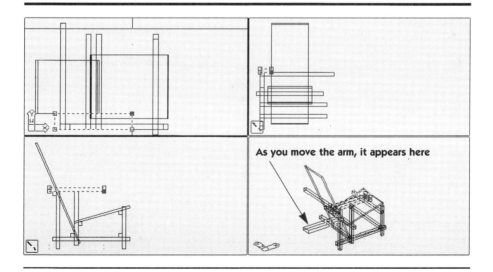

As you move the arm, it appears here

Figure 7.7: Moving the arm using the grip function

You know from 2D drawing that the Ortho mode forces the cursor to stay in a vertical or horizontal orientation. In this exercise, we saw that Ortho also keeps objects in a plane parallel to the current UCS (that is, while we were using grips to edit an object). This can be an important feature when working in multiple viewports.

Be aware, however, that if you use the Move or Copy tool, objects will not move out of their Z axis plane, regardless of whether the Ortho mode is on or off.

Working with viewports can be useful depending on the nature of your project. If you are modeling a fairly simple, rectilinear object, then viewports can be of tremendous help. Just remember that there are a few quirks you have to pay attention to:

◆ If you need to be accurate, use View ➤ Set UCS ➤ View to set the UCS parallel to the viewport you are working in.

◆ If you move objects with grips, check to be sure you aren't moving the object out of the plane of view.

◆ If you need to change a viewport display with Zoom or Pan, be sure to click on the viewport before you issue the command.

Now before you move on, you may want to finish this chair. The following images show the steps you need to take to complete it.

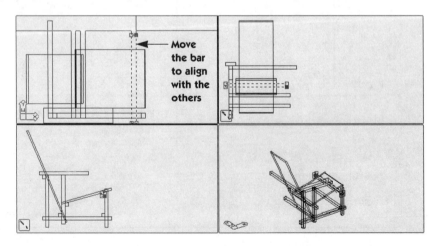

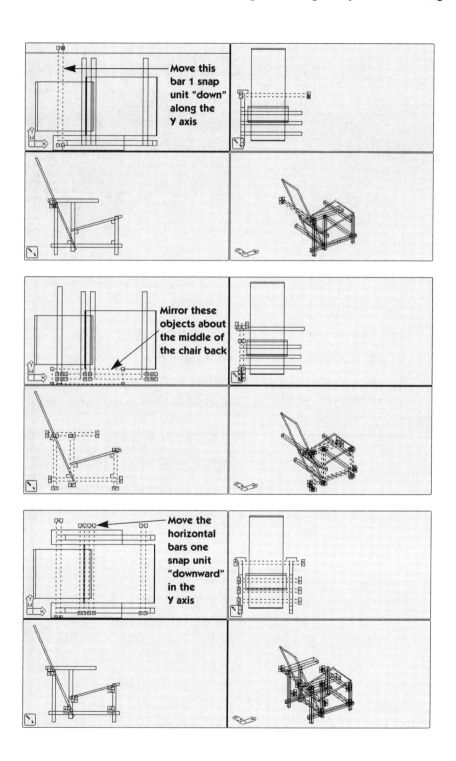

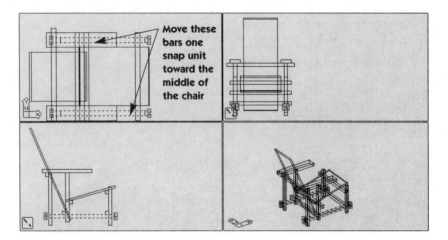

Before we end this section, you will need to know how to get back to a single viewport. Here's how it's done.

1. Click on the lower right viewport to make it active.

2. Choose View ➤ 3D Viewpoint Presets ➤ NE Isometric.

3. Choose View ➤ Tiled Viewports ➤ 1 Viewport. The active viewport enlarges to fill the drawing area, as shown in Figure 7.8.

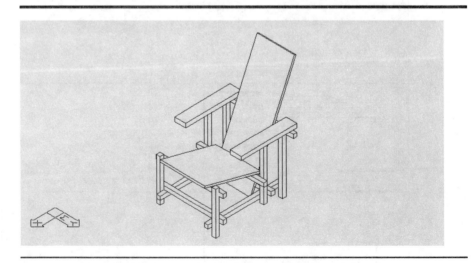

Figure 7.8: The Rvchair drawing viewed with a single viewport

◆ Using the 3D View Tripod

Up until now, you've used predefined 3D isometric views to navigate your models. You also saw in Chapter 2 how you can use the Viewpoint Presets dialog box to adjust your views and break away from the four fixed isometric views available on the pull-down menu. There are also two other methods for setting up non-perspective 3D views. The first of these that you'll look at is the *vector tripod*. This method uses two graphic devices, a vector tripod and circular target, to help you select a view. Try the following exercise to get firsthand experiences using this tool.

1. Open the `Portico.DWG` file you worked on in the last chapter.

2. Choose View ➤ 3D Viewpoint ➤ Tripod. Your screen will change to display the vector tripod and circular target. As you move your mouse, the tripod rotates and a small cross-hair cursor moves around in the circular target, as shown in Figure 7.9.

3. Carefully move the mouse so the cursor in the circular target is in the location shown in Figure 7.9, then press the left mouse button. You will return to a view of the portico similar to Figure 7.10.

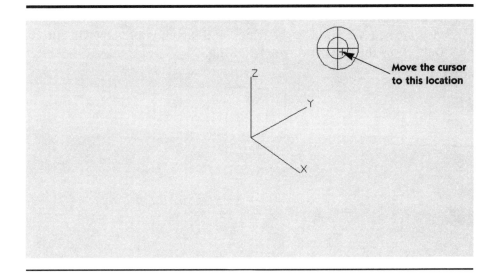

Figure 7.9: Setting up the tripod view

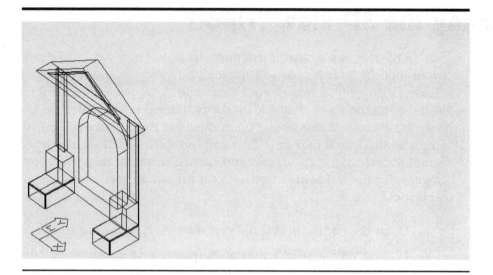

Figure 7.10: The resulting view of the portico

Of the two graphics, the circular target is the most useful. The tripod helps you visualize your viewpoint in relation to the model, but the circular target lets you determine your viewpoint location more precisely. The target also lets you determine the height of your viewpoint. Your viewpoint is always placed so that you view the entire drawing, regardless of the size and scale of your model. Just as with the predefined isometric views, whenever you use the tripod and target, your view will automatically show the extents of your drawing.

Understanding the Vector Tripod and Circular Target

You use the circular target in conjunction with the vector tripod to find out where you are in a plan or top view. You might think of the circular target as a dome over your model, as shown in Figure 7.11. As you move the cursor closer to the center of the target, your viewpoint is more directly centered above the model. As you move the cursor outward and away from the center, your viewpoint moves closer to the plane of the WCS and to a lower angle. The vector tripod gives a graphical representation of the actual view of your model, showing you the X, Y, and Z axis directions of the WCS.

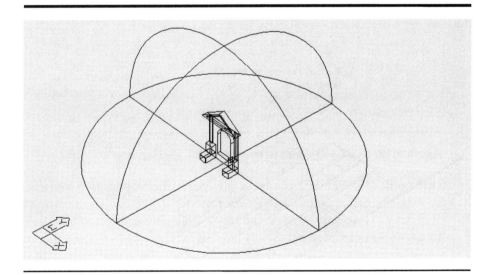

Figure 7.11: A representation of the circular target as a dome over your model

The circular target is divided into quadrants. Each division represents the X and Y axes of the WCS, with the top of the circle being the positive Y axis and the right edge of the target being the positive X axis. To get an approximation of the SW isometric view, you would select a point in the lower left quadrant of the target, as shown in Figure 7.12.

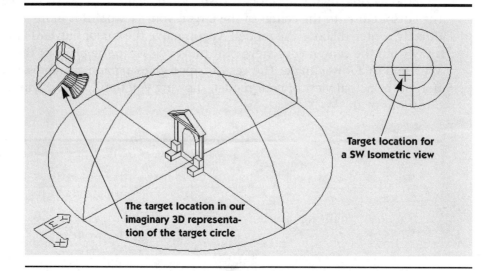

Figure 7.12: The X and Y axes in relation to the circular target

One quirk of the circular target is the way it shows you your vertical or Z-axis location as it relates to your model. You'll notice that the circle shows two concentric circles; the outer circle and a second circle halfway to the center of the target (see Figure 7.13). The region within the inner circle represents elevations above the plane of the WCS. When you select a point within that circle, you will be assured that your view will be from *above*, looking down on your model. The region between this inner circle and the outermost edge of the target represents the space *below* the plane of the WCS. If you select a point in this region, you will be looking up from below your model.

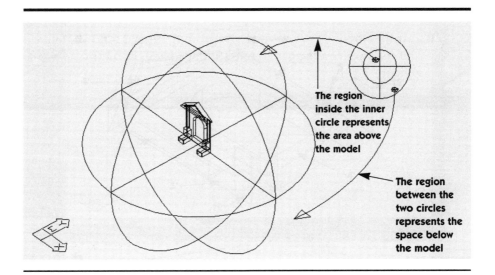

The region inside the inner circle represents the area above the model

The region between the two circles represents the space below the model

Figure 7.13: The relationship of the circles in the target and the location above and below your model

Using the vector tripod takes a little getting used to, but if you understand how it works, it can be a quick way to move around your model. With it, you can visually orient yourself to the X, Y, and Z axes.

Selecting a Viewpoint by Entering Coordinates

You have a second option of entering coordinates to determine your point of view. This option, called the *Vector* option, is a little deceptive since you aren't entering actual drawing coordinates. Instead, you must imagine your model as a *point* that fits in the *origin* of your coordinate system. The coordinates you enter represent the orientation of your viewpoint in relation to your entire model. Try the following exercise to get a firsthand glimpse of this option.

1. Choose View ➤ 3D Viewpoint ➤ Vector.

2. At the `Rotate/<View point>` prompt, enter **1,–1,1**↵. Your view of the portico changes to one similar to a SE isometric view (see Figure 7.14).

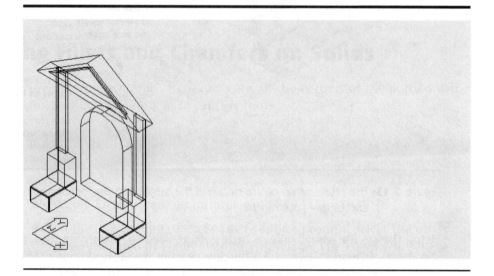

Figure 7.14: Your view of the portico after entering 1,–1,1 for the View ➤ Viewpoint ➤ Vector option

Consider the coordinate you entered in step 2. If you imagine yourself standing on a coordinate grid, and you place yourself at the coordinates 1,–1,1, you would see the origin below and to the left of you. You would then have an SE isometric view (see Figure 7.15). This is how the vector option works to set up your view—it uses a "virtual" coordinate system that has nothing to do with the actual coordinate system in your drawing.

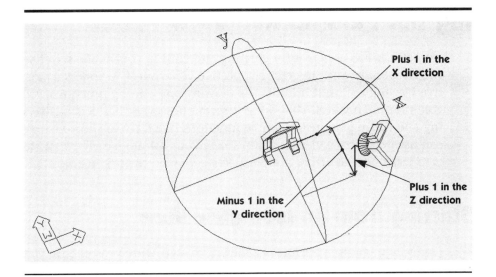

Figure 7.15: The "virtual" coordinate system used by the Vector option

The Vector option is actually at the root of all the isometric view tools. When you pick View ➤ 3D Viewpoint Presets ➤ SE Isometric, AutoCAD actually issues a command called Vpoint, which is the same command for all the viewpoint options, and enters the coordinates 1,–1,1. When you select View ➤ 3D Viewpoint ➤ Vector, you are also issuing the Vpoint command—only instead of AutoCAD automatically entering a coordinate, it awaits your input. If you press ↵ without entering any coordinates, you get the vector tripod!

> **Tip** *Chances are you will lean toward using the predefined isometric views and the Viewpoint Presets dialog box. They will suit virtually every need you will have for viewing your drawing in an isometric mode. The Tripod and Vector options, on the other hand, can be helpful shortcuts to those who spend the time to master them. They are simple, direct tools to setting up 3D views and they are worth spending some time to understand.*

◆ Using the Perspective View Tools

Isometric views are great for creating and editing your models, but you will eventually want to get a perspective view. AutoCAD offers a perspective viewing tool, but it limits the drawing and editing functions available from such views. That doesn't mean, however, that perspective viewing and editing are incompatible functions. We'll try to show how you can use perspective views to help shape your 3D models. The first step is to learn how to arrive at a perspective view in the first place.

Starting from an Isometric View

One way to get to a perspective view is to start with an isometric view. For the next exercise, you'll start from the current isometric view in the portico drawing, and move to a perspective view.

1. If you haven't already done so, open the portico drawing and choose View ➤ 3D Viewpoint Presets ➤ SE Isometric, then adjust your view so the portico is centered in the display.

2. Choose View ➤ 3D Dynamic View.

3. At the `Select object` prompt, select the triangular top and the two blocks at the base of the portico, then press ⏎ (see Figure 7.16). Notice that all the parts you didn't select disappear.

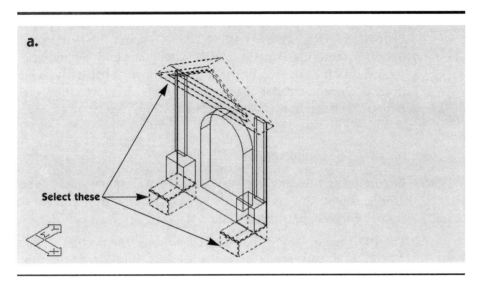

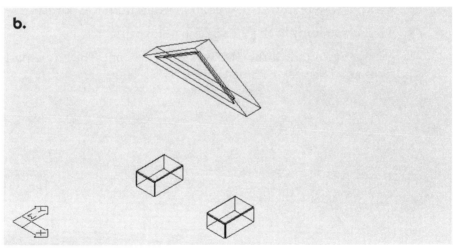

Figure 7.16: Selecting the portions of your drawing as references for the 3D Dynamic View tool

4. At the CAmera/TArget/Distance/POints/PAn/Zoom/TWist/ CLip/Hide/Off/Undo/ <eXit> prompt, select the Distance option by entering **D**↵. The portico disappears entirely and you see a slide bar at the top of the screen. This slide bar lets you graphically determine a distance from your point of view to the view target. You'll see how it works in the next exercise.

5. Besides using the slide bar, you can enter a distance value. Type **150'**↵. The portico comes into view. Notice that now you see the portico in perspective (see Figure 7.17a).

6. Enter **D**↵ again. Notice that now the view of the portico remains. As you slide your mouse from side to side, the slider at the top of the screen moves and the portico move in and out as if your viewpoint were moving closer and farther from the portico.

7. Press ↵ to return to the view you had in step 5.

8. Press ↵ again to exit the 3D Dynamic View tool. The entire portico appears in perspective (see Figure 7.17b).

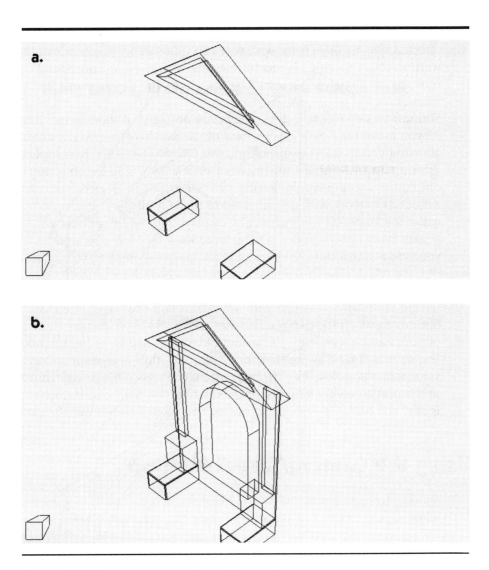

Figure 7.17: Your perspective view of the portico

Several things were happening in this exercise. First, in step 3, you selected specific objects to work with. To understand why you would want to select specific objects for viewing, you need to understand how the 3D Dynamic View tool works. Here's the explanation.

You saw in step 6 that AutoCAD lets you adjust your view in real time. As you moved the cursor, your view of the portico changed dynamically, allowing you to select just the right view. If you have a very complex drawing, this real-time adjustment of your view would become very difficult to accomplish. By letting you select specific objects, you allow AutoCAD to work with a smaller set of items to display, making it easier for AutoCAD to dynamically display changes in your view. Nearly every option in the 3D Dynamic View tool lets you adjust your view in real time.

The Distance option performs another function besides the obvious setting of distance between your viewpoint and the target: the Distance options turns on the perspective view mode. Had you chosen another option, Pan for example, you would have remained in isometric mode. You should also be aware that the Distance option defaults to a very low value when you first use it from an isometric view. This is why your view of the portico completely disappeared when you first used it (in step 4). It is as if you had your viewpoint one or two inches away from the portico.

Using the Camera/Target Method

Starting from an isometric view is helpful when you want to get an overall perspective view. But suppose you want to actually get *inside* an object. This is where perspective views are crucial. You cannot view the interior of an object using isometric views.

Now imagine yourself sitting next to a designer, or perhaps a client, and you want to show him or her what the design will look like.

To facilitate the setup of a perspective view, the 3D Dynamic View tool offers the Points option. This option works on a camera/target metaphor. You can select the camera and target locations by simply selecting points. The next exercise shows how this works.

1. Open the Savoye2a.DWG file. This is a 3D model similar to the one you created in previous chapters.

2. Click on the Hide tool in the Render toolbar to get a better view of the model.

3. Choose 3D Dynamic View, then select the ramp and the exterior wall as shown in Figure 7.18, and press ↵.

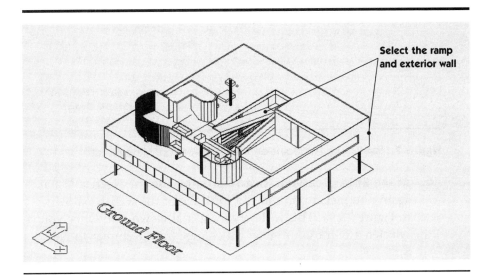

Figure 7.18: Selecting the objects to use for the 3D Dynamic view tool and selecting the points for the Points option

4. At the CAmera/TArget/Distance/POints/PAn/Zoom/TWist/ CLip/Hide/Off/Undo/ <eXit> prompt, enter **PO**↵ for the Points option.

5. At the Enter target point prompt, use the Nearest Osnap and pick the point on the ramp shown in Figure 7.19a. This is the point to which you will be looking.

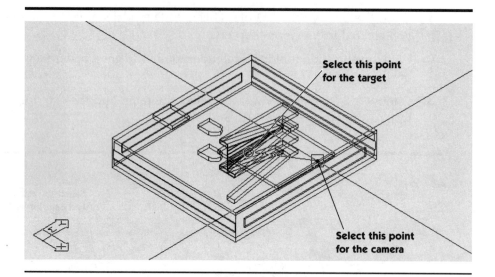

Figure 7.19a: Picking the point on the ramp for your view target

6. At the Enter camera point prompt, use the Nearest Osnap again and pick a point at the top edge of the wall, as shown in Figure 7.19a. This will be your initial viewpoint. Once you've selected a point your view will change to one similar to Figure 7.19b.

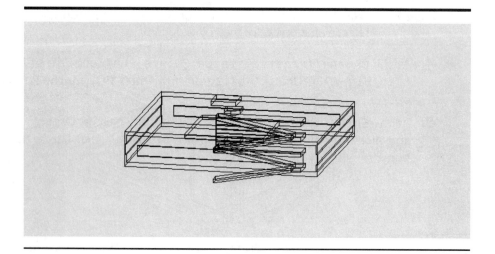

Figure 7.19b: The view after the Points option

Your view is not yet in perspective. Remember that the Distance option of the 3D Dynamic View tool turns on the perspective display. So let's continue by adjusting the distance between the camera and target points.

1. You should still be in the 3D Dynamic View tool. Type **D**⏎. Now as you move the cursor, you'll see the walls and ramp in perspective.

2. Press ⏎ to accept the default distance. You now have a perspective view.

3. Press ⏎ again to exit the 3D Dynamic View tool and to view the entire drawing.

4. The image is difficult to see due to the many layers of objects. Click on the Hide tool in the Render toolbar. You can now see the courtyard view more clearly (see Figure 7.20).

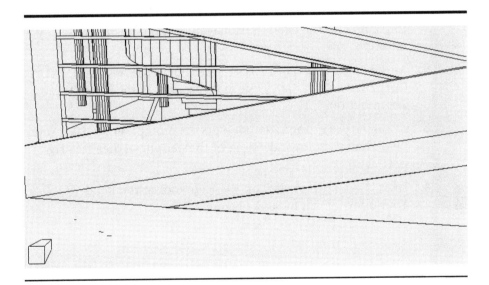

Figure 7.20: The perspective view of the Villa Savoye stairway

In this exercise, you only needed to issue the Distance option and accept the default distance. That distance is the one from the target point to the viewpoint you seleced in steps 4 and 5 of the previous exercise.

You might have also noticed that you didn't have to leave the 3D Dynamic View tool to use the Distance option. You can keep the tool active and make adjustments using any or all of the options until you arrive at the view you want.

Setting the Camera Focal Length

The view you have seems a bit narrow. You may feel you need to "pull back" the camera to view more of the building. Unfortunately, this would result in having a wall block your view. You can, however, change the *focal length* of your camera view to provide a more "wide angle" view. This is done with the Zoom option of the 3D Dynamic View tool. The following exercise illustrates how it works.

1. Choose 3D Dynamic View then enter **P**↵ (for Previous) to select the ramp and the exterior wall again. Press ↵ again to finish your selection.

2. At the `CAmera/TArget/Distance/POints/PAn/Zoom/TWist/CLip/Hide/Off/Undo/ <eXit>` prompt, enter **Z**↵ for the Zoom option.

3. At the `Adjust lenslength <50mm>` prompt, enter **30**↵. Your view changes to include more of the peripheral area (see Figure 7.21a).

4. Press ↵ again, then click on the Hide tool in the Render toolbar. Your drawing will look like Figure 7.21b.

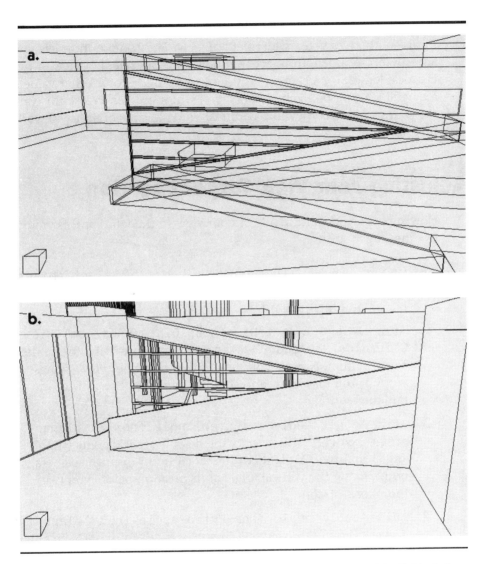

Figure 7.21: Adjusting the focal length of your camera to get a wider field of view

If you're familiar with cameras or telescopes, you know that a smaller focal length gives you a wider field of view. The Zoom option lets you adjust your focal length to accommodate a greater field of view. A typical focal length for a camera is 50mm, so AutoCAD offers that value as a default starting point. Invariably, you will want to decrease this value for your perspective viewing. For most work, a value of 35 to 40 works nicely.

Adjusting Your View Target Location

Now suppose you want to adjust your view to the left. For this, you will use the Target option.

1. Choose View ➤ 3D Dynamic View, then at the `Select object` prompt, type **P.** to select the previous objects (the walls and ramp), and then press .

2. At the `CAmera/TArget/Distance/POints/PAn/Zoom/TWist/ CLip/Hide/Off/Undo/ <eXit>` prompt, enter **TA.** to use the Target option. Now as you move the cursor, your view swings around. You may even find that you have lost the view of the building entirely.

3. At the `Toggle angle in/Enter angle from XY plane` prompt, enter . This accepts the default vertical angle (the angle from the XY plane) of the target point from the camera point, fixing the vertical angle at its position before you issue this Target option.

4. At the `Toggle angle from/Enter angle in XY plane from X axis` prompt, move your cursor from left to right. Notice that now the view motion is restricted to a horizontal one.

5. Adjust your view so it looks similar to Figure 7.22a, then press the left mouse button.

6. Press to exit the 3D Dynamic View option, then click on the Hide tool in the Render toolbar. Your view will look similar to Figure 7.22b.

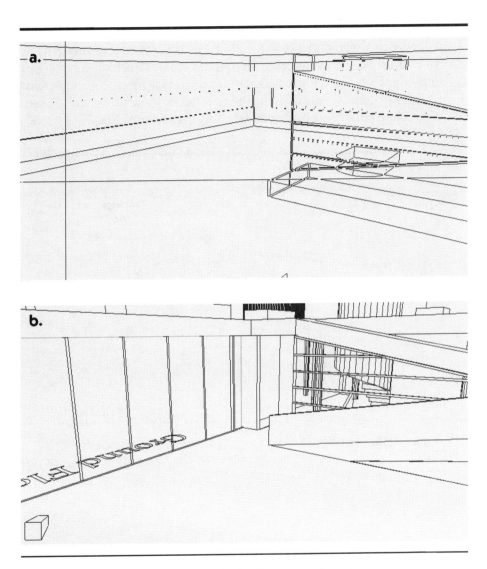

Figure 7.22: Adjusting the Target point for the perspective view

Let's take a moment to study what happened in the previous exercises. When you selected the Target option in step 2, you were suddenly able to rotate your camera around (see Figure 7.23). This had the effect of moving the target location. Once you pressed ↵ to accept the default, then your camera was fixed in the vertical axis and is now restricted to a rotation in the horizontal axis only (see Figure 7.24).

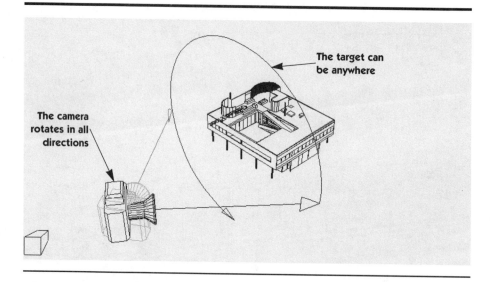

Figure 7.23: When first invoking the Target option, you are able to "rotate" the camera to any location. This can cause you to lose your view of the selected objects.

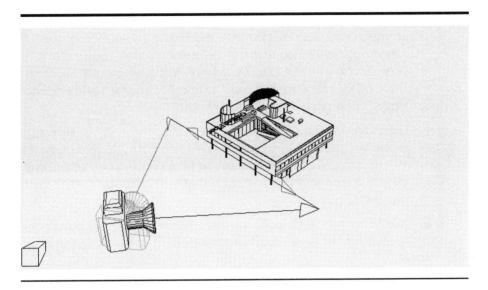

Figure 7.24: You press ↵ to fix the camera rotation angle in the vertical axis, so its rotational movement is in the horizontal axis only.

You can also fix the horizontal camera rotation in order to permit you to adjust the vertical rotation angle. The following exercise will demonstrate this.

1. Choose View ➤ 3D Dynamic View, then at the Select object prompt, type **P**↵ to select the previous objects (the walls and ramp), and then press ↵.

2. At the CAmera/TArget/Distance/POints/PAn/Zoom/TWist/ CLip/Hide/Off/Undo/ <eXit> prompt, enter **TA**↵ to use the Target option. Now as you move the cursor, your view swings around. As in the previous exercise, you may even find that you have lost the view of the building entirely.

3. At the `Toggle angle in/Enter angle from XY plane` prompt, enter **T**↵. This invokes the Toggle sub-option of the Target option. Notice that the prompt now says `Toggle angle from/Enter angle in XY plane from X axis`. "Enter angle in XY plane from X axis" is another way of saying "Choose a horizontal angle for your target point."

4. Enter ↵ again. This fixes the horizontal position of the target point to the position it was in before you started the Target option. Now as you move the cursor forward and backward, you can see your view move up and down. Notice that you cannot alter the view's horizontal position.

5. Adjust your view to look similar to Figure 7.25a, that is, so it includes more of the rooftop garden, then press the left mouse button.

6. Press ↵ again to exit the 3D Dynamic View tool, then click on the Hide tool in the Render toolbar. Your view will look similar to Figure 7.25b.

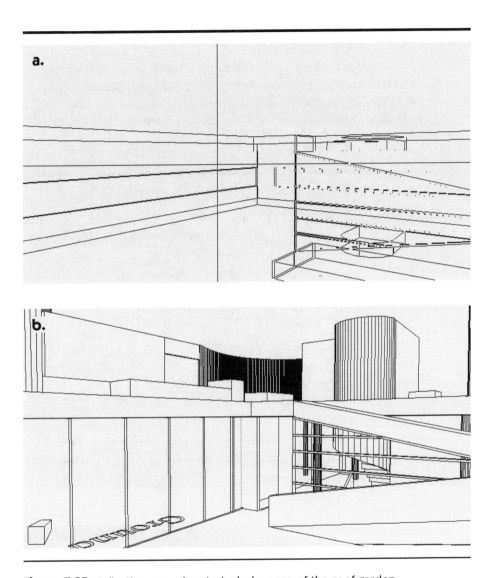

Figure 7.25: Adjusting your view to include more of the roof garden

The Toggle sub-option lets you determine the horizontal position of the viewpoint first. By entering **T**⏎⏎ in steps 3 and 4, you are telling AutoCAD that you want to fix the horizontal location of the target point at its last fixed location. Pressing ⏎ in step 4 essentially told AutoCAD to accept the default horizontal location of the target point. You are then free to set the vertical rotation angle of the camera as shown in Figure 7.26.

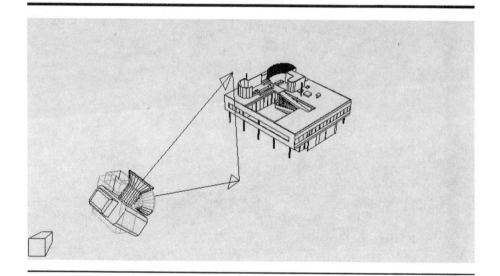

Figure 7.26: The Toggle sub-option of the Target option lets you fix the camera rotation to the vertical.

At first pass, the Target option seems rather cumbersome. With practice, however, it will become second nature and can provide a very quick method of adjusting your view.

Adjusting Your Camera Location

Now suppose your designer or client wants to move your point of view a bit to the right. For this adjustment, you will use the Camera option. Unlike the Target option, Camera moves the camera location.

1. Once again, choose View ➤ 3D Dynamic View, then at the `Select object` prompt type **P↵** to select the previous objects (the walls and ramp), and then press ↵.

2. At the `CAmera/TArget/Distance/POints/PAn/Zoom/TWist/ CLip/Hide/Off/Undo/ <eXit>` prompt, enter **CA↵** to use the Camera option. Now as you move the cursor, your view changes as if your target were fixed, but your point of view were moving.

3. At the `Toggle angle in/Enter angle from XY plane` prompt, enter ↵. This accepts the default vertical angle (the angle from the XY plane) of the camera point from the target point, fixing the vertical angle at its position before you issued this Camera option.

4. At the `Toggle angle from/Enter angle in XY plane from X axis` prompt, move your cursor from left to right. Notice that now the view motion is restricted to a horizontal one.

5. Adjust your view so it looks similar to Figure 7.27, then press the left mouse button.

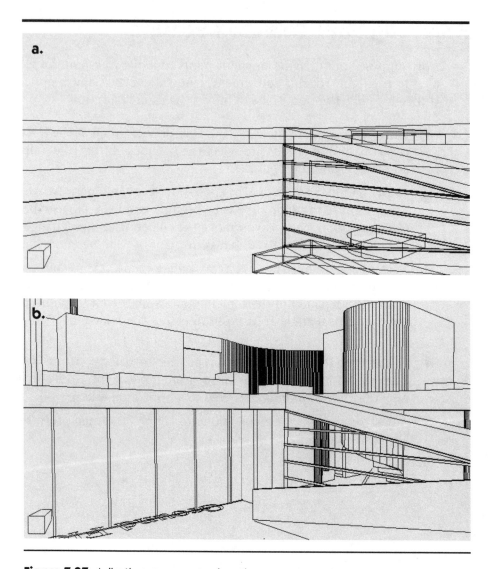

Figure 7.27: Adjusting your camera location

Just as with the Target option, the Camera option lets you adjust the vertical and horizontal position of the camera independently (see Figure 7.28). The Camera option also has a Toggle sub-option which allows you to fix the horizontal camera location before selecting the vertical position.

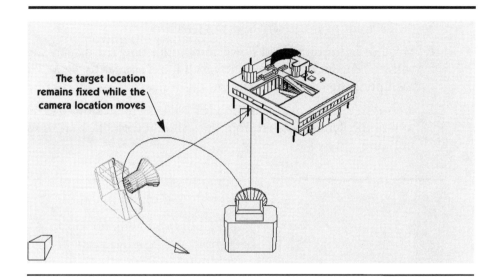

Figure 7.28: The Camera option lets you move the camera position. The Target location remains fixed.

Because, unlike the Target option, Camera won't send your view off the screen, you may find that you do not need to adjust the vertical and horizontal camera position independently. For example, in step 3, you could have moved the camera into position, adjusting both vertical and horizontal locations simultaneously with your mouse movement.

Panning Your View

Now suppose you want to shift both your viewpoint and camera location in the same direction—to the left and up. For this operation, you use the Pan option.

1. The 3D Dynamic View tool should still be active. Type **PA**↵ then pick a point near the center of the screen.

2. Move your cursor around slowly and notice how the display moves with the cursor. Adjust your view so it looks similar to Figure 7.29, then press the left mouse button.

3. Press ↵ to exit the 3D Dynamic View tool, then click on the Hide tool in the Render toolbar. Your view should look like that shown in Figure 7.30.

Figure 7.29: Your view after using the Pan option

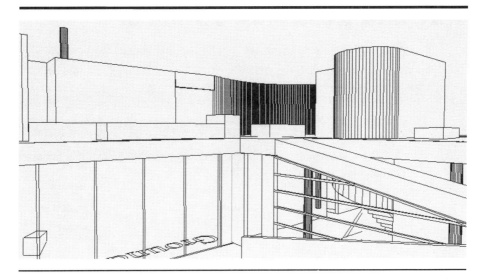

Figure 7.30: Your view with lines hidden after using the Pan option

The Pan option is a great tool for making fine adjustments to your view. As you saw in this exercise, you have a fairly fine control over the display.

Controlling Text Visibility

You may have noticed in the previous exercises that the Ground Floor label "bleeds through" your hidden-line perspective views of your model (Figure 7.27, Figure 7.30). There may be some instances where you will want text to appear in a 3D hidden-line view even when it is behind an object. However, if you do not want text to show, you have two options. You can place the text on a specific text layer and then turn it off when generating perspective views. The other is to give the text a non-zero thickness using the Properties tool. Whenever text has a thickness other than zero, it will act like any other surface object and will be hidden with the Hide tool.

◆ Saving and Restoring 3D Views

Now that you've got the perfect view, you will want to save it so you can easily return to it later. The View tools can be used to save 3D views as easily as 2D views. Here's how it's done.

1. Choose View ➤ Named Views. The View Control Dialog box appears.

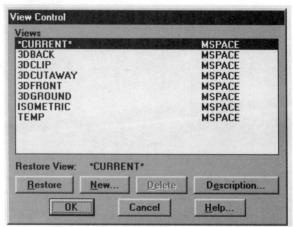

2. Click on the New button button in the bottom half of the dialog box. The Define New View dialog box appears.

3. In the New Name input box, enter **3Dcourt**, then click on the Save View button. You return to the View Control dialog box.

4. Notice that the new view name now appears in the list box. Click OK to exit the View Control dialog box.

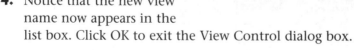

You may have noticed a few other view names in the list box in step 4. We've saved a few 3D views already, so we can demonstrate how views are recalled.

1. Choose View ➤ Named Views again.

2. At the View Control dialog box, click on *3Dfront* in the list box to highlight it.

3. Click on the Restore button, then click on OK.

4. You may get the prompt message "About to regen—proceed? <y>". Press ↵ to continue. Your view changes to display a 3D view of the front of the building (see Figure 7.31).

5. Open the View Control dialog box again and, this time, select the view you created in the previous exercises (*3Dcourt*).

6. Click on the Restore button and then OK. The view you created is restored.

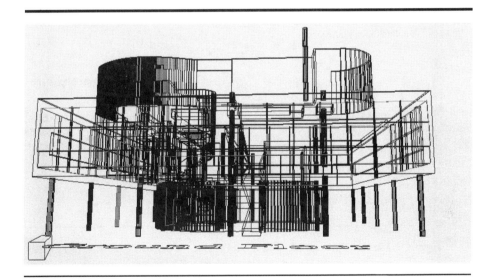

Figure 7.31: A 3D perspective view of the front of our building

◆ Hiding Foreground and Background Material

One of the more powerful tools available to you is a little known option of the 3D Dynamic View tool called *Clip*. This tool can be especially helpful to designers and architects who want to show an interior of a space in relation to the exterior. The Clip option hides a portion of your view so you can see interior portions of your model more clearly. Figure 7.32 shows you how the Clip option creates a "clipping plane" which determines which portion of your model is hidden.

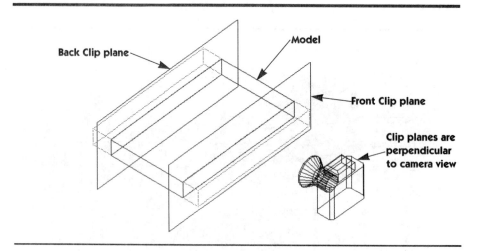

Figure 7.32: The Clip option of the 3D Dynamic View tool lets you hide foreground and background portions of your 3D model.

The following exercise will demonstrate how the Clip option can be used to generate a typical architectural cutaway view of our building. We've already set up a view from which you can begin.

1. First, restore the view we saved earlier called *3Dclip*: choose View ➤ Named Views. At the View Control dialog box, click on *3Dclip*, then click on the Restore button.

2. Click OK, then at the `Regen` prompt, press ↵. Your view shows a side of the building, as shown in Figure 7.33.

3. Choose View ➤ 3D Dynamic View.

4. At the `Select object` prompt, select the exterior walls of the second floor and a few columns, as shown in Figure 7.33, and then press ↵.

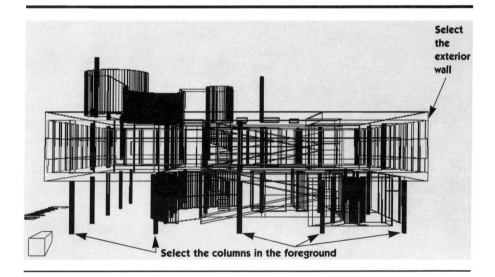

Figure 7.33: The 3Dclip view

5. At the CAmera/TArget/Distance/POints/PAn/Zoom/TWist/ CLip/Hide/Off/Undo/ <eXit> prompt, enter **CL↵**.

6. At the Back/Front/<off> prompt, type **F↵** to select the Front sub-option. You will see the Clip slide bar near the top of the drawing area (see Figure 7.34).

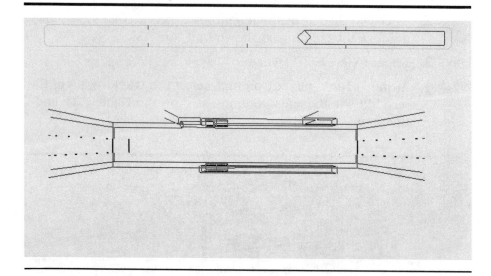

Figure 7.34: The 3D Dynamic View display with the Clip slidebar shown at the top

7. Move your mouse from right to left so the diamond in the slide bar is near the left side. Notice what happens to the walls as you move the slide bar.

8. When the diamond is in the approximate location shown in Figure 7.34, press the left mouse button. The slide bar disappears.

9. Press ↵ to exit the 3D Dynamic View tool, then click on the Hide tool in the Render toolbar. You will see a cutaway view of the building, as shown in Figure 7.35. As with all other views, you can save this cutaway view of the interior.

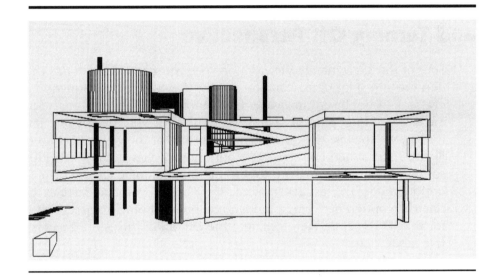

Figure 7.35: A hidden-line view of the building with the front portion cut away to reveal the interior of the building

You may have noticed other sub-options to the Clip option. The Back option shown in Step 6 of the previous exercise clips the back portion of the model. This can be helpful if you want to hide unwanted busyness in the background. The <off> option turns off any view clipping you may have set up.

◆ A Few More Things You Should Know

We've concentrated mostly on the 3D Dynamic View tool and have shown you the most commonly used options. There are a few other options and some restrictions that apply to this important 3D tool.

Twisting, Hiding, Undoing, and Turning Off Perspective

Four of the 3D Dynamic View options perform fairly simple tasks that don't require a lot of explanation in how they work. Their function, however, might not be entirely clear. I'd like to point them out briefly so you are aware of their purpose. The Twist option lets you rotate your view, as if you were to twist the camera about the axis of the view direction (see Figure 7.36). When you select this option, your view rotates with the cursor movement, allowing you to select a rotation angle visually. The Undo option undoes the last 3D Dynamic View option you may have executed. The Hide option performs a hidden-line removal of the objects you select for the 3D Dynamic View tool, and the Off option turns off the perspective mode view.

Figure 7.36: The cutaway view with the Twist option to rotate the view 30 degrees

What You Can't Do in a Perspective View

The perspective view is somewhat limiting as far as editing goes. You can select objects for most edits, but you can't select points. For example, you can use the Move tool and select objects in a perspective view, but you must enter base point and second point coordinates for the move through the keyboard; selecting points with the mouse will not work.

You also cannot use the Zoom or Pan tool in a perspective view. Those tools are available only for isometric and 2D views. Of course, you can use the 3D Dynamic View Pan, Distance, and Zoom functions to adjust your view in perspective. Still, once you've become accomplished at using the 3D Dynamic View tool, you can quickly switch from perspective view to isometric view during editing sessions to help you visualize your work as you go.

In the earlier part of this chapter, you saw how viewports can be used with 3D modeling. You might consider splitting your screen into two viewports—one for editing and one for viewing your model in 3D (see Figure 7.37). This way you can check your edits as you work without having to constantly switch from perspective to isometric and back.

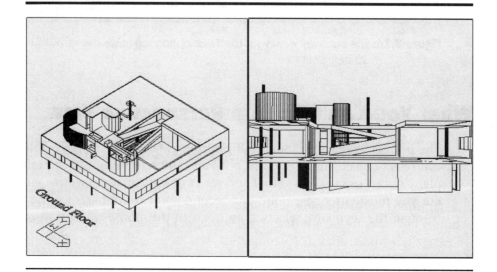

Figure 7.37: You can enhance your editing session by splitting your display into two viewports—one for a perspective view and the other for a "working" view of your model.

Adding Props to Aid View Creation

You've seen how you can use the Points option in the 3D Dynamic
View tool to select a camera and target point. At times it can be helpful to set up objects to facilitate exact locations for a camera and target
point. For example, if you want to get the view a person would see from
standing outside the building, you might place a vertical line at that
point. The height of the line would be the distance from the ground
plane to the eye level of the person (see Figure 7.38). You might also
place another line at the location of the target point, using the line's
endpoint for the actual target, as shown in Figure 7.38.

Using props such as lines to help select camera and target points can also
help you easily identify where your views were taken. To help locate the
props, you might also consider using viewports as shown in Figure 7.39.

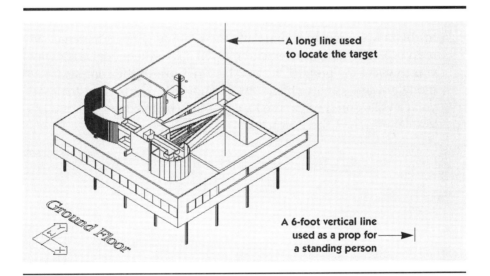

Figure 7.38: Using lines to set up and identify the camera and target points
of perspective views

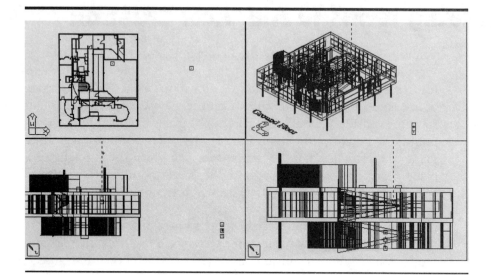

Figure 7.39: Using viewports to help position props

In the sample view in Figure 7.39, the props are lines. The target prop is an especially long line extending well above the model. This allows you to select the prop easily, as it becomes lost in the complexity of the model toward its bottom end. By extending it well beyond the model, you can click on it to expose its grips, thereby making its endpoints visible in each of the viewports.

◆ Getting Hard Copy Output

Chances are, you will use your perspective views as part of a presentation or perhaps as a background for a hand-rendered presentation. You have seen in Chapter 3 how you can use the Windows Clipboard to cut and paste views from AutoCAD to other graphics applications. You can also cut and paste perspective views from AutoCAD. Before we close this chapter, you will want to know about some of the options you have for *plotting* your perspective views.

Plotting a single Model Space view is easy enough. You select File ➤ Print, then make sure the Hide Lines checkbox is checked in the Plot Configuration dialog box.

When you want to plot a set of viewports from Paper Space, however, you will have to take a few steps before you plot to ensure that hidden lines are removed at plot time. The Floating Viewport option (Mview command) controls hidden-line removal in Paper Space viewports. The following exercise will step you through the creation and setup for hidden-line plots from Paper Space.

1. If you have closed the `Savoye2.DWG` file, open it again.

2. Choose View ➤ Paper Space. This places you in Paper Space. Since there are no viewports defined yet, your drawing area is blank.

3. Choose View ➤ Floating Viewports ➤ 4 Viewports. This option creates four floating viewports in Paper Space.

4. At the `Fit/<First Point>` prompt, enter **F**⏎. This causes AutoCAD to create four viewports of equal size to fit the extents of the drawing area. After a moment, you will see four identical views of the building (see Figure 7.40).

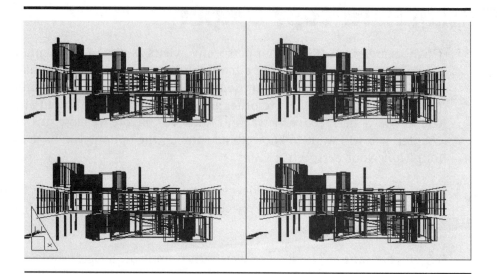

Figure 7.40: Four Paper Space viewports appear

5. Choose View ➤ Floating Model Space, then move the cursor to the lower right viewport. Notice that your cursor appears as a cross-hair there. This tells you that this viewport is the active one.

6. Click on the lower left viewport and choose View ➤ Named Views.

7. At the View Control dialog box, select 3Dground, then click on Restore.

8. Click OK. If you get the Regen warning message, press ↵. The viewport changes to show the 3Dground view (see Figure 7.41).

9. Repeat steps 6 through 8 for both of the top two viewports. You can restore any view from the list box you choose.

Tip *In step 9, when you are repeating the use of the View Control dialog box, you need only right-click on your mouse to open it again.*

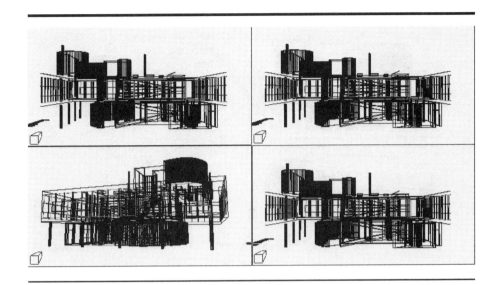

Figure 7.41: Restoring a saved view to the lower left viewport

Once you've got the layout of your Paper Space viewports set, you must turn on the Hideplot feature for each viewport.

1. Choose View ➤ Floating Viewports ➤ Hideplot. Notice that AutoCAD temporarily switches to Paper Space.

2. At the ON/OFF/Hideplot/Fit/2/3/4/Restore/<First Point>: _h ON/OFF prompt, enter **ON**↵.

3. At the Select objects prompt, use a crossing window and select the four viewports near the center of the screen (see Figure 7.42), then press ↵. While nothing appears to have happened, you have just set up all four views to plot without hidden lines at plot time.

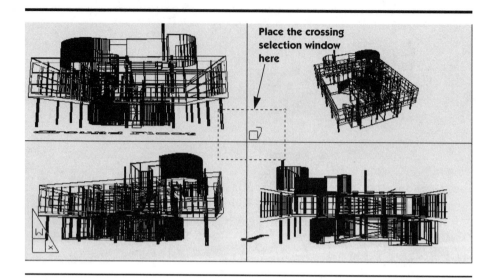

Figure 7.42: Selecting the four floating viewports using a crossing window

When plotting Paper Space viewports with their Hideplot option turned on, you need not have the Hide Lines checkbox checked in the Plot Configuration dialog box. AutoCAD automatically performs a hidden-line removal. You can check the results of Hideplot by using the Plot Preview option at plot time, as described in this next exercise.

1. First, make sure you are in Paper Space by choosing View ➤ Paper Space.

2. Choose File ➤ Print. The Plot Configuration dialog box appears.

3. In the Plot Preview button group toward the lower right corner of the dialog box, make sure the Full radio button is on, then click on the Preview button. After a minute or two, you'll see a preview of the plot as shown in Figure 7.43.

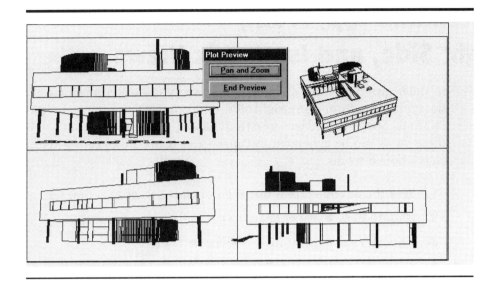

Figure 7.43: A preview of the Paper Space viewport plots with the Hideplot feature turned on

In this example, you selected all four viewports for hidden-line removal. You can be more selective about which viewports have their Hideplot feature turned on, however. For example, you may want to show a floor plan in one floating viewport; in such a case, you may not want hidden lines removed. You can turn off the Hideplot setting for a viewport by using the OFF option seen in step 2 of the above example.

◆ Automatic Top, Front, Right Side, and Isometric Views

In the beginning of this chapter, we showed you how you can create the typical four top, front, right side, and isometric mechanical views in Model Space. Before we close this chapter, we'd like to show you how these views can be generated in Paper Space using a tool called Mvsetup. Here's how it works.

1. Save the `Savoye2.DWG` file, then open the `Rvchair.DWG` file.

2. Choose View ➤ Paper Space to get to Paper Space mode.

3. Choose View ➤ Floating Viewports ➤ MV Setup.

4. At the `Align/Create/Scale viewports/Options/Title block/Undo` prompt, type **C**↵ to select the Create option.

5. At the `Delete objects/Undo/<Create viewports>` prompt, press ↵ to accept the default Create viewports. The AutoCAD Text Screen will pop up to display a list of four options:

   ```
   Available Mview viewport layout options:
   0: None
   1: Single
   2: Std. Engineering
   3: Array of Viewports
   Redisplay/<Number of entry to load>:
   ```

6. Type **2**↵ to select option 2, Std. Engineering.

7. At the `Bounding area for viewports. First point` prompt, select a point near the lower left corner of the drawing area.

8. At the `Other point` prompt, select a point in the upper right corner of the drawing area. This defines the area within which the four views will be placed.

9. At the next two prompts, `Distance between viewports in X. <0.0>:` and `Distance between viewports in Y. <0.0>:`, press ↵. These two prompts allow you to define a distance between the viewports. AutoCAD will proceed to generate the standard top, front, and right side views including an isometric view (see Figure 7.44).

10. Finally, at the `Align/Create/Scale viewports/Options/ Title block/Undo` prompt, press ↵ to exit the MV Setup tool.

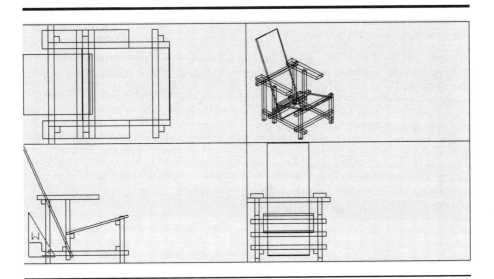

Figure 7.44: The views created by the Std. Engineering option of the MV Setup tool

Once you've got the views set up, you can switch to Floating Model Space (View ➤ Floating Model Space) and adjust the views. AutoCAD then acts in a way similar to the way it acts in Tiled Model Space, the mode you were working in in the first exercise in this chapter, using the `Rvchair` file. The Paper Space viewports act like the four views you set up in Model Space using View ➤ Tiled Viewports ➤ Layout.

Using Paper Space to set up multiple viewports has another advantage: You can easily resize and move the viewports individually. This means you can arrange the viewports in any configuration you want, even overlap them if you choose. Paper Space viewports act like typical AutoCAD objects—their properties can be edited using the Properties tool, and they can be moved, copied, scaled, and stretched using their corner grips.

◆ **Summary**

One of the rewards of working with 3D is that you get very quick feedback from your efforts. This is especially true when you are able to show others your work in a perspective view. I've shown you the tools you need to create and control perspective views in AutoCAD. I've also suggested that perspective can be a tool during preliminary design sessions. While it may seem a bit cumbersome at first, once you get used to the perspective tools, you will find that you can quickly arrive at a view you want.

We're approaching the end of the first part of this book. The next chapter will show you how you can start to render your computer model with color and light. You will then see how your construction methods impact your ability to produce computer renderings.

Rendering with
AutoVision

Computer rendering of 3D models has come a long way in a very short time. Just a few years ago, it took a workstation class computer many hours to render views similar to those you will produce in this chapter. Today, with faster hardware blurring the distinction between workstations and personal computers, and improved software like AutoVision and 3D Studio, 3D rendering is available to nearly anyone with a desktop computer. A typical PC set up to run AutoCAD will have no problem at all creating realistic images of products or buildings.

In this chapter, you'll learn how you can use AutoVision from Autodesk to produce rendered still images of your 3D models. AutoVision is an extension of the Render functions that are built into AutoCAD. You can add materials, control lighting, and even add landscaping and people to your models using AutoVision. You also have control over reflectance and transparency of objects and you can add bitmap backgrounds to help set the mood.

How to Get AutoVision

AutoVision is shipped with AutoCAD release 13. To use it, you need to install it from the AutoCAD release 13 CD-ROM or disk, then obtain a temporary authorization code from Autodesk. This authorization code allows you to try AutoVision for 30 days. After that, you need to purchase a permanent authorization code.

Before you begin the next section, be sure you have installed AutoVision and have obtained at least the temporary authorization code. Remember that once you have installed AutoVision and initialized it using the code, you have 30 days to use AutoVision. After that, AutoVision will no longer work. You cannot get another temporary authorization code.

You may want to wait to initialize AutoVision until you are ready to work through this chapter. That way you'll have plenty of time to try out the various features of AutoVision at your leisure, after our introduction.

◆ Things to Do before You Start

If you're like most of us and are working with a desktop PC instead of a high-powered workstation, you will want to take certain steps *before* you start working with AutoVision so you won't run into problems later. First, make sure you have assigned plenty of memory to be available to AutoCAD. AutoCAD likes to have lots of RAM, and when you add the overhead of AutoVision, you can bring your computer to a grinding halt working on large files.

Use the Environment tab in the Preferences dialog box to set the amount of memory allocated to AutoCAD. Set the value in the Memory input box to as high a value as you can. If you're running AutoCAD under Windows 95 or Windows NT—and I strongly suggest you do, because AutoVision balks frequently under Windows 3.x—try setting the value to 7 megabytes less than the maximum RAM capacity in your computer. (So for a system with 32 megabytes, you'd set AutoCAD to use 25 megabytes.)

NT users should allow at least 12 megabytes of memory for the operating system.

Also, make sure that you have lots of free disk space on the drive where Windows is installed. Having 100 megabytes of free disk space will ensure that you won't exceed your RAM capacity while rendering. This may sound like a lot, but remember, you are attempting to do with your desktop computer what only workstations were capable of a few years ago.

◆ Creating a Quick Study Rendering

You'll start by doing a preliminary rendering of the Facade model you created in Chapter 6. I've prepared a version of the Facade model that includes some additional objects.

1. Open the Facade3.DWG file from the Sample directory on the CD accompanying the book. You'll notice that we've added a few more elements like a ground plane and a neighboring building. We've also added a top to the building.

2. Choose AutoVis ➤ Render. The AutoVision Render dialog box appears. In time, you will become intimately familiar with this dialog box.

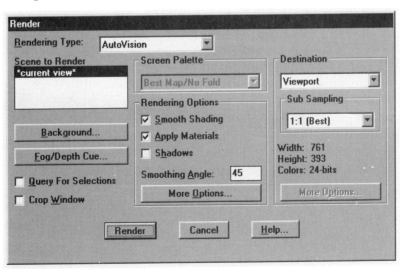

3. Click on the Render button. The model appears as a surface shaded model (see Figure 8.1)

Figure 8.1: The Facade drawing rendered using all the default settings

> **Note** *Once you've installed AutoVision, many of the functions on the standard AutoCAD Render toolbar invoke AutoVision tools of the same name, so you can continue to use AutoCAD's Render toolbar for AutoVision. You may, however, want the AutoVision toolbar up anyway, as it contains a few functions not found in the Render toolbar. To open the AutoVison toolbar, choose AutoVis ➤ AutoVis Toolbar.*

When you use the Render tool without any special settings, you get what is called a *Z buffer shaded model*. The surfaces are shaded in their color and the light source is, by default, from the camera location. This view is much like a hidden-line-removed view with color added to help distinguish surface orientation. You can actually get a similar view using the Shade tool in the standard AutoCAD Render toolbar.

Simulating the Sun Light Angle

The ability to add a Sun light source is one of AutoVision's key features. This is a frequently called for tool in the design of buildings in urban and suburban settings. Neighboring building owners usually want to know if your project will cast shadows over their homes or workplaces. The Sun option lets you accurately simulate the sun's location in relation to a model and its surrounding buildings. AutoVision also lets you set up multiple light sources other than the sun.

So let's add the sun to our model to give a better sense of the model's form and its relationship to its site.

1. Choose AutoVis ➤ Lights.

2. At the Lights dialog box, choose Distant Light from the drop-down list next to the New button (toward the bottom left).

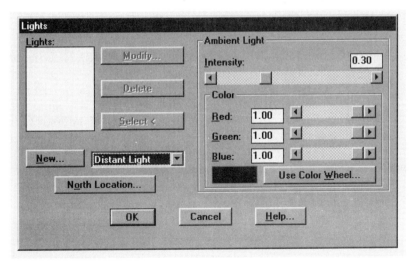

3. Click on the New button. The New Distant Light dialog box appears.

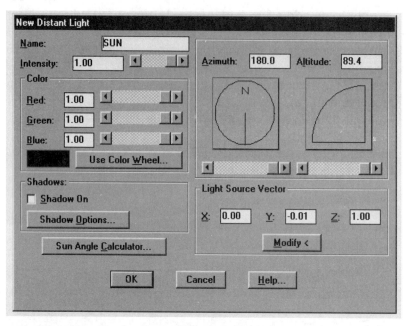

Tip *Whenever you are creating a new light or other object in AutoVision, you usually have to give it a name first, before you can do anything else. Regardless of how you type the name, AutoVision will automatically display it as all uppercase.*

4. Type **SUN**. The word *SUN* appears in the Name input box toward the top of the dialog box. This dialog box lets you control various aspects of the light source, such as color and location.

5. Since we want to simulate the sun in this example, click on the button labeled Sun Angle Calculator. The Sun Angle Calculator dialog box appears.

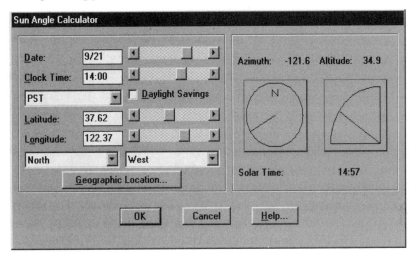

Notice that you have options for setting the date and time to determine the exact location of the sun. In addition, you have the option to indicate where true polar north is in relation to your model. AutoCAD assumes polar north is at the 90 degree position in the WCS.

6. One important factor for calculating the sun angle is finding your *model's* location. Click on the Geographic Location button. The Geographic Location dialog box appears. Here you can tell AutoCAD where your building is located in the world.

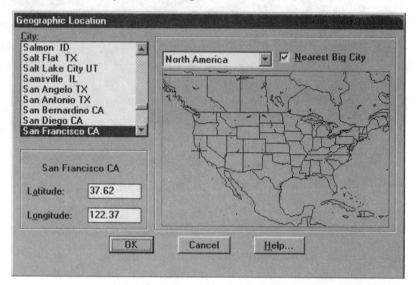

7. For the sake of this tutorial, let's suppose the Facade model is a building in San Francisco, California, USA. Make sure North America appears in the drop-down list above the map.

8. Locate and select *San Francisco CA*, which is listed in the scrolling list to the left. Notice that the values in the Latitude and Longitude input boxes below the list change to reflect the new location. For locations not listed, you can enter values manually in those input boxes.

9. Now click OK to return to the Sun Angle Calculator dialog box. Set the Date for **9/21** and the time for **14:00** hours. Notice that the graphic to the right of the dialog box adjusts to show the altitude and azimuth angle of the sun for the time you enter.

10. Click OK, then click OK again at the Lights dialog box.

11. Choose AutoVis ➤ Render, then click on the Render button in the Render dialog box. Your model will be shaded to reflect the sun's location (see Figure 8.2).

Figure 8.2: The Facade model with the sun light source added

Notice that the building itself looks darker than before, and that the ground plane is lighter. Remember that in the first rendering, the light source is the same as the camera location so the wall facing you receives more direct light. In this last rendering, the light source is at a glancing angle so the surface appears darker.

We mentioned that you can set the direction of polar north. This is accomplished by clicking on the North Location button in the Lights dialog box. When selected, this button opens the North Location dialog box shown in Figure 8.3. With this dialog box, you can set true north in any of three ways. You can click on the graphic to point to the direction; you can use the slide bar at the bottom to move the arrow of the graphic and adjust the value in the input box; or you can enter a value directly into the input box. You also have the option to indicate which UCS is used to set the north direction. For example, if you have already set a UCS to point to the true north direction, you need only select the UCS from the list and leave the angle at zero.

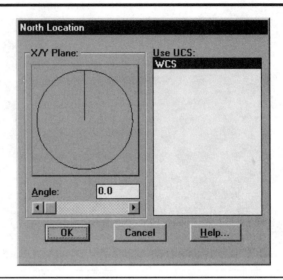

Figure 8.3: The North Location dialog box

Improving Display Accuracy with the FACETRES System Variable

At times when using the Render, Hide, or Shade tool, you might notice that solid or region arcs appear segmented rather than curved. This may be fine for producing layouts or backgrounds for hand-rendered drawings, but for final plots, you will want arcs and circles to appear as smooth curves. You can adjust the accuracy of your hidden, rendered, or shaded views by setting the Facetres system variable higher than its default .5 setting. For example, the Facade2 model has an arch that renders as a crude segmented arch. Setting Facetres to 1.5 forces AutoCAD to render the arch as a curve instead of a series of flat segments.

Adding Shadows

There is nothing like adding shadows to a 3D rendering to give the model a sense of realism. AutoVision offers three methods for casting shadows. The default method is called *Volumetric Shadows*. This method creates an approximation of how the shadows should look and takes a considerable amount of time when rendering more complex scenes. When using AutoVision's *Ray Trace* option (described later in this chapter), shadows will be generated using a method that simulates the way light rays travel. This method also takes time but produces the most accurate rendition of shadows. The third method, called *Shadow Maps*, offers the best speed but requires some adjustment to get good results. One option that Shadow Maps offers that the other methods don't is a soft-edge shadow. While shadow maps are generally less accurate than the other two methods, the soft edge option offers a level of realism not available in the other two methods.

In this chapter, you'll practice using the Ray Trace and Shadow Map method for casting shadows, starting with Shadow Maps in the following exercise. We won't use the Volumetric Shadows option, though you may want to explore it on your own.

What Is Ray Tracing?

To make a long, complicated story short, ray tracing simulates the way light works. And it does it in a sort of reverse way. Ray tracing analyzes the light path to each pixel of your display, tracing the light or "ray" from the pixel to the light origin as it bounces off objects in your model. Ray tracing takes into account the reflectivity and, in the case of glass, the refraction of light as it is affected by objects in the model. Since the more objects there are in a model the more surfaces there are to reflect light, ray tracing becomes more time-consuming as the number of objects increase. Also, since each pixel is analyzed, a greater image size increases the render time geometrically. By doubling the width and height of the view size, for example, you are essentially increasing the number of pixels by four times.

AutoVision offers Ray Tracing as an option for rendering both shadows and the entire scene. The ray trace options offer greater accuracy in exchange for slow rendering time. If you choose to select ray traced shadows, for example, you can expect at least a fourfold increase in rendering time. Rendering an entire scene can increase rendering time by an order of magnitude. Needless to say, if you are in a time crunch, you will want to save ray tracing just for the essential final renderings. Use AutoVision's other rendering options for study renderings or for situations that don't require the accuracy of ray tracing.

Tip   *When adding shadows, remember that you must turn on the Shadow option for both the Render dialog box and each light that is to cast a shadow.*

In the following exercise, you will use the Shadow Map method. It requires the most adjustments but yields the fastest rendering.

1. Choose AutoVis ➤ Lights.

2. At the Lights dialog box, make sure *Sun* is highlighted, then click Modify. The Modify Distant Light dialog box appears.

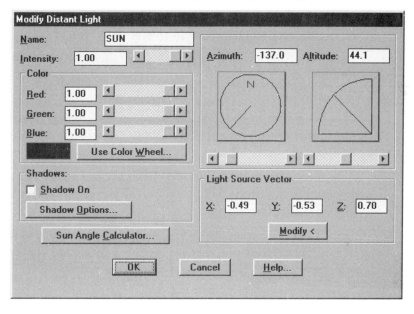

3. Click on the Shadow
On checkbox, then
click on the Shadow
Options button.
The Shadow Options
dialog box appears.

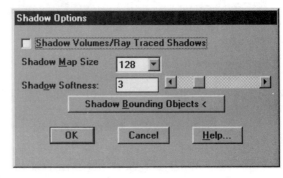

4. Click on the Shadow
Volumes/Ray Traced
Shadows checkbox
to remove the check-
mark. (The option is on by default.) Notice that the other options
become accessible when you do this.

5. Change the Shadow Map Size to 512 by selecting 512 from the
drop-down list.

6. Click on the Shadow Bounding Objects button. The dialog box
temporarily disappears to allow you to select objects from the
screen. This option allows you to select the objects you want to
cast shadows.

7. Select the entire Facade building. Take care not to select any of
the building next to it. When you are done, press ⏎. The Shadow
Options dialog box reappears.

8. Click OK to close the dialog box, then click OK at the Modify
Distant Light dialog box. It may take several seconds before the
dialog box closes.

9. When you get to the Lights dialog box, click OK to close it.

10. Click on the Render button in either the Render toolbar or the AutoVision toolbar.

11. At the Render dialog box, check the Shadows checkbox.

12. Click on the Render button. After a minute or two, the model appears rendered with shadows (see Figure 8.4).

Figure 8.4: The Facade drawing rendered with shadows using the Shadow Map method

Don't panic if the shadows don't appear correct. The Shadow Map method needs some adjustment before it will give the proper shadows. The default settings are appropriate for views of objects from a greater distance than our current view. The following exercise will show you what to do for "close-up" views.

1. Open the Render dialog box again, then click on the button labeled More Options. The AutoVision Render Options dialog box appears.

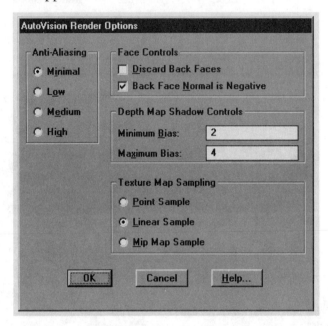

2. In the group labeled Depth Map Shadow Controls, change the Minimum Bias value from 2 to **.1**.

3. In the same group, change the Maximum Bias value from 4 to **.2**.

4. Click OK to close the dialog box, then click Render. Your next rendering will show more accurately drawn shadows (see Figure 8.5).

Figure 8.5: The rendered view with the shadow bias settings revised

The shadow still looks a bit rough. You can further refine the shadows'
appearance by increasing the Shadow Map size to greater than 512. This
setting can be found in the Shadow Options dialog box (discussed in step
4 of the exercise before the last one). Figure 8.6 shows the same rendering
with the shadow map size set to 1024. As you increase the map size, however, you also increase render time and the amount of RAM required to
render the view. If you don't have enough free disk space, you may find
that AutoVision will refuse to render the model. You will then have to
either free up some disk space or decrease the map size.

Figure 8.6: The rendered view with the Shadow Map size set to 1024

Notice that the shadow has a soft edge. You can control the softness of the shadow edge using the Shadow Options dialog box you saw in the exercise prior to the last one. The Shadow Softness input box and slide bar let you sharpen the shadow edge by decreasing the value, or soften it by increasing the value. The soft shadow is especially effective for renderings of building interiors or scenes where you are simulating artificial light.

Adding Materials

The rendering methods you've learned so far can be of enormous aid in your design effort. Simply being able to see how the sun affects your design can be of enormous help in selling your ideas, or in getting plans through a tough planning board review. But the look of the building is still kind of cartoonish. You can further enhance the rendering by adding *materials* to the objects in your model.

Let's suppose you want a granite-like finish to appear on the Facade model, and you want the building next to the Facade model to appear as a glass tower. The first step to adding materials is to aquire the materials from the materials *library*.

1. Choose AutoVis ➤ Materials. The Materials dialog box appears.

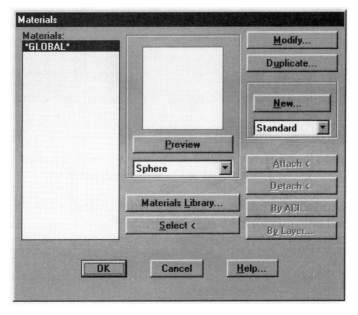

2. Click on the Materials Library button in the middle of the dialog box. The Materials Library dialog box appears.

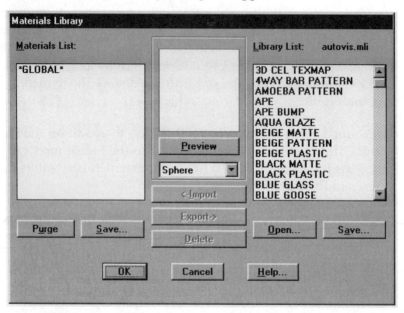

3. In the Library List box on the right side of the dialog box, find and select *Granite Pebbles* so it is highlighted. This is the material you will assign to the Facade.

4. Click on the Preview button in the middle of the dialog box. A view of the material appears on, by default, a sphere, giving you an idea of what the material looks like.

5. Click on the Import button. Notice that Granite Pebbles now appears in the Materials List box to the left. This list box is for showing the materials you've transferred to your drawing.

6. Locate *Glass* in the Library List to the right and select it. Click the Preview button again to see what it looks like. Notice that the preview shows a transparent sphere.

7. Click on the Import button again to make the Glass material available in the drawing, then click OK to exit the Materials Library dialog box.

Once you've aquired the materials, you can assign them to objects in your drawing.

1. At the Materials dialog box, highlight the Granite Pebbles item shown in the list to the left, then click on the Attach > button in the right half of the dialog box. The dialog box temporarily disappears, allowing you to select the objects you want to appear as Granite Pebbles.

2. Click on various parts of the Facade model, making sure to include the steps, columns, and arched entrance, then press ↵. You won't see any change in the model until you issue the Render command at the end of the exercise. For now, we'll continue with our second material. After a moment, the Materials dialog box appears again automatically.

3. Click on Glass from the Materials list.

4. This time you'll assign a material based on its layer. Click on the By Layer button to the right of the dialog box. The Attach By Layer dialog box appears.

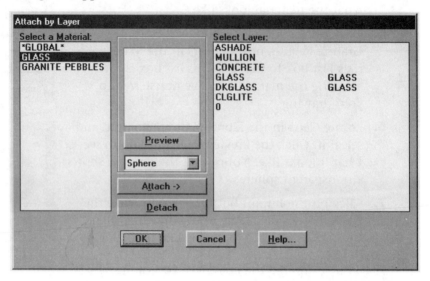

5. Select *Glass* and *Dkglass* from the Select Layer list to the right, then click on the Attach button. Notice that the word *Glass* now appears next to the Glass and Dkglass layer names you selected, indicating that the Glass material is now associated with those layers.

6. Click OK to exit the Attach By Layer dialog box, then click OK again to exit the Materials dialog box.

7. Choose AutoVis ➤ Render, then click on the Render button. You may want to take a break at this point, as the rendering will take a few minutes. When AutoVision is finished, your rendering will look like Figure 8.7.

Figure 8.7: The Facade model with the glass and granite pebbles materials added

Adjusting the Appearance of Materials

The Facade looks more like it has an army camouflage paint job instead of a granite finish, due to the immense size of the flakes in the granite. Also the glass of the office tower is a bit too transparent—it looks like the front and back walls have simply disappeared. Fortunately, you can make several adjustments to the materials. You will want to reduce the scale of the granite pebbles material so it is in line with the scale of the model. You will also want to darken the glass material so it looks more like the tinted glass used in modern office buildings. You'll start with the granite pebbles.

1. Choose AutoVis ➤ Materials.

2. At the Materials dialog box, select Granite Pebbles from the Materials list, then click on the Modify button. The Modify Granite Material dialog box appears.

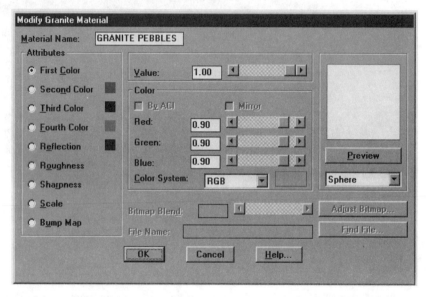

3. Click on the Scale radio button in the Attributes button group on the left side of the dialog box.

4. Change the Value input box near the top of the dialog box from .398 to **.01**. This will reduce the scale of the material.

5. Click on OK to return to the Materials dialog box.

The Modify Granite Materials dialog box offers a variety of options that let you control reflectivity, roughness, color, transparency, and of course, scale. Not all materials have the same options, as you'll see when you continue with the next exercise. The Help button on the Modify Granite Material dialog box will give a brief description of its options.

1. Select Glass from the Materials list, then click on the Modify button again. The Modify Standard Material dialog box appears.

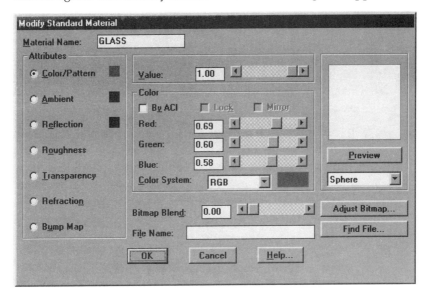

Notice that this dialog box offers a slightly different set of Attribute options from those offered in the Modify Granite Materials dialog box you edited in the previous exercise.

2. Select the Transparency radio button in the Attribute button group, then adjust the Value option downward to **.55**. This will have the effect of darkening the glass.

3. Select the Color/Pattern Attribute radio button, then, in the Color button group, adjust the red value to **.69**, the Green value to **.60** and the Blue to **.58**. This will give the glass a bronze tint.

4. Select *Cube* from the list box below the Preview button on the right side of the dialog box, then click on the Preview button to get a preview of the color settings.

Note   *Cube option in step 4 is available in any AutoVision dialog box that offers a preview.*

5. Click on OK in both the Standard Material and Materials dialog box to exit them.

6. Choose AutoVis ➤ Render, then click on the Render button to render the view with the new material settings. After a few minutes, your view will look something like Figure 8.8.

Figure 8.8: The Facade model after modifying the materials settings

Tip   *There are four basic types of materials: Standard, Marble, Granite, and Wood. Each type has its own set of characteristics that you can adjust. You can even create new materials based on one of the four primary types of materials.*

The granite surface of the Facade is a bit too strong. You can reduce the graininess of the granite by further editing the material settings.

1. Choose AutoVis ➤ Materials, select Granite Pebbles from the Materials list, and then choose Modify.

2. At the Modify Granite Material dialog box, click on the Sharpness Attribute radio button, then set the value input box to **.20**.

3. Click OK, then OK again at the Materials dialog box.

4. Choose AutoVis ➤ Render, then click on the Render button. Your rendering appears, after a few minutes, with a softer granite surface (see Figure 8.9).

Figure 8.9: The rendered image with a softer granite surface

◆ Adding a Background Scene

You could continue by adding and adjusting materials to the other parts of model, but let's try adding some interest to our view by adding a sky. This is done by controlling the *background*.

> **Note**   *In step 4 you can also choose from TIF, BMP, GIF, JPG, and PCX file formats for background images. See Chapter 12 for more on these file formats.*

1. Choose AutoVis ➤ Render, then at the Render dialog box, click on the button labeled Background. The Background dialog box appears.

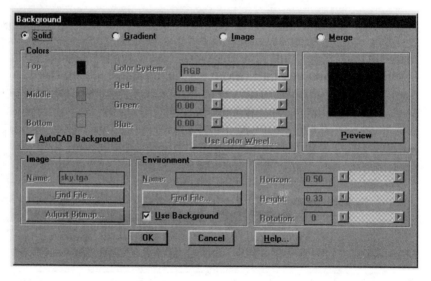

2. In the row of radio buttons across the top, find and click on Image. Notice that several of the options near the bottom of the dialog box are now available.

3. Click on the Find File button at the bottom left of the dialog box. The Background Image dialog box appears.

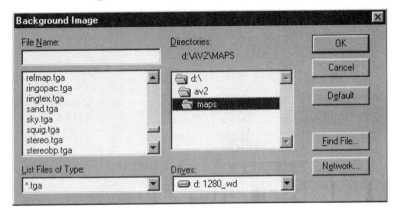

This is a typical AutoCAD file dialog box, set up to list by default all the .TGA bitmap files in your default AutoVision directory.

4. Use this dialog box to locate the Sky.TGA file in the AutoVision Maps subdirectory (av2\maps on the drive where AutoVision has been installed).

5. Once back at the Background Image, click on Preview to see what the file looks like. Sky.TGA is a bitmap image of a blue sky with clouds.

6. Click OK, then, once back at the Render dialog box, click on Render. The background appears behind the model, as shown in Figure 8.10.

Figure 8.10: The Facade model rendered with a sky bitmap image for a background

We chose to add a bitmap image for a background, but you can use other methods to generate a background. For example, you might prefer to use a gradient shade or color for the background. This can help give a sense of depth to the image (see Figure 8.11). You can, of course, add a single color to the background if you prefer.

To create a Gradient background, select the Gradient radio button at the top of the Background dialog box. You can then adjust the color for the top, middle, and bottom third of the background. AutoVision automatically blends the three colors from top to bottom to create the gradient colors.

Figure 8.11: The Facade model with a gradient color background

◆ Effects with Lighting

Up to now, you've only used one light source, called a *distant light*, to create a sun. You have two other light sources available to help simulate *point lights* and *spot lights*. This section will show you some examples of how with some imagination, you can perform any number of visual "tricks" with these light sources.

Simulating Interior Lights with a Single Point Light

Our current rendering shows a dead and lifeless-looking office building. It's missing a sense of activity. To help improve the image, you'll add some ceiling lights to the office building. I've already supplied the light fixtures in the form of square 3D faces arrayed just at the ceiling level of each floor, as shown in Figure 8.12. In this section, I'll show you how to make them appear illuminated.

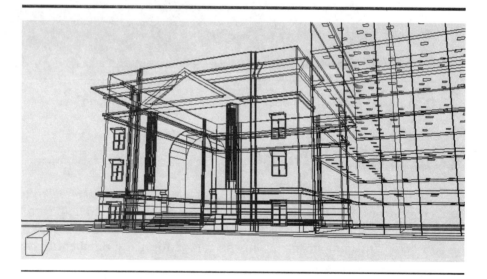

Figure 8.12: The 3D Face squares representing ceiling light fixtures

To create this effect, you'll employ a rendering "trick." You'll create the illusion of having the ceiling lights turned on by making them highly reflective, then shining a single light source at them so they all reflect the light. This way, they appear to have some brightness as if they were self-illuminated.

1. Start by assigning a reflective material to the squares. Choose AutoVis ➤ Materials ➤, then click on the Materials Library button.

2. At the Materials Library dialog box, locate and select *White Plastic* from the list on the right, then click on Import.

3. Click on OK to exit the Materials Library dialog box, then, at the Materials dialog box, highlight White Plastic in the list to the left and click on the By Layer button.

4. In the Attach By Layer dialog box, make sure White Plastic is highlighted in the Select A Material list to the left, then click on the *Clglite* layer in the Layer list to the right.

5. Click on the Attach –> button to attach the White Plastic material to the Clglite layer name in the Select Layer list.

6. Click OK to exit the Attach By Layer dialog box, then click OK to exit the Materials dialog box.

You now have a reflective white material assigned to the ceiling fixtures. But the reflective material alone will not give the effect of illuminated lights. You need a light source that can be reflected by the fixtures giving the impression of illumination. For this, you'll use a point light source.

1. Choose View ➤ 3D Viewpoint Presets ➤ SE Isometric to get an Isometric view of the model.

2. Zoom in to the base of the office building so your view is similar to Figure 8.13.

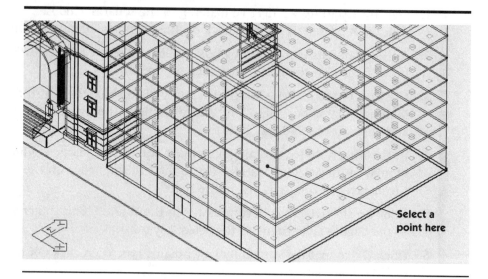

Select a
point here

Figure 8.13: Selecting the point light source location in the SW isometric view

3. Choose AutoVis ➤ Lights. Then at the Lights dialog box select *Point Light* from the New drop-down list, then click on the New button.

4. At the New Point Light dialog box, enter **Point1** for the light name, then enter **300** in the Intensity input box.

5. Click on the Modify button, then select a point at the very center of the office building base, as shown in Figure 8.13.

6. Click on OK to exit the New Point Light dialog box, then click on OK in the Lights dialog box.

7. Choose View ➤ Named Views, then at the Named Views dialog box, select 3Dfront and click the Restore button.

8. Click OK to exit the Named Views dialog box.

9. Click AutoVis ➤ Render, and at the Render dialog box, click on the Render button. After a minute, you will have a rendered view similar to Figure 8.14.

Figure 8.14: The rendered view with ceiling lights

The new point light in conjunction with the 3D face light fixture adds a sense of life and depth to the office building. Notice that despite the fact that the light is located inside the box representing the office core, the light manages to strike all the lights of all the floors, as if the floors and core were transparent. Since you didn't turn on the Shadow feature for the point light source, its light passes through all the objects in the model.

There is even light falling on the granite Facade building next door, illuminating the inside of the arched entrance. The point light from the center of the office building also casts light on the arched entrance. Though we didn't set out intentionally to light this area, it shows that with careful use of lighting, you can bring out some of the detail in the Facade model that might otherwise get lost with the single distant light source. For example, you might add some special detail to the arched entrance of the granite facade that wouldn't show up behind the shadow of the sun spotlight. Adding a point source light of the proper intensity would add some lighting to the entrance, as the point source did in our example, to illuminate the details that might normally be hidden by shadows.

Of course, you can use point light sources in a more traditional way, representing light bulbs or other nondirectional light sources. But by playing with light source location and shadow, you can create effects to help enhance your rendering.

Simulating a Night Scene with Spot Lights

Spot lights are lights that are directed. They are frequently used to provide emphasis and are usually used for interior views or product presentations. In this exercise, you'll set up a night view of the Facade model using spot lights to illuminate the Facade.

You'll start by setting up a view to help place the spot lights. Once they are placed, you make some adjustments to them to get a view you want.

> **Note** In step 6, make sure the Ortho mode is turned off. As you select the location for the spotlight, you should see a rubber-banding line from the light's target to the spotlight location as shown in Figure 8.15. Otherwise the light will be placed incorrectly and you will not see the spotlight on the building.

1. Choose View ➤ 3D Viewpoint Presets ➤ SE Isometric, then zoom into the Facade so your view looks similar to Figure 8.15.

2. Choose AutoVis ➤ Lights, then at the Lights dialog box, select Spotlight from the New drop-down list.

3. Click New, then at the New Spotlight dialog box, enter **Spot-L**. This designates a spotlight you will place on the left side of the Facade.

4. Enter **400** in the Intensity input box. Then click on the Modify button.

5. At the `Enter Target Location` prompt, use the Nearest Osnap and select the target point on the window indicated in Figure 8.15.

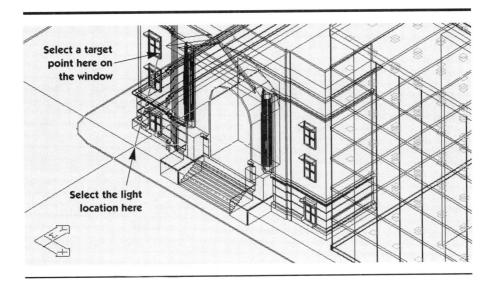

Select a target
point here on
the window

Select the light
location here

Figure 8.15: Selecting the points for the first spotlight

6. Make sure the Ortho mode is turned off, then at the Enter Light location prompt, select the light point indicated in Figure 8.15. Once you've selected the light location, the New Spotlight dialog box reappears.

7. Click OK, then at the Lights dialog box, click on New again to create another spotlight.

8. This time, enter **Spot-R** for the name, and set the intensity to **400** as before.

9. Click on the Modify button and select the target and light locations indicated in Figure 8.16. Remember to use the Nearest Osnap mode to select the target point on the window and turn off Ortho mode when selecting the spotlight location.

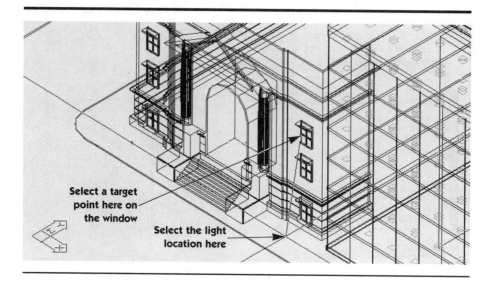

Figure 8.16: Selecting the points for the second spotlight

10. Click OK to exit the New Spotlight dialog box, then click OK again at the Lights dialog box. You now have two spotlights on your building.

11. Choose View ➤ Named Views and restore the 3Dfront view.

12. Render the model. (You already know how to do this by now). Your view will look similar to Figure 8.17.

Figure 8.17: The rendered view of the model with the spotlights

The rendered view has a number of problems. First, the Sun light source needs to be turned off. Second, the spot lights are too harsh. You can also see that the spot lights don't illuminate the center of the building, so we'll need to add some lighting at the entrance.

Controlling Lights with Scenes

The first problem we face is how to turn off the sun. One way you can do it is to set the sunlight Intensity value to zero using the Modify Distant Light dialog box. Another way is to set up a *scene*. AutoVision lets you combine different lights and views into named scenes. These scenes can then be quickly selected at render time so you don't have to adjust lighting or views every time you want a specific setup. Here's how it works.

1. Choose AutoVis ➤ Scene. You see the Scenes dialog box.

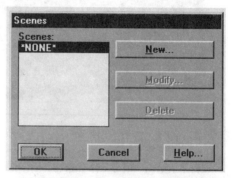

2. Click on New. The New Scene dialog box appears.

3. Enter **night** for the scene name. The name appears as all capitals (NIGHT) in the Scene Name input box.

4. Select 3DFRONT from the Views list and select SPOT-L, SPOT-R, and POINT1 from the Lights list.

5. Click OK. Notice that now you have NIGHT listed in the Scenes list in the Scenes dialog box.

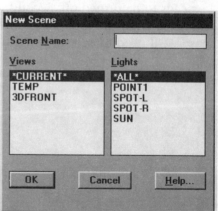

6. Click on New again, then type **day** at the New Scene dialog box. It shows up as DAY.

7. Select 3DFRONT from the Views list and SUN and POINT1 from the Lights list, then click OK. Click OK again to exit the Scene dialog box. You now have two scenes set up.

8. Now open the Render dialog box. Notice that you have DAY and NIGHT listed in the Scene To Render list box in the upper left of the Render dialog box.

9. Select Night, then click on the Render button. Your view will look like Figure 8.18.

Figure 8.18: Rendering the night scene excluding the SUN light source

We now see that without the SUN light source, our view is considerably darker. Let's continue by adding a few more light sources and adjusting some existing ones.

1. Choose View ➤ 3D Viewpoint Presets ➤ SE Isometric, then zoom into the office building so your view looks similar to Figure 8.19.

2. Choose AutoVis ➤ Lights, then use the new drop-down list and button to create a new point light.

3. Enter the name **point2**, and, using the Modify button, place it in the center of the office building in the same location as point1.

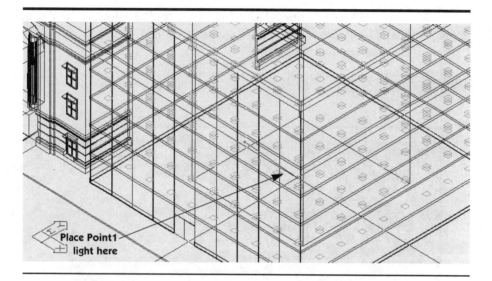

Place Point1
light here

Figure 8.19: Adding another point light source to the office building. This light source has a greater intensity for the night scene.

4. Give this new point light an intensity value of **500**, then click OK.

5. Create another point light source called **point3** and, using the .X, .Y, and .Z point selection filters, place it in the location shown in Figure 8.20, at the Facade entrance. Make sure you use the .X, .Y, and .Z point filters to select the location of the light, as shown in Figure 8.20.

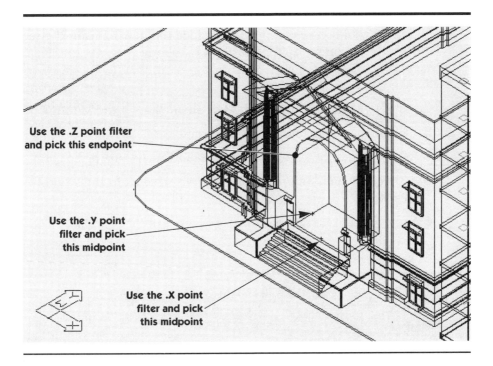

Use the .Z point filter and pick this endpoint

Use the .Y point filter and pick this midpoint

Use the .X point filter and pick this midpoint

Figure 8.20: Adding a point light source for the entrance to the Facade

Tip *You can use the scroll bars or the Pan button in the Standard toolbar to adjust your view to match Figure 8.20.*

6. Give Point3 an intensity of **150**.

7. Click OK, then at the Light dialog box, select the Spot-L light from the list and click on Modify.

8. At the Modify Spot Light dialog box, change the Falloff value in the upper right to **80**.

9. Repeat steps 7 and 8 for the Spot-R spotlight.

10. Click OK at the Modify Spotlight dialog box.

11. At the Light dialog box, increase the Ambient light intensity to **50**, then click OK.

You've got the new lights installed and the spot lights adjusted. Before you render your scene, you need to include the new lights in the second scene, the one you set up for the night rendering.

1. Choose AutoVis ➤ Scene.

2. Highlight *Night* in the Scenes list, then click on the Modify button.

3. Highlight *Point2* and *Point3*, then deselect *Point1* in the Lights list.

4. Click OK at both the Modify Scene and Scenes dialog box.

5. Choose Render and make sure *Night* is selected in the Scene To Render list.

6. Click on the Render button. Your view will look similar to Figure 8.21.

Figure 8.21: The night rendering with added lights and an increased falloff area for the spot lights

The new rendering is brighter. You can also see the effects of an increased falloff for the spot lights. They don't have the sharp edge they had in the first night rendering and the light is spread in a wider radius, illuminating more of the lower portion of the Facade.

You also see another by-product of using the Scene tools. You didn't have to return to the 3Dfront view to render the model. Since the 3Dfront view is included in the scene information, AutoVision automatically rendered the model from that view when the Night scene was selected. If you were to issue the Regen command now, you would see that AutoCAD still maintains the SE Isometric view.

Adding Reflections and Detail with Ray Tracing

You've been gradually building up the detail and realism in your renderings by adding light and materials. In this section, you'll learn how using a different rendering method can further enhance your renderings. Up until now, you've been using the standard AutoVision rendering method, but *ray tracing* can add even more interest to a rendering, especially in a model where reflective surfaces are prominent. In this section, you'll use the ray tracing method to render your model after making a few adjustments to the glass material.

Assigning a Mirror Attribute to Glass

Glass is a complex material to model in computer renderings. The AutoVision standard rendering method simply give glass a transparency with some "highlight" reflection. But glass has both refractive and reflective attributes, which makes it difficult to model. Since ray tracing models the way light works, it is especially well suited to rendering views that contain large glass areas.

To demonstrate what ray tracing can do, you'll use it to render the Facade model, which happens to contain an office building with a typical glass envelope. You'll start by making an adjustment to the glass material to make it appear more reflective.

Note *If your rendering doesn't look like the one in Figure 8.22, make sure you've set up the Day scene properly. Go back to the "Controlling Lights with Scenes" section and check to see if you have the correct set of lights selected for the Day scene.*

1. Choose AutoVis ➤ Materials, then at the Materials dialog box, highlight *Glass* in the list box and click on the Modify button.

2. Click on the Reflection radio button in the Attributes button group.

3. Click on the Mirror checkbox in the Color button group, then click on OK to close the Modify Standard Materials dialog box.

4. Click OK again at the Materials dialog box, then open the Render dialog box.

5. Choose AutoVis Raytrace from the Rendering Type list box near the top of the dialog box.

6. Click on the More Options button, then at the More Options dialog box, set the Minimum Bias setting to **.1** and the Maximum Bias setting to **.2**. Whenever you change the rendering type, you must reset these settings; AutoVision does not automatically transfer them to different rendering types.

7. Click OK to close the More Options dialog box, select *Day* from the Scene list, and then click on the Background button.

8. In the Background dialog box, make sure the Use Background checkbox is checked in the Environment button group, then click on the OK button.

9. Click on the Render button. Your view will look similar to Figure 8.22.

Figure 8.22: The Facade model rendered with the Ray trace method

The sky bitmap used as a background is faintly reflected in the glass of the office building. The office building has also gotten brighter from the reflection. Also notice the secondary reflection of the interior ceiling on the west interior wall of the office.

The brightness of the office building is a bit unrealistically overwhelming, so you will want to adjust the glass material to tone it down.

1. Choose AutoVis ➤ Materials, then with the Glass material highlighted, select Modify ➤.

2. At the Modify Standard Materials dialog box, make sure the Color/Pattern radio button is selected, then set the Value setting in the Color button group to **.20**. This will help darken the office building.

3. Click OK to close the Modify Standard Materials dialog box, then click OK at the Materials dialog box.

4. Render the scene again. Your view will look something like Figure 8.23.

Figure 8.23: The rendering with a lower Color/Pattern setting for the Glass material

You can further reduce the brightness of the office building by reducing the intensity value of the Point light source you added early in this chapter.

Getting a Sharp, Accurate Shadow with Ray Tracing

In the beginning of this chapter, I showed you how to use the Shadow Map method for casting shadows. Shadow maps offer the feature of allowing a soft edge shadow in exchange for accuracy. For exterior views, you may prefer a sharper shadow. The Facade example loses some detail using the Shadow Map method; in particular, the grooves in the base of the building disappear. By switching to the ray trace method for casting shadows, you can recover some detail.

1. Choose AutoVis ➤ Lights, then from the Lights list, select *Sun* and click on Modify.

2. At the Modify Distant Light dialog box, click on the Shadow Options button.

3. At the Shadow Options dialog box, click on Shadow Volumes/Ray Trace Shadows checkbox to place a checkmark there.

4. Click OK at all the dialog boxes successively to exit them and return to the AutoCAD view.

5. Render the view and this time select AutoVis Raytrace from the Rendering Type drop-down list near the top of the Render dialog box. Your view will look like Figure 8.24.

Figure 8.24: The model using the Shadow Volumes/Ray Trace Shadows option in the Modify Distant Light/Shadow Options dialog box

Notice that you can now see the rusticated base clearly. The Shadows also appear sharper, especially around the surface detail of the Facade model.

◆ Creating and Adjusting Texture Maps

You've already seen how you can assign a material to an object by adding the granite pebbles and glass materials to the buildings in the Facade3.DWG file. Many of these materials make use of bitmap image files to simulate textures. You can create your own surface textures or use bitmaps in other ways to help enhance your rendering. For example, you can include a photograph of existing buildings that may exist within the scene you are rendering.

Figure 8.25 shows a bitmap image that was scanned into the computer and edited using a popular paint program. Now imagine that this building is across the street from the Facade model, and you want to include it in the scene to show its relationship to your building. The following exercise will show you how it's done.

Figure 8.25: A photographic image of a building that was scanned into a computer and saved as a bitmap file

1. Click on Redraw from the Standard toolbar, then adjust your view so it looks like Figure 8.26.

2. Draw a line 133 feet long.

3. Change the thickness of the line to 80' using the Properties tool.

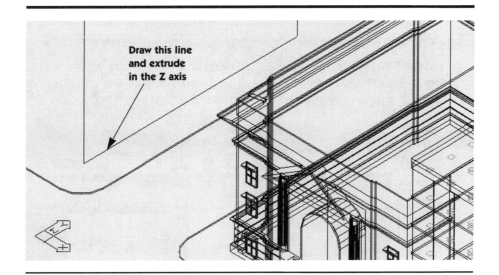

Draw this line and extrude in the Z axis

Figure 8.26: Adding an object to attach the bitmap image to

4. Choose AutoVis ➤ Materials, then at the Materials dialog box, click on New. Notice that the New Standard Materials dialog box is the same as the dialog box for the Glass material. The settings are not the same, however.

5. Enter **build1** for the material name.

6. Make sure the Color/Pattern radio button is selected, then click on the Find File button in the lower right corner of the dialog box.

7. Click on the *List Files of Type* drop-down list. Notice that you have several file types to choose from.

8. Choose *GIF* from the list, then locate the Market2.GIF file. This file comes with the other sample files from the disk accompanying the book.

9. Choose OK to exit this dialog box.

10. At the Materials dialog box, make sure *Build1* is selected in the Materials list, then click on the Attach button.

11. Select the line you added in step 1, then press ↵.

12. Click OK to exit the Materials dialog box, then render the scene. Your view will look like Figure 8.27.

Figure 8.27: Adding a bitmap image of a building to your rendering

The bitmap image does not appear properly in the rendered view. Instead, it looks like a vertical streak of colors. When you see this streaking, you know your bitmap image or material is not properly aligned with the object it is attached to. The following exercise introduces you to the tools you need to properly align a bitmap image to an object.

1. Redraw the screen, then choose AutoVis ➤ Mapping.

2. At the Select
Object prompt,
select the extruded
line you created
in the last exercise
and press ↵. The
Mapping dialog
box appears.

3. Click on the Adjust
Coordinates button.
The Adjust Planar
Coordinates dialog
box appears. Notice
the rectangle in the
graphic labeled
Center Position.

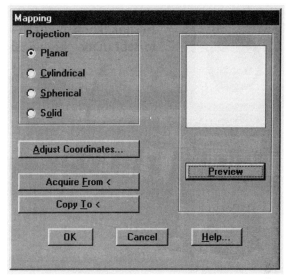

This shows the relationship of the bitmap image to the object
it has been assigned to. All you can see is a vertical line.

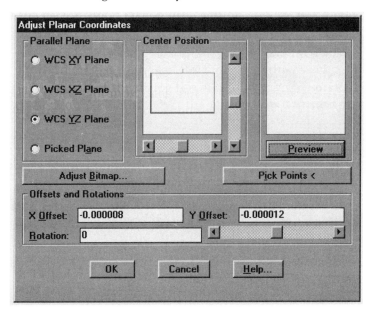

4. Click on the WCS YZ Plane radio button. (The plane defined
by the Y and Z axes is parallel to the surface on which you want
the bitmap to appear.)

5. Click on the Preview button. Now you can see how the bitmap will appear on the vertical surface. You now need to adjust the positioning of the bitmap.

6. First you will want to increase the size of the bitmap in relation to the surface so the image of the building completely covers the surface. To do this you will need one other dialog box. Click on the Adjust Bitmap button. The Adjust Object Bitmap Placement dialog box appears.

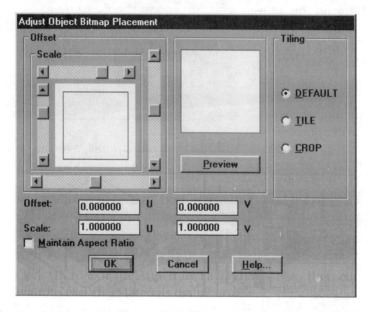

7. Enter **.95** in the Scale input box to the left of the U, then enter **.76** in the Scale input box to the left of the V. The U is the horizontal direction scale and the V is the vertical direction scale.

8. Click on the Preview button to view the effect of the scaling. Notice that the image is larger but still not centered vertically.

9. Use the Vertical Offset sliders to move the outer rectangle in the graphic upward, as shown in the following image, then click on the Preview button again. Now the image fits within the rectangle.

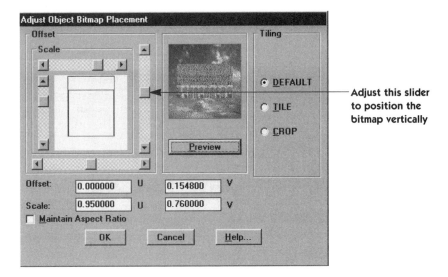

10. Click OK at each of the dialog boxes successively to close them, then render the model. Your view will look like Figure 8.28.

Figure 8.28: The rendered view with the bitmap image adjusted

Notice that now the image of the building across the street fits the object and there are no odd blank spaces. As you have seen in the previous exercise, the Adjust Object Bitmap Placement dialog box allows you to stretch the image vertically or horizontally in case the image is distorted and it needs to be fitted to an accurately drawn object.

Another option is to use a paint program to refine the bitmap image before it is used in AutoVision. AutoVision attempts to place the bitmap accurately on a surface, so if the bitmap is fairly clean and doesn't have any extra blank space around the edges, you can usually place it on an object without having to make any adjustments other than its orientation.

◆ Adding Landscape and People

There's nothing like adding landscaping to a rendering to create a sense of life and scale. Computer images in particular need landscape props since they tend to appear cold and somewhat lifeless. AutoVision offers a set of prebuilt landscape objects to help soften the appearance of your rendering. Let's see how we can add a few trees and people to the Facade model.

1. Choose View ➤ Redraw, then choose AutoVis ➤ Landscape New. The Landscape New dialog box appears.

2. Click on *Quaking Aspen* from the Library list, then click on Preview to view the item.

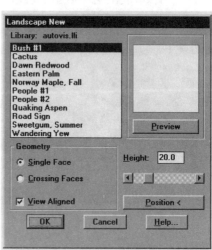

3. Use the slider just below the Preview button and change the Height value from 20 to **100**, the highest setting.

4. Click on the Position < button, then click on the point indicated in Figure 8.29a to place the tree in front of the buildings. You may have to adjust your view.

5. Click on the View Aligned checkbox to deselect this option. We'll explain later in this section what this option does.

6. Click OK. The tree appears as a rectangle with a text label telling you what it is, as shown in Figure 8.29b.

7. Copy the tree to the positions indicated in Figure 8.29b.

8. Now render the view. You will see a view similar to Figure 8.30.

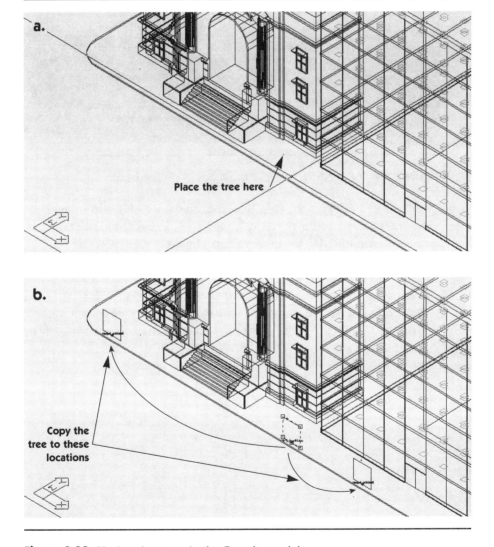

Figure 8.29: Placing the trees in the Facade model

Figure 8.30: The rendered view of the model with the trees

The trees you added are actually two-dimensional bitmap images. If you view the model from a glancing angle, the trees will look thinner; if you are perpendicular to them you might even see them edge-on. Two of the options in the Library New dialog box offer some options to reduce the 2D effect. The View Aligned option I asked you to turn off in step 5 forces the tree to be aligned to your point of view, so you never see the object edge-on. Another option, Crossing Faces, creates two images of the object to appear; each image crossed over the other, as shown in Figure 8.31.

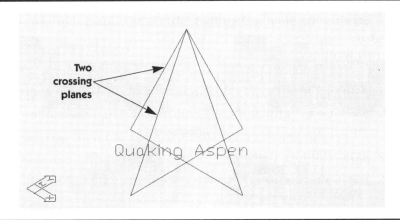

Figure 8.31: The Crossing Faces option used with a landscape object

New Object Types in AutoCAD

If you were to use the List tool to find out what the landscape objects were, you would find that some are called Plant, and some are called Person. Does AutoCAD r13 have some new object types we don't know about? The answer is...maybe.

Release 13 now allows third-party developers to add new object types that aren't native to the program itself. This is a fairly revolutionary idea. AutoVision uses this new capibility by adding Plants and People objects. There is a problem with adding new object types, however: you need the third-party application to view and edit the objects you create. When the application is not present, the new objects become what Autodesk calls "Zombies." For example, if you were to bring your `Facade3.DWG` file to another system with AutoCAD release 13 but with no AutoVision, you would see the plants and people, but you would not be able to view them in a rendering or edit them.

Nevertheless, the ability to add new object types to an AutoCAD drawing has some far-reaching implications. The possibilities for third-party developers is enormous, and you, the end user, will benefit in many ways. The Landscape tool in AutoVision is an example of what can be done.

There are a few things wrong with the rendering you see in Figure 8.31. The trees are too small—they look like bushes—and they appear to be shaded on the wrong side. This is easily fixed using standard AutoCAD editing tools.

1. Redraw the screen, then click on one of the trees to expose its grip.

2. Click on the grip at the base of the tree, then press ↵ twice to switch to the **ROTATE** grip mode.

3. Type **180**↵ to rotate the tree 180 degrees.

4. Click on the grip again, then press ↵ three times to switch to the **SCALE** grip mode.

5. Enter **2.4**↵ to increase the size of the tree 2.4 times.

6. Repeat these steps for each of the other trees.

7. Now for the people. Refer to Figure 8.32 when placing these third-party images. Choose AutoVis ➤ Library New and select *People #1* from the list.

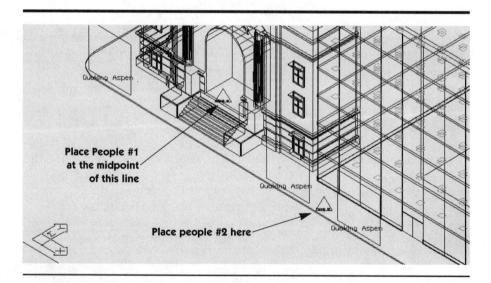

Figure 8.32: Placing people in the scene

8. Change the Height value to **66**, then use the Position button to place the people at the entrance of the Facade building. (Make sure you use the Nearest Osnap to place the people).

9. Repeat steps 7 and 8 to place *People #2* in front of the office building between the trees (see Figure 8.32).

10. Render the view. Your view will look similar to Figure 8.33.

Figure 8.33: The view after rendering with the trees adjusted and people added

The shadows of the trees now accord with the location of the sun and they are a size better suited to the model as a whole. Notice that the people are not lighted very well. This is because when you placed them, you did not turn off the View Align option. They are therefore facing your viewpoint, and so are tilted slightly away from the sun. This has the effect of darkening their image.

You can use AutoVis ➤ Landscape Edit to change the settings for landscape objects. You will be prompted to select an object. Once you do, you will see the Landscape Edit dialog box, which is identical to the Landscape New dialog box. From there, you can make changes to the settings for the selected landscape object.

◆ Rendering to the AutoVision Window

All through this chapter, you have been rendering to the AutoCAD drawing area. You can also render to a *file*, so you can recall the image at any time in any application, or you can render to the *AutoVision window*. From there, you have a number of options in dealing with the rendered image.

Rendering to the Window

The AutoVision window lets you control the resolution and color depth of your image. It also lets you save the images you render in the Windows .BMP format. Another advantage of the AutoVision window is that you can render several views and then compare them before you decide to save them.

1. Open the Render dialog box, then select Render Window from the Destination group in the upper right of the dialog box.

2. Click on Render. After a moment the AutoVision window will appear. It will then take a minute or two before the image finishes rendering and appears in the window.

Notice that the image is within its own window. If you render another view, that view will also appear in its own window, leaving the previous renderings undisturbed. You can use File ➤ Save to save the file as a .BMP file for later editing or printing, or you can print directly from the AutoVision window. You can also use the AutoVision window to cut and paste the image to another application, and to view saved rendered files in the .BMP format.

To set the size of renderings, you use the
File ➤ Option tool. This option opens
the Window Render Options dialog box.
Here you can choose from two standard
sizes or enter a custom size for your rendering.
You can also choose between 8-bit (256 colors)
and 24-bit (16 million colors) color depth.
Changes to these settings don't take effect
until you render another view.

Rendering Directly to a File

Rendering to the AutoVision window allows you to view and compare
your views before you save them. However, you can only save your views
in the .BMP format. If you plan to further edit the image in an image processing program, this may not be a problem. But if you want to use your
image file with a program that requires a specific file format, you may
want to render directly to a file. Here's how it's done.

1. Open the Render dialog box, then select File from the Destination
group in the upper right of the dialog box.

2. Choose More Options at the bottom of the Destination group. The File Output Configuration dialog box appears.

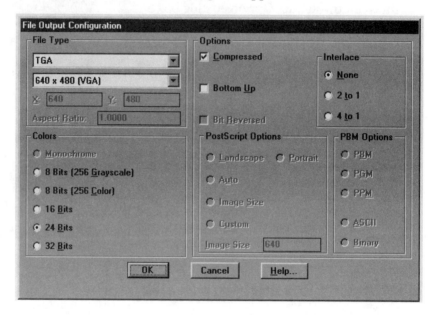

3. Click on the File Type drop-down list to see the options. You can save your image in GIF, TGA, TIFF, PCX, or even PostScript format. There are several other formats available also. You might also notice the other options available in the dialog box, such as Color Depth, Resolution, and Compression. Not all these options are available for all the file types. GIF, for example, is limited to 256 colors, so the other color options will not apply to GIF files.

4. Click on OK to return to the Render dialog box, then click on the Render button. The Rendering File dialog box appears, prompting you for a filename for your image.

5. Enter **Facade1**. AutoVision will add the filename extension for you.

6. Click OK and AutoVision proceeds to render to the file.

As AutoCAD renders to the file, it tells you in the command line how much of the image has been rendered.

◆ Tools to Improve Your Image and to Aid Editing

There will be times when you will be rushing to get a rendering done and won't want to wait for each trial rendering to become visible. AutoVision offers several tools that can save you time by limiting the resolution or area being rendered. Suppose you just want to render the area where you've added a tree to make sure it's in the right location. The following exercise will show you how to do this.

1. Choose View ➤ Named Views, then restore the 3Dfront view.

2. Open the Render dialog box, and set the Destination option to Viewport.

3. Click on the Crop Window checkbox to activate this option, then click on the Render button.

4. You are prompted to Pick Crop Window to Render. Select the area shown in Figure 8.34. Once you select the window, AutoVision renders only the area you selected.

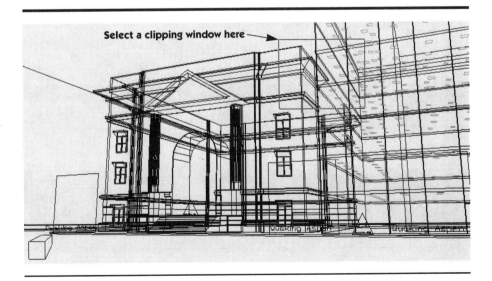

Figure 8.34: Selecting the crop window

The Crop Window option is a working tool; it is not available when File or Render Window are selected as destinations.

You can also select only specific objects to be included in the rendering. You do this by checking the Query For Selection checkbox in the Render dialog box. This option asks you to select a set of objects before it proceeds to render. You can render to all three destination options with Query For Selection turned on.

If you want to get a quick rendering with a reduced resolution, just to check composition, for instance, you can use the Sub Sampling option drop-down list. Try the following exercise to see how it works.

1. Open the Render dialog box, then open the Sub Sampling drop-down list.

2. Choose *3:1* from the list, make sure the Crop Window option is unchecked, then click on the Render button. Your view will render faster, but will look a bit crude at the lower resolution— see Figure 8.35.

Figure 8.35: A rendered view with the Sub Sampling option set to 3-to-1

The different ratios in the Sub Sampling option tell you how many pixels are being combined to reduce the resolution of the image. The 3:1 choice, for example, will combine three pixels into one to reduce the resolution to a third of the original.

◆ Smoothing Out the Rough Edges

Whereas the Sub Sampling option increases the jagged appearance of your rendering in the tradeoff for a *faster* rendering, the Anti-Aliasing option can actually improve the smoothness of edges and thereby increase the apparent resolution for your *final* rendering. This option, available through the Render dialog box, performs a kind of computer trick that reduces the jagged appearance of object edges. Anti-aliasing blends the color of two adjacent contrasting colors. This gives the effect of smoothing out the "stairstep" appearance of a computer-generated image. The improvement to your rendering can be striking. Try the following exercise to see firsthand what anti-aliasing can do.

1. Open the Render dialog box, then click on the More Options button.

2. In the Raytrace Rendering Options dialog box, click on the Medium radio button in the Anti-Aliasing button group, then click OK.

3. Select *1:1* from the Sub Sampling drop-down list, then click on the Render button. The rendering will take several minutes so you may want to take a break at this point. When the rendering is done, it will look similar to Figure 8.36.

Figure 8.36: A rendering with the Anti-Aliasing setting set to Medium

Notice that the edges of the buildings are much smoother. You can also see that the vertical mullions of the office building are more clearly defined. One negative point is that the texture effect of the Facade model has been reduced. You may have to increase the scale value for the Granite Pebbles material setting to bring the texture back.

As you can see from this exercise, you trade off rendering speed for a cleaner image. You will want to hold off from using the higher anti-aliasing settings until your final output.

◆ Summary

In this chapter, I've taken you on a guided tour of AutoVision, pointing out the main features of this product. I didn't go into the finer details of many of its features, as I have a limited amount of space, but you now have the basic knowledge from which you can build your rendering skills, and without too much effort, you can adapt much of what you've learned here to your own projects.

Computer rendering of 3D models is a craft that takes some time to master. You will want to take some time to experiment with these rendering tools to see first-hand the types of results you can expect. You might want to try different types of views, like an isometric or elevation view like that shown in Figure 8.37. With a bit more detail added, this rendered elevation could fit nicely into a set of renderings for a presentation.

Figure 8.37: A rendered view of the Facade model elevation

This brings to a close the AutoCAD portion of this book. You are now equipped to model virtually anything you may be called upon to build. In the next part of the book, you will learn how to use another very powerful rendering tool: 3D Studio. With 3D Studio, you can not only render still images, you can create animated walk-throughs—you can even generate files that you can walk through in real time.

Part Two:

Giving Life to Your World

Introducing 3D Studio

3D Studio is one of the world's most popular 3D modeling and animation programs. Like AutoCAD, it offers the power to do high-quality work on a desktop PC. It is used in a wide variety of industries from film to computer game creation. Chances are, if you have played a 3D computer game, you've seen a 3D Studio-created virtual environment.

3D Studio is a perfect companion to AutoCAD, filling in the areas of presentation and animation. AutoCAD, in turn, offers the ability to construct accurate 3D models based on 2D production or design drawings. You can use 3D Studio to create 3D objects, but its modeling functions are geared toward more free-form objects like plants and animals, or sculpted forms like automobiles and airplanes. Since the focus of this book is on AutoCAD 3D modeling, our discussion of 3D Studio will not cover 3D Studio's modeling tools in any great depth. Instead, we'll focus on how you can use 3D Studio to enhance your AutoCAD models by adding realism and motion.

We will look at 3D Studio version 4.0 for DOS. Its memory requirements are less restrictive than those of its big brother, 3D Studio MAX, which is for Windows NT. (You can check out Appendix C for a tutorial introduction to 3D Studio MAX.)

◆ Importing Your AutoCAD Model to 3D Studio

You have two options for importing AutoCAD files into 3D Studio. 3D Studio will read and write DXF files, which have become a standard data exchange file format for CAD drawings. AutoCAD release 13 also offers the ability to read and write 3D Studio's native 3DS file format. The 3DS format offers the advantage of preserving AutoCAD views so they appear in 3D Studio as *cameras* (you'll learn more about cameras later in this chapter). If you use AutoVision 2.0, you can also preserve materials assignments to objects in your model when transferring them to 3D Studio. Finally, with AutoCAD 3DS import and export tools, you can control what gets exported and imported, and how.

Exporting a 3DS File

You'll start by exporting the Savoye4.DWG file that is provided on the CD-ROM accompanying this book. This file is a version of the file you worked on in Chapter 5. You may recall that that file has a number of views already saved, so you'll see how those views are preserved when you later work on the file in 3D Studio.

AutoCAD's 3DS export tool has a restriction that can cause problems if you are not aware of it; it does not like to translate 3D solids or splines if they are contained in blocks. For this reason, you will want to explode any blocks you have in your drawing that might contain solids or splines. Once this is done, you can easily export your drawings to 3DS files.

There are, in fact, three blocks in the Savoye model that contain 3D solids and splines: the two stair blocks and the ramp. I've already exploded these blocks for you so you don't have to worry about it now. Just be aware of these limitations and, if you encounter any problems exporting AutoCAD files to 3DS format, check to see if you have any blocks containing splines or solids.

1. In AutoCAD, open the `Savoye4.DWG` file.

2. Choose File ➤ Export.

3. At the Data Export dialog box, open the *List Files of Type* drop-down list in the bottom left of the dialog box, then select **.3DS*.

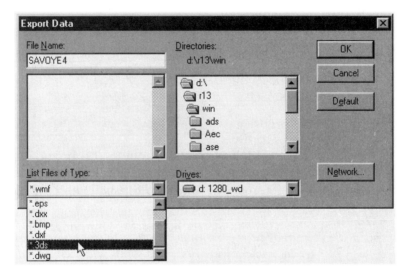

4. The File Name input box displays the name of the current file with the .3DS extension. Make sure you have selected an appropriate directory to store your 3DS file, then click OK.

5. Next, you are prompted to select the objects you want to export. Select the entire building, including the ground plane, which appears as a large rectangle at the base of the building.

6. Press ↵ when you have finished your selection. The 3D Studio File Export Options dialog box appears.

This dialog box lets you control how your model is translated to 3D Studio. We'll discuss these options in detail a bit later. For this exercise, go ahead and accept the default settings and click OK.

7. AutoCAD will work at producing the 3DS file, and as it does it will display messages in the command line. After a minute or two, AutoCAD will complete its task. When the command prompt returns, exit AutoCAD *without* saving the file.

Warning *3D Studio does not recognize splines and 3D Solids. If you use the DXF file format to export AutoCAD files to 3D Studio, explode any solids you have in your drawing first. The solids will then be reduced to a set of regions which 3D Studio can recognize.*

You now have a 3D Studio version of our model. Before we go on to 3D Studio, take a look at the 3D Studio File Export Options dialog box in step 6 of the previous exercise. You will want to know what these options do when you are transferring AutoCAD files to 3D Studio.

Grouping AutoCAD Objects into 3D Studio Objects

3D Studio does not organize objects in the same way as AutoCAD. What 3D Studio calls an object is more like groups or blocks in AutoCAD, that is, several objects are combined to form a larger object. The *Derive 3D Studio Objects From* radio button group offers a way to determine how AutoCAD objects are grouped to form 3D Studio objects.

In the exercise, you will use the default Layer option in this button group. This causes objects that are in separate layers in AutoCAD to be grouped together to form separate groups of objects in 3D Studio. This option is often the best, because by default the names of the objects in 3D Studio are then the same as those of their respective layers in AutoCAD; the names are easily recognizable. For example, if you decide to bring any objects from your model's Mullion layer into 3D Studio, they become a group of objects that is also called Mullion in 3D Studio. The other options do not assign AutoCAD names to objects when converting them into 3D Studio objects.

As you can see from the radio buttons, you also have the option to group objects by their AutoCAD color index or by their AutoCAD object type. Under some circumstances these last two options may be preferable, for example you may have organized your AutoCAD drawing so objects are assigned a color based on a material assignment you plan to give them.

Another option, *AutoCAD Blocks*, causes the translated file to maintain each block as a 3D Studio object. When this option is left unchecked, blocks are "exploded" and the components of the block are converted into objects based on the setting in the *Derive 3D Studio Objects From* radio button group.

Controlling How Smooth Objects Look

Nearly all curved 3D Surfaces in AutoCAD are actually built up of faceted meshes. These facets will show up as facets in a 3D Studio rendered image unless you apply what is called a *smoothing group*. When 3D Studio encounters an object that has a smoothing group applied to it, it evens out the facets of the object, giving the appearance of a smooth surface. You can apply smoothing groups while in 3D Studio. You can also have the smoothing group applied at translation time by having the Smoothing option checked.

The Degrees input box lets you determine when a smoothing group is applied based on the maximum angle between two surfaces. The default value is 30. This means that surfaces in a mesh, for example, whose difference in angle is less than 30 will be assigned a smoothing group and will appear smooth in 3D Studio renderings.

Joining Edges to Reduce Model Size

The last option in the dialog box is Welding. 3D Studio considers edges and vertices as objects. So when two surfaces are joined together, they share one edge. In AutoCAD, two 3D faces joined together, for example, still have two edges; one for each 3D face. The Weld option removes the extra edge between two surfaces, thereby reducing the 3D Studio file size and the time required to render it. The Threshold input box option lets you determine how close together two edges have to be before they are "welded."

Exporting Your Files through The DXF Format

You can also export a DXF file which can be later imported to 3D Studio. To produce a DXF file, choose File ➤ Export, then at the Data Export dialog box, choose *.dxf* from the *List Files of Type* drop-down list. You can then enter a new name in the File Name input box, or click OK to accept the default file name and settings. You are then asked for a value for the number of decimal places to be used in controlling the accuracy of the export. In most cases, you can accept the default value of 16. You also have the option to select specific objects for export, or to export a binary DXF file. The binary version of the file will be smaller.

◆ Getting Familiar with 3D Studio

This section guides you through your first look at 3D Studio 4. Think of it as a general tour through its features and don't worry about the details. Later chapters will fully describe the more common functions you will need to create renderings and animations.

Before we begin our tour, make sure you've set up 3D Studio to work on your system. Some computers may not have sufficient resources to allow for 3D Studio in a full-screen window under Windows 95, so you may have to temporarily exit Windows to run it. In this chapter I will assume you have configured your computer appropriately and know how to start 3D Studio on your own system.

Your First Look

Start up 3D Studio. You should see a screen like Figure 9.1. To the far right is the menu. An additional pull-down menu appears across the top of the screen when you move your cursor to the top. This arrangement may look vaguely familiar to longtime users of AutoCAD, as there are some similarities to the old DOS version of AutoCAD in the way the system works.

The Command Column

The list of options along the right side of the screen is called the *Command Column*. These are the tools you'll be using the most. They offer the rendering, object selection, lighting, materials, and camera editing tools. When you highlight and click on one of these options, you will see additional options appear below the list. For example, if you click on Lights, you will see Ambient, Omni, and Spot appear below the last item in the list, Display.

Notice that Omni and Spot are each followed by an ellipsis (...), which indicates that more options are available when you select them (see Figure 9.2). Also notice that these Lights options are indented slightly to show you that they are subheadings to the main options. The main options at the top of the list will always remain while the subheadings and their options change depending on which main option is selected.

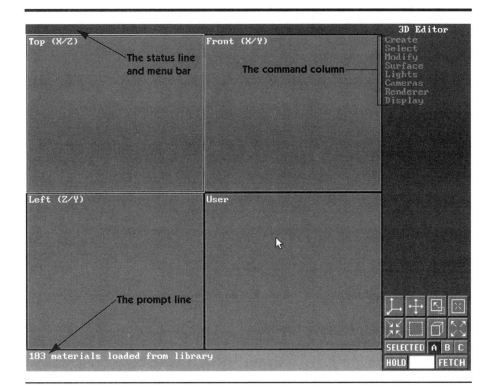

Figure 9.1: The 3D Studio screen

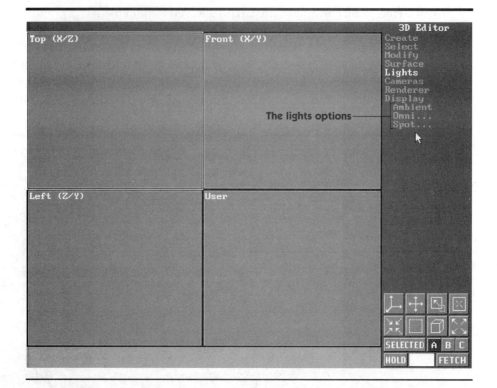

Figure 9.2: The 3D Studio command column with the Lights option selected

The Icon Panel

Toward the bottom, you'll see the icon panel (see Figure 9.3). The buttons in this panel control the viewports. With them, you can pan, zoom in or out, view the extents of a model, or switch to a full-screen view of a viewport. Two other buttons offer special features like isometric view control, similar to AutoCAD's viewpoint tripod, and an object origin control. The origin control button will be described later in this book.

Below the icon panel are two rows of text buttons. The Selected ABC buttons control object selection. The Hold and Fetch buttons act like the Undo command in AutoCAD. You might think of Hold as a placemarker, and Fetch as a "Return to Placemarker" tool.

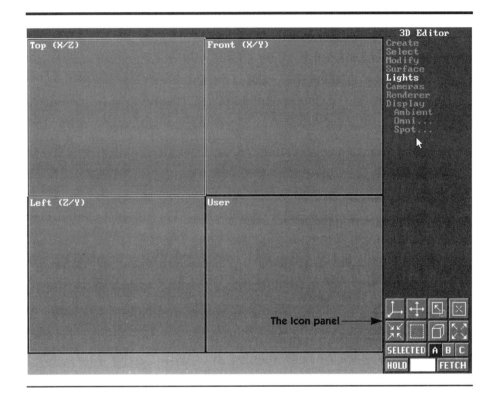

Figure 9.3: The 3D Studio icon panel

The Pull-Down Menus

At the top of the screen, you'll see a Status line. Right now it is blank, but as you work through the tutorials in this book, you will see important data regarding tools you are using. For example, whenever the cursor is placed in an active viewport, you'll see a coordinate readout in the Status line.

Place your cursor on the Status line, and you'll see a row of menu options. These are 3D Studio's pull-down menus. They offer general file and display controls, and mode settings. For example, you use the Files pull-down menu to open, save, import, and export files. The Info pull-down menu offers system information such as memory use and drawing size, and also allows you to set general program parameters such as where 3D Studio resources are kept.

The Viewports

You also see four viewports, each with a label across the top. These viewports display your model in orthographic top, front, and left side views, as well as a perspective or isometric view in the lower right corner (see Figure 9.4). Like AutoCAD viewports, you click on the viewport to make it active. You'll see this more clearly once you've opened a file.

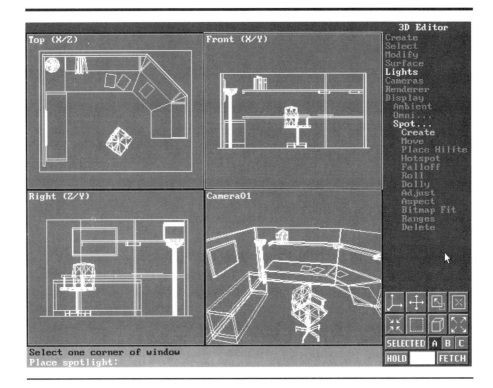

Figure 9.4: Views of an office cubicle

Note *An orthographic view is a view that is perpendicular to a surface of the object being viewed. A floor plan of a building could be considered an orthographic view of a building's floor. Building elevation drawings are an example of orthographic views of a building's sides.*

The Prompt Line

Finally, at the bottom of the screen is a prompt line. Like AutoCAD, you will see messages from time to time in this space. Unlike Auto-CAD, you don't have to respond by typing data into the prompt line. Your text responses always go into dialog boxes. Other graphical data entry is done through the cursor in the viewport. The Status line also plays an important role by "reading out" location, angle, and scale information.

Getting Quick Help

Generally, data input is through dialog boxes. Many functions have keyboard shortcuts, however. One of the most important shortcuts to know is the Help key. To get help, hold down the Alt key while clicking on an option. Try it now. Click on Lights ➤ Spot, for instance, to display the Spotlight options. Now Alt-click on Create. You see a Help message regarding this option. (see Figure 9.5).

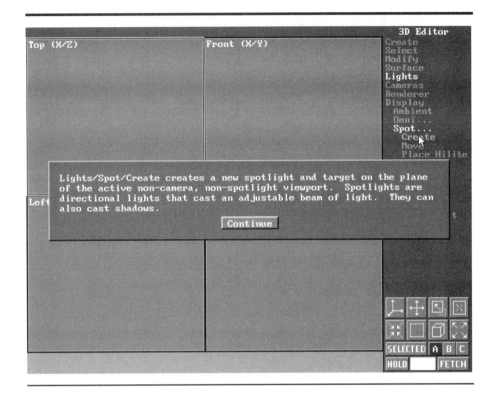

Figure 9.5: An example of 3D Studios Help messages

The Alt-click Help feature will work for pull-down menu options as well as the command-column options. The Help messages appear only for options that actually perform a function, however—you won't get a Help message when you Alt-click on an option that simply opens another list of options, like Lights or Cameras.

Modes of Operation

Another similarity between AutoCAD and 3D Studio is the way you use the tools. 3D Studio expects you to select the tool first, then select the object you want to affect with the tool. For example, if you want to move a camera in 3D Studio, you would first choose Cameras ➤ Move, then select the camera. This method of selecting the tool first is referred to as the Verb/Noun method and should be familiar to you by now.

But 3D Studio differs from AutoCAD in one major way. It is divided into several different *modes*, as follows:

◆ 2D Shaper

◆ 3D Lofter

◆ 3D Editor

◆ Keyframer

◆ Materials Editor

The 2D Shaper and 3D Lofter are used to create 3D models in 3D Studio. The 3D Editor (the mode you are in now) lets you set up lights, add materials, and place cameras. The Materials Editor lets you import materials to your model, and create new ones. The Keyframer gives you the tools to create an animation. You can get to these different modes through the Programs pull-down menu.

These five modes are like different programs that work similarly but present different tools, and, in some cases, different screen layouts. When you open 3D Studio for the first time, you see the 3D Editor. You'll spend most of your time here, and in the Keyframer. Since our focus is on using AutoCAD as a modeler instead of 3D Studio as a modeler, we won't spend much time on the finer points of the 2D Shaper and 3D Lofter modes. You will, however, spend a lot of time in the 3D Editor, Keyframer, and the Materials Editor.

The Keyframer looks nearly identical to the 3D Editor, with some variations. This is where you add movement to animate your model by moving your camera or objects through time. The Materials Editor lets you create new materials that you can assign to the parts of your models. You can also edit pre-existing materials.

◆ Importing and Viewing a File

Now let's import the model you exported in the beginning of this chapter.

1. If you opened the Help screen for the Lights ➤ Omni ➤ Create option, click on the Continue button.

2. Choose File ➤ Load from the pull-down menu. You'll see the Select Mesh to Load dialog box.

A mesh in 3D Studio is essentially the same thing as what we've been refering to as a model in AutoCAD. This dialog box may look a bit different from the standard File dialog boxes you are probably familiar with.

3. By default, 3D Studio shows a listing of files in the 3DS mesh subdirectory. If the Savoye4.3DS file is located on a drive other than the one indicated in the Dir: input box, select the drive letter from the buttons on the left side of the dialog box. Use the \ (Backslash) button to go to the root directory of the selected drive, or use the . . (double period) button to move up one directory.

4. Locate the Savoye4.3DS file and click on it. Its name appears in the Filename input box.

5. Click OK. The model appears in the four viewports.

6. Click on the Cameras option in the command column. You'll see a set of blue lines appear in each view (see Figure 9.6).

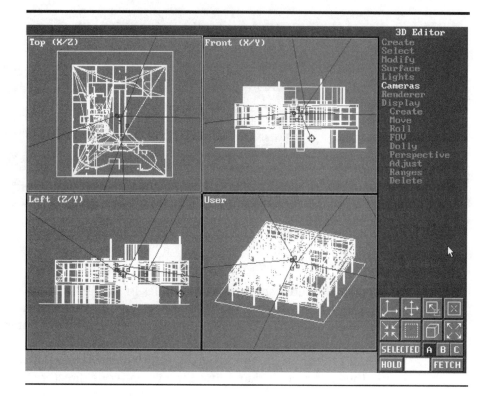

Figure 9.6: Our model in the 3D Studio viewports

Importing DXF Files

I'd like to point out that the Select Mesh To Load dialog box you saw in step 1 offers the option to import DXF files. You can click on the DXF button to list DXF files in the file list of the dialog box. You can then select a DXF file. Once you do, you are presented with another dialog box similar to the 3DS File Export Options dialog box you saw earlier in the first exercise of this chapter. From this dialog box, you can control how objects are translated into 3D Studio.

In some cases, the DXF file format is preferred over the 3DS file format. One very interesting quality of the DXF import is that closed polylines become surfaces in 3D Studio. This means that you can model surfaces using polyline outlines in AutoCAD, thereby reducing file size and modeling time. However, views are not transferred as they are when you export 3DS files directly from AutoCAD, nor can you transfer material settings from AutoVision rendered files. You must also remember to explode 3D Solids before you export DXF files.

When you import a DXF file into 3D Studio, you get a dialog box with the same options that are presented in the 3D Studio File Export Options dialog box shown in the first exercise of this chapter. You will also see one additional option called Unify Normals. We give a detailed description of normals in Chapter 11, but for now, just think of a normal as the reflective side of a surface. In 3D Studio, only one side of a surface reflects light. The Unify Normals option makes sure that all the light-reflecting sides of surfaces in an object are pointing the same way, usually outward.

Understanding the 3D Studio Camera

Besides the model, you see several blue lines with odd shapes at their endpoints. These are 3D Studio *cameras*. They were created when you used the File ➤ Export tool in AutoCAD, and they are the 3D Studio equivalent to the AutoCAD views that we created in Chapter 7. The cameras don't always appear when you open the file. That's why I asked you to select the Camera option in the previous exercise; by doing so, the cameras were made visible.

3D Studio cameras can be named so that each camera in the model corresponds to the AutoCAD view name. This next exercise shows you how you can bring up a view from a 3D Studio camera.

1. Click on the lower right viewport.

2. Type **C**. The Camera Selector dialog box appears.

3. Click on *3DGROUND* from the list, then click OK. The lower right view changes to the selected camera view (see Figure 9.7).

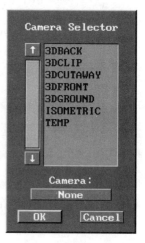

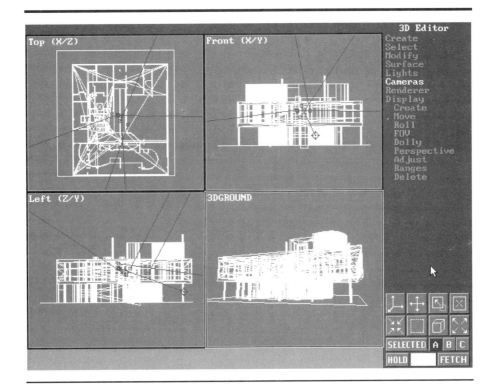

Figure 9.7: The 3DGROUND camera view

This view and its corresponding name are the same as the view of the same name in AutoCAD. Look at the other names in the list in step 2. You'll see that the names all match the names of views in the AutoCAD version of this file. You used some of these views in Chapter 7.

Adding a Camera

Before we move on to look at other tools, I'd like to show you how you can add more cameras in 3D Studio for those situations where no 3D Perspective views have been saved in the exported AutoCAD file.

1. Choose Cameras ➤ Create from the command column.

2. Click on the upper left viewport to make it active.

3. Notice the `Place Camera` message in the prompt area. Click on the point shown in Figure 9.8a.

4. The prompt line shows the message `Now place camera's target`. You also see a rubber-banding line from the point you selected in step 2. Click on the point shown in Figure 9.8b.

5. The Camera Defi-
nition dialog box
appears. Notice
that 3D Studio
has provided a
default name in
the Camera input
box in the upper

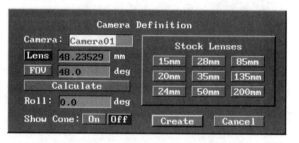

left corner of the dialog box. Type **Mycamera**. Your typing appears in the Camera input box, replacing the default name.

6. Click on the On button next to Show Cone. This displays a graphic that enables you to better visualize the view area that your camera will encompass.

7. Click Create. The dialog box disappears and you see the new camera. Notice the view cone attached to the camera graphic (see Figure 9.8c). Also notice the `Place Camera` message in the prompt line.

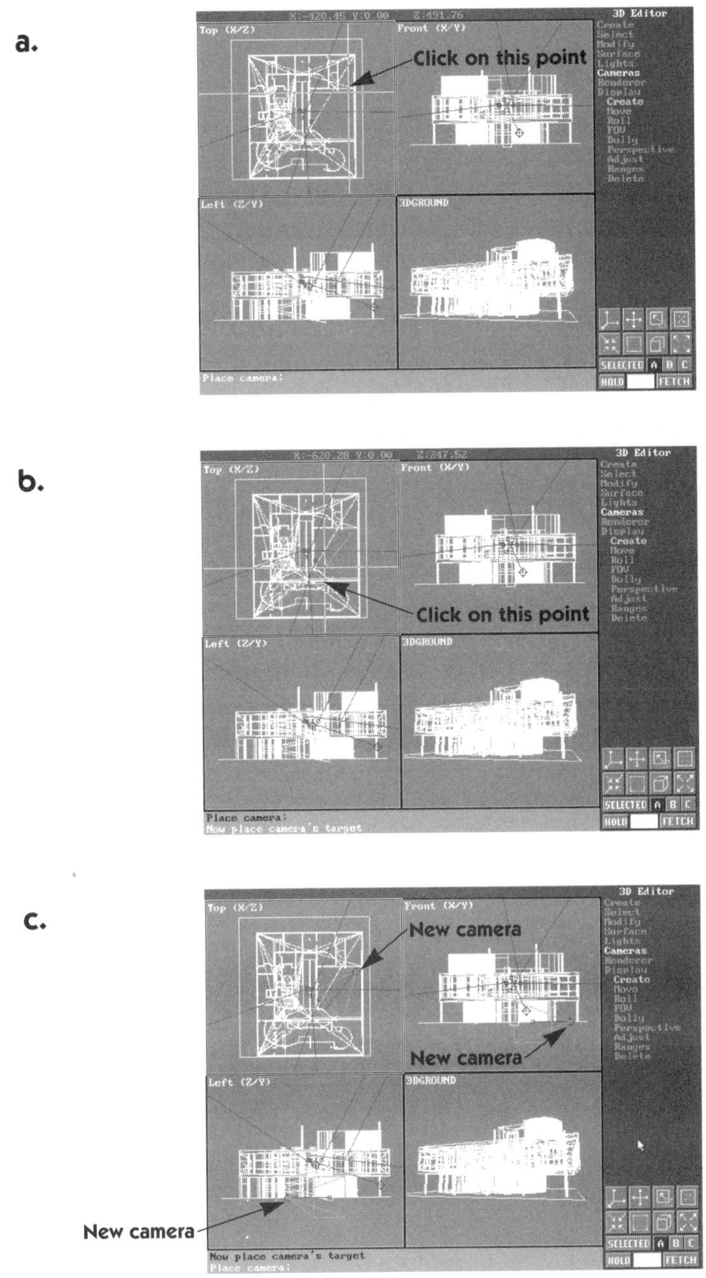

a.

b.

c.

Figure 9.8: The new camera with the view cone added

You can go on to add more cameras if you choose. 3D Studio remains in the last command until you choose another one.

Let's take a moment to study the Camera Definition dialog box in step 4. In addition to naming your camera, you have the option to define its focal length. You might recall from Chapter 7 that a camera's focal length determines its field of view. 3D Studio offers a default focal length of 48, which is close to the typical focal length found in most cameras. To the right, you can select from a set of pre-defined focal lengths. Or you can enter a focal length in the Lens input box.

Just below the Lens input box is the FOV (field of view) input box. If you prefer, you can enter the field of view in degrees instead of entering the focal length. If you prefer this approach, you click on the FOV button, then click on the Calculate button, and 3D Studio will calculate the focal length of the lens. This is a useful control to know about, because you can also use it to find out the field of view of a custom focal length you've entered: just click on the Lens button and then click on Calculate. The field of view value will appear next to the FOV button.

Finally, you can *rotate* your view using the Roll input box. This option is particularly helpful if you want to simulate a sense of motion in animations, though for architectural and product animations, this option is rarely used.

Editing a Camera's Settings

You can change any of the settings you see in the Camera Definition dialog box for any existing camera by clicking on Camera ➤ Adjust. Once this option is selected, you can select a camera and the Camera Definition dialog box will appear, allowing you to alter its values.

Adjusting the Camera Location

Next, you'll see how easy it is to adjust the camera location. You may recall in Chapter 7 that it took some work to adjust your camera viewpoint. 3D Studio offers a much easier way to set camera and target locations. This next exercise shows you how you can adjust the camera location.

1. Earlier, when you chose Camera from the command column, a set of camera options appeared below the main options in the menu. These are the Camera options. Click on Move from these options. (Notice the word *Move* is highlighted in yellow, telling you it is active.)

2. Click on the lower left viewport, then move your cursor over the viewport. Notice that the cursor turns into a box with four arrows emerging from it.

3. Click on the camera object shown in Figure 9.9a. The camera and its associated target are highlighted in yellow to help you visualize the camera's orientation.

4. Now as you move the cursor, the perspective view in the lower right viewport dynamically updates to show you how the new camera viewpoint looks. Notice that the geometry of the model is simplified in the perspective viewport.

5. Click on the point shown in Figure 9.9b. Your viewpoint becomes fixed as the camera is placed in its new location.

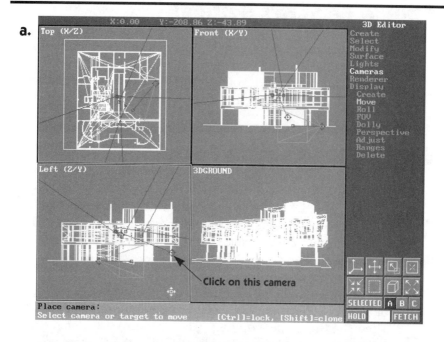

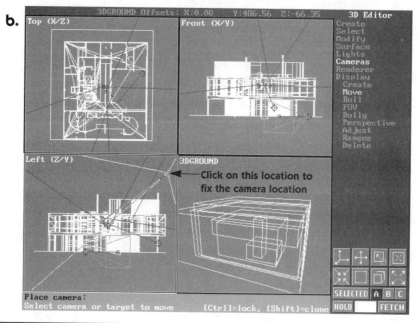

Figure 9.9: Moving the camera location

While moving the camera location, you get immediate feedback of how your view will look by watching the perspective viewport. Once you select the camera, you get immediate feedback as to the location of both the camera and target point.

Adjusting the Target

The perspective view is a bit too low in the viewport. You will want to lower the target point to center the view. Adjusting the target is just as easy as adjusting the camera. Try this exercise to move the target point downward.

1. Notice that the word Move in the command column is highlighted in yellow. This tells you that this option is still active, which means that you can click on another camera or a target to move it. Click on the upper left viewport to make it active.

2. Click on the target point shown in Figure 9.10a. The camera you moved earlier will be highlighted in yellow to show you which camera you've selected. If you happen to select the wrong camera, right-click and then try your selection again.

3. Once you've selected the correct target, move the target around and notice how the perspective view changes. Move the target until your perspective view looks similar to the one in Figure 9.10b, then click on that point.

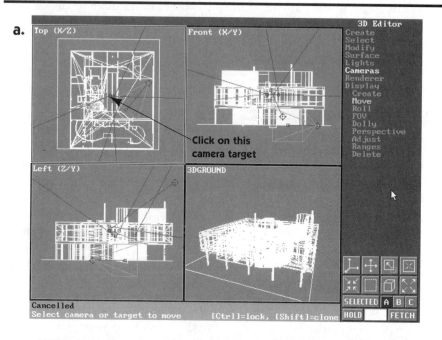

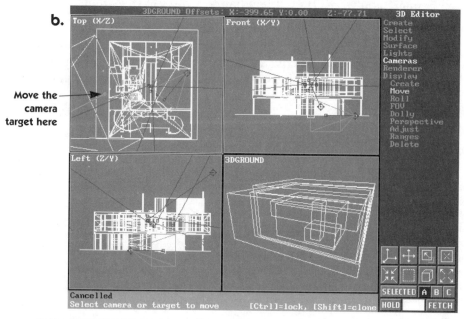

Figure 9.10: Moving the camera target location

In this exercise, you adjusted the target location in the plan view of the building in the upper left viewport. Don't let this suggest that you are limited to working in a single viewport, however—you can use any viewport you want when moving your camera or target.

Adjusting Your View with the Icon Panel Tools

The target points are crowded in the interior of the building, so it becomes a bit more difficult to select the target you want. As we explained in step 2 of the previous exercise, if you happen to select the wrong target or camera, you can right-click on the mouse to deselect the object. But sometimes the camera or target points will be so crowded that you will want to get a closer look to make your selection easier. Let's take a look at the tools needed to get around in your drawing.

Using a Zoom Window

To get a close-up view of a particular portion of your model, you use the Zoom Window button. This button works exactly like AutoCAD's Zoom Window tool.

1. Click on the dotted square icon in the icon panel.

   This is the 3D Studio equivalent of a Zoom Window. The icon turns red to indicate that it is active. Also notice that the Move option is no longer highlighted.

2. Click on the lower left viewport to make it active

3. Place a window just as you would do with the AutoCAD Zoom Window tool, in the area shown in Figure 9.11a. The view enlarges.

4. Click on the Move option in the command column to make it active again, then click on the target point shown in Figure 9.11b. Your target point may not be exactly where it is shown in this figure. The point is, you want to locate and select the target of the camera from a different viewport.

5. Move the cursor to the left until it touches the edge of the viewport. Notice that the view pans to the right to accommodate your moving target.

6. Move the cursor to the right edge of the viewport to return to the previous view.

7. Now suppose you decide you don't want to move the target point after all. Right-click on your mouse to exit the Move camera tool without changing anything.

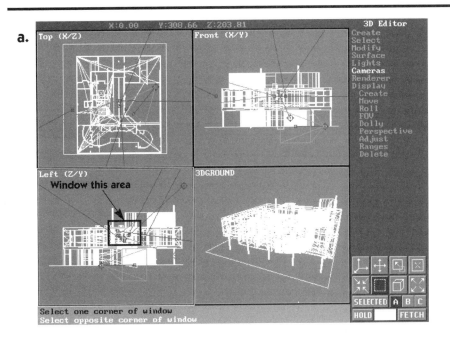

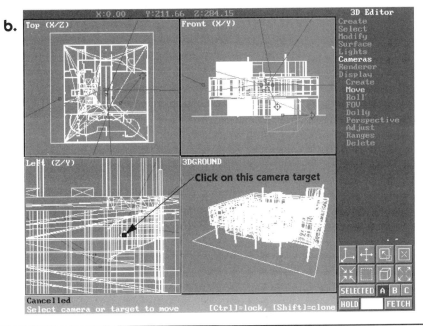

Figure 9.11: Using a Zoom window

You've seen two tools in action here: the Zoom Window tool in the icon panel, and the automatic panning of your view when you reach the edge of the viewport. As mentioned above, the Zoom Window tool is very similar to AutoCAD Zoom Window. The automatic panning feature offers a convenient way to "nudge" your view when you need to pick a location that is outside the current view.

Panning a View

3D Studio also offers a View Pan tool which acts just like AutoCAD's Pan tool. Its icon looks like a cross with arrows at each end.

1. Click on the Pan button in the icon panel.

2. In the active viewport, click on the two points shown in Figure 9.12. Your view moves the distance and direction you indicate with the selected points.

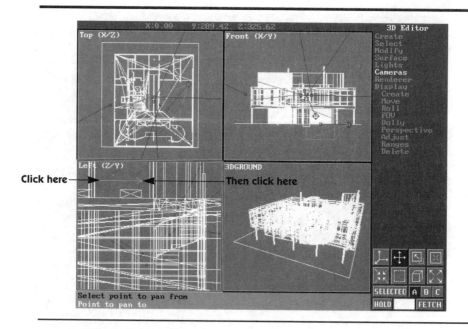

Figure 9.12: Using the Pan tool

You should feel right at home with the Zoom Window and Pan buttons. The only caveat to using these tools is that you may accidentally access the automatic panning feature by getting too close to the edge of the viewport while selecting points, even while using the Pan tool.

Zooming In and Out

After having enlarged a view, you frequently need to return to an overall view to make changes elsewhere in the model or to just get an overall picture of the changes you've made. To zoom out, you use the tool with the outward pointing arrow.

1. Click on the Zoom Out button in the icon panel.

   Your view changes to include more of the building.

2. Now right-click on the Zoom Out button again. All three orthographic views change to show even more of the model. When you right-click on the Zoom Out button, all the views except for perspective views zoom out.

3. Right-click on the Zoom In button. This is the button with the arrows pointing inward.

   Now all the orthogonal views enlarge or "zoom in."

4. Click on the Zoom In button with the left mouse button. The view in the single active viewport enlarges.

The Zoom In and Zoom Out buttons are fairly typical in graphics programs. They let you enlarge or reduce the size of a view by a fixed amount. AutoCAD Release 13 also has similar tools in the Standard tool-bar. 3D Studio adds a slight variation to these tools by allowing the right-click, which causes the tool to act on all orthographic views.

Viewing the Model's Extents

Now suppose you want to see the entire model in each of the orthographic viewports so you can make changes to one of the other cameras.
This would be the equivalent of a Zoom Extents operation in AutoCAD.

1. Click on the perspective view, then type **C** to open the Camera
   Selector dialog box.

2. Select the Isometric view from the list then click OK. Now suppose
   you want to adjust this view, but the camera for this view is outside of all the orthographic viewports.

3. Right-click on the button with the cube icon.

   The three orthographic views zoom out to show
   the entire model, including all the cameras.

4. Now click on the Move option in the command
   column, then click on the upper right viewport.

5. Click on the upper right viewport to make it active.

6. Click on the camera as shown in Figure 9.13. Now as you move the
   camera, your perspective view adjusts to your new camera location.

7. Right-click to cancel the camera move.

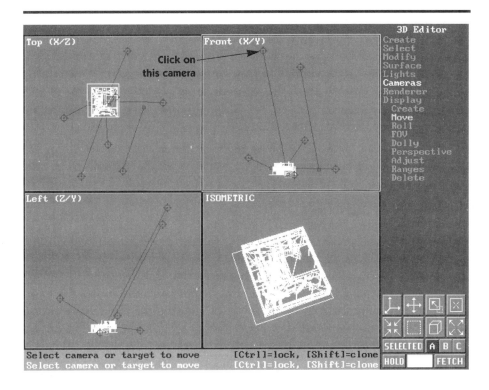

Figure 9.13: Selecting the camera to move. Once selected, the Isometric view changes while the camera moves.

As with the Zoom In and Zoom Out buttons the Zoom Extents button can be selected with either the left or right mouse button. In the example, you use the right button to affect all the orthographic viewports. The left mouse button will affect the active viewport only.

◆ Adding Lights

You're very close to being ready to render your first 3D Studio image. But you still need to create at least one light source. Unlike the AutoCAD Renderer or AutoVision, there is no default light source in 3D Studio. Fortunately, creating a light is a fairly easy operation. It is similar to the way cameras are created.

3D Studio offers three light types: ambient, omni, and spot.

◆ Ambient light is the general lighting of the model. You might think of it in terms of the lighting you get on an overcast day— the light seems to come from all around with no distinct direction.

◆ Omni lights are point source lights, like a light bulb with no shade or cover. The light from an omni light spreads out in all directions.

◆ The spotlight is a directed light. It produces the same effect as a flashlight in that the light can be pointed toward an object or in a general direction as shown in Figure 9.14. Spotlights are the only light source that will cast shadows in 3D Studio.

Figure 9.14: The image on the left represents a typical omni light. It is a point light source spreading light in all directions. The image on the right is a spotlight with a distinct source and target or direction. (By the way, these models were created in AutoCAD and imported into 3D Studio.)

Adding a Spotlight to Simulate the Sun

If you worked through the tutorials in Chapter 8, you know that AutoVision offers a light source that can simulate the sun's location. Unfortunately, 3D Studio version 4 doesn't offer such a light source. You can simulate the sun, however, using a spotlight placed at a fairly large distance from the model. 3D Studio lets you control the intensity as well as the "spread" of the spotlight. You can focus the light down to a very narrow beam like the headlights of a car, or you can spread the light out in a wide angle like the light from a desk lamp.

Note *The process for adding an Omni light is nearly identical to adding a Spotlight. The main difference is that an Omni light doesn't require a target point. The Omni light options are not as extensive, either.*

Start by adding a spotlight, as follows.

1. Choose Lights ➤ Spot ➤ Create.

2. Click on the upper left viewport, the one that shows the plan view of the model.

3. The prompt line shows `Place Spotlight`. Click on a point in the lower left corner of the viewport, as shown in Figure 9.15a.

4. As you move the cursor, you see a rubber-banding line from the point you selected. The prompt line shows the message `Now place spotlight target`. Pick a point in the center of the model plan, as shown in Figure 9.15b. The Spotlight Definition dialog box appears.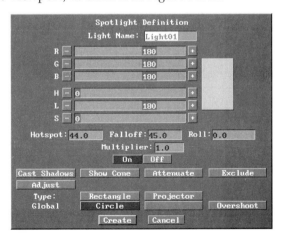

5. Type **SUN** to name this light.

6. Click on Create. The spotlight appears in all the viewports.

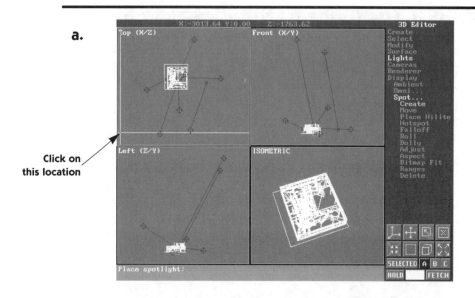

a.

Click on this location

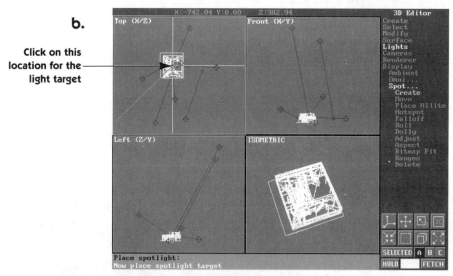

b.

Click on this location for the light target

Figure 9.15: Adding the Spotlight

As you can see from the Spotlight Definition dialog box, you have quite a few options available to control the characteristics of a spotlight. For now, you've taken the default settings; you can return at any time to make changes.

Moving a Spotlight

Notice that in the two side views (the lower left and upper right viewports) the spotlight appears horizontal. 3D Studio places the light and the light target points at the zero coordinate of the Z axis. You must then move them into position. Let's move the spotlight to a point high in the sky.

1. Choose Lights ➤ Spot ➤ Move from the command column.

2. Click on the lower left viewport to make it active, then click on the spotlight as shown in Figure 9.16a. Notice that once you've selected the spotlight, you see a cone appear. This cone indicates the direction and spread of the spotlight and helps you get a better idea of how your model is illuminated.

3. Move the light to the position shown in Figure 9.16b, then click on that point.

4. Now click on the spotlight's target point and move it to a location at the top of the model and click on that point (see Figure 9.16c).

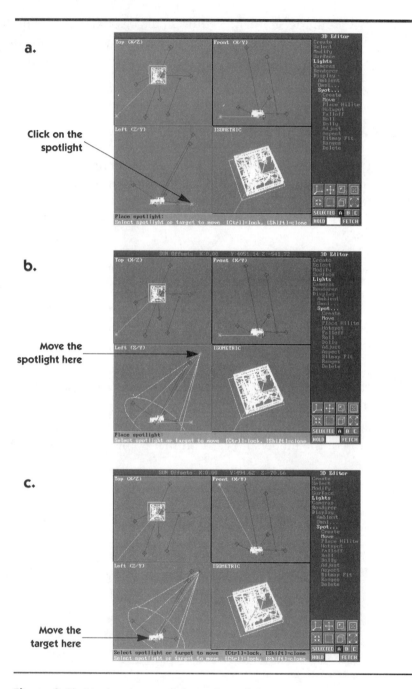

Figure 9.16: Moving the spotlight and spotlight target

As you can see from this exercise, moving the spotlight is similar to moving a camera.

Editing a Spotlight

Once you've placed the spotlight in its new position, the light cone disappears. You can turn it on so it appears all the time by editing the spotlight settings.

1. Choose Lights ➤ Spot ➤ Adjust, then click on the spotlight you just added. You can click on either the light or the light's target when using the Adjust option.

2. At the Spotlight Definition dialog box, click on the button labeled Show Cone, then click on OK. The light cone appears in the viewports.

Here you see that you can edit the settings for the spotlight using the Adjust option.

Now take a moment to look at the Spotlight Definition dialog box. From here, you can control the light intensity as well as the color of the light. You can also control whether the light casts shadows and even which objects it is to affect.

You'll come back to this dialog box and work with it frequently, but for this first tour of 3D Studio, we'll move on to see how to get a rendered view.

◆ Rendering a View

Now let's render the view to see what we've done.

1. Click on the Isometric view, then type **C**.

2. Choose 3Dground from the Camera Selection dialog box, then click OK.

3. Choose Renderer ➤ Render View. Notice the message in the prompt line, `Select Viewport to Render`.

4. Click on the lower right viewport. The Render Still Image dialog box opens.

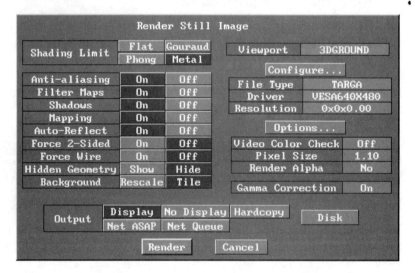

You have several settings you can make to control your rendered view. You'll learn about these options later in this and other chapters. For now, let's take the default settings.

5. Click Render. You'll see the Render dialog box display a series of messages. As it does, it shows a graphic telling you how long each process takes. When 3D Studio is finished, you see the rendered image (see Figure 9.17).

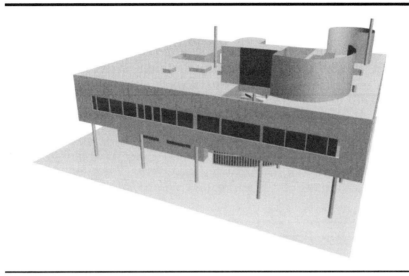

Figure 9.17: The first rendered view in 3D Studio

Since you didn't add materials to the model yet, the rendering appears with the default materials assigned to all surfaces. This rendered image doesn't look great. The process of creating a finished rendering or animation involves a repeated cycle of rendering, adjusting, and rendering again, until you've reached a look you are pleased with.

As you progress through the chapters in this part of the book, you'll learn this process firsthand. We'll explain the method for adding materials and further enhancing the rendered image in the next chapter. But for now, let's continue with our tour.

◆ Creating a Quick Study Animation

Before we conclude this chapter, I'd like to show you how to move to another 3D Studio mode or program, to use the animation facilities. So far, you've used the tools in the 3D Editor of 3D Studio. The construction of animations takes place primarily in the Keyframer.

1. To get to the Keyframer, choose Programs ➤ Keyframer from the pull-down menu. The Keyframer screen doesn't look much different from the 3D Editor screen (see Figure 9.18). The main difference is in the contents of the command column and the prompt line.

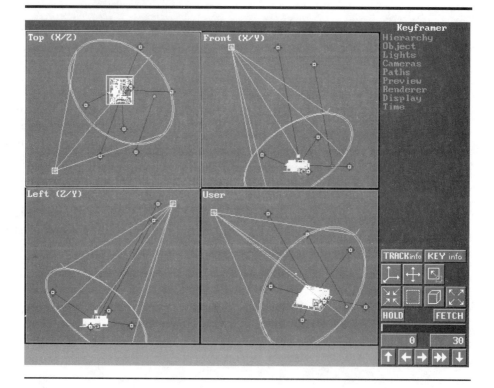

Figure 9.18: The Keyframer screen

2. Move the cursor down to the prompt line. Notice that the prompt line changes to display a slidebar.

3. Click and drag the button labeled *0* (zero) (it's found in the left side of the slidebar) across the bottom of the screen to the far right (see Figure 9.19). Notice that the number in the slidebar changes as it slides across. When it gets to the far right, the number reads *30*. You also see a red bar in the icon palette and two sets of numbers, one of which changes as you slide the button.

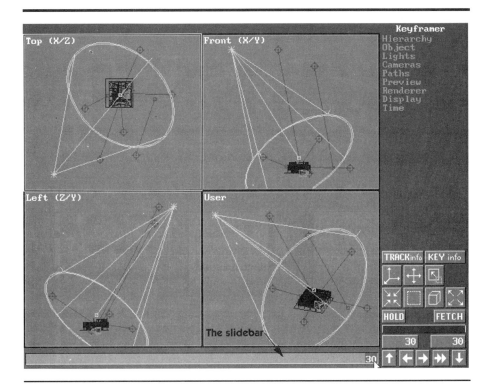

Figure 9.19: Moving the slidebar in the prompt line

Adding Camera Motion

3D Studio starts out by giving you 30 frames of an animation sequence. The slidebar you just used lets you move through the frames quickly.

> **Note**   *You can increase the number in the slidebar by using the Time option in the command column. For this presentation, you'll stick with the 30 frames, which is equivalent to one second of animation time.*

To get a better picture of how the Keyframer works, let's add some motion to the model.

1. Click on the lower right viewport, then type **C**. Notice that you get the camera selection dialog box just as you did in the 3D Editor.

2. Choose 3Dfront and click OK.

3. Choose Camera ➤ Move from the command column.

4. Click on the camera shown in Figure 9.20a. This is the camera that controls the view in the lower right viewport.

5. Move the camera to the location shown in Figure 9.20b so your view in the perspective viewport looks similar to the one in Figure 9.20b. Select that point.

6. Now click and drag the button in the slider at the bottom of the screen. Move it slowly to the left and watch what happens to the perspective view. The view changes dynamically as you move the bar. Also notice that the camera in the upper left viewport also moves, showing you its location at each frame.

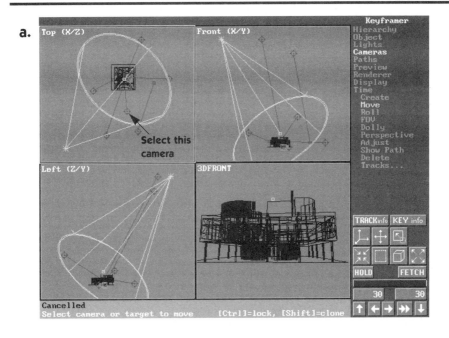

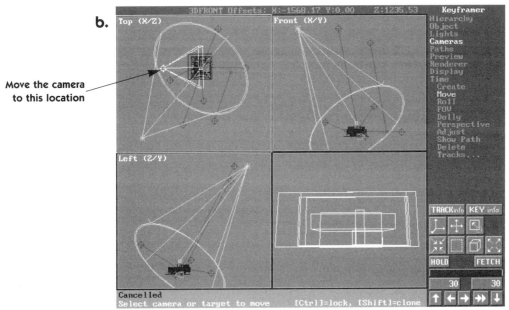

Figure 9.20: Selecting the camera to move

You have just created a camera motion by simply selecting a frame using the slidebar, which you did in the exercise prior to the last one, then positioning the camera to the new location for that frame.

Adjusting the Camera Path

If you study the animated perspective view as you move the slidebar back and forth, you may notice that you alternately move closer to the building then move away. Let's assume you don't want that effect, and that you want the camera to stay a fairly consistent distance from the model. You can add an additional control point called a *keyframe* that will adjust your camera path so it maintains the same distance from your model through the animation. Keyframes are points along the camera path that direct the motion of the camera. In AutoCAD terms, you can think of the camera path as a spline or smooth polyline, and the keyframe as a control point or node on that polyline.

Here's how you add a keyframe to a camera path.

1. Move the slidebar so it is in the middle position and it shows the number 15, as shown in Figure 9.21a. Notice that the Camera ➤ Move option is still active.

2. Click on the same camera you moved in the previous exercise and move it downward to the location shown in Figure 9.21b. Check that your perspective view is similar to the one shown in Figure 9.21b.

3. Now click and drag the slider again across the full width of the slidebar. Notice that now the view stays at a more consistent distance from the model. Also notice how the camera moves in the upper left viewport. It travels in an arc path instead of a straight line.

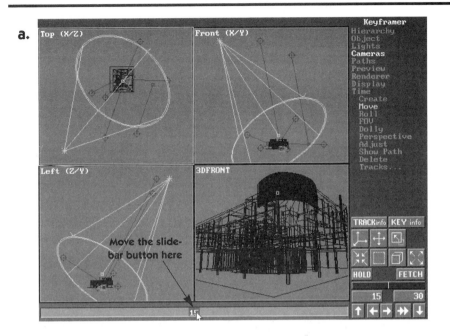

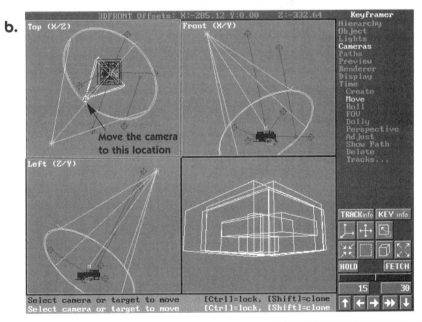

Figure 9.21: Creating a keyframe

You might also notice that as the camera moves across the 15th frame, it turns white and you see a dot. This tells you that a keyframe exists at that point.

You can better visualize the camera path by making it visible.

1. Choose Path ➤ Show/Hide.

2. The prompt line shows the message Select object to show or hide path. Click on the camera you've been editing. The camera path appears on each of the orthographic views (see Figure 9.22).

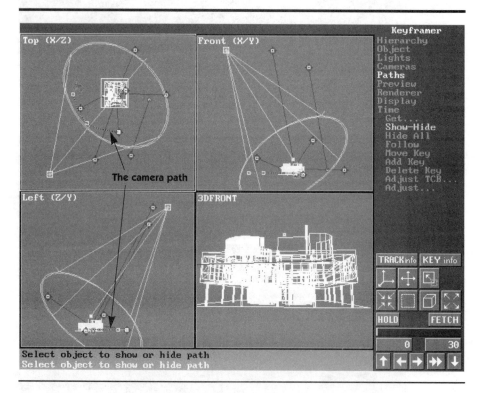

Figure 9.22: The camera path made visible

You can turn off the path visibility by repeating these last steps. The Show/Hide option acts like a toggle that turns the path visibility on or off depending on its current state.

If you look closely at the path, you'll notice a series of yellow dots. These dots represent the location of each frame in the animation. Since we currently have 30 frames, you will see 30 dots.

Once you've established the keyframes of your animation (the beginning and end frames are also keyframes) you can edit them to further refine your camera motion. You'll see how that's done in a later chapter. For now, let's get a preview of this animation.

Creating a Preview Animation

I've already mentioned that the rendering process involves a repeated cycle of rendering and adjusting your model. Animations also follow a similar cycle of adjusting camera paths and previewing the resulting animation. You can often get a fairly good idea of how your animation will look, just by using the slider in the slidebar at the bottom of the screen. You can also create a quick study animation just to see if your camera motion is the way you want it. Here's how to create a preview animation.

1. Choose Preview ➤ Make from the command column.

2. At the `Select viewport to Preview` prompt, click on the perspective view in the lower right corner of the screen. The Make Preview dialog box appears.

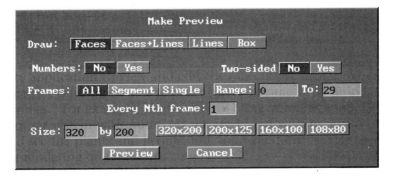

3. Click on the Preview button. You will first see a red bar showing you 3D Studio's progress as it creates the preview animation file. When it's finished, you'll see the preview.

4. Right-click on your mouse to exit the preview.

The preview is crude, but it does show you your camera motion. The model itself is not rendered fully, nor are the lights shown in their proper setting. The main purpose of the preview is to give you a sense of your camera motion, which is, at this point, fairly crude and jerky.

If you look at the Make Preview dialog box, you see that you have several options that control the preview animation. You can have the animation display the frame number by setting the Numbers option to Yes, or you can control the size of the animation using the Size input boxes. You'll get a closer look at these options later in this book.

As you work further into the following chapters, you learn how to take control of the camera to create a smooth, professional looking walk-through of your model. For now, save your file and exit 3D Studio.

1. Choose File ➤ Save. The Select a Mesh File To Save dialog box appears.

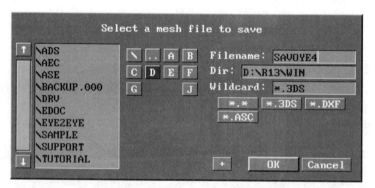

2. Change the name in the Filename input box to **SAVOYE5**, then click OK, which saves this file as Savoye5.3DS.

3. Click on File ➤ Quit to exit 3D Studio.

The Select a Mesh File To Save dialog box doubles as a Save and SaveAs dialog box. When you attempt to save a file that already exists, you are prompted to make sure you want to overwrite the previously saved file.

◆ Summary

This concludes our introductory tour of 3D Studio. As you can see, it has many similarities to AutoCAD in the way it works. And while its interface is somewhat odd by today's standards, it is consistent, so once you've learned the basics, it's fairly easy to progress.

In the next chapter, you'll focus on creating a finished rendering by learning how to apply materials and how to edit them when they aren't exactly what you need. In later chapters, you'll also look at the options you have for file output.

Editing Objects and Assigning Materials

Note *In Chapter 9, you spent most of your efforts familiarizing your-self with 3D Studio's interface. In this chapter, you'll get a chance to delve deeper into its workings by learning how to* edit *objects in your model. You'll also learn how you can assign* materials *to objects to add more realism to your renderings.*

You may wonder to what extent you can make changes to a model once it has been imported to 3D Studio. Editing objects in 3D Studio is a bit different from editing in AutoCAD. For on thing, objects are not organized or defined in the same way. In AutoCAD, you have arcs, lines, circles, and other distinct object types. In 3D Studio, objects are whole groups of surfaces, vertexes, and elements combined to form a single 3D shape.

Selecting objects for editing is also different in 3D Studio than it is in AutoCAD. The key to understanding the selection process in 3D Studio is knowing what kinds of pieces make up an object. Unlike AutoCAD, in 3D Studio objects are built on a *hierarchy* of object *components*.

◆ Understanding 3D Studio Objects

If you click on the Modify option in the 3D Studio command column, you will see a list of the following items: Vertex, Edge, Face, Element, and Object. This list shows, in ascending order, the hierarchy of components that make up an object in 3D Studio. In other words, objects in 3D Studio are composed of elements, which are composed of faces, which can be composed of edges and vertexes. For the most part, objects are the largest components of 3D Studio models.

When you exported the building to a 3D Studio file in Chapter 9, you had the opportunity to determine how the AutoCAD model would be converted to 3D Studio objects. You took the default Layer option, so all the objects on the Ext-wall layer, for example, became an object called Ext-wall in 3D Studio, and all the objects on the column layer became a single object called Columns, and so on.

Let's take a look at each of the 3D Studio object components, starting with the most basic one, the vertex.

Vertex

The *vertex* in 3D Studio is similar to a vertex in an AutoCAD polyline in that it defines a point in space. But unlike a vertex in a polyline, a 3D Studio vertex is an object that can be selected and edited. It is the smallest component of a 3D Studio model. Vertexes are needed to construct faces; faces are actually dependent on vertexes to exist. In fact, if you delete a vertex, all the faces associated with the vertex will also be deleted.

Faces and Edges

A *face* in 3D Studio is a triangular surface capable of reflecting light. You can think of a face as the equivalent of a 3D face in AutoCAD with the difference of having one less side. When you translate an AutoCAD drawing into 3D Studio, a single 3D face from AutoCAD usually becomes two 3D Studio faces with a vertex at each corner (see Figure 10.1). In addition, an edge is added.

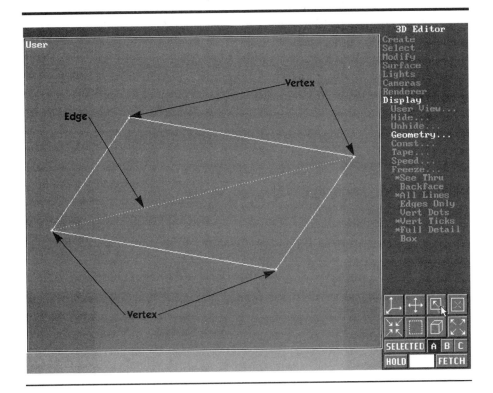

Figure 10.1: An AutoCAD 3D face that has been converted into a 3D Studio face. The Vertexes and Edge have been made visible using the Display ➤ Geometry options.

Edges are not actually distinct objects like faces and vertexes, but they do have certain properties that you can control. For example, the edge created when a AutoCAD 3D face is converted to two 3D Studio faces can be made visible or invisible. By default, the edge of such a pair of faces is made invisible to reduce visual clutter.

Another property of edges is that they can be *shared* by two faces. Using our AutoCAD-to-3D Studio example again, a translated 3D face will have a single shared edge. If several faces of an object are close together, they may be joined to share other edges as well. For example, one of the options you encounter when importing AutoCAD models into 3D Studio is the Weld Faces option, which lets you determine whether edges are shared between adjoining faces. By sharing edges, you can reduce the size of a 3D Studio model.

> **Note**   As with vertexes, deleting edges removes their associated faces.

Elements

Elements are 3D Studio components that fall hierarchically between complete objects and individual faces. They are groups of faces that form a sub-component of an object. For example, although all the columns in the model you imported are considered collectively as one object, each individual column is an element, composed of a set of faces and vertexes.

Elements can be thought of as objects in their own right, that happen to be part of a greater object. If needed, you can convert an element into an object using the Create ➤ Element ➤ Detach option in the command column.

Objects

Objects in 3D Studio are like objects in the real world. For example, you usually think of a vase as a single object, and not as you would consider a vase in AutoCAD, which would be as a collection of arcs, polylines, and 3D faces. So 3D Studio objects are whole items. Objects always have names, so whenever you create a new object in 3D Studio, you are asked to give it a name. (You'll see this in a later exercise).

◆ Creating and Editing in the 3D Editor

Now that you have some background as to what 3D Studio objects are about, let's try adding a new object and editing a pre-existing object. When you rendered the building in Chapter 9, the rendered image looked like it was floating in space. We need to add a ground plane to overcome this unwanted effect.

Creating a Box to Represent the Ground Plane

To represent the ground plane, you'll use a 3D Studio box. The creation of a box in 3D Studio is very similar to creating a box in AutoCAD. You first define the general outline using a rectangle, then you determine the depth of the box.

1. Start 3D Studio and load the Savoye5.3DS file.
2. Right-click on the Zoom Extents button in the icon panel.

3. Click on the upper left viewport, then zoom out so your view looks like Figure 10.2a.

4. Choose Create ➤ Box from the command column.

5. At the `Place one corner of box` prompt, click on the upper left viewport to make it active, then click on the point shown in Figure 10.2a.

6. At the `Place Opposite corner of box` prompt, select the point shown in Figure 10.2b.

7. At the `Click in viewport to define length of box` prompt, click on the upper right viewport and then click on the two points shown in Figure 10.2c. Notice that once you pick the first point, the Status line at the top of the screen shows you the distance from that point to your current cursor location. The distance between the two points will determine the thickness of the box.

Note *In this case, the thickness (mentioned in step 7) is not too important since you are really only going to see the top surface of this box representing the ground plane.*

8. Once you select the two points, the Name For New Object dialog box appears.

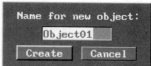

9. 3D Studio offers an object name of Object01. Type **Ground** for the name, then click on the Create button. The ground plane appears.

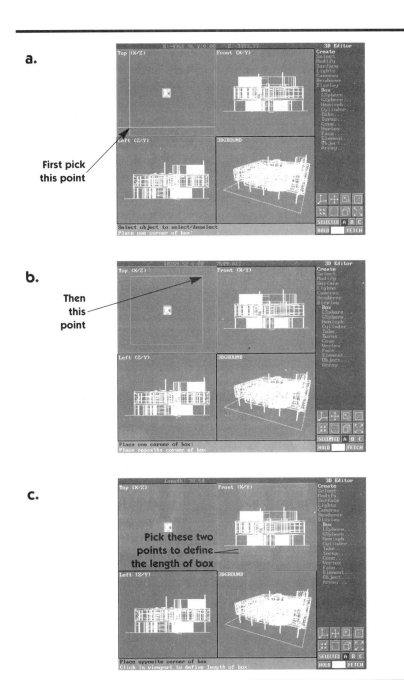

Figure 10.2: Constructing the ground plane

You may have noticed the other objects listed in the command column in step 2. Most of the objects are fairly self-explanatory. You can easily create those objects by following the prompts, and they are similar to the objects available in AutoCAD. A few of the other options offer some special editing tools you'll want to know about, such as detaching elements and performing Boolean operations on objects. You'll see how these things work a bit later. For now, let's move on and see how to change the size of the object you just created.

Scaling an Object

Notice that you can still see the edge of the new Ground object in the distance. To make the ground seem more like the earth, you will need to enlarge it considerably. The following exercise shows you how you can *scale* (enlarge or shrink) an object for such purposes.

> **Note** *Just as with the moving of cameras and lights, you can right-click the mouse to terminate the current editing function. If you decide you do not want to scale a selected object after you've already selected it, right-click the mouse.*

1. Choose Modify ➤ Object ➤ 2D Scale.

2. At the `Select Object to scale` prompt, click on the upper left viewport. Notice that your cursor turns into the same icon you saw in Chapter 9 when you were moving cameras and lights.

3. Click on the rectangle you just created. Now as you move the mouse from left to right, the rectangle changes in size. Also notice that the Status line dynamically displays the scale factor as you move the mouse.

4. Press the Tab key, then move the cursor. Notice that now the scaling is restricted to the X axis only.

5. Press the Tab key again. Now the scaling is restricted to the Y axis.

6. Press the Tab key a third time.

7. Move the mouse to the right until the Status line shows 400%, then left-click your mouse.

The 2D Scale option only scales the selected object in the two axes displayed in the selected viewport. The third axis, in this case the thickness of the ground plane, is not affected. You also saw how the Tab key can be used to further restrict the direction of scaling to either the X or Y axis.

The 3D Scale option works the same way as the 2D Scale option, with the additional scaling of the third axis.

Moving an Object

Now you have a larger ground area so your model won't look like it's floating in space when you render it. At this point, you will want to make sure that the new Ground object doesn't interfere with the base of the building. The base is the smaller rectangle on the ground level. This rectangle represents a gravel material that is part of the design of the building.

Highlighting an Object

First, let's highlight the new Ground object to help us distinguish it from the rest of the model.

1. Choose Select ➤ Object ➤ Single. Now as you move the cursor over the active viewport, you see a small square similar to the AutoCAD selection cursor.

2. Click on the upper right viewport, then click on the new Ground object as shown in Figure 10.3. It is highlighted in red to indicate that it has been selected.

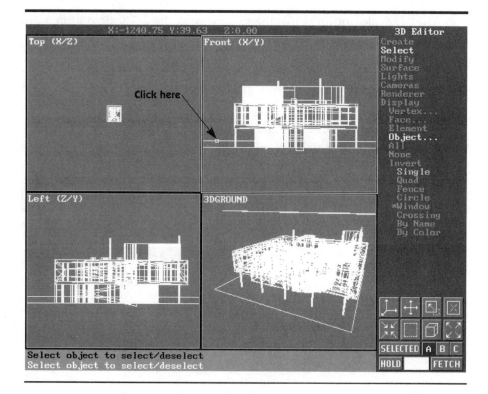

Figure 10.3: Selecting the new Ground object

The Select options let you select objects before you edit them. This is useful in situations where it is difficult to select the object you want to edit, or if you want to edit groups of objects together. In this brief exercise, you didn't actually use it for that purpose. Instead, you use the Select option to simply highlight the Ground object, making it more easy to identify when you enlarge your view of the base of the building in the next exercise. Later in this chapter, you'll learn how to use the Select options to actually select objects for editing.

Restraining Motion

Now that you can clearly distinguish the Ground object from the rest of the model, you can get a closer look at the base of the model to see what's going on.

> **Warning**   *As you move the cursor in step 3, take care not to move your mouse too fast or in too wide a motion. You may recall in Chapter 9 that 3D Studio has an Automatic Pan feature. Even when you cannot see the cursor, the Automatic Pan feature can still shift your view if you move your mouse too far from the original pick point.*

1. Use the Zoom tool in the icon panel and zoom into the base of the column in the upper right viewport, as shown in Figure 10.4a. You can see the base of the building represented as a single line, since you are looking at it edge-on. Notice that the highlighted Ground object surrounds the base of the building. To make sure the base is still visible when you next render the model, you will want to move the Ground object downward.

2. Choose Modify ➤ Object ➤ Move.

3. Click on the Ground object (see Figure 10.4b). Now as you move your mouse, you move the Ground object with it.

4. Since you only want to move the Ground object *downward*, you might want to restrict the movement to the vertical axis. You can restrain the movement of the cursor using the Tab key.

5. Press the Tab key twice and notice what happens. In the Status line as you move the cursor, only the Y value changes. This tells you that your movement is restricted to the Y axis of your current viewport.

6. Press the Tab key again and move the Ground object downward so it is just below the base of the building as shown in Figure 10.4c.

7. Click on this point.

8. Choose View ➤ Redraw to clean up the screen.

9. Now press the Tab key three more times, each time noticing what happens to the cursor.

In steps 5 through 8, you saw how the Tab key lets you restrain the movement of an object in either the up and down or side to side direction. You can think of the Tab key as the 3D Studio equivalent of AutoCAD's Ortho mode. The Tab key works in any situation where you see the Move cursor, which is the square cursor with the arrows pointing outward. If you press the Tab key before you select the object to move, you will see the cursor change to show the direction of restraint (see Figure 10.5).

a.

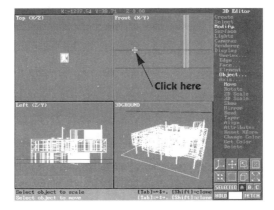

b.

c.

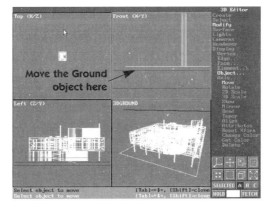

Figure 10.4: Moving the Ground object

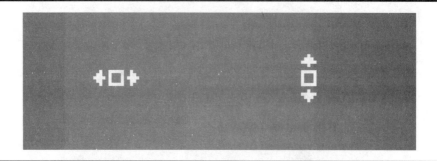

Figure 10.5: The cursor as it appears when motion is restrained horizontally (left) and vertically (right)

Since the cursor disappears once you select the object, you don't see the cursor change shape, but you still have the motion restraint.

Making a Copy

As you moved the Ground object in the previous exercise, you may have noticed the [Shift]=Clone message in the prompt line.

This message is telling you that if you hold down the Shift key as you select an object to be moved, it will be copied instead of moved. Try it in the next exercise by making a copy of the Ground object.

1. With the Modify ➤ Object ➤ Move option still highlighted, click on the lower left viewport, then Shift-click on the Ground object.

2. Move the object upward to the position shown in Figure 10.6, then click on that point. The Name For New Object dialog box appears.

Notice that 3D Studio offers a name for you. The name uses the name of the original object with the addition of a two-digit number. You can enter a different name if you want.

3. For this exercise, click the Create button to accept the default name. A copy of the Ground object appears in the location you selected (see Figure 10.6).

4. Save this file to use in the next set of exercises.

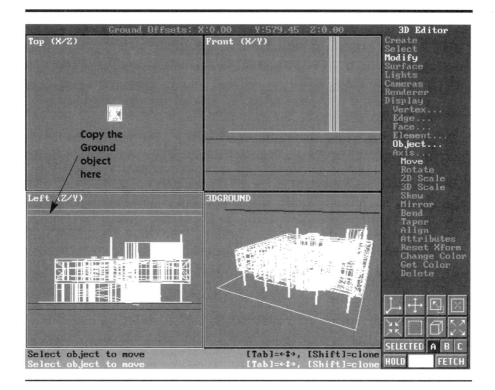

Figure 10.6: Copying the Ground Object

Using a Shift-click on an object to make a copy is not limited to the Modify ➤ Object ➤ Move option. It works in any Move option that appears in the command column. For example, you can choose Cameras ➤ Move, then Shift-click on a camera to copy it. The same applies to the Lights ➤ Spot or Omni ➤ Move option.

Selecting Groups of Objects or Single Elements and Faces

You may have noticed that the Move option allowed you to select only one object. But suppose you wanted to move several objects together at one time. To do this, you need to use the Select options.

You used the Select ➤ Object ➤ Single option to highlight the Ground object making it more easily distinguishable from the rest of the model. But the Select options also let you select multiple objects before using the Modify options. They also allow you to select combinations of vertexes, faces, elements, and objects for later editing.

The following exercise will use the Ground object and its copy to demonstrate how you can select multiple objects. You'll also see how the Hold and Fetch options are used to save and undo your work.

1. If the file you saved in the last exercise is not open, open it now, and then click on the Hold button at the bottom of the icon panel. This button is similar to the File ➤ Save option, only it doesn't save to the current filename. Instead, it saves your current file in a temporary holding file. You'll see how you restore a file that was saved with Hold in the next exercise.

2. Now choose Select ➤ Object ➤ Single and click on the original Ground object, which is currently highlighted.

3. Whoops—When you select an object that is already selected, it is deselected, so click on the Ground object again. You will want it selected so you can see how you can select and edit multiple items in 3D Studio.

4. Click on the Zoom Extents button.

5. Click on the Quad option from the command column. The Quad option is equivalent to the Window Selection option in AutoCAD.

6. Place a window around the copy of the Ground object. Notice that you now have two objects selected.

7. Hold down the Alt key and window the copy of the Ground object. The copy is now deselected.

8. Now choose Select ➤ Element and, in the upper right viewport, select the column. Now you have an element and an object highlighted.

You can continue to select more objects and faces using the Select ➤ Object options. Now let's see how you can edit a selection of different items.

1. Click on the Zoom Out button.

2. Now choose Select ➤ Face ➤ Quad, and window the area shown in Figure 10.7a. Now you have a combination of objects, elements and faces selected.

3. Choose Modify ➤ Face ➤ Move.

4. Click on the button labeled Selected at the bottom of the icon panel. The button turns red to indicate that it is active.

5. Click on a point in the upper right viewport as shown in Figure 10.7b. You see a rectangle representing the selected items. The Status line indicates the distance of displacement as you move your mouse. In this situation, since you cannot see the entire set of selected objects, the Status line helps you determine the direction and distance of your move.

6. Press the Tab key to restrain the motion to the X axis, then move the cursor until the Status line shows X:-60.00 or some distance close to this and click at that point. The columns, ground, and faces move to the new location as shown in Figure 10.7c.

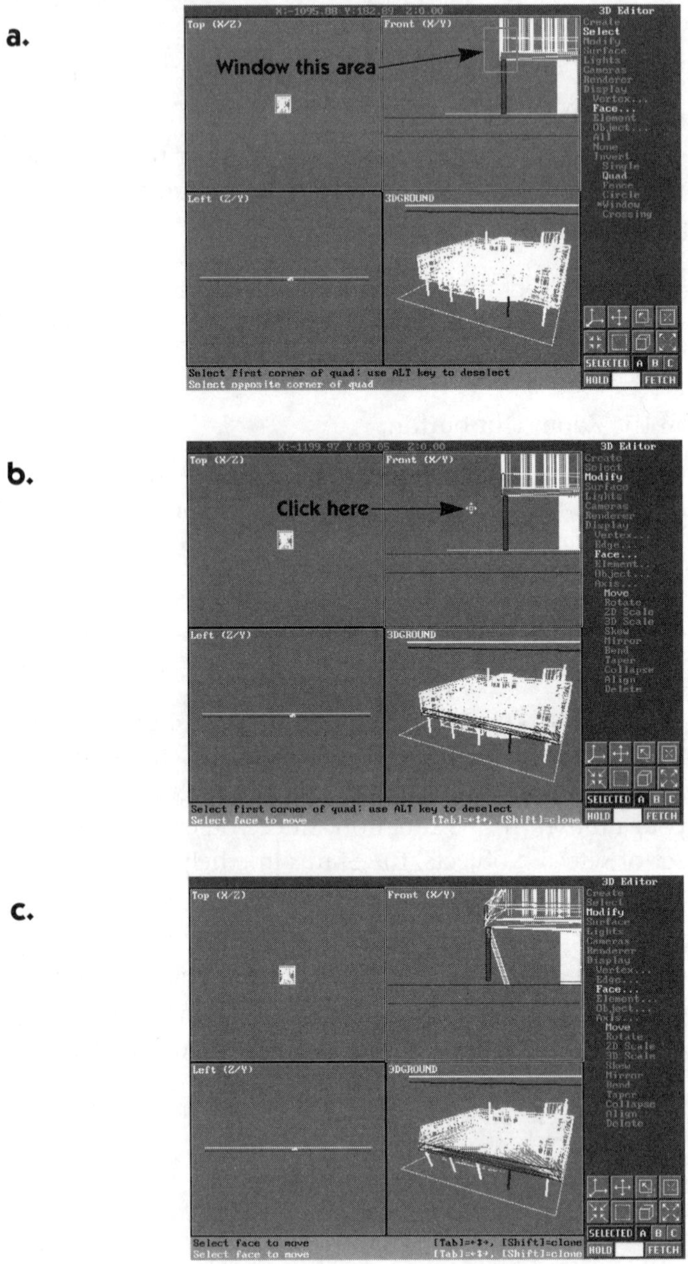

Figure 10.7: Moving a selected set of faces and objects

7. Click on two more points to move the selection again. You can repeat the option as many times as you need.

8. You don't really want to keep these changes, so click on the Fetch button at the bottom of the icon panel to restore the model to its condition before you started the previous exercise.

9. 3D Studio displays a box asking if you want to restore the hold buffer. Click Yes to restore the model to its earlier condition.

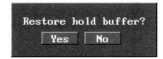

Notice that the faces that adjoin the face you selected also move with the selection set. They move with the selection because they share edges with the face you selected earlier. If they did not share an edge, then only the selected face would have moved, leaving adjoining faces undisturbed.

In step 1 of the last exercise, you used the Modify ➤ Face ➤ Move option. When you move a selection that is a combination of faces and objects, you must use this option. On the other hand, if your selection is made up only of objects, you can use the Modify ➤ Object ➤ Move option. Also be aware that Elements cannot be used as a selection option when using the Selected button in the icon panel. If you select Modify ➤ Element and then attempt to click on the Selected button in the icon panel, you will find that the button will not activate. You must use the Faces option when moving a selected set of elements.

Using Endpoint Osnaps in 3D Studio

When moving 3D Studio elements around, you may find the need to join endpoints and vertexes exactly. 3D Studio has an equivalent to the AutoCAD Endpoint Object Snap called Vertex Snap. To activate it, you press the Alt+V key combination. You will then see a yellow V appear in the upper right corner of the screen, indicating that Vertex Snap is active. Then, whenever you see the 3D Studio selection cursor (the square with arrows pointing outward), you can click on a vertex and you will know that you have selected the exact vertex location. Since you don't get any immediate feedback, this tool takes a little getting used to.

Detaching Faces and Converting Them to New Objects

There will be times when you will want to detach a face from an object so you can assign a separate material to it. This is a fairly common situation, so it is worth practicing it at least once. Try the following exercise to separate some faces from the Int-wall object in the current model.

1. Set up your views to match those shown in Figure 10.8a.

2. Choose Select ➤ Object ➤ Single, then click on a wall on the roof garden, as shown in Figure 10.8a. Notice that the roof garden walls are part of the interior walls as one object.

3. Choose Select ➤ None to clear the selections you may have.

4. Choose Select ➤ Faces ➤ Quad from the command column, then click on the Crossing option just below the Quad option. Notice that the asterisk moves from Window to Crossing.

5. Window the area shown in Figure 10.8b. Notice that the walls on the roof are selected.

a.

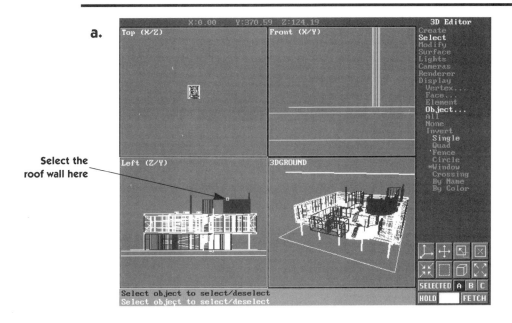

Select the
roof wall here

b.

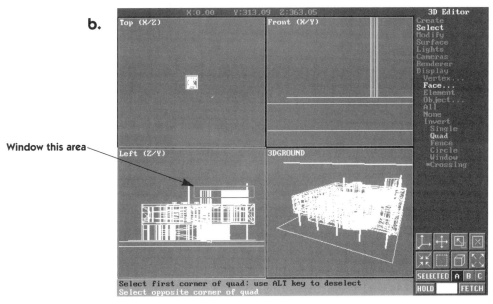

Window this area

Figure 10.8: Selecting the roof walls first with a single pick, then with a crossing
window

The Crossing mode you selected in step 5 acts like the AutoCAD Crossing selection option. It selects objects that are not only within the selection window, but also crossing through it. There is one key difference, however. In 3D Studio, you must include in the selection window at least one set of vertexes associated with the faces you want to select.

Now that you've selected a set of faces, you can detach them and convert them to a new object.

1. Choose Create ➤ Faces ➤ Detach.

2. Click on the Selected button in the icon panel, then click anywhere in the lower left viewport, but not on an object.

3. You see the message Detach selected faces? Click OK.

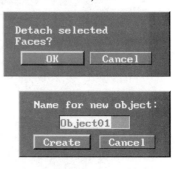

4. In the Name For New Object dialog box, enter **Roofwall** and then click Create. The Roof walls are now a separate object.

5. Choose Select ➤ Object ➤ Single, then click on a roof wall. Notice that the walls of the roof are now a single object by themselves.

Deleting an Object

I asked you to make a copy of the Ground object to show you how the Move command doubles as the Copy command and also to show you how you can select objects and elements in a model. You don't really need it, so we'll use the copy to demonstrate how you delete objects from your model.

1. Choose Modify ➤ Objects ➤ Delete.

2. Click on the copy of the Ground object. You see the Delete warning box.

3. Click OK. The copy disappears.

You can use the Modify ➤ Faces ➤ Delete option to delete a set of items that include a mix of faces, elements, and objects. If you delete faces from a model, you will be asked if you also want to delete the associated vertexes. You would normally want to delete the vertexes as well, unless you plan to save them as markers for some future object.

Now that you've moved the Ground object so it doesn't interfere with the base of the building, let's render a view to see how it looks.

1. Click on the perspective view, then type **C**.
2. Select 3Dfront from the Camera selector dialog box, then click OK.
3. Choose Renderer ➤ Render View, then click on the perspective view.
4. At the Render Still Image dialog box, click Render. After a moment, you'll get a view similar to Figure 10.9.

Figure 10.9: The rendered view of the building with the ground plane

In this section, you've seen how the selection process works and how elements in 3D Studio can be edited. We've barely scratched the surface of the editing capabilities of the 3D Editor. In this section, we've given you the basic knowledge that you'll need to get started in rendering your models and in making minor adjustments to your models. Since all the editing functions operate similarly, you can have the confidence to explore new and unfamiliar tools in the 3D Editor on your own.

◆ Enhancing the Model with Materials

As you can see from the last rendering, the model is still quite cartoon-like. Once you've set up a light and a camera or two, you can start adding materials to the model to give it a more lifelike appearance.

If you worked through the AutoVision tutorial in Chapter 8, you saw how materials can add life to a model. The Materials feature of 3D Studio let you simulate surface color, texture, transparency, and even reflectance and roughness or bumpiness. You also have a great deal of control over these features through the Materials Editor. Before you actually start using materials, however, let's look at some basic issues you'll need to be aware of.

Understanding Bitmaps

To simulate a surface material, 3D Studio offers the Surface Materials Library. This is a library of simulated materials you can assign to objects. Each material contains properties such as color, reflectance, transparency, and roughness. Many materials also make use of image maps or "bitmaps" to simulate the look of complex surfaces like marble, wood, or brick.

A bitmap is an image file that shows a graphic sample of the material. A common bitmap image is marble. Another is brick. You might think of a material that uses bitmaps as a kind of decal or sticker that is placed on a surface.

There are actually seven ways to use bitmaps in the properties of a material:

- ◆ Texture maps
- ◆ Bump maps
- ◆ Opacity maps
- ◆ Specular maps
- ◆ Shininess maps
- ◆ Self-Illumination maps
- ◆ Reflection maps

Texture maps are the most common use of bitmaps. The following describes all the types of bitmaps you can have in 3D Studio.

Texture Maps

Brick is an example of a material available in 3D Studio that is a *texture* map. Whenever you assign the Brick material to an object, 3D Studio pastes a bitmap image of a brick wall to the object when it is rendered, so the objects looks like a brick surface (see Figure 10.10).

Figure 10.10: An example of a bitmap image (left) used as a texture map to simulate a brick wall

Bump Maps

You can also simulate a *bumpy* texture using grayscale bitmap images. Figure 10.11 shows a 2D bitmap image and an objects rendered with a material that uses the bitmap to simulate a bumpy surface. 3D Studio converts the different intensities of light and dark tones of the grayscale bitmap into high and low points on the bumpy surface. Color bitmaps can also be used for bump maps, though the color information itself is not used; just as with grayscale images, it is the intensity of the color that determines the bumpy texture.

Figure 10.11: A bumpy surface can be simulated using a grayscale bitmap, as shown at left. The light portions of the bitmap translate to high points in the bumpy surface while the darker portions of the bitmap translate to low points.

Opacity Maps

Opacity maps make use of grayscale bitmap images to control opacity and transparency. For example, you can turn a solid surface into an intricate filigree using an opacity map as shown in Figure 10.12.

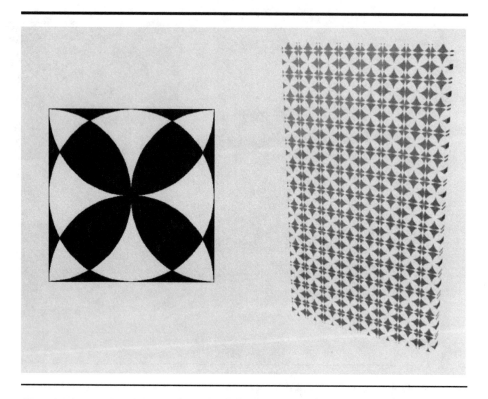

Figure 10.12: A single blank surface can be made to appear quite intricate using opacity maps. The bitmap image to the left was used to turn a simple rectangular object into an intricate screen.

Specular Maps

Specular maps (see Figure 10.13) are full-color image bitmaps that only appear in specular highlights of a surface. This type of map would be used to add subtle complexity to a material, like imperfections in a shiny surface.

Shininess Map

Shininess maps are gray-scale bitmaps that control the shininess of a surface by virtue of the bitmaps' grayscale intensity, with white being the shiniest and black the dullest (see Figure 10.13). Like Specular maps, shininess maps can be used to add complexity to a material's appearance.

Self-Illumination Maps

You can create materials that appear to glow using the self-illumination feature. A Self-illumination map (see Figure 10.13) is a grayscale bitmap image that lets you shape the "glow" of a surface based on the bitmap's grayscale intensity. White is the brightest glow while black is no glow at all.

Reflection Map

A reflection map is a special type of bitmap assignment. It is used where you want a material that appears to be reflective, like a glass office building or a lake or pond. The bitmap image you use will "move" just as reflections move when you pass by a reflective surface—see Figure 10.13.

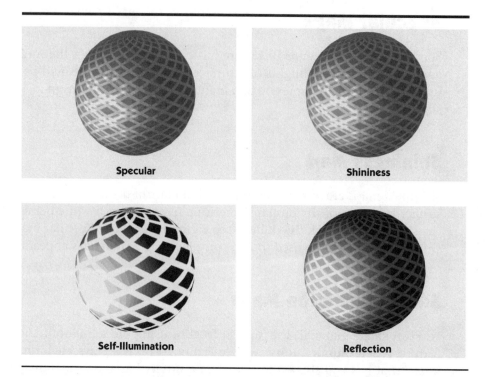

Figure 10.13: Samples of Specular, Shininess, Self-Illumination, and Reflection maps

Surface Properties

There are some materials that rely solely on the properties of color, reflectance, and transparency. Glass is a material that doesn't use a bitmap. Instead, it uses transparency and reflectance to simulate the appearance of glass. Unlike the Brick material, Glass doesn't require an image or pattern to simulate the appearance of glass (see Figure 10.14).

Figure 10.14: Examples of surface materials that do not require bitmaps

Most materials are a mixture of texture, bump, or opacity maps and properties like color, reflectance, or transparency. Bitmaps and material properties are combined to simulate detail you would otherwise find impossible to recreate through surface or solid modeling alone (see Figure 10.15).

Figure 10.15: A simple rectangular object with a single surface material that makes use of all the different types of maps and properties available in 3D Studio

◆ Adding Materials to Objects

For our tutorial, you'll start by selecting a few standard materials from a list and applying them to the model. Then after checking the appearance of the material with another rendering, you'll look at ways to adjust the material to better suit your model.

The glass in the model appears as an opaque blue material. 3D Studio offers a glass material that is both transparent and shiny. In the next exercise, you'll add the glass material to the model.

1. Choose Surface ➤ Material ➤ Choose. The Material Selector dialog box appears.

2. Use the scroll bar to the left to scroll down the list and locate Glass (or GLASS, as the case may be).

3. Highlight GLASS, then click on OK.

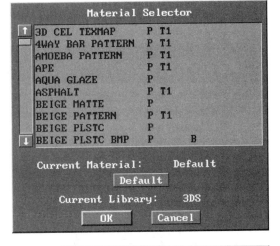

4. Choose Surface ➤ Material ➤ Assign ➤ By Name. The *Assign "GLASS" to:* dialog box appears.

5. Click on GLASS from this list. Notice that an asterisk appears next to the name. This indicates that the Glass material is assigned to the material called Glass. Remember that when you

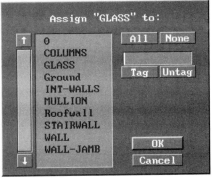

exported this file, objects were grouped by layer name. All the objects that were on the Glass layer in AutoCAD are now combined into an object called Glass in 3D Studio.

6. Click OK. A warning message pops up asking if you want to Assign material "GLASS" to tagged objects?. Click OK.

7. Now choose Renderer ➤ Render View, then click on the perspective view.

8. At the Render Still Image dialog box, click on the Render button. After a few moments, you'll see an image similar to Figure 10.16.

Figure 10.16: The building rendered with a glass material added

You've just added a material to an object. Through the method just shown, you can add materials based on the objects name. If you prefer, you can select objects from a viewport instead of from a list. To do this, you would use the Surfaces ➤ Materials ➤ Assign ➤ Object option in the command column. You can also assign materials to elements or even faces, instead of to complete objects. You may want to use the Select option described later in this chapter when assigning materials to elements or faces.

Now let's get back to the tutorial. The glass is transparent to the point that you don't even know it's there. We'll show you how to make adjustments to a material in the next section. For now, let's try adding another material to the model, but this time you'll select an object directly from a viewport.

Adding Materials Mapping

As I explained earlier, the glass material is a material that does not make use of a bitmap image. When you add a material that does use bitmaps, you need to tell 3D Studio how to align or map the bitmap to the object you want the material assigned to.

In the next exercise, you will add a material to the Ground object to make it seem more like a grassy lawn. The material you will use, Green Vines, uses a bitmap image to give the appearance of foliage.

As part of the exercise, you will assign a surface map to the Ground object to establish the orientation and size of the bitmap in relation to the object.

1. Choose Surface ➤ Material ➤ Choose.

2. At the Materials Selector dialog box, find and select Green Vines, then click OK.

3. Choose Surface ➤ Material ➤ Assign ➤ Object, then click on the Ground object you created earlier in this chapter.

4. At the *Assign "Green Vines" to:* dialog box, make sure you are assigning the material to Ground, then click OK.

5. Choose Renderer ➤ Render View, then click on the perspective view.

6. Click Render in the Render Still Scene dialog box. You get a warning dialog box.

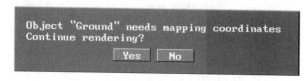

This dialog box reminds you that you need to apply mapping coordinates to the Ground object if you want to control the results, but asks if you want it to go ahead and render anyway.

7. Click No on the dialog box to stop the rendering process; we'll take its advice and apply the coordinates before we continue.

Mapping coordinates tell 3D Studio how to align texture maps to an object. This message is saying, in essence, that 3D Studio doesn't know how to orient the Green Vines texture map to the object's surface.

Now let's see how we apply a mapping coordinate to an object.

1. Choose Surfaces ➤ Mapping ➤ Type. Notice the options that appear in the command column: Planar, Spherical, and Cylindrical.

2. Make sure Planar is selected by clicking on it. You can tell it is selected by the asterisk that appears in front of it.

3. Now choose Adjust from the Surfaces ➤ Mapping options. You see a new set of options appear.

4. Click on View Align from the new list in the command column.

5. At the `Click in viewport to align map icon` prompt, click in the plan view of the model in the upper left viewport to make it active, then click in the viewport again. If you look very carefully at the viewport you will see a yellow and green icon appear with a point (see Figure 10.18a).

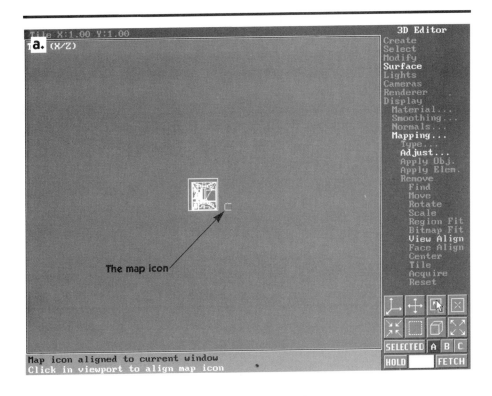

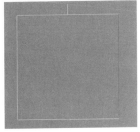

Figure 10.17: *Top:* The area covered by the bitmap image is shown by an icon in the upper left viewport. *Bottom:* Detail of the icon.

This icon represents the area covered by the bitmap image used in the Green Vines image (see Figure 10.17). It is a visual aid for showing you the scale and orientation of the mapping coordinates. I'll explain this icon in more detail after this exercise.

6. Choose Apply Obj. from the Surface ➤ Mapping options in the command column, then click on the Ground object. The Apply Mapping Coordinates dialog box appears.

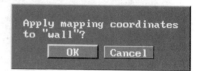

7. Click OK to accept the mapping coordinate assignment.

8. Choose Renderer ➤ Render View, then click on the perspective view.

9. Click Render in the Render Still Scene dialog box. After a few moments your model appears rendered (see Figure 10.18b).

Figure 10.18: The model rendered with the Ground surface material

◆ Understanding Mapping Coordinates

The mapping coordinate you added in the last exercise told 3D Studio the size, location, and orientation of the material on the object it is assigned to. At render time, the image is usually applied to the object in a repeated or "tiled" fashion. You can also set a material to apply the bitmap just once, as with a label on a wine bottle.

What Happened When You Added the Mapping Coordinate

The map icon you saw in step 5 is a visual representation of the mapping coordinates. Its shape and color are aids in helping you see the bitmap's orientation more clearly. The point at the top of the icon represents the top, while the green shows the right side. These indicators can tell you at a glance whether the bitmap image of the material you are using is upside-down, mirrored, or backward in relation to the object to which the coordinates are being applied (see Figure 10.19).

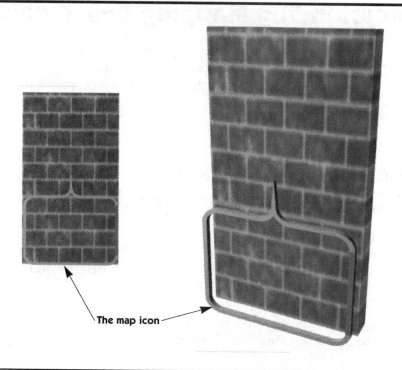

The map icon

Figure 10.19: The map icon in relation to a material bitmap

The orientation of the bitmap in this exercise is really not that important, but it can be important for texture maps that do have a specific orientation like a brick pattern, or a single image such as a wine label or a road sign.

Figure 10.20a shows the map icon in relation to the Ground object. As it appears in step 5, the icon represents the outline of the bitmap image associated with the Green Vines material. Figure 10.20b shows the relationship of the map icon and the bitmap image, as well as the resulting rendered Ground object as seen from the top view.

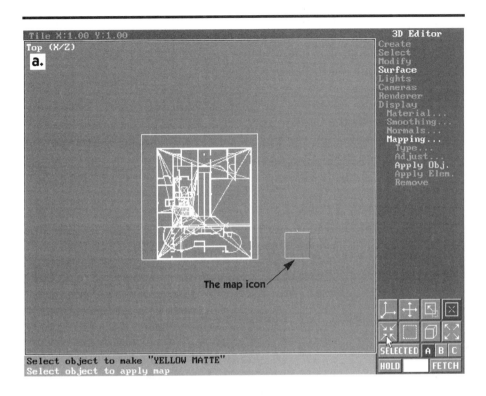

The map icon

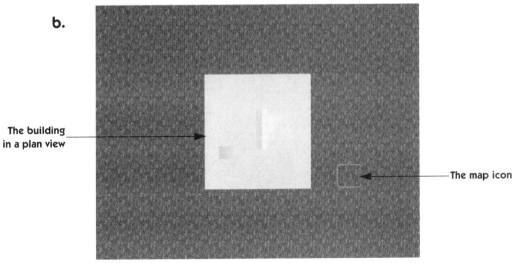

The building
in a plan view

The map icon

Figure 10.20: A comparison of the map icon and the actual bitmap image as it is
applied to the Ground object

Notice that the map icon shows the approximate size of the bitmap in relation to the object to which it is being applied. When the model is rendered, multiple copies of the image are then applied over the entire surface of the object like tiles on a kitchen counter.

You can alter the size and orientation of the map icon, which in turn alters the way the bitmap is applied to the object (see Figure 10.21). But once the mapping is applied to an object, it doesn't change until the mapping is altered and reapplied. For example, you can rotate and scale the map icon, but unless you use the Surface ➤ Mapping ➤ Apply Obj. option from the command column, and assign the new mapping coordinates to the object, the object will maintain its old mapping coordinates. This allows you to apply different mapping coordinates to different objects without affecting each other's mapping coordinate.

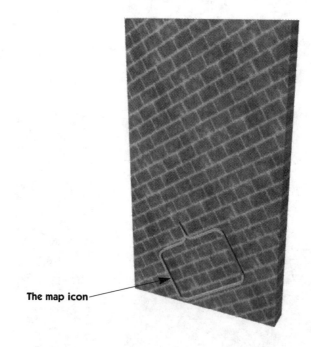

The map icon

Figure 10.21: Changing the mapping coordinates and reassigning them to the object will alter the object's appearance. This is a rendering of the brick wall example with the mapping scaled down and rotated.

Finding the Map Icon

In step 4 of the last exercise, you selected an option called View Align from the Surface ➤ Mapping options. This option turned the map icon around to be parallel with the selected view. This is significant because mapping coordinates can get lost easily in a model. The View Align option offers a quick way to orient the map icon, and therefore the mapping coordinates, to a particular orientation as defined by a view.

Another important tool for finding the map icon is the Surface ➤ Mapping ➤ Adjust ➤ Find option. This option changes the scale of the map icon to fill the currently active viewport. You use it by first selecting the viewport in which you want to locate the map icon, then choosing Surfaces ➤ Mapping ➤ Adjust ➤ Find. You see a dialog box asking if you really want to "Rescale map icon to viewport." Once you click OK, the map icon is scaled to fit the viewport. When used together, View Align and Find can help you quickly locate the map icon.

Adjusting the Map Icon

You have a number of options to control the size, shape and orientation of the map icon. These will be crucial to your ability to accurately place materials on an object or face. Table 10.1 provides descriptions of all the Surface ➤ Mapping ➤ Adjust options as they appear in the command column.

Table 10.1: The Command Column's Surface ➤ Mapping ➤ Adjust Options

Option	Description
Find	Changes the scale of the map icon to fill the currently active viewport. You use it by first selecting the viewport in which you want to locate the map icon, then choose the option.
Move	Lets you move the map icon around in your model. As with moving objects, camera, and lights, you can restrain the movement with the Tab key.
Rotate	Lets you rotate the map icon. You are shown the rotation angle in the Status line at the top of the screen for greater accuracy.
Scale	Allows you to scale the map icon. You are shown the scale percentage in the Status line at the top of the screen as you adjust the map icon size.
Region Fit	Lets you fit the map icon to a specific rectangular area. This is useful for situations where you want a texture map to fit exactly over an object, like an aerial photograph on a 3D topographical map. When you choose this option you are prompted to select two points. These two points define the opposite corners of the map icon. The process is similar to selecting a zoom window or creating a rectangle in AutoCAD. Since this option lets you select any two points, it will stretch and distort the map icon in either the X or Y axis. To orient the map icon right-side-up, pick two points over the region starting with the upper left corner (see Figure 10.22).

Table 10.1: The Command Column's Surface ➤ Mapping ➤ Adjust Options (continued)

Option	Description
Bitmap Fit	Adjusts the map icon's proportion to fit the shape of a particular bitmap image. This option is helpful if your material definition uses a bitmap that is not square, and you want a better idea of its shape as you assign the mapping coordinates to objects. Before you use this option, you must know the name of the bitmap file used by the material in question.
View Align	Aligns the map icon to a viewport. See the description in the earlier section.
Face Align	Aligns the map icon to a selected face.
Center	Centers the map icon on an object's surface.
Tile	Similar to Scale, only this option lets you set the number of times the bitmap image is repeated within the map icon (see Figure 10.23).
Acquire	Sets the map icon to match the mapping coordinates of an object that already has mapping coordinates assigned to it.
Reset	Resets the map icon to the 3D Studio default size and orientation.

a.

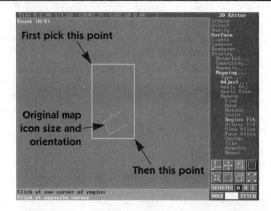

b.

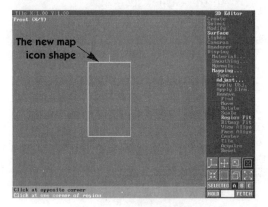

c.

Figure 10.22: Using the Region Fit option to fit a brick texture map to the entire surface of the brick wall sample. The bottom image shows the rendered result.

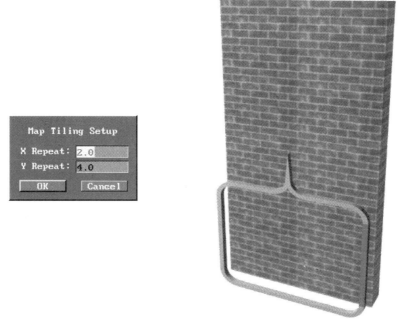

Figure 10.23: The Tile option allows you to set multiple images within the map icon area. In this example, the icon map size is the same as in Figure 10.19 but the Map Tiling options have been changed to 2 for the X axis and 4 for the Y axis, as shown in the dialog box at left.

Understanding the Different Types of Mapping

The first thing I asked you to do in the last exercise was to set the surface mapping *type*. The default is Planar. As you might guess from its name, this type maps the bitmap image to a planar or flat surface as shown in Figure 10.23. This option projects a flat image onto a surface. While this may sound fairly simplistic, you have a great deal of flexibility in how that map is placed on a surface, by aligning the map icon in a variety of different ways. Figure 10.24 shows how the same texture map can be projected onto a box with different effects.

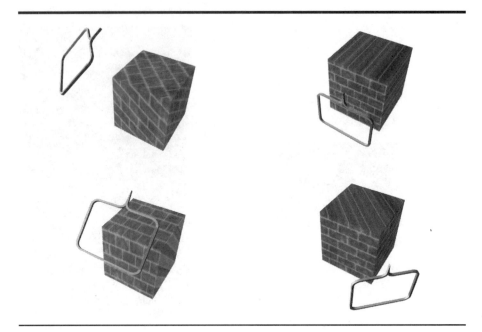

Figure 10.24: A box with mapping coordinates oriented in different ways. The texture map is identical in each example.

But what do you do if you want to map an image to a cylindrical or spherical object? 3D Studio offers the Cylindrical and Spherical map types to facilitate nonplanar surfaces.

The Cylindrical type curves the bitmap into a cylindrical shape, then projects the map outward from the center of the cylinder. Naturally, you would normally use this type of mapping on cylindrical objects. You should also generally place such a map in the center of the object.

When you choose this mapping type, the map icon changes to a cylindrical one as shown in Figure 10.25a. You would then place this map in the center of a cylindrical object, and assign it to the object. You can also distort the map by moving the map icon closer to one side or the other, or rotating the map so it isn't aligned with the object.

a.

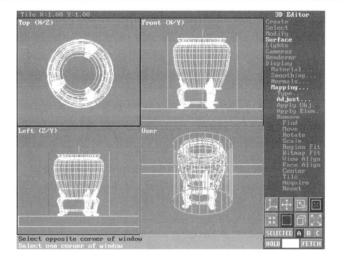

b.

Figure 10.25: A view of the map icon when using the Cylindrical mapping type, along with a sample of an object that uses this mapping type

The Spherical mapping type curves the bitmap into a spherical shape, then projects the map outward in all directions. One use of this mapping type is a model of the earth. You could use the Spherical mapping type to place a flat map of the earth on a sphere.

As with the Cylindrical mapping type, the map icon changes to a different shape when the Spherical mapping type is chosen, as shown in Figure 10.26. You would place this map in the center of the spherical shape that requires mapping. As with the other two map types, you can distort the map by placing the map icon closer to one side of the object.

Figure 10.26: A view of the map icon when using the Spherical mapping type, along with a sample of an object that uses this type

While we've suggested that you use each map type with its corresponding object shape, you can achieve some unusual effects by mixing map types with different surfaces. For example, if you use a planar map on a cylinder, the image is stretched as it is projected toward the edge of cylinder as shown in Figure 10.27.

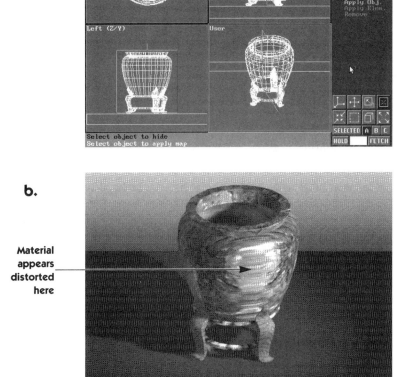

Figure 10.27: A sample of a planar map used on a cylindrical surface

The mapping coordinate tools we've been discussing give you a high degree of control over the way your material assignments affect your model. Like a lot of 3D Studio tools, your skill in using them will develop over time. Like any craft, practice makes perfect!

◆ Editing Materials

The last time you rendered your Villa Savoye model, the glass was virtually invisible and the ground color and texture looked too strong and unnatural. In this section, you'll learn how to use the Materials Editor to adjust both the Glass and Green Vines materials to improve your image.

Adjusting Bitmap Strength

We'll start our exploration of the Materials Editor by making a few changes to the Green Vines material. In the last rendering, the ground looked unnatural. Let's adjust the material so it looks a bit more like grass. You might think of the Materials Editor as a very big Properties dialog box that enables you to control the properties of materials.

1. Choose Programs ➤ Materials from the pull-down menu. Your screen will change to display the Materials Editor.

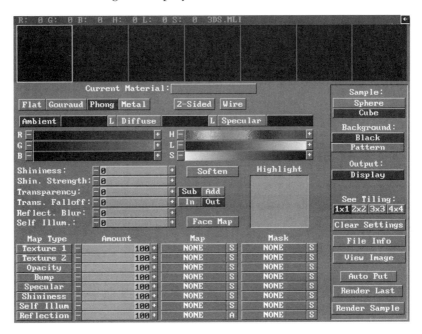

This screen is quite different from the 3D Editor, but the functions are fairly easy to understand once you've gone through them.

2. Move the cursor to the top of the screen. Notice that, just as in the 3D Editor, a pull-down menu bar appears.

3. The first thing you need to do is retrieve the Green Vines material from the model. From the pull-down menu, choose Material ➤ Get From Scene, which brings up the Get Material From Scene dialog box.

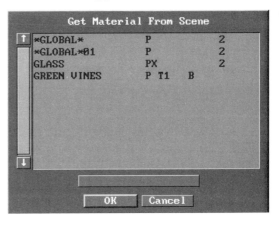

4. Click on Green Vines from the list, then click OK. You will see a sample of green vines appear in the upper left corner.

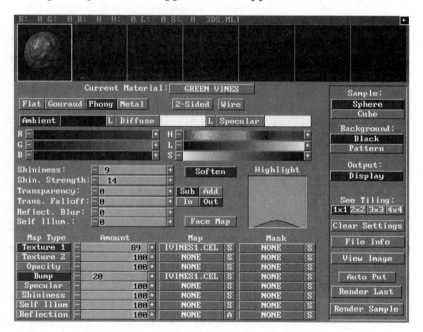

The sample shows the Green Vines material on a spherical surface. In your model, however, you will be using this material on a flat surface. You can get a preview image on a cube instead of a sphere, which will be preferable for your model. Here's how to change the preview image.

1. In the right side of the screen, you see a column of options under the heading Sample. Click on the button labeled Cube to highlight it.

2. At the bottom of this column, click on Render Sample. The sample appears on a cube.

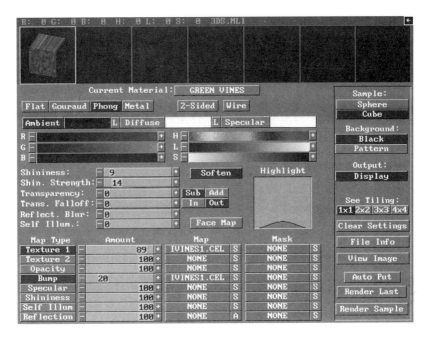

Now the sample gives us a better idea of what the Green Vines material looks like, and it certainly looks similar to the sample in our model. This material is a bit too strong for our purposes, however. We need to tone it down for our ground plane. Here's how we do it.

1. Click and drag the sample image from the far left to the next box to the right.

2. You see a dialog box asking you if you want to copy the material.

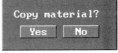

Click Yes. You see a copy of the material in the second box from the left. This gives us a copy of the material settings that we can play with without affecting the original settings. It also lets us compare two settings side-by-side. As you can see from all the frames available, you can make many copies and variations.

3. In the lower left corner of the screen, you see a column of sliders under the heading Amount. To the left, you see another column under the heading Map Type. Underneath the Amount column, move the Texture 1 slider to the left. As you move it, notice that the number displayed within the slider changes.

4. Place the slider so the number shows 20. By doing this, you have decreased the strength of the Texture Map1 map type to less than a quarter of its original value of 89.

5. Click on the Render Sample button again. The sample shows that the colors aren't so strong. It now appears grayer and less mottled.

When you reduced the strength of the texture map in step 4, you reduced the amount of color in the material. This is because the bitmap image used for the texture is a color image, and reducing its strength reduces its color.

Before we go on, take a look over the other options in the bottom third of the screen.

Map Type	Amount		Map		Mask	
Texture 1	−	20	+	IVINES1.CEL	S	NONE	S
Texture 2	−	100	+	NONE	S	NONE	S
Opacity	−	100	+	NONE	S	NONE	S
Bump	−	20	+	IVINES1.CEL	S	NONE	S
Specular	−	100	+	NONE	S	NONE	S
Shininess	−	100	+	NONE	S	NONE	S
Self Illum	−	100	+	NONE	S	NONE	S
Reflection	−	100	+	NONE	A	NONE	S

In the Map Type column, you see the options we discussed earlier in the introduction to this section. You've also seen firsthand how the Amount column affects the material in the previous exercise. The Map column lets you select the actual bitmap file for the map type listed on the left. The Mask column lets you select a masking bitmap for the map type. This last option lets you use a grayscale bitmap to vary the intensity of the main bitmap listed under the Map column. In the Mask bitmap, white lets the full intensity of the main bitmap through, gray decreases intensity, and black completely blocks intensity.

Adjusting the Material Color

We don't want the ground to appear as gray as the sample shows, since we are trying to simulate a grassy field. With the strength of the Texture map diminished, you can add color using the color slide bars that are just below the sample images.

Using the Color Slidebars

You'll start by adjusting the colors for the Ambient light setting.

1. Click on the Ambient button at the upper left side of the screen.

2. Click and drag the cursor over the slidebar labeled L near the middle of the screen. Notice that a white bar on the slide bar follows your motion.

3. Adjust the H and S slidebars so the white bar is in the position shown below. Notice that the color of the bar next to the Ambient button changes to a new color.

4. Click on the Render Sample button to see what the new settings do to the material.

The H, L, and S of the slidebars stand for Hue, Luminance, and Strength. The Hue slider controls the actual color as displayed on the slide bar itself. The Luminance slider controls the brightness of the color. The Strength slider controls the strength of the color set in the Hue slide bar. With the Strength slider all the way to the left, the color remains gray. Moving the Strength slider to the right increases the strength of the color selected in the Hue slide bar.

You can also control color using the R, G, and B (Red, Green, and Blue) sliders to the left of the H, L, S sliders. You may notice that these sliders move automatically as you move the H, L, and S sliders.

Copying Color Settings

The material is still too gray. Let's try adding color to the Diffuse setting, which appears next to the Ambient setting. This time, instead of using the slide bar, you'll simply copy the Ambient setting.

1. Click and hold the color bar next to the Ambient button.

2. Drag the cursor away from the bar. Notice that a rectangle appears and moves with the cursor.

3. Place your cursor on the bar next to the Diffuse button. The color from the Ambient setting is copied to the Diffuse setting.

4. Click on the Render Sample button to see the result.

You may be wondering what the differences between the Ambient, Diffuse, and Specular color settings are, especially after changing the Ambient setting with little effect. These three color settings control the intensity and color of the light being *reflected* from a surface for each type of light they refer to. Hence, the Ambient setting controls the intensity and color of reflected ambient light. Ambient lighting is the general lighting in a model and can be adjusted in the Lights ➤ Ambient option. Right now, it is set so low that the changes you copied over to the Diffuse button have little effect; there isn't enough ambient light to be reflected.

The Diffuse setting controls the color and intensity of reflected omni or spot lights. Since spot lights are the predominant light source in the model in the exercise, the Diffuse setting has the greatest effect on the overall color of the material.

The Specular setting controls the color and intensity of any specular reflection from omni or spotlights. It controls the color of the "hot spot" from reflected lights. This setting has little effect on surfaces that have little or no reflectance.

By adjusting these different color settings, you can create some very realistic materials. They are especially helpful in creating metallic materials.

Moving the New Material to the 3D Editor

Now more of the material sample shows a green color. Let's place this new version of Green Vines back into the model and render it to see if it's what we want.

1. Click on the button labeled Green Vines near the top of the screen. The New Name For Material dialog box appears.

2. Type **Green Grass** and click OK.

3. To show you that you still have a copy of the old material, Green Vines, click on the sample view in the far left. Notice that the name in the Current Materials button changes back to Green Vines, and the color settings revert to the original values.

4. Click on the second sample from the left to return to the material you just created, Green Grass.

5. Choose Material ➤ Put To Current from the pull-down menu. The New Current Material Name dialog box appears with the name Green Grass.

6. Click OK, then choose Programs ➤ 3D Editor from the pull-down menu.

7. Choose Surface ➤ Material ➤ Assign ➤ Object. Notice that the prompt line shows the prompt `Select object to make "Green Grass"`.

8. Click on the Ground object.

9. At the Assign dialog box, click OK.

Now you are ready to render your view again to check the Green Grass material. You don't necessarily want to render the whole image. You have the option to render just a portion of the image to save time. Here's how it's done.

1. Choose Renderer ➤ Render Region.

2. In the lower right viewport, window the ground region shown in Figure 10.28.

3. At the Render dialog box, click on Render. After the rendering messages, you see the image shown at the bottom of Figure 10.28.

a.

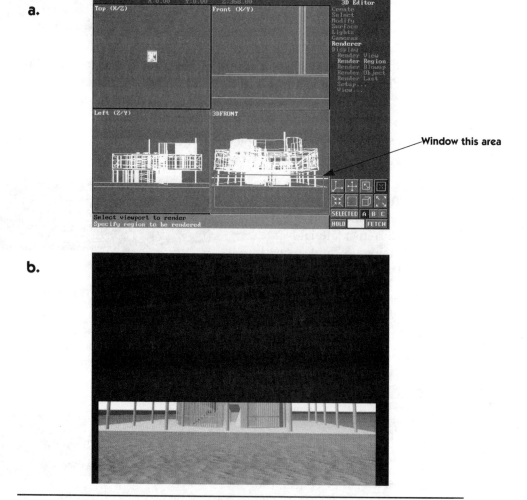

Window this area

b.

Figure 10.28: Windowing the region shown above lets you render just the "Green Grass" ground material

As you've gathered, rendering in 3D Studio is a cyclical process of rendering, adjusting, then rendering again. By allowing you to render your model in portions, the program can reduce the time you spend in these revision cycles.

You may have noticed a few other Render options. Here's a list with a brief description.

Render Blowup   Similar to Render Region, but instead of rendering to the same size as the overall view, expands the region you select to fill the screen.

Render Object   Renders only the objects you select.

Render Last   Repeats the last rendering option you used with any changes you may have made to the model.

Adjusting Color and Transparency

In the last section, you were introduced to several of the basic tools in the Materials Editor. In this section, you'll continue your exploration of the Materials Editor by making adjustments to the glass material.

In previous full-screen renderings, the glass appeared to have disappeared entirely from the model, because the current glass material is a bit too transparent. The following exercise will demonstrate how transparency can be controlled.

1. Choose Program ➤ Materials to return to the Materials Editor.

2. Click on the next blank sample image box at the top of the screen to the right of the Green Grass sample.

3. Choose Material ➤ Get From Scene.

4. At the Get Material From Scene dialog box, choose GLASS, then click OK.

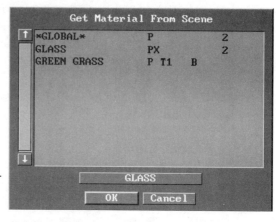

5. Notice that, if the current rendered sample box shows anything at all at this point, it is very faint. To help visualize transparent materials, 3D Studio offers a background for the sample.

6. In the column of options to the right side of the screen, choose Pattern under the Background heading.

7. Click on Render Sample again. You see a colored checkerboard pattern appear in the sample box. If you look very carefully, you'll see that there is indeed a sample image, but it's very faint.

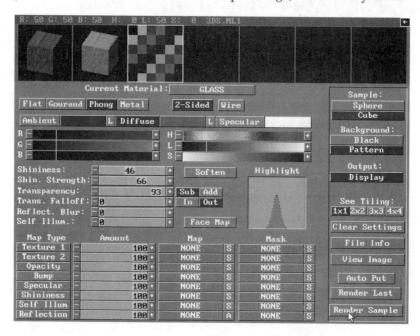

We already know from our rendering that the glass material is perhaps a bit too transparent, and the sample rendering confirms this for us. Let's try decreasing its transparency so the glass can be detected in the rendered view.

1. In the column of slide bars in the middle left of the screen, locate the one labeled Transparency.

2. Move this slider to the left until its value reads 66.

3. Now click on Render Sample. A clearly defined image appears in the sample box.

Now let's add a bit more color to the glass to help us to detect it in the rendering.

1. Click on the Diffuse button just above the color slide bars.

2. Move the H, L, and S sliders so they look similar to the settings shown below. Once you've made the settings, the Diffuse box shows a very slight blue tint.

3. Click on the Render Sample button again. Now the sample also shows a very slight blue tint.

Now let's place the adjusted glass material back into the model. In the exercise with the Green Grass material, you placed a new material into the model. In this exercise, you'll replace an existing material.

1. Choose Material ➤ Put To Scene. 3D Studio brings up a message asking you to confirm that you want to replace an existing material with the new settings.

2. Click OK.

3. Choose Program ➤ 3D Editor.

4. Choose Renderer ➤ Render View, then go ahead and render the perspective view. You will have a rendering similar to Figure 10.29.

5. Since this is the last exercise of this chapter, save the file as
Savoye6. You will continue editing this file in the next chapter.

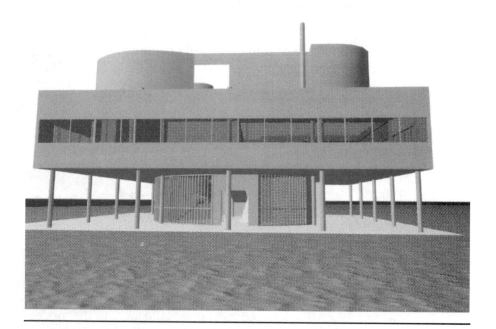

Figure 10.29: The rendering with the glass material adjusted

The glass is now more apparent, though still quite subtle. Notice that
you didn't have to reassign the material to the glass. Since you replaced
the old glass material with the new one, 3D Studio now uses the new
materials properties when it renders the model.

Mapping Materials to All the Faces of an Object

Before we close this chapter, I'd like to discuss one problem with mapping coordinates, and offer a solution. You may have noticed back in Figure 10.24 that when an object receives a mapping coordinate, the texture is projected through the object. Faces that are perpendicular to the mapping coordinate face show streaks instead of the texture map. In many situations, you will want the map to appear on all the different faces of the object. To allow for this situation, 3D Studio offers the Face Map option in the Materials Editor (see Figure 10.30).

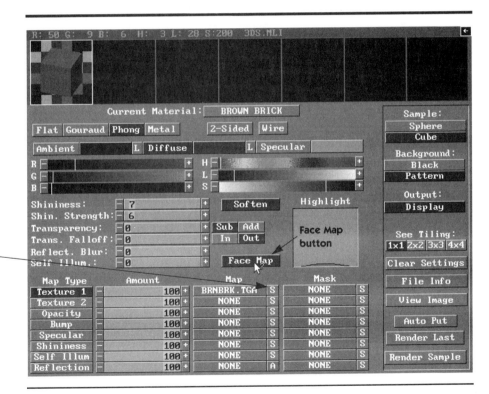

Figure 10.30: The Materials Editor with the Face Map option selected

When this option is selected, the material will be projected onto each face of the object as shown in Figure 10.31. Unfortunately, the Face Map option ignores any mapping coordinates you may have applied to the object, so it is more difficult to control the orientation of the material. In situations where you need absolute control of the orientation of the material, you may need to detach the faces of the object and assign mapping coordinates and materials to each face individually.

Figure 10.31: A sample rendering using the brick material with the Face Map option turned on

If the image orientation isn't a problem but the scaling is, you do have the option to change the scaling of the material when using the Face Map option. To do this, you click on the button labeled S next to the Map option button, the one that determines which bitmap file to use for the material (see Figure 10.30). When you click on the S button, you see the Mapping Parameters dialog box shown in Figure 10.32.

Mapping Parameters

Tile   Decal   Both   Ignore Map Alpha

Filtering: Pyramidal Summed Area

Blur: —   10   +

Mirror   Negative

U Scale: 0.25   V Scale: 0.25
U Offset: 0.0   V Offset: 0.0

Rotation Angle: 0.0

Source: RGB   RGB Luma Tint Alpha Tint
         RGB Tint

OK   Cancel

Figure 10.32: The Mapping Parameters dialog box

This dialog box offers the U Scale and V scale options. These two options let you set the scale of the bitmap image in relation to the surface it is being assigned to. In Figure 10.32 the U and V scales are set to .25, which causes the bitmap to be reduced to one quarter of its normal size. Figure 10.33 shows the result of this setting on the same object that was shown in Figure 10.31.

Figure 10.33: The object rendered with the brick material's Mapping Parameters U and V scale setting set to 0.25

The brick sample shows how orientation is affected by the Face Map option. Other materials like square tiles or sand and stucco textures would not pose the problem of improper orientation.

◆ Summary

You haven't quite finished your rendering, but you've gotten a good start. In this chapter, I've introduced to you the different ways you can edit your model. You've seen that by making changes to materials, you can greatly alter the appearance of your rendering. The Materials Editor is a powerful tool, so you will want to get as familiar with it as possible.

Chapter 11 takes you deeper into the Materials Editor's features. There, you'll also learn more about lighting and how to add a background scene.

Controlling Lights and Materials

In the last two chapters, you were shown the basic operations of the 3D Editor and the Materials Editor. You even got to do a crude animation. In this chapter, you'll concentrate on the same editors to develop a better understanding of how they work. Once you've mastered their use, there won't be anything you can't model or render!

You'll start by making some adjustments to the model in the 3D Editor, adding a background scene and adjusting some lights. Next, you'll focus on the Materials Editor by creating some props and further editing some existing materials. Toward the end of the chapter, you'll learn some new ways of editing and creating objects in 3D Studio. You'll wrap things up by creating a night scene.

◆ Adding a Background

In the movie industry, artists are employed to produce background images (called mattes) to simulate a special environment, in order to fool you into thinking a scene was shot in mountainous terrain, in the middle of an ocean, or inside a space station, when in fact it was shot on a sound stage in Hollywood. You can employ a similar technique using 3D Studio's Background option.

The following exercise will show you how you can quickly add a sky to your model by adding a bitmap image for a background.

1. Start 3D Studio and load Savoye5.3DS.

2. Choose Renderer ➤ Setup ➤ Background. The Background Method dialog box appears.

3. Click on the button labeled Bitmap so it becomes highlighted.

4. Click on the blank bar to the right of the Bitmap button. The Bitmap For Rendered Background dialog box appears.

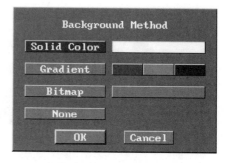

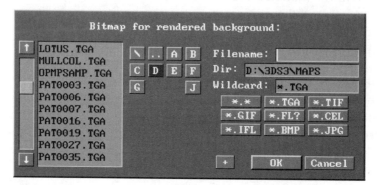

Notice the set of buttons to the lower right. These indicate the bitmap file types you can use for this option.

5. Click on the button labeled *.JPG. This is a typical file name extension for JPEG compressed bitmap image files.

6. In the scrolling list to the left, locate SUNSET.JPG and click on it. SUNSET.JPG appears in the Filename input box in the upper right.

7. Click OK, then click OK at the Background Method dialog box.

8. Render the perspective view. Your rendering will look similar to Figure 11.1.

Figure 11.1: The model rendered with a background image

Matching Your Perspective View to a Background

One key advantage of being able to add a background is that you can place your model in a photograph of a real site. If you convert your photograph into a computer image file, preferably in a format that is listed in the Bitmap For Rendered Background dialog box seen in the previous exercise, you can then assign it as a background for your rendering.

Another advantage to using a background is that it can help reduce rendering time. If your model contains objects in the background that do not change, you might consider rendering them separately, then using them as a background. That way, 3D Studio won't have to render them as 3D objects every time you render your model.

To match the perspective view of your model to the background image, you can have 3D Studio display a simplified grayscale version of the background in the Perspective viewport. Here's how it's done.

1. Choose Views ➤ See Backgrnd. After a few moments, a grayscale facsimile of the background image will appear in the viewport.

2. Make camera adjustments until your model perspective view matches the background perspective. In addition, you have some limited control over the facsimile image using the Views ➤ Adj Backgrnd option in the pull-down menu.

If you've created a background scene from objects in your model, and you want to "turn off" those objects, you can do so by following these steps:

1. Choose Display ➤ Hide ➤ Object from the command column.

2. Click on individual objects you want to hide from your rendering, or click on By Name or By Color in the command column to select objects to hide by name or color. Also notice that you can hide cameras and lights.

To restore objects that have been hidden, choose Display ➤ Unhide, then select the appropriate option from those that appear at the bottom of the command column. For example, Display ➤ Unhide ➤ All will unhide all hidden objects.

◆ Adding Effects with Light and Shadow

You've seen how a single spotlight can be used to simulate the Sun.
You can also use lighting to add emphasis or provide a sense of drama.
Shadows can be controlled to provide a seemingly sharp, strong light
source or a softer, more diffuse interior light. In this section, you'll take
a look at some of the more commonly used lighting options.

Adding Shadows

You will want to add some shadows to the model to give it a bit more
depth and realism. Also, you can add some highlight to the glass so it
stands out a bit more clearly.

First let's turn on some shadows.

1. Choose Lights ➤ Spot ➤ Adjust.
2. Click on the spotlight you created to represent the Sun.
3. At the Spotlight Definition dialog box, click on the Cast Shadow
   button in the lower left.
4. Click OK.
5. Render the perspective view. You see an image similar to
   Figure 11.2.

Figure 11.2: The rendered model with shadows turned on

The shadows appear in our model, but they seem to have missed the columns. They are a bit too "soft" for our model. To sharpen the shadow, you have several options. If you find that shadows start to pull away from columns, as in the last rendering, you can decrease the shadow *bias*. Here's how it's done.

1. Choose Renderer ➤ Setup ➤ Shadows. The Global Shadow Control dialog box appears.

> Global Shadow Control
> Light: (Global)
>
> Map bias: 2.0   Ray trace bias: 0.2
> Map size: 300
> Map sample range: 5.0
>
> Shadow Maps   Ray Trace
>
> OK   Cancel

2. In the Map Bias input box, change the value from 2.0 to **.2**.

3. Click OK, then render the model again using the Render View option. You see a view similar to Figure 11.3.

Figure 11.3: The shadows rendered with a Map bias setting at .2

Sharpening Shadows

If you look carefully, you see that the shadows for the columns are now forming. The next thing you will want to do is sharpen the shadow. Two options in the Global Shadow Control dialog box will help you accomplish this: Map Size and Map Sample Range.

Map Size controls the resolution of the 3D Studio *shadow map*. A shadow map is a temporary bitmap image of the shadows cast by objects in the model. You never actually see this bitmap. 3D Studio uses it, however, to calculate where the shadows will appear and what they will look like. If the shadow map is a small size, it creates a shadow that is rough around the edges, like a low-resolution rendering. A larger shadow map makes for a more detailed shadow. If the shadow map size is too great, of course, it will consume greater amounts of memory and add to the amount of time it takes to render.

Map Sample Range controls the softness of the edge of the shadow. A smaller map sample value makes for a sharper shadow.

1. Choose Renderer ➤ Setup ➤ Shadows.
2. In the Map Size input box, change the value from 300 to **1024**.
3. In the Map Sample Range input box, change the value from 5 to **3**.
4. Click OK, then render the model again using the Render Object option. You see a view similar to Figure 11.4.

Figure 11.4: The shadows rendered with a larger shadow map and lower map sample range

In the last exercise, you saw how you can sharpen the shadow edge by increasing the shadow map size and reducing the map sample range in the Global Shadow Control dialog box. Another way to sharpen the shadow is to minimize the difference between the spotlight's Hotspot and Falloff values. These control the softness of the edge of a spotlight where it strikes a surface. Figure 11.5 shows two samples of a spotlight, with the hotspot and falloff at different distances.

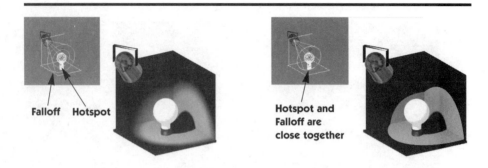

Falloff   Hotspot

Hotspot and
Falloff are
close together

Figure 11.5: The effects of distances between a spotlight's hotspot and falloff

You can change the Hotspot and Falloff settings using the Lights ➤ Spot ➤ Adjust option. This opens the Spotlight Definition dialog box as shown in Figure 11.6. Notice the two hotspot and falloff settings pointed out in the figure. You can also use the Lights ➤ Spot ➤ Hotspot option to visually set the hotspot and falloff on your model.

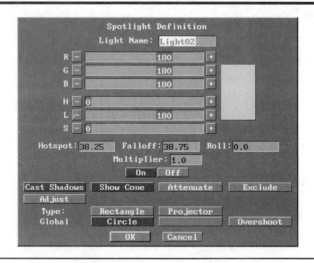

Figure 11.6: Hotspot and Falloff settings in the Spotlight Definition dialog box

If you want the shadows to be as sharp as possible, to simulate a bright sunlit day for example, you can switch to a Ray Trace shadow. These shadows take much longer to render, so you will want to use this option sparingly.

1. Choose Renderer ➤ Setup ➤ Shadows. The Global Shadow Control dialog box appears.

2. Click on the Ray Trace button. Neither the Shadow Map Size or Map Sample Range setting have any effect on Ray Traced shadows.

3. Click OK, then choose Renderer ➤ Render View and click on the perspective view. After a minute or two, your rendered image will appear with sharp, distinct shadow edges (see Figure 11.7).

4. IMPORTANT: In order the keep the rendering time down for the rest of this chapter, open the Global Shadow Control dialog box again and click on the Shadow Maps button to turn off the Ray Trace shadow option.

Figure 11.7: A rendering of the building using Ray Traced shadows

If you prefer, you can control shadows on a light-by-light basis, instead of using a global setting. To do this, choose Lights ➤ Spot ➤ Adjust, then click on the light that is casting the shadow. At the Spotlight Definition dialog box, click on the Adjust button just below the Cast Shadow button. The Local Shadow Control dialog box appears. This dialog box is identical to the Global Shadow Control dialog box except that it has the addition of the Use Global Settings button. By clicking on the Shadow Maps button to highlight it, you turn the control of shadows over to the settings in the Local Shadow Control dialog box.

Note *If it seems like the changes you are making in the Global Shadow Control dialog box don't have any effect, check the Local Shadow Control dialog box for the light in question. (While having both local and global control over shadows is helpful, it can also lead to confusion if not carefully used.)*

Adding a Highlight

By adding a highlight, you will be able to see that there is indeed glass in the windows, and it adds bit of interest to the rendering.

1. Choose Lights ➤ Omni ➤ Create.

2. Pick a place for this new Omni light anywhere in the plan view toward the front of the building (see Figure 11.8a).

3. At the Light Definition dialog box, move the Luminance (L) slider down to around **80** (we don't want the highlight to be too strong) and then click on Create.

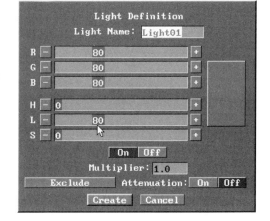

4. Click on Lights ➤ Omni ➤ Place Hilite.

5. At the `Click at point to receive highlight` prompt, click on the point shown in Figure 11.8b in the perspective view. In a moment you'll see the prompt message "Click on a light source for highlight."

6. Click on the Omni light you just created. Another moment will pass as 3D Studio moves the selected light to a proper location to create the desired highlight.

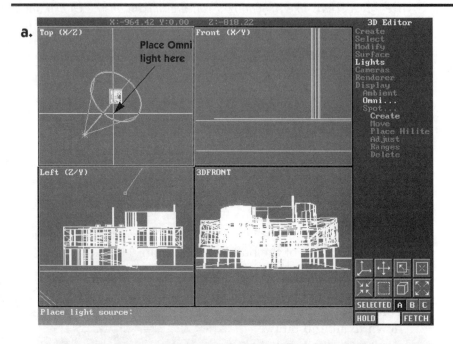

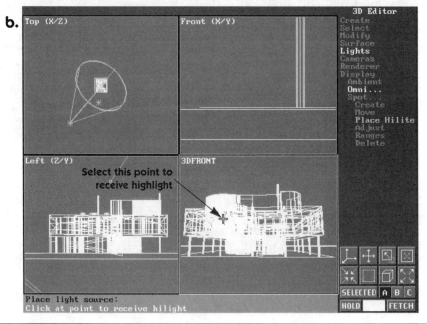

Figure 11.8: Placing an Omni light and locating the highlight

You don't want the highlight light source to affect anything other than the glass, otherwise the surfaces will appear too bright. You can control what gets light and what doesn't by using the Adjust option.

1. Choose Lights ➤ Omni ➤ Adjust.

2. Click on the Omni light you added in the last exercise.

3. At the Light Definition dialog box, click on the button labeled Exclude. The Exclude Objects dialog box appears.

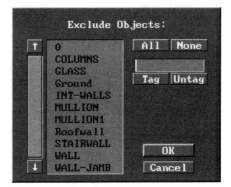

4. Click on the All button. Notice that an asterisk appears on every item in the list of objects to the left.

5. Click on Glass from the list to deselect it. The asterisk is removed from Glass. You've just set up the light to highlight only the glass by excluding all other objects.

6. Click OK, then click OK again at the Light Definition dialog box.

7. Render the entire perspective scene. You'll see a view similar to Figure 11.9.

Figure 11.9: The model rendered with a highlight on the glass

The Spotlight also has a similar option that allows you to control what objects are affected by the light source. While the highlight is not placed correctly for the Sun angle, it is soft enough to enhance the appearance of the glass without being too obtrusive.

By controlling highlights and the objects that lights effect, you can simulate a wide variety of lighting conditions.

◆ Adding Props

In the last chapter, you learned how to use the Materials Editor to make adjustments to materials. In this section, you'll look at ways to create materials from scratch. We'll focus on creating *trees* that we'll add to the building model.

You can approach building trees in two ways: you can model them leaf for leaf, or you can project a image of a tree onto a flat surface (similar to the trees you used in Chapter 8). If you are creating a model you intend to animate with camera locations that are close to the trees and foliage, you may want to consider modeling trees with more detail. On the other hand, if you are creating a model for a still image, or if the camera motion of your animation doesn't get too close to the trees, you can usually get by with flat projections.

There are a few programs available that will generate natural foliage for you, if you need that kind of detail. The following exercise shows you how to use bitmap images of trees to create a projected, flat tree. Among other things, you'll learn how to use *opacity maps* to create a shape from a plain rectangle.

> ***Note***   *For the following exercises you will need some files from the AutoVision installation. If you haven't already installed AutoVision from your AutoCAD R13 CD-ROM, do so now. If you prefer, you can just copy the contents of the* \Maps *subdirectory of the AutoCAD CD-ROM installation disk onto your computer's main hard drive.*

Adding a Map Path to Help 3D Studio Find Bitmaps

Before you do anything, you must first tell 3D Studio where to look for bitmap image files. 3D Studio already knows that it must look in the \3ds4\Maps directory, but you can also direct it to look in other directories. This is helpful for keeping maps separated on a project-by-project basis, or if you simply have so many maps you want to organize them by subdirectories.

> **Note** *The listings you see in the dialog boxes below will be somewhat different from what you see on your screen. This is due to different installations and should not affect the tutorial.*

1. Choose Info ➤ Configure from the pull-down menu. You see the Program Configuration dialog box.

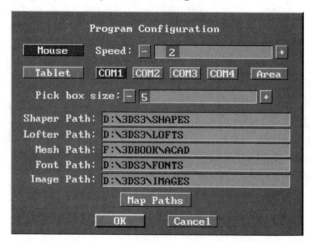

2. Click on the button labeled Map Paths. The Specify Map Paths dialog box appears.

3. Click on the Add button at the bottom of the dialog box.

4. Click on the location just below the last item on the list (click in a blank space). You see the Add Map Path dialog box.

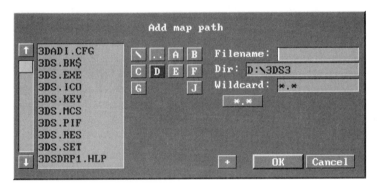

5. Use the dialog box to locate the \AV2\Maps directory. You don't want anything showing in the Filename input box. You only want the directory name to appear in the Dir input box.

6. When you've accomplished this, click OK at all the dialog boxes to close them.

Saving a Map Path Permanently

If you use Info ➤ Configure to specify a map path, 3D Studio will not remember it from one session to the next. If you think you will be using a map path in all of your 3D Studio work, you can make it permanent by adding it to a special 3D Studio configuration file called 3DS.SET. This is a text file, found in the 3D Studio directory, that 3D Studio uses to set itself up.

To make a map path permanent, open the 3DS.SET file with any text editor such as the Windows Notepad, then locate the line that reads:

```
MAP-PATH = "MAPS"
```

This is the default permanent map path. Below this, you will see a listing of other alternate map paths. You'll notice that these alternatives all start with a semicolon. The semicolon indicates that these items are not active, and are to be ignored by 3D Studio at startup time.

If you want to include another map path besides "MAPS" you can add another line below MAP-PATH = "MAPS". For example, to include the AutoVision map directory \AV2\MAPS, add a line that reads:

```
MAP-PATH = "d:\AV2\MAPS"
```

below the first map path. (The *d* should be replaced by the letter of the drive where you've installed AutoVision.) Save the file with this new map path. The next time you start 3D Studio, it will include d:\AV2\MAPS automatically in its map paths.

Autodesk recommends that you not add too many listings to your map paths, as having more than one map path tends to increase rendering time.

If you only want to store a map path for a particular project, you can use File ➤ Save Project from the 3D Editor pull-down menu. This saves your 3D Studio model as a file with the .PRJ filename extension instead of the typical .3DS extension. Project files store not only the geometry and materials data of your model, but also any settings you have made in 3D Studio up to the time you save the project. You can open project files using File ➤ Open Project from the pull-down menu.

Creating a Tree Material

Now you are ready to create some trees using image bitmap files from the AutoVision maps. In this section you will learn how to apply a combination of texture maps and opacity maps to simulate a tree.

1. Choose Programs ➤ Materials to go to the Materials Editor.

2. In the column of buttons under Map, toward the bottom of the screen, click on the top button that corresponds to the Texture 1 row.

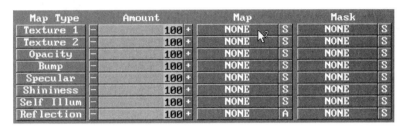

3. The Select Texture Map dialog box appears. Use this dialog box to locate and select 8TREE32L.TGA from the \AV2\Maps directory, then click OK. The name 8TREE32L.TGA will appear on the Map button.

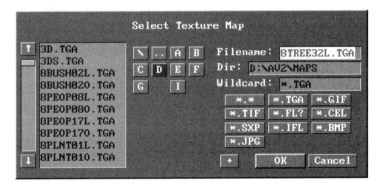

4. Get a preview of this file by clicking and dragging the
8TREE32L.TGA button over to the View Image button in
the column of buttons to the far right. Depending on how
you have 3D Studio configured, you may see the following
warning.

If you see this message, click on the Resize
button. The bitmap file image appears on
the screen.

5. Right-click on the mouse to return to the
Materials Editor.

6. In the column of buttons to the far right,
click on Cube and Pattern, then click on
Render Sample. You see the sample of the
tree as it might appear on a surface.

You now have the beginnings of a tree, but, as
the rendered sample shows, it looks like a picture
of a tree plastered on the side of a black box. You
need to remove the portions of the box that are
black. To do this, you use an *opacity map*, as discussed next.

Hiding Unwanted Surfaces with Opacity Maps

An opacity map is a grayscale bitmap image that tells 3D Studio which part of the surface is opaque and which part is transparent. Black will become completely transparent while white will turn completely opaque.

To see how this works, look at Figure 11.10. To the left you see an opacity map. The middle figure shows a simple rectangle in 3D Studio without a material assigned to it. The figure to the far right shows the same rectangle that is assigned a material using the opacity map at left. Notice that the portions of the opacity map that are black appear invisible in the rectangle.

Opacity map	**Object**	**Object with opacity map**

Figure 11.10: A sample of an opacity map, and an object to which it is assigned

You can also use shades of gray to simulate a semi-transparent material or to gradually change the transparency of a surface. Color images can be used for opacity maps as well, though it's easier to visualize how grayscale images are translated into opaque surfaces.

Now that you have an understanding of what opacity maps are, let's add one to our tree material.

1. Look for the button in the Maps column that corresponds to the Opacity button row. (This would be the third button down from the top of the Map column.)

2. Click on this button, and as in the last exercise, locate the `\AV2\Maps` directory.

3. Find the file named `8TREE320.TGA` and click on it. This is the opacity bitmap image associated with the 8TREE32L.TGA file you located in the last exercise.

4. Click OK, then click and drag this button to the View Image button to see what it looks like.

    Compare this image to the one you saw in the previous exercise. Notice that it is the outline of the same tree.

5. Now click on Render Sample. Notice that now the sample shows the tree without the black box surrounding the image.

6. Click on the box labeled Current Material, then enter the name **Tree01** and click OK.

7. Choose Material ➤ Put To Current from the pull-down menu, then click OK at the New Current Material name dialog box. The current material is now Tree01.

You've just created a material that, when applied to an object, will appear as a tree. Now you'll need to create an object for the Tree01 material. This will be a simple, vertical rectangle.

1. Choose Program ➤ 3D Editor.

2. Click on the upper right viewport, then use the Zoom Out button and Pan tool in the Icon panel to approximate the view shown in Figure 11.11.

3. Click on the upper left viewport and zoom in to the area shown in Figure 11.11.

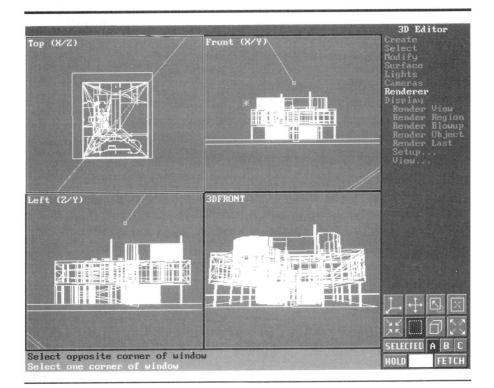

Figure 11.11: Setting up your views to add the tree object

4. Choose Create ➤ Box, then, in the upper right viewport, place the first two points of the box as the rectangle shown in Figure 11.12a. This will be the front profile of the tree.

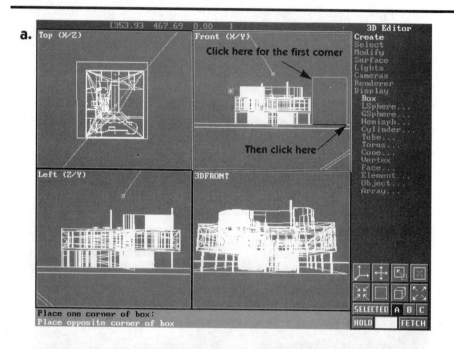

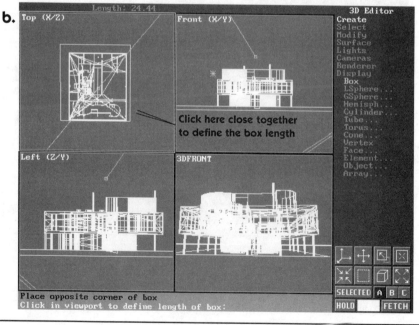

Figure 11.12: Creating a box to represent the tree

5. For the length of the box, click on the upper left viewport and click on the two points shown close together in Figure 11.12b. You want the box representing the tree to be a thin one, like a two-dimensional plane. If it's too thick, it may interfere with other objects in the view.

6. At the Name for new object dialog box, enter **Tree01**, then click Create. The box appears in all the views.

The next step is to add the material and the mapping coordinates.

1. Choose Surface ➤ Material ➤ Assign ➤ Object, then click on the rectangle you just created.

2. At the Assign Tree01 Material To dialog box, click on OK to accept Tree01. (Remember that you made the current material Tree01 just before you exited the Materials Editor, so Treeo1 is the current default material.)

3. Now click on Surface ➤ Mapping ➤ Adjust ➤ Region Fit.

4. At the `Click on one corner of region` prompt, In the upper right viewport, click on the upper left corner of the rectangle you just created, as shown in Figure 11.13.

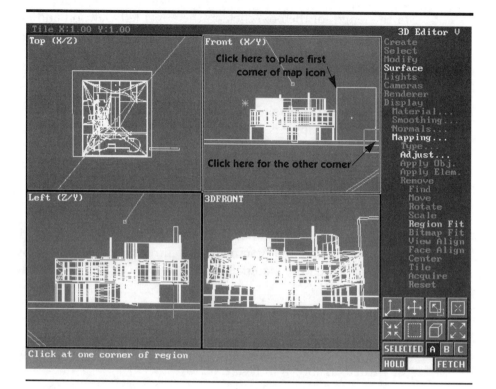

Figure 11.13: Fitting the map icon to the Tree1 object

5. At the Click at opposite corner prompt, select the other corner of the rectangle (also shown in Figure 11.13).

6. Now the map is stretched to fit over the rectangle. The last step is to make sure the new mapping coordinates are assigned to the Tree01 object.

7. Choose Surface ➤ Mapping ➤ Apply Obj., then click on the Tree01 object. At the Apply Mapping? message, click OK.

Now it's time to render. Let's switch the shadow method back to Shadow Map from Ray Tracing first.

1. Choose Renderer ➤ Setup ➤ Shadows.

2. At the Global Shadow Control dialog box, click on the Shadow Maps button, then click OK.

3. Now render the perspective view. Be sure the Shading Limit is set to Metal and that the Anti-aliasing, Filter Maps, Shadows, and Mapping settings are all turned on before you start the rendering. The tree appears in the view (see Figure 11.14).

Figure 11.14: The tree as part of the rendering

The tree is off the screen, but you can get a glimpse of it at the far right. The scene still looks a bit bare, so in the next exercise, you'll make copies of the tree to give the impression that the building is surrounded by a grove of trees. In so doing, you'll see that copies of objects maintain their material assignments.

1. Choose Modify ➤ Object ➤ Move, then, in the upper left viewport, Shift-click on the Tree01 object.

2. Place a copy of Tree01 on the opposite side of the house as shown in Figure 11.15a. At the Name For New Object dialog box, click Create to accept the default name **Tree02**. A copy of the tree appears.

3. Repeat step 2 to make several more copies. Use Figure 11.15b as a guide to placing the trees.

4. Render the perspective view again. You will have a view similar to Figure 11.15c.

5. Save the file to disk.

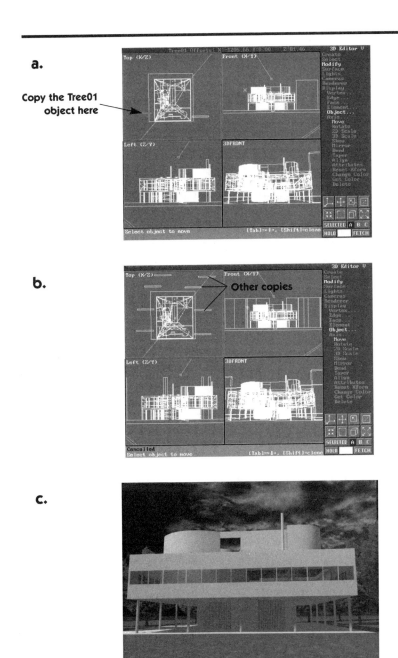

Figure 11.15: Making more copies of the tree

The trees really help give the rendering a realistic appearance. You can further enhance the rendering by varying the size of each tree and rotating the trees 180 degrees so that some of them appear as mirror images. This adds a bit more variety and makes it a little less obvious that the trees are identical. Of course, you can create different types of trees in the Materials Editor and add them to the scene.

The method we've shown you here for creating and adding trees will also work for adding text or signage to a model. Or you can use this method to add people. Again, Photoshop will aid you in creating the texture and opacity maps for people. If you don't want to create your own, there are many third-party sources for texture maps and models. Here is a partial list of companies that provide texture maps and models for 3D Studio.

> Acuris 3-D Models
> 1098 Washington Crossing Rd.
> Washington Crossing, PA 18977
> 800-652-2874
>
> Cyberprops
> 1202 West Olympic Blvd., Suite #101
> Santa Monica, CA 90404
> 310-314-2171
>
> Ketiv Software
> 6601 NE 78th Court, A-8
> Portland, OR 97218
> 800-458-0690
>
> Viewpoint DataLabs Int'l
> 625 South State Street
> Orem, UT 84058
> 800-328-2738

In addition to texture maps, these companies also offer prebuilt 3D objects such as furniture, cars, appliances, cabinetry, and animals. If you are in a hurry to build scenes quickly, you will want to check out the library of objects offered by these and other companies.

Adjusting an Object to a Bitmap Shape

In general, you will find it easier to align a bitmap image to an object, as you did earlier for the tree. But sometimes you may find it necessary to match the object's shape to a bitmap's shape. For example, you may create a material that uses bitmap images of people standing. To avoid distorting the shape of the people, you would want to match the object to the bitmap as closely as possible (see Figure 11.16).

Figure 11.16: Two renderings with people used as bitmaps. The image to the left has distorted the people.

To do this, choose Surface ➤ Mapping ➤ Adjust ➤ Bitmap Fit. You'll see a file dialog box called Select Bitmap For Aspect Ratio Fit. Locate the bitmap file associated with the material that uses the bitmap. Once selected, you return to the 3D Studio screen and the map icon will be adjusted to fit the aspect ratio of the selected bitmap.

Once you have the new map icon, you can adjust your object to fit as closely as you can to the map icon shape. This is a bit tricky since the map icon disappears when you use the Modify or Create options. You'll have to alternate between editing the object and viewing the map icon. You may not be able to get an absolutely accurate match, but you can get close and then use the Region Fit option described in the previous exercise to align the map exactly to the object.

Using Bump Maps

Before we move on to the next section, let's take a quick look at *bump maps*. In Chapter 10, you saw a sample of a bump map in Figure 10.11. It showed how a grayscale image creates the impression of a bumpy surface. The material you assigned to the Ground object also makes use of a bump map that gives the ground a rippled appearance.

In the following exercise, you'll modify the ground material to make the ground appear more like a rolling surface as opposed to a ripply one.

1. Choose Program ➤ Materials.

2. At the Materials Editor, Choose Materials ➤ Get From Scene from the pull-down menu

3. At the Get Material From Scene dialog box, choose Green Grass, then click OK.

4. Click on the top Map button labeled Ivines1.CEL.

5. At the Select Texture Map dialog box, locate `Clover.TGA`, select it, and click OK. (`Clover.TGA` is a sample file included with the other AutoCAD and 3D Studio files on the CD that comes with this book.)

6. Click and drag the Clover.TGA button to the View Image button at the right of the screen. You see a sample of this new texture map.

7. Right-click on your mouse to return to the Materials Editor.

8. Set the Amount slider for Texture 1 to **75**. This will reduce the strength of the bitmap image a little, as it's a bit too dark for our rendering.

Map Type	Amount	Map		Mask	
Texture 1	75	CLOVER.TGA	S	NONE	S
Texture 2	100	NONE	S	NONE	S
Opacity	100	NONE	S	NONE	S
Bump	15	IVINES1.CEL	S	NONE	S
Specular	100	NONE	S	NONE	S
Shininess	100	NONE	S	NONE	S
Self Illum	100	NONE	S	NONE	S
Reflection	100	NONE	A	NONE	S

9. Set the Amount slider for the Bump map to **15**. This will reduce the strength of the bump map, lessening the apparent height of the bumps in the rendering.

So far, you've added a new texture map to the Green Grass material and reduced the bumpiness a bit. The next set of steps will show you how you can alter the scale of the bump map.

1. Click on the button labeled S next to the Ivines1.CEL button of the Bump map row. The Mapping Parameters dialog box appears.

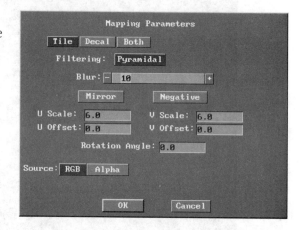

2. Change the U Scale and V Scale input boxes to **6**. This will enlarge the bump map up to six times its current size, and will spread the bumps out and make them appear less like ripples in water or sand on a beach.

3. Click OK, then choose Material ➤ Put To Scene.

4. At the warning message, click OK.

5. Choose Program ➤ 3D Editor and render the perspective view. You will see that the ground now looks more like a field of clover and the surface bumpiness is less extreme (see Figure 11.17).

Figure 11.17: The building rendered with a new texture map (Bump map setting)

Animating Materials

There are animation files available for use in 3D Studio. These can be fun to incorporate into your projects. A classic use of an animation is a changing sky used as a background; you can also have fun assigning an animation file to a material and using that material as a television screen within your model.

Your choices for animated materials when selecting image files for texture maps in the Materials Editor are *Flic files* and *Targa sequences*. Flic files are single files that contain a complete animation. Targa sequences are sets of files, with each file containing the image for a single *frame* of an animation (see Chapter 12 for more on animation frames). The files in a Targa sequence will be named so that the first four characters in the filename are the same for all the files in the sequence, while the next four characters are used for a number representing the frame's location in the sequence.

Selecting animated Flic files for a material is simply a matter of choosing the *.FL? button in the Select Texture Map dialog box when you're selecting a texture map image file. Selecting Targa sequences is a bit trickier.

1. Choose *.TGA in the Select Texture Map dialog box.

2. Locate and select the first file of a Targa sequence that looks interesting to you (FILE0000.TGA, for example). The name then appears in the Filename input box.

3. Change the name in the Filename input box by replacing the last four digits in the filename with an asterisk. (In our example, you would type **FILE*.TGA**.) 3D Studio will then know that you have selected a Targa sequence and not just a single image file.

It is important to retain the first four characters of the Targa sequence filename before you add the asterisk. If you use any less than four or any more than four, 3D Studio will not use the sequence. The sequence also must be in the map path discussed earlier.

Backgrounds can also be animated by specifying Targa sequence files in this way.

NOTE: There are also computer video devices that will allow you to perform "rotoscoping" to add live video to your materials or backgrounds. Rotoscoping is a means of "grabbing" sequential frames from a professional video recorder and incorporating them in your animation. To perform rotoscoping, you need both a computer device that will precisely control the video deck, plus another device that can translate the video signal from the deck into a computer file.

◆ Setting Up a New Scene

We've been focusing on an exterior view of the model. Now it's time to see how we can create a more intimate view of the building. Next, you'll set up a camera and light to get a view of the second-floor courtyard. In the process you'll have a chance to become more familiar with lighting and editing.

Adjusting a Camera

Start by adjusting the camera you created in Chapter 10.

1. In the lower left viewport, use the Zoom Window tool to enlarge the view of the building (see Figure 11.18).

2. In the upper left viewport, use the Zoom Window tool again to enlarge the lower right corner of the plan view as shown in Figure 11.18.

3. Choose Camera ➤ Move, then click on the camera shown in Figure 11.18 in the upper left viewport.

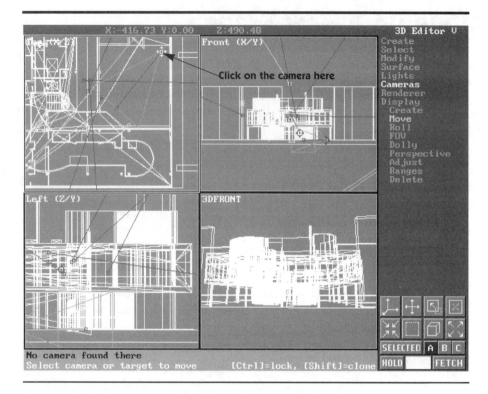

Figure 11.18: Enlarging the side and top view of the building

4. Move the camera to the position shown in Figure 11.19.

5. Click on the camera target and move it into the position shown in Figure 11.19.

6. Click on the lower left viewport and move the camera and target so they are in the position shown in Figure 11.19.

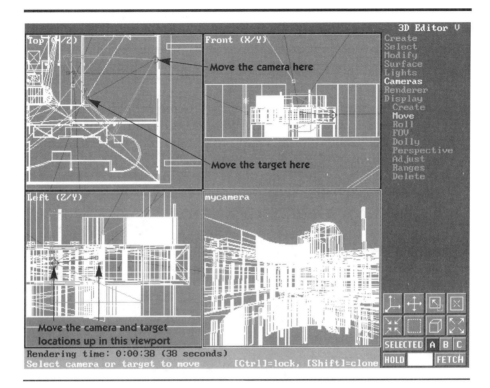

Figure 11.19: Moving the camera

7. Choose Cameras ➤ Adjust from the command column, then click on the camera you just moved.

8. At the Camera Definition dialog box, click on 35mm from the Stock Lenses button group.

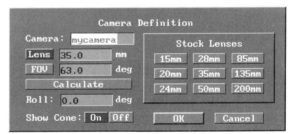

9. Click OK. This will give your view a wider field.

10. Click on the lower right viewport, then type **C**.

11. In the Camera Selector dialog box, choose Mycamera, then click OK. Your perspective view will change to one similar to Figure 11.19. If your view isn't exactly the same as the one shown, you can adjust it by clicking in the perspective view and adjusting it with your mouse.

12. Now render the perspective view. Choose Renderer ➤ Render View and click on the perspective view. At the Render dialog box, click on the Render button. After a minute or two, you will see a rendering similar to Figure 11.20.

Figure 11.20: The rendered view

Copying the Sun

The rendered image is mostly in shadow, so you cannot see any detail. Also, all the surfaces have been assigned the default material; you haven't actually assigned a material to any part of the building. You'll want to move the light source so more of the courtyard is visible. To do this, you can make a copy of the current Sun spotlight in a new position to provide light for your new view. Here's how to copy a light.

1. Click on Lights in the command column to make the lights visible.

2. Click on the upper left viewport to make it active, then click on the Zoom Out button in the Icon panel until you see the Sun spotlight.

3. Choose Lights ➤ Spot ➤ Move, then Shift-click on the Sun spotlight. Remember that Shift-clicking on an object during the Move option causes 3D Studio to make a copy instead of just moving the object.

4. Move the cursor so the new light is in the position shown in Figure 11.21, then left-click the mouse to fix the position.

5. At the Name For New Object dialog box, click on the Create button to accept the default name for the new spotlight.

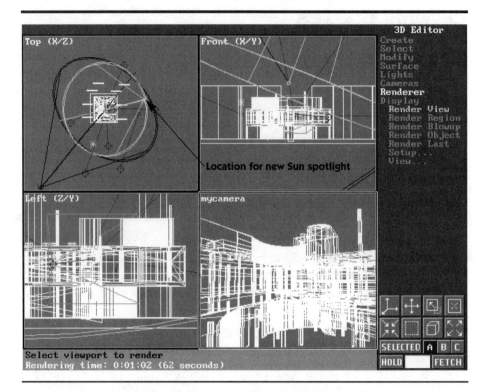

Figure 11.21: Creating a copy of the Sun spotlight

The new spotlight has all the same settings as the original, so you don't have to make any adjustments for shadows or intensity.

Notice that when you made the copy of the Sun spotlight, the light location was moved but the target location remained in the same location as the original spotlight location. You can move the target independently at a later time if you need to.

You don't want two suns shining on your model, so you will want to turn off the original Sun spotlight for the current view.

1. Choose Lights ➤ Spot ➤ Adjust, then click on the original Sun spotlight. The Spotlight Definition dialog box appears.

2. Click on the Off button toward the lower middle half of the dialog box, then click OK. Notice how the spotlight is now black. This shows you that it is off.

3. Render the perspective view again. Now you can see more of the courtyard and details, as in Figure 11.22.

Figure 11.22: The courtyard view rendered with a new spotlight for the Sun location

Detaching a Surface to Add a Separate Material

When you import an AutoCAD model into 3D Studio, all the objects are assigned a default material. This default material is gray in color and has a low reflectance. Currently, all of the building, with the exception of the glass, is assigned this default material.

To help delineate the rendering, you can add a tile pattern material to the floor. To do this, however, you must first detach the floor from the rest of the building, because the floor is part of the exterior wall. Here's how to detach a surface.

1. Click on the upper right viewport, then zoom out until the building just fills the viewport.

2. Click on the Full Screen Toggle button in the Icon panel to make the viewport fill the screen. This will help you select the faces of the floor in the next two steps.

3. Choose Select ➤ Face ➤ Quad from the command column.

4. Place a window around the area of the ground floor shown in Figure 11.23.

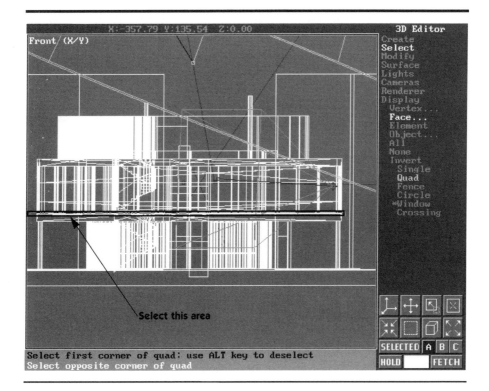

Figure 11.23: Selecting the floor faces

5. Click on the Full Screen Toggle button again to return to the four viewports setup.

6. Choose Create ➤ Face ➤ Detach, then click on the Selected button in the Icon panel to highlight it.

7. Don't click *on* anything in the upper right viewport, but do click somewhere within that viewport. When using the Selected button, you do not want to select an object. Once you've clicked in the viewport, you will see the Detach Selected Faces? message.

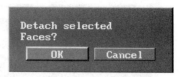

Click OK.

8. Next you see the Name For New Object dialog box.

9. Enter **Floor01** for the new object name, then click OK. The floor surface is now a separate object with the name Floor01.

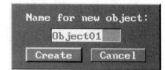

Now you can assign a material to the floor without affecting the other parts of the building.

1. Choose Surface ➤ Material ➤ Choose.

2. At the Material Selector dialog box, choose Tile Greygranite, then click on OK.

3. Choose Surface ➤ Material ➤ Assign ➤ By Name.

4. At the Assign Material To dialog box, click on Floor01 from the list, then click OK.

5. Now assign a mapping coordinate to the floor. In the upper left viewport, zoom into the building so you have a view similar to the one shown in Figure 11.24.

6. With the upper left viewport active, choose Surface ➤ Mapping ➤ Adjust ➤ View Align.

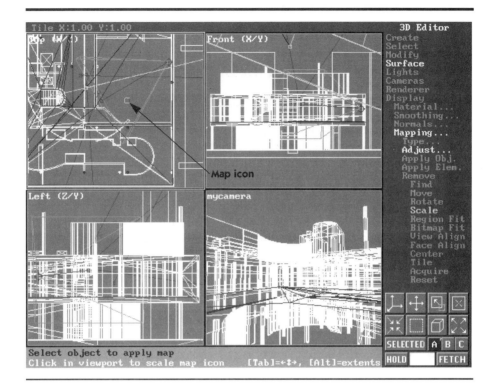

Figure 11.24: Adjusting the plan view and resizing the map icon for the floor

The map appears in the view, but it is no longer square. You may recall that in an earlier exercise, you used the Region Fit option to force the map to fit the Tree01 object. 3D Studio maintains the last mapping icon shape until you modify it further. Let's make the map icon square again, which is its default shape.

> ***Note*** *If you cannot find the map icon, choose Surface ➤ Mapping ➤ Adjust ➤ View Align, then click in the viewport where you want to locate the map icon. Next choose Surface ➤ Mapping ➤ Adjust ➤ Find. The map icon will appear to fill the viewport.*

1. Choose Surface ➤ Mapping ➤ Adjust ➤ Reset. This brings up the Reset dialog box.

2. Click on Aspect Ratio. This will reshape the map icon back to a square.

3. Choose Surface ➤ Mapping ➤ Adjust ➤ Scale, and scale the map icon down to the size shown in Figure 11.24.

The size of the map icon indicates the size of the individual tiles in the material. Don't worry about being exact at this point.

1. Choose Select ➤ Object ➤ By Name, then click on Floor01 in the list box of the Select Object By Name dialog box. Click OK.

2. Choose Surface ➤ Mapping ➤ Apply Obj., then click on the Selected button in the Icon panel.

3. Click on the active viewport (but not *on* an object).

4. At the Apply Mapping Coordinated? message, click OK.

5. Now render the perspective view. You will have a rendering similar to Figure 11.25.

Figure 11.25: The rendered view of the courtyard with the new floor material

You could continue to select and separate faces into other objects to add more detail to the rendering. For example, you might detach the window mullions and add a metallic material to them. We don't have the space in this book to walk you through the addition of more materials, so you may want to do this as an exercise on your own.

◆ Missing Surface, Normals

At times, you will render a model only to find that some of the faces disappear. You know the faces are there because you can see them in the wireframe mode. Where do they go at render time?

To understand why surfaces disappear, you need to know one basic fact about 3D computer models: *Surfaces have only one visible side that reflects light*. The other side of a surface does not reflect light at all. This may sound crazy, but it's true for virtually all 3D computer rendering programs.

You can determine which side of a face reflects light by finding the surface's *normal*. A normal is a vector pointing away from the face; the direction of the normal is determined by the way the face is created. Figure 11.26 shows a typical face and its normal. The order in which the vertexes of the face were chosen at creation time determines the direction of the normal. The normal points away from the side of the face that reflects light.

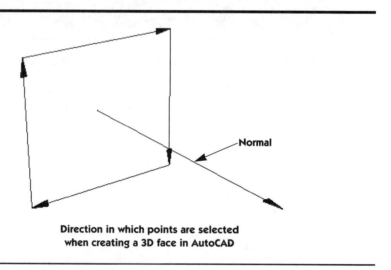

**Direction in which points are selected
when creating a 3D face in AutoCAD**

Figure 11.26: A normal in relation to a face in 3D Studio

AutoCAD doesn't really pay much attention to normals, so frequently files imported into 3D Studio from AutoCAD will have faces turned in different ways. The result is a rendering with "black holes" appearing at random.

There are three ways to deal with normals in a model.

◆ You can choose Surface ➤ Normals ➤ Face Flip, then select a specific face to "flip" its normal to point in the direction you want. This can be time-consuming if you model has many faces that are not oriented correctly.

◆ *Or* you can assign to the object, element, or face a material that is two-sided. When you look at the Materials Editor, you will see a button labeled 2-Sided near the top of the screen. When this is checked for a material, the surface will act like a double-sided surface with normals pointing out in both directions.

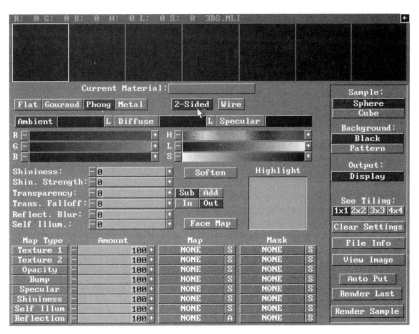

◆ *Or* you can select the Render Both Sides button in the Render dialog box. This option causes 3D Studio to render every surface as if it were two-sided. The problem with this option is that it increases rendering time.

The best method is the second one, of assigning a two-sided material to the object that has normals pointing in the wrong direction. It still increases rendering time, but since it isn't adding a two-sided surface to all the objects in your model, the impact isn't as great as in the third option.

By the way, the default surface that 3D Studio applies to imported and new objects is a two-sided material.

◆ Adjusting the Smooth Appearance of Objects

3D Studio is capable of rendering faceted objects as smooth surfaces. For example, even though the sphere in Figure 11.27 is really made up of flat surfaces, 3D Studio makes it appear as a smooth object. This smoothing is accomplished by "blending" the shading between surfaces.

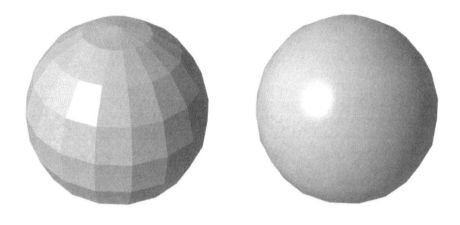

Figure 11.27: A faceted sphere appears as a smooth sphere in 3D Studio.

Note *The outline of the sphere in Figure 11.27 still appears faceted. While smoothing does wonders on faceted surfaces, it cannot smooth the outline. To reduce the faceted edge outline, you must model the object with more facets, or adjust your view or the placement of the object so the faceted outline is not so apparent.*

In all the rendered views of the courtyard, the wall of the stairwell on the roof appears faceted. It *should*, however, appear as a smooth curve, even though it is made up of a series of flat segments. 3D Studio's *smoothing groups* are useful for surfaces such as this one. Here's how to apply a smoothing group to an object.

1. Choose Surface ➤ Smoothing ➤ Object ➤ Auto Smoothing.

2. Click on the roof garden wall as shown in Figure 11.28. You see the Auto Smooth dialog box appears.

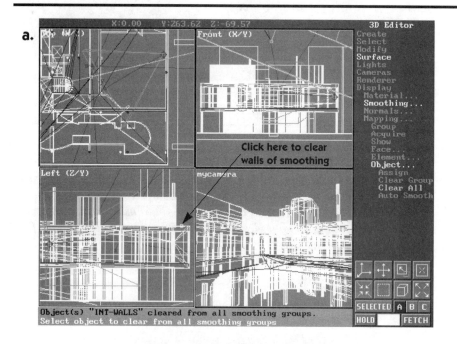

Figure 11.28: Click on the roof garden wall to bring up the Auto Smoothing dialog box.

Notice that the Angle value in the dialog box shows 30. This tells 3D Studio to blend or smooth out two adjacent flat surfaces when the angle between them is equal to or less than 30 degrees. You can enter another value or accept the default value of 30.

3. Click OK to accept the default.

Sometimes, 3D Studio applies smoothing groups to objects that don't require smoothing. The effect is an odd-looking rendering with surfaces casting shadows in an odd way or reflecting light in an odd way. In fact, if you look at the last rendered view of the building, you'll see that it has some odd shading around the walls surrounding the courtyard. This is indicative of an erroneous smoothing group being applied to what should be plain flat surfaces. To remove smoothing from an object, do the following.

1. Select Surface ➤ Smoothing ➤ Object ➤ Clear All. You are then prompted to select the object you want to clear from all smoothing groups.

2. Click on the exterior wall of the second floor in the lower left viewport.

3. Now render the perspective view. Notice that now the roof wall around the stairwell no longer appears faceted (see Figure 11.29).

Figure 11.29: The courtyard rendered with smoothing applied to the roof wall, but removed from the courtyard walls

Smoothing groups are one of the more esoteric tools of 3D Studio. For the most part, the tools we've shown you here are all you need for applying and detaching smoothing from objects. With them, you can control smoothing to a very high degree. Unfortunately, we don't have the space in this book to go into more detail about smoothing groups. The 3D Studio reference manual and tutorial are excellent for finding out more about smoothing groups.

◆ Creating a Night Scene

At times, you may want to simulate a night scene of an existing model. Night scenes offer some dramatic appeal and can often help emphasize parts of your design that might otherwise go unnoticed.

In this section you'll add some lights and modify others to see firsthand how lighting can be controlled in 3D Studio.

1. First, turn off all the current lights, then set up your viewport to allow you to place the new omni lights shown in Figure 11.30 more easily.

2. In the upper left viewport. Zoom out so you can see the Sun spotlight. To do this, click on the Zoom Out button twice in the Icon panel.

3. Choose Lights ➤ Spot ➤ Adjust, then click on the second Sun spotlight you created in the prior set of exercises.

4. At the Spotlight Definition dialog box, click on the Off button (to turn it off), then click OK.

5. In the upper left viewport, zoom back in to the previous view by clicking on the Zoom In button twice in the Icon panel.

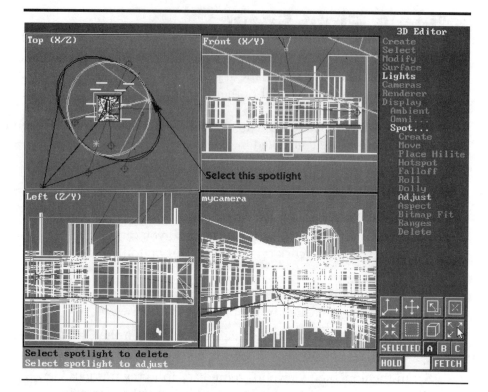

Figure 11.30: Selecting the second Sun spotlight to turn it off

Now you are ready to start adding lights for a night scene. In this next example, you will add a spotlight to generate some shadows in the court-yard. You will also add some Omni lights to add some general interior lighting. This will give the impression of a twilight condition.

1. Choose Lights ➤ Omni ➤ Create.

2. In the upper left viewport, place an Omni light at the location shown in Figure 11.31. You'll see the Light Definition dialog box appear.

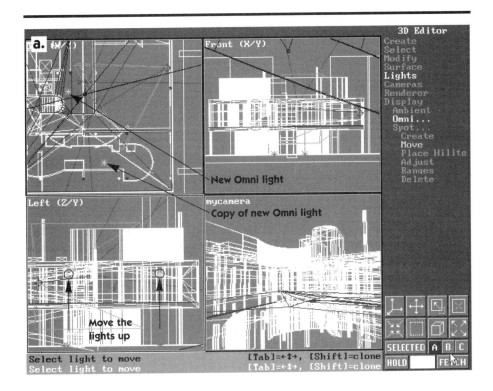

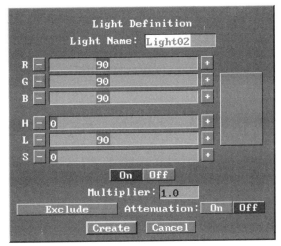

Figure 11.31: Adding the Omni lights to the second floor interior

3. At the dialog box, move the L (luminance) slider to the left until it shows **90**, then click Create.

4. Choose Lights ➤ Omni ➤ Move, then Shift-click on the light you just created.

5. Place a second light in the location shown in Figure 11.31 and, when the Name For New Object dialog box appears, click Create.

6. Choose Lights ➤ Omni ➤ Move, then, in the lower left viewport, move the two lights you just created (move them vertically from the ground level to the position shown in Figure 11.31).

You've just placed two Omni lights in the second floor interior. These lights will provide general lighting to the objects inside the building, giving the impression of lights being on inside the building. You can place these light more accurately to simulate the precise location of fixtures, but for now, let's move on to placing a spotlight for our shadows.

1. Choose Lights ➤ Spot ➤ Create.

2. In the upper left viewport, place the spotlight and spotlight target in the locations shown in Figure 11.32. The Spotlight Definition dialog box appears.

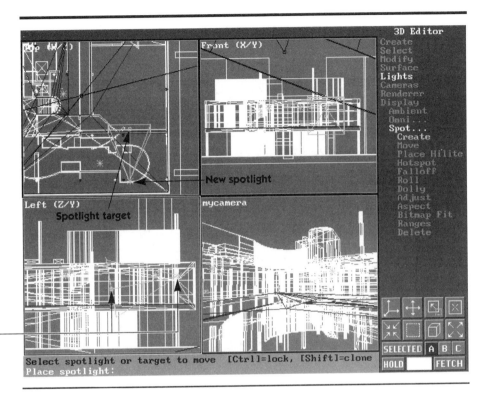

Figure 11.32: Adding a spotlight and adjusting its location

3. Adjust the L slider to **180** and click on the Show Cone button.

4. Click on the Rectangle option and the Cast Shadow button.

5. Click on the Create button. Notice that the spotlight shows a rectangular light cone instead of a round one. This is a result of choosing the Rectangle option in the Spotlight Definition dialog box.

6. Choose Lights ➤ Spot ➤ Move, then, in the lower left viewport, move the light and its target to the location shown in Figure 11.32.

7. Now render the perspective scene. You see a rendering similar to Figure 11.33.

Figure 11.33: The rendering after adding new lights and turning off the Sun
spotlight

It's an interesting view, but there are a few things wrong with it. First
of all, the roof garden walls are too strongly lit. The Omni lights do not
cast shadows. Everything in the scene is affected by them. You will need
to exclude the roof garden walls from being affected by the Omni lights.

By the same token, the spotlight, which we included in order to cast
shadows, doesn't seem to be doing its job. The reason for this is that the
glass, while transparent, is acting like an opaque surface, preventing the
spotlight light from casting any shadows through it. To prevent the glass
object from blocking the shadow-casting light, you need to change an
attribute of the glass object so it doesn't cast shadows of its own.

1. Choose Lights ➤ Omni ➤ Adjust, then click on one of the Omni lights.

2. At the Light Definition dialog box, click on Exclude. The Exclude objects dialog box appears.

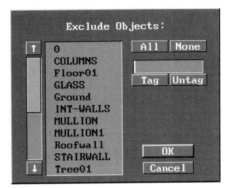

3. Click on Roofwall from the list in the dialog box, then click OK.

4. Click OK at the Light Definition dialog box.

5. Repeat steps 1 through 4 for the second Omni light, excluding the roofwall object from its light.

You've excluded the roof garden walls from reflecting the light from the Omni lights. The next step is to adjust the glass objects so they don't cast shadows.

1. Choose Select ➤ None to clear any selections you may currently have.

2. Choose Select ➤ Object ➤ By Name, then at the Select Objects by Name dialog box, choose Glass and click OK. This step will help you easily locate the glass object.

3. Choose Modify ➤ Object ➤ Attributes, then carefully click on the highlighted glass object in the Perspective viewport as shown in Figure 11.34. The Object Attributes dialog box appears.

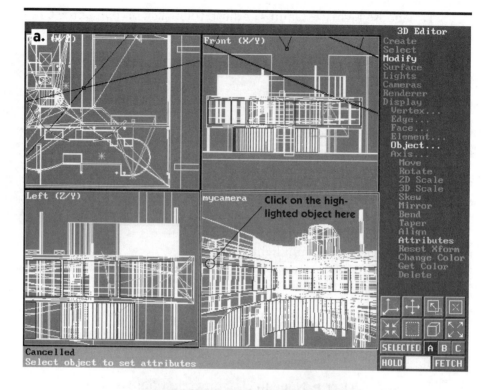

Figure 11.34: Selecting the glass in the Perspective viewport brings up the Object Attributes dialog box.

4. Make sure the name of the material shows up as GLASS. If it doesn't, click on Cancel and try selecting the glass again.

5. Once you've got the Glass Object Attributes dialog box set as described, click on the button labeled Cast Shadows so it is no longer highlighted, then click OK.

6. Render the scene. You will see a view similar to Figure 11.35.

Figure 11.35: The rendering of the courtyard with the Roofwall object excluded from the Omni lights and the Glass object excluded from the spotlight

Now we're getting closer to what we might really expect to see in this scene. But the spotlight isn't casting a complete shadow. It's not casting light on parts of the ramp and the wall by the ramp. Let's see how you can adjust the spread of a rectangular light to fit the lighted area.

1. Choose Lights ➤ Spot ➤ Hotspot, then click on the spotlight in the upper left viewport.

2. Adjust the hotspot outward so the light cone looks like Figure 11.36a, then left-click.

3. Choose Lights ➤ Spot ➤ Aspect, then click on the spotlight in the upper right viewport. Notice that now as you move your mouse to the right, the light cone shrinks in the X axis. As you move your mouse to the left, it shrinks in the Y axis.

4. Adjust the light cone so it looks like the one in Figure 11.36b, then left-click.

5. Choose Lights ➤ Spot ➤ Move, then, in the lower left viewport, adjust the light target position so it looks more like Figure 11.36b. For the effect we're looking for, let the light cone just graze the courtyard window opening.

6. Choose Lights ➤ Ambient. The Ambient Light Definition dialog box appears.

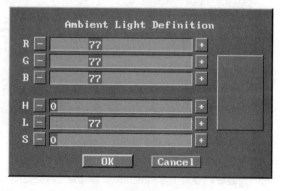

7. Set the L slider to **40**, then click OK. Since this is a night scene, there will be little ambient light. We're leaving some ambient light to give some definition to the roof walls.

8. Now render the perspective view. You will see a view similar to Figure 11.37.

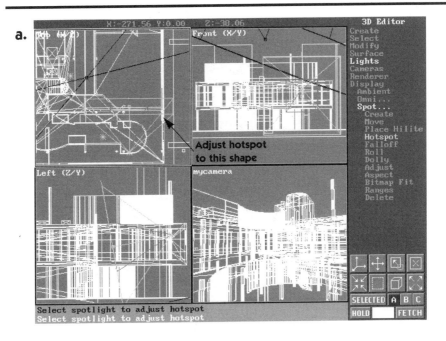

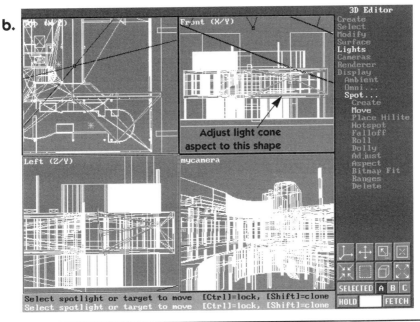

Figure 11.36: Adjusting the spotlight hotspot and aspect ratio

Figure 11.37: The rendering after adjusting the lights

As you can see from the rendering, the spotlight gives the impression of a bright light shining from the room to the left. You could further add furniture, and other props to give the view a more lived-in appearance. You might also add an exterior spotlight or two to highlight certain areas of the exterior. And as a final touch, you could add a starry sky to the background (see Figure 11.38).

You could continue to add and adjust lighting until you get the perfect scene. As you practice with this and other models, you will get a feel for the amount of lighting needed to accomplish a certain task. As I've mentioned before, computer rendering, like other art forms, takes some practice to master. There aren't any hard, fast rules. So let your imagination run for a while and perhaps you will discover some new techniques for creating the perfect rendering.

Figure 11.38: The courtyard view with a few additional props and a different background

◈ Editing Objects at Odd Angles

In all our exercises so far, the surfaces have all been at right angles to each other. In this type of model, it's fairly easy to align the map icon to the surface. But what about surfaces that don't conform to a top, front, and right-side view? In this section you'll learn some simple tools to help you with the more interesting shapes you may end up designing.

Applying Mapping Coordinates to Surfaces at Odd Angles

You've seen how you can align the *map icon* to a viewport. This is fine for models that have all their surfaces aligned with the standard viewports. Now suppose you want to align the map icon to a surface that isn't parallel to any of the viewports. How do you do that? You create a viewport that is aligned with the surface.

To align a map icon to a surface, you need to know about the *User* viewport. The User viewport is similar to the isometric views available in AutoCAD. It offers a non-perspective 3D view of your model. In fact, a User viewport even offers the 3D Tripod, similar to the one you see in AutoCAD when using the View ➤ Rotate option.

To explore the User viewport and aligning viewports to a surface, first create a new file with an object you can work with.

1. Choose File ➤ New. At the New All dialog box, make sure that only the New All button is highlighted, then click OK.

2. Choose Create ➤ Lspheres ➤ Values.

3. At the Set Lat-Long Sphere Segments dialog box, move the slider to the left to set the Segments value to **8**, then click OK.

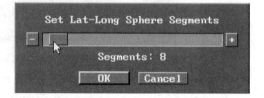

4. Choose Create ➤ Lspheres ➤ Faceted, then click on the upper left viewport to make it active.

5. Click on the center of the viewport to set the center of the Lsphere (see Figure 11.39).

6. At the `Set radius` prompt, choose the point shown in Figure 11.39.

7. At the `Name for new object` prompt, go ahead and accept the default name and press Create. You now have a faceted sphere.

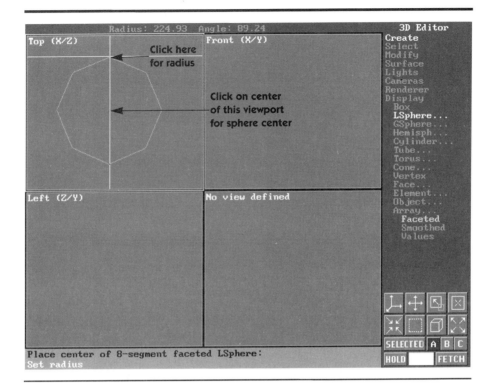

Figure 11.39: Drawing a faceted sphere

This faceted sphere will give you a good sample of an object whose surfaces are not parallel to the view plane. Notice that where you usually have a perspective view in the lower right viewport, you see the words *No View Defined*. There are no cameras in this new file to define a perspective view. The next exercise shows you how to set up a User view in that viewport.

1. Click on the lower right viewport to make it active.

2. Hold your mouse still and type **U**. A coordinates tripod appears, similar to the one you see in AutoCAD.

3. Move your mouse around and notice how the tripod moves. Set up the tripod so it looks similar to Figure 11.40a, then press the left mouse key. Your User viewport will look similar to Figure 11.40b.

4. Use the Zoom Out and Pan buttons in the Icon panel to set up the User view to look like Figure 11.40c.

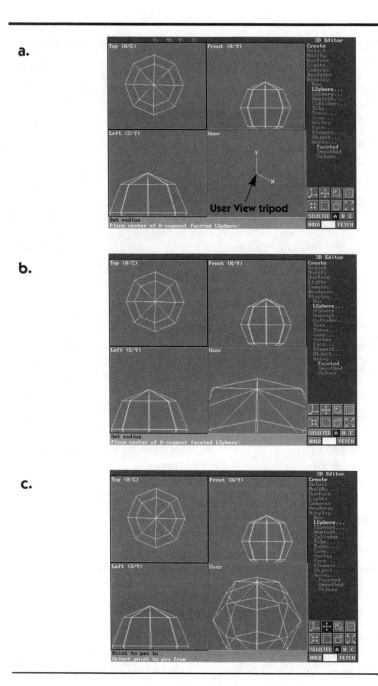

Figure 11.40: Creating and controlling a User viewport

Now suppose you wanted to place a map icon on one of the faces of the sphere. The first step is to align a viewport to the desired face. To do this, you use the User View feature of 3D Studio. User View is a view similar to the Isometric views you used in AutoCAD.

1. Choose Display ➤ User View ➤ Align.

2. Click on the vertex shown in Figure 11.41a. Now as you move the cursor you see a blue outline jump between each face associated with the vertex you selected.

3. Move your mouse so the face shown in Figure 11.41b is highlighted with the blue outline, then left-click your mouse. Your User view will change so that the face you selected is parallel to the User view.

4. Choose Display ➤ User View ➤ Show.

Notice that you see a cyan-colored polygon in the other three views. This polygon represents the orientation of the current User view in relation to the object.

Now you can go ahead and use the Surface ➤ Mapping options to add a mapping coordinate to the selected surface.

1. Choose Surface ➤ Mapping ➤ Adjust ➤ View Align.

2. Click on the User viewport. The map icon is aligned with the selected surface.

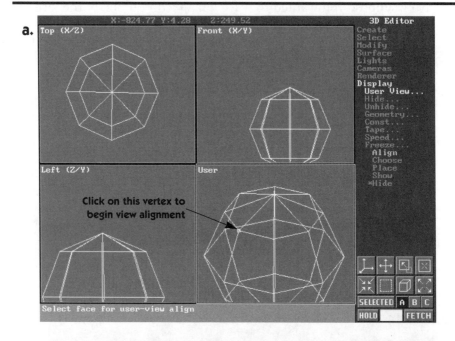

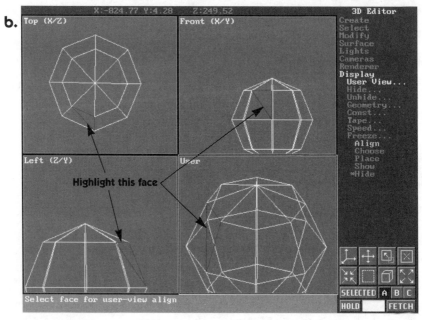

Figure 11.41: Aligning the User view to a surface of an object

You can also use User viewports to align objects to a surface. Once you've set up a User view to be parallel to a surface as described in this section, you can use any Create ➤ Object option to create an object on the User view plane. That User view plane is actually on the surface you selected in the previous exercise, and new objects will use that plane as their base. You might think of the Display ➤ User View ➤ Align option as the 3D Studio equivalent of AutoCAD's UCS.

Now suppose you want to align an object to the User view you created earlier. This would be helpful in moving objects from one orientation to another so that they are aligned to a specific surface.

1. Choose Create ➤ Hemisph ➤ Faceted. This creates a hemisphere shape.

2. For the Hemisphere object, use the User viewport and click on the center of the face that is aligned with the viewport, as shown in Figure 11.42a.

3. For the radius of the hemisphere, select the point shown in Figure 11.42b. The size isn't that important as we are only using the hemisphere to demonstrate how to align an object to a surface.

4. At the Name For New Object dialog box, click on Create. The hemisphere appears on the surface.

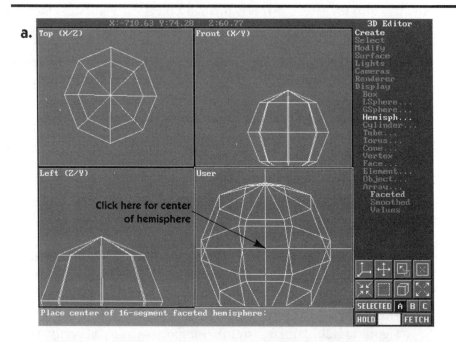

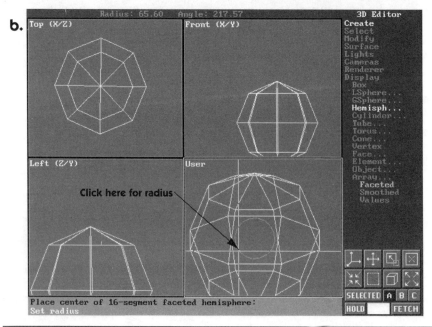

Figure 11.42: Drawing the hemisphere

This hemisphere shows us that when you create an object in the User viewport, it is aligned with the viewport plane and the surface to which the viewport plane is aligned.

Now we'll use this hemisphere to see how you can align it to a different surface of the larger sphere. The next step is to select the surface to which you want to align the object.

1. Choose Display ➤ User View ➤ Align, then click on the vertex shown in Figure 11.43a. This is a vertex adjoining the surface to which you want to move the hemisphere.

2. When you see the blue highlighted triangle as shown in Figure 11.43b, left-click your mouse. This will be the target surface.

The User view changes to be parallel to the surface you selected. Notice that the hemisphere is off to one side. The next step is to actually move the hemisphere to the selected surface.

1. Choose Modify ➤ Object ➤ Align.

2. Click on a vertex at the base of the hemisphere as shown in Figure 11.44a. A blue face outline appears just as before when you used the User View ➤ Align option.

3. Set the blue face outline to indicate a face on the base of the hemisphere as shown in Figure 11.44b, then left-click the mouse. This brings up the Align Method dialog box. This dialog box lets you choose which side of the selected surface you want facing toward you in the User view. Usually you will want the normals facing toward you, but in this case you actually want the surface facing away from you, since you selected the base of the hemisphere for alignment.

a.

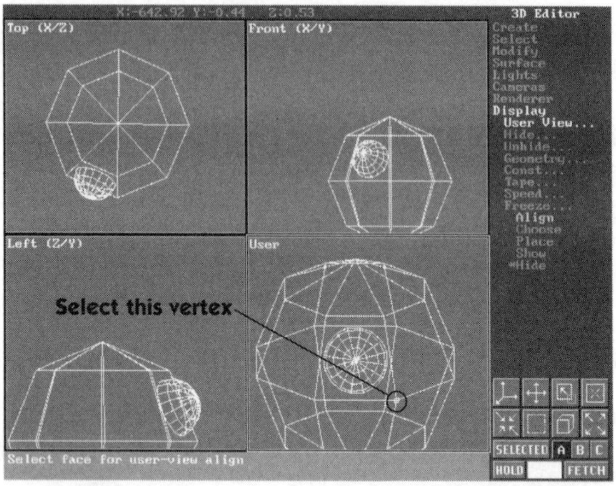

b.

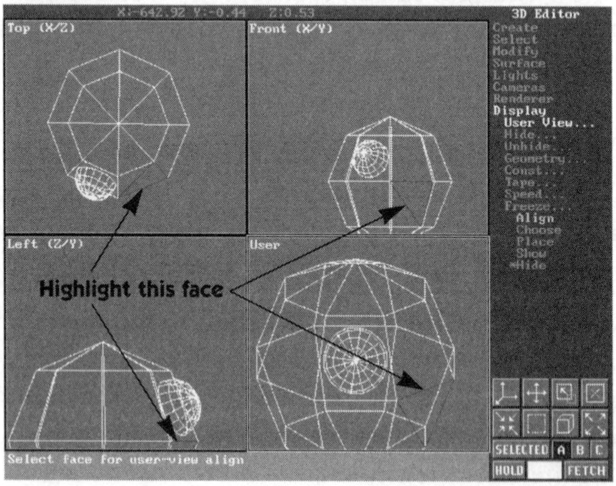

Figure 11.43: Selecting the surface to which you want the hemisphere aligned

a.

Select this vertex
at the base of
the hemisphere

b.

Select this face
at the base of
the hemisphere

c.

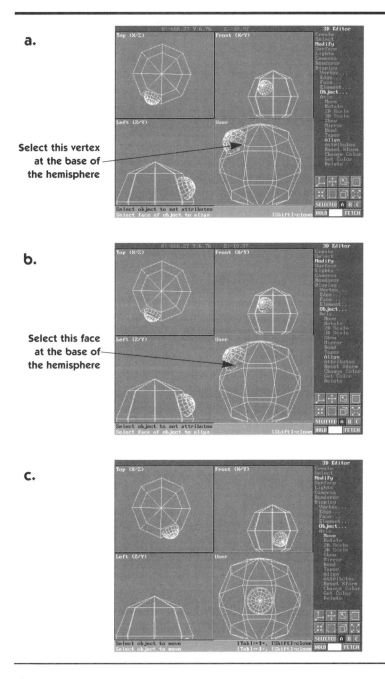

Figure 11.44: Selecting the surface of the hemisphere that is to be aligned with
the current User view

4. Click on the Facing Away button. The hemisphere jumps into an orientation that is parallel to the User view, and therefore parallel to the surface of the sphere you chose in the previous exercise.

5. Choose Modify ➤ Object ➤ Move, and move the hemisphere into position over the facet of the sphere.

To summarize the method of aligning an object to a surface: First you align the User view to the surface to which you want your object aligned, by using Display ➤ User View ➤ Align. Next, you align the object to the User view, by using Modify ➤ Object ➤ Align. The common plane to which the surface and the object are aligned is the User view. In one case, the User view is aligned to an object. In the other, the object is aligned to the User view.

Controlling Object Visibility

Our example of aligning objects and views is a fairly simple model of just two objects. But what happens in models that contain hundred of objects that may interfere with your editing? If you find a drawing too crowded, you can temporarily turn off the visibility of objects in much the same way as you would turn off layers in AutoCAD. Choose Display ➤ Hide ➤ By Name. You will see the Hide Objects dialog box.

This dialog box lists all the objects in your drawing by name. Click on the names in the list box to place an asterisk next to the objects you want hidden. When you click OK, the asterisked objects will be hidden.

You can also choose Display ➤ Hide ➤ Face, Element, or Object to hide these classes of items by selecting them from the screen.

To *unhide* objects, use the Display ➤ Unhide options. Don't forget to unhide objects you want rendered with the scene!

Controlling the Predefined Viewports

Actually, any viewport can be the User viewport. You can even have more than one User viewport: for each viewport you want to use as a User viewport, simply click on that viewport to make it active, and then type **U**.

You can restore a viewport to its standard orthographic view by first making it active, then typing the first letter of its name. For example, for the Top view, you click on the upper right viewport, then type **T**.

Here is a listing of all the views available in each viewport.

Back	Front	Spotlight
Bottom	Left	Top
Camera	Right	User

◆ Adding Text

Eventually, you will have the task of adding text to a model. For example, you may have to add the name of a hotel to an entrance, or an office building will require a name displayed in addition to its street address. These are instances where 3D Studio modeling tools are invaluable.

So here's a brief tutorial on how to add text to your models. It's short, and doesn't cover all the nuances of tools you are about to use, but it's enough to get you going and will cover most if not all situations where text is required for a model.

For text, you will use two modes of 3D Studio you haven't used before: the 2D Shaper and 3D Lofter. I'll show you just the basics to do text.

1. Load the `Textsmpl.3DS` file.

2. Click on the upper right viewport to make it active. This step is necessary because the 2D Shaper will use the active 3D Editor viewport for a background image. You will use this background to help you determine the size and orientation of the text.

Now let's go to the 2D Shaper. The first step is to acquire the background image.

1. Choose Program ➤ 2D Shaper.

2. Choose Display ➤ 3D Display ➤ Choose from the command column. You will see the Display Objects dialog box. This dialog box lets you select the object to be displayed as a background in the 2D Shaper window.

3. Choose 0 (zero) from the list. This is the facade model to which you will add text.

4. Click OK, then click on the On choice from the command column. You will see the bottom corner of the building appear on the screen in a light gray tone.

5. Use the Icon panel tools to adjust your view to look more like Figure 11.45.

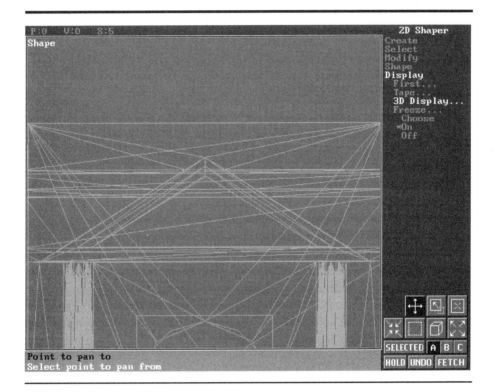

Figure 11.45: The 2D Shaper screen with a background image of the building

You may remember at the beginning of this section, I asked you to make the upper right viewport active. The background you see is determined by the active viewport in the 3D Editor.

Now you are ready to begin adding text. This is a three-step process of selecting the font, entering the text, and, finally, placing the text.

1. Choose Create ➤ Text ➤ Font. The Font File dialog box appears. You can select from the font library included with 3D Studio, or you can use your own library of PostScript fonts.

2. Choose Swisslte.FNT from the list of fonts, then click OK.

3. The next step is to enter the text you want to display. Choose Create ➤ Text ➤ Enter. The Enter Text dialog box appears.

4. Type **LIBRARY** then click OK. Although nothing happens on the screen, 3D Studio remembers what you entered.

5. Choose Create ➤ Text ➤ Place. You see the message Click at one corner of text region in the prompt. You also see [Ctrl] = Correct Aspect. This last message tells you that you must hold the Ctrl key when selecting the first corner of the text region if you want to place the text with the correct aspect ratio.

6. Hold the Ctrl key down and select the first point shown in Figure 11.46 for your text region. Now as you move the mouse, you see a rectangle follow your motion. This is the text region.

7. Select the second point of the region as shown in Figure 11.46. The text appears in the screen.

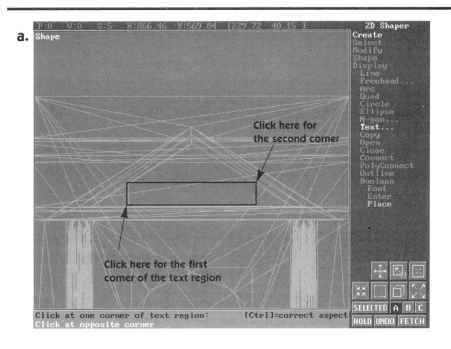

Figure 11.46: Placing the text region in the 2D Shaper

The text is not like the text in AutoCAD. The characters are actually 2D polygon outlines and not text as you know it in AutoCAD. Once you place the text in the 2D Shaper screen, you cannot edit it. Also, you are limited in the amount of text you can add at one time. This will depend on the complexity of the font, but the limit is about one short sentence.

If you have a lot of text, you can build it up with several smaller text portions, then arrange the text the way you want using the 2D Shaper editing tools.

You've now created 2D polygons in the Shaper, but you're not finished yet. The next step is to use the 3D Lofter to extrude or "loft" the shape into the third dimension. The 3D Lofter will extrude a 2D polygon along a path which can be set up in many different ways. For example, you can extrude a 2D polygon shape through a corkscrew path to create a spring. I won't go into the details of how to use the 3D Shaper now, however. You'll concentrate on getting the text into your model.

To get the 2D polygon shape into the 3D Lofter, you must first assign the objects you want to send to the Lofter.

1. Choose Select ➤ Vertex ➤ Quad, then place a selection window around the text, just as you would place a selection window in AutoCAD. The text is highlighted in red.

2. Choose Shape ➤ Assign, then click on the Selected button in the Icon panel.

3. Click on a blank space in the 2D Shaper viewport. The text is highlighted in yellow, indicating the polygons that will be sent to the Lofter when called for. This will become clearer in the next exercise.

It may seem like you've gone through a lot of steps just to select a set of objects. While you selected all the objects in the 3D Lofter (the background cannot be selected), there are times when you may only want to select a few of the objects in the Shaper to send to the Lofter. For example, say you have several 2D shapes you want to "loft," but you want each shape lofted to a different height. Since the Lofter will loft everything it receives from the Shaper to the same height, you would have to send the 2D shapes to the 3D Lofter according to the dimension to which you want them lofted.

Now let's see firsthand how the Lofter works.

1. Choose Program ➤ 3D Lofter. You see the screen shown in Figure 11.47.

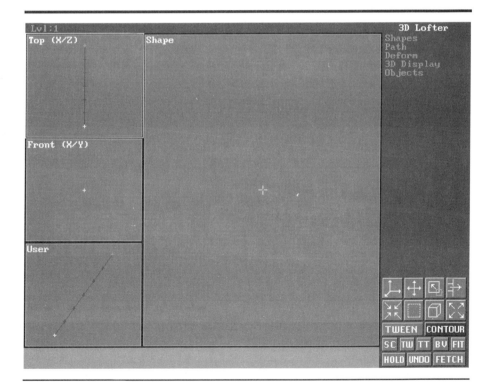

Figure 11.47: The 3D Lofter screen

2. Choose Shapes ➤ Get ➤ Shaper. The text polygons appear in the main viewport.

3. Right-click on the Zoom Extents button in the toolbar. The text appears in all the other viewports. (The text may be too small to be recognizable in the viewports to the left.)

4. Click on Path ➤ Move Vertex, then click on the upper left viewport.

5. Press the Tab key twice so the cursor changes to show two arrows pointing up and down.

6. Click on the top vertex of the extrusion path as shown in Figure 11.48. The extrusion path is the blue vertical line shown in the left viewports. It shows you how the polygons will be lofted, its entire length being the length of the loft.

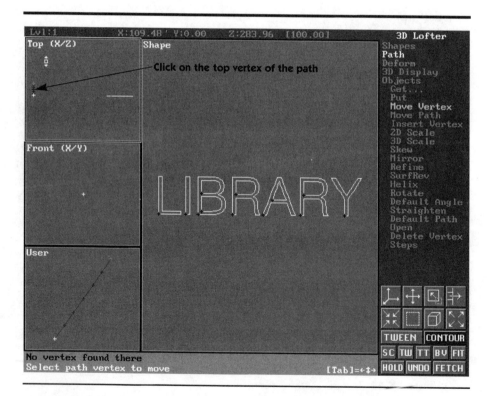

Figure 11.48: Selecting the vertex of the extrusion path

7. Carefully move it downward so the Z-xis readout in the Status line shows a value around **20**. You can see the extrusion length as indicated by the entire length of the extrusion path. I've asked you to set the Z value at 20, but this is really an arbitrary value I'm suggesting just for demonstration purposes.

8. Now choose Objects ➤ Make. The Object Lofting Controls dialog box appears.

9. Enter **Text01** for Object Name, then click Create. You'll see another dialog box listing the status of the object creation. When it's done, though, nothing will appear to have changed.

10. Choose Preview from the command column. The Preview Controls dialog box appears.

11. Click the Preview button. You'll see the front and back faces of the newly extruded object appear.

The dialog box you encountered in step 8 lets you control a variety of features of the object you are lofting. You can control whether the ends of the loft are open or closed, and you can control how maps are assigned to the extrusion. You'll find an excellent description of these features in the standard documentation that comes with 3D Studio. For now, let's finish adding the text to your 3D model.

Now for the final step of moving your newly created text into place.

1. Choose Program ➤ 3D Editor. You see the text appear in each viewport, though it is in the wrong location.

2. Choose Modify ➤ Object ➤ Move, then click on the text in the upper left viewport.

3. Move the text so it is in the triangular portion of the building facade.

4. Use the Zoom Window button to enlarge the entry area of the facade in the upper left viewport, then move the text into position.

5. Render the view to see how the text looks in the building facade. It should look like Figure 11.49.

Figure 11.49: The text extruded, rendered in the Facade model

◆ Summary

In this chapter, you got a more detailed look at lighting and materials in 3D Studio. I also provided some instruction on editing in different surface planes and in creating text. By now, you should have a pretty good grasp of how 3D Studio works.

The most enjoyable part of using 3D Studio is in the experimentation. So while you have the time to experiment, play with the buildings I've provided with this book. Try out some of the other texture maps to see how they work.

In the next chapter you'll explore the world of animation. There, you'll find that if an object can be moved or adjusted in the 3D Editor, it can be animated.

Creating an Animation

Perhaps the most interesting and fun part of using 3D Studio is creating an animated presentation of your design. Animation can really bring your designs to life by adding motion over time.

Time is really the key ingredient to animation. This may sound a bit simplistic, but it will become clear as you work through the tutorials in this chapter that you need to pay at least as much attention to the interaction of your objects through *time* as you devote to moving them through *space*. As you gather more experience animating your work, you'll start to develop an almost intuitive sense for what I call the *timespace* of your model: the ten to twenty seconds of each animated segment you create. You'll become intimately familiar with this timespace as you move and adjust the elements of your model. So as you work through this chapter, be aware of how time is always the key component of everything you do.

Each move of the camera, each change in light intensity, and each movement you put an object through must be choreographed carefully to create a natural-looking flow through time. In this chapter I'll show you the basic tools you need to accomplish this. You will be working primarily with the Keyframer program within 3D Studio.

◆ Understanding the World of Video Time

Have you ever seen, perhaps when you were a child, a special type of book called a *flipbook*? These are books that show a crude animation when you riffle the pages with your thumb. To be more precise, a flipbook is a series of pages displaying a sequence of still pictures arranged in such a way that, when the book is "flipped through," each image is quickly replaced with its successor, one after another, giving the impression of motion within a single image. Today, you can purchase software that will create flipbooks for you from stock cartoon character poses or from images you create yourself. You could probably even create a flipbook of your 3D Studio animation.

Flipbooks demonstrate, in a crude way, how television and film work. To give the impression of motion, your television is really flashing a series of still images at you. These still images replace each other so fast that your mind doesn't perceive them individually, but rather interprets them as a smooth stream of motion, just as it perceives the sequence of images presented by a flipbook.

In the USA, we use what is called the *NTSC standard* for television. This standard determines, among other things, the number of times a second these still images appear on your TV. The rate of images per second, or the *frame rate* as it is more commonly called, is 29.97 frames per second. We usually round this up to 30 frames per second for discussion purposes, but to be absolutely accurate, it is 29.97 FPS. This means that your TV displays one whole picture or *frame* each 1/29.97th of a second. So for 10 seconds, you will see 297.7 separate pictures. (The two European standards, called PAL and SECAM, uses 24 frames per second.)

As you work in 3D Studio, you can think of each of these frames as a unit of time. For the sake of our discussion, I'll round this unit of time to 1/30th of a second. So 30 frames is equal to one second. This will become more apparent as you work through the tutorials.

◆ Creating Camera Motion

In Chapter 9, you were shown a brief glimpse of the *Keyframer*. There, you created a short test animation that moved the camera around your building. In this section, you'll pick up from where you left off in Chapter 9 and begin to refine the camera motion.

1. Load the file called `Savoye7.3DS`.

2. Choose Program ➤ Keyframer.

3. Move your cursor to the bottom of the screen below the view-ports and notice what happens to the command prompt (see Figure 12.1).

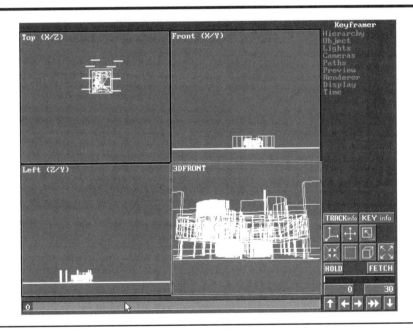

Figure 12.1: The Keyframer Screen with the cursor resting below the viewports

You see the *Frame slider* at the bottom of the screen. This slider lets you find a specific point in time in your animation; you use it by sliding the button in the slider. Initially, you are given 30 frames, or one second's worth of time. Try the slider out.

1. Click on Cameras from the command column. The cameras in this model appear in the viewports (see Figure 12.2).

2. Click and drag the button on the Frame slider, moving it from side to side. Notice how the number in the slider changes. Also notice that there is a red graphic bar indicating your current frame location in the overall scheme of things. Just below the bar is a button to the left that shows your exact frame number.

3. Move the slider to the far right. Though you'll notice that the number stops at 30, you aren't limited to 30 frames. You can increase the number of total frames through some of the tools in the Keyframer command column and Icon panel. You'll see how this is done a bit later.

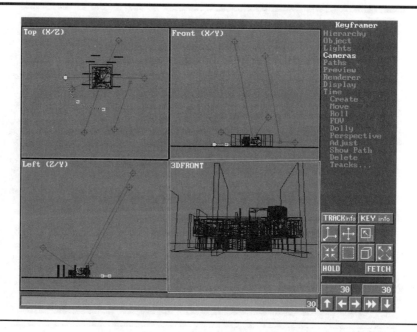

Figure 12.2: The camera path and keyframes appear once you select Cameras from the command column.

If you followed along with the exercises in Chapter 9, you saw how you can move a camera through time. To summarize that chapter's section on the Keyframer, the Frame slider was set to 30, then the camera was moved to a location that viewed the "back" side of the building. The original location of the camera remained while a second location was created at frame 30. In the file you have currently open, you can see the camera location as you move the slider to frame 30.

◆ **Understanding Keyframes**

The exercise in Chapter 9 further demonstrated that you can add what is called a *keyframe* to the camera path. The keyframe is a point along the path that can be manipulated in a number of ways to adjust your camera motion. It appears as a small white square on the camera path. In Chapter 9, a keyframe was created in the middle of the set of frames, frame 15, and then it was moved so the camera path curved around the building.

The simplest adjustment you can make to a keyframe is to move it. Notice that there are already keyframes at the beginning and end of the camera path. These are automatically created as soon as you set the Frame slider to a frame greater than 0 and move the camera. Let's try changing the view of the last frame of this camera path by moving the end keyframe.

1. Choose Paths ➤ Move Key.

2. In the upper left viewport, click on the keyframe shown in Figure 12.3a.

3. Move the keyframe to the location shown in Figure 12.3b. Notice what happens to the camera path.

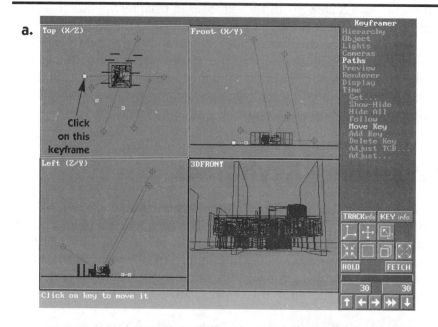

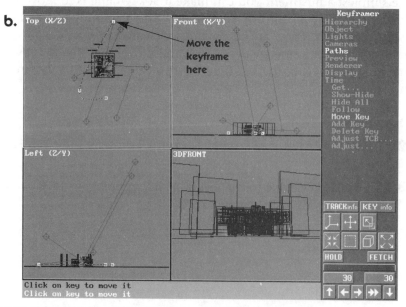

Figure 12.3: Moving the keyframe for frame 30, the last frame

The yellow dots on the camera path show you graphically the location of the camera at each frame. They also show you the change in speed of your camera over time.

Notice that after moving the last keyframe, the yellow dots are spread apart between the middle keyframe at frame 15 and the last frame at frame 30. This tells you that the camera motion is faster between frame 15 and 30 than it is between frame 0 and 15. You know this because the distance between frames is greater from frame 15 to 30 than it is between frames 0 to 15. You can visualize this clearly by creating a preview animation.

You might also notice that the camera path now crosses directly through some trees. To smooth out the camera motion, and to avoid the trees, you will want to move the middle keyframe at frame 15.

1. With Paths ➤ Move Key still selected, click on the middle key-frame and move it to the location shown in Figure 12.4, placing it halfway between the beginning and end of the camera path. Notice that by placing the keyframe here, the yellow dots appear to be more uniformly distributed over the camera path.

2. Choose Preview ➤ Make, then click on the Perspective viewport. The Make Preview dialog box appears.

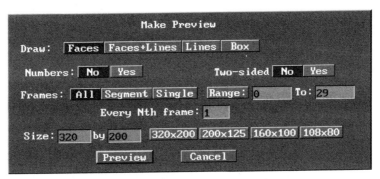

3. Click on the Preview button. The Generating preview message appears, showing 3D Studio's progress as it creates the preview. Once it's done, the preview is displayed.

4. Right-click on the mouse to stop the preview animation.

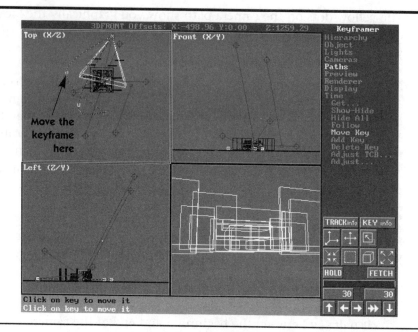

Figure 12.4: Selecting the middle keyframe to move it

The preview shows that your camera motion is too fast. Also, the beginning and end are rather abrupt. First let's see how to slow down the animation by increasing the number of frames in the animation.

Before we move on, I'd like to clarify the difference between moving the camera and moving a keyframe. You can create motion in the Keyframer by selecting a point in time (which is the same as selecting a frame using the Frame slider), then moving a 3D Studio object such as a light, camera, or model object. In doing so, you create a keyframe for that object in that particular frame. You've also moved the object from one place to another over time. The keyframe in turn can be moved using the Paths ➤ Move Key option in the command column. Moving the keyframe changes the location of the object at that particular frame, but it doesn't create any new keyframes.

Increasing the Number of Frames in an Animation Segment

In the beginning of this chapter, I mentioned that the standard frame rate for video is about 30 frames per second. Since this is a fixed quantity, the only way to lengthen the time in our building animation is to increase the number of frames. Right now, we have 30 frames, equivalent to 1 second of animation. Let's see what we need to do to increase our current path to 90 frames.

1. Choose Time ➤ Scale Segment. The Scale Segment Length dialog box appears.

2. Type **90** to change the 30 to 90 in the Scale To input box.

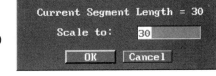

3. Click OK. Notice that the number of yellow dots in the path have increased.

4. Move the cursor to the Frame slider at the bottom of the screen. Notice that the maximum number of frames has increased to 90.

5. Create another preview of the animation.

The animation is now slower. The term *Segment* in the option *Scale Segment* refers to a set of frames within your animation. By default, *all* the frames in a new animation are considered the set of frames in the segment. You can, however, define a smaller segment within the overall animation, to which you can add frames without affecting the rest of the animation. You'll see how that works in the next section. Right now, let's see how to smooth out the beginning and end of the camera path so it doesn't seem so abrupt.

Accelerating and Decelerating the Camera Motion Smoothly

You don't want the camera to just suddenly start moving at its full rate; if it did, your animation would seem jarring. You want the camera motion to start out slowly and then increase speed, as if you were in a car starting out from a stop light. The same is true for the end of the camera path. You want to slow down gradually and not stop instantly. You can control the acceleration and deceleration of the camera using the KEY Info button just above the Icon panel.

1. Click on the button labeled KEY Info just above the Icon panel in the lower right of the screen.

2. In the upper left viewport, click on the keyframe at the beginning of the camera path (see Figure 12.5). The KEY Info dialog box appears.

   As you can see, there are quite a few options in this dialog box. It offers all the controls available for keyframes.

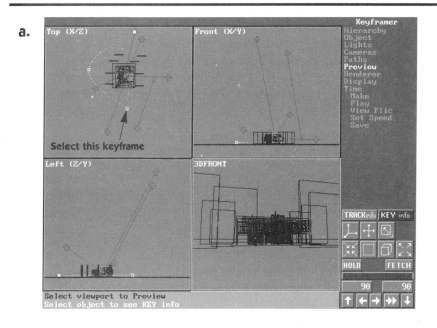

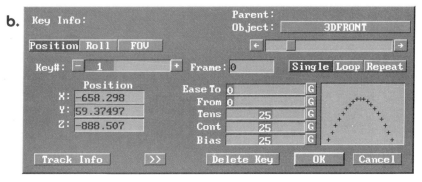

Figure 12.5: Selecting the starting keyframe brings up the KEY Info dialog box

3. Near the lower middle portion of the dialog box, you will see a group of sliders labeled Ease To, From, Tens, Cont, and Bias. Click and drag the From slider button to the middle of the slider so it aligns with the Tens button just below it. As you move the button, watch what happens to the graphic to the right of the sliders. The little X marks on the arch "bunch up" on the right side of the arch's peak.

4. Adjust the From slider button until it shows the number **25**.

5. Click OK, then click on the full-screen toggle button to enlarge the upper left viewport. You'll notice that the yellow dots are arranged more closely together at the beginning of the path and gradually spread apart as you get further from the beginning keyframe (see Figure 12.6).

6. Click on the Full Screen toggle to return to the four-viewport view, then create a preview of the perspective camera viewport to see the effect of changes you just made.

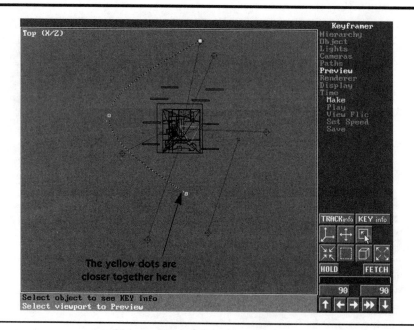

Figure 12.6: Notice how the yellow dots are closer together at the beginning keyframe of the camera path.

You will notice that now the beginning of the animation starts out in a gradual acceleration from a stop. The "bunching up" of yellow dots at the starting keyframe shows you that the frames at the beginning are closer together. As the frames move away from the starting keyframe they gradually spread apart, traversing a greater distance with each frame until a uniform frame to frame distance is reached. The net effect of all this is a smooth acceleration from the camera starting point.

The graphic showing the arch in the KEY Info dialog box shows a sample keyframe in relation to the path. The arch represents time, with the peak of the arch showing the current keyframe. Time moves from left to right in the graphic, so when the X's bunch up on the *right* side, you know the frames are closer together in time *after* the keyframe.

Other Ways of Controlling Speed

If your animation is strictly for video or film, you have no alternative to controlling speed other than increasing or decreasing the number of frames in a segment. On the other hand, if you plan to have your animation shown exclusively on a computer monitor, you have other options.

Most video playback programs for computers allow you to vary the frame rate of your animation up or down from the typical 15 frames per second. In practice, 15 frames per second is perhaps the slowest frame rate you will want. Any slower and you will notice the jerkiness between frames.

There is also a hardware approach, available with some computers, to varying the speed for certain types of animation files. With such a system, you can play back a full 30 frames per second, or decrease the frame rate to slow the animation down.

Now let's adjust the ending keyframe to decelerate the camera motion gradually.

1. Click on the KEY Info button again, then click on the last keyframe of the camera path near the top of the viewport (see Figure 12.7).

2. At the KEY Info dialog box, move the Ease To slider button to where it reads 25. Notice that the X's on the graphic "bunch up" on the left side of the arch's peak.

3. Click OK. Now you will see the yellow dots arranged more closely together near the ending keyframe, as shown in Figure 12.7.

4. Click on the Full Screen toggle button again to restore the four-viewport arrangement.

5. Create another preview animation to see the effects of the Ease To setting.

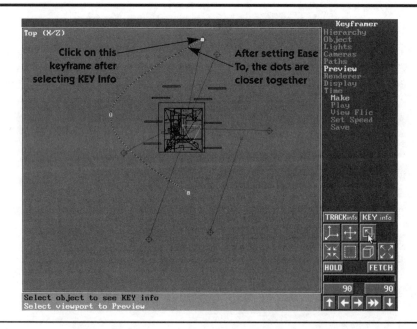

Figure 12.7: Selecting the last keyframe of the camera path. Notice how the yellow dots are closer together at the last keyframe after you change the Ease To setting in the KEY Info dialog box.

In this second exercise, you adjusted the frame rate for the end of the camera path in a way similar to the beginning. Instead of starting out closer together and spreading apart, however, the frames start at their maximum distance apart then gradually become closer together as they approach the ending keyframe. The net effect is a deceleration of the camera motion.

Editing Keyframes

Keyframes are not set in stone and it's a good thing they aren't. A recurring theme in this part of the book is the cycle of editing, testing, then editing again. This process applies to keyframes as much as it does to editing materials and lights in the 3D Editor.

In the following set of exercises, you will add more keyframes and then adjust them to further understand how they work. You'll focus on the Camera keyframes, but as you will learn later, these changes can be applied to keyframes for other objects in your model, such as the lights and objects.

Moving a Keyframe's Location in Time

The camera path still comes a bit too close to the trees. This in turn blocks out the view of the building. Let's add another keyframe to the camera path so we can pull the path further away from the trees.

1. Choose Paths ➤ Add Key, then click on the camera path at the point shown in Figure 12.8a.

2. Choose Paths ➤ Move Key, then move the new keyframe and the keyframe just before it as shown in Figure 12.8b.

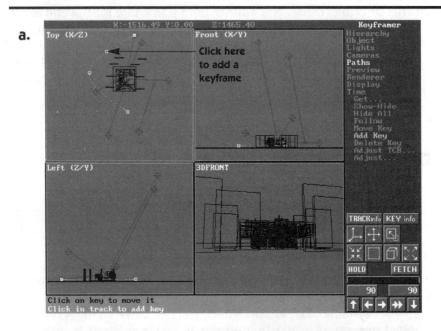

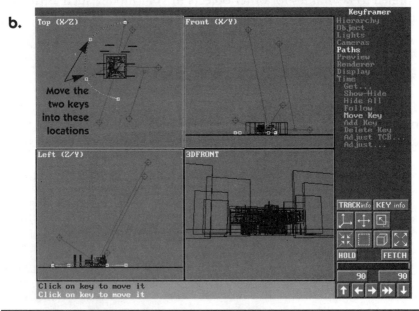

Figure 12.8: Adding and moving a keyframe

Take a moment to study the distribution of the yellow dots along the camera path. They are once again unevenly distributed over the path; they are crowded at the beginning and spaced out in the later half of the path. This will create an animation that will start out slowly and then suddenly speed up. You'll want to "move" the keyframes in *time*, but not necessarily in *space*. By moving the keyframes in time, say by moving the first keyframe to frame 30, for example, you can smooth out the motion of the animation. Here's how it's done.

1. Choose Paths ➤ Adjust ➤ Key Time.

2. Click on the keyframe shown in Figure 12.9a.

3. Now move the mouse from left to right and notice what happens to the yellow dots.

The keyframe does not move, but the yellow dots representing the frames of the camera motion move through the keyframe. Also notice that the Status line at the top of the screen shows the exact frame number for the keyframe, by displaying `Key time = frame #`. Here you see that you get both numerical and visual feedback regarding the location of the keyframe in time.

4. Adjust the yellow dots (by moving the mouse left or right) so they look similar to Figure 12.9B, and the Status line shows `Key time = 36`.

5. Click on the new keyframe and adjust the key time so the Status line shows `Key time = 60`.

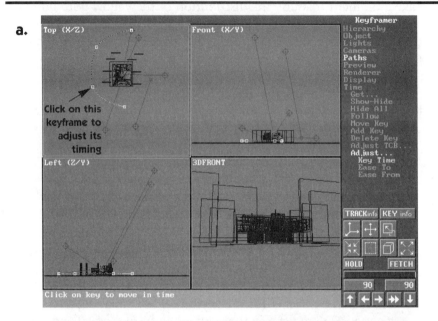

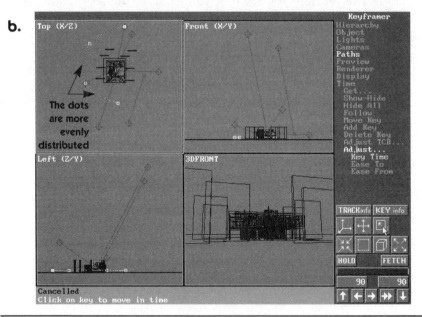

Figure 12.9: Adjusting the keyframe's position in time

Here you saw that you can visually adjust the keyframe's position in time without affecting its physical location. Another way to change a keyframe's position in time is to use the KEY Info dialog box.

1. Click on the KEY Info button, then click on the new keyframe that is second from the end on the path.

2. Make a note of the value in the Frame input box located just above the sliders, then change that value to **75**.

3. Click OK. Now look at the yellow dots in the camera path. Notice that they are crowded below the new keyframe and are spaced out above it toward the last keyframe (see Figure 12.10).

4. Click on the KEY Info button again, select the new keyframe, then return the Frame value to where it was before you changed it in step 2 (around **60**).

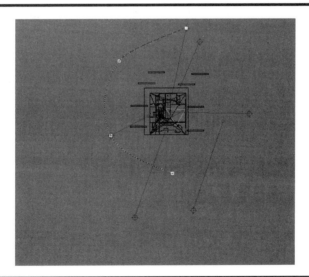

Figure 12.10: The camera path after adjusting the keyframe's frame location using the KEY Info dialog box

> **Tip**   *You may find yourself in a situation where you must synchronize the motion of a camera or other object to sound. The Frame input box in the KEY Info dialog box lets you select an exact keyframe location in time thereby allowing you to set the exact point at which certain sounds and actions must coincide.*

◆ Adding More Frames for Additional Camera Motion

Now let's suppose we want to add some additional *camera motion* to our current animation. It may seem as though we've already used up all the available frames for the tour around the building. As I alluded to earlier, though, you can add additional frames at the beginning or end of any segment of frames.

Adding Frames to the End of a Segment

Adding frames to the end of a segment is a fairly straightforward operation. Here's how it's done.

1. Move the Frame slider to the far right so it reads **90**. This isn't essential to adding new frames, but it will help demonstrate what happens when you do add frames.

2. Choose Time ➤ Total Frames. The Set Number Of Frames dialog box appears.

3. Type **120** to replace the 90 in the Number input box, then click OK. It appears that nothing happens.

4. Move your cursor to the Frame slider at the bottom of the screen. Notice that frame 90, which was at the end of the slider before, has now moved to the left (see Figure 12.11). This tells you that you now have an additional set of frames to play with beyond frame 90.

5. Move the Frame slider all the way to the right again. The Slider button shows 120, telling you that you now have 120 total frames.

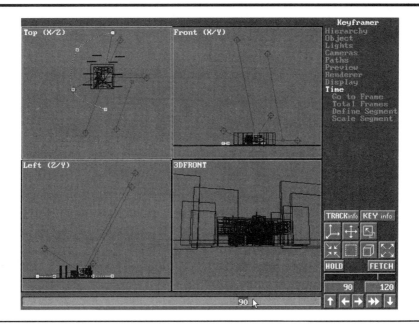

Figure 12.11: The Frame slider after increasing the total number of frames in the animation

While you added more frames to the animation through the Total Frames option, the additional frames had no effect on the existing frames. The number of frames in the camera path did not change. You simply added more frames to the animation which you are currently not utilizing.

Now let's make use of those extra frames.

1. If you haven't done so already, move the Frame slider all the way to the right so it reads **120**.

2. Make sure the upper left viewport is active, and click on the Full-Screen toggle button.

3. Choose Cameras ➤ Move from the command column and move the camera to the position shown in Figure 12.12. Notice that the path now continues around what was the last keyframe to the new one you just created by moving the camera.

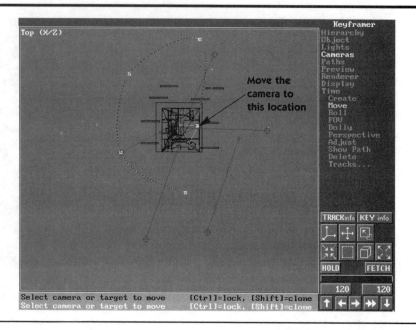

Figure 12.12: Moving the camera to create a new keyframe

Remember that one way to create a new keyframe is to select a new frame number and then move the camera (or other 3D Studio object). In this case, you added more time, then set the Frame slider to the new end of the segment and moved the camera.

Your view at the end seems a bit low. To give the animation a bit more interest, move the keyframes vertically to give the sense of flying up over the building.

1. Click on the Full-Screen toggle button to restore the four-viewports arrangement.

2. Choose Paths ➤ Move Key.

3. Click on the lower left viewport to make it active, then click on the Full-Screen toggle button again to enlarge this view.

4. Press the Tab key twice to restrain the move to a vertical one.

5. Move each keyframe vertically to match the ones in Figure 12.13.

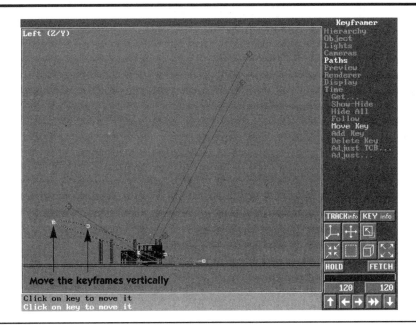

Figure 12.13: Moving the keyframes vertically creates a sense of flying up over the building.

If you gradually move the Frame slider from the far left to right, you get a sense of the motion while you watch the perspective view.

Adjusting the Camera Motion through a Keyframe

Now that you've added a new ending keyframe, the keyframe that used to be last needs a bit of work.

The path through the keyframe at frame 90 swerves out, then curves toward the new ending keyframe. This kind of camera motion might be fine for a funhouse ride, but suppose you want something a little more restrained. For example, you may want the camera to pause at keyframe 90 before it proceeds to the ending keyframe. You can control how a path's motion traverses a keyframe by adjusting the *Continuity* setting, which lets you determine whether the path passes smoothly through a keyframe or makes a sharp turn.

1. Click on the Full-Screen toggle button to return to the four viewports.

2. Choose Paths ➤ Adjust TCB ➤ Continuity.

3. Click on the keyframe at frame 90, as shown in Figure 12.14a. Now as you move your mouse from left to right, you see the camera path change from a smooth curve around the keyframe to a sharp bend. Also notice that the Status line at the top of the screen shows the continuity value as Continuity = #.

4. Use your mouse to adjust the path so it looks similar to the one in Figure 12.14b and the Status line shows Continuity = 4, then left-click the mouse.

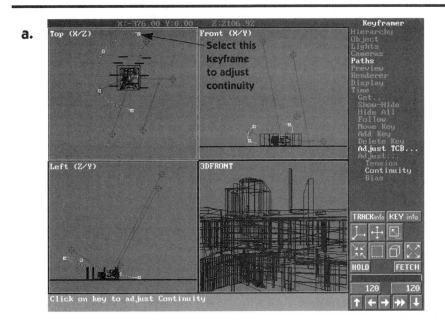

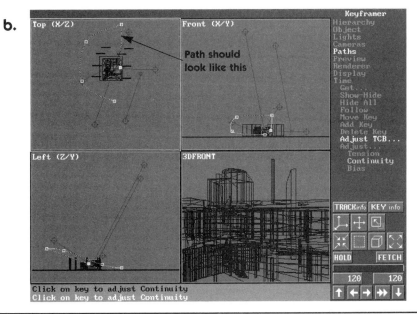

Figure 12.14: Selecting the keyframe to edit and adjusting its continuity setting

5. Now click on the KEY Info button and click on the same keyframe at frame 90. Notice the Cont slider in the dialog box is now set lower than the default setting of 25. You can adjust the continuity here as well, by making changes to this slider, but the Paths ➤ Adjust TCB ➤ Continuity option you used above, offers a way to manipulate the path visually.

6. Adjust the From slider so it is set to **25**, then click OK.

7. Now do a quick check of the camera motion by moving the Frame slider from the far left to the right and watching the perspective view. Notice how the camera seems to pause at frame 90 before it proceeds to move into the building.

You might think that this sharp bend will cause the camera to make an abrupt change at frame 90, but remember that you are working with time as well as actual physical location. Since you set the Ease To and From settings to 25 at the keyframe on frame 90, the transition seems smooth. By making the path a sharp bend, you eliminate the swaying motion of the camera.

You'll want to set the Ease To setting for the last frame so the camera decelerates smoothly to a stop. This time, you'll use the command column to change this setting.

1. Choose Paths ➤ Adjust ➤ Ease To.

2. Click on the last keyframe in the path, as shown in Figure 12.15.

3. As you move the cursor from left to right, notice that the Status line at the top of the screen displays the Ease To value. These values are the same as the ones found in the KEY Info dialog box for the Ease To slider.

4. Move the mouse until the Status line shows Ease To = 25, then left-click your mouse.

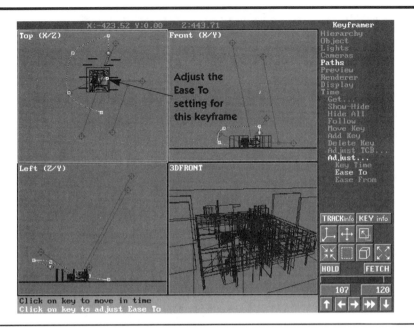

Figure 12.15: Selecting a keyframe to adjust its Ease To setting

As you can see from these exercises, many of the options in the command column are duplicated in the KEY Info dialog box. While it may seem redundant, there will be times when the dialog box will be easier to use than the command column. This is especially true when you want to change the setting for a keyframe that you cannot see from your current view, or when you want to make several changes at one time to a keyframe. The command column options, on the other hand, allow you to visualize the changes more easily.

Increasing the Number of Frames between a Selected Set of Frames

You saw earlier how you can increase the number of frames to increase the overall time or slow down the animation. You can use the same option to slow down the camera motion through a specific group of frames. To do this, you must first define the group of frames you want to slow down.

I've been referring to the entire animation as a segment, but you can actually specify a subset of frames to be a segment which you can expand or contract. Here's how it's done. For our example, you will increase the number of frames between frame 90 and the end of the camera path, frame 120.

1. Choose Time ➤ Define Segment. The Define Active Segment dialog box appears.

2. In the Start input box, enter **90** to define the beginning frame for the segment. Notice that the end frame is already set to 120, which is the last frame in the animation.

3. Click OK. Notice that now you only see frames 90 to 120 in the camera path (see Figure 12.16). Also note that the bar graphic below the Icon panel only shows part of the time line in red. This tells you at a glance that only a portion of all the animation's frames is currently active.

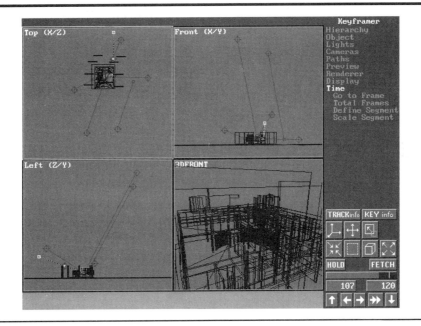

Figure 12.16: The camera path after defining a time segment

Next you will increase the number of frames in this segment to slow the camera motion.

1. Choose Scale Segment. The Scale Segment Length dialog box appears.

2. Enter **60** to change the segment length from 30 to 60.

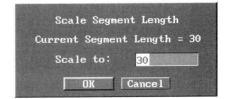

3. Click OK. Notice that the yellow dots increase in number.

Now you will restore all the frames to take a look at how the additional changes affect the camera motion.

1. Choose Time ➤ Define Segment.

2. Click on the All button in the dialog box. Notice that the value in the Start input box changes to 0.

3. Click OK. The entire camera path appears.

4. Now move the Frame slider from left to right to see how the new camera motion looks.

5. If you like, you may create a preview animation at this point to get an even better idea of how the camera motion looks.

Adding Frames to the Beginning of a Segment

You've seen how to add time to the end of a time segment. Now let's look at how you add time to the beginning. You've already been exposed to some of the tools to do this. Here, I'll introduce the TRACK Info button and dialog box.

1. Choose TRACK Info, then click on the camera path. The TRACK Info dialog box appears (see Figure 12.17).

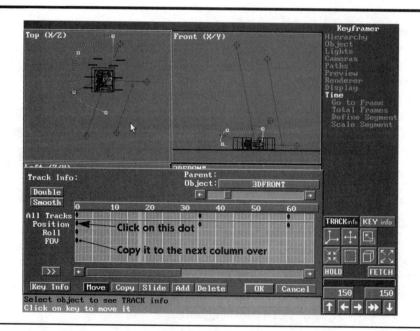

Figure 12.17: The TRACK Info dialog box

This dialog box shows you the keyframes of the camera path along a time line. With this dialog box, you can copy, move, add, or delete a keyframe anywhere along the time line. You can also create new keyframes to control other types of camera behavior over time, like field of view and rotation.

2. Click on the Copy button at the bottom of the dialog box.

3. Click on the black dot next to the Position label at the far left of the time line (see Figure 12.17). Now as you move the mouse, you see two yellow dots move with it along the time line.

4. Drag the yellow dots into the next column to the right (the frame 1 position), and click the mouse to leave them there. Each column represents one frame, so you've just copied the Position properties of the first keyframe at frame 0 to frame 1.

5. Now click OK to exit the dialog box.

Take a moment to look at Figure 12.17. As you can see, the TRACK Info dialog box is a tool that will allow you to duplicate or move specific keyframe *properties*. In the previous exercise, you duplicated the Position property of the first keyframe. This action created a new keyframe in the same location as the original starting keyframe.

Notice that there are other properties listed to the left of the time line, such as Roll and Field of View. Keyframes associated with other types of objects will display properties appropriate to them. For example, a light will display Color, Hotspot, Falloff, and Roll. These are all light properties that you can change over time. You can copy these properties to other existing keyframes, or you can create new keyframes to control these properties, just as you have done in the last exercise.

At frame 1 you now have a new keyframe that is a copy of the properties of keyframe 0, the beginning keyframe. Since they are so close together, you can't really see the new keyframe in any of the views, but it is there, as the next exercise will demonstrate.

1. Choose Time ➤ Define Segment.

2. In the Define Active Segment dialog box, click on the End input box and change its value to **1**.

3. Click OK.

4. Make sure the Frame slider is on 0, then choose Paths ➤ Move Key.

5. Click on the beginning keyframe, as shown in Figure 12.18a.

6. Move the keyframe to the position shown in Figure 12.18b. Notice that now you can see the second keyframe. Also notice that there are no yellow dots between the two keyframes, because there are no intermediate frames.

7. Choose Time ➤ Scale Segment, then at the Scale Segment Length dialog box, enter **40** and click OK.

8. Choose Time ➤ Define Segment, then, at the Define Active Segment dialog, click All, and then click OK.

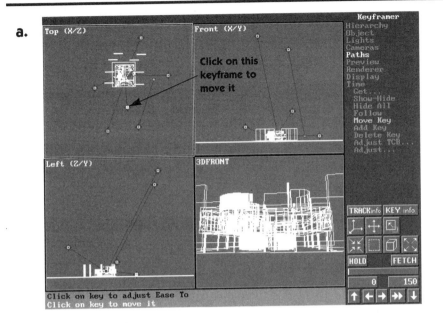

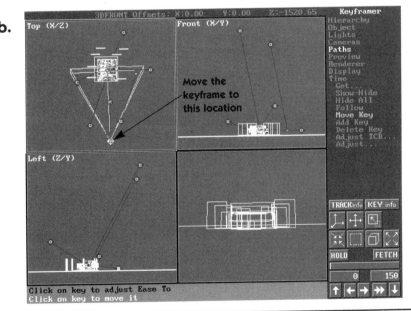

Figure 12.18: Moving the beginning keyframe to a new position

Now you have some additional time at the beginning of the animation. In this situation, you added camera motion first by moving frame 0 from its original location to one further away from the building, then you added the additional time between keyframes 0 and 1.

To finish this first portion of the animation, let's adjust the new second keyframe so that the camera motion will be smoother.

1. Click on the KEY Info button, then click on the second keyframe as shown in Figure 12.19.

2. At the KEY Info dialog box, set the Ease To slider to **25**.

3. Set the Cont slider to **5**. These settings are similar to the second-to-last keyframe where the camera pauses before it moves into the courtyard of the building.

4. Click OK.

5. Create a preview of the animation now, to check the camera motion.

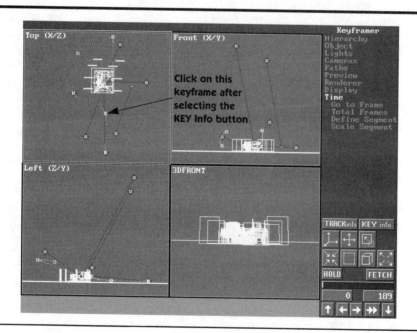

Figure 12.19: Selecting the keyframe to set the continuity of the path

Throughout this chapter, I've asked you to create preview animations or to use the Frame slider to check your camera motion. The next section will show you some new ways to preview the motion in your model.

Other Options for Previewing Your Motion

At the end of Chapter 9, you learned how to create a preview animation that gives you a pretty good sense of the speed and overall time of your animation. You've also seen in this chapter how you can use the Frame slider to get an idea of the camera motion by manually sliding the bar at a slow rate and watching the result in the perspective view.

A third way to study the motion in your animation is to use the Playback buttons located at the bottom of the command column, below the Icon panel.

These buttons work like buttons on a VCR:

◆ The first, upward-pointing button moves you to the first frame of the active segment. The last, downward-pointing button moves you to the last frame.

◆ The left-pointing single arrow moves you backward one frame at a time. The right-pointing single arrow moves you forward one frame at a time.

◆ The button with the right-pointing *double* arrow, also called the *Playback button*, plays the active segment in a continuous loop. It enlarges the currently active viewport and shows you the motion of objects from the perspective of that viewport.

The playback is useful for getting an idea of how your animation is working. The playback speed is not at a full 30 fps, but it can still give you an idea of what's happening in your animation.

Try it out on what you've got so far.

1. Click on the perspective view to make it active.

2. Click on the Playback button below the Icon panel and watch the playback for a few seconds.

3. Right-click on your mouse to stop the playback.

The animation is played back at a fairly slow speed. You can alter the way your view is displayed to help improve the speed somewhat, as demonstrated in this next exercise.

1. Choose Display ➤ Speed ➤ Fastdraw. Notice that an asterisk appears next to Fastdraw in the command column, indicating that it is the option currently selected. Also notice what happens to the perspective view. It looks less well defined (see Figure 12.20).

2. Click on the Playback button. The playback speed is now a bit faster.

3. Right-click on your mouse to stop the playback.

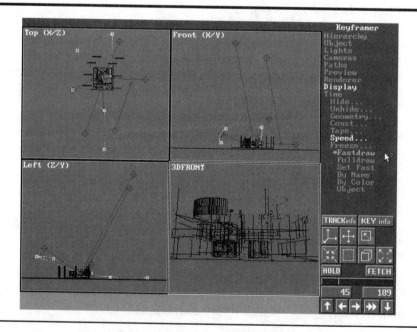

Figure 12.20: The perspective view using the Fastdraw setting

You can increase the speed even more by using *boxes* to represent the objects in your model. This spares 3D Studio from having to use resources to show the details of the model's appearance.

1. Choose Display ➤ Geometry ➤ Box. Notice that an asterisk appears next to the box to tell you that it is now the current option. Also notice what happens to the display in the perspective view. All the objects now appear as boxes.

2. Now click on the Playback button. The playback speed is much faster now.

3. Right-click on your mouse to stop the playback.

4. For normal editing, you will want to set the display back to its previous setting (Full Detail). Choose Display ➤ Geometry ➤ Full Detail.

5. Also choose Display ➤ Speed ➤ Full Draw to return to the original settings.

As you've just seen, these different options offer a variety of ways of previewing your animation. These tools will let you get a sense of the motion in the animation at each change you make. They are an aid to refining your animation, so make liberal use of them!

◆ Moving the Camera Target through Time

So far in this chapter, you've touched on all the major editing activities you might run into while creating a camera *path*. You can also make changes to the camera target. The target can be manipulated independently of the camera it is attached to.

1. In the upper left viewport, use Figure 12.21a as a a reference to enlarge your view of the building courtyard so it looks like Figure 12.21b.

2. Move the Frame slider to the far right (to the last frame) so you can see the camera in the viewport.

3. Choose Camera ➤ Adjust, then click on the camera (see Figure 12.21b).

4. In the Camera definition dialog box, click the Show Cone On button, then click OK. This will help you locate the target for this camera.

5. Choose Camera ➤ Move, then move the camera target to the location shown in Figure 12.21c.

6. Choose Paths ➤ Show-Hide, then click on the camera target you just moved. You'll see its short path appear (see Figure 12.22).

7. Finally, choose Paths ➤ Move Key and move the last keyframe for the camera to the location shown in Figure 12.21c.

a.

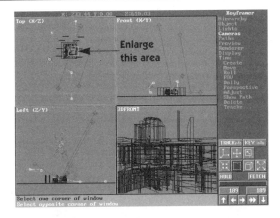

b.

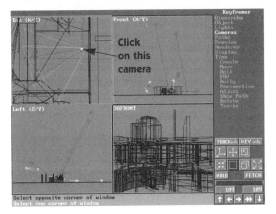

c.

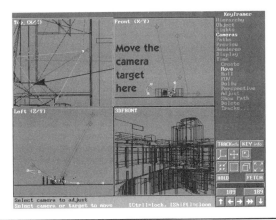

Figure 12.21: Moving the camera target

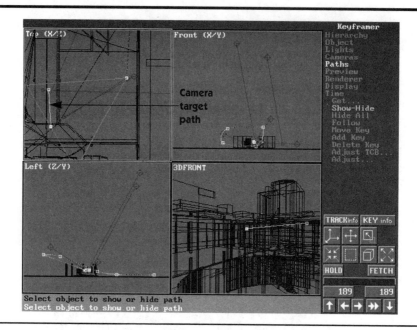

Figure 12.22: The camera target path

Now you've created a motion for your target. The target has just two keyframes at each end of its path. Just as with the camera path, you can adjust the keyframes with the Ease To and Ease From settings, as well as with Continuity. Remember that when you start to add camera target motion, you will need to pay attention to its effect on the overall animation. If part of the animation seems too "jerky" and you've adjusted everything for the camera path, check the target path for abrupt changes. The target motion is often forgotten as the cause of erratic camera motion.

◆ Controlling Lights over Time

In this section, you'll learn that you can move a light over time in the same way as you move a camera. You'll also learn how properties of a light, such as intensity, can also be made to change over time.

In the first exercise, you'll move one of the Sun spotlights over time in conjunction with the camera motion. This will give the effect of a time-lapse video, since this "Sun" will be moving fairly rapidly. You wouldn't normally do this in an architectural walk-through, but we're doing it here to further demonstrate how to manipulate your animation through time.

1. In the upper left viewport, zoom out so you can see the view of the building plan as shown in Figure 12.23a.

2. Set the Frame slider to the end of the animation.

3. Choose Lights ➤ Spot ➤ Adjust, then click on the spotlight shown in Figure 12.23a. The Spotlight Definition dialog box appears.

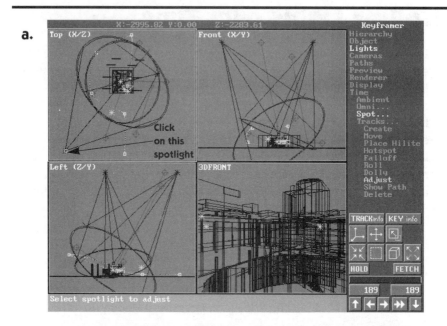

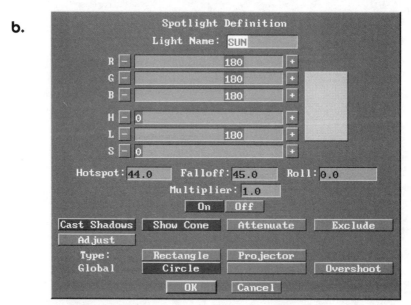

Figure 12.23a: Setting up to move the Sun spotlight

4. At the Spotlight Definition dialog box, click on the On button to turn this light on, then click OK.

5. Choose Lights ➤ Spot ➤ Move and, in the upper left viewport, move the light to the position shown in Figure 12.23b, near the second Sun spotlight.

6. Move the Frame slider back and forth to see the motion of the spotlight.

7. To make the spotlight path visible, choose Paths ➤ Show-Hide, then click on the spotlight.

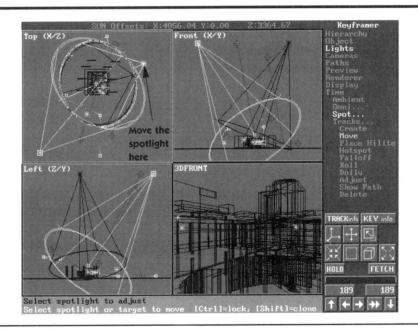

Figure 12.23b: Moving the Sun spotlight

You can now see the path of the Sun spotlight. It currently traverses this path over the entire length of the animation. But suppose you want the Sun to start its motion at frame 100 instead of frame 0. For this, you'll use the KEY Info dialog box again.

1. Click on the KEY Info button, then click on the first keyframe of the spotlight in the lower left corner of the viewport.

2. At the KEY Info dialog box, change the Frame input box from its current value of 0 to **100**.

3. Click OK.

4. Now move the Frame slider from 0 to the end to see how the spotlight moves.

The spotlight now waits until frame 100 before it starts to move. You can also tell that the timing for the spotlight is different simply by the number of yellow dots along its path. Its motion doesn't start until frame 100, which reduces the total number of frames in its path.

In this example, you altered the time associated with the beginning of the motion for the spotlight. You can use the same procedure for any object and keyframe.

Changing Light Intensity over Time

Suppose you want to fade the sunlight while simultaneously brightening the interior lights, to duplicate the effect of what happens to most houses every evening. In addition, let's suppose you want this done at the end of the viewing of the courtyard, while the camera is no longer moving. To accomplish this, you'll use several of the tools you've already worked with.

1. First add some time to the end of the animation by choosing Time ➤ Total Frames.

2. At the Set Number of Frames dialog box, change the number to **250**. This will add about two seconds of time to the end.

3. Click on TRACK Info, then click on the spotlight path.

4. In the TRACK Info dialog box, move the Timeline slider, just below the time line, all the way to the right. Notice that the numbers above the line move as you move the slider. They indicate the frame number.

5. Click on the Copy button at the bottom of the dialog box so the button is highlighted, then click on the black dot in the row labeled Color (see Figure 12.24a). These black dots represent the last keyframe for the spotlight path. Now as you move the cursor, two yellow dots follow and you see a readout of the selected dot's location in the Status line.

6. Click on the location shown in Figure 12.24b to place a copy of the Color property at frame number 230.

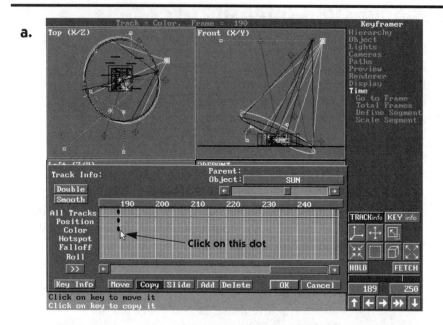

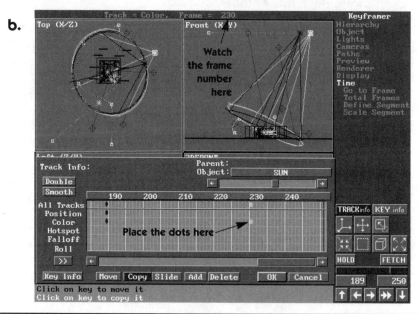

Figure 12.24: Selecting and copying the Color property to create a new spotlight keyframe

You've just created a new keyframe for the light. This new keyframe is in the same position as the last keyframe for the spotlight path. Since it's in the exact same location as the original, it would be difficult to select it visually in the viewport. But all the keyframes in the model can be accessed easily from the TRACK Info dialog box, regardless of whether they are overlapping or not, as you will see in the next exercise.

Now let's adjust the last spotlight keyframe to turn the light down.

1. Click on KEY Info at the bottom of the dialog box so the button is highlighted.

2. Click on one of the black dots representing the copy of the Color property keyframe you just created at frame 230. You see the KEY Info dialog box for that frame.

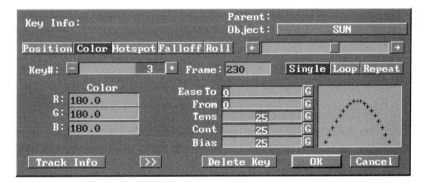

3. You want the spotlight to be off at this point in the spotlight's path. There is no Off button, but you can reduce the intensity to 0 by changing all the color input boxes in the left side of the dialog box to 0. Click on the box labeled R, then change the value to **0** (zero).

4. Press the Tab key to move to the next color input box labeled G, then enter **0** again.

5. Repeat step 4 to change the B input box to **0**. Now the light intensity for this last keyframe is 0, essentially turning off the spotlight at this point in time.

6. Click OK to exit the KEY Info dialog.

Take a moment to study the dialog box shown in step 2 of the previous exercise. Notice that in the upper portion of the dialog box, you have buttons labeled Position, Color, Hotspot, Falloff, and Roll. Currently the Color button is highlighted. This tells you that the changes you make in this dialog box will affect the color property of the spotlight. The Frame number shows the frame associated with this keyframe.

The Key # slider shows which of the three spotlight keyframes you are currently editing. You can use the Key # slider to move to another keyframe if you so choose. This Key # slider will only let you select from the keyframes that have the currently selected property (Color) available for editing.

Since the preview options in the Keyframer don't offer ways to show lighting, the effects of lighting over time won't be apparent until you actually render this file as an animation.

◆ Render File Output Options

Now let's take a look at the rendering options for the Keyframer. The options aren't really much different from those available for the 3D Editor. There are some additions, however, that allow you to select a range of frames to render, as well as an additional file format specifically for animations.

Creating a Study Animation

In the following exercise, you'll create an animation file to be viewed in 3D Studio. It won't be a finished product by any means. In fact, it will seem nearly as crude as the preview animation you created earlier in this chapter. The advantage to using the Renderer output, however, is that you will be able to see the lighting change over time.

The first animation you'll do will focus on the last few frames of the animation, to ascertain that the spotlight is indeed dimming at the end.

1. Choose Renderer ➤ Render View, then click on the Perspective viewport. The Render Animation dialog box appears.

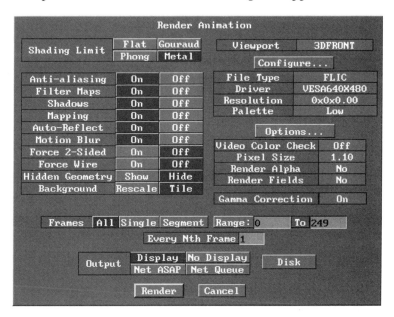

Notice that the options are quite similar to the Render options in the 3D Editor.

2. Click on the Off button for the following options: Anti-aliasing, Filter maps, Shadows, Mapping, Auto-Reflect, and Motion Blur. All these options would increase the amount of time required for rendering, and, for now, all we want is a quick animation that will show us what the lights are doing.

3. Click on Flat in the Shading Limit button group near the top of the dialog box. This option produces the simplest shading.

4. Now click on the button labeled Range in the lower half of the dialog box.

5. In the input box next to the Range button, change the value from 0 to **200**. This forces 3D Studio to render just the last frames starting at frame 200.

6. Make sure the button labeled Disk is highlighted by clicking on it. It should now be red indicating that it is active.

You're nearly ready to render, but one important step now is to select an output file format.

1. Click on the Configure button in the upper right corner of the dialog box. The Device Configuration dialog box appears.

This dialog box allows you to select the type of file you want for your animation, as well as the file resolution.

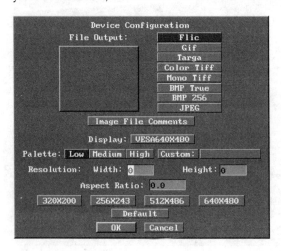

2. Notice that *Flic* is highlighted at the top of the column of buttons. This is an animation-file format specifically designed for playback on a computer. (See the discussion on file format at the end of this chapter.)

3. Click on the button labeled 320×200 in the lower half of the dialog box.

4. Click OK. You return to the Render Animation dialog.

5. Click Render. The Save Rendered Animation To File dialog box appears.

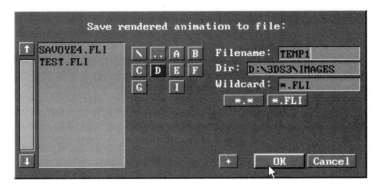

Note *The information shown in the list box of the Save Rendered Animation dialog box will differ from computer to computer. Don't be alarmed if you see different files listed.*

6. Enter **Temp1** in the Filename input box. Notice that 3D Studio shows the \3ds4\Images subdirectory (or \3ds3\Images if you've upgraded 3D Studio from the earlier version and kept the old directory name). 3D Studio places animation files in this subdirectory by default. You can, of course, select a different sub-directory. For this example, go ahead and use the default.

7. Click OK. 3D Studio will proceed to render the frames.

3D Studio may take several minutes to render all the frames. When it has finished, 3D Studio returns to the Keyframer.

Now you can view the rendered animation from the Keyframer.

1. Choose Preview ➤ View Flic. The Select Flic File To Load dialog box appears.

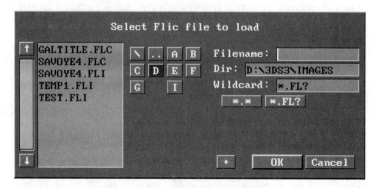

Notice that this dialog box automatically displays the contents of the \3ds4\Images subdirectory.

2. Click on Temp1.FLI then click OK. You see the animation play back on the screen.

The animation plays back in a loop until you press the right mouse button. If you followed the instructions to the tutorials carefully, you see the lights dimming.

As you can see, the animation is still pretty crude, but at least we can tell whether the lights are doing what we want them to.

Creating a Quick Overall Study Animation

Now suppose you want to get a quick view of the overall animation, to make sure everything is working as planned. In the next exercise you'll adjust some of the frame output settings to limit the number of frames that are animated. This will help reduce the total animation time so you'll see the results more quickly.

1. Choose Renderer ➤ Render View, then click on the perspective view again.

2. At the Render Animation dialog box, click on the button labeled All in the Frames button group.

3. In the Every Nth Frame input box just below the Frames button group, change the value to **2**. This causes the Renderer to render every second frame instead of each frame.

4. Click Render. The Save Rendered Animation To File dialog box appears.

5. Enter **Temp2** in the Filename input box, then click OK.

3D Studio will take several minutes to render these frames. You might want to take a little break at this point and return in a few minutes. When 3D Studio has finished rendering, it returns to the Keyframer screen.

Before you view the second animation, you will want to change the playback speed to compensate for the fact that the animation contains every other frame instead of every frame.

1. Choose Preview ➤ Set Speed. The Preview Playback Speed dialog box appears.

2. Enter **15** in the Frames Per Second input box. Since your animation contains every other frame, you will want to play it back at a slower rate to approximate the actual speed of the final animation. If you play it back at the full 30fps, it will appear at twice the normal speed.

3. Click OK to exit the dialog box.

4. Choose Preview ➤ View Flic.

5. At the Select Flic File To Load dialog box, select `Temp2.FLI`, then click OK. The entire animation plays back.

This animation is still crude and a bit jerky, but it does convey a sense of how the final animation will appear. It also shows us some problems that need fixing. The next section addresses those problems and looks for solutions.

◆ Working with Backgrounds and Props

You probably noticed that the trees appear as boxes. You turned off many of the rendering features that made the trees appear so lifelike in Chapter 10. You may have also noticed that the background stayed the same while the rest of the animation moved by. This shows us that the background does not move with the camera. It remains the same no matter where you are in the model. The flat trees and background may have been satisfactory in a single image, but now that you've added motion, you find that they produce some odd results. This section will show you some ways of dealing with backgrounds and props that will give your animated renderings a sense of realism. You'll start with the background.

> ***Tip*** *You may run into a situation where a bitmap image you used as a background appears in a tile pattern in the final rendering instead of as a single image. This is caused by a mismatch between the resolution of the background image and the output resolution of your rendering. If this happens, change the Background setting in the Render Animation dialog box to Rescale. (The default is Tile.)*

Creating a Credible Background

There are ways of producing an animated background; unfortunately, we won't have time to discuss those methods in detail in this book. We can, however, employ some other modeling methods to create a background that follows the rest of the model.

In animations such as this one, where you are showing an outdoor flyby of a building, the background can be a simple gradient from bottom to top. Such a background will not appear to be static since there are no objects in the background to define a point of reference as the camera moves.

1. Choose Renderer ➤ Setup ➤ Background. The Background Method dialog box appears.

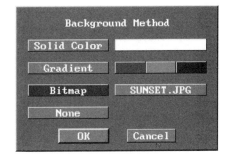

This is the same Background Method dialog box you saw in Chapter 10 when you first added the sky background.

2. Click on the button labeled Gradient.

3. Click on the color bar next to the Gradient color bar. The Define Gradient Colors dialog box appears.

4. Click on the graphic in the lower left that shows the gradient colors. Now the arrow pointing to the middle color box on the right moves up and down with the mouse.

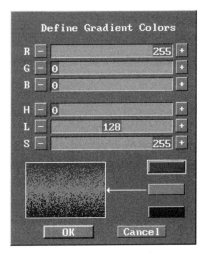

5. Move your mouse so the arrow looks similar to the one shown below, then left-click your mouse. The gradient color changes to follow the arrow.

6. Click on the middle green color bar to make it active. You can tell it is selected and active by the white outline around it.

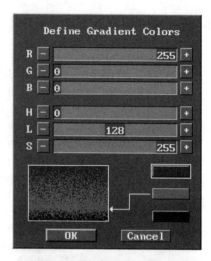

7. Move the color sliders in the upper half of the dialog box so they match the settings shown here.

This produces a dark gray color for the mid to lower third of the gradient color.

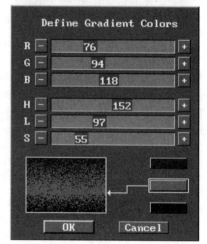

8. Click on the Top color bar, then move the color sliders to match the settings shown below.

9. Finally, click on the bottom color bar, then set the color sliders to **0**.

10. Click OK, then click OK again at the Background Method dialog.

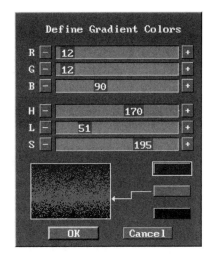

Now let's take a look at what the new rendering will look like. Before you can render, you must make sure that the AutoVision \AV2\Maps directory is in the map path. Otherwise you will see a series of error messages telling you that 3D Studio cannot find map images. Use Info ➤ Configure … to locate \AV2\MAPS in the Map Path. If you need help doing this, refer to the section entitled "Adding a Map Path to Help 3D Studio Find Bitmaps" in the previous chapter.

1. Move the Frame slider to frame 0. You will render this frame to see what the new background looks like.

2. Choose Renderer ➤ Render View, then click on the perspective view.

3. Click on the On button for the Anti-aliasing, Filter maps, Shadows, Mapping, Auto-Reflect, and Motion Blur options to turn these features back on.

4. Click on the button labeled Single in the Frames button group. (You only want to render a single frame and this is the button that will do it.)

5. Click on the button labeled Metal in the Shading Limit button group. This will shade the model at the highest-quality level.

6. Click on the Disk button to turn it off. (You don't necessarily want to save this rendering to disk since we're only using it here to check our background.)

7. Click Render. A message appears asking you if you really want to render to the screen only. Click OK.

After a few moments, you will see the rendered view appear on your screen (see Figure 12.25). It may appear smaller than you are used to, or it may appear at a lower resolution. This is because you haven't yet set the rendering resolution back to the default, 640×480, in the Device Configuration dialog box.

Figure 12.25: A rendered view of the model with a new gradient background

The new background looks like a typical clear sky with a gray horizon. It won't matter that the background remains the same throughout the animation, since the gradient colors won't "give away" the fact that they are not moving with the camera.

Using a Texture Map and Hemisphere for the Sky

The gradient background offers the illusion of a clear sky, but what if you want to add some clouds? You can simulate a cloudy sky by adding a flattened dome over your model, then assigning a texture map to the dome that uses a bitmap of a cloudy sky. Here's how it's done.

First you'll add the hemisphere object.

1. Choose Program ➤ 3D Editor.

2. Click on the upper left viewport to make it active.

3. Click on the Zoom Extents button to view the entire plan of the building.

4. Choose Create ➤ Hemisph ➤ Smooth.

5. At the `Place center of 16-segment smoothed hemisphere` prompt, click on the building (see Figure 12.26).

6. Click on the edge of the ground object to define the hemisphere's diameter (see Figure 12.26).

7. At the `Name For New Object` prompt, enter **Sky**, then click Create.

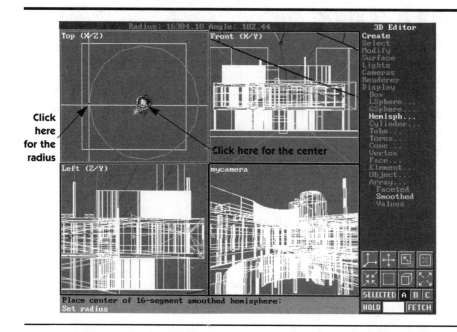

Figure 12.26: Creating the Sky hemisphere

Now that you have the sky object, the next thing to do is to create a material to map to it.

1. From the pull-down menu, choose Program ➤ Materials.

2. Click on the Map button across from the Texture 1 row in the Texture Map button group.

Map Type	Amount			Map		Mask	
Texture 1	—	100	+	NONE	S	NONE	S
Texture 2	—	100	+	NONE	S	NONE	S
Opacity	—	100	+	NONE	S	NONE	S
Bump	—	100	+	NONE	S	NONE	S
Specular	—	100	+	NONE	S	NONE	S
Shininess	—	100	+	NONE	S	NONE	S
Self Illum	—	100	+	NONE	S	NONE	S
Reflection	—	100	+	NONE	A	NONE	S

3. At the Select Texture Map dialog box, click on the button labeled .JPG, then select SKY.JPG in the list box and click OK.

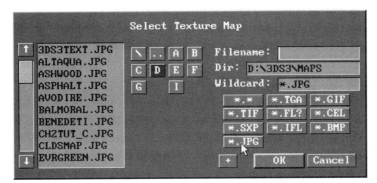

4. Back at the Materials Editor, click on the Current Material input box, then at the New Name For Material dialog box, enter **Sky**.

5. Choose Material ➤ Put to Current.

6. At the New Current Material dialog box, click OK.

The last step is to add the material and a mapping coordinate to the sky object.

1. Choose Program ➤ 3D Editor.

2. Choose Surface ➤ Normals ➤ Object Flip, then click on the hemisphere.

3. At the Flip Normals Of Object "Sky" dialog box, click OK.

Remembering that the direction of the normals determine the side of the object that reflects light, you want to flip the normals of the sky hemisphere, because the normals of a hemisphere point outward by default. In this case you want them pointing inward to show the sky texture map on the inside of the hemisphere, where all your views take place.

1. Click on the upper right viewport, then click on the Zoom Extents button to get a complete view of the sky hemisphere.

2. Choose Surface ➤ Mapping ➤ Adjust ➤ Region Fit.

3. Click on the two points shown in Figure 12.27 to place a planar mapping coordinate on the entire surface of the hemisphere.

4. Choose Surface ➤ Mapping ➤ Apply Object, then click on the hemisphere to apply the mapping coordinate to the sky object.

5. Choose OK at the Apply mapping dialog box.

6. Choose Surface ➤ Material ➤ Assign ➤ Object, and click on the hemisphere.

7. At the Assign Sky To Object dialog, click OK.

8. While in the 3D Editor, choose Modify ➤ Object ➤ Move, then move the sky hemisphere downward slightly so its base is not aligned with the ground object.

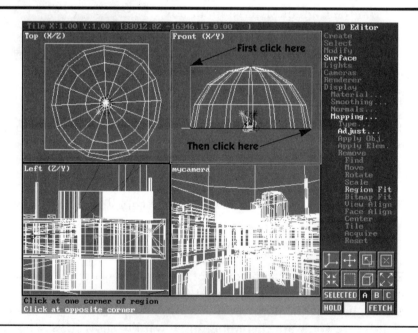

Figure 12.27: Adding the mapping coordinates to the sky hemisphere

> **Note**   *One anomaly in 3D Studio is that if the hemisphere is aligned with the ground object, the ground will render as if it had the sky material (instead of the green grass material) assigned to it. Also, if the hemisphere is too high, the light from the Sun spotlight stops at the region defined by the bottom edge of the hemisphere. This is why I asked you to move the hemisphere downward in step 8.*

Even though the sky object is half a sphere, you used a planar mapping coordinate. The planar mapping will prevent the sky bitmap from "curling" at a center point, something the other two map types tend to do. The planar mapping coordinate will distort the sky in the left and right sides of the hemisphere when viewed from the upper right viewport, but the distortion is not too noticeable.

Now return to the Keyframer and render a frame to see how the new sky looks.

1. Choose Program ➤ Keyframer.

2. Make sure you are at frame 0, then choose Renderer ➤ Render View.

3. Click on the Perspective viewport.

4. At the Render Animation dialog box, make sure the Single button is selected in the Frames button group.

5. Click on the Configure button.

6. At the Configure dialog box, click on the button labeled 640×480, then click OK.

7. Click on Render, then at the Render To Screen Only? message, click OK. You will see a view similar to Figure 12.28.

Figure 12.28: The model rendered with a sky

Since the sky bitmap is now assigned to an object in the model, it will remain fixed in relation to the rest of the model. The net effect will be that the sky will appropriately follow the rest of the objects in the scene as the camera moves along its path.

Animating Materials

You've seen how you can use static bitmap images for texture maps in the Materials Editor. You can also use animated Flic files or sequential bitmap files for texture maps. For example, you could create an animation of the sky moving across the screen, then use that animation in place of a static bitmap for the Map option in the Texture Map settings of the Materials Editor.

The Renderer ➤ Setup ➤ Background option also allows the use of animations for backgrounds. See "Animation File Output" later in this chapter for more on animation files.

Making the Trees Appear in 3D in the Animation

As I mentioned earlier, the trees look fine as long as you render a view that shows them face-forward. When you see them from the side, however, as in frame 100, you see that they are really just flat planes. You can employ a common 3D animation trick to at least reduce this problem.

The trick is to create a second tree that crosses through the first, like two intersecting planes as shown below. Such an arrangement gives the impression that the tree is indeed three-dimensional instead of just a flat plane. Here's how to make the change in the building model to add the extra plane to each tree.

1. Choose Program ➤ 3D Editor.

2. In the upper left viewport, zoom into the building so you can see all of the trees (see Figure 12.29).

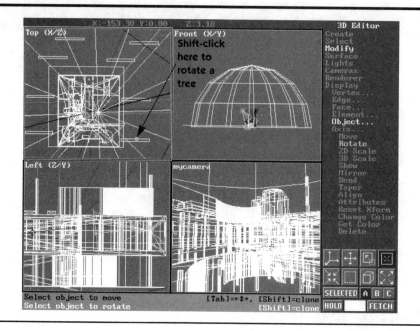

Figure 12.29: Making copies of the trees that cross through the original trees

3. Click on the Local Axis icon in the Icon panel. This icon forces certain editing options to use the selected object's local origin (as opposed to the global origin of the model).

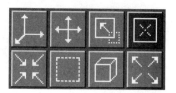

4. Choose Modify ➤ Object ➤ Rotate, then Shift-click on one of the trees as shown in Figure 12.29.

> **Tip** *After choosing Modify ➤ Object ➤ Rotate, type **A** to force the angle of rotation to 10-degree increments. This will make it easier in the next step to rotate the trees to exactly 90 degrees.*

5. Rotate the tree 90 degrees so the original and the copy form a cross, then click the left mouse button. The Name For New Object dialog box appears with a suggested name.

6. Click on Create at the dialog box to accept the suggested name.

7. Repeat steps 4 and 5 for each tree.

Note *The Keyframer also has an Object ➤ Rotate option, but as with all edits in the Keyframer, rotating objects are time-dependent. This means that by rotating an object in the Keyframer, the object will actually appear to rotate over time in your animation. Also, the Object ➤ Rotate option in the Keyframer can be toggled with the Tab key to change the rotation axis.*

In step 3, you used the Local Axis icon to rotate the tree about its own axis. Had you not used this option, the tree would rotate about the global origin of the model as though it were on a merry-go-round. The global origin is similar to the origin in the WCS in AutoCAD.

Now that you've got the trees in the form of a cross, you will want to turn off their ability to receive shadows, because any shadows cast by the crossing planes will draw attention to the fact that they *are* crossed planes. You want to minimize the planar appearance as much as possible.

1. Choose Modify ➤ Object ➤ Attributes, then click on one of the trees.

2. At the Object Attributes dialog box, click on Receive Shadows to turn off that option.

3. Click OK to exit the dialog box.

4. Repeat steps 2 and 3 for all the rest of the trees.

Now the trees will cast shadows but will not receive them. The next step is to return to the Keyframer and look at the effects of your work.

1. Choose Program ➤ Keyframe.

2. Set the Frame slider to frame 90.

3. Choose Renderer ➤ Render View, then click on the Perspective viewport.

4. At the Render Animation dialog box, make sure Single is selected in the Frames button group, then click Render.

5. Click OK at the Render To Screen? message. After a minute or two, you will see a view similar to Figure 12.30.

Figure 12.30: The rendered view of the trees after adding copies that cross

Now the trees look a bit less like false-front buildings. You can further improve the simulation of trees by changing the opacity map for the tree so its foliage isn't completely solid. Figure 12.31 shows the opacity map modified in a paint program to "break up" the solid areas of the tree. By reducing the tree's opacity, it softens the tree's flat appearance.

Figure 12.31: A sample of the opacity bitmap before and after adding gray tones

Adding a Moving Car

Before we leave this chapter, you will want to know how to animate an object in your model. In this last set of exercises, you'll use a box to represent a car to see how you can make an object move smoothly in an animation.

1. Choose Program ➤ 3D Editor.

2. In the two left viewports, adjust your views so they look similar to the ones in Figure 12.32.

3. Choose Create ➤ Box.

4. Draw the two corners of the box in the upper right viewport as shown in Figure 12.32. The size isn't that important at this point, as we're just using the box to represent a car.

5. For the Length of the box, select the two points shown in Figure 12.32 in the lower left viewport.

6. At the Name For New Object dialog box, type **Car**, then click on the Create button.

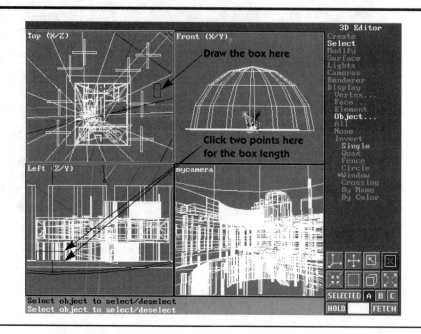

Figure 12.32: Creating a box to represent a car

Next, you'll add motion to the box.

1. Now return to the Keyframer by choosing Program ➤ Keyframer.

2. Move the Frame slider to frame 90.

3. Enlarge the view in the upper left viewport so it looks similar to Figure 12.33a.

4. Move the box to the location shown in Figure 12.33a.

5. Choose Paths ➤ Show-Hide, then click on the box.

6. Choose Paths ➤ Add Key and select the point on the box's path (the point shown in Figure 12.33b).

7. Select Paths ➤ Move Key and move the new key to the point shown in Figure 12.33c.

8. Now move the slider from 0 to 90.

a.

b.

c.

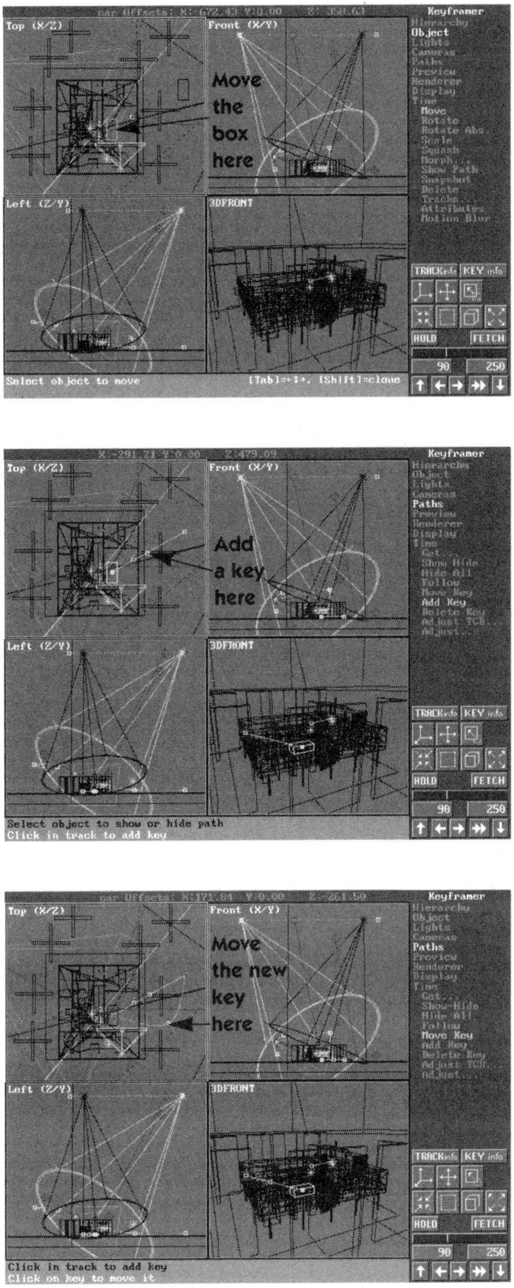

Figure 12.33: Adding motion and adjusting the path to the box

Notice that the box moves along the path as you might want it to, but the box maintains its orientation; it doesn't turn with the path the way we might expect a car to turn. To remedy this situation, you need to apply the Paths ➤ Follow option.

1. Choose Paths ➤ Follow, then click on the box's path. The Follow Path dialog box appears.

2. Enter **0** in the Max Bank Angle input box and make sure the Yes box is checked (it is checked by default).

3. Click OK, then move the Frame slider from 0 to 90 again. Notice that now the box follows the orientation of the path.

Now the box moves along the path *and* turns along with it, just as a car would turn into a driveway.

In step 2, you changed the Max Bank Angle in the Follow Path dialog box to 0, but you didn't change the Yes setting. Even though you didn't actually "bank" the object, as an airplane would tilt or lean in a turn, the Banking option must be on before the object will follow the path orientation. You would set the banking angle to a value greater than 0 for a flying object such as an airplane or a bird.

You can also edit the box's path just as you have edited the path for the camera by changing the Ease To, From, and Continuity settings at each keyframe.

◆ Creating a Final Animation

Note *I've created an animated Flic file of the model used in this chapter. You can find it, along with the other sample tutorial files, on the CD accompanying the book. Use Preview ➤ View Flic in the 3D Studio Keyframer command column to view the file, or install the Autodesk animation player (also on the CD-ROM) to view the file in Windows.*

When you are ready to create your final animation, you can follow the steps shown next.

1. Choose Renderer ➤ Render View.

2. Click on the Perspective viewport.

3. At the Render Animation dialog box, make sure the Anti-aliasing, Filter maps, Shadows, Mapping, Auto-Reflect, and Motion Blur settings are on, and that the Metal option in the Shading Limit button group is selected.

4. Make sure All is selected in the Frames button group.

5. Make sure the Every Nth Frame input box shows 1 to render every frame.

6. This time, make sure Disk is selected.

7. Click on Configure, then at the Device Configuration dialog box, select the file type you want and the image resolution (see the next section on rendering file formats, "The Animation File Output Options," for more on these options).

8. Click OK at the Device Configuration dialog box, then click Render at the Render Animation dialog box.

Tip *As it renders, the Render Animation dialog box will change to display the current rendering settings as well as the number of the frame it is currently busy rendering. It will also display a message at the top telling you what 3D Studio is currently doing. A horizontal bar appears just below the message, showing you how much of the current process is complete.*

9. Wait until 3D Studio is done creating the animation files. You'll know it's done when 3D Studio closes the Render dialog box and returns to the keyframe screen.

Warning   *The time you have to wait for the rendering can be anywhere from an hour or two to several days(!) depending on the complexity of your animation and its length. Most of the time, you will create animated segments that will be around 15 to 30 seconds long.*

You or an editor (that is, an editing program) would then edit these segments into a complete animation. In Chapter 14 you'll learn about the different ways you can get your animation onto video tape. I'll discuss editing your animated segments in Chapter 15. There you'll learn how you can use your desktop PC to put together a set of animated segments into a finished product. You'll also learn about different ways of viewing your animation on your PC. For now, we'll finish this chapter with a look at file output options.

◆ The Animation File Output Options

Before we end this chapter, you'll want to know about the animation file formats. Most of these formats are the same as those for single still images, with a few twists.

You have several options for animation file output, each with its advantages and disadvantages. The following sections describe each option.

Flic

This is Autodesk's own animation file format. It is limited to 256 colors and image sizes of 320×200 and 640×480. The 320×200 resolution files can have a .FLC or .FLI filename extension. The 640×480 resolution files will only have the .FLC extension. Flic files are single files that contain the entire animation. They can be quite large, with a typical 10-second animation taking approximately 15 megabytes.

You need the Autodesk animation player to view files in this format.

The playback rate will vary depending on the power of your computer and the speed of your hard drive. The smaller image size (320×200) will play back faster, and for test animation this can be more than adequate.

Gif

This is a highly compressed image-file format that is limited to 256 colors. If you render to this format, you will get a series of bitmap images, one for each frame of animation, instead of one large file.

This file format is popular because it can be sent easily via modems over telecommunication lines. If you surf the Internet, chances are you've see images in this format.

Gif files are not often used for animations since they duplicate the color depth of the Flic file format.

Targa

This is perhaps the most universally accepted format for high-quality animation. Like the Gif file format, it produces a single file for each frame. Since a typical Targa file is close to a megabyte in size, you will use up disk space in a hurry using this format. Still, it is the format of choice when you want the best quality. It offers a wide variety of resolutions and provides color depth to well over 16 million colors.

Color and Mono Tiff

These file formats offer high-quality color or monochrome output. They are similar to the Targa format for quality, but because there are so many different variations of this format, it isn't as popular as the Targa format. This format also produces one file per frame of animation.

BMP True and 256

The BMP format is the native Windows image format. It is not as universally used as the Targa format, but all Windows graphics programs can read BMP files. True refers to *True-color*, or more than 16 million colors.

JPEG

This format is a highly compressed true-color file format. Like the GIF format, JPEG is frequently used where color images need to be sent over telecommunication lines. The advantage of JPEG is that it is a True-color format offering very high quality images at a reduced file size. One drawback to JPEG files is their tendency to be distorted due to the methods used to compress the image.

True Color vs. 256 Colors

Three of the formats—Flic, GIF, and BMP—offer 256-color output. You can get some very impressive still images from 256 colors, but when you start to use animation, the color limitation starts to create problems. One major problem is something called *color banding*, which occurs when an image has a color gradient. Instead of a smooth transition of colors over a surface (as gradients are supposed to have), you see bands, as shown in Figure 12.34. The effect is similar to the Posterize option in many paint programs.

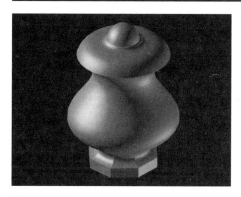

Figure 12.34: Two images rendered in 3D Studio. The one on the left shows what the image should look like under good conditions. The one on the right shows color banding caused by a limited color palette.

This color banding may be fine for limited applications such as previewing animations, but you will want to use true-color output for your finished product. True-color images, such as those offered by Targa, Tiff, BMP True, and JPEG files, do not suffer from banding. They also offer smoother edges on models with lots of straight edges. If you don't need the absolute best quality, you might consider the JPEG output option. It provides high resolution and true color in a small file size. You can render a 10-second animation with JPEG files with less than 40 megabytes of disk space in some cases. Most graphics and desktop video editing software today can read JPEG files.

File Naming in Animations

When you choose any of the file formats other than Flic, 3D Studio generates a file for each frame of your animation. The name of each frame is given a number so that their sequence can be easily determined by other programs.

3D Studio will only use the first four characters of the name you provide at the Animation File Name dialog box. For the rest of the name, 3D Studio will add a number. For example, if you enter the name Savoye for the animation file output using the Targa file format, 3D Studio will create a set of files with the name Savo0000.TGA, Savo0001.TGA, Savo0002.TGA, and so on.

This is true even if you are rendering only one frame of your animation. For single frames, 3D Studio will truncate the name to the first four characters, then attach the frame number to the name. For example, if you render frame 100 from the Savoye7 file, you will get a file named savo0100.TGA.

Choosing an Image Size

Still image sizes will vary depending on the medium of presentation: 1024×768 is a good resolution for 8×10-inch prints, for example, and larger, poster-size prints will require much larger resolutions. The resolution for video animations, on the other hand, is determined by the type of device you are using to record to video tape; it will usually not exceed 752×480. For example, if you are using a traditional step-frame recording method that records a single frame at a time directly to videotape, and you are using a specialized TV Video display device, such as the Truevision Targa Plus display card, you would typically render to an image size of 512×486.

Animating for film requires much higher resolutions, simply because the typical theater screen is so large.

If you intend to have your animation played back on computers only, you can keep the resolution down to one of those used for video. I'll discuss video resolutions in more detail in Chapter 14.

Other File Options

Besides the formats I've described here, there are also digital video formats, such as the Windows AVI formats, MPEG1 and MPEG2, and Motion JPEG, to name a few. In addition, there are some proprietary formats that come from non-linear video editing products. These file options, while not directly supported by 3D Studio, are usually supported through what are called *plug-ins*. Plug-ins are external programs that attach themselves to a program (for example, to 3D Studio) to add more functionality. Such file-output plug-ins are provided by hardware manufacturers who support these formats for their computer video editing hardware. For example, a hardware product called the MARS2 from Darim Inc. adds MPEG video compression for 3D Studio through a software plug-in. I'll discuss these digital video formats in more detail in Chapters 14 and 15.

Summary

This concludes our animation tutorials for 3D Studio. There are many issues I didn't touch on, such as network rendering to help speed up your renders, character animation, and the use of 3D Studio's Video Post feature to aid in the editing of animations. My intent is to show you the basic tools you'll need to get up and running with 3D Studio. The tutorial and reference that come with 3D Studio are good sources for delving deeper into this great program.

Also, I'll discuss what to do with the animations in Chapters 14, 15, and 16. In these chapters, you'll learn about the ins and outs of video, video editing, and, in Chapter 16, how you can use 3D Studio to create Virtual Reality worlds.

In the next chapter, you'll learn how you can use Photoshop to help enhance the renderings you produce with AutoCAD and 3D Studio. You'll also look at ways you can use Photoshop to create image bitmaps for 3D Studio materials.

Part Three:

Getting a Final Product

Exploring Photoshop

Photoshop has become the image editing program of choice for the print and pre-press trade. It offers many tools specifically designed for the print professional. It is also frequently used in conjunction with 3D modeling to add backgrounds, color, light, and other useful effects.

In this chapter, you'll focus on how to use Photoshop to enhance images of your 3D models, first by rendering preliminary line drawings of your 3D AutoCAD models, then by learning how to use the program to give a much more natural look to your renderings. With just a little experience with Photoshop, you can produce 3D models that appear like hand-painted illustrations rather than hard-edged computer simulations.

> **Note**   *If you don't already have Photoshop 3.0, you can use the tryout version included with this book. The tryout version works the same as the full, commercial version in almost every way, with the exception that the tryout version will not let you print or save your work.*

◆ Taking Your First Look

If you've ever used a Windows paint program before, then Photoshop will seem familiar to you. Many of its tools are similar to those found in the most basic paint programs. Of course, Photoshop's tools go well beyond the basics.

In this first section, you'll take a quick tour of Photoshop before you actually begin work. Figure 13.1 shows some common elements of the basic Photoshop screen. (This is not the default appearance, so don't worry if the first time you open Photoshop you don't see this arrangement.)

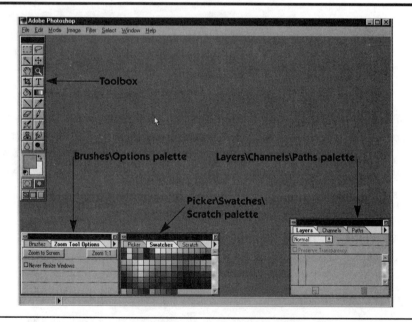

Figure 13.1: The Photoshop window

The Palettes

Let's take a moment to get familiar with the Photoshop screen. On the left side of the screen is the Toolbox, containing tools for painting, editing, and viewing images. The tools are described in Figure 13.2.

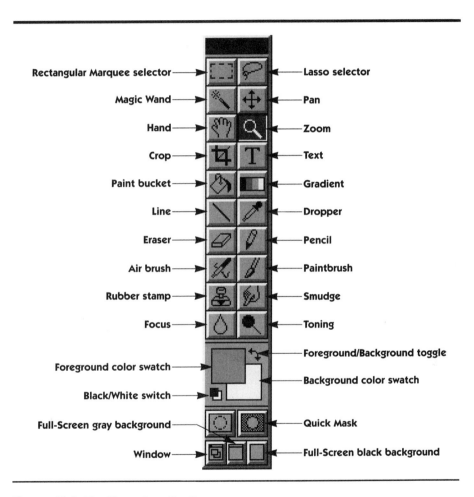

Figure 13.2: The Photoshop Toolbox

Here you'll find some of the more common painting tools, such as a rectangular selection tool (called the Rectangular Marquee Selector in Photoshop), a text tool, a paintbrush, a paintbucket (for solid fills), and a magnifying glass (for zooms). Toward the bottom of the Toolbox is a pair of overlapping color swatches for showing you the currently active foreground and background colors. There are other tools too, that may be less familiar to you, such as the Gradient tool and the Dropper.

The Brushes and Options palette controls the settings for various tools in the Toolbox. The tab showing in the image here shows options for the Zoom tool, which, if you'll refer back to Figure 13.1, is the currently selected tool in the Toolbox. When another tool is selected in the Toolbox, this tab will 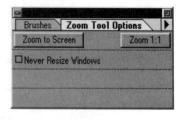 change to show different options accordingly. The other tab in this palette, the Brushes tab, offers settings for the tools that use brushes, for such values as brush width, shape, and opacity.

The Picker\Swatches\Scratch palette controls color selection and adjustment. Here, you can select colors for paint functions such as solid and gradient fills, pen strokes, airbrush, and paint. This palette offers several ways to select colors, which you will see later in this chapter.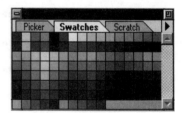

The Layers\Channels\Paths palette
controls a wide array of selection and
drawing tools. This palette offers some
important tools for editing and organizing
your work in Photoshop, as you will see
in the first part of this chapter.

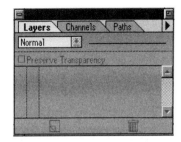

Accessing Additional Palettes

In addition to the Toolbox and the palettes shown so far are other
palettes that you can access by clicking on Photoshop's Window
menu, selecting Palette, and then selecting the Show/Hide option
with the palette name.

There are ten palettes. Two in particular will will come in quite handy
the more you work in Photoshop:

- ◆ The Info palette provides information about the image, including
  its color makeup and settings.

- ◆ The Commands palette is customizable in that you can have it
  display the commands you use the most often, thus making them
  easily available. Not only can you access your favorite commands
  on this palette, you can give them key shortcuts as well.

◆ Trying a Few Tools

Now that you're a bit more familiar with the screen, it's time to try out a few things. This first exercise is intended to give you a feel for how the tools work. You'll start by examining an image from the 3D ground-floor plan you drew in Chapter 3.

If you're starting this chapter from the "Exporting Your View to Other Applications" exercise in Chapter 3:

1. Choose File ➤ New. The New File dialog box appears.

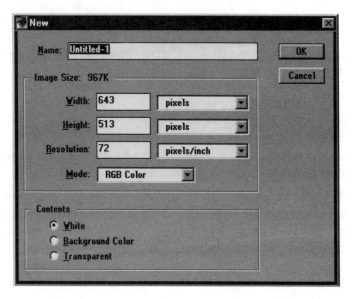

2. Go ahead and accept the default settings for this dialog box and click OK.

3. Choose Edit ➤ Paste. The image you copied from AutoCAD appears in the window.

Photoshop automatically sizes a new file to the size of the Clipboard contents, so in step 3 all you needed to do was to paste the image from AutoCAD into the new, blank image. It fits perfectly.

If you're starting this chapter from any point other than Chapter 3:

1. Choose File ➤ Open. The Open dialog box appears.

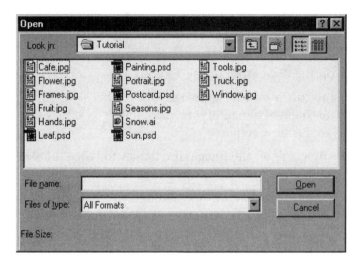

2. Locate and select the `Savoye.JPG` file from the `Sample` directory on the CD accompanying this book, then click Open. The ground-floor plan appears in a window.

Adjusting Your View

This first exercise will show you how to use a fairly common tool in paint programs: the Zoom tool (the one with the magnifying glass icon). The Zoom tool lets you zoom in and out of your image, like the Zoom tool in AutoCAD.

1. Make sure your window is maximized in Photoshop. If it's too small, click on the Maximize button in the window containing the ground-floor plan. The window will enlarge to fill the Photoshop window.

2. Click on the Zoom tool in the Toolbox.

3. Place the cursor on the 3D image. Notice that your cursor is in the shape of a magnifying glass, telling you that the Zoom tool is now active.

4. Click anywhere on the image. It enlarges to twice the size it was compared to when it was opened.

Now the image should be large enough to work with. If portions of the image are blocked by palettes, you can rearrange the palettes to get them out of the way.

5. To reduce your view, hold the Alt key down while clicking on your image with the Zoom tool.

Tip   *To get the* largest *view that will fit in the window, double-click on the Zoom tool in the Toolbox.*

Masking an Area and Adding a Gradient Fill

Next you'll use the Magic Wand tool to select the ground area, then you'll uses the Gradient tool to add a gradient fill to that area.

1. Click on the Magic Wand tool in the Toolbox.

2. Move the cursor to the image and notice that the cursor has changed into a magic wand.

3. Click on the portion of the image shown in Figure 13.3a. The white area is outlined by what older Adobe program-mers refer to as a "marching ants" (dashed) outline, which shows you the area that has been selected for editing. Areas outside the area bounded by the "marching ants" are masked off and won't be affected by painting, brushing or filling.

4. Shift-click on the area shown in Figure 13.3b. In doing this, you have selected an additional area to be editable. Notice that you see a message at the bottom of the Photoshop window that says "Add to existing selection."

5. Now click (notice I said *click*, not *Shift*-click) on the area shown in Figure 13.3c. Notice that when you click instead of Shift-clicking, your previous selection is dropped and the new one is selected.

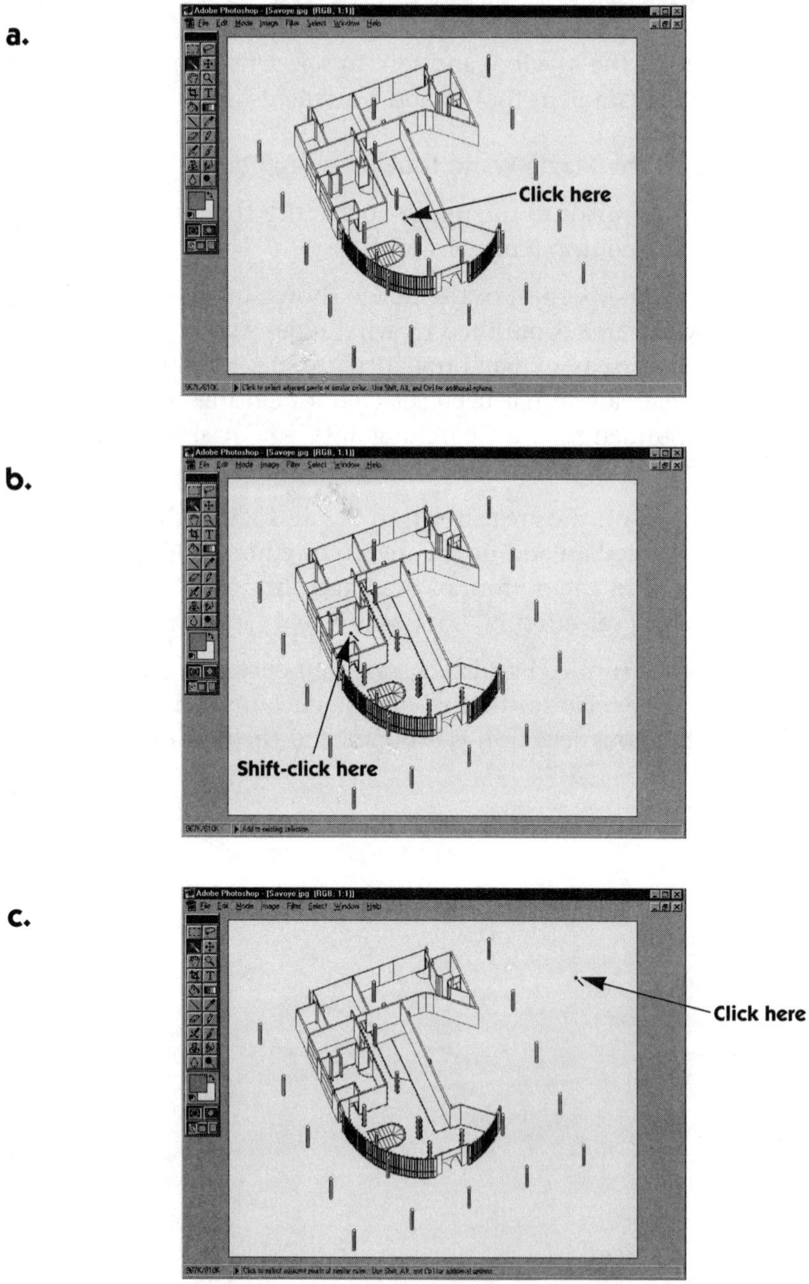

a.

b.

c.

Figure 13.3: Selecting areas with the Magic Wand tool

You can Shift-click on multiple areas to include them as part of your paintable area, masking out all other areas. If you accidentally select an area, you can Ctrl-click on it to deselect it. This is an important feature of the Magic Wand tool, as you will see later in this chapter.

Now let's see how the Gradient tool works.

1. Click on the Gradient tool in the Toolbox.

2. Now click and hold on a point near the very top of the image. A rubber-banding line appears from the point you select to wherever you move the pointer.

3. Drag to a point near the bottom of the image, and click. A gradient fill appears in the image in the area bounded by the "marching ants" (see Figure 13.4).

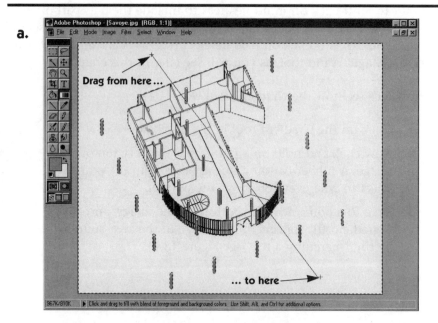

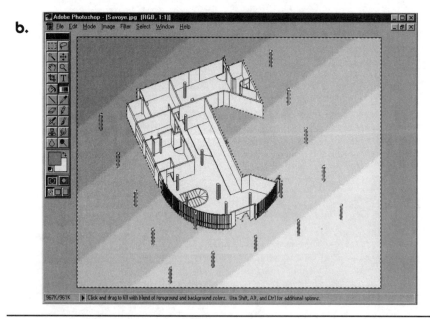

Figure 13.4: Adding the gradient fill

You've quickly "painted" an area using two key tools in Photoshop: the Magic Wand and the Gradient tool. You'll use the Gradient tool frequently in this chapter, so let's take a moment to get more familiar with it.

As you've seen, the Gradient tool places a gradient shade in the area you click in. The color of the gradient fill is determined by the foreground and background colors selected in the color swatches at the bottom of the Toolbox. The direction and degree of gradation depends on where you select the two points. Try the following to see how different selections affect the gradient fill.

1. Choose Edit ➤ Undo Gradient Tool to remove the gradient color you created above.

2. With the Gradient tool still active (that is, still selected on the Toolbox), click and drag to create a gradient between the two points shown in Figure 13.5. This time, because the two points are closer together, the gradient is less spread out, and because the two points are on a diagonal, the gradient is in a diagonal direction.

3. Choose Edit ➤ Undo Gradient Tool to remove the gradient fill. We won't need it in our next exercise.

a.
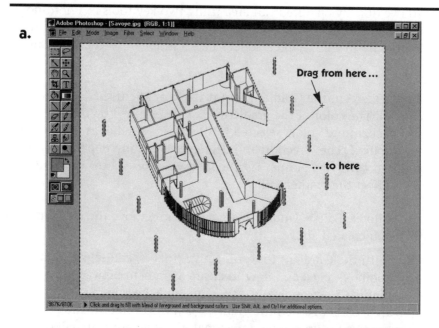

b.
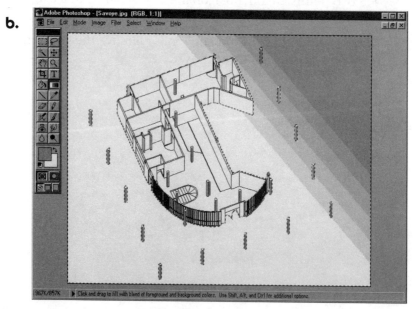

Figure 13.5: Selecting a different gradation

Right now, the gradient color is gray. You'll get a chance to adjust the color settings for the Gradient tool a bit later in the chapter.

◆ Setting Up Selections

One of the features that really sets Photoshop apart from other paint programs is its collection of tools for helping you organize your work. It offers a set of highly sophisticated masking functions, and offers a layering tool similar to AutoCAD's layers.

The purpose of these tools is to help you maintain a high degree of adaptability in your editing. For example, in a typical paint program, you might start to build up colors and modify your original image, but after a while, become dissatisfied with the progress of your work, and have to start over from scratch. Photoshop, with its selection and layering tools, gives you greater flexibility so that if you find you have made a mistake, you can easily revise your work without having to start over.

By offering layers on which you can segregate different aspects of your work, you have the freedom to experiment more freely. And by offering a broad set of masking and selection tools, you can easily select portions of your image to control what gets edited and what is untouched.

In the previous section, you used the Magic Wand tool to select an area. In the next set of exercises, you'll extend your knowledge of selections by learning how to store and recall them. You'll also look at ways to combine selections.

First let's see how you can save a selection for later retrieval.

1. Choose Select ➤ Save Selection. The Save Selection dialog box appears.

2. Notice the reference to a *channel* in this dialog box. I'll discuss channels shortly. For now, just click OK.

You've just saved the mask selection, which you can recall at any time, even after you've made other selections with the Magic Wand. Now let's see how to give that selection a meaningful name.

1. In the Layers\Channels\Paths palette, click on the Channels tab. You'll see the options in the palette change to show the channel list.

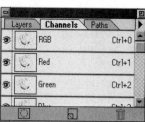

2. Use the scroll bar to the right to scroll to the bottom of the channels list.

3. You will see an item labeled #4 at the bottom of the list. Double-click on that channel name. The Channel Options dialog box appears.

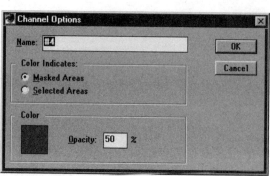

4. In the dialog box, enter **Landscape** in the Name input box. This will be the name for this selection.

5. Click OK to close the dialog box. Now notice that the name Landscape appears in the Layers\Channels\Paths palette.

When you saved the selection in the exercise prior to the last one, you created a new *channel* in the current file. That channel is then displayed in the Channels tab of the Layers\Channels\Paths palette.

You might think of the channels as slots in the image file, slots that store the separate color components of the image. The Savoye.JPG file is an RGB file, so it uses one channel for each of the colors red, green, and blue. You may have noticed the red, green, and blue channels in the Channels list in step 1 of the previous exercise. In addition to the RGB channels, you can create other channels, called *alpha channels*, to store other graphic data that is not directly displayed with the image. In this case, you are storing selections.

> **Note**   *Alpha channels add a great deal to the file size of an image, so you will want to use them sparingly. See the section on "Saving a Path" and "Converting a Selection to a Path" for information on how to reduce the size of files that have lots of stored selection channels.*

> **Note**   *Take another look at the Channel Options dialog box in step 3. The* Color Indicates: *button group offers two options: Masked area and Selected area. The default is Masked area. This tells us that the area in black is the masked area. Had you clicked on the Selected area button, then you would see the black and white areas reversed.*

If you look at your figure now, you see the selection area with the masked area shown in black. Don't be alarmed, your 3D image is still there. It's just being hidden by the current display of the new Landscape selection channel. Next you'll see how to restore your old view.

CMYK, RGB, Indexed Colors

In our exercises the image you are working with is in *RGB* mode. There are actually several modes you can work with in Photoshop, but for our discussion in this chapter, we'll concentrate on the CMYK, RGB, and Indexed Color modes as these are the modes you are most likely to be working with in conjunction with your 3D Work.

You can find out what mode you are in by clicking on the Mode menu to see which mode is checked. Images in the RGB mode are composed of 3 channels. These channels represent three basic components of colored light: Red, Green, and Blue (RGB). From these colors you can, by adding them together in varying intensities, create all colors. Since white, the color containing the whole spectrum, is created by adding these colors together at full intensity, they are called Additive colors. In this mode, black is simply the absence of all colors. Additive colors are typically used where a light source is used to create images, such as a television or computer monitor.

If this were an image destined for a printing press, you would more likely use the *CMYK* color mode. In a CMYK image there would be 4 channels, one each for Cyan, Magenta, Yellow, and Black (the K comes from the K in Black). These are the four colors printers are talking about when they use the term "four-color process". Unlike televisions and computer monitors, print media rely on light *reflected* off of paper to produce colors. A red pigment on a white background, for example, absorbs all the other colors of the spectrum and reflects only red. Since the four colors of cyan, magenta, yellow, and black absorb or subtract colors from the spectrum, they are called Subtractive. The CMYK color mode is most commonly used in the graphic arts and print industry.

A third method for representing color uses the *Indexed Color* mode. Indexed Color images are single-channel images that use what is called a *look-up table* containing 256 colors. Through this look-up table, each pixel in the image is assigned its own color instead of combining varying intensities of the three or four primary colors of multiple channels. This mode is able to store color information quite efficiently, and is used when the image is intended for computer presentations and Web-page art where small file size is important. Photoshop's filters will not work on Indexed Color files so you need to convert Indexed Color images to RGB before the filters can be used. This is easily done by selecting Mode ➤ RGB from the Photoshop pull-down menu.

Understanding the Channel Options

As you work with Photoshop, your display will change depending on the tools you are using. This can be a source of confusion if you don't understand the modal behavior of Photoshop. Let's examine how the Channels options work in the Layers\Channels\Paths palette.

Right now, you should still be in the Channels palette with the Landscape alpha channel selected as the current, active channel. You made this channel current when you double-clicked on it to open the Channel Options dialog box. You can tell it is current because it is highlighted in the list of channels in the palette. The main part of the Photoshop window shows what that selected channel looks like. With the channel active, you can make adjustments to it using the paint tools in the Toolbox. For example, you could feather the edge of the mask using the Airbrush or Toning tools. Making adjustments to the channel, however, has no effect on the actual image.

Now let's imagine that you want to get back to work on your image and don't want to make changes to the Landscape channel mask. Here's how you return to the previous view of the 3D ground floor to see how the image actually looks.

1. In the Layers\Channels\Paths palette, move the slide bar at the right to the very top.

2. Click on the RGB channel in the list. The ground-floor plan appears and the selection mask appears as a red tone over the building area (see Figure 13.6).

3. Move the slide bar back down to the bottom, then click on the eye icon next to the Landscape channel. The red screen disappears.

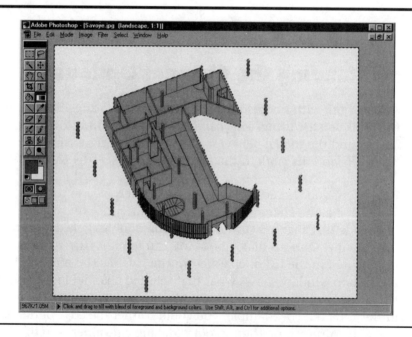

Figure 13.6: The image after choosing the RGB channel from the Channels palette

Note *You generally edit all three RGB channels at once, hence the RGB selection option in the Channels list. In some cases, after you have more experience, you might want to edit just one of the color components. This is an advanced topic, however, which is beyond the scope of this book.*

By clicking on the space to the left of a channel, you make that channel visible or invisible. When it is made visible, you see an eye icon in the space. By clicking on the name in the list, you make that channel the current active channel, as in step 2 of the last exercise. To get a normal view of your image, you need to make the top RGB channel in the list current, and turn off the alpha channels. The RGB channel at the top of the Channels list turns on all three red, green, and blue color channels at once. Unlike the alpha channels, making changes to the red, green, and blue channels will affect your image.

Before you turned off the Landscape alpha channel in step 3 of the last exercise, you saw the channel displayed as a red overlay on the image. By being able to see the channel in this way, you are able to make a visual check of the areas that are masked.

By the way, Photoshop uses the red transparent color of the mask to simulate the appearance of a material called *rubylith*. Rubylith is a photographic masking material frequently used in the print industry. It is a translucent red plastic material on a clear mylar backing. The red material is easily cut and peeled to expose the clear mylar. By cutting and removing the red portion of rubylith, a graphic artist can create photographic masks since the clear mylar lets light through while the red does not.

Inverting (Reversing) a Mask

You can still see the original selection on your image. You haven't done anything to remove it yet so it remains on the screen. Next, you'll invert the selection so it masks off the landscape area and exposes only the building—the opposite of the Landscape selection you saved in the last set of exercises. Once you've done this, you'll save the inverted selection as another channel.

1. Choose Selection ➤ Inverse. It's very subtle, but if you look carefully, you will notice that the selection now only outlines portions of the building. You can tell, however, that the selection no longer includes the landscape because the "marching ants" are not enclosing the outer border of the image.

2. Choose Selection ➤ Save Selection.

3. At the Save Selection dialog box, click OK.

4. In the Layers\Channels\Paths palette, locate #5 at the bottom of the list and double-click on it. This opens the Channel Options dialog box and makes the #5 channel the current active channel.

5. In the Channel Options dialog box, enter **Building** in the Name input box, then click OK.

6. In the Channels palette, scroll up the list to the top and click on the box to the far left of the channel labeled RGB at the top of the list. You now see the "rubylith" mask covering the landscape area. Here you can visualize how the mask really looks (see Figure 13.7).

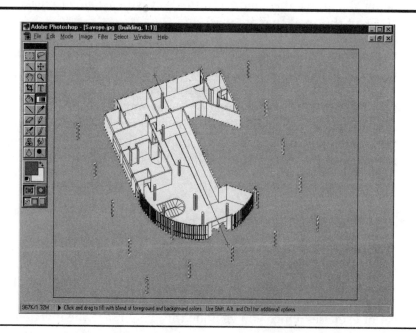

Figure 13.7: The red color indicates where the masked areas are.

In step 6 you made the RGB channels visible without making them active. Your current channel is still the Building channel. Any editing you do with the toolbox tools will affect only this channel.

You now have two alpha channels, Landscape and Building, that are storing selections. If you save your file at this point and exit Photoshop, the selection information will be stored with the file for later retrieval.

Restoring a Mask

Now let's see how you can restore a previously saved mask selection.

1. In the Layers\Channels\Paths palette list, click on the RGB channel to make it the current channel. Remember, that the RGB channel is the one you want active when you are actually working on your image.

2. Scroll down the list of channels to the bottom, then click on the eye icon on the left side of the building channel listing. This will turn off the Building channel's visibility. The red mask disappears.

3. Choose Selection ➤ Load Selection. The Load Selection dialog box appears.

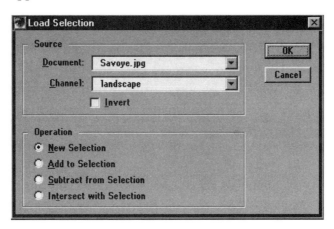

4. In the Channel drop-down list, make sure Landscape is selected. Remember that Landscape is the name you gave to the first channel you created, the one that stores the selection for the landscape of the drawing.

5. In the Operation button group, make sure New Selection is checked, then click OK. The Landscape selection is restored, replacing the inverse selection you created in the last exercise.

Take a moment to examine the Load Selection dialog box you saw in step 1 of the previous exercise. Notice that you have several options in the Operation button group. These options let you combine any current selection with saved selections. This allows you to create entirely new selections that are composites of two other selections. You'll get a chance to practice using some of these options later.

Using the Quick Mask Tool

Masking is used in virtually every visual medium from painting to air brushing to photo retouching. It is perhaps the single most time-consuming activity in your creative work, however. Fortunately, Photoshop offers a rich set of tools to quickly create masks.

One masking tool you will want to know about is the Quick Mask tool. This tool is accessed through two buttons at the bottom of the toolbox (see the keyed Toolbox graphic at the beginning of this chapter). The Quick Mask tool lets you quickly edit an existing mask using the paint and draw tools of the toolbox.

When you click on the right button while a selection is active, you will see the "rubylith" mask of the selection. Further, while the Quick Mask tool is active, you can add to or subtract from the mask using the tools in the Toolbox. For example, you can use the Smudge tool to soften the edge of a mask, or use the Line tool to mask a linear detail in the image.

When you have finished editing the mask, click on the left button of the Quick Mask tool and proceed with your edits. As with all other selections, you can store, as channels, selections that were edited with the Quick Mask tool. As mentioned earlier, you can also edit stored selections by making them active in the Channels tab of the Layers\Channels\Paths palette.

◆ Drawing within a Selection Using Paths

> ***Tip***   *You can quickly deselect a selection by choosing the Rectangular Marquee Selector tool or the Lasso Selector tool, and then clicking once on the image in a selected area.*

You've seen how easily the Magic Wand tool selects outlined areas for you. You can also use the Rectangular Marquee Selector and Lasso Selector tools to mask and select areas within your image. The Rectangular Marquee Selector tool lets you select a rectangular region (it can also be modified to select circular or elliptical regions). The Lasso Selector tool lets you draw a "free-hand" selection. But what if you want to select an irregular-shape area using straight lines instead of the sometimes difficult to draw free-hand technique? In the next exercise you'll explore the Path tools to outline a gravel base area that will surround the ground-floor plan.

Paths serve a double duty. They let you draw an irregular selection area with much greater accuracy than the Lasso Selector tool permits. They also let you draw fairly accurate curves and lines in your image. When you first create a path, it doesn't add anything to your image; you must take specific steps to "draw" the path to the image or create a selection with the path. This may sound like a limitation, but it actually gives you enormous flexibility in both drawing and selecting areas.

Using the Path Tools

Imagine that you just now realized that you forgot to draw a gravel base for the building. You *could* go back to AutoCAD to add the boundary for the base in AutoCAD and then import the image to Photoshop again, but you've already done some work on it in Photoshop and you don't want to have to re-create your work.

Fortunately Photoshop offers the Path tools. These are vector-line drawing tools similar to those used in Adobe Illustrator and CorelDraw. If you've used either of these programs, you'll be familiar with the Path tool.

Let's use the Path tool to add the base of the building.

1. Click on the Paths tab in the Layers\Channels\Paths palette. The palette changes to show the different path options.

2. Click on the first pen icon from the left.

3. Select the four points in the sequence shown in Figure 13.8, and then click on the first point you picked to close your selection of points.

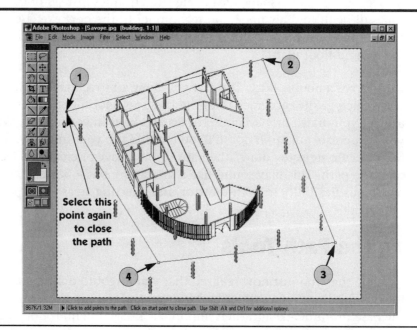

Figure 13.8: Selecting points to draw the outline of the gravel base

Now you have an outline with anchor points at each corner. I've asked you to draw the outline in a somewhat crude way because it would be difficult for you to draw the base accurately on the first try. Fortunately, you can easily move the anchor points at the corners of the outline using the arrow cursor.

1. Select the arrow icon from the Paths palette.

2. Click and drag the corner shown in Figure 13.9a to move it into position.

3. Use the arrow cursor to move the other corners into position so that the outline looks like Figure 13.9b.

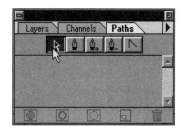

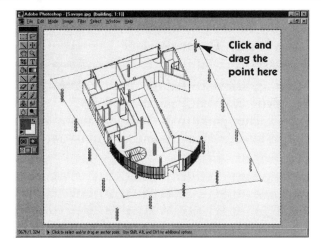

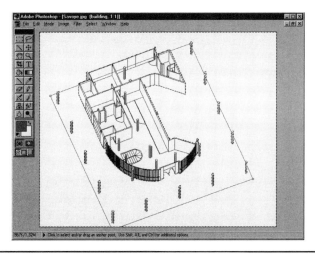

Figure 13.9: Adjusting the outline using the arrow cursor

Editing a Path

Now suppose you want the back side of the path to be a curve. You can add a anchor point to the line representing the back side of the base, then pull the new anchor point to turn the straight line into a curve. The following exercise demonstrates this.

1. Click on the pen icon that has the plus sign next to it.

2. Click on the outline toward the back of the building, as shown in Figure 13.10a. The new anchor point appears.

3. Click on the arrow icon in the Paths palette, then click and drag the new anchor point to the location shown in Figure 13.10b. The line turns into an arc and some additional anchor points appear.

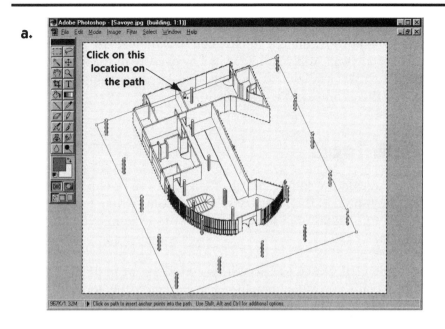

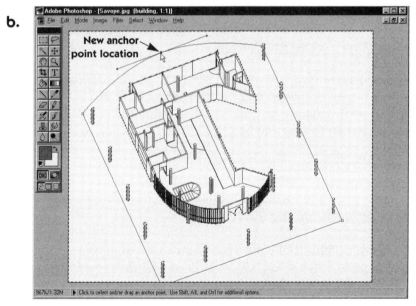

Figure 13.10: Adding a new anchor point and moving it to create a curve

The additional anchor points along the arc allow you to make subtle changes to the curve of the path. These new anchor points do not become part of your image. In fact, you haven't actually affected your image in any way. You've only created a *boundary* in the form of the path which you can convert to either lines or a selection area. You'll see how this is done in the next section.

The Path Tools

While we're on the subject of Path tools, here is a brief presentation of all the tools and their purposes. We won't have time to explore each one in a tutorial fashion, so you may want to experiment with them on your own.

The Arrow tool is used to select points on paths, or to drag anchor points for reshaping paths. You can select this tool at any time by holding down the Ctrl key when a path, paint, or edit tool is selected.

The Pen tool is used to draw smooth-edged lines or curves. Pressing the T key selects this tool.

The Insert Point tool lets you add points to an existing path. You select this tool when you are using the Arrow tool by Ctrl+Alt while clicking on a path. When using the Pen tool you can switch to this tool by pressing Ctrl and clicking.

The Remove Point tool removes points in a path without breaking the path. Ctrl+Alt-clicking on a point will accomplish the same when the Arrow tool is selected. Ctrl-clicking will do the same when using the Pen tool.

The Convert Point tool converts a point to a corner or a smooth point when you click on it. Press Ctrl to access this tool when the Arrow tool is selected.

Converting a Path into a Line in the Image

So far, you've created a path, but a path by itself doesn't affect your image in any way. Like the selections you stored as channels, the paths lie "dormant" until you are ready to apply them.

In the next exercise, you'll convert the path into a line in your image.

1. If you haven't done so already, make sure the RGB channel is selected as the current channel in the Channels tab list.

2. In the Brushes\Options palette, click on the Brushes tab and select a brush width.

3. In the Paths tab of the Layers\Channels\Paths palette, click on the right-pointing arrow to the right of the palette. The Paths flyout menu appears.

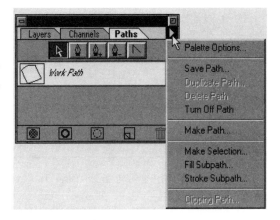

4. Select Stroke Subpath from the flyout menu. The Stroke Subpath dialog box appears.

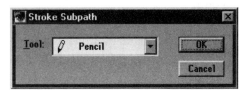

The Tool drop-down list lets you select from the different tools in the Toolbox. For this example you'll use the default Pencil tool to draw a fine line.

5. Click OK. Photoshop will take a moment, then the outline will appear in your image.

6. Click on the Layers tab in the Layers\Channels\Paths palette to view your image. You will see an image similar to Figure 13.11.

By moving to either the Channels or Layers tab, you hide the Path tools and the paths' appearance in the image.

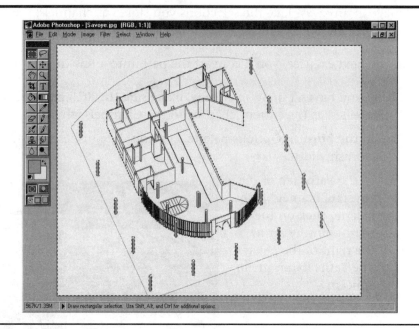

Figure 13.11: The image after using the Stroke Subpath option

As you can see from this example, you can add line work to your image quite easily with the Path tools. Since you don't commit the line work to your image until your path is set correctly, you don't have to worry about correcting mistakes later. If you've worked with other paint programs, you know how difficult it can be to make corrections to line work.

Converting a Path into a Selection

As I mentioned earlier, paths serve double duty in their ability to both add line work and create selections. In the following exercise, you'll create a selection from the same path you used to draw the lines.

1. First undo the line you created in the last exercise, by choosing Edit ➤ Undo Stroke Subpath. I'm asking you to do this so you can see the effects of the new selection you are about to make.

2. Click on the Paths tab in the Layers\Channels\Paths palette. Notice that the path is still there, even though you removed the line from the image.

3. Click on the right-pointing arrow to open the Paths flyout menu and select Make Selection. The Make Selection dialog box appears.

4. Click OK to accept the default settings. A selection appears in line with the path.

5. Click on the Layers tab in the Layers\Channels\Paths palette to get a better look at the selection.

This path will be useful in adding a separate tone over the gravel base area, but it needs a bit more work so that it will mask the building area. You'll learn how to combine selection masks a bit later in this chapter. For now, you'll learn how to save a path.

Saving a Path

You can save this new selection as a channel just as you saved the Landscape and Building selections. But you don't really need to save it as a selection, because you can save the path instead. Paths take up less storage space than channels, so if you create a selection using a path, you may prefer to save the path in favor of saving the selection generated from it.

1. Click on the Paths tab in the Layers\Channels\Paths palette again.

2. Open the
Paths flyout
and select
Save Path.
The Save
Path dialog
box appears.

3. Enter **Base** in the Name input box, then click OK.

Your path is now saved with the name *Base*. Now let's see how to create
a new path.

1. Open the
Paths flyout
menu, then
click on the
New Path
option. The
New Path dialog box opens.

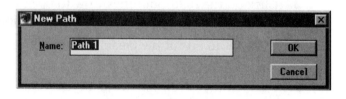

2. Click OK to accept the default settings. Notice that now you have
another item listed in the Paths palette: Path 1.

3. Click back and forth between the Path 1 listing and the Base
Path listing in the Paths palette. Notice that when you click on
the Base Path listing, the base path appears, and when you click
on the Path 1 listing, the base path *dis*appears.

You can now create another path that is separate from the first one you
created.

Converting a Selection into a Path

Saved selections are extremely helpful; however, you may find that if you must save lots of selections, your Photoshop file will become quite large. You can, however, convert selections into paths. Since paths are much less space consuming, they will help keep your file size down. In addition, if you find you need to make fine adjustments to a selection, converting it into a path lets you make those adjustments manually using the Path tools. Once you've made your adjustments to the selection that you've converted to a path, you can then reconvert the path back to a selection.

Here's how you can convert a selection into a path. In this exercise, you will recall the building selection, then convert it into a path.

> **Tip** *Once a path is selected, you can delete the path by pressing the Delete key.*

1. Choose Select ➤ Load Selection from the pull-down menu.

2. At the Load Selection dialog box, choose Building from the Channels drop-down list, then click OK. The building selection appears.

3. Open the Paths flyout menu from the Paths palette, then choose Make Path. The Make Path dialog box appears.

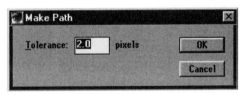

4. At the Make Path dialog box, click OK to accept the default tolerance value. Nothing seems to happen.

5. Select the arrow tool in the Paths palette, then click on the outline of the building as shown in Figure 13.12a. The anchor points of the path appear, showing you that you do indeed have a path.

6. Click and drag the cursor to the location shown in Figure 13.12b. Notice that a marquee appears.

7. Move the cursor so that the marquee surrounds three of the columns, as shown in Figure 13.12b, then release the mouse button. You see that the columns are also outlined with paths.

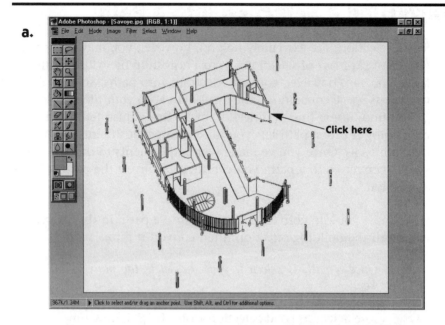

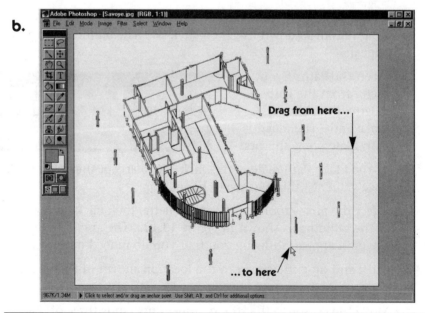

Figure 13.12: Selecting the paths to make them visible

In step 4, you saw a setting called Tolerance. This setting lets you determine how closely the new path will conform to the selection. A higher value will produce fewer anchor points and a smoother rendition of the selection. A lower value will increase the number of anchor points and produce a more accurate reproduction of the selection.

Once you've created a path from a selection, you can save it for future use or edit the path to make changes to the selection. Don't forget that to convert a path back into a selection, you must use the Make Selection option in the Paths flyout menu.

Using Layers and Combining Selections

We've spent a lot of time on selections and haven't really done any drawing yet. In this section, you'll finally add some tone to your image and, in the process, learn how to combine two selections to isolate a specific area of your image. You'll use a combination of a path and a stored selection to create a mask for the gravel base of the building. In addition, you'll see how to use a layer in Photoshop.

Creating a Layer

The first operation you'll perform is to create a layer in which to place your additional work. You've already got a base layer, called the Background layer. The Background layer contains the original line drawing image you imported from AutoCAD. By creating a new layer and placing your work on it, you will leave the original artwork untouched.

1. Click on the Layers tab in the Layers\Channels\Paths palette.

2. Click on the New Layer icon at the bottom of the palette.

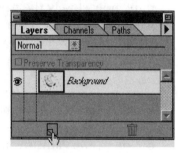

The New Layer dialog box appears.

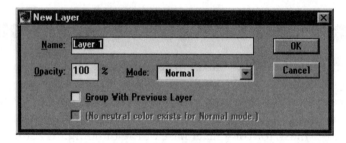

3. In the Name input box, enter **Gravel Base**, then click OK. You now have a new layer. Notice that in the Layers palette, you see the Gravel Base layer listed above the Background layer.

Layers in Photoshop and layers in AutoCAD work in a suprisingly similar way. You can think of the Layers palette as the Photoshop equivalent of the Layer drop-down list in AutoCAD. You can select layers to be active from here. You can also make layers visible or invisible by clicking on the eye icon to the far left of the layer list.

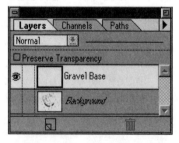

To make a layer current and active, click on its name from the list. As in AutoCAD, only one layer is current at a time.

Combining Selections

Now that you have a new layer, let's add a gray tone to the gravel base area. You currently have a path that defines the overall gravel base, but you need to exclude, or mask out, the portions of the gravel base path that are occupied by the building.

In the following exercise, you will create a new selection mask by combining the path with the previously saved landscape selection.

1. Click on the Paths tab of the Layers\Channels\Paths palette.

2. Move the vertical slider to the top of the list and click on the Base path to make it current.

3. Choose Make Selection from the Paths flyout menu.

4. At the Make Selection dialog box, make sure New Selection is selected in the Operations button group, then click OK.

5. Click on the Layers tab in the Layers\Channels\Paths palette. This gives you a clear view of your image as it stands so far.

6. Choose Select ➤ Load Selection.

7. At the Load Selection dialog box, make sure Landscape is selected in the Channel drop-down list.

8. In the Operations button group, click on the Intersect With Selection option, then click OK. After a brief pause, you will see the selection change from a simple polygon outlining the entire gravel area, to one that masks the building around the gravel area (see Figure 13.13).

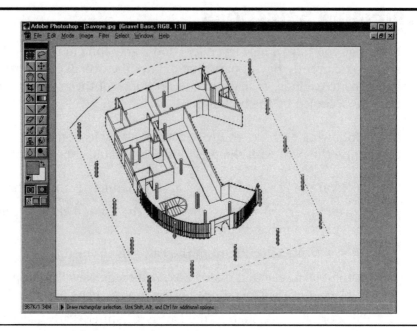

Figure 13.13: The intersection of the gravel area and the Landscape selection channel

Here you saw how you can combine two selections together to get a single selection of the area you want. If the Operations options seem familiar, it is because they offer Boolean operations, the same type of operations you saw in Chapter 6. This time, instead of using Boolean operations on objects, you are using them to construct selection masks.

Now that you've got some selections stored, let's add some color to your image.

◆ Using Color

You've already seen how the Gradient tool works. Let's continue to use it to add a tone to the gravel area over which you've created a mask, then add a green gradient over the outlying areas.

Using the Picker in the Color Palette

In this first exercise, you'll see how you can select a color from the Picker tab of the Color palette.

1. Make sure you are on the Gravel Base layer by clicking on the Layer tab of the Layers\Channels\Paths palette and clicking on Gravel Base in the list.

2. Click on the Gradient tool in the Toolbox.

3. In the Brush\Options palette, set the opacity slider to **40%**. This allows some of the background colors to appear as you'll see later in this exercise.

4. Select the two points as shown in Figure 13.14.

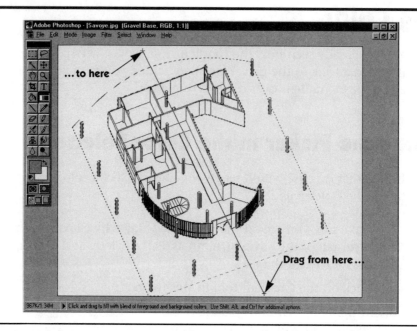

Figure 13.14: Selecting points to add the gradient colors

5. Choose Select ➤ Load Selection.

6. At the Load Selection dialog box, make sure Landscape is selected in the Channel drop-down list, and that the New Selection button is selected, then click OK.

7. Move your cursor to the bottom portion of the color palette containing the Picker\Swatches\Scratch tabs. Notice that your cursor changes to a "dropper" icon.

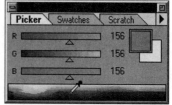

8. Click and drag the dropper icon over the colors and notice what happens to the RGB sliders and the color swatches in the Toolbox. They dynamically change as you click and drag the dropper. When you release the mouse button, the color that the dropper selected last becomes the default color.

9. Click and drag the dropper so you see a light green color in the swatch. Try to match the slider settings shown here. You don't have to be exact.

10. With the Gradient tool selected, click on the two points shown in Figure 13.15. Notice that the gradient adds a tint to the gravel area as well as to the overall ground area.

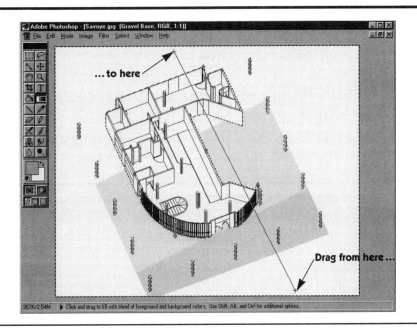

Figure 13.15: Selecting points to add the gradient colors

You could have removed the gravel base area from your selection so the gradient fill didn't affect it. But adding some of the color of the background to the gravel helps blend the surface colors.

The colors were blended because the opacity of the gradient fill is set to 40 percent. This allows colors in the background to show through. You can set the opacity of the Gradient tool by using the Opacity slider in the Gradient tool options palette.

Fine-Tuning a Color

Now you're ready to start adding colors to the actual building. Here you will add a solid color to the floor area and, in the process, you'll see how you can fine-tune a color using the Color Picker dialog box.

> **Note** The Magic Wand tool in step 4 will not work across layers, so in step 3 you must make the Background layer active to select areas bounded by the line work. If you stay in the Building layer and attempt to select the floor area with the Magic Wand, the entire image area will be selected.

1. In the Layers\Channels\Paths palette, click on the Layers tab.

2. Click on the New Layer icon and create a new layer called Building Color.

3. Make the Background layer the active one by clicking on it from the list of layers.

4. Select the Magic Wand tool from the Toolbox, then click on the floor area shown in Figure 13.16.

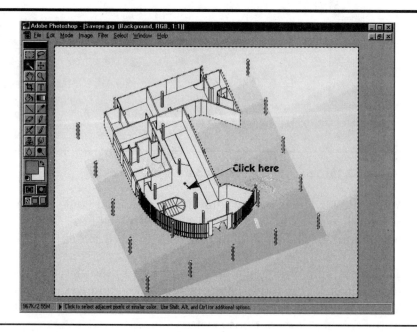

Figure 13.16: Selecting the area to be painted

5. In the Color palette, use the slidebars to approximate the color settings shown here.

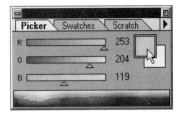

6. Next, click on the foreground color swatch at the far right of the color palette as shown in the previous graphic. The Color Picker dialog box appears.

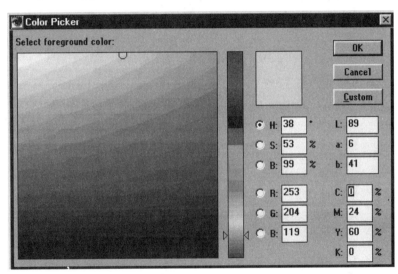

Note As you move the cursor around, you may notice a triangle with an exclamation point appear in the upper right corner of the dialog box. This is a warning that the color you are currently on is a non-printable color, that is, a color that cannot be reproduced in the CMYK color mode.

This dialog box lets you fine-tune the selected color over a range of intensities. The largest portion of the dialog box is taken by the color field. The upper right corner of the color field offers the greatest color intensity. As you move to the left, the color intensity fades. As you move down, the brightness is diminished.

To the right of the color field is a vertical bar that lets you select a different color. You can also enter values for the different color modes such as RGB or HSB (Hue, Saturation, and Brightness).

Now let's adjust the color from the color field.

1. Move the cursor into the color field. Notice that it changes to a circle.

2. Click on the location shown in Figure 13.17. This is a bit less intense than the original color.

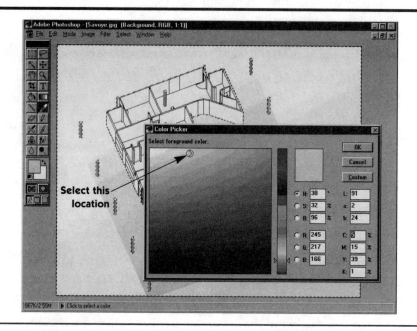

Figure 13.17: Selecting a color from the Color Picker dialog box

3. Click OK.

4. Go back to the Layers\Channels\Paths palette and select the Building Color layer to make it current.

5. Click on the Paint Bucket tool in the Toolbox.

6. Click on the selected area shown in Figure 13.18. The floor area receives the selected color.

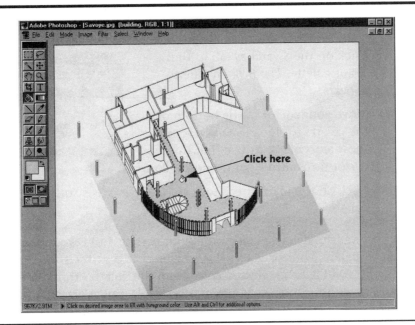

Figure 13.18: Adding color to the floor

You've used the Picker tab in the Color palette to select a color, and, in a new project, this may be the best tool. As you work with Photoshop, however, you will want to be able to store your favorite colors somewhere. You might also want to test your colors before you commit them to your image. The following describes a couple of other tools that will become handy while working with Photoshop.

Using the Swatches Tab to Store Favorite Colors

The Swatches tab in the Color palette offers a set of the more common colors you might use. You might think of it as a place where you keep your favorite colors. You can save and recall a set of swatches using the Swatches flyout.

Suppose, for example, you want to save the current color you've used to color the ground, in case you need to duplicate it later.

1. Click on the Swatches tab in the Color palette. The Swatch palette appears.

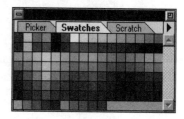

2. Move your cursor to the bottom of the palette to the area that doesn't show any colors. Notice that the cursor turns into a paint bucket icon.

3. Click on the blank area. Your color appears as a square in the palette.

If you want to delete a color from your palette, hold down the Ctrl key while making your selection. The cursor changes to scissors, indicating that you will cut the selected color from the palette. To replace a color, hold down the Shift key while making a selection. Finally, to insert a color within the array of color swatches, instead of at the end, hold down both the Shift and the Alt key while clicking on the location for the swatch.

Selecting a color from the Swatch palette is simply a matter of placing the dropper icon on a color swatch, then clicking on it.

Testing Your Brushes and Colors

You will find that you want to test a brush or color before committing it to your image. This is especially true if you are new to Photoshop. A common practice is to test brushes and colors directly on the image and then use the Undo option in the Edit menu to remove the test. But this can be a dangerous practice. Fortunately, Photoshop provides a scratch area for you to test your brushes and colors before you commit them to the image.

To access the scratch area, choose the Scratch tab in the Color palette. You'll see some colors appear.

◆ Once you have the scratch palette in view, you can paint, airbrush, or use any tool to see its effect. The colors are there to allow you to test the effect of tools that don't paint colors, such as the Smudge tool.

◆ If you prefer to use a blank test area, choose Clear from the Scratch Color flyout.

Using Foreground and Background Colors with Gradients

Photoshop, like many paint programs, offers you control over both the foreground and background colors. You might think of the foreground colors as those that you paint with. The background color is the color of the blank surface of your image—it is the color that will appear if you erase or clear a portion of your image.

As you have seen, you can adjust the foreground color away from its default black. The background color can also be modified. The Gradient tool makes use of the background color to determine which two colors to blend.

The following exercise demonstrates how the Gradient tool uses the background color.

1. In the Colors palette, select the Picker tab and click on the Background Color swatch shown here. Notice that the swatch gets a double border.

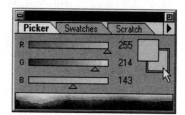

2. Adjust the RGB sliders to match the settings shown in the previous graphic.

3. Now click on the Foreground Color swatch as shown here. The double border switches to the foreground swatch.

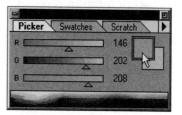

4. Adjust the RGB sliders to match shown in this graphic.

5. In the Layers\Channels\Paths palette, select the Background layer to set for the Magic Wand tool.

6. Select the Magic Wand tool from the Toolbox, then click and Shift-click on the areas shown in Figure 13.19a.

7. Go back to the Building Color layer.

8. Select the Gradient tool and select the points shown in Figure 13.19b. Note that the two points define a vector that is perpendicular to the lines that define the top and bottom edges of the wall. A gradient fill appears on the back walls.

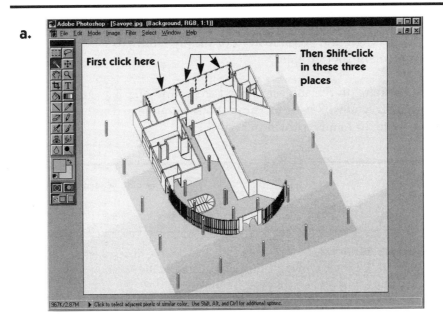

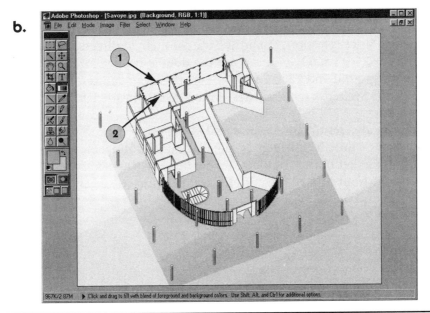

Figure 13.19: Making a Magic Wand selection and adding a gradient fill

Although the figures in this book don't show the colors, the gradient fill on your machine should now produce a transition from the foreground to the background color, instead of simply fading to white as in the previous gradient fill examples.

While we're on the subject of the Foreground and Background Color swatches, you will want to know about a couple of Toolbox options that can come in handy, shown in Figure 13.20.

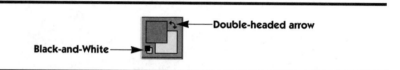

Figure 13.20: The black-and-white icon and double-headed arrow for toggling settings in the Color Swatch area of the Toolbox

You can quickly reverse the foreground and background colors by clicking on the double-headed arrow in the upper right corner of the Color Swatch area in the Toolbox. This is especially useful for recalling background colors from the Swatches tab of the Picker\Swatches\Scratch palette. Since selections from the Swatches tab go directly to the Foreground Color swatch, you can use the double-headed arrow to switch the foreground and background colors, then you can select a color from the Swatches tab and click on the double-headed arrow again.

You can also set the foreground and background back to their default black and white by clicking on the black-and-white icon that is below and to the left of the swatches. Before you use the black-and-white icon, you may want to save the current swatch colors in the Swatches tab of the Colors palette.

◆ Importing Bitmaps to Add Props

In the AutoVision and 3D Studio tutorials preceding this chapter, you saw how you can import bitmap images to add *props*, such as people and landscaping. Photoshop is quite at home performing this type of work. In this section, you'll learn how you can easily add landscaping to your image. In the process, you will see how you can manipulate an image to give it a less photographic look to match the appearance of your image.

Importing Plants

Perhaps one of the more time-consuming operations in creating a rendered image is adding landscaping. In the following example, you'll see how you can use existing bitmap images of bushes to add landscaping to your image. You'll use some of the bitmap images from AutoVision in this exercise, so make sure you've installed that program before you proceed.

You'll start by creating a layer for the plants.

1. Click on the Layers tab in the Layers\Channels\Paths palette.
2. Open the Layers flyout menu and select New Layer.
3. At the New Layer dialog box, enter **Plant** for the name, then click OK.
4. Make sure the Plant layer is the current one.

Now you are ready to import some plants.

1. Choose File ➤ Open.
2. At the Open dialog box, locate the \AutoVision\Maps directory.
3. Locate and select the file called 8bush021.TGA then click OK. You see the file in a separate Photoshop window (see Figure 13.21).

Figure 13.21: The 8bush02l.TGA file opened in Photoshop

The image is a bit large for your building image, so you'll want to scale it down. First scale it down roughly. Later you'll get a chance to make other adjustments to its size after you've imported it into the building image.

1. Click on the Magic Wand tool, then click on the black outlying area in the bush image. The black area is selected.

2. Choose Select ➤ Inverse to invert the selection (so you have the bush selected).

3. Now choose Image ➤ Effects ➤ Scale. Look very closely and you'll see a gray rectangle surrounding the image. The rectangle will have anchor points at its corners (see Figure 13.22a). As you move the cursor over the image, you'll see a cursor icon that looks like a circle with a line through it.

Note   *The Image ➤ Effects ➤ Scale option lets you resize selections. Another option, Image ➤ Image Size, lets you scale the entire image through a dialog box.*

4. Bring the cursor to the upper left anchor point. It turns into an arrow (see Figure 13.22a).

5. Place the arrow cursor on the upper left anchor point and drag it. The rectangle follows the cursor.

6. While still dragging the rectangle, hold the Shift key down. The rectangle is now restrained to its original width-to-height ratio.

7. Adjust the size of the rectangle so it is approximately one quarter of its original size, then release the mouse button. Your image will look similar to Figure 13.22b.

8. Now if you move the cursor into the selected image area, you'll notice a hammer icon. With the hammer icon showing, left-click your mouse.

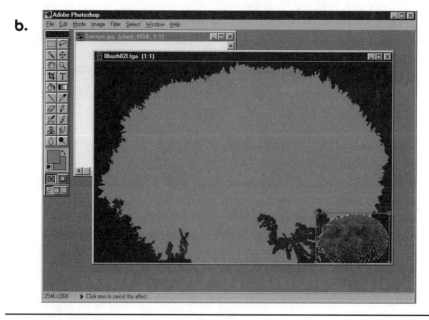

Figure 13.22: Changing the scale of the bush

The hammer icon tells you that you can either accept the current size or continue to resize the image. In step 8, you accepted the new size by clicking on a point inside the selection area.

Now let's import the bush into the building image.

1. Choose Edit ➤ Copy to copy the selection to the Windows Clipboard.

2. Switch back to the building file by selecting it from the Window pull-down menu, or by clicking on its window border.

3. Enlarge the building image window by clicking on the Maximize button in the upper right corner of the window.

4. Choose Edit ➤ Paste. The bush appears in the window.

The bush is a bit too big, and its colors are too strong compared to the building image. You've already seen how you can adjust a selection's size. Now let's see how to adjust its brightness and contrast.

1. Choose Image ➤ Adjust ➤ Brightness/Contrast. The Brightness/Contrast dialog box appears.

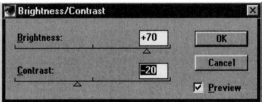

2. Move the Brightness slider to the right until the Brightness input box shows **70**.

3. Move the Contrast slider to the left so the Contrast input box shows **–20**, then click OK.

4. Choose Image ➤ Effects ➤ Scale, then use the anchor points of the image scale rectangle to adjust the size to about half of its current size. Remember to click on the hammer icon to accept the new size.

Now you have a single bush that is about the right size and shade for the building image. The final step is to copy this new version of the bush to the Clipboard, then paste it back into the image multiple times.

> **Tip**   *Sometimes when you press Ctrl+V to paste the bush into your image, it may appear that the pasting is not occurring. This can happen when Photoshop pastes a copy directly on the original. The original will emerge from behind the pasted image, however, when you click and drag the pasted bush to a new location.*

1. First, move the bush to the upper right corner of the image. Move the cursor on top of the bush (it should still be selected) so that the arrow cursor appears.

2. Click and drag the bush to the upper corner of the image area as shown in Figure 13.23a.

3. For a change use the keyboard to copy the selection to the Clipboard. To do this, press Ctrl+C while the bush is selected.

4. Use the keyboard to paste a copy of the bush into the image by pressing Ctrl+V. The original bush is deselected and a copy appears. The copy is now selected (see Figure 13.23b).

5. Click and drag the copy to a position overlapping the original as shown in Figure 13.23c.

6. Press Ctrl+V again. Another copy appears. Move it to a new position.

7. Continue to press Ctrl+V to add more bushes. As you add them, arrange them so your image appears similar to Figure 13.24.

a.

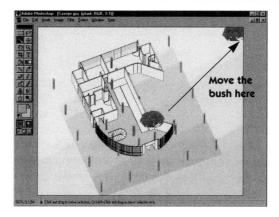

b.

c.

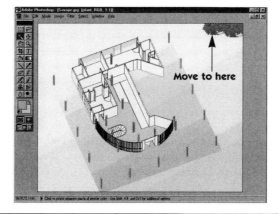

Figure 13.23: Adding bushes to your image

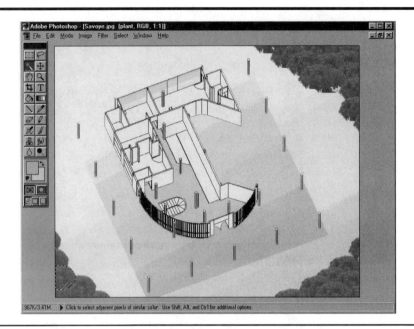

Figure 13.24: The final arrangement of bushes in the building image

As you can see from this exercise, you can import and then adjust an image of a plant to fit your building's image. This process will work for images of people and trees as well. I gave an example of editing the brightness and contrast of the pasted image, but you can make other adjustments, such as color balance and hue/saturation. These options are found in the Image ➤ Adjust menu.

◈ Importing 3D Studio Images

You may find that you want to overlay or composite several 3D Studio renderings to arrive at a desired affect. For example, say you want to place several objects rendered in 3D Studio over a photographic image of a jungle background.

You can employ the methods described in this chapter, under "Importing Bitmaps to Add Props," but as long as you are using 3D Studio to create the props in the first place, you can take advantage of 3D Studio's ability to generate alpha channels, thereby simplifying the selection process. Here's what you do.

1. When rendering your "prop" in 3D Studio, make sure you are rendering to a blank background.

2. In the Render dialog box, open the Render Options dialog box, then make sure the Render Alpha option is set to Yes (a full description of this procedure can be found in Chapter 15 under "Creating Alpha Channels in 3D Studio").

3. Render your image as a Targa file.

By selecting the Render Alpha option, you've directed 3D Studio to include an alpha channel in the image file from which you can obtain an exact selection area. The next step is to open Photoshop to complete your composite work.

1. Open the rendered prop image in Photoshop.

2. Choose Select ➤ Load Selection. You'll see the prop outlined with the "marching ants" selection box. You may need to choose Select ➤ Inverse to invert the selection.

Remember that Select ➤ Load Selection creates a selection from the alpha channel. Since you rendered the prop using the Alpha Channel option in 3D Studio, the prop image file already has the alpha channel available to convert to a selection. By utilizing the alpha channel generated by 3D Studio, you are assured of an accurate selection.

Now the last step is to actually cut and paste the selection into your background.

1. Use the Edit ➤ Copy option to copy the prop to the Clipboard.
2. Go to the background image into which you will paste the prop.
3. Create a layer to receive the prop.
4. Paste the prop into the Background image.

The alpha channel created in 3D Studio contains transparency information for portions of an image that may not be 100-percent transparent. So using a 3D Studio-generated alpha channel can often be the only way to capture all the transparency information from a rendering.

For more on the topic of utilizing 3D Studio alpha channels, see "Creating Alpha Channels in 3D Studio" in Chapter 15.

◆ **Adding Text**

In addition to props, you may also find a need to add text to your image. Photoshop does an excellent job of blending text with bitmap images.

Suppose you want to label some of the areas of the ground floor. Try the following exercise to see how it's done.

1. Create a new layer called **Text** and make it current (you should know how to do this by now). It is very helpful to keep your text on a separate layer in case you need to delete and replace text later.

2. Click on the Text tool in the Toolbox.

3. Move the cursor over to the image. Notice that the cursor now shows the standard I-beam cursor for text.

4. Click on the point shown in Figure 13.25. The Type Tool dialog box appears.

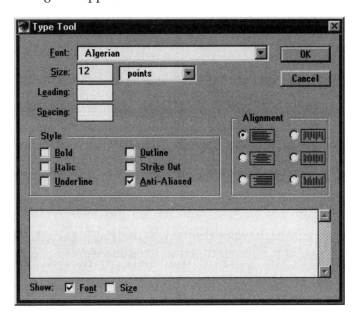

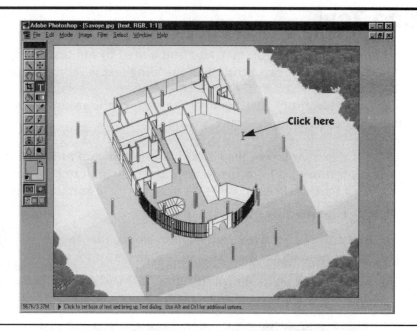

Figure 13.25: Selecting the point to place the text

Take a moment to study this dialog box. It offers many of the more common options found in word processing programs, such as alignment, font, and font size, as well as leading (the space between lines of text) and spacing (the space between characters in a line). The large box at the bottom is the input box for entering your text. You can enter single lines of text or entire paragraphs.

1. Type **Car Port**. Your typing appears in the text input box at the bottom of the dialog box.

2. Select Arial from the Font drop-down list, then click OK. The text appears at the location you selected in step 3 of the previous exercise.

Notice that the text is selected. You can move it or delete it while it is selected. The text at this stage of our exercise looks a bit small, so let's delete it and replace it with larger text.

1. Press the Delete key. The text disappears. The Delete key will delete anything that is selected.

2. Click on the same location again to place the text. The Type Tools dialog box appears again. Notice that it still shows the same option settings you used for the previous text, including the text itself.

3. Change the 12 in the Size input box to **24**, then click OK. The text appears in a larger size.

Now you will want to reposition the text. In typical Photoshop fashion, you can move a selection by placing the cursor on the selection until you see an arrow cursor. You then click and drag the selection. It is a bit trickier for text, however.

1. Place the cursor on the first character of the text, until it turns into an arrow.

2. Click and drag the text to the left until it's in the location shown in Figure 13.26.

3. To place the text permanently in the image, click on any location in the image away from the text. The text is now in place.

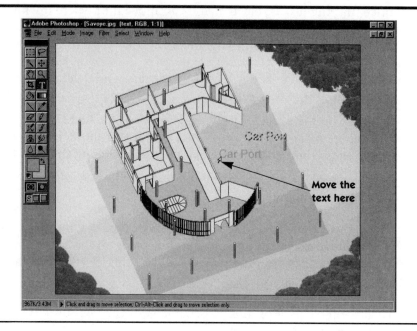

Figure 13.26: Moving the text to a new location

Notice that the text is in the same color as the current foreground color. You will want to make sure the current color is appropriate for your text before you start placing it in your image.

Since the text is on its own layer, you can easily rearrange the text location using the Rectangular Marquee Selector tool. Just make sure that your current layer is the Text layer before attempting to make changes to the text.

There is much more you can do to this image. You can add more labels, people, and trees, for example. Figure 13.27 shows an example of the image with some additional props and labels.

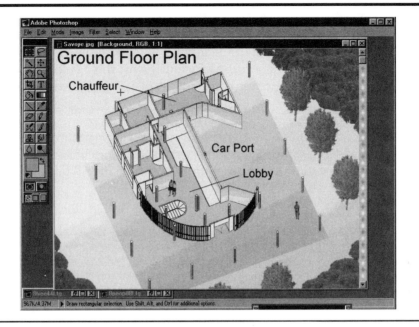

Figure 13.27: A more finished version of the ground floor image

You might want to experiment with this image on your own to practice some of the things you've learned in this section.

◆ File Formats in Photoshop

This brings us to the end of the ground floor example. If you are using the tryout version of Photoshop included with this book, you won't be able to save your work, but you'll still want to be aware of File options in Photoshop.

You can save a file in a variety of formats, including many of those supported by 3D Studio, but to preserve the channels and paths you've created, you will want to save your file in the native Photoshop format.

1. Choose File ➤ Save As. The Save As dialog box appears.

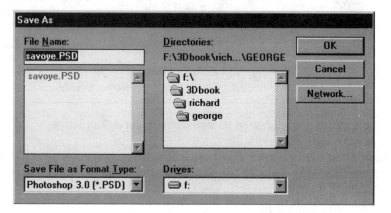

2. Open the Save File As Format Type drop-down list and select Photoshop 3.0 (*.PSD).

3. Enter a name for your file in the Name input box, then click OK.

If you intend to send your file to a service bureau to have it printed, you can usually use the Photoshop .PSD file format. You can use the Targa file format (*.TGA) instead, though this format will not save path information.

If you want to send your file to someone but you want to save on the file size, you can use the File ➤ Save As Copy option. This gives you the option to discard the alpha channels in your image. If you have a lot of alpha channel information, you can reduce the file size by discarding it for transport.

Adding Effects

Computer 3D renderings like those produced by AutoVision and 3D Studio can be amazingly lifelike. But all too often I hear users comment that while they like what these tools offer, they don't always want a photo-realistic rendering. Frequently, users want a softer, less-formal looking image that doesn't give their client the impression that their design is "etched in stone."

Photoshop can be of great assistance when you want to take the "edge" off of your 3D rendering. In this final section, you'll look at ways you can use Photoshop to "soften" images from AutoCAD, AutoVision, and 3D Studio.

A Hand-Drawn Look to Line Drawings

Perhaps the most frequently asked question from designers working in AutoCAD is "How can I get an AutoCAD perspective line drawing to look like it was hand-drawn?" At first, this sounds a bit crazy. Why would anyone want to turn a nearly perfect line drawing of a perspective into a hand-drawn image? But there are many reasons for wanting this, many of which revolve around personal preference.

Of course, most users know that you *can* use Photoshop to produce a hand-drawn effect. It's perhaps the main reason why most of you reading this book are interested in the program. Here's how you can do it.

1. Open the sample file called `Lineart.JPG`. This is a hidden-line view of the Facade model you saw in Chapters 6 and 8.

2. Choose Image ➤ Image Size. The Image Size dialog box appears.

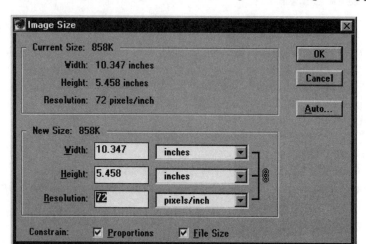

3. In the Width input box, enter **15**.

4. Make sure the File Size option at the bottom of the dialog box is unchecked, then click OK. By leaving the File Size option unchecked, you allow Photoshop to increase the resolution of the image. By default, Photoshop will anti-alias the image when it is enlarged, so that the gagged appearance of line work is not exaggerated.

5. Now choose Filter ➤ Stylize ➤ Diffuse. The Diffuse dialog box appears and line work in the image changes.

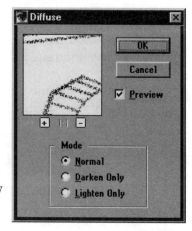

6. Click on the Darken Only button to see its effect. The lines darken.

7. Click on the Lighten Only button and click OK.

8. Click on the Zoom tool and Alt-click on the image to zoom out. Your view will look like Figure 13.28.

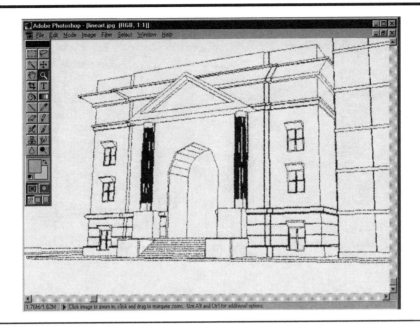

Figure 13.28: The line drawing after using the Diffuse filter

By enlarging the image size in step 3, you diluted the effects of the Diffuse filter. Otherwise the line work would have gotten much thicker.

The line drawing now looks more like it was done with a soft pencil on watercolor paper. You can use the Filter ➤ Pixelate ➤ Crystallize tool to create a "pen-on-paper-napkin" effect (see Figure 13.29).

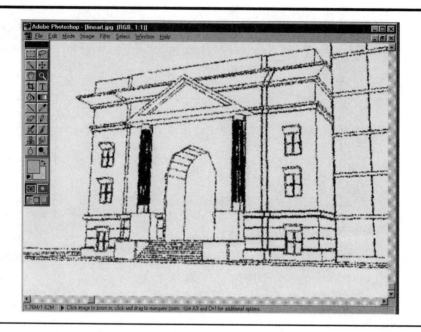

Figure 13.29: The line drawing again using the Crystallize filter

Adding a Painterly Effect

Now let's look at what you can do to soften a color image. Photoshop offers a wide range of filters that can add interest to your 3D computer renderings. And if you don't find what you need in the standard filters, you can purchase plug-ins to Photoshop that offer a wide range of effects.

Let's try out a few of the standard effects to see what can be done.

1. Close the current file (you can save it if you like), then open the Savoye10.JPG sample file from the CD accompanying this book.

2. Use the Zoom tool to enlarge the view.

3. Choose Filter ➤ Noise ➤ Add Noise. The Add Noise dialog box appears and the image changes.

4. Move the Amount slider to 40 and watch what happens to the image. The amount of "noise" changes.

5. Click OK to accept the amount. Your image will look similar to Figure 13.30.

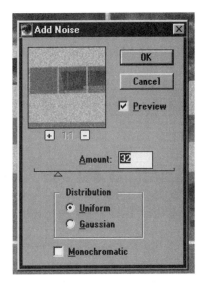

Figure 13.30: The Noise filter applied to a rendering from 3D Studio

Here you have an effect similar to a mezzotint print. Photoshop actually provides a Mezzotint filter, but it may be too strong for your images.

In addition to the filters you've seen so far, you may want to try the Wind, Pointillize, and Unsharp Mask filters. Another very interesting effect is the one given by the Watercolor plug-in filter from Adobe's Gallery Effects, a separate Adobe product.

Adding a Paper Texture Effect

Another effect that is popular is the paper texture. By applying a patterned texture to your image, like the texture of certain art papers, you can create the impression of surface texture.

The following example shows how you can quickly apply a scanned or computer-generated paper texture to your image.

1. With an image file open, choose Mode ➤ RGB. (This step is unnecessary if the image is already in RGB mode.) I chose a rendering to which I'd applied a Vignette effect.

2. Create a new channel called Texture.

3. Open the image file of the texture. I've supplied a file called Canvas.tga for you to try out.

4. Choose Select ➤ All to select the entire canvas texture.

5. Choose Edit ➤ Copy.

6. Return to the image you are working on, then choose Edit ➤ Paste to paste the texture into your new Texture channel.

7. In the Channels tab, click on the RGB channel at the top of the list.

At this point, you've just created a channel and added some material to it. The image itself has not been affected. The next step is to apply an effect to the image that will bring out the texture in the newly added channel.

1. Choose Filter ➤ Render ➤ Lighting Effects. The Lighting Effects dialog box appears.

2. In the Texture Channel button group drop-down list toward the bottom of the dialog box, select Texture. This is the channel you just created.

3. Again in the Texture Channel button group, move the Height slider to the left until the Mountainous value is at **4**.

4. In the Light Type button group, set the Intensity to **8**.

5. In the Preview window to the left, click and hold the bottom left anchor point of graphic representing the spotlight.

6. Drag the anchor point so the spotlight area becomes a circle, as shown in Figure 13.31a.

7. Click OK. After a moment, your image will show a texture as shown in Figure 13.31b.

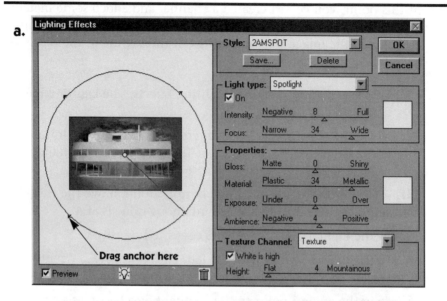

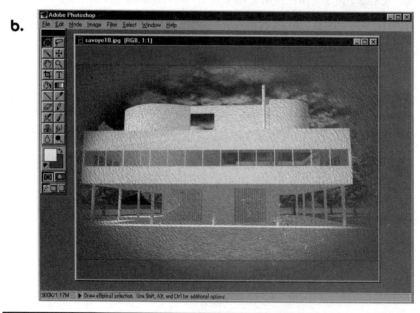

Figure 13.31: A rendering from 3D Studio with an added paper texture

The Lighting Effects filter offers a variety of different controls such as lighting intensity, types of lights, and "bumpiness" of texture. You may want to experiment with this filter on your own.

You can get a lens flare effect from 3D Studio using Autodesk's Flare plug-in on a still image or an animation. With Photoshop's Lens Flare filter, you can add the same effect to a still image. Figure 13.32 shows an example of an image with a lens flare added in Photoshop.

Figure 13.32: An image with a lens flare effect added

Adding a Quick Background

At times, you might want to be able to just create a quick 3D Studio rendering and save it to add a background to it later. Photoshop's ability to select specific areas of an image with the Magic Wand tool can make quick work of adding a background. Here's how it's done.

1. Open the Backgrnd.PCX sample file.

2. Open the Sky.TGA map file in the AutoVision subdirectory \AV2\Maps.

3. Choose Select ➤ All to select all of the Sky image.

4. Choose Edit ➤ Copy to copy the image to the Clipboard.

5. Go back to the Backgrnd.PCX sample file, then choose the Magic Wand tool.

6. Shift-click on the areas shown in Figure 13.33a.

7. Choose Edit ➤ Paste Into. The sky is pasted into the selected areas only.

8. Move the Sky image to the upper left corner, then choose Image ➤ Effects ➤ Scale.

9. Click and drag the lower right corner's anchor point down and to the right so the Sky image fills the background.

10. With the hammer cursor visible, click on the image to fix the sky background into place.

a.

Shift-click on these areas

b.

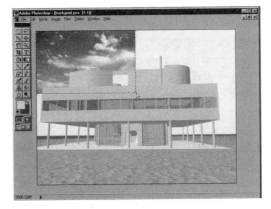

c.

Figure 13.33: Adding a bitmap image of the sky to the background of 3D Studio rendering

As a final touch to this view, you can choose Image ➤ Map ➤ Posterize. You see the Posterize dialog box. You can reduce the level of colors in the image to the number shown in the Levels input box, giving your rendering a painted look.

Photoshop as a 3D Studio Companion

Aside from the editing features presented in this chapter, you can use Photoshop to generate textures for 3D Studio. For example, you can easily convert scanned photographs of people and landscapes into bitmap images for props in 3D Studio. Use the Magic Wand or Path tool to separate and remove the background from the person or plant in the image, then save the selection to create the opacity map for the image.

Another use of Photoshop is to actually paint textures from scratch for those situations where you can't find a "canned" texture you like. The paper texture used in the earlier section was actually created in Photoshop using a combination of Noise, Blur, and Emboss filters on a blank, new file.

You can also use Photoshop in conjunction with AutoCAD to quickly generate 3D props. The train, bus, and people mover in the 3D Studio rendering shown in Figure 13.34 were all created by first modeling their shapes in AutoCAD, then cutting and pasting profiles of the model into Photoshop. There, the windows, striping, and text were added. The side of the engine was taken from a photograph, and enhanced in Photoshop.

Even though the 3D models themselves were very simple, they give the impression of being fairly detailed, due to the visual information added by the bitmaps.

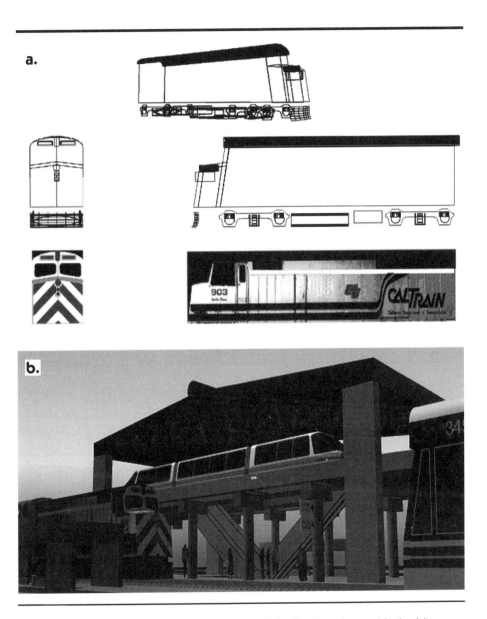

Figure 13.34: The top panel shows the AutoCAD drawing along with the bitmap images created and edited in Photoshop. The bottom panel shows a 3D Studio rendering with the train (lower left) using the bitmaps from Photoshop.

◆ Summary

Photoshop is a program with a great deal of depth. Even though I've attempted to show you the tools you are most likely to use in your rendering efforts, this chapter still only scratches the surface of Photoshop's potential for enhancing your computer images. Hopefully you will be motivated to learn the other tools as you need them. Experiment with the tools you know. Many of the effects in the later sections of this chapter were created as a result of experimentation.

In the next chapter, we'll jump into the world of video. You'll learn the basics of video engineering so you will better understand the tools that go into creating animations.

Transferring Your Animations to Video

As you began to explore 3D Studio's animation capabilities in Chapter 11, you started by creating *flic files* from 3D Studio and viewing them on your computer monitor. Once you start comparing your creations to animations created by other means, however, you're sure to notice that flic files do not produce the greatest quality image available. You'll eventually want to see your work in the best possible light, which means you'll want to translate your animations into full-color *television video*. But moving your 3D Studio animations from computer to television is no simple task, because television video is quite different from computer video.

This chapter is intended to help you bridge the gap between computers and television. I'll first explain how television gets its pictures. You'll need to know this in order to maximize the quality of your 3D Studio output from the outset. I'll also discuss some of the hardware available to translate your computer animation to videotape, and which video formats are best for different purposes. Along the way, you'll learn some of the terms used in the video industry, and their significance to your work as an animator.

◆ Introduction to Video

Television was originally devised as a means of transmitting live visual information over the airwaves in a way similar to radio. The inventors devised a way to convert visual information into a modulated signal that could be transmitted through the air, just like others had done with sound and radio signals. The receiver of this signal, a television set, then converted the signal into a series of pictures, which in turn appeared as a black-and-white moving image.

Today, the method remains virtually the same as when it was first devised, only now color and stereo sound have been added, and standards have been set up so that television manufacturers could design their sets to receive the same broadcast signal regardless of where it was used. Those standards are known as the NTSC standards in North America and Japan. Europe has two of its own sets of standards, known as PAL and SECAM.

The NTSC standard were established in the early 1950s. They dictate how visual information should be encoded into broadcast signals and how those signals should in turn be converted back into visual information. NTSC stands for the National Television System Committee. For this discussion, we'll focus on the NTSC standards.

How Television Gets Its Pictures

You're probably aware that motion pictures are actually sequences of still images that are flashed on a screen so rapidly that they appear to be in motion. For film, these pictures are shown to us at a rate of 24 frames per second. In NTSC Video, that rate is 29.98 pictures per second (compare that to 25 per second under the European standards). Actually, to use the correct term, in video the pictures are called *frames*. If you've gone through the 3D Studio tutorial in Chapter 12, then you are already familiar with the idea of frames.

Understanding a Video Frame

While motion pictures and video both use sequential frames to create the sense of motion, the way each medium displays a frame is quite different. In motion pictures, each frame is like a photograph and the entire frame is displayed at once. In video, each frame is actually drawn onto a screen—and over a very short period of time: 1/29.98th of a second to be exact.

The frame in a TV monitor is created by electron beams that range across the face of the television screen (see Figure 14.1). In 1/29.98th of a second, these electron beams zigzag across the screen 525 times to produce a picture. As the beams strike the screen, they excite the electrons in the screen's special coating, which produces light. The intensity of the beams controls the intensity of that light, thus, to produce a picture, the beams vary in intensity as they range across the screen. Higher intensities produce bright spots on the screen while lower intensities produce darker spots. The net result is an image that changes as the intensity changes.

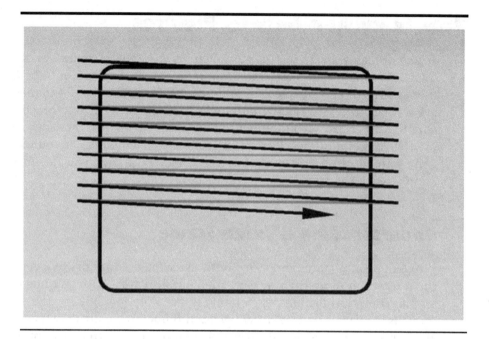

Figure 14.1: Scan lines in a television monitor

These scan lines are most apparent in old black-and-white televisions. If you've ever placed your nose up to one of these old sets, you'd actually see the scan lines. Furthermore, you'd see that each line varied in shades of gray across the screen (see Figure 14.2).

Figure 14.2: A magnified view of an old black-and-white television screen

In today's typical color television, there are actually three beams that scan across the screen, one for each color in the RGB color model. You may recall from the last chapter that the RGB color model is an additive one. By combining varying intensities of red, green, and blue, you can produce an almost infinite number of colors. The beams in a color TV monitor vary in intensity just as the beams in a black-and-white TV do, and the three beams scan the screen to produce full-color video images (see Figure 14.3).

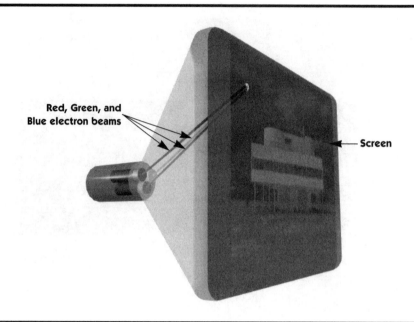

Red, Green, and Blue electron beams

Screen

Figure 14.3: A cross-section of a color television tube, with the three electron beams

How Television Resolution Is Determined

The number of scan lines in a television is fixed at 525 horizontal scan lines. However, not all of these lines are used for visual information. The actual number of scan lines devoted to the picture is 486. The remaining scan lines are used to convey non-visual electronic information to your TV monitor. You might think of these lines as being analogous to the vertical resolution of a computer monitor.

If you've ever seen the picture on your TV slowly scroll vertically while trying to tune into a weak station, you've see these non-visual scan lines. They look like a blank bar across the screen. The information these scan lines carry are the *equalizing pulse* and the *sync pulse*, though other information can also be carried such as closed-caption data or teletext information. The equalization and sync pulse can actually be seen if you were to look at this blank area carefully (see Figure 14.4).

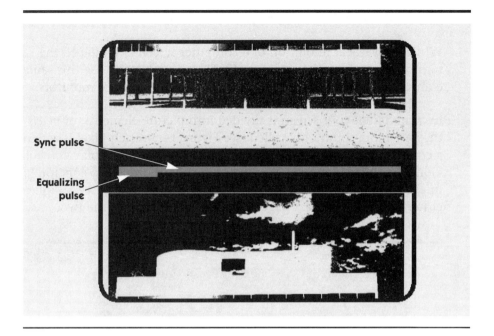

Figure 14.4: A graphic representation of a TV monitor showing the equalizing and sync pulses. The equalizing pulse is called a *hammerhead* because of its shape.

The purposes of these pulses are significant, and when you really get involved with your video quality, you'll want to know more about them. But for our discussion here, just know that they are there to help stabilize your TV image. They are like the sprockets in a filmstrip, helping to maintain a steady rate of film through a projector. In the case of the video frame, they tell your television where a frame begins and ends, among other things.

Horizontal Television Resolution

While the vertical resolution of a computer screen is similar to the number of horizontal scan lines of a TV, we can't really use this same comparison when describing horizontal resolution in TV monitors.

In a computer, your screen is divided into picture elements, or *pixels* as they are more commonly called (see Figure 14.5). Each pixel is assigned a color, usually one of 256 colors available from your display controller. (Some high-end computer displays offer over 16 million colors for Targa image files.) When all the pixels are viewed at once, you see an image, either a graphic or a text page or some combination of the two.

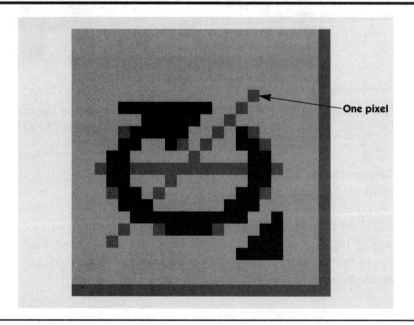

Figure 14.5: An enlarged view of an icon from Windows 95 showing the pixels making up the icon

Computers are designed to portray static images with a limited amount of movement. Televisions, on the other hand were designed from the ground up to display moving images. Instead of methodically defining each individual pixel of an array of pixels, as in a computer, television produces a constant stream of ever-changing light intensity that repaints the entire screen every 29.98th of a second.

In a television, the scan lines race across the screen of a TV to create an image. As I mentioned earlier, the scan line varies in intensity as it races across the screen, in order to produce the various colors on the screen. The number of times the intensity changes as it scans would be similar to the number we use to express the horizontal resolution of a computer monitor; however, since the variation is not fixed to any particular amount per scan line, it is difficult to give as specific a number as we give for the horizontal resolution of a computer display.

To better understand horizontal resolution in video, we'll look at an image that is often used to test a TV's ability to reproduce an image clearly. Figure 14.6 shows a comparison of how a series of black and white vertical stripes might be generated on a computer monitor versus how it would be generated on a television.

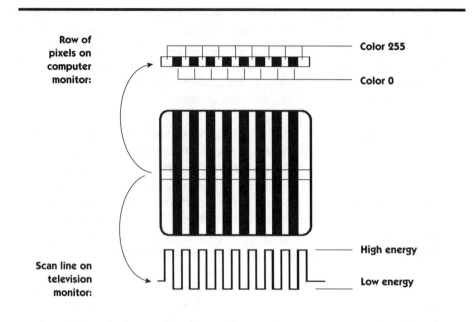

Figure 14.6: The top panel shows how a single row of a black-and-white pattern would be drawn in pixels on a computer monitor. The lower panel shows how it is generated onto a television monitor by means of changing the scan intensity.

Figure 14.6 points out an interesting difference between the two methods for displaying an image. The change in color from black to white in the computer is a matter of changing a color value, which boils down to changing a numerical value in the computer display memory. The television, on the other hand, requires the scan line intensity to change quite rapidly as it scans across the screen. The rate at which the television is able to change from one intensity to another over time determines the resolution of the television.

For example, suppose we make the spacing between the vertical bars very small, so that there are now more bars on the screen. For the television, the change in intensity of the scan line has to increase in frequency as the spacing becomes smaller and the number of bars increases. Remember that the scan line traverses the width of the screen in a fixed amount of time, 0.00013 seconds to be precise. The computer, on the other hand, needs only to rearrange the value of the pixels in its display system.

So, the horizontal resolution of a television monitor is really determined by its capacity to modulate the scan line over a fixed interval of time. This is quite a bit like the ability of a stereo system to reproduce high-frequency sounds. The higher the frequency a stereo system is able to reproduce accurately, the higher we rate the system. The greater the frequency a scan line is able to produce, the more horizontal "resolution" we get from the video image.

Translating Computer Files into Full-Motion Video

The previous discussion might lead you to believe that converting a set of computer images into a video stream is a complicated process. Fortunately, there are many products available that are capable of making the conversion fairly painless for computer 3D animators. In this section, I'll discuss some of the common devices in use today for converting computer files into video clips. But before I do that, it would be helpful to offer you an overview of the process of getting a series of still frames from your computer to videotape. Figure 14.7 shows a schematic view of a typical setup for recording computer image files from 3D Studio to a videotape recorder.

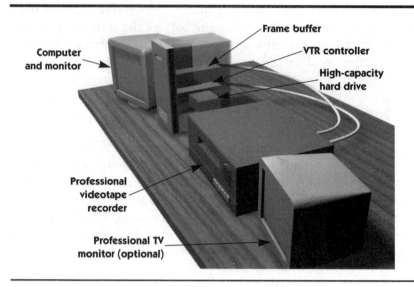

Figure 14.7: A schematic view of a setup for converting still frames from a computer to a video stream on videotape

It takes only a few devices to record video frames onto videotape. The devices are the *frame buffer* and the *VTR controller* (installable inside your computer), the videotape recorder itself (the *VTR*), and, optionally, a professional television monitor. Both the the frame buffer and the VTR controller are computer add-on cards; they are plugged into a computer's expansion slots. The computer itself can be a fairly low-end 486 50MHz machine, with a standard VGA display and 8MB of RAM.

Now let's see how these parts work together to create an animation.

Converting Files into Video Clips

Traditionally, video animators use a method called *step-frame recording* to transcribe computer-generated frames onto videotape. In this method, each frame of an animation is "laid down" on videotape one at a time. To use an analogy, imagine a filmstrip, with its individual pictures strung out along its length. Step-frame recording essentially places the animation frames in a similar sequence on videotape. A computer provides the video image to be recorded and also controls the video recording equipment. Here's a step-by-step description of the process.

Step-Frame Recording Simplified

The first step in the process is to go to the VTR controller software to tell the VTR controller the "In point" for your animation. This is the exact location on the tape where the animation is to start. Once you've done this, you can begin the recording process, which takes the following steps.

1. The frame buffer reads a computer image file, then sends the image to the VTR.

2. The VTR controller backs the tape up to a point roughly 10 seconds before the location of the actual frame. This is called a *pre-roll*. The VTR controller then starts the tape in forward motion, using that 10 seconds' worth of tape to accelerate the tape up to full speed.

3. As the tape reaches the point where the frame is to be inserted, the VTR controller tells the VTR to record the image being sent to it by the frame buffer.

4. The tape continues to roll for a second or two after the frame is recorded, then stops.

5. The frame buffer reads the next image file in the sequence and the process is repeated for every frame of the animation.

Once you've set up your computer with the necessary cards and software, you can just let the VTR controller software take over; it will continue to perform the steps described here until all the frames of your animation have been recorded. All you need to do is wait. After an hour or two (or three) your animation is on videotape ready to be viewed in real time.

Now let's take a closer look at each of the devices used in step frame recording.

The VTR Controller

The VTR Controller is like the conductor in an orchestra. It tells the VTR when to start, stop, and pre-roll. It also tells the VTR to record at the precise moment when the frame location is reached on the videotape. One of the more popular VTR controllers is the DiaQuest 422 Plus.

The Professional Videotape Recorder

The VTR in your conversion setup must be a professional-level videotape recorder that includes a *time code generator* as part of its circuitry. A time code generator places a special code on the tape that serves as a sort of indexing system. The time code can be read by the VTR to locate specific frames.

> **Note**   When you purchase blank tapes for a professional VTR, you usually need to add the initial time code by "blackening" the tape. This is a process where you record a black screen or color bar onto the tape to place the time code on the tape. It's a bit like formatting a disk or backup tape before copying data onto it.

The time code is presented to you via the VTR in a standardized way, showing hours, minutes, seconds, and frames, as in the following example:

```
01:30:45:29
```

This example shows a frame location of 1 hour, 30 minutes, 45 seconds, and 29 frames from the beginning of the time code. This is the SMPTE standard format for representing a frame "address" on videotape. (SMPTE is the acronym for Society of Motion Picture and Television Engineers, the acronym is pronounced "Simptee.")

The Frame Buffer

As mentioned earlier, the frame buffer is a computer add-in device, usually in the form of a card that fits into an internal slot. It reads a computer image file and then translates it into a video signal that can be sent to a video recorder or monitor.

Frame buffers come in a variety of grades, with each grade producing a different level of image quality and image resolution. The very lowest grade frame buffer would be something called a *scan converter* that attaches to your computer's video output and splits the signal so that you can view your computer programs on both your computer monitor and on a television. These converters are most frequently used for computer presentations, not for recording your animations to videotape. You can use such devices, however, to record real-time playback of flic files (I'll discuss real-time recording solutions in the next chapter), but they are not recommended for anything but the lowest-quality animations.

Mid-level frame buffers include devices like the *Truevision Targa Plus*. This device is dedicated to encoding your computer images into a high-quality video signal that can be understood by video devices. The Targa Plus requires you to render your image frames to a TGA file format at a resolution of 512×486. Although I've called this a mid-level frame buffer, you can use it to produce high-quality video clips. Some users believe that for field-rendered animations (I'll discuss field rendering in a later section), the Targa Plus is actually superior to its more expensive cousin, the *AT Vista board*.

The higher grades of frame buffers include products that are able to encode much higher resolution images. The *Truevision AT Vista*, for example, allows you to render TGA files to a resolution of 1024×486. It produces a very sharp, clear picture and is an excellent choice for architectural or industrial design visualization.

Recording Directly to Tape from 3D Studio

The description above of step-frame recording assumes you've already recorded all of your frames onto your hard drive and are now ready to record them to videotape. It is not the only sequence you could take for rendering and recording your animation, but it is the sequence that is preferred. If you wish, you can take a different approach and skip the step of recording your images to your hard drive. That is, you can have 3D Studio record your animation directly to the VTR, provided that the VTR controller offers the software drivers that will connect it with 3D Studio. You save on hard disk storage, but you pay in terms of adding considerable time to 3D Studio's animation rendering, since each frame you render would now require the additional time of the pre-roll and actual recording on the VTR (including the extra couple of seconds after the recording).

Another possible drawback to rendering directly to video is that it eliminates the possibility of using 3D Studio's network rendering capabilities. Network rendering can improve rendering time by distributing the rendering of frames to separate computers. That is, it sets up the rendering process in such a way that each computer on the network renders an individual frame. To render directly to a VTR, however, all the frames must be rendered from one computer running 3D Studio; in addition, each frame must be rendered in sequence, one right after the other. Network rendering is not set up to render frames sequentially, nor does it allow for the step-frame recording of each frame as it is rendered.

With today's hard drive prices falling relatively quickly, it pays to increase your storage capacity to *store* your animation frames rather than to try to render directly to the VTR. An added advantage to rendering to a hard drive is related to the fact that step-frame recording from the hard drive to the VTR can occasionally cause glitches, in the form of corrupted frames. As long as you still have the original TGA files on your hard drive, you can easily replace any frame that does not translate properly to videotape.

The recording is taken care of by the VTR controller. You usually don't have to do anything but wait. As you might imagine, the recording process can take several hours, but, depending on the type of VTR and frame buffer you use, you can get a very high quality video from such an arrangement. The video quality will depend on the condition of your VTR, the recording format you use, and the quality of the video signal coming from your frame buffer. We'll take a closer look at these last two considerations next.

Video Formats

When it comes to discussing video formats, the recording medium and the format are considered one and the same, so when I mention formats here, I'm really referring to a physical tape and a system as well. In the home consumer market, most of us are familiar with basically two formats: VHS and 8-millimeter. But in the world of professional video, there are many more formats available, each with its own advantages and disadvantages. This section provides a summary of tape formats that you, as an animator, will want to know about. To help you better understand the differences in these formats, let's start with a brief look at how color was introduced to television.

Color and Video

In the mid 1930s the FCC determined the range where video signals could be placed in the "air-waves." Originally, since television "resolution" was limited, and there was no color, the amount of the allotted bandwidth (or space on the airwaves) used in early television was quite small. Few people believed the entire bandwidth would ever be used or even needed. This is similar to the idea in the early 1980s that 640K was more than adequate for personal computers. As video resolution increased, more of the bandwidth was used; then when color was added, a separate portion of the bandwidth was used to carry color information, further crowding the video bandwidth.

> **Note**   *Color information, or* chrominance, *is actually encoded into the Luminance information of a video signal, but a detailed discussion of how this is done goes beyond the scope of this book. For a more in-depth discussion of this topic, along with a discussion of video signal testing methods, refer to* NTSC Video Measurements: The Basics, *available from Tektronix, Inc., Measurement Business Division, in Santa Clara, California.*

This leads us to our current situation: The video bandwidth is saturated. Much effort has been made to squeeze more information into the current limited bandwidth, but video bandwidth remains pretty much as it was in the early 1950s when color was first introduced. Today the color portion of the video signal is called the *Chrominance* component. The other component, called *Luminance*, carries the brightness information and is similar to the original black-and-white signal of pre-color television.

The NTSC standard mentioned at the beginning of this chapter specifies how chrominance should be encoded with luminance to form a compact signal. Unfortunately, a by-product of the Chrominance+Luminance encoding is a type of interference called "chromacrawl." This effect, which is most obvious in the reds and blues, can be characterized as a "bleeding" of colors from their true location in a video image.

Chrominance, Luminance, and Formats

One way to reduce the effects of "chromacrawl" is to keep the Chrominance and Luminance signals separate. You may have seen the term Y/C in reference to S-video connectors found in S-VHS or Hi-8 video decks and on computer-to-video translators. Video engineers use Y to symbolize Luminance (using an X,Y coordinate system) and C to symbolize Color, hence the term Y/C. When you see an S-video connector on a video deck, it generally means that the luminance signal is carried over a channel that is separate from the channel used to carry the color signal.

In contrast, a typical *composite* signal jumbles all the video signals into one carrier signal, which in turn muddies the video image. This composite signal is the lowest common denominator in the NTSC Video world. This is the type of signal carried through the air waves and between your consumer VHS deck to your TV monitor, usually in the form of an RCA jack.

Y/C separation in the "professional consumer" level (or "prosumer" level) of video hardware, such as S-VHS and Hi-8, offers a step up in quality from the typical consumer-level video products. When you get into the high-end, professional formats, you will find that the signal is further separated into Red, Green, and Blue color channels. Devices that are capable of distributing the video signal in separate RGB channels are called *component* (as opposed to *composite*) systems.

> **Note** *The Y/C separation provided by the S-video connector is actually considered a pseudo component system because, while it doesn't fully separate the video signal into its RGB color components, it does separate luminance and chrominance.*

By keeping the different components of a video signal separate, you get a sharper video image with less "chromacrawl." If you compare a video image produced on a component-based format with one from a composite-base format, you see a distinct blurring of reds in the composite format.

> **Note** *There is another format, called D2, which is a* digital *composite format. While its ability to maintain good quality after many copies (due to its digital nature) is superior to nearly all other tape formats, D2's composite nature reduces its ability to offer sharp color rendition compared to component formats such as Betacam SP and D1.*

So we find a variety of video formats offering three ways of conveying a video signal: component, pseudo-component, and composite. Now let's look at the specific formats and how they differ.

Finding the Best Format

There are really two components to video production: *acquisition* and *editing*. A format good for one may not be well-suited to the other. Acquisition requires portability and convenience. Editing requires robustness and generational stability. You need the right tool for the job, and the job may require different tools at different times. If you talk to ten different videographers, you'll probably get ten different opinions on what is the best video format. Table 14.1 describes the most common formats, with the formats giving the highest-quality results at the top of the list.

Table 14.1: The Most Common Video Formats

Format	Description
D1	Digital, component, high-resolution, used primarily for video editing.
D2	Digital, composite, high-resolution, used for editing.
Betacam SP	Analog, component, high-resolution, used for acquisition and editing.
Umatic SP	Analog, component, medium-resolution, used for editing.
Hi-8	Analog, Y/C, medium-resolution, used for acquisition and editing.
S-VHS	Analog, Y/C, medium-resolution, used for editing.
8mm	Analog, composite, low-resolution, used for the home market.
VHS	Analog, composite, low-resolution, used for the home market.

These formats can be roughly divided into three categories: broadcast, industrial/prosumer, and consumer. There is some overlap among the categories. For example, D1 through Umatic SP could all be considered broadcast-level formats, the highest level in quality, but Umatic SP is frequently used at the industrial level as well. Hi-8 and S-VHS are also used at the industrial level, but they are also available in consumer-level products such as home VCRs and video cameras.

Formats for Acquisition

Acquisition simply means recording video with a portable camera. In a very short time, video cameras have become a major consumer market. And the quality level of some of the consumer products is quite good. Here's a brief rundown on formats used most frequently for acquisition.

Let's start at the bottom of the list and work our way up. The lowest common denominator is the VHS format, which JVC invented and propagated through heavy advertising and support. It is not considered to be a very good system, but it is widely available. Even though Sony introduced the superior Beta format early on, when the consumer video market was still young, JVC just did a better job of marketing and supporting VHS, and the rest is history. The 8-millimeter consumer-level cameras, which offer a more compact and convenient size, didn't become available until much later.

Mid-level formats in use for acquisition are S-VHS, Hi-8, and 3/4" Umatic SP. Hi-8 is perhaps the most popular with videographers and journalists because it can produce a good quality image and is extremely portable. It also holds color better than its competing format does, S-VHS. Also, while Hi-8 is said to produce "drop-outs," in reality, tape quality plays a big role in Hi-8 video performance. S-VHS and 3/4" Umatic SP seem to follow behind Hi-8 in popularity for acquisition. S-VHS is bulkier than Hi-8, as is 3/4" Umatic SP.

S-VHS vs. Hi-8

At a glance, output from both S-VHS and Hi-8 look pretty good and they are comparable in price. But one video engineer I talked to didn't even think S-VHS was a viable medium. He regarded Hi-8 as a reasonable medium because it is highly portable. It also produced a good video signal, which is important when you ask it to work in conjunction with other video formats.

In fact, a Hi-8 video signal matches the quality of the digital D2 format in most respects—except one: signal-to-noise ratio. Here is where Hi-8 really shows the limitations of its small format. A poor signal-to-noise ratio shows up as a kind of flickering. This flickering can best be seen on a blue screen.

To see the effects of poor signal-to-noise, try recording a blue screen on a VHS deck, then play it back. Instead of a uniform, smooth blue, you will see the color "dance" and flicker.

One more thing: If you plan to use Hi-8, make sure you use good-quality, short-length tape. The shorter tapes are more robust because a thicker base is used. Also, avoid using the first and last several minutes of the tape, as these are where the tape is most likely to stretch.

At the high end of the acquisition list, Betacam SP is *the* standard broadcast-level acquisition medium. The cameras, while not exactly small, are manageable and they produce the best image available without going to a digital format. Video material acquired through Betacam SP holds up well over many generations of edits, making it an excellent medium for editing.

Formats for Editing

Betacam SP is not only the standard broadcast-level acquisition format, it is the favored editing format as well. With Betacam SP's all-around high marks, it's no wonder it is the industry standard.

D1, the next step up, is strictly an editing format. It has the best generational stability and it is a component system. It is also a digital format, meaning that the visual information is stored as binary numbers. In the field, a news videographer will use Betacam or even Hi-8 to acquire images, then dub those tapes to D1 for editing. By the way, most of the non-news programs you see on TV are shot on 35mm or even 16mm film, then dubbed to D1. (Film does a much better job at capturing subtle color differences.)

D2, also a digital format, suffers from being a composite format. In some instances D2 does not look as good as Betacam SP. But both D1 and D2 offer superior digital registration, making these two formats the best for overlaying video images. Overlaying is a process whereby different video sources are merged on top of each other to produce a video montage or other video special effects.

The Best Format for Animation

While the issues of acquisition vs. editing are important to videographers, they aren't quite so important to computer animators. Most of us will want to stick to the best format for *editing*.

> **Note** *Services that convert computer animation files to D1 format will usually offer computer-to-Betacam SP or Digital Betacam as well.*

The ideal process is to record directly to D1. Provided you have the right equipment, you can have a service bureau do this for you. The process for converting your .TGA files to D1 goes as follows: You would first generate your animation frames in TGA format, then back them up on a tape. The type of tape backup you use would depend on the service bureau that makes the conversion from the backup. Once you have the D1 tape, you would need to rent studio time to edit and transcribe your animation to a more portable format like Betacam SP.

The next-best option is to use a Betacam SP. Most of us may not even be able to detect the differences between material from a D1 tape and a Betacam SP tape, and chances are, you won't be editing down so many generations that you'll notice any image degradation. Also, it's cheaper to rent facilities for editing in Betacam SP than for D1. If you have a Targa or Vista frame buffer, a VTR controller, and the software to control the deck, you can rent a Betacam SP deck with a time code generator for around $350/day (price as this book is being published, mid-1996). If you are planning to use a video capture board (discussed in the next chapter), then you won't necessarily need a VTR with a time code generator. You can use a stripped-down Betacam SP deck, which is less costly to rent or even to own.

If you're on a budget but you'd like to own your own equipment, Hi-8 and Umatic SP are not bad alternatives for industrial-level work. S-VHS is also used frequently by animators, though it doesn't hold color as well as Hi-8.

◆ Video Quality Testing

I've discussed various issues regarding video quality as it relates to the hardware used to present and record it. But there is one topic that touches on all aspects of video quality, and that is *video testing*.

Video quality might seem at first glance to be a fairly subjective thing. It either looks good on the monitor or it doesn't. But video equipment is really quite forgiving when it receives a poor video signal. Today's modern consumer video equipment will do its best to give you a clear picture. Also, variations from television to television can greatly affect the way a video looks. If your animation video is producing a marginal video signal, it can still look pretty good on your monitor, but may not look so good on another system. Furthermore, a video image may degrade rapidly after only one copy. The only way to really be sure your video is at its best is to check the signal from your source material: your original videotape.

You may have heard the term "broadcast quality." Some believe that broadcast quality is synonymous with the Betacam SP format. This may be true to some degree, but having a video recorded on Betacam SP doesn't guarantee that your video will be as good as some of the finest things you've ever seen broadcast. The true meaning of this term is that your video produces a signal that conforms to NTSC standards, period. The reason this is important is that conformance to the NTSC standards guarantees that your video will look the way you intended it to on the widest possible range of video equipment. It also means that your video won't be rejected (at least not for technical reasons) by a television station or production facility when it comes time to broadcast your animation to the world. NTSC conformance is the first test of any video destined for broadcast.

Why should a production facility care about conformance to a standard? Well, when video is edited, it must go through a myriad of electronic circuits and equipment, each adding a bit of distortion to the original signal. The equipment itself expects the signal to behave a certain way; otherwise distortions may be magnified. When a video source conforms to the NTSC standards, then people editing your work can be confident that the final product will be as close to the original work as possible. But if the source material does not conform, then it's anybody's guess as to where the image will be once it's edited. So quality assurance in the video industry starts with a tape that produces a broadcast-quality signal.

Conforming to the NTSC standards means testing a video signal on two very common pieces of professional video equipment: a *waveform monitor* and a *vectorscope* (see Figure 14.8). These two devices test, among other things, the chrominance and luminance signal we discussed earlier. The waveform monitor is used to look at the signal in general, while the vectorscope is used to examine the chrominance portion of a signal. Both of these devices can detect problems in a video signal that may not surface immediately on a video monitor.

Figure 14.8: A rendition of a waveform monitor and vectorscope

I won't go into any detail on how these devices are used, but don't feel intimidated by their names. You can learn how to use these devices in an afternoon. The point is, the waveform monitor and vectorscope are your keys to producing broadcast-quality video. If you intend to produce animations for the professional video market, you will want to at least be familiar with these devices and perhaps even own them at some point. Remember that in the world of professional video, quality can and will be measured. No matter how good your video may look on your own monitor, its quality and acceptability depends on whether it is up to the NTSC standards.

◈ Video and 3D Studio

A lot of this chapter has covered video in a general way, and having a deeper understanding of video can only enhance your 3D work. But there are some specific issues we can discuss as they relate to 3D Studio animations. In this section, you'll look at two options in 3D Studio that are closely tied to the video medium. These options are *field rendering* and *Gamma correction*.

Field vs. Frame Rendering

You know that there are only 525 scan lines in a television monitor, but I haven't told you yet that those 525 lines are divided into two sets of lines, called *fields* in the NTSC standard, that are 262.5 lines each. 262.5? How do you get half a scan line in a field? Figure 14.9 shows how these two fields are drawn onto a screen.

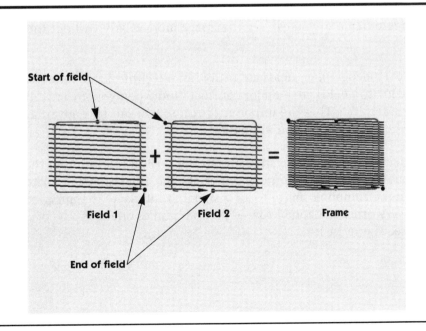

Figure 14.9: Two fields are drawn to make a complete frame.

A frame is created by first drawing one field in 1/59.94th of a second, then the other field in the next 1/59.94th of a second. The lines of one field are drawn between the lines of the other. This intertwining of two fields is called *interlacing*.

We normally think of video as 29.98 frames per second at 525 scan lines per frame. But you could also think of NTSC video as 59.94 fields per second at 262.5 scan lines per field. So far, we've been talking about frames as if they were a complete picture, but in fact, one frame contains enough information for two complete pictures. Now, for all intents and purposes, a field contains a complete picture, so you could say the NTSC standard is actually closer to 60 low-resolution pictures per second instead of the approximately 30 images (frames) per second we were speaking of earlier.

In some less expensive VCRs that have a freeze-frame feature, you can see the effect of the two fields, especially when you freeze the frame of an action scene: the screen seems to vibrate back and forth. This jittery effect is caused by the two interlaced fields showing two slightly different pictures. Some VCR's provide a feature that eliminates one field from a freeze frame so you can see the image more clearly without the jittery effect.

To a videographer, fields are really just a technical side note. But to an animator, fields are a major consideration when you are creating your masterpiece. They are important because you can take advantage of them when you render your animations.

Fields have a direct relationship to the vertical resolution of the computer image. When a frame buffer like the Truevision Targa Plus translates a computer image to a TV signal, it interlaces the image so that every other horizontal row of pixels becomes one scan line of a field (see Figure 14.10).

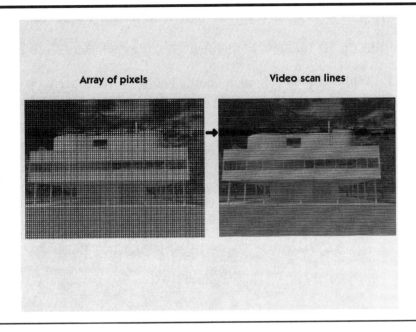

Figure 14.10: Converting rows of pixels into scan lines in a field. One row of pixels is converted to one scan line.

In my discussions of 3D Studio in Chapter 12, I always gave examples of rendering each *frame*. But you also have the option to have 3D Studio render *fields* separately. Two fields of the same frame of a fast-action scene can be slightly different in their content due to any motion that occurs in the 1/59.94th of a second between fields. So if you have an animation that contains a lot of motion, you will want to render fields instead of frames. By rendering fields, your animation will be smoother. On the other hand, if your animation is a fairly slow one without any quick action or motion, you can save some rendering time by rendering frames. Saving rendering time can be important for time-critical projects. The time difference between rendering fields and rendering frames can be significant.

Setting Up 3D Studio to Render Fields

Setting up 3D Studio to render fields is fairly easy. Here's how it's done.

1. While in the Keyframer, choose Renderer ➤ Render View,
   and select the viewport to render in order to open the Render
   Animation dialog box.

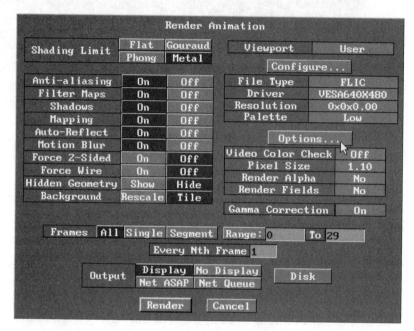

2. Click on the Options button. The Render Options dialog box appears.

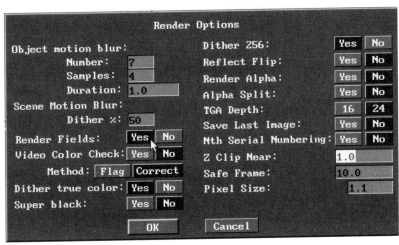

3. In the column of options to the left, locate Render Fields, and click on the Yes button.

4. Click OK to exit the Render Options dialog box, make sure the Disk button is selected, then click Render to begin rendering your frames.

5. As the frames render, you will see messages in the bottom of the dialog box telling you as each frame is being rendered.

As 3D Studio renders fields, you will notice that each field is rendered individually, as if it were a frame. Once both fields of a frame are rendered, then the frame is saved as a file. Since 3D Studio must *transform* the model for each field, it takes longer to render such frames. (Transform in this sense means making adjustments to each moving part of the animation for the field or frame.)

> ***Warning*** *Be aware that field rendering is only significant for* video. It *will distort the appearance of animations destined for* computer *viewing, such as Flic files or TGA files destined to be converted to the AVI format. (AVI files can contain field-rendered Targa files, however.)*

Understanding Gamma Correction

In very simple terms, *gamma* means *brightness*. 3D Studio offers the Gamma Correction dialog box to help correct differences in the brightness between various video systems.

Gamma correction is basically a way of standardizing the brightness between your computer and video monitors. There are many variables that can affect the brightness of a monitor, including the settings for brightness and contrast, the software drivers used for 3D Studio, and even the ambient light in your room. Not only are there differences from one computer monitor to the next, there are even greater differences between computer monitors and video monitors. Gamma correction provides a means of ensuring that what you see on your computer screen will be as close as possible to what you see in your final video output.

Turning On and Adjusting Gamma Correction

There are several ways, depending on your hardware, to set gamma correction. If you have a frame buffer installed in your computer, such as the Truevision Targa Plus, setting gamma can be fairly simple. Here is a description of the steps for setting the gamma correction in such a system.

1. Choose Info ➤ Gamma Control. The Gamma Control dialog box appears.

2. Click on the On button to turn on gamma correction.

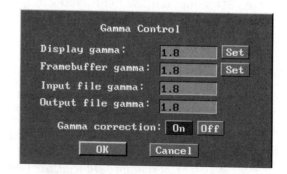

3. Click on the Set button next to the Display Gamma input box. You see the Display Gamma dialog box.

4. Move the slider at the bottom of the dialog box until the gray square in the middle of the graphic matches (blends with) the background black-and-white checkerboard.

5. Click OK.

The next step is a bit trickier. You want to perform the same steps as in the previous exercise, but this time you click on the Set button next to the Framebuffer gamma input box. You can then adjust the slider in the Framebuffer dialog box to match the grays in your video monitor.

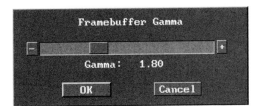

Note   *If you are using a professional video monitor, use a standard color bar to adjust the monitor first before you attempt to adjust the Framebuffer gamma correction setting in 3D Studio. Color bars are usually available in the frame buffer software. See your frame buffer manual for details.*

Make Sure Only ONE of Your Pieces Is Using Gamma Correction

If it happens that your Framebuffer setting appears correct with the gamma set to 1.0, then chances are your frame buffer has its own gamma correction turned on. You don't want gamma correction to be performed twice; it can cause distortions in your image. Exit 3D Studio and turn off the gamma correction in your frame buffer. (Consult your frame buffer manual to find out how to do this. Frame buffer gamma controls are usually set through software.)

After you've turned off gamma control in your frame buffer, return to 3D Studio, open the Gamma Control dialog box again, and click on the Framebuffer Gamma Set button to adjust the gamma for the frame buffer. Be aware that VTRs may also have gamma correction circuitry, so before you actually record your animations to tape, make sure the VTR you are using does not have gamma control turned on.

Setting Gamma for Imported Files

If you're importing gamma-corrected images for backgrounds or materials, you may find that their brightness is set incorrectly. The Gamma Control dialog box offers the Input File gamma setting to allow you to "de-gamma correct" imported images. This setting will require some trial-and-error testing on your part unless you know the amount of gamma correction that was applied to the image.

Setting Gamma for Output Files

Finally, the Gamma Control dialog box lets you set the gamma correction for your output files. This again is a trial-and-error process, of rendering an image and then comparing its video output to the image rendered on your computer screen. If you're not using a frame buffer, but are using a video-capture device such as the PAR board, this is really the only way you can check gamma correction. To help simplify this process, you can use the `Testpat.GIF` file provided with 3D Studio. Assign `Testpat.GIF` as a background, then render to both a file and the screen. You can then compare the grays in each monitor and adjust the Output gamma setting. You may have to do this several times to get the adjustment right.

Set Gamma to 1 For Printed Material

The 3D Studio documentation recommends that you set up your gamma correction once, then leave it on always, perhaps checking it periodically as your hardware ages. But if you are rendering single images destined for a printer, you will want to change the Output Files gamma setting to 1.0 before you create your final rendering file; otherwise you may find that the printed version of your rendering is too dark.

Just Make the Settings Once

Setting the gamma correction can take some time and a little tinkering with your video equipment. But once you do it, you needn't do it again. You should, however, check the settings from time to time, as the brightness of monitors tends to fall off with continuous use.

You will most likely need to reset the gamma settings if you ever replace your computer or video monitor (since, as we mentioned earlier, no two devices will display the same image with the same degree of brightness). Remember to calibrate your video monitor to a color bar before you adjust the 3D Studio gamma settings. Also, the newer the equipment, the more often you should check the gamma settings, because the brightness of video monitors falls off most rapidly when they are new.

Video Legal Colors

In an earlier discussion, I mentioned a problem called chromacrawl that is a result, in part, of the crowded NTSC bandwidth. This problem can be a very serious one, especially if you have intense, highly saturated colors in your animation. In general, you will want to keep color intensity from getting too "hot" by using "video legal" colors. There isn't any particular setting or chart I can point to that will describe what these "video legal" colors are, but 3D Studio can help you locate them in a rendering using the Video Color Check option in the Rendering Options dialog box. Here's how to use it.

1. If you are rendering an animation, render a small flic file and view it to determine which frame contains the brightest, most intense colors.

2. In the Keyframer, go to the frame you found in step 1, then choose Renderer ➤ Render View.

3. Click on the perspective view of the frame. The Render Animation dialog box appears.

4. Click on the Options button. The Render Options dialog box appears.

5. Locate the Video Color Check option in the left column of options and click on Yes to turn this option on.

6. Click OK, then select Single from the Frames button group.

7. Click on Render. Your image is rendered in the usual way, but if there are any colors that are not "video legal" colors, they will appear as black spots.

You may want to create two image files from this scene: one with Video Color Check turned on and the other with it turned off. That way you will be able to compare the two images to see which colors are the problem colors. Once you find them you can then make adjustments to your model to compensate for the colors.

In general, highly saturated reds and blues will cause problems, so try to keep these colors toned down. Another way to check these colors is to import the brightest frame into Photoshop, then apply the Filter ➤ Video ➤ NTSC Colors option to the image. This option will "tone down" any colors that are too saturated for NTSC video, and you will see the difference in the image.

> **Note** *Before you can use any of the Photoshop filters, your image must be in RGB or CMYK mode. You can set the mode by choosing Mode ➤ RGB from the Photoshop pull-down menu while the file is open.*

◆ Setting Your Monitor to SMPTE Standards

I've mentioned that before you actually set gamma correction for your video monitor, you will want to calibrate it first. This means you will want to do a visual adjustment of your monitor's chroma, hue, and brightness. The purpose of this, once again, is to ensure that you are working within video standards, so that your animation won't look completely different on someone else's video system.

> **Note** *These steps assume you are using a professional video monitor, not a consumer-level television. Consumer televisions do not offer the controls required to perform the calibration.*

To calibrate your monitor, you use the SMPTE color bar (shown in Figure 14.11; unfortunately, we can't show this picture in color). Frequently, the color bars are included with frame buffers. You can also obtain shareware video testing software from forums on CompuServe. One in particular, called NTSCTSTS, offers a whole series of tests and screen patterns.

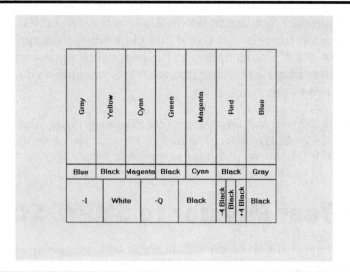

Figure 14.11: A diagram showing the SMPTE color bars used for calibrating a professional video monitor

Once you've got the SMPTE colors displayed on your video monitor through the frame buffer, take the following steps.

1. Turn off the red and green colors on your monitor. Most professional monitors have switches that do this; some even have a single switch that turns off the red and green colors at one time. Once you've done this, you'll see that the cyan, magenta, and blue bars are now all blue of different intensities.

2. Use the chroma controls to match either of the outer blue chroma set bars to the main color bar above it (see Figure 14.12a).

3. Use the hue control to match either of the middle blue chroma set bars to the main blue above it (see Figure 14.12b).

4. Turn the red and green colors back on, then adjust the brightness so the +4 black bar is just visible and the –4 black bar is not visible (see Figure 14.12c).

I've suggested using the shareware provided with this book, but many of the frame buffers come with their own color bars. By calibrating your monitor in this way, you can ensure that what you see will be close to what others will see on their monitors.

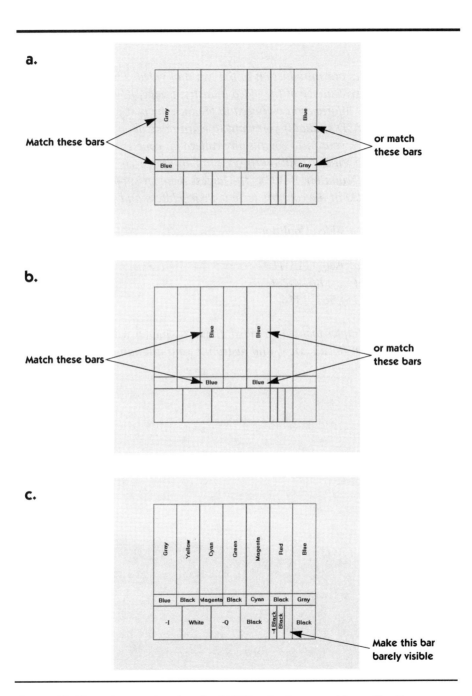

Figure 14.12: A diagram showing the SMPTE color bars used for calibrating a professional video monitor

◆ Summary

This concludes our introduction to the world of video. This is by no means a comprehensive survey of the video industry. I hope, however, that I have given you the information you need to produce the best possible animation you can with 3D studio. If you want to learn more about the art and science of video, check your local community college for courses. You can also contact The Bay Area Video Coalition (BAVC) in San Francisco, California for other sources of information. BAVC is the largest member-supported, nonprofit center for video in the country. Here is their address and phone number:

Bay Area Video Coalition
1111 17th Street @ Mississippi
San Francisco, CA 94107
Phone: (415) 861-3286
Fax: (415) 861-4316

While this chapter focused on video, the next chapter will concentrate on using your computer to edit, view, and distribute your animations.

Using Computer Video

The last chapter discussed methods for converting your 3D Studio animation to videotape. In this chapter, you'll look at how you can assemble and view your animations directly with your computer. Computer video, or *desktop video* as it is often called, is growing by leaps and bounds. It can aid in the production of traditional broadcast video and it can be used for multimedia production and presentations.

I'll start by giving you some background information concerning traditional editing methods that are still used by people in the video industry. Then I'll move on to presenting computer applications in video, including a discussion on video compression. Midway through the chapter you'll get to follow along as we create some video frames and use Adobe Premiere 4.0 to turn your frames into files you can view on your computer.

The very first order of business is to look at the reasons for using a computer for video in the first place.

◆ Real-Time Recording Systems

In recent years, products called *video capture boards* have appeared on the market to enable you to convert your animation frames into a video that can be played back in real time from your computer's hard disk instead of from videotape. Because they obviate the need for videotape, they coincidentally replace the need for the step-frame method discussed in the last chapter. These systems also enable you to capture live video and "digitize" it into a computer format.

What are the biggest reasons for switching to a digital video recorder for your animations instead of converting to video via the step-frame method?

One big reason is convenience. It's far easier and faster to convert a series of animated frames to video using a video capture device than it is to use the traditional step-frame method. In the case of the PAR board discussed in this chapter, for example, it is simply a matter of copying a Targa file sequence to the PAR-dedicated hard drive.

Another reason is editing. But to understand how video on a computer can help with editing, it will help to know a bit about how video editing works in the first place.

Some Popular Video Capture Boards

Two video capture boards that have become popular among PC animators are the *Perception Video Recorder* (*PVR*) and the *Personal Animation Recorder* (*PAR*). Both of these devices are manufactured by a company called Digital Processing Systems Inc.

The PVR and PAR are add-in boards that connect to the internal slots of a PC. They are capable of converting a Targa sequence of an animation into a video stream that can be recorded directly to videotape in real time. With these devices you don't have to use the step-frame method to record animation (described in Chapter 14); the time savings, in terms of time required for conversion, is dramatic. Also, you don't need the use of an expensive frame-accurate VTR as you do with step-frame recording.

Both devices require dedicated hard drives onto which they record the animation. The PVR requires SCSI drives; the PAR uses fast IDE drives.

Truevision, the makers of the Targa frame buffers described in the previous chapter, also makes a set of digital video recorders called the *Targa 1000* and the *Targa 2000*. The Targa 1000 competes with the PAR and the PVR in price, while the Targa 2000 is a more expensive, "high-end" system. Both products require high-speed hard drives.

Finally, if you think MPEG is the way to go for your animations, you may want to consider the *MARS2* MPEG encoder from Darim Vision Co., Ltd. This device will turn your animation into an MPEG 1 or MPEG 2 video file without the need for a dedicated hard drive (see the "Notes on MPEG Compression" discussion later in this chapter).

A-B Roll Editing

The traditional method of editing videotape requires someone in the role of editor to plan a video sequence, down to the last frame. He or she then joins video segments end-to-end, adding transitions, voice-overs, sound effects, and more. The segments may come from different parts of a video-tape, or even from different tapes.

The editor works with a script as a guide and assembles the video from the beginning to the end in a sequential, linear fashion (because the tape format itself is linear). You might imagine a videotape edit to be like adding cars to a freight train, with each car being another piece of the raw video footage. It's easy enough to add cars one at a time to the end of the train, but you can't add a car to the middle of the train without some difficulty.

A common editing method, called *A-B roll editing*, uses two VTRs to access the segments of video from the source material. Segments that are supposed to blend into another segment must be available on separate sources, so that the editor can play the end of one segment and the beginning of the next at the same time to control the degree of transition. Both sources are synchronized, then played simultaneously; the editor adds the transition from one source to the other when desired. The output from the two source VTRs, including the transitions, are recorded onto a third VTR.

> **Note**   *If you are part of a team producing a video that contains your animations, you may be asked to produce two copies so that the editor can perform an A-B roll edit.*

A-B roll editing is a laborious process that requires the editor to make several copies of original video footage. Since the copies are then used to create a third edited copy, the final product is often a 5th- or 6th-generation copy, which means that its quality has degraded.

But the real problem occurs when, at the last minute, the editor needs to insert or replace a segment within a nearly completed video. The editor cannot simply "splice in" the new segment as you might do with film. Once the video is placed on the tape, you cannot "lift and move" portions of it. The editor must either re-edit the entire video or use the final edited version as one of the source tapes to produce a new final tape, and in doing so, reduce the quality of the video.

The Digital Video Advantage

Videotape is a linear format. In order to get to a location on the tape, you must move through the tape until you get to the point you want. Computer video eliminates the linear nature of video editing and gives you direct access to the portion of the video you want, when you want it. Instead of having to fast-forward or reverse a tape, you can access frames and segments in a more direct manner. Computer video also allows you to perform cut-and-paste operations in a way similar to word processors. This reduces the need to make multiple copies of source material.

Even when you do find the need to copy video material, the copies do not degrade the original video image. You can copy whole video segments or parts of a segment fairly easily and in less time. And finally, you can insert segments in the middle of a finished video without having to re-edit the entire video or losing quality. This is a direct benefit of the nonlinear quality of computer video.

On-Line vs. Off-Line Editing

The advantages of computer non-linear video editing are great, but there is one major drawback. *Encoding* video into a computer format causes quality loss (see the next section, "Squeezing Video onto a Hard Drive"). But through a method called *off-line editing*, you can take advantage of computer video editing without giving up quality.

The traditional A-B roll editing described earlier is a form of what is called on-line editing, in which you edit the video material directly. The method called off-line editing allows you to use a computer to edit a *facsimile* of your original video. The facsimile contains all the information of the original video, including its SMPTE time code from the source videotape. When you complete your edits on your computer, you create what is called an *edit decision list*, or *EDL*. This is a text file that contains all the information about the clip locations, sequences, and special-effects transitions used in your final computer-edited facsimile. When you take this EDL to a post-production service, they can assemble the final video by combining the facsimile's information with the source videotape.

Although off-line editing is the preferred method for using nonlinear computer editing techniques with live video footage, animators are in the fortunate position of *not* having to deal with EDL and post-production services; if their animation material is already on a computer in a digital format, they can take advantage of nonlinear editing tools. Provided you have digital video recording equipment and it produces decent output, you can go directly to tape from your nonlinear editing software, eliminating the need to produce EDLs or going to a post-production facility to create your final tape. The next section offers an introduction to computer video to help you better understand what it has to offer.

◆ Squeezing Video onto a Hard Drive

The key to computer video is file compression. Without some means of reducing the size of video images, computers could not be used to produce video. Let's take a closer look at why compression is so important.

When you start to render animations in full video resolution, you find that a single frame takes quite a bit of hard disk space. A typical 512×486 resolution 24-bit image takes about 800K of disk space. A higher resolution, say 752×480, as required by the PAR animation recorder, takes 1MB. You can imagine how quickly your animations will fill up your hard drive at a megabyte a frame. At that rate, a mere 10 seconds of animation, or 300 frames, requires 300MB of disk space.

But aside from sheer size of these video frames, the ability of the computer to actually open and display these frames as video would require a data *rate* of around 30MB per second. Even by today's standards (mid-1996), this data rate is nearly impossible to achieve on a desktop computer.

This is where compression comes in. If you can get the file size down for each frame, you can store more video and reduce the rate of data the computer needs to pump out.

Compression Usually Means Loss of Quality

In Chapter 12, I mentioned one file format that offers full color at a high resolution and a relatively small file size. JPEG is a standardized method for compressing image files, and it has become quite common. If you've use the World Wide Web, chances are you've seen at least a few JPEG images.

JPEG compresses files by throwing away redundant information. Unfortunately, the moment you throw away any image information you start to lose image quality. JPEG does allow you to control the amount of compression, however. The lower the compression, the better the image quality.

There are image compression schemes specifically designed for video. The one called *Motion JPEG* has become a popular format for the higher-quality video capture boards. Motion JPEG applies compression to each frame of an animation, which also results in a loss of quality, but since we only see each image for an instant, the loss of information is not as apparent as it might be if we viewed each frame individually.

Video purists tend to shy away from video capture devices because of this loss in quality. However, to the untrained eye, the output from a good-quality video capture device looks every bit as good as video from a VTR.

Interframe Compression vs. Intraframe Compression

Another popular video compression scheme is called *MPEG*. This scheme offers a much higher compression rate than Motion JPEG, and it has a growing following among digital video enthusiasts. In fact, MPEG is being used commercially in the satellite distribution of video to homes and it is being considered as a means for conveying High-Definition TV (HDTV) video. (HDTV is the next-generation television format, with a screen proportion that resembles the wider screens used in movie theaters.)

MPEG offers as much as a 200-to-1 compression ratio. File sizes are so small that full-length VHS-quality videos can be distributed on CD-ROMs. The smaller size also means that the data rate required to play back MPEG video is fairly low, low enough in fact to play back easily on most desktop computers, provided the computer is equipped with hardware to decode the MPEG information. You will see MPEG playback hardware built into many of the PCs being sold today. Perhaps one great advantage to MPEG is that it is a format that can be used for both high-quality video output and computer-only playback.

MPEG achieves its high compression rate because it performs what is called *interframe compression*. Unlike Motion JPEG, which compresses each individual frame (*intraframe compression*), MPEG looks at a series of frames to see not only what information is redundant within each frame, but what is redundant over several frames. It then attempts to throw out this redundant material that occurs over a set of frames. MPEG is not the only compression scheme that does this, but it manages to do it without an unbearable loss in quality.

There are advantages to both interframe and intraframe compression schemes, so you should choose the compression scheme that works best for what you want to do. Interframe compression schemes like MPEG generally do not allow editing, simply because a frame is not an independent item in this scheme. There are some systems that offer MPEG editing by converting MPEG files into a format that is editable with video editing software, but with such systems, there is some image degradation due to the translation from one compression scheme to another. Motion JPEG doesn't suffer as much from this problem, because each individual frame is accessible. Though some image degradation is unavoidable with compression schemes, the problem is reduced with Motion JPEG.

There are many other video compression methods available, all of which degrade the video quality to some degree. Some of the methods are geared toward presenting video only on a computer. Quick Time, Indeo, and Cinepak are three popular schemes that, although originally designed to let users display full-motion video on their computer monitors, have evolved to feature television video output as well.

Notes on MPEG Compression

There are actually several different versions of MPEG. The most common are MPEG 1 and MPEG 2. The main difference between these two versions is resolution; MPEG 1 displays a maximum resolution of 352×240-pixel NTSC image (352×288 for PAL), while MPEG 2 displays a maximum resolution of 720×480 NTSC (720×576 for PAL). Also, since MPEG 2 contains enough information for a full 486 NTSC scan lines, it can reproduce video fields.

MPEG compression for live video usually requires expensive hardware, but if you are using 3D Studio, a relatively inexpensive product called the MARS2 from Darim Vision Co., Ltd. can convert your animations directly to MPEG 2 files and play them back in real-time. The output from the MARS2 product is quite good and compares favorably with output from the PAR product mentioned earlier. It offers composite, Y/C, and RGB component output. It is also an excellent tool for producing material destined for computer conveyance and playback or for simply getting a high-quality preview of your work. The MARS 2 can also capture and compress output from Adobe Premiere and other MCI-compatible Windows products.

With computers becoming more powerful, software MPEG compression and decompression solutions are becoming more practical, especially for animation. On the CD that comes with this book I've included a demo version of Darim Vision's MCI MPEG compression drivers for Windows 95 and Windows NT. These drivers will let you experiment with MPEG compression using video editing software like Adobe Premiere and in:synch Razor Pro. See Appendix B for details on their use and installation.

The output quality of computer video is constantly improving. There are high-end versions of video capture boards that are designed for professional broadcasters. In fact, there is something of a revolution occurring in the video industry as professional-level equipment moves into digital formats such as Digital Betacam on the professional level and DVD (Digital Versatile Disk, a laser storage format that uses MPEG to store video) on the consumer level.

◆ Compiling and Editing Your Animations

Now that you have a little background into desktop video, you can start to explore ways to assemble and view your 3D Studio animations. In this section, you'll look at how to create sequential Targa files that will become the raw material for your animation assembly and editing. Once you have animation files, you will see how you can use software to convert those frames into a video you can view from your computer or transfer to videotape.

Creating Video Frames

As you work with animations, you'll find that you can easily fill up your hard drive. If you plan to do some serious work with animation, plan on purchasing a large multi-gigabyte hard drive for storage. You may want to consider a high-capacity tape backup system too. Even if your projects are only a few seconds long, the hard drive space will save you time and frustration in the long run.

So before you begin, be sure you have at least 100MB of free space to store your frames. While this may seem like a lot, in fact you won't even be rendering to full video frame sizes. Instead you will be working with a reduced frame size of 320×240.

> **Note** *If you don't want to render frames now, you can use the ones I've provided on the CD accompanying this book. Locate the* `\Animate` *directory on the CD and copy it to a hard drive that has at least 100MB free. You can then skip this section and begin with "Introducing Adobe Premiere."*

You'll also want to reserve doing this exercise for a time when you won't be needing your computer. You might consider doing this exercise when you can leave your computer overnight or while you are away for several hours.

Once you've got the space ready, do the following.

1. Set up a directory called `Animate` to store your animation files.

2. Start 3D Studio, then choose Info ➤ Configure. The Program Configuration dialog box appears.

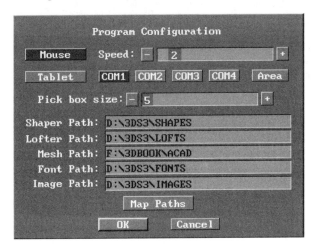

3. Click on the Map Path button to open the Specify Map Paths dialog box.

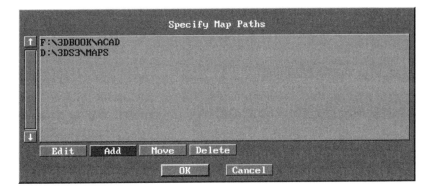

4. Make sure the Add button is selected, then click on the space just below the last item in the list box. The Add Map Path dialog box appears.

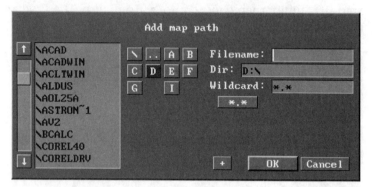

5. Locate the \AV2\Maps directory. This is the AutoVision Maps directory. You should have this directory on your computer after installing the AutoVision software from your AutoCAD disk.

6. Once the AutoVision Maps directory appears in the Dir: input box, click OK.

7. Click OK at the Specify Map Paths and Program Configuration dialog boxes to close them.

The preceding steps are necessary to tell 3D Studio where to find the texture map image files for the trees in the file you are about to render.

Now you're ready to open the file and prepare it for rendering.

1. Open the CH12.3DS file from the CD that comes with this book.

2. Choose Program ➤ Keyframer to go to Keyframer mode.

3. Choose Renderer ➤ Render View, then click on the Perspective viewport.

4. At the Render Animation dialog box, click on the Configure button. The Device Configuration dialog box appears.

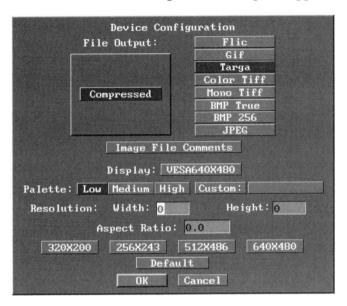

5. In the column of buttons in the upper half of the dialog box, select Targa to create a Targa sequence.

6. Click on the Display button. The Select Display Driver dialog appears.

7. Choose Null from the list, then click OK. You return to the Device Configuration dialog box.

8. In the Resolution Width input box, enter **320**.

9. In the Resolution Height input box, enter **240**.

10. In the Aspect Ratio input box, enter **1**.

11. Click OK to exit the Configure Device dialog box.

By entering a frame resolution of 320×240, you are creating a file that won't take too much space but won't sacrifice too much in the way of image quality. This resolution is really a sort of borderline resolution that is almost at the quality of VHS videotape yet can be played back on a Pentium-class computer without too much strain on the system.

I also asked you to set the Display Driver dialog to Null so 3D Studio won't waste time displaying each frame as it renders. (Also, if this option is set to a displayable option, the resolution input box options will be reset to the resolution of your display, and that's something we'd rather control for ourselves at this point.)

Now let's go ahead and render the frames. This is the part that will take some time.

1. Click on the Disk button in the Render Animation dialog box. The button should then be highlighted.

2. Make sure the All button is selected in the Frames button group and also make sure that Every Nth Frame is set to 1.

3. Finally, check your Render Animations dialog box against Figure 15.1 to make sure the settings match. (Don't worry about the Gamma setting at this time. See Chapter 14 for more on the Gamma setting).

4. Click on Render. The Save Rendered Animation To File dialog box appears.

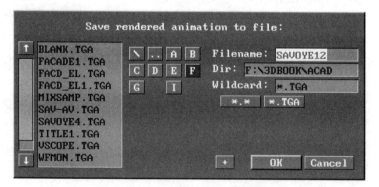

5. Locate the `Animate` directory you set up in the first part of this exercise, then select it and click OK. 3D Studio will start to render the frames.

On an Intel Pentium 90-based system with 32MB of RAM, your animation will take approximately five hours to render completely.

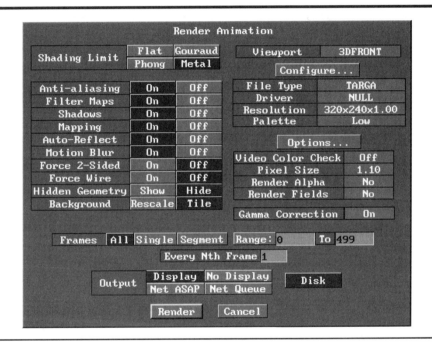

Figure 15.1: The settings for the Render Animation dialog box in 3D Studio

There's one last thing I'll ask you to do to set up your files for Adobe Premiere. Create two more directories in the Animate directory, calling them **First** and **Second**. Move the first 260 files to the `\Animate\First` directory, then move the remaining 240 files to the `\Animate\Second` directory. By dividing your animation into two directories, you'll have two segments to work with in Premiere.

Once your animation is rendered and organized into separate directories, you are ready to move on and assemble your frames into video streams. In the next section, you will be introduced to a program that can be an indispensable tool in your work with animations.

◆ Introducing Adobe Premiere 4.0

There are a number of desktop video editing programs available on the market. Adobe Premiere is perhaps the best known of them. Another popular product is in:synch's Razor Pro for Windows 3.1 and Windows 95, and Razor Mach III for Windows NT. In this section, you'll get a firsthand look at Adobe Premiere. You'll use it to compile and edit your animation into a form that you can view on your computer. Let's start by looking at the Premiere Screen layout.

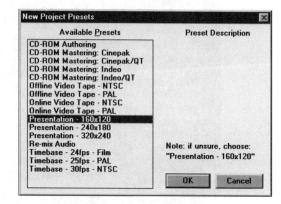

1. After installing Adobe Premiere, start it by choosing Start ➤ Programs ➤ Adobe ➤ Premiere 4.0. Premiere will start up with its screen splash. You'll then see the New Project Presets dialog box.

This dialog box offers a set of predefined Premiere settings. They can be altered at a later time; you can also create your own presets.

2. Choose Timebase - 30fps - NTSC. Next, you'll see a window similar to Figure 15.2.

3. Take a moment to look over Figure 15.2 as it compares to your screen.

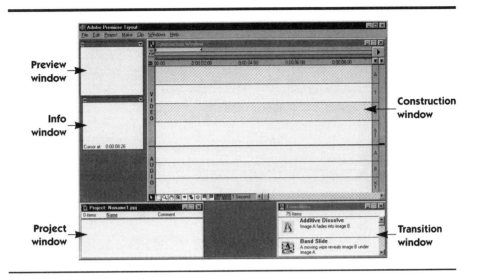

Figure 15.2: The Adobe Premiere 4.0 window

You see five windows within the main Premiere window. Here is a run-down of these windows and what they are for. The last one described here is illustrated in Figure 15.3.

Preview	Lets you preview individual frames of a video "clip." I'll discuss clips a bit later in this section.
Info	Shows you text-related information about a video clip, a WAV sound file, a still image, or whatever file you have currently selected.
Project	This is where you keep all of your video resources, from sound files to video clips. You can think of this window as a file folder or drawer where you store all the items you want to use in a video project.
Transition	This is where the various video special-effect transitions are stored.
Construction	This is the workspace in Premiere. This is where you will do most of the work of editing, overlaying, and compiling of your animation. There are several components to this window as shown in Figure 15.3.

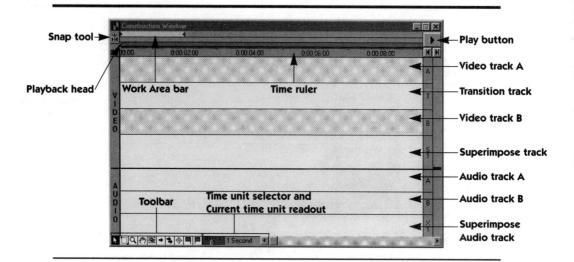

Figure 15.3: The Construction window and its components

As you work through this chapter, the functions of these windows will become more clear. You may want to refer to Figure 15.3 from time to time as you follow along with the tutorials. Right now, let's get a general overview of how Premiere works.

Drop-Frame vs. Non-Drop-Frame Time Code

In Chapter 14, we mentioned that the true frame rate of NTSC video is 29.98 fps. In Premiere, this is rounded up to 30 fps for clarity and convenience, since the SMPTE time code is in whole hours, minutes, seconds, and frames. Unfortunately, the SMPTE time code can add some complexity and confusion to your work, since there is a discrepancy between the actual time of a video and the time code.

To compensate for this discrepancy, the Society of Motion Picture and Television Engineers devised what is called the drop-frame format. In this format, two frame counts are dropped for 9 of every 10 minutes. No frames are actually removed; just their count is dropped. In non-drop-frame format, the time code discrepancy is ignored, which leads to the actual duration of the video being inaccurate.

It's important to be aware of this NTSC oddity, since an animation that shows a SMPTE non-drop-frame time code as 00:15:00:00 will actually be 15 minutes and 1 second.

Organizing Your Work

In Premiere, your work is organized on a project basis. In fact, the Premiere file is called a *project file*. A project might consists of several video clips, still images, and sound files from a variety of sources. The main Premiere project file keeps track of the many different files that will go into your final video. The project file also keeps track of the editing you do on the source material, as well as the settings you use for importing and exporting material.

Types of Files You Can Use, and Where to Keep Them

You can use a wide variety of file types with Premiere. I asked you to render your animation to the TGA format, which is fairly universal. You could have used the BMP format, or even rendered a Flic file. Premiere will read these and other graphic and animation file formats, including Windows AVI, QuickTime, JPEG, Photoshop .PSD, Macintosh PICT, and TIF. For sound, Premiere will accept Windows WAV files and Audio Interchange AIF file formats.

Premiere doesn't really care where files are stored, but to keep yourself organized, you may want to create a project directory that is divided into the different components of your project.

Importing 3D Studio Frames

Now let's see how we can import a series of animated frames into Premiere.

1. Choose File ➤ Import ➤ File. The File Import dialog box opens.

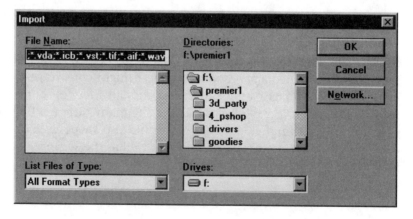

2. Open the List Files Of Type drop-down list at the bottom of the dialog box.

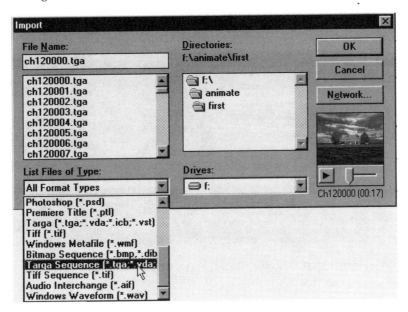

3. Locate Targa Sequence and select it. Be sure you don't select the plain Targa option.

4. Locate the \Animate\First directory, where the first set of your Targa animation files are stored. You will see the TGA animation files in the list box to the left.

5. Select the first frame of the animation (the file named
ch120000.TGA), then wait a second. A thumbnail view
of the first frame appears in the lower right corner of the
dialog box.

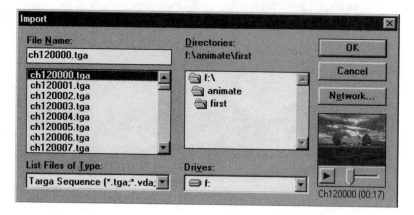

Notice that the thumbnail has a slider. You can move the slider
to view the sequence.

6. Now click OK. The frame appears in the Project window.

Let's stop here a moment to look at the newly imported frames as they
appear in the Project window. You see a thumbnail of the first frame. You
also see some text information indicating that this is an animation with
a duration of 4 minutes and 20 seconds and a resolution of 320×240. The
duration doesn't seem right for the number of frames you have. This is
because Premiere assumes a 1-frame-per-second frame rate for imported
sequential frames. You will need to adjust the frame rate to one appropriate to this animation. Here's how it's done.

1. Click on the imported clip in the Project window to select it and
make it active.

2. Choose Clip ➤ Speed from the
the pull-down menu. The Clip
Speed dialog box appears.

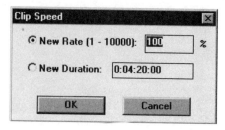

The speed is set to 100 percent.
This means the speed is 100
percent of 1 frame per second.

To increase this to the standard 30 frames per second you have to multiply this value by 30.

3. Enter **3000** in the New Rate input box, then click OK. Notice that now the duration is more in line with what you would expect from 260 frames.

Let's continue by adding a still frame to our project. Here's how to import one of your animated frames as a still.

1. Choose File ➤ Import ➤ File.

2. At the Import dialog box, open the List Files Of Type drop-down list then select *Targa (*.tga, *.vda, *.icb, *.vst).*

3. In the file list, select `ch120000.TGA`, then click OK. The file appears in the Project window.

You'll use this frame in the editing exercise later in this chapter. Notice that the item in the Project window tells you that it is a still frame with a duration of 1 second. This is the default duration for single frames. You can change the duration at any time, as you'll see later.

Let's add one more clip to your project. This time you'll bring in the second half of the animation as a second clip.

1. Choose File ➤ Import ➤ File. The File Import dialog box opens.

2. Open the List Files Of Type drop-down list at the bottom of the dialog box.

3. Locate Targa Sequence and select it.

4. In the Directory list, locate the `\Animate\Second` directory.

5. Select the first frame of the animation (the file named `ch120260.TGA`), then click OK. The frame appears in the Project window.

Just as with the first animation clip you imported, the speed is set to Low. Now set the speed for the second clip, this time using the pop-up menu.

1. Right-click on the newly imported clip. The Clip pop-up menu appears.

2. Select Speed from the pop-up menu. The Speed dialog box appears. This is the same one that appears when you choose Clip ➤ Speed from the pull-down menu.

3. Set the speed to 3000% as you did with the first animation clip, then click OK.

The options on the pop-up menu are all operations you can perform on clips. You can also right-click on clips and other items in the Construction window to access similar pop-up menus.

You now have a set of items to work with to create a video. You can add more items to the Project window at any time, including sound files.

By now, you may be anxious to see how your animation turned out. The next exercise will show you how you can preview your imported frames as video clips.

Previewing Your Animation

Now that you've got the frames into Premiere, you can get your first look at it as an animated clip. To do this, you must first place the clip in the Construction window. You also need to set the yellow slider at the top of the window to indicate which part of the Construction window you want to have previewed.

1. In the Project window, move the slider so you can see the first animation clip you imported (Ch120000.TGA).

2. Place the cursor over the thumbnail image of Ch120000.TGA. Notice that it turns into a hand.

3. From the Project window, click and drag the thumbnail image of the imported clip to the top row of the Construction window. The clip appears as a strip (see Figure 15.4a).

4. Place the cursor on the right-hand red arrow of the yellow band of the Work Area bar (at the top of the Construction window).

5. Click and drag the arrow to the right so it aligns with the right edge of the clip (see Figure 15.4b).

6. Now, if you are using a full version of Premiere, and not the tryout version that comes on the CD with this book, save the current project as a Premiere project named **Savoye.ppj**. Premiere will not create a preview unless you save the project. (The tryout version that comes with this book does not require a save.)

7. Choose Project ➤ Preview. Premiere will take a minute or two to create the preview, then it will appear in the Preview window.

8. Choose Project ➤ Preview again. This time Premiere doesn't have to recompile the preview.

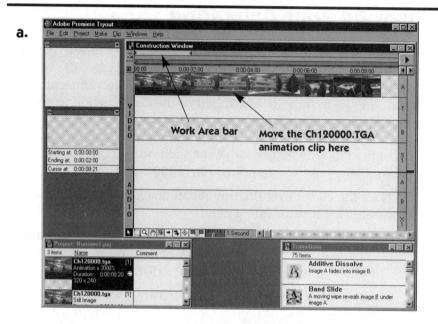

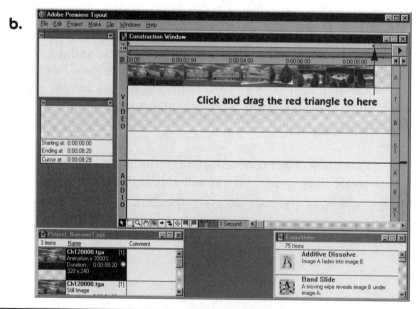

Figure 15.4: Placing the animation clip in the Construction window and adjusting the Work Area bar

Now you've seen how you can import and preview a sequence of frames from 3D Studio, and if this were all you needed you would be close to being done. But Premiere offers much more. Let's see how it can be used to combine or rearrange clips.

Editing with Premiere

The preview shows us that the beginning of the animation starts right into motion. Now suppose you want to add approximately a second's worth of still frames in the beginning before the motion starts. Let's also suppose that you want to take the second half of the animation and reverse it, then add it to the first half with a cross-fade.

In this section, you'll explore the possibilities of editing your animation with Premiere. You'll see how you might use Premiere to help put together a more interesting animation and save some rendering time as well.

Adding a Still Sequence

In Chapter 12, you set up an entire animation in the Keyframer in such a way that there were no segments where no activity took place. Either the camera was in motion or the lights were changing. This is a good goal to shoot for, because you don't really want to waste 3D Studio rendering time on still shots; you would simply be taking up time to render the same frame several times. A video editor can add the still frames later, as long as you specify where those frames should be.

Now you will play the role of editor and add about a second's worth of still frames to the beginning of the current project. Here's how it's done.

1. In the Construction window, click and drag the animation clip to the right. Watch the Info window and move the clip until the Starting At item shows 0:00:01:00, then release the mouse button. This places the start of the clip at 1 second.

2. Now click and drag the still frame, thumbnail view of
`Savo0000.TGA` from the Project window to the beginning
of the clip in the Construction window. You've just added
a second's worth of still frames to the beginning of the
project.

You can change the duration of the still
frame by selecting it in the Project window
or the Construction window, then choosing
Clip ➤ Duration. The Duration dialog box
appears.

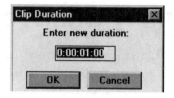

Enter a new duration length and click OK. If you want to increase the
duration, you must first move the animated clip to the right to give
the still clip more room. Once you've increased the time, you can
move the animated clip back to join the end of the still clip.

Now let's see how we can get a quick preview of the addition.

1. Place the cursor on the gray band
just above the time line in the Construction window, in the position
shown here.

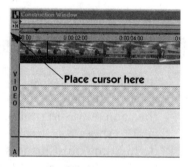

The cursor turns into a downward
pointing triangle. This is the Playback head. It functions like a Jog
Shuttle on a VCR or VTR.

2. Click and slowly drag the cursor to the right and watch the Preview window. Notice that the animation is played back. This bar
acts like the Frame slider in the Keyframer of 3D Studio, displaying
your animation as you move the slider.

> ***Note***   *If you move the slider over a transition that hasn't been previewed
> you'll see a large red X in the preview window. This indicates that while the
> transition may have been placed, it has not yet been "compiled," or
> processed and saved to disk. Once it is compiled, which is accomplished by
> previewing or making a movie, then you see a square indicating the portion
> of the clip that contains an effect or transition.*

As you move the slider, you can see that you now have about a second's worth of still frames in the beginning of the animation. Imagine having to render or even just copy these frames thirty times and you can see that Premiere has saved you some effort.

Making Changes to Your Construction Window View

By now, your still frames and the clip are crowding your view. To get a bigger picture of your project, you can use the Zoom tool. The Zoom tool works the same as the Zoom tool in Adobe Photoshop and many other Windows programs. But instead of actually enlarging or reducing a view, you are enlarging and reducing a "window of time," increasing or decreasing the visible time interval you can see of your project.

1. Click on the Zoom tool's magnifying glass icon at the bottom of the Construction window.

2. Move the cursor over the Construction window and, while holding down the Alt key, click mouse. The view zooms out to show more of the clip.

3. Place the cursor on the end of the clip and click on it. Your view zooms in to the end portion of the clip.

4. Now Alt-click in the window again to view the overall clip.

Another tool for adjusting your view is the time unit selector, next to the toolbar at the bottom of the Construction window. This tool lets you determine the units of increment shown in the time ruler at the top of the Construction window, and it also changes the view of the project.

1. Click and drag the time unit selector to the right and notice the time readout just to the right of it. The readout changes to indicate the new time unit.

2. Slide the time selector to the left until the readout shows 1 second, then let go of the mouse button. The Construction window returns to its original view.

3. Now set the time unit selector to 2 seconds for the next operation.

4. Click on the Arrow icon in the tool-bar at the bottom of the Construction window to return to the selection mode.

Select the arrow

Adding a New Clip
with a Cross-Fade Transition

Earlier in this chapter, I described an editing method called A-B roll editing. You may have noticed that to the right of the Construction window, you see the labels A and B. These indicate the two sources, A and B, that editors normally associate with videotape. Now we see their computer equivalent as time lines in the Construction window. This method of showing the A and B sources has been adopted by many other computer video editing programs besides Premiere.

So far, you've just used the A source. Generally, you can do this as long as you are just making straight cuts between clips. A straight cut means going from one clip to another without any special transition.

Now suppose you want to add another animated clip with a *cross-dissolve* (also referred to as a *cross-fade*), a transition where one clip fades out while another fades in over the first. For this type of transition, you will have to make use of the B track.

Adding a Transition

In the following exercise, you'll add the second half of the animation to the Construction window, then add a cross-dissolve transition. "Adding a transition" means, in effect, specifying what kind of transition you want between the clips. In the following steps, you'll overlap the two clips by 10 frames and add the transition to the overlap. To make things more interesting, you'll also reverse the second clip.

1. In the Project window, locate the animation clip that starts with frame Ch120260.TGA.

2. Click and drag this frame from the Project window to the B track of the Construction window.

3. Click and drag the track so it begins at approximately 00:09:05, as shown in Figure 15.5. You can use the Info window to help you locate the beginning of the clip in the time line.

Info	
Ch120260.tga [1]	
Animation x 3000%	
Duration: 0:00:07:15	
320 x 240	
Starting at: 0:00:09:05	
Ending at: 0:00:16:20	
Cursor at: 0:00:09:05	

4. In the Transition window, use the scroll bar to the right to scroll down the list of transitions to Cross-Dissolve.

5. Place the cursor on the Cross-Dissolve transition. It turns into a hand icon.

6. Click and drag the Cross-Dissolve transition to the track labeled T (for Transition) between the A and B tracks and place it between the end of the clip in track A and the beginning of the clip in track B (see Figure 15.5b). The transition will automatically fit between the beginning of the B track and the end of the A track.

Note *In general, you will want to have your clips overlap for transitions, as the overlapped material is used in the transition. If you do not overlap the clips, the transitions will not have any effect.*

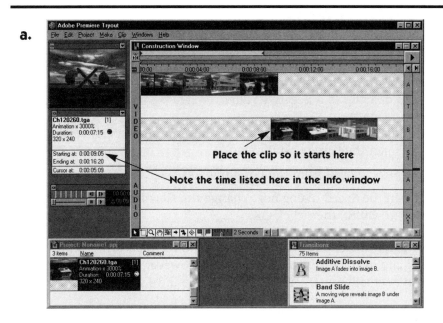

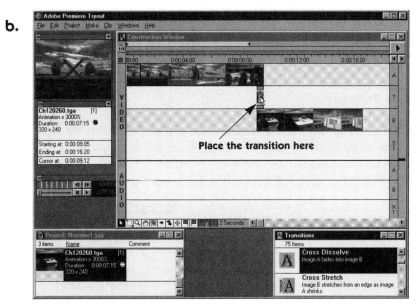

Figure 15.5: Adding the second clip to the Construction window

Reversing a Clip

Now you've got two clips joined with a cross-dissolve transition. You could do a preview now to see how it looks, but before we do that, let's see how to reverse the direction of a clip. This is done by changing the speed of a clip to a negative value.

1. Right-click on the clip in track B to simultaneously select it and open the Clip pop-up menu.

2. Select Speed from the Pop-up menu.

3. In the Speed dialog box, change the New Rate input box from 3000 to **–3000**, then click OK.

Although the clip now shows –3000 in the Project window, the thumbnail clip in the Construction window, however, does not change. You won't actually see the reversal of the clip until you do a preview.

Considering Fields in Clips

If you've rendered your Targa sequence with the Field option turned on in 3D Studio, you'll want to reverse what is called the *field dominance* at the same time that you reverse the direction of a clip. The following steps show you how.

> **Note** *The sample animation files you've been working with are low-resolution 320×240 images, thus they are not field-rendered.*

1. Select the reversed clip in the Construction window.

2. Choose Clip ➤ Field Options. The Field Options dialog box appears.

3. Click on the Reverse Field Dominance checkbox, then click OK.

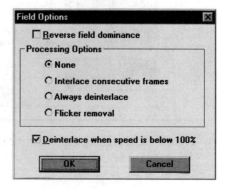

Remember that fields are like frames, so if you reverse a clip, you will want the order in which the fields are presented reversed also.

If you are mixing live video that was captured to your computer, and the field dominance of the live video is not the same as your animations, this option can be used to set the field dominance the same for all of your clips.

In addition to the Field Dominance option, you have other field-related settings you can use in the Field Options dialog box, as described in the following list.

None	Turns off field processing.
Interlace Consecutive Frames	Turns a sequence of non-interlaced frames into a sequence of fields, so a set of 60 frames becomes 30 frames of two fields each.
Always Deinterlace	Averages fields of a frame into a single, non-interlaced frame. This can be useful if you are converting a field-rendered animation into an animation destined for computer playback.
Flicker Removal	Blends any bright horizontal line of one pixel with the pixels above and below it to reduce flickering.
Deinterlace Fields When Speed is Below 100%	Does the same thing as Always Deinterlace for clips that have been reduced in speed below the default 100% setting.

Previewing Your Animation

You could do a preview of the whole animation to see how it looks so far, but for now, let's see how you can preview just the transition. You can move the Work Area bar, the yellow bar at the top of the window, to a new position over the transition. This bar determines how much of the project is previewed when you use the Preview command.

> **Note** *You can use the Playback head to preview a transition after a preview has been made, but not before.*

1. Move the cursor to the middle of the yellow bar.

2. Click and drag the bar so it is over the transition as shown in Figure 15.6.

3. Choose Project ➤ Preview. Premiere will take a minute or two to construct the preview, then it is displayed in the Preview window.

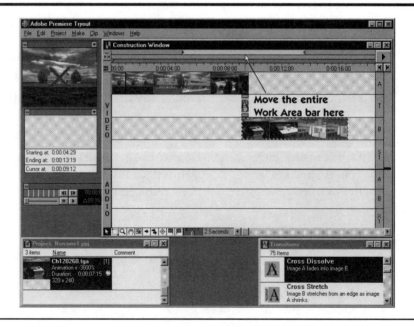

Figure 15.6: Moving the Work Area bar

Notice that the preview shows that the second clip is indeed reversed, playing from the end instead of from the beginning (remember, the scene in the courtyard is at the end of your animation).

Adjusting Transitions

Before you move on, you'll want to know how to modify transitions you've added to your project. Perhaps the most important thing to know is how to set a transition from track B to track A. When you added a transition in one of the above exercises, you simply placed the transition in the transition track between the end of the A track and the beginning of the B track. The default transition "direction" is to fade out track A and to fade in track B.

Sooner or later, you will find yourself in a situation where you want to transition to another clip behind the B track. To do this you would add a third clip in the A track and then add another transition between the second clip and the last clip. Now comes the important part: At that point you will want to make sure that the transition fades the B track out and fades the A track in. This is the opposite direction from the previous transition exercise where track A fades out and track B fades in.

To reverse the transition direction, take the following steps.

1. Double-click on the transition you've placed in the Construction window. The Transition Settings dialog box appears. Note the animated thumbnail example in its lower right corner. It shows you how the transition looks and it indicates the direction of the transition by showing you the letter of the tracks.

2. In the animated thumbnail, click on the arrow just to the left of the animation. It changes direction. This arrow shows you the direction of the transition, whether it is from A to B (a downward pointing arrow) or B to A (an upward pointing arrow). And as you have just seen, it also allows you to switch the direction of the transition.

The checkbox labeled Show Actual Source lets you view your clips in the two larger thumbnails in the dialog box. Other options vary depending on the transition. You may want to experiment with other transitions and their settings after you've worked through this tutorial.

If you find that the transitions Premiere supplies do not suit your needs, you can purchase "plug-in" transitions from third-party vendors such as Kai's Power Tools.

Trimming a Clip Down

Now let's suppose you decide that you don't want to use the last second's worth of the first clip. You can control the portion of a clip that is used in your project by using the Clip window. This is a window that displays clips in its own window. Here's how it works.

1. Double-click on the clip in track A. The Clip window appears (see Figure 15.7).

2. In the lower left corner of the window, move the slider until the time code display shows 00:00:07:20. You can get close to the correct time using the slider, then use the Job control above the slider to "zero in" on the 00:00:07:20 time. This is the point in the clip where you will end the clip.

   Note   *You can also select the exact time code by placing the cursor over the current location readout, then clicking on it. You can then enter a time code through the keyboard. The clip will then move to that position.*

3. Click on the Out button. This tells Premiere that you want to stop the display of the clip at the current location. The clip will shorten in the Construction window.

4. Close the window to return to the Construction window.

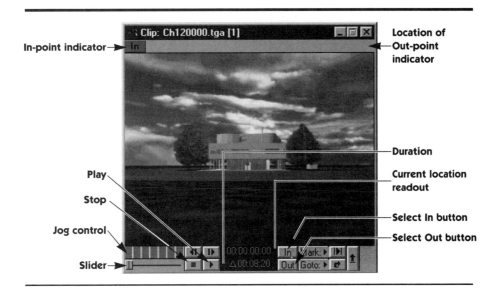

Figure 15.7: The Clip window

Using the Snap Tools to Align Clips and Transitions

Now you need to rearrange the transition and the second clip to align with the trimmed-down first clip. To aid in the alignment, you'll use the Snap tool.

1. Click on the Snap Tool so it shows the outward pointing lines and the arrow turns red. These lines indicate that the tool is active.

2. Move the transition to the left so it is in line with the new end of the first clip. Notice how it snaps into place (see Figure 15.8a).

3. Move the second clip so it is in line with the beginning of the transition. It too snaps into place (see Figure 15.8b).

4. Adjust the Work Area bar to include the transition, and create another preview by choosing Project ➤ Preview.

a.

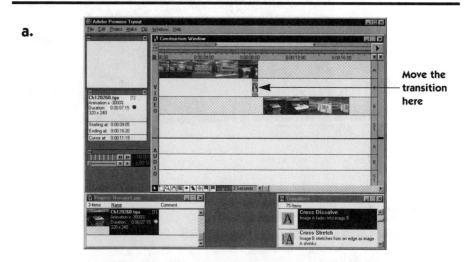

Move the
transition
here

b.

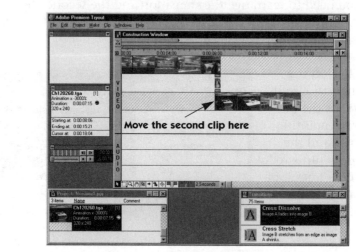

Move the second clip here

Figure 15.8: Moving the transition and second clip into place

You haven't actually discarded any of the first clip; you've just set a marker called the Out point to tell Premiere to ignore everything in the clip past that point.

Another marker called the In point lets you control where to begin the clip. Setting the In point is similar to setting the Out point. You open the Clip window by double-clicking on a clip. Next, you locate the frame on which to begin the clip, and then you click on the In button.

If you want to reset the Out point back to the true end of the clip, for example, double-click on the clip, move the slider to the far right to get to the end of the clip, then click on the Out button.

> **Note**   *Setting the In and Out point of a* reversed *clip is a bit trickier. You will first have to un-reverse the clip, then set the In and Out points. Once they are set, you would then have to re-reverse the clip. Since the clip is reversed, the In point becomes the Out point and the Out point becomes the In point.*

You can also set the In and Out points of a clip in the Construction window using the In and Out tools in the toolbar. These tools look like left- and right-pointing flags.

The In-point tool — ... — The Out-point tool

The left-pointing flag sets the In point and the right-pointing flag sets the Out point. To use these tools, click on them, then click on the point in the clip in the Construction window where you want to place the point.

Adding Sound

Filmmakers have known for a long time that sound plays a crucial role in a presentation. In this next exercise, you'll add a pre-existing sound file to your animation. You'll also see how you can adjust the volume over time to fade the sound out toward the end.

1. Choose File ➤ Import ➤ File.

2. In the Import dialog box, open the List Files Of Type drop-down list and select Windows Waveform (*.wav).

3. Locate and select the Techno.wav file in the \Animate directory where you've stored the sample files from this book.

4. Click OK. The Techno.wav file is now in the Project window.

5. Click and drag Techno.wav from the Project window to Audio track 1 as shown in Figure 15.9a.

6. Move the Work Area bar to the far left, then adjust its length by clicking and dragging the red triangle at the right end to the 4-second mark (see Figure 15.9b).

7. Choose Project ➤ Preview. After a moment, you'll hear the sound file and see the animation.

   Note   *Your computer must be equipped with multimedia sound capabilities before you can hear the sound from the Sample.wav file.*

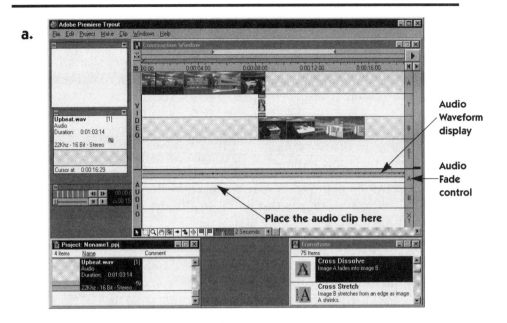

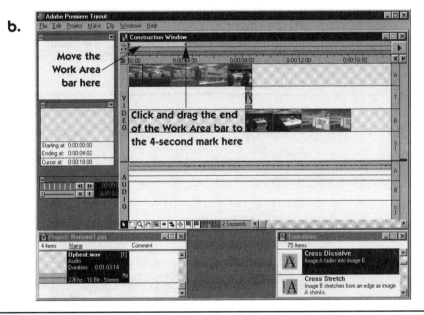

Figure 15.9: Placing the sound file into the A sound track

This sound file is considerably longer than your project. You can set the In and Out points of a sound clip just as you can with a video clip. In the following exercise, you'll use the Out Point tool in the toolbar to set the Out point of the sound clip. Also, to keep the sound from ending abruptly at that point, you'll adjust the sound track to fade out by means of the Volume control.

1. Click on the Out Point icon in the Construction window toolbar.

2. Click on audio track A at the location shown in Figure 15.10. You've now set the Out point. Notice that the audio track ends where you selected the Out point.

3. To fade the audio track out, place the cursor on the Audio Fade control section of the audio track (the strip just below the graphic of the audio track). The cursor changes into a pointing hand.

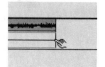

4. Place the pointing hand on the small dot at the Out point of the track, as shown in Figure 15.11a.

5. Click and drag the dot down to the bottom of the Audio Fade control section (See Figure 15.11b).

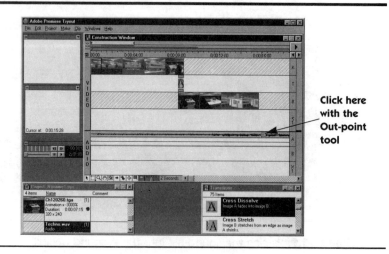

Click here with the Out-point tool

Figure 15.10: Setting the Out point for the audio track

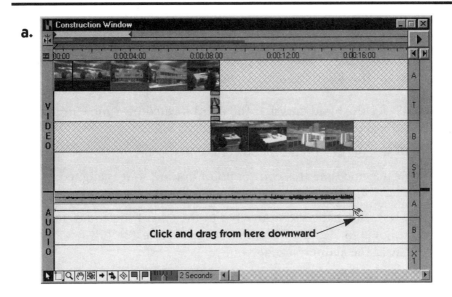

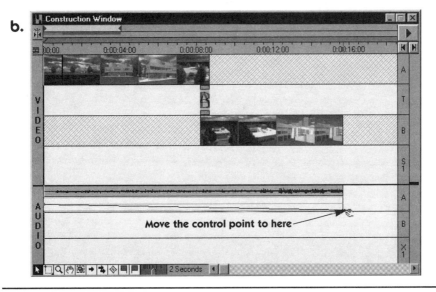

Figure 15.11: Adjusting the Audio Fade control

You now have the volume set to decrease gradually over the entire length of the project, which is not exactly what you may have had in mind. You need to add a control point on the Audio Fade control to raise and maintain the volume of the audio track until the appropriate moment when you want the audio to start to fade.

1. Place the hand cursor at the point located near the Out point of the audio track, as shown in Figure 15.12a.

2. Click on this point. A control point appears.

3. Click and drag this control point upward so it is aligned with the level line in the Audio Fade control section (see Figure 15.12b).

4. Now move the Work Area bar to the end of the audio track as shown in Figure 15.12c, then choose Project ➤ Preview. You'll hear the audio track fade out.

   Note   *To delete an unwanted control point in the Audio Fade control, click and drag the point out of the audio track area.*

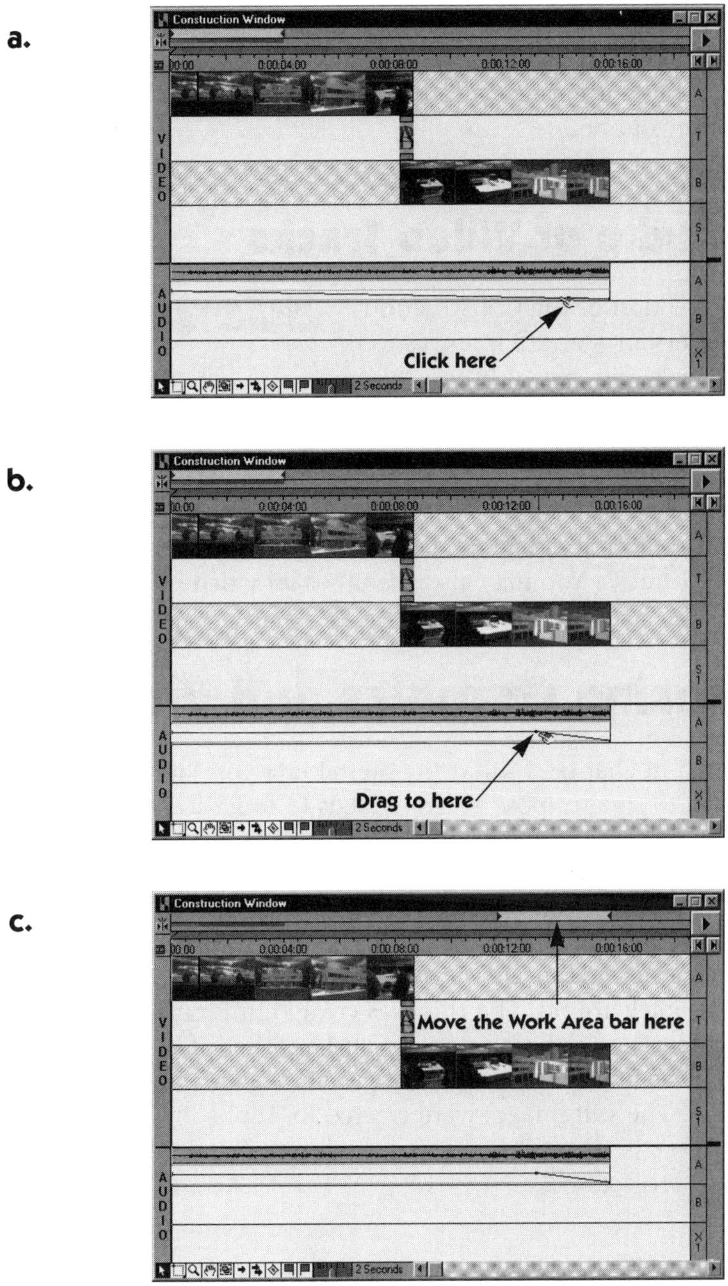

a.

b.

c.

Figure 15.12: Adding a control point to the Audio Fade control

You can also control the volume of the audio track between control points using the Fade Adjustment tool. Shift-click and drag the Audio Fade control line up or down to increase or decrease the volume.

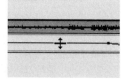

Adding Audio or Video Tracks

The audio section of the Construction window offers an A and B track, as well as an X1 track. You can add more audio or video tracks by selecting Projects ➤ Add/Delete Tracks, which brings up the Add/Delete Tracks dialog box.

Additional audio tracks will be designated as X2, X3, X4, and so on up to a total of 99 tracks. You may also use up to 99 video tracks.

✦ Superimposing Graphics and Video

I mentioned in chapter 14 that the digital tape formats D1 and D2 can be used to superimpose several videos in order to create special effects. You can also superimpose several video sources in Premiere. For example, you may want to overlay a title on the beginning or end of your animation.

I've created an animated title in the AVI format that simply fades out from a blue background. The title was created in Premiere by assembling two still images: one of a blue screen and another of a blue screen with black text. The blue in each case is a pure blue, with no red or green component. The still images were created in Adobe Photoshop. The following exercise shows you how you can overlay this title onto the current project.

1. Choose File ➤ Import ➤ File.

2. At the Import dialog box, open the List Files Of Type drop-down list and select AVI Movie(*.avi).

3. Locate the Sample files and select `Samplttl.AVI`.

4. Click OK to place `Samplttl.AVI` into the Project window.

5. Click and drag `Samplttl.AVI` to the S1 Video track. This is a track reserved for overlays.

6. Right-click on the clip in the S1 track, then, at the pop-up menu, select Transparency. The Transparency Settings dialog box appears (see Figure 15.13).

7. Open the Key Type drop-down menu, then select Blue Screen from the list. The options here let you determine which part of your overlay becomes transparent. In this situation, you want the Blue background to be transparent, so you should select Blue Screen.

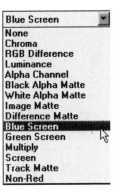

8. In the upper right corner, click on the Page Peel icon.

   A preview of the overlay title appears with the animation behind it.

9. Click OK.

10. Move the yellow Work Area bar over the first three seconds of the animation and create a preview.

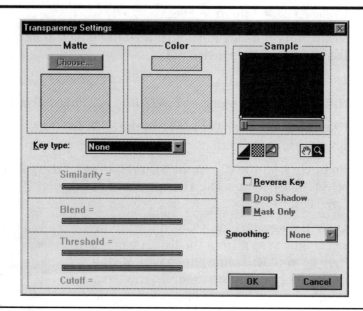

Figure 15.13: The Transparency Setting dialog box

As you've seen from this example, you can use the overlay track to super-impose one video clip over another. You can also superimpose still images as well. Although you currently see only one S1 overlay track, you can add several more if needed by using the Projects ➤ Add/Delete Tracks command in the pull-down menu.

You used the Blue Screen Key Type option in the exercise. The following briefly describes the other options available. The term *Key* means how the transparency is related to the superimposed image. For example, in the previous exercise the transparency was keyed to the blue back-ground, so any area that was blue became transparent.

Table 15.1: Key Type Options

None	No Image Keying
Chroma	Keying to a selected color using a dropper icon cursor.
RGB Difference	Similar to Chroma but with limited slider control.
Luminance	Lets you key to a gray scale value.
Alpha Channel	Uses alpha channel information to determine transparency. See the discussion "Using Alpha Channels with Superimposed Clips" below.
Black Alpha Matte	Similar to Alpha Channel but is designed to work best with images that have had alpha channels created using a black background.
White Alpha Matte	Similar to Alpha Channel but is designed to work best with images that have had alpha channels created over a white background.
Image Matte	Lets you superimpose a third, intermediate image behind the current superimposed track. The main image in Track A or B is filtered through this third image. Use the Choose button in the Matte button group to select an image file.
Difference Matte	Keys out areas that are similar between the superimposed track and the main A or B track, leaving the differences opaque.
Blue Screen	Keys out blue.
Green Screen	Keys out green.
Multiply	Keys out lighter areas of the superimposed image.
Screen	Applies the superimposed image over the A or B video track so that its lighter colors appear to screen the A or B track.
Track Matte	Similar to Image Matte, but instead of selecting an image file, you select a second Superimpose track. (You can add additional Superimpose tracks using Project ➤ Add/Delete Track.)
Not Red	Similar to Blue Screen and Green screen but offers finer control through sliders.

Using Alpha Channels with Superimposed Clips

In Chapter 13 I discussed alpha channels and their use as a storage area for masks. You can take advantage of alpha channels in Premiere when you add a superimposed video. Premiere will read the alpha channel and use the information there to determine which part of the superimposed track becomes transparent.

You may ask why you would bother with the alpha channel when, as you've seen from the exercise, you can overlay images using a blue background. The advantage to using the alpha channel becomes clear when you try to superimpose a color or grayscale image over another video track. In the border between the superimposed image and the background, you'll see blank or off-color pixels which can detract from the image (see Figure 15.14).

Poor matching of a superimposed image causes problems along the edge of the image

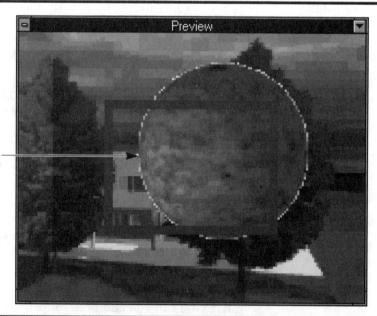

Figure 15.14: An enlarged view of a multi-color image superimposed over a video track using the Blue Screen option in the Transparency Settings dialog box

The edge of the superimposed image is anti-aliased, which means the colors were blended with the background to smooth the edge and reduce the stairstep effect that can be seen in some computer images (see Figure 15.15).

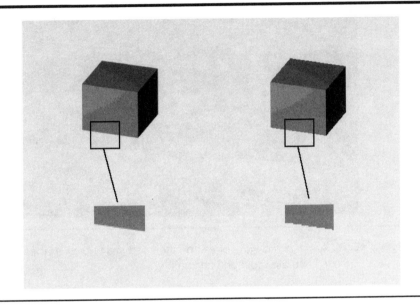

Figure 15.15: Anti-aliased and aliased samples of an image

An alpha channel can be created that contains a mask that is also anti-aliased. When an anti-aliased alpha mask is applied to a superimposed image, the result is a smooth-looking overlay as shown in Figure 15.16.

Figure 15.16: An enlarged view of a superimposed image over a video track using an anti-aliased alpha channel

Creating Alpha Channels in 3D Studio

The alpha channel is especially important if you plan to create animated superimposed video tracks. For example, instead of a using a static title at the beginning of your animation, you may want to create flying letters that appear over your animation.

Adding anti-alias alpha information to a 3D Studio animation is simply a matter of making sure the Render-Alpha option is turned on at render time. Here are the specific steps you need to take.

1. Set up your animation with a black background.

2. In the Keyframer, choose Renderer ➤ Render View, then click on the Perspective Camera viewport.

3. At the Render Animation dialog box, click on the Configure button.

4. At the Device Configuration dialog box, make sure you select Targa as the file output format. Targa files can contain alpha channel information.

5. Click OK, then click the Options button.

6. At the Render Options dialog box, click on Yes next to the Render-Alpha label. Make sure Alpha-Split is set to No.

7. Make sure the TGA-Depth setting is set to 24.

8. Click OK, then proceed to render your animation to disk.

3D Studio will automatically create the alpha information, which in turn can be used by Premiere when you superimpose your animation over a video clip.

You can import the 3D Studio animation into Premiere in the normal way (Targa Sequence), then place the animation in the Superimpose track of the Construction window. Once you do this, take the following steps to make use of the alpha channel.

1. Right-click on the animated clip in the Superimpose track, then select Transparency from the pop-up menu.

2. At the Transparency Settings dialog box, choose Alpha Channel from the Key Type drop-down list.

3. Click OK.

The superimposed animation will appear without any stray, odd looking pixels.

> **Note** *There are other methods for adding motion and animated titles in Adobe Premiere. Our focus here, however, is using 3D Studio animations with Premiere so I haven't discussed animation methods available directly in Premiere. Refer to Chapter 10 of the Premiere manual for information on special effects in Premiere.*

◆ Making a Movie

Once you have finished compiling and editing your animation, you can make your video files. The first step is to *save* your final project. Remember that the Premiere project file (*.PPJ) stores all the settings you made in the Construction window and also points to the imported files you've used as clips. It doesn't actually store any of the source material, so you will have to make sure the source material is also backed up.

Once you've saved your Premiere project, take the following steps to create your movie.

> **Note**   *If you are using the Tryout version of Premiere, read through this exercise to get the concepts. You won't be able to do the exercise, however, since the Tryout version won't let you save or create output.*

1. Before you start, make sure you have adequate room on your hard drive to store the output from Premiere. Video files can be quite large, and you already know that a Targa sequence is extremely space-consuming.

2. Choose Make ➤ Make Movie. The Make Movie dialog box appears.

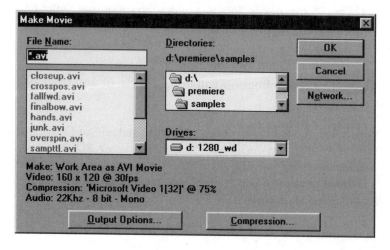

3. Click on the Output Options button at the bottom of the dialog box. The Project Output Options dialog box appears.

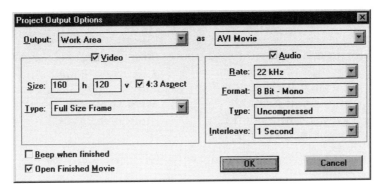

4. In the Size input boxes, enter the desired size of your video frames. Generally you will want these settings to match your original source material's resolution.

5. In the Output drop-down list, select the part of your project you want to turn into frames. You can use either the Work Area setting (set using the Work Area bar) or the entire project.

6. In the As drop-down list (to the right of the Output drop-down list), select the file format. To maintain the best level of quality, you may want to keep your work as a Targa sequence. You can then export the sequence to a video capture card, such as the PAR or PVR, or some other format, such as MPEG through an MPEG translator. Of course, you can also choose AVI, the standard PC video format.

7. Once you've made the settings in the Output Options dialog box, click OK.

8. At the Make Movie dialog box, enter a name for you new Targa sequence, then click OK.

The AVI File Format

If your animation is destined for computer presentation, use the AVI file format. (AVI, which stands for Audio Video Interleave, is the standard Windows file format for digital video.) AVI allows you to select from a variety of compression methods (including MPEG if you have an MPEG MCI driver) for your animation file. Here's a rundown of the most common compression methods for AVI:

Cinepak is designed for high-quality video playback from a computer.

Intel Indeo is designed for high-compression ratios and is best suited for multimedia applications. Indeo is similar to Cinepak in quality and compression.

Intel Indeo RAW applies no compression to a video. Use this format if you want to keep your Targa animations at their highest level of quality but want to use the AVI format.

Microsoft RLE is designed to keep file sizes down by reducing the color depth. It is primarily designed for 8-bit animations.

Microsoft Video is similar to RLE in that it reduces the color depth of the file. It is designed for 8- and 16-bit animations and video.

None applies no compression at all to your file. Like the Intel Indeo RAW format, you would use this to store Targa files at their best level of quality, sacrificing disk storage space.

◆ Speeding Things Up with Miniatures

In the previous exercises, you've been using Targa files that are 320×240. This is not the optimum size for high-quality video work. You will want to render your 3D Studio animations to at least 512×480 if you plan to put your animations on videotape. But using frames of this size can bog down the performance of Premiere. Fortunately, Premiere offers an option that lets you work with smaller versions of your original Targa sequences.

The Make Miniature command in Premiere creates a Targa sequence of reduced resolution from your original Targa sequence. You can then work with those smaller files, called miniatures, to edit your video. When you are ready to create your final output from Premiere, you use the Refind Files command in the Project pull-down menu to replace the miniatures with the original, high-resolution files. Here are the specific steps to creating miniatures and refinding files.

Creating Miniatures

The process of creating miniatures is fairly simple. Make sure, however, that you have enough free disk space before you start.

1. Choose Files ➤ Tools ➤ Miniatures. The Select Directory dialog box appears.

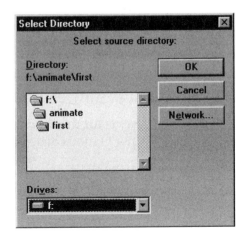

2. Make sure the directory containing the original high-resolution Targa sequence is selected, then click OK. The Create Miniatures Directory dialog box appears.

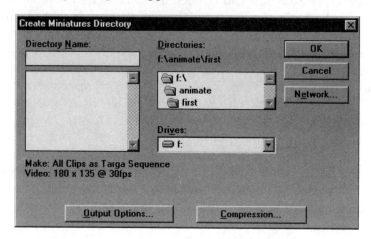

Note that the directory listing in the middle of the dialog box shows the directory you selected in step 2. Premiere creates a subdirectory below the directory containing the original files, then places the miniatures there.

> **Warning**   *When Premiere creates miniatures, it creates a low-resolution copy of the Targa sequence using the original names. This is why they need to be in a separate directory.*

Also notice that at the bottom of the dialog box, you have the Output Options and Compression buttons available. These buttons function in the same way as those found in the Make Movie dialog box in the previous section.

1. Enter a name for the new directory, then click on Output Options. The Output Options dialog box appears.

2. Enter a resolution for your miniatures, then select Targa Sequence from the As drop-down list.

3. Click OK, then click OK at the Create Miniatures Directory dialog box. You'll see the Making Miniatures dialog box display the files as they are being converted.

Note *Another way to make miniatures is to simply import the original clips into Premiere, then use the Make ➤ Make Movie option to create a low-resolution Targa sequence.*

Using the Original Hi-Res Files for Final Output

Once you've created the miniatures, you can use them in place of the original high-resolution files to do your editing work. When you are done with your work and ready to create your Targa sequence output, you can then replace the miniatures with the original high-resolution files. You can also use the Refind File command as follows.

1. In the Project window, select the clip whose source is the miniature Targa sequence.

2. Choose Project ➤ Refind Files. You will see a message warning you that you cannot undo the current operation.

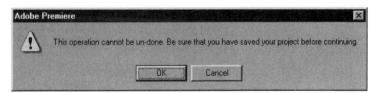

3. Click OK. The Locate File dialog box appears.

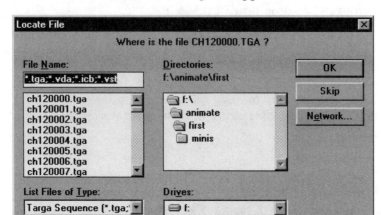

At the top of the dialog box, you will see a message that reads "where is the file *filename.tga?*" The name I show in italics here will be the name of the first file of the Targa Sequence.

4. Using the Directories and File Name list boxes, locate the original high-resolution file for the first frame of the sequence and select it.

5. Click OK. Premiere will reassign the high-resolution files to the clip.

Once you've reassigned the high-resolution files, you can go ahead and create your output Targa sequence.

◆ Creating Presets

In the beginning of the Premiere tutorial, I showed you how you can choose from several preset options. These options determine the following items:

◆ Timebase (SMPTE drop or non-drop frame, PAL/SECAM, or film)

◆ Default frames per second

◆ Method of compression for output

◆ Type of output file

◆ Resolution of output

◆ Audio output

◆ Preview settings

These items can be adjusted at any time using the commands in the Make pull-down menu, however, the presets offer a convenient way to save some time.

You can review the settings of the presets, and create some custom presets by opening the Presets dialog box. Try the following exercise to familiarize yourself with the presets.

1. Choose Make ➤ Presets. This brings up the Presets dialog box.

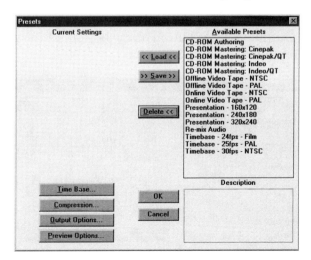

2. In the list to the right, click on Timebase - 30fps - NTSC to select it.

3. Click on the Load button in the middle of the dialog box. This brings up a listing of the settings for the selected item in the column to the left.

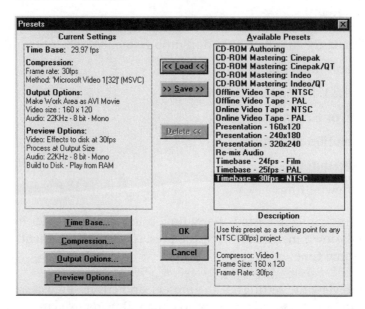

You can change any of the settings shown in left list box using the buttons at the bottom. For example, suppose you want to change the output options to Targa Sequence at 752×480. This would be an appropriate setting if your project is destined for a PVR video capture board.

1. Click on the Output Options button at the bottom of the dialog box. The Output Options dialog appears.

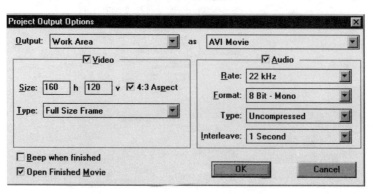

2. Change the Size input boxes in the Video button group to **752** and **480**.

3. Select Targa Sequence from the As drop-down list.

4. Click OK. You return to the Presets dialog box.

5. Now click the >>Save>> button. The Preset Name dialog box appears.

6. Enter the name **Targa Sequence Output** in the Name For This Preset input box.

7. Enter **Use this for 3D Studio Animations** in the Description For This Preset input box.

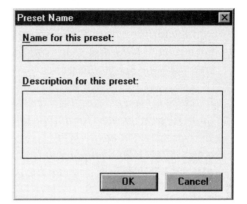

8. Click OK. The new preset is displayed in the list to the right.

From now on, you can select your newly created preset whenever you start a new project in Premiere.

◆ Summary

You've taken a introductory tour of Premiere 4.0 in this chapter. I've tried to focus on those features that will be of benefit to 3D Studio users but I've just scratched the surface of what Premiere has to offer. You can use Premiere as an off-line video editing tool if you prefer, or you can keep all your material in a digital format until you are ready to lay it down on tape. As long as you have enough hard disk space you can do a lot of editing on your own to further enhance your 3D Studio work.

In addition, you can use Premiere to produce your animation in formats other than Targa sequences for output to videotape. With additional hardware and software you can create MPEG compressed video files ready for playback from a CD-ROM. With computer video formats such as Autodesk Animator Pro files, AVI, and QuickTime, you can include synchronized sound.

But Premiere isn't the only program that offers these capabilities. in:synch's Razor Mach III and Razor Pro are two popular video editing programs for the personal computer. These programs are tightly integrated with the PAR and PVR video capture board mentioned earlier in this chapter. By working closely with hardware, the Razor products offer greatly enhanced speed in conjunction with a reduced file size. This means you can work with your animations directly in the PAR/PVR environment without the extra burden of worrying about file management.

In the next and final chapter, you'll look at some emerging trends in computer presentation techniques. You'll learn how you can make use of virtual reality to present your 3D models. You'll also see how you might take advantage of the Internet to help deliver your presentations to your clients.

Presentations on Computers Only

Computers can offer ways of interacting with 3D models that television cannot. With television, you are pretty much at the mercy of what is being presented. Computers, on the other hand, let you view documents in a nonlinear and interactive way. You can watch a video stream, or stop it in the middle to examine a particular view. For 3D models, virtual reality tools allow you to take a stroll through your ideas in real time.

Multimedia tools can help us pull together the different computer-generated material associated with a design project to create an interactive presentation. Still images, animated clips, and even virtual reality can be packaged into a multimedia application that can communicate your design ideas more thoroughly.

In this chapter, you'll look at some of the programs available that will allow you to create the raw material for computer presentations. You'll start by looking at Autodesk's Animator Studio, which offers the ability to edit and output still images as well as animations. You'll then move on to virtual reality to learn how you can easily convert AutoCAD and 3D Studio models into computer "environments" you can walk-through in real time.

◆ A Look at Autodesk Animator Studio

Autodesk's Animator Studio is a unique product that combines the functionality of Adobe Photoshop and Adobe Premiere into one product. It is aimed at users who want to quickly produce animation and presentation material for computers. In this section, you'll get a quick tour of this product by creating a quick animated clip of the Facade project from Chapter 8. First, let's look at the layout of Animator Studio screen.

> **Note**   *This tutorial uses Animator Studio release 1.1. This release has many desirable improvements over release 1.0. If you are using release 1.0, you can get a free upgrade to 1.1 from Autodesk. Contact your vendor for details.*

Start Animator Studio by choosing Start ➤ Programs ➤ Autodesk Multimedia ➤ Animator Studio. (Windows 3.x users should open the Autodesk Multimedia program group and double-click on the Animator Studio icon.) You see the screen splash, then the four windows of Animator Studio appear (see Figure 16.1).

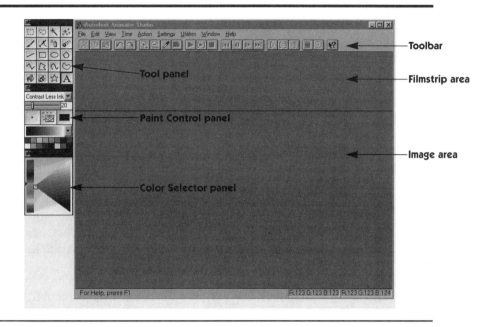

Figure 16.1: The Animator Studio screen layout

The Tool panel contains a set of tools you typically find in a paint program, with some additional tools geared toward 2D animation, such as the Sprite tool.

The Paint Control panel offers a set of paint effects in a drop-down menu as well as a Paint Strength slider, Brush Size control, Foreground/Background selector, Gradient selector, and a Color Swatch.

The Color Selector panel lets you select colors from a color triangle and slide bar.

The Main window is your work area. As you will see, it displays individual frames of an animation as well as a sequence of frames in a timeline format.

Importing Still Images

> **Note** *You can easily import Targa sequences by selecting Targa in the List Files Of Type drop-down list in the File Open dialog box, then selecting the first frame of a Targa sequence. Animator Studio will automatically detect the fact that it is a sequence and will import the other frames automatically. You can then save the sequence as an AVI file or otherwise edit as explained in this section.*

In this section, you'll create a short clip that shows the wireframe AutoCAD drawing of the Facade model from Chapter 8, cross-dissolving into a finished rendering from AutoVision. You'll also look at how you can add an animated title.

Importing and Resizing a Still Image

The first step in creating the animated clip is to import the still image and convert it into an animation of a series of frames.

1. Choose File ➤ Open. The File Open dialog box appears. This is a typical Windows File dialog box.

2. Locate and select the file named Cover1.TIF in the sample files directory you created for this book (see Appendix B).

3. Click OK to open the file. This brings up the Key Color dialog box.

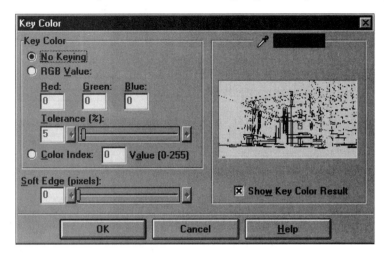

This dialog box lets you select a color for transparency keying, similar to Premiere's Superimpose Transparency command.

4. We don't really want to key anything in this exercise, so click OK to import the image as is. This brings up a message telling you that Animator Studio is converting the file into a movie. When it is done, you see the image plus three frames at the top of the main window.

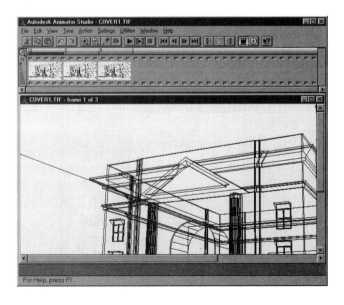

Notice that Animator Studio automatically converted the still image into a "movie." You can still save the image as a single frame if you so choose, but Animator assumes you want to create a movie clip, so that is what you get.

The image you imported is of a much higher resolution than you need. Next, you'll reduce the size of the image.

1. Choose Utilities ➤ Create Resized. The Create Resized movie dialog box appears.

2. Make sure the Keep Aspect Ratio checkbox is checked.

3. In the Width input box, enter **320**, then press ⏎. Notice that the value in the Height input box changes to 174 to maintain the aspect ratio.

4. Click OK to exit the dialog box. A Resizing message box appears, showing you that it is working to create a new movie resized to your specifications. After a moment, the new, smaller movie appears.

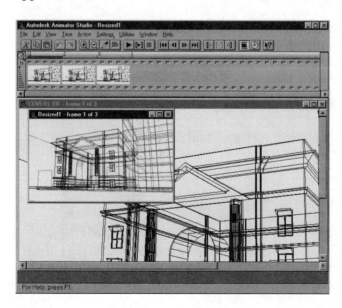

5. Animator created a copy of the original `Cover1.TIF` file. You
don't need the original, so click on the larger of the two images
and choose File ➤ Close. The resized copy of the file remains.

Adding Frames to the Movie

The copy of our original file is given the default name of `Resized1`.
Since you haven't saved it yet, Animator Studio doesn't know what file
format it should be in. You'll take care of that later. The next step is to
turn `Resized1` into an animation clip of 30 frames.

1. Choose Settings ➤
Movie Length.
The Movie
Length dialog
box appears.

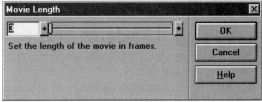

2. Type **30** for 30 frames.
The number appears in the input box to the far left. You can also
use the slider to select a frame count.

3. Click OK. The filmstrip at the top of the window expands to show
more frames.

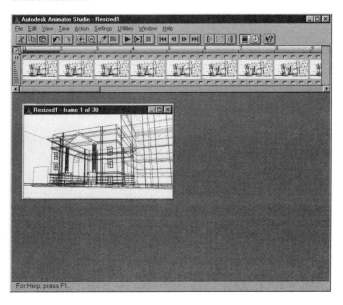

4. Now save the file as a Windows AVI file. Choose File ➤ Save As. A typical Windows Save As dialog box appears.

5. In the Save File As Type drop-down list, locate and select Windows AVI.

6. In the File Name input box, enter **cover1**, then click OK to save the file.

The additional frames you added in steps 2 and 3 are simply duplicates of the single still image; if you were to play the movie, you would see no motion. You need the extra frames, however, to add the transition effect from one image to another.

Adding a Fade-in and Fade-out Effect

Before you move to the next part, you need to add a fade-in and fade-out effect to this movie. Here's how it's done.

You must first define a segment of the clip in which you want apply the effect, as follows.

1. Choose Time ➤ Define Segment. The Define Segment dialog box appears.

2. Leave the First Frame input box as 1.

3. Enter **10** in the Last Frame input box, then click on OK.

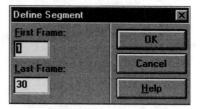

By defining a segment, you are just selecting a segment of time in which you want to apply effects. You aren't deleting any frames.

The next step is to apply the effect.

1. Choose Utilities ➤ Fade Segment In.

2. The Fade Segment In message appears as it creates the effect. When it is done, you see the first four frames change. Frame 1 is completely black. As the frames progress to the right, they become lighter until you can see the entire image.

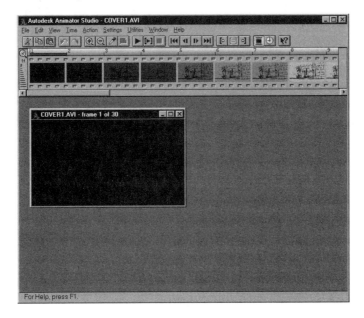

3. Choose Time ➤ Define Segment again, but this time enter **21** for the first frame, change the Last Frame input box to **30**, then click OK. Nothing seems to happen, but if you look at the filmstrip area, you notice that the bar at the top of the strip, showing the frame numbers, is now gray.

4. Choose Utilities ➤ Fade Segment Out. This brings up a message telling you that Animator Studio is fading the frames.

5. When it is done, move the slide bar below the filmstrip to the far right. You see the last ten frames fade to black.

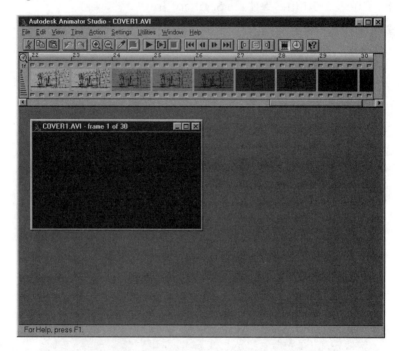

Joining Two Clips

In order to create a cross-dissolve animation, you will need to create a second AVI file of the rendered image of the Facade model. The steps to accomplish this are identical to those you've already taken, so to avoid repetition, I've provided an AVI file all ready to be joined with the current one.

In the next exercise, you'll open this second movie clip and join it to the first, creating a cross-dissolve. Before you actually merge the two files, you need to make sure that both clips have the appropriate transparency.

Start by loading the second clip.

1. Choose File ➤ Open.

2. Locate and select `Cover2.AVI` from the sample files, then click
OK. The first frame of the clip appears in the main window, and
you see the rest of the clip in the filmstrip above.

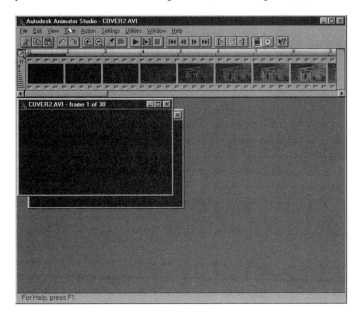

3. The first clip is still loaded and available, but the current clip is the
one you just opened. You can switch between clips by clicking on
the first frame of the desired clip displayed in the main window.
Click on the view of the `Cover1.AVI` clip. Notice that the filmstrip
changes to show `Cover1.AVI`. This tells you that this clip is now
the active one.

Setting Up Transparency of Clips

Before you join the clips, you need to set their background alpha value to zero. This makes the background completely transparent. In this case, the background is the black color of the transition.

1. Choose Settings ➤
   Background.
   The Background
   Color dialog box
   appears.

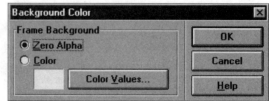

2. Make sure the Zero
   Alpha radio button is selected, then click OK. This makes the black background color completely transparent. This is necessary for the transition.

3. Click on the Cover2.AVI window to make it active.

4. Repeat steps 1 and 2 to make the background black color transparent in the Cover2.AVI clip.

Selecting a Segment for Editing

Now you are ready to join the clips together. First you will switch to time mode; then you'll select the entire second clip. By switching to time mode, you are able to perform edits across several or all the frames of a clip. Then you will copy the clip to the Windows Clipboard to get ready to paste it into the first clip.

1. Make sure the Cover2.AVI window is active.

2. Click on the Time Mode
   button in the button
   Toolbar or select Time ➤
   Time Mode.

3. Choose Time ➤ Put All
   Of Movie In Segment.

4. Choose Edit ➤ Select All Of Segment. You'll see the "marching ants" surround the Cover2.AVI windows.

5. Choose Edit ➤ Copy Selection.

In steps 3 and 4, you made sure that the entire clip was selected, for otherwise only the selected frames would be copied to the Windows Clipboard.

Now you are ready to complete the joining process. You must first select the frame into which you want to paste the second clip. You also need to make room for the second clip by increasing the number of frames in the receiving movie.

1. Click on the Cover1.AVI window to make it active.

2. Click on the Time Mode icon in the Toolbar.

3. Move the slider below the filmstrip to the far right. This lets you view the last several frames of the movie.

4. Click on frame 21 in the filmstrip (see Figure 16.2). This makes frame 21 the current frame. Notice that the Cover1.AVI frame window indicates which frame is current.

5. To extend the length of the Cover1.AVI, choose Settings ➤ Movie Length.

6. At the Movie Length dialog, enter **50**. You need a total of 50 frames in order to accept the incoming clip from the Windows Clipboard.

7. Click OK.

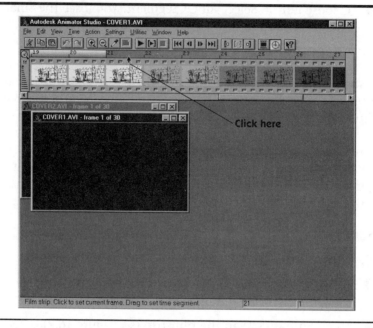

Figure 16.2: Selecting a frame in the timeline

Pasting a Clip

Now you are ready to place the clip from the Windows Clipboard. Pasting a clip in Animator Studio is a process that diverges somewhat from the typical "cut and paste" routine.

1. Choose Edit ➤ Paste. You'll see a diamond appear at the center of the Cover1.AVI window and you'll see the edge of the window blink continuously. This tells you that the Cover2.AVI clip has been temporarily placed in the current clip.

2. To complete the placement of the Cover2.AVI clip, choose Action ➤ Render. The Render message appears.

3. Move the filmstrip slider to the far right. You see the `Cover2.AVI` clip at the end.

4. Now click on the Play button in the Toolbar. You see your animation play back in the `Cover1.AVI` window.

5. Click on the red Stop Play button in the Toolbar to stop the animation.

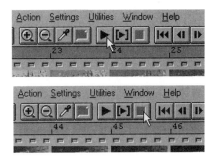

In step 2, you had to specifically choose Action ➤ Render to finally place `Cover2.AVI` from the Clipboard into the `Cover1.AVI` movie. This is because Animator Studio offers the option to set the location of the incoming clip before you commit it to `Cover1.AVI`. You can make position adjustments in step 1, when you see the blinking border and diamond shape.

Adding Scrolling Text

Animator Studio offers a quick way to add animated text to your project. In this section you'll add some text that will scroll from the bottom to the top as the clip plays. In addition, the text will be made to appear in a perspective mode.

The first step is to set up the text to behave the way you want it to.

1. Double-click on the Text tool in the Tool panel.

The Text dialog box appears.

2. Make sure the Align Center radio button is selected. As you might guess, this option lets you determine how the text is aligned.

3. Click on the Time Action tab at the top of the dialog box. The options change to show the time options.

4. In the Titling Effects button group, make sure Scroll is selected.

5. In the Scroll Direction button group, make sure the Up option is selected. This and the option mentioned in step 4 cause the text to scroll up.

6. In the Scroll Extent button group, make sure Start Out, End Out is selected. This option makes the text start completely out of the frame at the beginning and end completely out at the end. (The Start In, End Out option, on the other hand, would cause the text to appear in the middle of the frame at the start.)

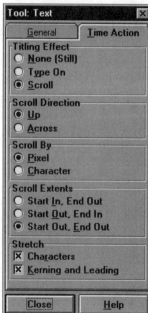

7. Click Close to close the dialog box.

Now you are ready to place the text. Like placing a clip from the Windows Clipboard, placing text includes an extra Render step. This allows you to alter the appearance of the text, as you'll see in the following exercise.

1. First, select the segment in which the text is to appear. Choose Time ➤ Define Segment.

2. At the Define Segment dialog box, enter **10** for the first frame and **40** for the last frame, then click OK. This keeps the scrolling text out of the fade-in and fade-out portions of the animation.

3. Click on frame 10 in the timeline. Use the slider if you need to locate frame 10.

4. With the Text tool selected, move the cursor over the Cover1.AVI window. Notice that the cursor appears as a cross with the letter A next to it. This tells you that you can place a text marquee in the window.

5. Click and drag from the point shown in Figure 16.3 to place the text marquee.

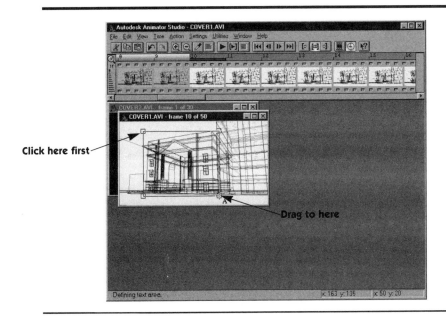

Figure 16.3: Placing the text box in the Cover1.AVI window

6. When you let go of the mouse, the Edit Text dialog box appears.

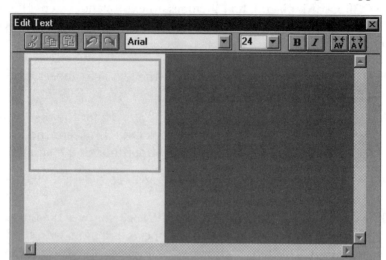

7. Enter the following: **From AutoCAD wireframe to AutoVision rendered image** (or enter whatever text you like of approximately the same length).

8. Select Arial from the Font drop-down list and 24 from the Point Size list, then click OK.

9. Choose Color Ink from the Paint Control panel's drop-down list.

10. Click on the red color in the Paint Control panel's color swatches.

You could go ahead and select Action ➤ Render to add the text to the clip. But to make things a bit more interesting, let's make the text appear to be in perspective.

1. Choose Action ➤ Float. This will let you edit the block of text you just created.

2. Choose Action ➤ Rotate. Notice that the text box now appears with some additional control points (see Figure 16.4a).

3. Click and drag the control point on the left side of the box. As you move the cursor, the box rotates as if it were a 3D object.

4. Rotate it to the position shown in Figure 16.4b.

5. Now click and drag the control point in the lower right corner of the text box. As you move the cursor, the entire box rotates clockwise or counterclockwise.

6. Use the corner control point to position the text box as shown in Figure 16.4c.

a.

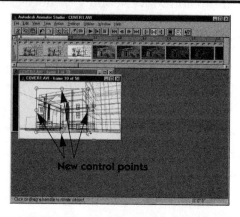

b.

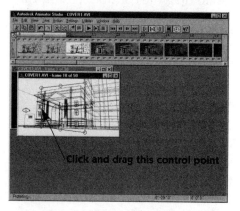

c.

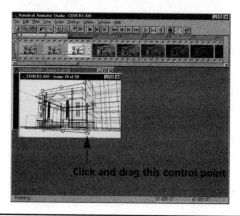

Figure 16.4: Adjusting the orientation of the text using the control points and the Action ➤ Rotate option

You are now ready to commit the text to the animated clip.

1. Choose Action ➤ Render.

2. The Render message box appears.

3. When Animator Studio is finished rendering, click on the Play button to see the results.

4. When you finish viewing the animation, click on the red Stop Play button.

If you don't like the results of your text placement, you can modify it by floating the text box and making changes. Here's how it's done.

1. Choose frame 10 in the filmstrip.

2. Choose Action ➤ Float. The text box appears again in the Cover1.AVI window.

3. Choose Action ➤ Modify, then right-click on the text box. The Edit Text dialog box appears again, allowing you to make changes to the text, font, and font size.

4. Click on OK to close the dialog box.

You can use the Action ➤ Rotate option to make adjustments to the rotation of the text, or you can use the Paint Control panel to change the text color. When you are done, you can choose Action ➤ Render again to see your changes.

There's Much More

As with Adobe Photoshop and Premiere, there is a great deal more to Animator Studio than I've shown here. You can learn more about Animator Studio by using its Help feature and by going through the tutorials provided in its documentation. If you're looking for a general tool for editing your animations or for creating materials for 3D Studio, check out Autodesk's Animator Studio.

Animator Studio is primarily a 2D animation package aimed at multi-media and computer playback. Such animations can add impact to a presentation, or they can help tell a story, but they are generally not interactive. In the next section, you'll look at some virtual reality tools that can really bring your 3D models to life and allow for a much higher degree of interactivity between your model and your audience.

◆ Taking a Look at Virtual Reality

Virtual Reality (VR) is the name given to any computer-generated environment in which you can "place" yourself and freely move around in real time. Some of the first applications of VR were flight simulators designed to help train pilots. As interest in VR has grown, applications have been developed for using VR in the design industry and to help architects visualize and *experience* spaces.

In its early days, VR was a high-tech tool accessible to only the few government agencies and big companies that could afford it. But as personal computers became more powerful, its use caught on in the home computer game world. Now, a technology that was once thought of as exotic seems fairly commonplace, especially to computer game users. VR has also become a prominent part of the Internet and World Wide Web. Through the Virtual Reality Modeling Language (VRML, pronounced "vermal"), VR has become cheap and easily accessible to the general public.

VRML became a reality through the efforts of a handful of people closely involved with the development of virtual reality and the World Wide Web. They sought a means of conveying 3D worlds through the World Wide Web and found what they were looking for in a system developed by Silicon Graphics, Inc. That system, called Open Inventor, was a programming library for use in creating 3D applications. A subset of Open Inventor was developed, and placed in the public domain through the good graces of Silicon Graphics. That subset is at the root of a software specification called VRML 1.0.

In this chapter, you'll explore the ways you can make use of VR through some of the VRML 1.0 tools that are freely available. You'll start by converting a sample model from AutoCAD into a virtual environment through which you can walk or fly.

AutoCAD to VRML

Just a few years ago, doing a virtual reality walk-through of an AutoCAD 3D model was an expensive proposition. It required special display hardware with lots of memory. Today, there is software that makes the special hardware unnecessary. Not only that, but the software is fairly inexpensive.

In this section, you'll see how you can convert a 3D AutoCAD model into a VRML file format that can then be easily viewed and "walked through." You'll start by exporting a modified version of the Savoye4.DWG sample file, called Sav1VRML.DWG. This file contains some additional surfaces, like flooring in the second floor and a green ground-floor plane representing grass.

> **Note** *Poorly aligned normals in a 3D model can drastically affect the model's appearance. For this reason, you will want to pay close attention to the normals when you create your VR files, particularly those that originate in AutoCAD. Once you've created the VR file, walk through it with a browser to see if any surfaces are missing. If there are, go back to the original .DWG or .3DS file and reverse the normal for that surface. For more information on normals, see "Missing Surface, Normals" in Chapter 11.*

Exporting from AutoCAD

The first step in getting the building model into a VRML format is to export Sav1VRML.DWG into a 3D Studio file format. The translator application you will use can read 3D Studio files.

1. Open AutoCAD, then open the Sav1VRML.DWG sample file. You will see an Isometric view of the building.

2. Choose File ➤ Export.

3. At the File Export dialog box, a typical Windows File dialog box, choose *.3DS from the List Files Of Type drop-down list.

4. Make sure that the file input box shows Sav1VRML.3DS, then click OK.

5. At the Select Objects prompt, type **All** and then press ↵ twice. This selects the entire model.

6. At the 3D Studio File Export options, make sure Layer is selected in the Derive 3D Studio Objects From button group. Autosmoothing and Autowelding should also be checked.

7. Click OK to begin the export. After a moment, AutoCAD will create a 3D Studio file.

Translating the Intermediate 3DS File

The next step is to convert the 3DS file into a WRL file, the file format for VRML. This step requires the use of a program called Wcvt2pov. This is a freeware program written by Keith Rule, a computer 3D wizard. His program provides translation between several 3D file formats.

> **Note**   *You might notice that Wcvt2pov also imports AutoCAD DXF files. Unfortunately, the version of Wcvt2pov I've included on the CD with this book does not support DXF files from AutoCAD release 13, so I've elected to use 3D Studio files instead. Keith Rule is working on other translators. You can visit his Web page at* `http://www.europa.com/~keithr` *to get his latest translators.*

Consult Appendix B of this book to find out how to install and set up this program. Once you have it installed, do the following.

1. Close AutoCAD, then start Wcvt2pov by double-clicking on the `Wcvt2pov.EXE` file in the directory where you have installed it. You'll see the window shown in Figure 16.5a.

2. Choose File ➤ Open ➤ 3D Studio. A typical File Open dialog box appears.

3. Locate and select `Sav_VRML.3DS`, then click OK. The building will appear in the window (see Figure 16.5b).

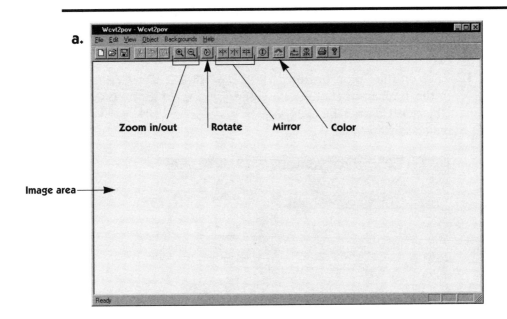

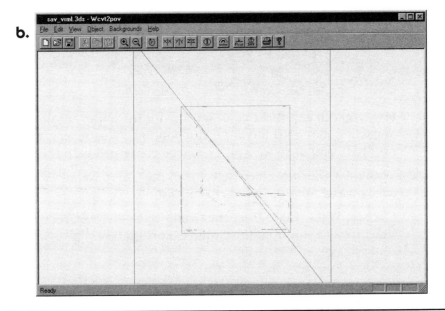

Figure 16.5: The Wcvt2pov window

The next step is to modify the color of the components of the model. This will help it become more visible both in Wcvt2pov and in the VRML browser you will use later.

1. Click on the Colors button in the Toolbar, or choose Object ➤ Colors. The Colors dialog box appears.

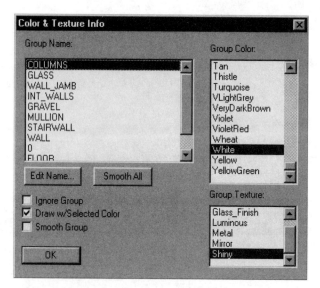

Here you can adjust the color settings for the objects in the model. You will notice a list box for texture options. These have no effect on VRML output so we won't really be concerned with them.

2. With the COLUMN object selected in the Group Name list box, click on Red from the Group Colors list box.

3. Click on WALL_JAMB from the Group Name list box, then select VLightGray again from the Group Colors list box.

4. Continue to go down the list of group names, setting each object to the color listed here:

Group	Color
GRAVEL	Gray
STAIR	Tan
INT_WALLS	LightGray
RAMP	Tan
MULLION	LightBlue
STAIRWALL	Tan
GRASS	Green
ROOF	Gray50
WALL	VLightGray
RAIL	LtBlue
CHAIR1,2,3,4	Thistle
RUG	Turquoise
FLOOR	Brown

5. When you've finished, click OK. You will be better able to see the model in the window.

If you look carefully, you'll notice that your current view is from underneath the model and that the model is mirrored along the vertical axis. You will want to set your view so you are looking at the building from the side. By orienting the building in this way, you will be better able to move through the building when you view it through the VRML browser application.

1. To mirror the model to the appropriate orientation, first click on the Y-axis mirror button.

(Or you could choose Object ➤ Mirror ➤ Y Axis.)

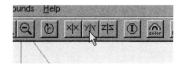

2. Next choose Object ➤ Rotate. The Rotate X, Y, Z dialog box appears.

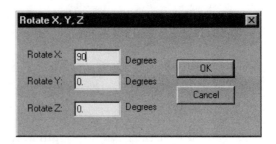

3. Enter **90** in the Rotate X input box. This will rotate the model in the X axis 90 degrees so your view is normal to an exterior wall.

4. Click OK. You will see a perspective view of the model from one of its sides.

Now you are ready to create a VRML file.

1. Choose File ➤ Save As ➤ VRML 1.0. A typical Windows Save As dialog box appears.

2. In the File Name input box, enter **Sav_VRML.WRL**, then click Save. You now have a VRML file.

Walking through Your Building

To get into your VRML model, you will need a VRML *browser*. There are many such browsers, some of which are helper applications to your main World Wide Web browser and do not appear until the main browser encounters a VRML file.

I've included a beta version of a stand-alone VRML browser called WorldView, from Intervista Software Corp. This browser is capable of operating independently of a World Wide Web browser. With WorldView, you can view VRML files on the Web or on your own computer. You can also have two independent views open at once: one of a Web page and one of a virtual 3D environment.

Before you get started, install WorldView from the CD accompanying this book. See Appendix B for installation instructions.

Note *The version of WorldView supplied with this book is programmed to stop working after May of 1996. The providers of the program (Intervista Software Corp.) have assured me that you can still use it for the purposes of this tutorial, however, by first changing your computer's date setting back to April 1996. (You do this using the Date/Time tool in the Windows Control Panel.) To get the latest version, access the Intervista Web site at* www.intervista.com. *In addition, you need Windows 95 or Windows NT to use WorldView.*

Once you've installed WorldView, do the following to get used to moving within the browser.

1. Exit Wcvt2pov and start WorldView by selecting Start ➤ Programs ➤ WorldView ➤ WorldView. The WorldView window opens, showing you a rotating globe (see Figure 16.6).

Figure 16.6: The WorldView window

2. To get closer to the globe, click and drag your mouse slowly from the center of the window upward. When you've gotten as close as you want, release your mouse button.

3. To move away from the globe, click and drag downward. The amount you drag your mouse determines the speed of your move inward or outward.

4. Try alternating between moving in and moving out by clicking and dragging upward then downward.

5. Move to the left by clicking and dragging the mouse to the left. You can simultaneously move to the right and out by clicking and dragging to the lower right. You can return to the opening view of your model by clicking on the Restore View button.

Note *If it looks like a surface is missing in your model, chances are its normal needs to be reversed. As a workaround, you can set WorldView to show both sides of the surfaces in your model regardless of their normals' orientations. Choose Options ➤ Preference, then, in the Advanced tab of the Preferences dialog box, make sure there is a checkmark in Generate Polygon Back Faces checkbox. Click OK to exit the dialog box, then click on the Reload button on the toolbar. Be aware, however, as you are creating your VR models, that not all VRML browsers will have this "show both sides" feature.*

The globe you see spinning is a VRML file. WorldView allows you to have an object rotate as you view it. As you can see from this exercise, it takes a bit of practice moving around in a virtual world. After a few minutes, though, you'll find it an interesting experience.

So far, you've used WorldView's default navigation tool to move in and out and left and right. Other tools let you move up and down, straighten your view, or rotate your model. You'll get a chance to use those other tools, but first, set up WorldView for a tour of your own model.

1. Choose Simulation ➤ Quality ➤ Good (Flat Shading). This will prevent WorldView from attempting to smooth the Sav_VRML file, which is mostly flat planes.

2. Choose Simulation ➤ Quality ➤ Quality When Moving ➤ Good. This setting determines how your model appears as you are moving through it.

3. Finally, for the purposes of this exercise, make sure Simulation ➤ Prevent Collision is not checked.

Now you are ready to view your model.

1. Choose File ➤ Open. This brings up an Open Location dialog box.

Since WorldView is primarily intended to be used as a WWW/ VRML browser, this dialog box is presented to allow you to enter a Web page address, otherwise known as a URL (*Uniform Resource Locator*).

2. We don't want to visit a WWW site right now, so click on the button labeled Open Local File. A standard Windows File dialog box appears.

3. Locate and select Sav_VRML.WRL, then click Open. Your model appears in the WorldView window (see Figure 16.7).

4. Click and drag the mouse from the center of the window upward in order to zoom in to the model.

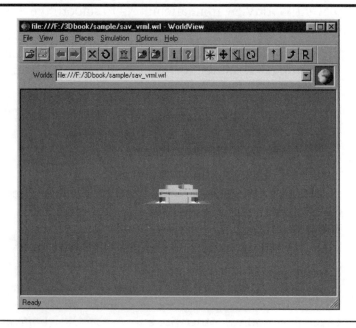

Figure 16.7: The Sav_VRML.WRL file in WorldView. To zoom in to this image, click on it and drag it upward.

Rotating Your View around the Model

Now let's try rotating the model to get a view from a different angle.

1. Click on the Inspect button in the Toolbar. This is the button that looks like two rotating arrows.

2. Slowly click and drag the mouse from the center of the window to the right. As you drag the mouse, the building rotates.

Note *The side of the building appears dark. You can adjust the lighting to some degree by selecting Options ➤ Preferences. You'll see the Preferences dialog box. Here you can set the Use A Default Light setting by selecting from Never, Best Guess, and Always. As you'll see later, you have better control over lighting in 3D Studio.*

3. Keep rotating the building until you get a view similar to Figure 16.8a. If the building ends up tilted, click on the Straighten Up button on the Toolbar.

4. Click on the Navigate button. This button is on by default whenever you open a new file.

5. Click and drag the mouse from the center upward to move into the courtyard of the building.

6. Stop when your view looks like Figure 16.8b.

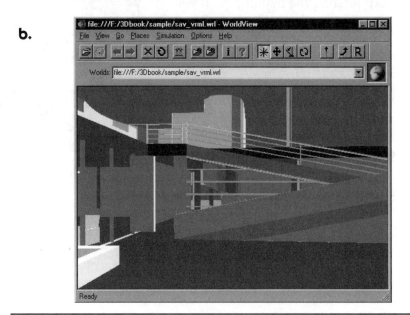

Figure 16.8: Navigate around the Sav_VRML.WRL model to see the view shown at top here, then zoom in by dragging the image upward on screen.

Panning across Your Model

Now let's move to the lower floor using the Pan tool. The WorldView Pan tool is similar to the Pan tool in the AutoCAD 3D Dynamic View command. It moves both the camera and target points.

1. Click on the Pan tool.

2. Click and drag the mouse from the center of the window upward. As you move the mouse, your viewpoint moves downward.

3. Continue to move your mouse upward until you move through the floor and you see the view shown in Figure 16.9a.

4. Now click and drag the mouse to the right until you see the entrance to the ground floor lobby (see Figure 16.9b).

a.

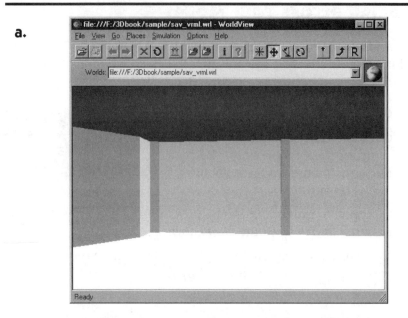

b.

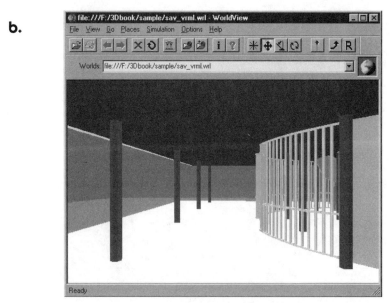

Figure 16.9: Panning your view to the ground floor entrance

As you can see, you are able to move through the model using the Navigate and Pan buttons. After you've had some practice, you may want to try moving through the interior of the model to see what it is like. Remember to go slow at first, and if your view starts to get tilted, use the Straighten Up tool. If you want to get back to the original starting viewpoint, click on the Restore View button.

Creating a VRML World in 3D Studio

The VRML 3D model from AutoCAD is fairly plain and somewhat cartoonish, but you can get a fair impression of the space inside the model using WorldView. VRML does allow for texture mapping, which can bring an added sense of reality to a space. In fact, by simplifying the actual geometry of the model and using texture maps to suggest detail, you can create some very interesting spaces without having to create large VRML files.

On the CD that comes with this book, Autodesk has provided version 1.2 of its VRML plug-in for use with 3D Studio 4.0. You can use this plug-in to attach texture maps to objects in a 3D Model. The method is slightly different from the usual way of attaching materials, however, as we'll see in the following section. (If you find this plug-in useful, consider buying the current version now available directly from Autodesk, which has more features and works with 3D Studio Max as well.)

Using Bitmaps to "Fake" Detail

In the following exercise, you'll use 3D Studio to add texture maps to a very simple model of a plaza or square created in AutoCAD. The model is made up of simple extruded lines and regions (see Figure 16.10).

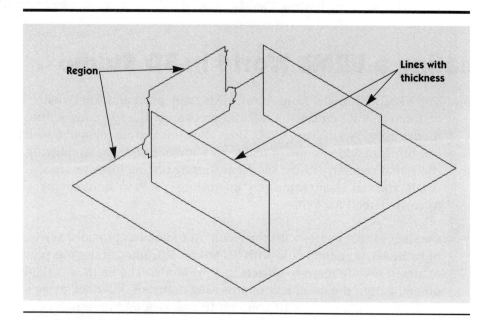

Figure 16.10: An isometric view of the AutoCAD model to be used for the following exercise

The vertical planes will receive bitmap images of buildings to create a "false front" effect. The oddly shaped vertical plane is a region, which will become the Facade building from Chapter 6.

I've already converted the file to a 3D Studio file called `Square.3DS`. You'll use this file in the following tutorial, along with the VRML plug-in from Autodesk. Before you start, make sure you've installed the VRML plug-in. See Appendix B for details.

Adding Mapping Coordinates

Just as with typical 3D Studio models, you will need to apply mapping coordinates to objects that will receive texture maps. First you'll add a texture map to the library facade, which is the odd-shaped surface in the center of the upper left viewport.

1. Open 3D Studio 4.0, then open the Square.3DS sample file. You'll see the model appear in your viewports.

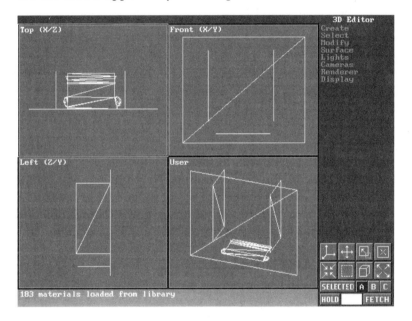

The first thing you might notice is the unusual arrangement of the model. The front view shows what normally would be the top view. VRML starts with a "top-down" view by default, so if you plan to export your models to VRML, make sure you've arranged the model with the Front viewport showing the "plan" of your model.

2. Select Surfaces ➤ Mapping ➤ Adjust ➤ View Align, then click on the upper left viewport to align the map icon to the view. You won't see the map icon, as it is larger than the current view in the viewport.

3. Zoom in to the viewport so it looks similar to Figure 16.11. You'll want a closer look at the center object, which is the library facade, so that you can apply a mapping coordinate to it in the following steps.

4. Choose Surfaces ➤ Mapping ➤ Adjust ➤ Region Fit, then select the two points shown in Figure 16.11.

5. Choose Surfaces ➤ Mapping ➤ Apply Obj, then select the center object.

6. At the Apply Mapping Coordinates To "LIB1" dialog box, click Yes.

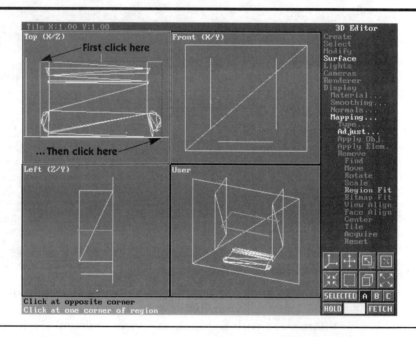

Figure 16.11: Adding the mapping coordinates to the library facade

Next, add the mapping coordinates for the two rectangles on either side of the center library facade.

1. Choose Surfaces ➤ Mapping ➤ Adjust ➤ View Align, then click on the lower left viewport to align the map icon to the view.

2. Choose Surfaces ➤ Mapping ➤ Adjust ➤ Region Fit, then select the two points shown in Figure 16.12.

3. Choose Surfaces ➤ Mapping ➤ Apply Obj, then select the rectangle shown in Figure 16.12. This rectangle represent a building that borders the square.

4. At the Apply Mapping Coordinates To "MARK1" dialog box, choose Yes.

5. Click on the other rectangle shown in Figure 16.12 (Mark2) to assign the mapping coordinates to it as well.

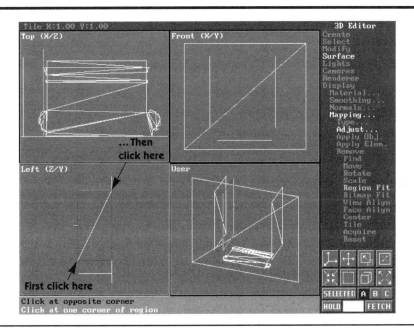

Figure 16.12: Adding the mapping coordinates to the two side-building facades

Finally, you'll want to add mapping coordinates to the ground plane so you can apply a texture map to it. (In addition, you'll need to add lights.) VRML files can contain point-source light information to help illuminate surfaces in your model.

1. By now you should have a feel for the method of applying mapping coordinates. Add the mapping coordinates to the ground plane in the upper right viewport, as shown in Figure 16.13a.

2. Choose Lights ➤ Omni ➤ Create, then, in the upper right viewport, click on the location shown in Figure 16.13b. The Light Definition dialog box appears.

3. Set the L slider all the way to the right so the slider reads **255**, then click OK.

4. Choose Lights ➤ Omni ➤ Move, then in the upper left viewport, move the Omni light you just created to the position shown in Figure 16.13c. This will help illuminate all the surfaces of the model.

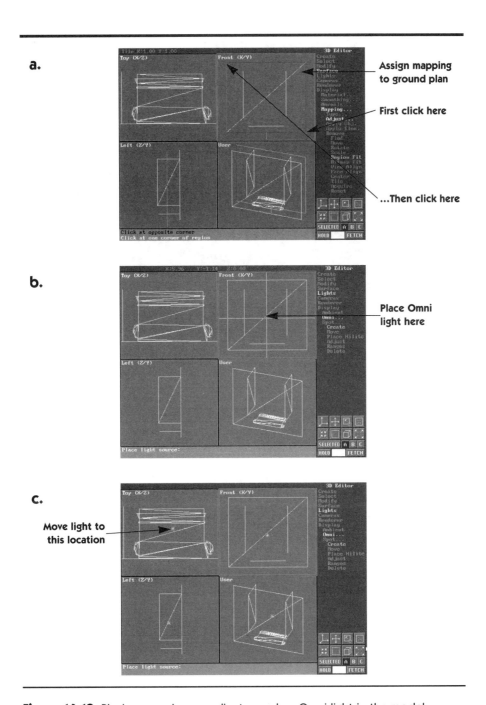

Figure 16.13: Placing mapping coordinates and an Omni light in the model

Assigning Image Bitmaps

Now you're ready to create the VRML file from the 3D Studio model. Notice that you haven't yet added any texture maps to your model, just the mapping coordinates. For VRML output from 3D Studio, you will add the textures through the VRML plug-in (see Figure 16.14).

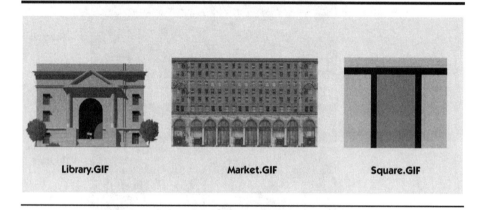

Library.GIF   Market.GIF   Square.GIF

Figure 16.14: The image maps used in the VRML model of the square

1. Choose Program ➤ PXP Loader from the pull-down menu. The PXP Selector dialog box appears.

2. Locate VRML in the list. If you don't see it, that means you haven't installed the VRML plug-in yet. (See Appendix B for installation instructions.)

3. Click OK. The 3DS VRML Plug-in dialog box appears.

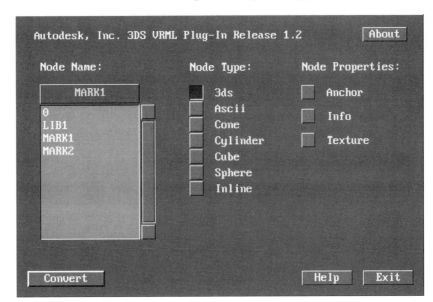

4. In the list on the left, click on Lib1 to select it. This is the object in the model that represents the library facade.

5. Click on the Texture button on the right. The Enter A File Name Or URL dialog box appears.

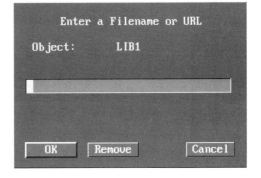

6. Enter **library.gif** in the input box, then click OK. You've just attached a bitmap image called Library.GIF to the library facade object in the model.

7. Next, click on Mark1 in the Node Name list, then click on the texture button. Mark1 is the name of one of the rectangular objects in the model.

8. At the Enter A File Name dialog box, enter **Market.GIF**, then click OK.

9. Repeat steps 7 and 8 for the item labeled Mark2 in the Node Name list. Use the same `Market.GIF` file for Mark2's bitmap image.

10. Finally, assign the file named `Square.GIF` to the 0 item in the list.

Note   *You may have noticed that the image files used as texture maps are GIF files. GIF and JPEG files are the most commonly used image file formats for the World Wide Web and can also be used in VRML files for textures.*

Adding a URL Link

You've added all the texture maps to your model and could go ahead and export the model to the VRML format. But there is one other VRML feature you can exploit through the VRML plug-in. You can add a *link* to another VRML world, or to another type of data (like an audio or video clip), or to a Web site. In the following exercise, you'll add a link to the VRML building you created with Wcvt2pov earlier in this chapter.

1. While in the VRML dialog box, click on the Lib1 item in the Node Name list.

2. Click on the Anchor button. The WWW Anchor Group Node dialog box appears.

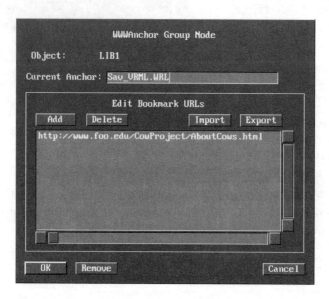

3. In the input box at the very top of the dialog, enter **Sav_VRML.WRL**. As an alternate, you could enter a Web site address (URL) here. For our demonstration, you'll use a local (that is, "located on your own machine") VRML file.

4. Click OK to exit the dialog box.

Converting to VRML

Now you're finally ready to convert the file to a VRML format.

1. Choose Convert from the VRML dialog box. The Select Nodes To Convert dialog box appears.

2. Click on the All button in the upper right of the dialog box. Notice that the Node Name list shows asterisks in front of all the items in the list.

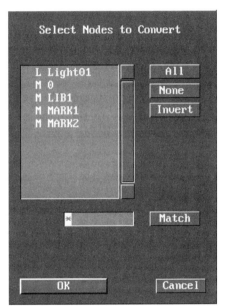

3. Click OK. The Select An Output File dialog box appears with the default name of Square.WRL. Make sure you are saving the file to the same directory where the other sample files from this book are stored, then click OK to accept the name. After a moment, you will notice some disk activity on your computer, but no indication that 3D Studio has done anything.

4. Click Cancel at the Select Nodes To Convert dialog box, then click Exit at the Main VRML Plug-in dialog box.

5. Save the current file, then exit to Windows.

In step 3, I asked you to save the file to the directory that contains the samples from this book. I did this because unless you specify otherwise, VRML browsers will assume that the bitmap files used in a WRL file are located in the same directory as the WRL file. Since you didn't specify a directory when you specified the bitmap filenames, you will want the bitmap files to be in the same location as the main VRML file.

Viewing the Square File and Its Links

The next step is to check the file to see if you really have a model with bitmap images attached.

> **Note**   *Remember to set the Date/Time settings on your system back to April 1996 before attempting to run WorldView. (Also remember to set the date back to the current date after leaving WorldView!)*

1. Open WorldView.

2. Choose File ➤ Open.

3. At the Open Location dialog box, choose Open Local File.

4. At the File dialog box, locate and select `Square.WRL`.

5. Click OK. `Square.WRL` appears in the WorldView windows (see Figure 16.15).

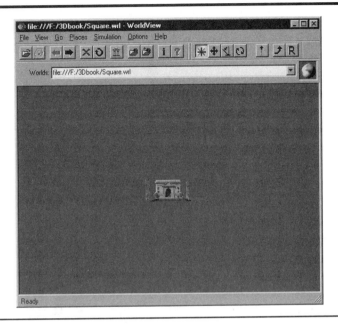

Figure 16.15: The Square.WRL as seen from WorldView

6. Use the Navigate tool to move forward into the model. Notice how the bitmaps of the buildings give the impression of a three-dimensional surface.

7. Move in close to the library facade; then, without clicking your mouse, place the cursor on top of the building. Notice that the cursor turns into a pointing hand icon. This tells you that the library facade has a link to another object.

8. Now click on the library. WorldView will open the Sav_VRML.WRL file.

9. To return to the Square.WRL file, click on the left-pointing arrow in the Toolbar.

The model you just edited is extremely simple. You can copy some of the facade surfaces and add some lights to make the buildings appear more solid in the VRML environment, as shown in Figure 16.16.

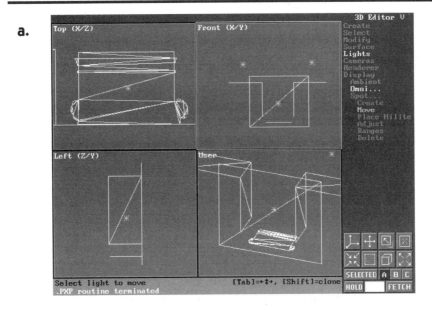

Figure 16.16: Lights and surfaces added in 3D Studio, and the WorldView view of the additional surfaces

I mentioned in the exercise of the prior heading "Adding a URL Link" that you could have entered a Web site address for an anchor. Suppose, for example, you entered **http://www.autodesk.com** instead of Sav_VRML.WRL in that exercise. When you clicked on the library facade in WorldView, WorldView would have started your Web browser and attempted to "log on" to the Autodesk Web site.

Other 3D Studio VRML Plug-in Options

> ***Note***   *VRML refers to objects as* nodes, *hence the term in the VRML Plug-in dialog box. When you are working with 3D Studio and VRML, just remember that* node *equals* objects.

You have a variety of other options in the VRML Plug-in dialog box that were not covered in the tutorial. Many of these options are designed to help simplify your model and to reduce the model's file size. With VRML you want as small a file as you can get, because when you're working with the World Wide Web the files are usually being sent over phone lines. Table 16.1 lists some of those options and what they do. These options affect the selected item in the Node Name list.

Table 16.1: Options in 3D Studio's VRML Plug-in Dialog Box

Option	Purpose
3DS	This is the default you used in the exercises. It maintains the 3D Studio object geometry.
ASCII	Converts the selected item into ASCII text. A dialog box opens that allows you to enter the desired text.
Cone	Converts the selected node into a VRML cone. A dialog box opens to allow you to specify the dimensions of the cone.
Cylinder	Converts the selected node into a VRML cylinder. A dialog box opens to allow you to specify the dimensions of the cylinder.
Cube	Converts the selected node to a VRML cube. A dialog box opens to allow you to specify the dimensions of the cube.
Sphere	Converts the selected node into a VRML Sphere. A dialog box opens to allow you to specify the dimensions of the sphere.
Inline	Converts the selected node into what is called an Inline object, an object that references another VRML file that is to be loaded at the same time as the current one. (The idea is similar to AutoCAD Xref files that are not part of the current open file but are loaded along with the current file.) A dialog box opens to allow you to specify the name of the VRML inline file you wish to have loaded in place of the node.

Modeling for Animations vs. Virtual Reality

While I've shown how you can use the same model for Virtual Reality that you used to create a "canned" animation, you need to be aware that modeling for VR requires different standards from those needed for modeling for a video animation. Here are some points to keep in mind when you are creating your VR models:

◆ Keep the polygon count down as low as possible on your model. The more complex your model is (that is, the more polygons there are), the slower it will respond while you are "walking" through it. Complex models will also take longer to download over phone lines, something to keep in mind if you are planning to place your model on a Web site.

◆ Keep the texture map files small. You may have to go through some trial and error to get a decent appearance on the texture maps while keeping the file size down.

◆ Avoid shapes that require smooth shading. There will be a trade-off between smoothness and the number of polygons you want to use in a model. Again, this will take some trial and error to see what works best.

◆ As mentioned earlier, pay attention to normals in your model. Normals are easier to control in 3D Studio, so you may want to use 3D Studio to adjust normals if you need to.

VR is *very* processor-intensive, and you have to remember that not everyone who views your model has a Pentium 166 with 32MB of RAM. A lot also depends on the browser being used to view the VR model, so if you are putting your models on a Web site, you won't have much control over who uses what browser. It's best to play it safe by building efficient models with properly aligned normals.

The Possibilities

You've seen how you can create a VRML space either by converting a fairly detailed 3D model into the VRML format or by creating simple shapes and mapping images to them. You aren't limited to one or the other, however. You can add image maps to a complex model to further enhance its realism, or you can add more model detail to a simple model.

So far, you've looked at your 3D models at face value. That is, you've viewed them as a representation of something you might want to construct in the real world or that already exists. But you might also want to consider how VRML can help you present your ideas in other ways. For example, you might design a VRML room with a number of virtual artifacts, each linked to a document describing your design project. Depending on the Web browser you use, you could link sound files and animated clips to objects in your virtual room. With VRML, you can easily devise a control panel with buttons that transport you to other VRML worlds or to other Web pages. You could create a "virtual gallery" of your projects, and even include a virtual docent.

◆ Putting It All Together with the World Wide Web

Throughout this book, you've seen how you can generate pieces of a presentation. But we haven't really touched on ways to pull those pieces into an organized, final presentation. For many 3D users, the presentation may take the form of the traditional paper renderings mounted on boards and lined up on a wall. But since your material is created on a computer to begin with, you may want to consider delivering your presentation through a computer-based medium.

Multimedia and 3D

When we think of computer presentations, we think of multimedia. There are certainly many multimedia authoring tools available that allow you to quickly pull together a presentation from a set of images, animations, text, and VRML files. Products like Astound from Gold Disk offer basic multimedia authoring capabilities to help you quickly build a professional-looking presentation. If you want to produce a bigger production or perhaps author a game, MacroMedia Director is considered one of the best high-end programs.

Another way to pull your work together into a single "package" is to use a World Wide Web browser like Netscape or Mosaic. Though such products were not necessarily designed as multimedia tools, if you've ever used the World Wide Web, you begin to realize that it is really a kind of multimedia environment. A primitive level of interactivity is afforded by offering hypertext links to other parts of a document or to entirely different Web sites. Helper applications, similar to VRML browsers, can allow you to access sound and even a limited amount of animation over the Web. Cornell University's CUSeeMe adjunct to the Web even lets you view a live video "feed" from nearly anywhere in the world.

Multimedia on the Web

The idea of the World Wide Web as a multimedia environment has not been lost on the producers of Web content. Web extensions like VRML and Sun Microsystems' Java are adding a new level of interactivity to Web sites, as more and more sites are starting to include animated graphics and sound. An added benefit of using Web-related tools to help present your ideas is that once you've gotten a presentation together, you can use it on a freestanding computer or publish it on the Web. A third and perhaps even faster-growing option is to publish your presentation on a company-wide Internet network, otherwise known as an *Intranet*.

> **Note** *An Intranet network uses existing Internet and World Wide Web tools to help distribute information on demand to those who need it within a company or organization. Unlike the very public Internet, an Intranet is restricted to local and wide area networks that have already been set up within a company. Intranet networks can also include consultants, business partners, and even clients through high-speed data/telephone lines such as ISDN and T1. Public access to an Intranet is tightly controlled or even nonexistent.*

The World Wide Web offers a completely new way of using a computer, but it is based on the lowest common denominator in the computer world: ASCII text. Web pages are really fairly simple text files that include codes that describe how the text in the page is supposed to look. Other codes determine the placement of graphics files within the text, while still others provide links to documents in another location. Even VRML files are text files that describe geometry.

The codes that make up a Web page, while not really hard to understand, can be a bit confusing and difficult to work with. Fortunately, there are many software offerings that will "desktop publish" your Web page for you. All you need to do is arrange the text and graphics and select fonts and font sizes, and the program adds the appropriate special codes, called *HyperText Markup Language* or *HTML*, to your document. Products like Quarterdeck's Web Author are like plug-ins to word processors that add HTML tools. There are also low-end offerings like Web Wizard from CompuServe that can quickly generate simple Web pages for you.

At the time I'm writing this, with the popularity of Java growing, multimedia software makers are planning programs that will allow non-programmers to add interactivity to their Web sites. One of the first of such products is Autodesk's HyperWire. HyperWire takes the idea of a Web page "desktop publishing" program one step further, and lets you create interactive Web pages based on Java, without actually having to know how to program. If you want to see firsthand what HyperWire has to offer, you can download a "sneak preview" version from the Kinetix Web site at `http://www.ktx.com`.

What Is Java, Anyway?

Java is a computer programming language derived from the popular C++ object-oriented language. It was developed by Sun Microsystems as a completely hardware-independent version of C++. This is significant because C has always been a language closely tied to hardware.

Instead of accessing your computer's hardware directly, Java relies on a "virtual" computer. This virtual computer is basically a program that sits quietly in the background and provides the link between Java and your particular hardware. This virtual computer currently exists as an integral part of Web browsers like Netscape 2.0 and Sun Microsystems' own Hot Java. A Java program will run on a Windows machine, a Mac, a Sun Microsystems workstation, and a host of other systems without having to create specific versions of the program for each system.

Java is only one way of getting your multimedia presentation across the Web. A growing number of software companies are creating plug-ins to Web browsers that will allow you to view their proprietary binary file formats without actually owning their software. For example, both Gold Disk (the makers of Astound) and Macromedia (the makers of Director) offer plug-ins to Netscape 2.0 that allow users to view Astound and Director presentations that are embedded in Web pages. A plug-in called Cool-Fusion by Iterated Systems lets you view a Windows AVI animation file as it is being downloaded. Another plug-in called Action by Open2u lets you view MPEG video streams while on line. Even Autodesk offers a plug-in that allows you to publish your AutoCAD 2D drawings on the Web so that you can use the Web as a design collaboration medium. Autodesk's Kinetix division has Topper, a tool that brings the next generation of VRML to Web pages by adding motion and animation ("object behaviors") to VRML files.

Peering into the Future

In the early 70s, I had the good fortune to take a course on computer applications in architecture from Nicholas Negroponte, the founder of MIT's Media Lab and professor of Media Technology. At that time, he predicted that computers would become almost commodity items; cheap and freely accessible. It sounded implausible at the very least, especially since the only computer I'd ever used was a huge, monstrous machine in the basement of the math building. Now, a little over 20 years later, we have personal computers, many times more powerful than that math building monster, being sold alongside stereos and big screen TVs. I mention this because Nicholas Negroponte is still making predictions, so perhaps this time we should listen very carefully. If you are interested in the topics covered in this chapter, I urge you to read his book *Being Digital*, published by Vintage Books (1995). He is also a regular columnist for *Wired* magazine.

The Web beyond Multimedia

The personal computer is becoming a tool for collaboration, and the Internet and World Wide Web are showing us the way. Right now, the Web is changing from a strictly one-way street to a two-way boulevard where all the cars have car phones and built-in entertainment systems. In the not too distant future, you will not only be able to present your design ideas over common communication lines, you will interactively work out design problems in 3D from across the street or across a continent. You may even take on a virtual persona in a multi-participant 3D virtual environment as you work. That virtual environment will be built by creative people who know how to use the tools presented in this book.

◆ Summary

I hope you find this book useful beyond your initial reading. I've attempted to create something that will be helpful to the AutoCAD 3D user regardless of whether you are a professional designer or a student trying to find a career path. By including discussions of programs besides AutoCAD, I've given you a more complete picture of computer 3D and how you can exploit it.

Thanks for purchasing Mastering AutoCAD 3D. If you have comments or questions, feel free to contact me at:
gomura@sirius.com

or at:
76515,1250@compuserve.com

You can also visit my Web page at:
http://wyp.net/users/omura/aec.htm

Best of luck to you in your virtual future.

Appendices

Appendix A

Software Installation Notes

You'll find here steps for installing the main programs to the recommended Windows 95 or Windows NT machine.

Software installation is fairly straightforward for most of the applications discussed in this book. In this appendix, I offer instructions for installing the main programs: *AutoCAD* release 13 revision C4, *AutoVision* 2.0, and *3D Studio* 4.0. For help installing the Adobe Photoshop and Premiere tryout software found on the accompanying CD, consult Appendix B.

3D modeling is one of the most computer-intensive applications you can find. It should be no surprise, then, that we expect that you will have a high-capacity system. You will need a fair amount of RAM and disk storage space.

Minimum Requirements:

486DX/66 processor

16 Megabytes of RAM (24 minimum for Windows NT)

Windows 95 or Windows NT

High-capacity hard disk with at least 200 Megabytes free

High-resolution 1024×758×256 color monitor

CD-ROM drive

Mouse or tablet

These are *minimum* requirements; they should be raised if you are considering some serious 3D work (like, doing it for money, on a deadline, for instance).

On the software side, I expect that you are using a true 32-bit operating system such as Windows 95 or Windows NT. I do *not* recommend using Windows 3.1 for this memory- and resource-intensive work.

With one exception, all of the tutorials in this book were created using AutoCAD release 13 revision C4 running under Windows 95. In later chapters I also used AutoVision 2.0 running under Windows 95, and 3D Studio 4.0 running as a DOS application under Windows 95. (The exception is Appendix C, where I use 3D Studio MAX running under Windows NT.)

> **Note**   *3D Studio 4.0, which I present in Part Two (Chapters 9 through 12), is a DOS program; no Windows 95 version exists. For this book, I simply set it up as a DOS application under Windows 95. (Windows NT users can use the 3D Studio Max version of the program, but be warned that it is quite different from the version I discuss in Part Two. I provide a brief introduction to the similarities and differences between the two programs in Appendix C.)*

Installing AutoCAD 13

To install your AutoCAD r13 software for Windows 95, run the Setup.EXE application on the install disk that comes with the program. It's a typical Windows installation. Here are the steps.

1. Place the installation disk in drive A or B, whichever is appropriate for the disk size.

2. From the Windows 95 Taskbar, Choose Start ➤ Run.

3. At the Run dialog box, enter **A:\setup** (or **B:\setup** as appropriate), then click OK.

4. Follow the instructions on the screen to complete the installation.

Configuring AutoCAD

When you first run AutoCAD, you will be asked to configure your system for peripheral hardware. If you have any doubts, select the defaults presented for device options. You can always change them later using Options ➤ Configure from AutoCAD's pull-down menu.

Have Your Authorization Code Ready

During the configuration, you will also be asked for your authorization code. You can run AutoCAD for 30 days without the authorization code, but after that time AutoCAD will not run. To obtain an authorization code, you need to contact the Autodesk Authorization Center. Their phone number is listed in the documentation you received with the AutoCAD package.

♦ Installing AutoVision 2.0

AutoVision 2.0, the program I discuss in Chapter 8, is included as a trial version in your AutoCAD r13 package. AutoVision requires a bit more work to install than most Windows programs. First you need to install the software on your hard drive, then you need to configure AutoCAD so it knows where to look for AutoVision. Remember that AutoVision is an add-on to AutoCAD and runs inside it. Also, AutoVision will not run without an authorization code. Before you attempt to run AutoVision, obtain the authorization code as described below.

Installing AutoVision 2.0 on Your Hard Drive

Installing AutoVision on your computer is like installing any other Windows 95 program.

1. Place the AutoCAD r13 CD in your CD-ROM drive.
2. Choose Start ➤ Run from the Windows 95 Taskbar.
3. At the Run dialog box, enter *d:***autovis****setup** (replacing *d* here with the drive letter of your CD-ROM drive).
4. Follow the instructions on screen for installing AutoVision. When you are asked for a directory name for AutoVision, I recommend you use **AV2**.

Configuring AutoCAD for AutoVision

Once AutoVision is installed on your hard drive, you need to make some configuration changes to AutoCAD. The following describes the steps required to set up AutoCAD to use AutoVision. Read these instructions very carefully.

1. Start AutoCAD.
2. Choose Options ➤ Preferences. The Preferences dialog box appears.
3. Click on the Environment tab. The Environment options appear.

4. Click on the Support input box, then press the End key to get to the end of the listing in the input box.

5. Add the following line to the end of the Support input box's information:

> **;*d*:\av2\avwin;d:\av2\avis_sup**

(where *d* is the drive letter for the drive you installed AutoVision to).

6. Click on the Render tab. The Render options appear.

7. Click on the Map File Path input box and enter the following:

> ***d*:\av2\maps;d:\av2\tutorial**

(where, as before, *d* is the drive letter where AutoVision is installed).

8. Click OK, then restart AutoCAD.

Once you've taken these steps, you'll need to do one more very important thing: obtain an authorization code.

Have Your Authorization Code Ready

> ***Warning*** *Don't call for your AutoVision authorization code until you're actually ready to work with the program—the version that comes with AutoCAD r13 gives only a 30-day trial version. For the best use of your time with the program, then, don't try to run the program until you are ready for Chapter 8.*

When you first attempt to run AutoVision by selecting any of the Render options in AutoCAD, you will be asked for your authorization code, so before you start with Chapter 8, have your authorization code ready. If you are using the tryout version of AutoVision that comes with Auto-CAD, you can obtain a temporary authorization code by contacting the Autodesk Authorization Code Department. Their phone number is listed in the documentation you received with AutoCAD.

Have your AutoCAD serial number on hand as they will ask for it. The temporary code allows you to run AutoVision for 30 days, after which you will need to purchase a full license to run AutoVision. With the full license, you will receive additional documentation and more material image maps. You will also be required to obtain another, permanent authorization code.

♦ 3D Studio 4.0 Installation Notes

Although I use 3D Studio under Windows 95, there is no version of 3D Studio created specifically *for* Windows 95. Version 4.0 of this program, which I present in Chapters 9 and later, is a DOS program, so you will need to run the Install.EXE program on the 3D Studio installation disk from a DOS prompt. After you install the program, you will have to run it as a full-screen DOS program under Windows 95. Here are the basic steps you need to follow.

To install the program, place the 3D Studio CD in your CD-ROM drive and place the install disk in your floppy drive. Then, from the DOS prompt, type **a:install** or **b:install**, as appropriate. Follow the instructions that appear on the screen.

In order to run 3D Studio in a full-screen window under Windows 95, you must make a couple of minor modifications to your Windows setup. Take the following steps after installing 3D Studio.

1. Locate the file Pharlap.386 in the 3D Studio directory. (By default, 3D Studio will have been placed in a directory called \3ds4.)

2. Copy Pharlap.386 into your Windows directory.

3. Open the file System.INI with a text editor. (System.INI is located in your Windows directory.)

4. Scroll down the file until you see a line that reads [386Enh].

5. Below the [386Enh] heading, add the following line:

   device=pharlap.386

6. Save System.INI, then restart Windows.

Next, you need to set up a shortcut for 3D Studio so that you can access it from the Windows 95 Taskbar. This is a standard Windows procedure; check your Windows documentation or the Windows Help system if you need instructions.

Problems with the 3D Studio "Hardware Lock" and Windows 95

3D Studio requires a device called a "hardware lock." This is a unit about 3 inches square that plugs into the printer port of your computer. Without it, 3D Studio will not run. The hardware lock is intended to reduce the pirate use of 3D Studio: copying the program disks is not so difficult, but reproducing the lock *is*. Unfortunately, the hardware lock can cause some problems when attempting to run 3D Studio from Windows 95.

Some products designed for Windows 95, such as advanced printers, backup drives, and scanners, use the printer port in such a way that they need to "poll" the port at certain intervals. Unfortunately, if that the port is being polled by one of the other products, you will receive error messages regarding the printer port. If this happens to you when you're attempting to run 3D Studio, check to see what devices you have installed on that port, and consult the manufacturer of the other devices to see if you can disable their polling features.

Setting Up 3D Studio 4.0 under Windows NT 3.5

Autodesk makes no claim to 3D Studio 4.0's ability to run under Windows NT. If you are using Windows NT and want to do 3D modeling with AutoCAD, you should upgrade to the NT version, *3D Studio MAX*. I present instructions for installing and using it in Appendix C.

◆ Windows Display Driver Conflicts and 3D Studio 4.0

Even after successfully installing 3D Studio under Windows 95, you may encounter problems with conflicting display drivers. They will show up when you attempt to open the Materials Editor in 3D Studio. You will see a garbled screen or perhaps just a blank screen, and 3D Studio will not respond.

If you run into these types of problems, first try setting your display driver settings to VESA (that is, if your display hardware supports the VESA standard). If that doesn't help, you may want to experiment with the display drivers in 3D Studio until you find one that works. Due to the large number of different display options, I cannot give a more thorough discussion of this topic here, other than the general steps below.

To open the 3D Studio display configuration system, do the following:

1. Open a DOS window.

2. Go to the 3D Studio directory.

3. Enter **3ds vibcfg**↵ at the DOS prompt. The Vibrant display driver configuration screen opens.

4. Make the adjustments that seem appropriate for your system, then exit the configuration screen to go to 3D Studio.

5. In 3D Studio, choose Program ➤ Material.

If the Materials Editor screen opens and your computer continues to function, you are OK. Otherwise, you'll have to press Alt+Tab to toggle back to Windows and close 3D Studio from there by right-clicking on the 3D Studio button in the Taskbar and then clicking Close. You will get a warning message asking if you really want to close the program; choose Yes.

> **Tip**   *If you have a CompuServe account, you may be able to find others who have solved the display driver problem for you. Check out the Autodesk Asoft forum—log on to CompuServe and then enter* **GO ASOFT**.

◆ Setting Up AutoCAD for 3D-to-2D Conversions

In Chapter 3, I mention that you can convert a 3D model into an AutoCAD 2D line drawing for the purposes of editing and "cleaning up" for purposes of line-art presentations. In order to do this, you must configure AutoCAD to plot to DXB files. (DXB files are Autodesk's own file format for exporting to plotters.)

Here are the steps necessary to set up AutoCAD to produce DXB files.

1. While in AutoCAD, Choose Options ➤ Configure. The AutoCAD text window appears and you'll see the message `Press RETURN to continue`.

2. Press ↵. You'll see a numbered listing of configuration options.

3. Enter **5**↵ to select the Configure Plotter option. Another numbered listing of plotter configuration options appears.

4. Enter **1**↵ to select Add A Plotter Configuration. Another numbered listing appears of available plotters.

5. Enter **2**↵ to select the option *AutoCAD File Output Formats (Pre 4.1) - By Autodesk, Inc.*

6. At the Supported Models numbered list, enter **2**↵ to select AutoCAD DXB File.

7. At the `Maximum horizontal (X) plot size in drawing units <11.0000>:` prompt, enter **30**↵.

8. At the `Plotter steps per drawing unit <1000.0000>:` prompt, press ↵ to accept the default.

9. At the `Maximum vertical (Y) plot size in drawing units <8.5000>:` prompt, enter **30**↵. You will see a listing of the default settings for this AutoCAD DXB plotter configuration.

10. At the `Do you want to change anything? (No/Yes/File) <N>:` prompt, press ↵ to accept the default settings. You can always change them later.

11. At the `Enter a description for this plotter:` prompt, enter a description you like or press ⏎ to accept the default description AutoCAD provides. You won't see the AutoCAD default description until you actually attempt to plot something.

12. Next you return to the Plotter Configuration menu listing. Press ⏎ to accept the default option (Exit To Configuration Menu).

13. You return to the general Configuration menu. Press ⏎ again to accept the default option (Exit To Drawing Editor). You get the following message:

> `If you answer N to the following question, all`
> `configuration changes you have just made will`
> `be discarded. Keep configuration changes? <Y>`

Go ahead and press ⏎ to accept the new configuration changes.

Now you are ready to convert your 3D model into a 2D line drawing.

1. Set up your 3D view. You can plot from either Tiled Model Space or from Paper Space.

2. Choose File ➤ Print. The Plot Configuration dialog box appears.

3. Click on the Device And Default Selection button in the upper left corner of the dialog box. The Device And Default Selection dialog box appears.

4. Click on the item in the list entitled *AutoCAD File Output Formats. (Pre 4.1) - By Autodesk, Inc.* (or click on the description you entered in step 11 of the previous set of instructions).

5. Click OK.

6. Click on the File Name button, then enter a name and location for your DXB plot file.

7. Click OK, then click OK to create the file.

8. Once the plot is complete, close the current file and open a new one.

9. At the command prompt, enter **DXBIN**⏎.

10. Locate and select the plot file you just created, then click OK. A 2D line drawing of your 3D model will appear.

◆ AutoCAD-to-3D Studio File-Transfer Issues

In Chapter 9, I show how to convert an AutoCAD file to a 3D Studio file using AutoCAD's File ➤ Export (3DSOUT) option. Two other issues should be brought out regarding file transfers from AutoCAD to 3D Studio. The first deals with curved objects such as arc and circles.

Controlling the Smoothness of Arcs and Cylinders

When using the File ➤ Export option in AutoCAD, extruded arcs and circles are simplified into faceted shapes. Depending on certain conditions, this can cause objects like columns and tubes to appear "boxy" and less smooth. To avoid this, you can use the Facetres system variable to improve the smoothness of exported shapes.

In Chapter 9 I explained that Facetres can improve the smoothness of curved surfaces in AutoVision. It also affects 3D Studio exports. Facetres is normally set to 0.05 and has a range from 0.01 to 10.0. If you find that curved surfaces exported to 3D Studio appear too "boxy," then increase the Facetres system variable. Note that you can use AutoCAD's Render tool to check the smoothness of arcs and circles. Also note that Facetres is dependent on your display resolution and view. When exporting AutoCAD files to 3DS, set your AutoCAD window to fill your screen and zoom in on your model so it fills the screen.

Adjusting the Normals of AutoCAD Faces

In Chapter 16, I mentioned that you have to pay close attention to the normals in the surfaces of your AutoCAD model when exporting your model for VRML. I mentioned that you can check your model by "walking through" it with a VRML browser like WorldView, then noting any "missing" faces. Once you've identified the missing faces you can use 3D Studio or AutoCAD to "flip" the face's normal.

In 3D Studio, you can easily flip the normal of a face by first selecting it, then selecting Surface ➤ Normals ➤ Face Flip from the command column. 3D Studio 4.0 also has a tool that will let you locate the errant face. If you select Display ➤ Geometry ➤ Backface from the command column, 3D Studio will show faces that have normals pointing *toward* you as outlines. Faces that have normals pointing *away* from you will be displayed with pointers at their vertex points.

If you don't have 3D Studio, you will have to use AutoCAD to reverse the face normal. Using AutoCAD is a bit more involved. The best approach here is to import the exported 3DS file you created as the intermediate VRML transfer file. Take the following steps to do this.

1. In AutoCAD, choose File ➤ Import.
2. At the Import File dialog box, choose *.3ds from the List Files Of Type drop-down list, then locate the file that need fixing.
3. Next, you will see the 3D Studio Import File Options dialog box. Click on the Add All button, then click OK. AutoCAD will take a minute or two to import the file.
4. Use the Explode command to explode the imported file.
5. Type **Splframe**↵ at the command prompt, then enter **1** to make all of the face edges visible.

You can now locate the "missing" face and reverse its normal by erasing it and then redrawing it using a 3D Face. Remember that as you draw the 3D Face, you must select the points in a clockwise direction to make the normal point toward you.

Appendix B

Using the Companion CD

This appendix discusses installing and running the files and programs you can find on the CD. This is where you will find information on installing tryout software, shareware, freeware, and sample files. I'll start with the sample files.

◆ The Sample Files

The files mentioned throughout the tutorials in the book can be found on the CD in a directory called \sample. Whenever you find a reference to a named file in the book, this is where you can find it.

For convenience, you may want to copy the entire directory onto your computer's hard drive so you have ready access to the sample files at all times.

In addition, I've included the Targa sequence files for Chapter 15 in two directories called \Animate\first and \Animate\Second. These were separated only because of the sheer volume of these files. You may want to leave them on the CD until you start working on Chapter 15. You will also find other files related to Chapter 15 in the \Animate parent directory.

◆ Adobe Tryout Products

The CD contains "tryout" versions of three Adobe products: Photoshop 3.0.5, Premiere 4.0, and Streamline 3.0. These tryout versions offer all the functionality of their commercially available siblings except for the fact that you can't save or print with them. (Actually, the tryout version of Streamline *does* let you print; you just can't save or use the Clipboard with it.) Photoshop can be installed directly from the CD, but Premiere requires that you copy the installation files onto your computer before you install it.

Installing Adobe Photoshop

To install the Adobe Photoshop Tryout software first make sure you have at least 8MB of free space on your hard disk. Locate the Setup.EXE file in the \Adobe\Photoshp\Disk1 directory in the CD, then double-click on it. Follow the instructions that appear on your screen. You can use the Windows 95 Explorer to find the file, or for Windows NT or Windows 3.1, use the File Manager. After Photoshop has been installed, take some time to read the PSReadMe.WRI document that appears with the Photoshop program file. (If you accepted the installation program's suggestions, you'll find the program files under your Win32App directory.)

Installing Adobe Premiere

To install the Adobe Premiere tryout software, first make sure you have at least 22MB of free disk space on your hard drive. Locate the \Adobe\Premiere directory on the CD (using the Windows 95 Explorer, or the File Manager for Windows NT or Windows 3.1), then click and drag the entire \Premiere directory onto your hard drive. Next, locate the Setup.EXE program in the \Premiere\Disk1 directory on your hard drive and double-click on it. Follow the instructions that appear.

After Premiere has been installed, take some time to read the
`ReadMe.WRI` document that appears with the Premiere program file.

Installing Adobe Streamline

Adobe Streamline is a graphics file conversion program. It is especially
useful to AutoCAD users because with it, you can convert bitmap image
files, such as PCX, TIFF, or Macintosh Paint (PNT) files into AutoCAD
DXF vector files. This can be helpful for importing scanned maps, logos,
or other types of image files into AutoCAD. It can also be useful in
matching 3D models to photographic images.

To install the Streamline tryout, go to the `\Adobe\Strmline` directory
of the CD and double-click on the `Slsetup.EXE` file. You can use the
Windows 95 Explorer to find the file, or use the File Manager if you're
using Windows NT or Windows 3.1. Follow the instructions given by the
installation program. After the program has been installed, take a few
minutes to peruse the `readmesl.WRI` file.

◆ DVMPEG

DVMPEG is a set of MPEG Windows drivers from Darim Vision Co., Ltd.
that enable you to create MPEG video and audio files directly from any
Windows program that supports Windows MCI and Video For Windows.
They've provided a demo beta version of the DVMPEG drivers that will
let you record five seconds (150 frames) of MPEG 1 or MPEG 2 video and
audio. These demo drivers are for Windows 95 and Windows NT. Once
installed, these drivers will let you create MPEG-compressed video files.

DVMPEG supports the following MPEG formats:

- ◆ MPEG 1 system layer (ISO/IEC 11172-1)
- ◆ MPEG 1 video (ISO/IEC 11172-2)
- ◆ MPEG 1 layer II audio (ISO/IEC 11172-3)
- ◆ MPEG 2 Main Profile @ Main Level (ISO/IEC 13818-21)

Darim recommends that you check the Darim Web page for the latest version before you install these demos. Their Web page address is:

```
http://darvision.kaist.ac.kr
```

To install the DVMPEG drivers in Windows 95, create a temporary directory on your hard drive and copy into it the contents of the CD's `\Software\DVMPEG\Win95` directory. Then, in the Windows 95 Explorer, go to the new directory on your hard drive and right-click on `DVMPEG.INF`. Choose Install from the menu that appears.

For more information, read the `Readme.TXT` file in the `\software\VMPEG\Win95` directory and the longer `DVMPEG32.DOC` located in the parent `\software\DVMPEG` directory.

◆ Razor Demo

I've included a demo version of Razor from in:sync. Razor is a video editing program similar to Adobe Premiere. It is currently available in two versions, Razor Pro for Windows 95/Windows 3.1 and Razor Mach III for Windows NT.

The demo version of Razor most closely resembles Razor Pro. It is a black-and-white-only version that does allow file saves. To use it, simply copy the `\Software\Razor` folder to your hard drive. Locate the `Avedit.exe` file and double-click on it to start the program.

◆ 3D Studio 4.0 VRML Plug-in

In Chapter 16, I discuss the use of 3D Studio as a VRML world-building tool. Before you start the tutorial in that chapter, make sure you've installed this 3D Studio VRML plug-in. To do this, copy the contents of `\Software\3ds4vrml` into your 3D Studio `\process` subdirectory, and read the text document files that are in the `\3ds4vrml` directory. This plug-in works only with 3D Studio 4.0.

◆ Intervista WorldView

WorldView is a VRML browser described in Chapter 16. It allows you to explore VRML world files on the World Wide Web, or from your own computer. To install it, first create a directory called \Wrldview on your hard disk, then copy the contents of the \Software\ Wrldview directory into your \Wrldview directory. Double-click on the Install.exe file in the \WrldView directory on your computer.

This version of WorldView is a beta release and is timed to be disabled after April 1996. The creators of the program authorize you to set your computer date back to April 1996 before you attempt to use it. You can do this by opening the Date/Time tool in the Windows Control Panel.

If you want the latest version of WorldView, log on to the Intervista Web page at www.intervista.com.

◆ Wcvt2pov

Wcvt2pov is a tool for converting 3D file formats. In Chapter 16, I describe how it can be used to convert an AutoCAD 3D drawing into a VRML world file. To use it, copy the contents of \Software\ wcvt2pov onto your hard drive. Once you've done this, you can simply double-click on the Wcvt2pov.EXE file to run the program.

◆ AutoLISP

As you work with AutoCAD 3D, you may find that some limitations are quite annoying. I've written a few AutoLISP utilities to help ease your 3D work in AutoCAD. These tools are Splinep.LSP, Tube.LSP, 3Dpedit.LSP, and a set of utilities designed to work together called Eye2eye.

Splinep.lsp will extrude a shape along a spline in 3D space. This will allow you to easily create curved tubular shapes, like auto exhaust pipes and motorcycle frames. Tube.LSP creates a simple straight tube based on a pre-existing line. 3Dpedit.LSP lets you easily edit polylines that are not parallel to the current user coordinate system. Eye2eye offers a more intuitive way of viewing your 3D model in perspective mode.

To install these utilities, copy the contents of \autolisp into the \support subdirectory of your AutoCAD directory. For example, if AutoCAD is installed in a directory called \r13\win then you should copy the files from the \autolisp directory of the CD to the \r13\ win\support subdirectory on your computer.

Once you've copied them, you can load them during any AutoCAD session by doing the following:

1. Choose Tools ➤ Applications from the AutoCAD pull-down menu.
2. At the *Load AutoLISP, ADS and ARX Files* dialog box, choose File.
3. At the *Select AutoLISP, ADS and ARX Files* dialog box, locate and select the appropriate AutoLISP file, then click OK. You will return to the *Load AutoLISP, ADS and ARX Files* dialog box. In the list box you will see the name of the file you just selected.
4. Select the filename from the list, then click the Load button.
5. Enter the name of the utility at the command prompt.
6. Answer the prompts that follow.

Once you've loaded a file in this way, the utilities will be available to load from the *Load AutoLISP, ADS and ARX Files* dialog box. The following sections describe how each of the utilities work.

Splinep

To use Splinep, you must first have a spline drawn, plus a profile of the shape you want to extrude along the spline. The profile can be a circle, arc, spline or polyline. Once you have these ready, do the following.

1. At the command prompt, enter **splinep**⏎.

2. At the `Pick profile for extrusion:` prompt, pick the object you want to extrude.

3. At the `Select insertion point for profile` prompt, select a point defining its base or insertion point. This is the point that Splinep will use to align to the extrusion path.

4. At the `Pick path for extrusion:` prompt, click on the spline curve you set up as the extrusion path.

5. At the `Pick orientation point:` prompt, pick a point to orient the profile. (This is only important if you are using an irregular-shape polygon for the profile. You will want to experiment with this option to see which location works best for a given profile.)

6. At the `Enter number of segments:` prompt, enter the number of segments you will want for the extrusion. A low number will give the extrusion a blocky appearance. A higher number will make it appear smoother.

7. At the `Enter size increment:` prompt, enter a value only if you want to "flare" the extrusion like a trumpet horn. Otherwise you can simply press ⏎.

You'll see the Please wait message, and then the extrusion will appear.

Tube

Tube is useful for drawing trusses. It simply creates a circular tube over a line. You must first have a 3D line representation of the truss before you start. Once you've got that, do the following:

1. Enter **tube↵** at the command prompt.

2. At the `Enter tube radius <1.0>:` prompt, enter a radius for your tube.

3. At the `Select object` prompt, select the line representing the centerline of the tube. The tube will be drawn.

3Dpedit

This utility is the simplest of all. After loading 3Dpedit, you enter **3Dpedit** at the command prompt, then select the polyline you wish to edit. The Edit Polyline tool is issued and you are ready to edit the polyline.

Eye2eye

Eye2eye is a set of AutoLISP utilities that aid the viewing of 3D models in AutoCAD. If you find you are struggling with the AutoCAD Dview command, these utilities will be of benefit to you.

Eye2eye is based on the idea of using a camera and target object to control your perspective views. I call the camera and target objects *eyes*, hence the name Eye2eye. To set up a view, you simply place the camera, or EYETO block (see Figure B.1), where you want your point of view. You then place the target, or EYEFROM block, where you want your center of attention. You then use Eye2eye's SHOWEYE command to display the perspective.

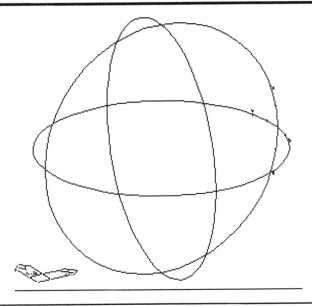

Figure B.1: The EYETO block used with Eye2eye

The following list gives a brief description of all of the Eye2eye commands:

SHOWEYE displays the current eye-target perspective view in the current viewport. Be sure to have the desired viewport active before using this command.

FINDEYE draws a temporary vector between the camera and target points to help locate these points.

CROSSEYE displays a view that reverses the camera and target locations.

MTARG moves the target location. You must be using an orthogonal view for this command.

MEYE moves the camera location. You must be using an orthogonal view for this command.

SETEYE allows you to turn the perspective mode on or off, to set camera "focal length," to turn the camera and target objects on or off, to pan the perspective view, or to set up multiple viewport for Eye2eye.

PANEYE lets you pan the perspective view. This is useful for fine-tuning your perspective view.

MATCHEYE sets the camera and target objects to the current perspective view. You must be working in a perspective viewport to use this command. This command is useful when you've changed your view using methods outside of the Eye2eye command set (i.e., using the Dview command).

Installing Eye2eye

Locate the following list of files on the \software\autolisp subdirectory of the CD.

Eye2eye.lsp

Eyeto.dwg

Eyefrom.dwg

Eye2eye.wri (these instructions)

Mview.scr

Ddsetup.lsp

Ddsetup.dcl

Copy the entire contents of this subdirectory to the \Support subdirectory of AutoCAD release 13. Alternately, you can create a separate subdirectory for these files, then add that subdirectory path to the AutoCAD Support environment setting in the AutoCAD Preferences dialog box.

Using Eye2eye

Eye2eye assumes that you have a fairly good grasp of AutoCAD's 3D functions and the use of Paper Space viewports. It is best suited as a tool for viewing your model after you've created the basic massing.

Once you have a 3D model built, load the Eye2eye utilities by entering the following at the command prompt:

(load "eye2eye")

You can alternatively choose Tools ➤ Applications, then, at the dialog box, click on the File button and locate and load the Eye2eye.lsp file.

After you've loaded Eye2eye, set up multiple viewports by doing the following.

1. Go to the World Coordinate System, then type **SETEYE**↵ at the command prompt.

2. Since this is the first time you are using Eye2eye, you are prompted to pick a camera point. Do so. Don't worry about the exact placement of your camera just yet; you will get a chance to adjust its location later. The camera object, a block called EYETO, appears.

3. Next, you are prompted to select a target location. Do so. As with the camera location, it isn't important to place the target in an exact location at this time. You can easily adjust it later.

4. At the Perspective Off/ON/Focal length/Pan/Hide eyes/ Show eyes/setUp vports: prompt, type **U**↵.

Eye2eye will switch to Paper Space, then set up four viewports: one large viewport (to the right) for your perspective view and three smaller viewports (to the left) for your top, front, and left-side orthogonal views. You will use the orthogonal views to manipulate the camera and target points (see Figure B.2). You are now ready to use the Eye2eye utilities.

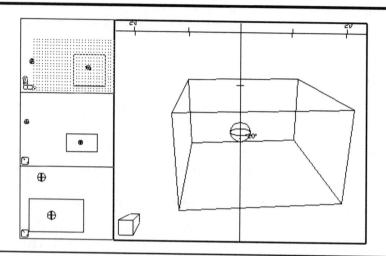

Figure B.2: A sample of the viewport arrangement created by Eye2eye's SETEYE command

Since your views are in Paper Space, you can easily enlarge or resize a view for easy editing. Just remember that while using the Eye2eye utilities, you must be in Tiled Model Space.

Using Eye2eye for Model Construction

If you want to use Eye2eye as a tool to help you construct your 3D model, be sure you set up your Model Space work area before you proceed with the above steps. You can use the Ddsetup utility provided with Eye2eye to accomplish this. To use Ddsetup, go to the command prompt and type

> **(load "ddsetup").**↵
> **DDSETUP.**↵

A dialog box appears from which you can choose a unit style, sheet size, and scale. Once you've selected the appropriate options, click OK. The drawing is then set up according to your selections. You will also see the grid dots. They are set to represent 1-inch intervals at your final plot size.

You can now set up Eye2eye as described above.

Setting the Eyes

Try moving the camera and target objects in the orthogonal views. You can use the MEYE and MTARG commands to help you locate the camera and target objects. When you use these commands, a temporary red and green vector is drawn to show you the location of the camera and target. The red portion of the vector shows the direction of the camera while the green portion shows the direction of the target. Use the REDRAW command to remove the vectors. (They are not true AutoCAD objects and will not plot.)

MTARG and MEYE work just like the MOVE command except that you don't have to select an object; the camera (MEYE) or target (MTARG) is automatically selected. You need only select the base point and second point for the move. You can also use the standard AutoCAD MOVE command to move the camera and target.

Once you've placed the camera and target to your liking, make the large viewport active (by clicking on it), then type **SHOWEYE**↵. A perspective view based on the camera-target locations is displayed. You can then use the AutoCAD View command to save your view or go on to make minor adjustments. For example, you can use the PANEYE command to adjust your perspective view before saving it.

Controlling the Eyes

You will notice some lines and numbers on the perspective view. These are parts of the camera object showing you the angle below or above horizontal in 10-degree increments. You can turn off the display of camera and target objects by using the Hide Eyes option of the SETEYE command. To turn them back on again, use the Show Eyes option. Alternately, you can simply turn the EYES layer on or off. The EYES layer is the layer on which the EYETO and EYEFROM blocks were constructed.

3D Studio MAX
for 3D Studio 4.0 Users

If you are working in the Windows NT environment, you'll want to take a look at 3D Studio MAX, Autodesk's 3D modeling, rendering, and animation program for Windows NT. 3D Studio MAX is an entirely new program, built from the ground up as a 32-bit Windows NT application. Of course, it has many of the same tools as the DOS version of 3D Studio, but it goes well beyond them in all areas.

A thorough coverage of 3D Studio MAX, which I'll call MAX from here on, would take several volumes of text. This appendix is intended only as an introductory guide to MAX, and it's intended for readers already familiar with 3D Studio 4.0 (the program we used extensively in Part Two of this book). In particular, I'll show you how to find the tools we used in the DOS-version tutorials in Part Two of this book, so you can get a head start in learning this powerful new program.

As you read and work through this appendix, keep in mind the following points:

♦ MAX has combined the different program modules of 3D Studio 4.0 into one environment.

♦ MAX employs a hierarchical structure for nearly everything. This reflects its object-oriented architecture.

♦ 3D Studio 4.0 tools exist under MAX but are often implemented differently.

♦ Right-clicking on objects and options often brings up shortcuts to features.

This appendix starts with a tutorial showing the basic functions of MAX and then switches over to some general descriptions of various processes you will want to know about. As you work through this appendix, you'll see many options that will be new to you. I'll concentrate only on those options that relate to tools you've used in this book.

♦ Introducing 3D Studio MAX

Perhaps the biggest barrier to learning MAX is simply the way tools are set up, especially if you are already used to 3D Studio 4.0. So let's start with a look at the 3D Studio MAX screen.

Open the Kinetix program group and double-click on 3D Studio MAX. The 3D Studio MAX window appears (see Figure C.1).

> **Note** *Kinetix is the multimedia division of Autodesk.*

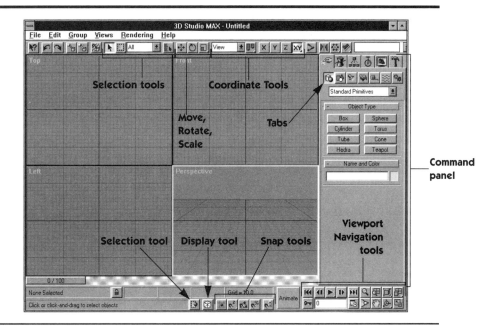

Figure C.1: The 3D Studio MAX screen

The layout might appear vaguely similar to the older 3D Studio 4.0 screen. The general areas of the screen serve similar functions as before. At the top, you see the Menu bar. To the right, you have what is called the command panels section.

Along the top, you see a Toolbar that is entirely new for 3D Studio. As in other Windows applications, the Toolbar duplicates some of the commands found in the pull-down menus, while others are unique.

At the bottom, you have some new tools mixed in with some familiar ones. First of all, you see a Frame slider. In the DOS version of 3D Studio, the Frame slider appears only in the Keyframer section of the program. This illustrates an important difference between the two versions: unlike the DOS version, MAX is not divided into different modules. All the tools are accessible within an integrated environment.

At the bottom you also see a series of magnet icons. These are Snap tools similar to AutoCAD's Object Snap tools. In the lower right corner, the Tool panel is replaced with the Viewport Navigation controls.

The Menu Pan Tool

MAX is designed to be used in a maximized window of at least 1024×768 resolution. Even then, some of the tool panels are too large to fit in the allotted space. For example, the current MAX window does not show the entire Toolbar. To allow access to parts of a tool panel or Toolbar that might not currently be visible in the window, MAX supplies the *Menu Pan tool*.

1. Place the cursor over the gray area between any two buttons in the Toolbar. It turns into a hand icon.

2. Click and drag the Toolbar to the left. Notice that more buttons now appear at the right of the Toolbar.

This is a slight departure from the usual Windows interface we're used to. Be aware of this tool as you explore MAX, so you don't miss any details that may be lurking in some hidden place.

The Command Panels

Another slight departure from the standard Windows interface is the Command panels section. MAX replaces the older text-based command column from its DOS cousin with a set of command *panels*, which are tabbed groups of icons. You can get a ToolTip description of each command tab by simply placing the arrow cursor on the tab and letting it rest there for a moment.

1. Place the cursor on the Display tab, the one that is second from the right in the Command panels section. (It's the one that looks like a computer screen with shapes being displayed.) The *Display* ToolTip appears.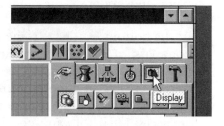

2. Click on the icon. The command panel changes to show the Display options. Move the cursor to the blank area of the Display command panel just below the Invert button. It turns into a Menu Pan tool.

3. Click and drag the mouse upward. Notice that the panel moves up to reveal more options.

At first the command panels appear a bit alien to 3D Studio 4.0 users, but a quick look at the ToolTips reveals that at least some of the older 3D Studio 4.0 tools are duplicated here. Create, Modify, Hierarchy, and Display are commands that have 3D Studio 4.0 command-column equivalents. Motion and Utilities are new, but even they at least contain some tools that the version 4.0 users will be familiar with.

The Viewport Navigation Controls

Another set of tools that resemble, but do not duplicate, their 3D Studio 4.0 counterparts are the *viewport navigation* controls.

These controls let you adjust your view in each viewport. A glance at the ToolTips for each button shows you that there are indeed some similarities. Even the icons look similar to the Tool panel icons of 3D Studio 4.0, and they work in a similar way, except for, perhaps, the Zoom tool. There's also a new tool called the Arc Rotate tool, that lets you adjust your camera orientation. The buttons that are available depend on the type of active viewport.

◆ Trying Out Some Tools

In this section, you'll explore MAX by creating some shapes and seeing firsthand how to get around. You'll start by creating a rectangular box. Here, you'll see more similarities and differences from 3D Studio 4.0.

Creating a Box

1. Click on the Create tab in the command panels section.

   Notice the row of buttons along the top of the Create command panel. It offers all the categories of objects you know about from 3D Studio 4.0, such as Lights, Cameras, Shapes, and Geometry. It also adds some new objects like Helpers, Space Warps, and Systems. We won't get into the new objects in this tour, however, since we're mostly concerned about similarities between version 4.0 and MAX.

2. Click on the Geometry button.

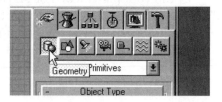

   Note   If you're not starting MAX from scratch, you might not be able to see the following button options in the Geometry command panel. To see the correct set of options, select Standard Primitives from the Subcategory drop-down list below the panel.

3. In the Object Type button group below the command panels, click on the Box button. Notice that a new set of options appears in the lower half of the command panels section of the screen. This echoes the way that we displayed text options in 3D Studio 4.0's command column back in Part Two.

4. Click on the upper left viewport to make it active. Notice that the cursor shows a small cross-hair cursor.

5. Drag the cursor to the location shown in Figure C.2 and let go. The top view of the rectangle remains fixed, but notice what happens in the other three viewports as you move the mouse. The height of the box changes as you move the mouse. Also, the Y input box in the command panels section displays the changing Y dimension of the box as you move the mouse.

6. Move your mouse so the Height input box shows a value near **12**, then click.

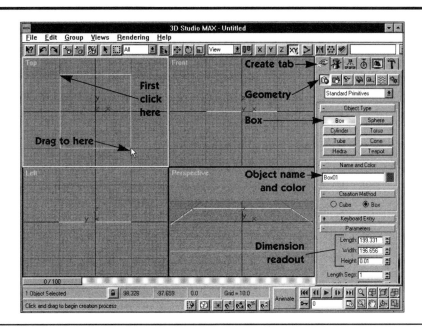

Figure C.2: Creating a rectangular box

You've just created a box in MAX. You can make changes to the dimension of the box by entering exact values into the Length, Width, and Height input boxes of the Parameters flyout in the command panel section, or clicking and dragging on the up and down arrow buttons next to the input boxes, called spinners, to adjust the box's dimensions. The spinners work by clicking and dragging on them either upward or down.

1. In the command panel, next to the Height input box, click and drag the spinner upward. Notice that the value in the input box increases.

2. Use the spinner to set the Height value close to **15**.

Creating a Dome

Now let's try drawing a dome. This operation is similar to the method for creating a box.

1. Click on the Sphere button.

2. Click and drag on the center of the box in the upper left viewport. The sphere appears.

3. Drag the radius of the sphere out to the edge of the rectangle as shown in Figure C.3, then let go. You now have a full sphere. Now let's reduce the sphere to a hemisphere.

4. In the command panel, make sure the Chop radio button is selected in the Parameters flyout.

5. Locate the Hemisphere input box in the Parameters flyout, then place the arrow cursor on the Hemisphere spinner and click and drag upward. The value in the hemisphere input box increases, and the sphere in the viewport begins to disappear from the bottom up.

6. Continue to adjust the spinner until the Hemisphere input box reads **0.50** and the sphere becomes a hemisphere.

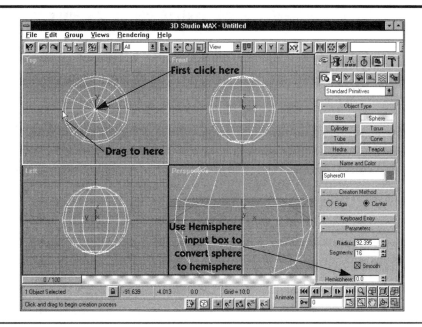

Figure C.3: Creating a dome

You can see from these examples that MAX has a high degree of inter-activity. You can control objects you create better than you could with the 3D Studio 4.0.

Object Properties

Once you've created an object, you can adjust some of its attributes by selecting the object first in the command panel, then right-clicking on it. You then see a pop-up menu from which you can select Properties. You then see the Object Properties dialog box. This dialog box includes those options you normally associate with the object's attributes in 3D Studio 4.0, such as Cast Shadows and Receive Shadows.

Moving, Copying, Rotating and Scaling

You can perform basic editing like
moving, rotating, and scaling, by first
selecting an object, then selecting the
Move, Rotate, or Scale tool on the Toolbar.

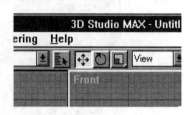

Once an object and tool are selected, you
can click and drag the object to make these
basic edits. To make copies, you can use the familiar 3D Studio 4.0 Shift-
click technique on the object. For more elaborate edits, you will use the
Modify tab on the command panel.

Zooming and Rotating Your View

The Viewport Navigation tools offer many of the same functions as 3D
Studio 4.0. For example, the Zoom Extents and Zoom Extents All tools
act like their 3D Studio 4.0 counterparts. The Zoom tool operates slightly
differently.

1. Click on the Zoom tool in the
Navigation Controls panel.

2. Click and drag the Zoom icon
upward in the Perspective viewport.
Notice that you move closer to the objects.

3. Click and drag downward from the center. You move away from
the objects.

If you've done the tutorial on the WorldView VRML browser in Chapter 16, you'll feel at home with the new way the Zoom tool works in MAX. Another tool that is similar to the VRML browser is the Arc Rotate tool.

1. With the perspective view still current, click on the Arc Rotate button in the Viewport Navigation Control panel.

   A circle graphic with control handles at quadrant points appears in the Perspective viewport.

2. Click and drag inside the circle. The view rotates.

3. Click and drag the top control handle on the graphic. Notice how the view's rotation is restricted to an up-and-down motion.

4. Right-click to turn off the Arc Rotate tool.

Getting a Shaded View

So far, you've been working with a wireframe view similar to the 3D Studio 4.0 view. You can also set MAX to show you your work in a *shaded* view to help you better visualize what's going on.

1. Right-click on the Perspective label (in the upper left corner of the Perspective viewport. A pop-up menu appears.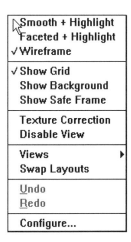

2. Select Smooth + Highlight. Your perspective view changes to show a smooth shaded version of the objects with the specular highlights.

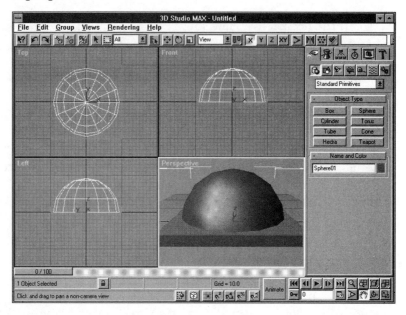

◆ Adding Lights

To add a light to a scene, you use the Create tab of the command panel. You may recall from the first time you saw this that the Create tab has buttons to create all the same categories of object that are available in 3D Studio 4.0, plus a few more.

1. Click on the Create tab of the command panel.

2. Click on the Lights button

3. The panel changes to show four different light types: Omni, Directional, Target Spot, and Free Spot.

4. Click on Target Spot. This is the tool that acts most like the Spotlight tool in 3D Studio 4.0.

5. In the Top view, click and drag on the point shown in Figure C.4: As you drag the mouse, the target for the light appears. The first point you click on become the light location.

6. Place the target in the location shown in Figure C.4.

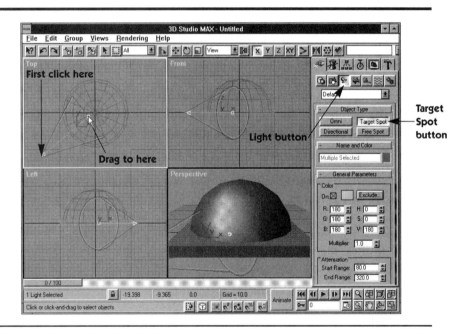

Figure C.4: Placing the light

Setting the Lights Parameters

Once the light is placed, you adjust its name and color in the Name and Color flyout in the command panel. You can edit the name or accept the default name that MAX gives you. If you click on the color swatch next to the light name, the Object Color

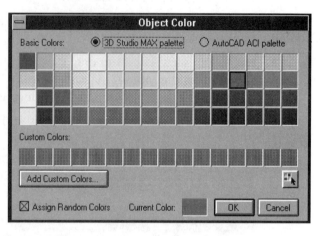

dialog box appears, allowing you to select a color for this light.

You can create a custom color from a Color Selector dialog box by clicking on the Add Custom Colors button.

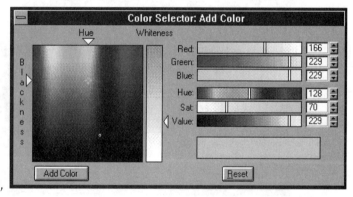

Other settings, such as Hotspot, Falloff (in the Spotlight Parameters flyout), and shadow controls (in the Shadow Parameters flyout) can be found below the Name and Color flyout. You can use the Menu Pan tool to scroll downward and view these options if they are hidden from you.

Let's set the light intensity up to maximum.

1. Click on the Modify tab.

2. Click on the light you just created. Notice that its name and color appear at the top of the Modify command panel.

3. Use the Menu Pan tool to scroll the command panel up so you can see the General Parameters flyout.

4. Change the V (for Value) setting to read **255**. You can either enter the value into the input box, or use the spinner to the right of the input box.

Moving Objects: Adjusting the Light's Position

In 3D Studio 4.0, you could easily adjust the location of a spotlight by choosing Lights ➤ Spotlight ➤ Move, then moving the light in the appropriate viewport. This operation is slightly different in MAX, mainly due to MAX's new X, Y, and Z *restriction tools*. The following demonstrates the procedure.

1. Make sure you are in the Modify tab of the command panel.

2. In the Front viewport, click on the newly created light to select it, then take a close look at the Axis Tripod icon that appears on the screen/viewport. The axis icon shows the X, Y, and Z axes of the selected object.

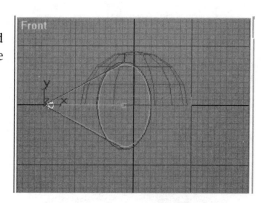

The Axis Tripod icon shows red in the X and Y axes and black in the Z axis. The red indicates the axes within which your movement is restricted. You can change this by using the

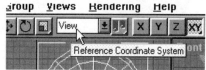

buttons labeled X, Y, Z, and the XZ flyout. You can also change the orientation of the axes based on the "World" coordinates, the "Screen" coordinates, or a variety of other references. These other coordinate systems can be accessed through the Reference Coordinate System (if you're looking for information on this in the manual, it is referred to as the Transform Coordinate System) drop-down list from the Toolbar.

1. Open the Reference Coordinate System drop-down list, and make sure View is selected. Make note of the other options in this list.

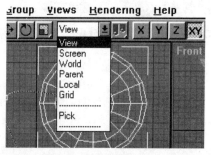

2. Click on the Restrict To Y button in the Toolbar.

Notice that now the Y axis is red in the Axis icon while the X and Z are black.

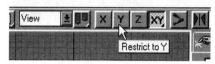

3. Now click on the Move tool in the Toolbar.

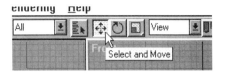

Click and drag the light vertically in the Front viewport to the location shown in Figure C.5.

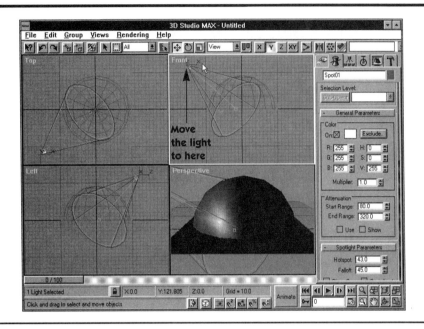

Figure C.5: Moving the light vertically

The restriction tools add an extra step when moving objects in your model. While they may seem like a nuisance at first, they enable you to do a good deal of your editing in the perspective view so you don't have to rely on the orthogonal views. You may want to experiment with working purely in the perspective view using the X, Y, and Z restriction tools at a later time. Now let's see how cameras are added.

◆ Adding a Camera

Adding cameras to a scene is similar to adding lights. You add the camera first, then make adjustments in its position.

1. Click on the Create tab in the command panel.

2. Click on the Cameras button.

3. Click on the Target button. A new set of parameters appears in the command panel. Notice that low in the panel there is a set of lens focal lengths. There is also a Lens and FOV input box. These options duplicate the ones found in the Camera Type dialog box in 3D Studio 4.0.

4. In the Top viewport, click and drag the mouse to place the camera and target points as shown in Figure C.6.

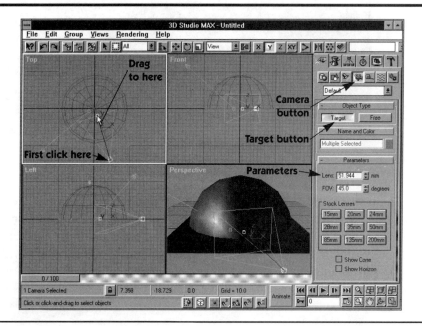

Figure C.6: Adding a camera

Using Filters to Select Objects

The next step is to adjust the camera's location as you might do in 3D Studio 4.0. But MAX adds a new tool that will help you more easily control the selection of the camera points in your model. Often cameras become enmeshed in the geometry of a model and so they become difficult to select. Selection filters help ease this problem as shown in the next exercise.

1. Select the camera, then click on the Move button.

2. Click on the Modify tab.

3. In the Front view, with the Restrict To Y button selected in the Toolbar, click and drag the camera to the location shown in Figure C.7.

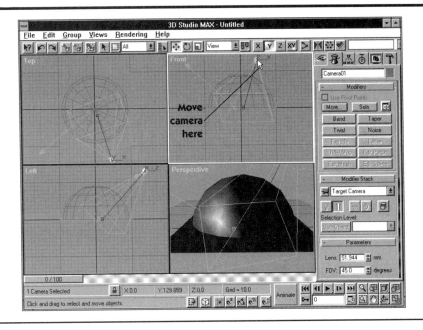

Figure C.7: Placing the camera in a new position

4. Now try to click and drag the camera target. If you're lucky, you might select the target, but it is more likely that you will end up moving the hemisphere. In the following steps you'll see how the restriction tools can make this a lot easier to do successfully.

5. If you accidentally moved the hemisphere in the previous step, choose Edit ➤ Undo Move or click on the Undo button in the Toolbar.

6. Open the Selection Filter drop-down list from the Toolbar.

7. Click on Cameras from the list.

8. Now click and drag the target point in the Front viewport. With the Cameras filter on, MAX selects only the camera, and ignores other objects.

The Selection Filter is great in helping you select specific types of objects, but it may take a little getting used to. If you have problems selecting objects, check the Selection Filter first and set it to All when in doubt.

Getting the Camera View in the Perspective Viewport

To get the camera view into the Perspective viewport, you use the pop-up menu that appears when you right-click on the viewport title.

1. Right-click on the word *Perspective* in the upper left corner of the Perspective viewport. A pop-up menu appears.

2. Choose Views ➤ Camera01. Your view changes to the camera view.

3. Click on the Dolly Camera tool in the
Navigation Control panel, then click
and drag downward in the Camera01
viewport to get a better view of your

model. Notice that the camera moves in the other viewports as you
"dolly" back.

With a camera view selected for this viewport, the Zoom tool in the
Navigation Control panel changes to a Dolly Camera button. This tool
acts exactly like the Zoom tool, with the additional effect of adjusting
the camera position to match the view.

◆ Adding Materials

As you have seen so far, MAX has gotten away from a modal method
of editing, where you must use several different modules to create your
model. Instead, MAX has a more unified modeling environment. The
Material Editor in MAX really shows how this change helps improve
your ability to get work done, as you'll see next.

Opening the Material Editor
and Assigning Materials

The first step in using the Material Editor is finding it in the first place.

1. If you cannot see the entire Toolbar at the top of the window, then
click and drag it to the left using the Toolbar's Menu Pan tool.

2. Next, click on the Material Editor
button.

The Material Editor dialog box appears.

3. Click on the cyan-colored sphere in the lower left of the six sample images.

4. In the main MAX window, click on Pick from the Reference Coordinate System drop-down list, then click on the hemisphere to select it. The Pick option allows you to select an object.

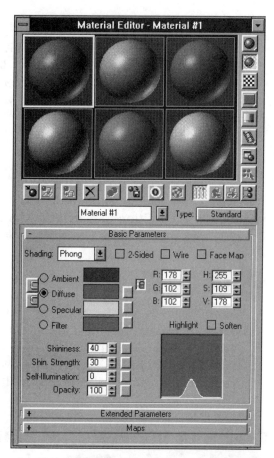

5. In the Material Editor dialog box, click on the Assign Material To Selection button.

Notice that the hemisphere has changed to the material selected in the Material Editor.

Take a moment to examine the Material Editor dialog box. Under the Basic Parameters flyout, you see the same options found in the Materials Editor of 3D Studio 4.0. They are just arranged in a different way. The only things missing are the Texture Map options.

Adding Texture Maps

To access the Texture Map options, you need to open the Maps flyout panel.

1. Click on the Maps button at the bottom of the dialog box. The Maps options appear (see Figure C.8).

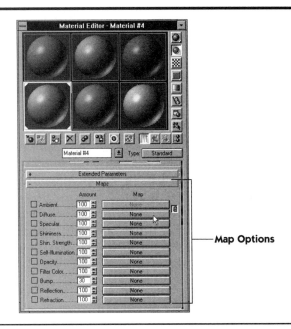

Figure C.8: More maps options

2. Click on the button labeled None under the Maps column (across from the Diffuse options as shown in Figure C.8). The Material/Map Browser dialog box appears.

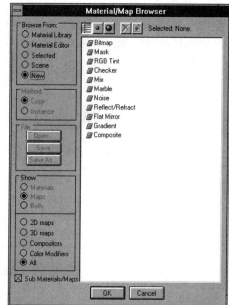

3. Double-click on the Bitmap option at the top of the list. This brings up a new set of Bitmap Parameters in the Material Editor window.

4. Click on the bar labeled Bitmap. This brings up a typical File dialog box.

5. Locate `Evrgren2.JPG` and select it, then click OK. Notice that the current sample now has the `Evrgren2.JPG` bitmap.

6. Click on the Assign Material To Selection button. Nothing appears to happen. You won't see the effects of a texture map material until you do a preview rendering of your model. As with 3D Studio 4.0, you also need to assign mapping coordinates to any object that has a bitmap material assigned to it.

Note *If you want to remove a texture bitmap from a material definition, follow steps 1 and 2 above, then click on None in the Material/Map Browser dialog box. None appears as an option when a bitmap has been assigned to the material.*

After you selected the material from the Material Browser in step 4, the options in the Material Editor dialog box changed to show the bitmap parameters for Tex #1. This is just the name MAX gives the first texture you add to the materials definition; it's like a subsection of the main material, which in this case is simply called Material #4. You can return to the main material settings by choosing Material #4 in the Material Name drop-down list.

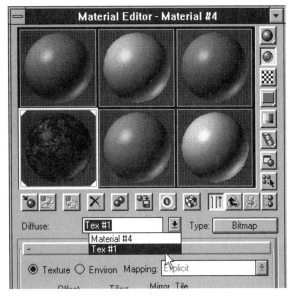

The Material Editor in MAX is a much richer environment and could take some time to master, but it still contains the basic tools you are familiar with from 3D Studio 4.0.

> **Note** *This concludes the tutorial portion of this appendix. The following sections will describe other basic features you will want to know about, especially in regard to the chapters that cover 3D Studio 4.0 in this book.*

◆ Selecting Objects, Faces, and Vertexes

Object selection in MAX maintains some similarities to 3D Studio 4.0. The main differences are in the location of the selection tools. There are also some differences in the way you select components of an object, such as faces and vertexes. I'd like to point out some of the other selection features of MAX so you will be aware of them as you begin to build and edit your own models.

Selecting Objects

3D Studio 4.0 offered the Select options in the command column. Those options are now part of MAX's pull-down menu. If you click on Edit from the menu bar, you'll see that many of the Select options are there.

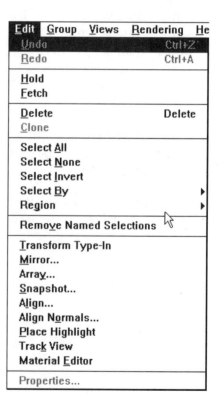

In addition, the Edit ➤ Select By option offers the option to select objects by color or by name. You can also get directly to the Select Objects dialog box by clicking on the Select By Name button in the Toolbar.

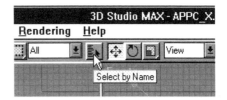

The Edit ➤ Select By ➤ Name option opens a dialog box that lets you filter and select objects like you would in 3D Studio 4.0.

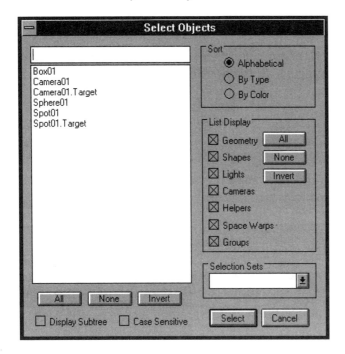

Note that selected objects appear in white in wireframe mode, not red as in 3D Studio 4.0. If your viewport is set to show objects shaded (or Shade Selected is checked in Views pull-down menu), you'll see white "corner marks" surrounding the selected object.

Selecting Faces, Vertexes, and Edges

In Chapter 11, I described a method for selecting and detaching faces of an object to turn them into separate objects. At the time, the reason I had you do this was that we needed to assign a separate material to one of the surfaces of the object. (Note that you can assign materials to faces *without* detaching them into separate objects; I was just using the exercise to show you one way of doing it.) To accomplish this same operation in MAX, you will have to follow a different process. Here are the steps you need to take to select a set of faces for editing.

1. Click on the Modify tab in the command panel.

2. Click on the object containing the faces you want to edit. This selects the entire object. The options in the command panel will change to reflect the type of object you have selected.

3. Choose Edit mesh from the Modifiers flyout in the command panel.

4. Click on Sub-Object button in Selection Level group.

5. Choose Face from the Selection Level drop-down list. As you can see from the list, you can also select vertexes and edges.

6. Click on the Crossing Selection toggle button at the bottom of the MAX window. This changes the selection method to Window Selection.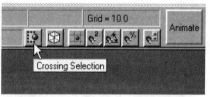

7. Place a selection window around the desired faces in the appropriate viewport.

8. Choose Detach from the Miscellaneous button group near the bottom of the Modify command panel. This brings up the Detach dialog box.

9. At the Detach dialog box, enter a name for new detached object in the Detach As input box.

The Crossing Selection/Window Selection tool mentioned in step 6 replaces the Quad and Crossing Selection options of 3D Studio 4.0. You can also select these options from the MAX menu bar by choosing Edit ➤ Region.

◆ Mapping Coordinates

Just as with 3D Studio 4.0, you will need to apply mapping coordinates to objects that have texture maps assigned to them. Mapping coordinates are already assigned to objects created within MAX, but if you have imported an AutoCAD model, you will need to add mapping coordinates to any objects within it that will receive materials with texture maps.

Viewing the Map Icon

> **Note** *If you are editing the map icon, you may want to turn off shading in all the viewports. Shading may hide the map icon if the icon is small and located within the geometry of the object.*

In 3D Studio 4.0, mapping coordinates are facilitated through the map icon. A similar object called a *gizmo* is available in MAX. Actually, the term in MAX refers to a collection of objects that "frame" objects like lights, cameras, and mapping coordinates to facilitate their editing.

To view a map gizmo, take the following steps.

1. Click on the Modify tab of the command panel.
2. Select the object whose mapping coordinates you wish to edit.

3. In the command panel, click on the UVW Map button in the Modifiers flyout.

4. In the Selection Level group, click on Sub-Object.

5. In the Selection Level drop-down list, make sure Gizmo is selected. The map icon appears in the viewports.

Note that the map icon options you are familiar with in 3D Studio 4.0 appear in the Parameters flyout of the command panel once you select the UVW Map button in step 3. These include the mapping types: Planar, Cylindrical, Spherical, etc.

Editing the Mapping Gizmo

> **Note**   *If you want to use the Selection Filter to select a gizmo, use the Helpers option in the Selection Filter drop-down list.*

Once you have the mapping gizmo displayed, you can use the Move, Rotate, and Scale tools in the Toolbar to make adjustments.

You needn't reassign the mapping coordinate to the object as in 3D Studio 4.0, for the map is a part of the object.

You might notice the U, V, and W options in the Parameters section of the command panel. These refer to the local coordinates of the map, similar to X, Y, and Z coordinates designation we're so used to. U and V are the X and Y equivalents for the map, and W is equivalent to the Z axis. U, V, and W are used to differentiate mapping coordinates from the typical coordinates used for locating points in a model. (The designation of U, V, and W come from the last three letters in the alphabet *before* X, Y, and Z.)

When a material that requires mapping coordinates is assigned to a rectangular object, it is usually assigned what is called a Box mapping. This means that all six sides have their surfaces mapped with the image. The map is also stretched to fit each surface of the box. This differs from 3D Studio 4.0, which assigns the map to just one surface and projects the map through the object. For this reason, you may find that you don't need to make as many adjustments to your material maps.

Smoothing Groups and Normals

While we're on the subject of material maps, you'll want to know how to access smoothing groups and normals. These options can be found by clicking on the More button in the Modify tab of the command panel. This opens the Modifiers dialog box.

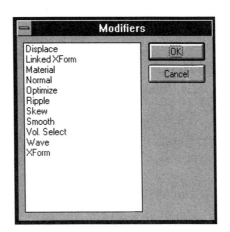

Here, you can select Smooth to edit the smoothing group assigned to an object, or you can select Normal to unify or flip normals in an object.

◆ Animation

> **Note**   *To edit the position of an object, make sure the Sub-Object button in the Modify command panel is not selected.*

In 3D Studio 4.0, the Keyframer is the program you use to add motion. Coincidentally, the Keyframer's appearance is nearly identical to the 3D Editor. MAX eliminates the redundancies between the Keyframer and the 3D Editor and turns

the Keyframer into a single Animate button at the bottom of the MAX window.

When the Animate button is selected, you are, for all intents and purposes, in the Keyframer of MAX. You can then add animated motion by moving to a non-zero frame, and you can move objects just as you would in 3D Studio 4.0. You can go to different frames by using the Frame slider (called the Time slider in MAX) or by entering a number in the Frame counter below and to the right of the slider. You can preview your animation using the Time controls which are similar to 3D Studio 4.0's.

Making Keyframes and Paths Visible

While animating objects in MAX is fairly similar to the process you would follow in 3D Studio 4.0, editing Keyframes and displaying paths is somewhat different. MAX places less emphasis on the paths than does 3D Studio 4.0. The paths do still play a role, however.

To make the motion path and keyframes of an object visible after motion has been added to a model, take the following steps.

1. Click on the Motion tab in the command panel.

2. Click on the object whose motion you wish to view.

3. Click on the Trajectories button. The path will become visible (see Figure C.9).

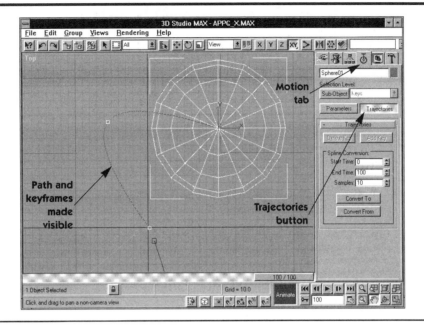

Figure C.9: The path of an object becomes visible when you select the Trajectories button in the Motion tab of the command panel.

Adding and Deleting Keyframes

Once you've made the path visible, you can make adjustments to the path by using the Edit tools on the keyframe points along the path, just as with 3D Studio 4.0. You can also delete or add keyframes by taking the following steps.

1. In the Motion command panel, with an object selected and its path showing (with the Trajectories button selected), click on the Sub-Object button in the Selection Level group to make it active.

2. Make sure Keys is selected in the Selection Level drop-down list.

Once you do this, the Delete Key and Add Key buttons are available to you. To add a keyframe, you need only click on Add Key, then click on the location on the path where you want a new keyframe.

Making Adjustments to Keyframes

You can make adjustments to keyframes with Ease To and Ease From, just as you did in 3D Studio 4.0, using a Key Info dialog box. But getting to the Key Info dialog box is quite different in MAX.

1. With the Sub-Object button selected in the Motion command panel, and the path and keyframes visible in the viewports, click on the desired keyframe. The X, Y, and Z coordinates (the Axis Tripod icon) of the keyframe are visible.

2. Right-click on the selected keyframe. A pop-up menu appears.

3. Select Key Info from the menu. The Key Info dialog box appears.

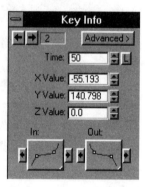

Notice that the Key Info dialog box is quite different from its equivalent in 3D Studio 4.0. For example, MAX offers many more tools for controlling keyframes. A discussion of these tools would not be appropriate for this discussion; however, I can show you how you can set up MAX to display the tool options 3D Studio 4.0 users are more familiar with.

Setting Up the Key Info Dialog to Show TCB Options

In Chapter 12, you saw how you can control the motion of a camera through the keyframes by using the Ease To, Ease From, Continuity, and Bias settings of the Key Info dialog box. MAX has not done away with these options. They are just moved one level deeper in the system of keyframe options. You can access these tools, known as the Time, Continuity, and Bias tools (TCB), by following these instructions.

> ***Note*** *In step 3, your view of the Track View window will look different depending on the number and types of objects in your model.*

1. Click on the Track View button in the Toolbar.

   The Track View 1 dialog box appears. This is similar to the TRACK Info dialog box in 3D Studio 4.0, with the addition of the Track View hierarchy list to the left (see Figure C.10a). This hierarchy list looks similar to the directory list of the Windows 95 Explorer or of many backup utilities.

2. Look down the list of options until you see Objects, then click on the square with the plus sign on it. The list expands to reveal more items in the hierarchy (see Figure C.10b).

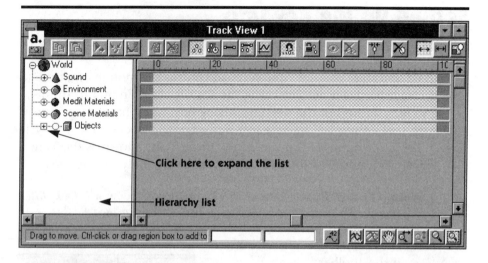

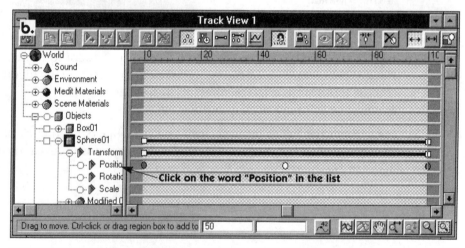

Figure C.10: Viewing the Track information for objects in your model

3. Click on the plus sign associated with the object that has motion in your model. You'll see more items listed, including Transform and Position.

4. Click on the Position item in the list (so the word Position is highlighted).

5. Click on the Assign Controller button in the Track View toolbar.

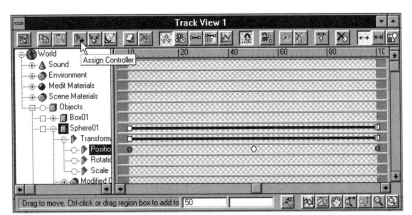

The Replace Position Controller dialog box appears.

6. Select TCB Position from the list, then click OK. This makes the TCB options available in the Key Info dialog box you saw in the previous example. You can also click on Make Default. This option will make the TCB position the default for all objects, not just the one you are currently adjusting.

7. Exit the Track View dialog box.

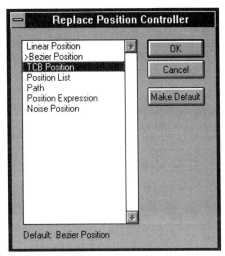

Now you can make adjustments to the keyframes in a way more familiar to 3D Studio 4.0 users.

1. Close the Track View window.

2. Select the Motion tab from the command panel,

3. Select the object whose keyframe you wish to edit.

4. Click on the Trajectories button to make the path visible.

5. Click on the Sub-Object button to make it active, and make sure Key is selected in the Selection Level drop-down list.

6. Click on the keyframe you wish to edit, then right-click on it to open the pop-up menu.

7. Select Key Info from the menu. The Key Info dialog box appears with the TCB options 3D Studio 4.0 users are more familiar with.

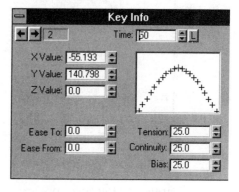

As mentioned in step 6 of the previous example, you can make the TCB options the default for all the objects in your model, if you so choose. You may want to do this if you are already a seasoned 3D Studio 4.0 user, but don't overlook the other keyframe options available.

Adding and Scaling Time

In Chapter 12, you were shown how to add time to an animation, as well as how to *scale* time to reduce or increase its speed. MAX offers the same options in a simplified form.

To *add* time, do the following:

1. Click on the Time button at the bottom of the MAX window.

The Time Configuration dialog box appears.

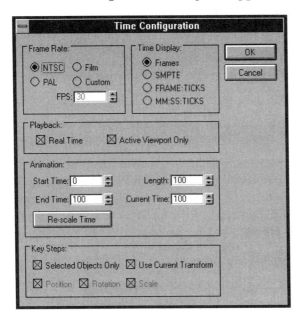

2. Enter the new length of your animation in the Length input box, then click OK.

To select and *scale* a segment do the following:

1. Click on the Time Configuration button to open the Time Configuration dialog box.

2. Click on the Re-scale Time button. The Re-scale Time dialog box appears.

3. In the Start Time input box, enter the frame number of the first frame of the segment you wish to scale.

4. In the End Time input box, enter the last frame number of the segment you wish to scale.

5. OR, in the Length input box, enter the new length you want the segment to be.

6. Click OK, then click OK at the Time Configuration dialog box.

Adjusting an Object's Motion in Time

Adding time to the beginning of an animation in 3D Studio 4.0 takes a little work. MAX has greatly simplified this task. You first increase the total number of frames in the animation as described in the previous example, then you use the Track View dialog box as described below to move the entire track for the object later in time (that is, further to the right on a time line).

1. Once you've increased the overall amount of time for your animation, click on the Track View button to open the Track View dialog box (see Figure C.11).

2. Click on the plus button next to the Objects category in the Hierarchy list. The list expands to show the objects and their corresponding time lines (see Figure C.11).

3. Locate the object you wish to push later in time, then place the cursor on its time track so it shows a double-headed cursor.

4. Click and drag the time track to the right to move its entire motion later through time in the animation.

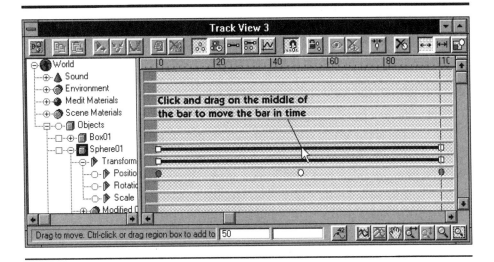

Figure C.11: The Track View with the objects timeline visible

You can also expand the duration of the object's motion by clicking and dragging either of the control points at the end of the object's time track. When you place the cursor on one of these control points, the cursor turns into a single-headed arrow, indicating that you can click and drag the control point.

You might also notice the dots in the time line (see Figure C.11). These dots represent the keyframes in the track. You can right-click on these dots to open the Key Info dialog box. In addition, you can right-click on the object name in the hierarchy list to open the Key Info dialog box.

You'll find that once you've created an animation (at least two keyframes), you can also use the View Track dialog box to control light intensity over time. Here are the steps to take to get to a lights keyframe from the View Track dialog box.

1. Open the View Track dialog box.

2. Locate the word Objects in the Heirarchy list, then click on the plus sign to the left of it. The list expands to show more information.

3. Locate the name of the light you want to edit, then click on the plus sign to the right of it. The list expands to show the attributes of that object. For example, if you have made the selected light change in intensity over time, you will see the keyframes indicated as dots, called keys, in a row next to the Color attribute of the selected light.

4. Right-click on one of the keys. You will see the Key Info dialog box with light color settings

You can then adjust the color in the dialog box to set the light's intensity, for example. Once you have the color keys displayed in the View Track dialog box, you can also add, delete, and move the keys in a way similar to the Key Info dialog box in 3DS 4.0.

◆ Rendering Your Model

You have two options for rendering your model. You can either do a full rendering, which offers options similar to those of 3D Studio 4.0, or you can do a *Quick Render*. If you choose a Quick Render, you will see an abbreviated form of the Rendering message dialog box, plus the Quick Render window (see Figure C.12).

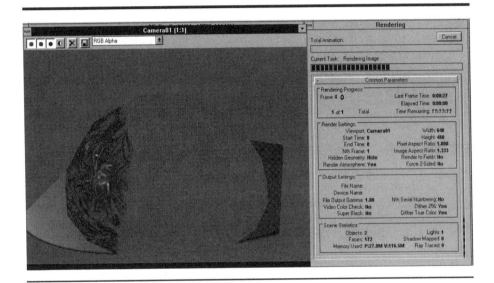

Figure C.12: The Quick Render window and message dialog box

Both Render Scene and Quick Render can be found on the Toolbar to the far right. Their buttons look like the Render buttons in AutoCAD.

◆ Opening 3DS 4.0 and DXF Files

3D Studio MAX has its own file format, with the extension .MAX. If you want to open files created in 3D Studio 4.0 or earlier, you will need to use the File ➤ Import option in MAX. You will get a typical File dialog box from which you can select either 3D Studio 4.0 3DS files, PRJ (project) files, or AutoCAD DXF files. If you are importing DXF files, you will see additional dialog boxes similar to the ones that appear in 3DS 4.0 for importing DXF files.

MAX's File ➤ Export command lets you export native MAX files to 3DS and DXF formats. Be aware, however, that the appearance of materials and lighting may change when materials are imported and exported from MAX.

◆ Summary

3D Studio MAX is an incredibly rich 3D environment designed to compete head-to-head with "high-end" workstation class animation programs. I hope that this little tour will help you get a start with this product. Remember that MAX is really a very different program from 3D Studio 4.0, and that I've mainly touched on a few similarities in this appendix. To really get familiar with the power of MAX, you will want to work with the tutorials in the MAX documentation set.

Index

Note to the Reader: Throughout this index **boldface** page numbers indicate primary discussions of a topic. *Italicized* page numbers indicate illustrations.

t
t(

About the CD

This CD contains a wealth of data, utility, and program files to help you explore the world of 3D. On this CD you'll find:

◆ All of the files you'll need to complete the exercises in this book. You can start most of the tutorials in the book with a file or two from the CD's Sample directory.

◆ Special tryout versions of *Adobe Photoshop* and *Adobe Premiere*. These are fully functional versions, with the exception that the Save and Print facilities have been disabled.

◆ A tryout version of *Adobe Streamline*, a graphics file conversion program that lets AutoCAD users convert bitmap image files to AutoCAD DXF vector files. This can be helpful for importing scanned maps, logos, or other types of image files into AutoCAD. This tryout version lets you do everything the retail version does, except for saving artwork files and for Clipboard cutting and pasting.

◆ *Wcvt2pov*, a translation program that will enable AutoCAD and 3D Studio users to convert their models to a format that can be "walked through" in real time, without the need for special hardware. Wcvt2pov is a freeware program.

◆ *3D Studio 4.0 VRML 1.2 plug-in*, courtesy of Autodesk, Inc. Used in the tutorials in Chapter 16, this plug-in helps you explore the use of 3D Studio as a VRML world-building tool.

◆ A beta version of *WorldView* by Intervista Software Corp. WorldView is a virtual reality "browser" program that lets you navigate through virtual worlds on the Internet or on your own computer.

◆ A demo of Darim Vision Co.'s *DVMPEG* compression drivers for Windows 95 and Windows NT, which provide you with the ability to create highly compressed MPEG video and audio streams from your existing movie or animation. (DVMPEG is copyright 1995 Darim Vision Co., Ltd. Their WWW address is http://darvision.kaist.ac.kr)

◆ A demo version of in:sync Corp.'s *Razor*, a video editing program similar to Adobe Premiere. The demo is a black-and-white-only version of the retail product.

◆ A set of AutoLISP utilities that can help you work in AutoCAD with a minimum of frustration. *Eye2eye* is a collection of tools designed to help you visualize your models more easily. *Splinep* and *Tube* are helpful for constructing complex shapes.

ɔ find out more about the CD, check out Appendix B. There you will find installa-
ɔn instructions and more detailed information about the CD's contents. Please refer
the file LICENSE.TXT for program copyright and license information.